How Research Has Changed American Schools

A History from 1840 to the Present

Robert M. W. Travers

Western Michigan University

Mythos Press
P.O. Box 589
Kalamazoo, Michigan 49005

Printed in the United States of America

ISBN 0-9609682-0-2

Library of Congress Catalog Card Number 82-62326

Mythos Press
P.O. Box 589
Kalamazoo
Michigan, 49005

Printing: 1 2 3 4 5 6 7 8 Year: 3 4 5 6 7 8 9

To

Edward Lee Thorndike

to whom I owe so much

Preface

During the century covered by the main body of this volume, an immense amount of knowledge was accumulated that resulted in important changes in education. During that century, the entire conception of education changed in the minds of those who operated the schools. A 12-year-old in 1840 might have been given a printed sermon as an exercise in reading, but the materials chosen as a reading assignment for a child a century later would have been selected on a vastly more sophisticated basis. A book designed for a child in the middle of our own century would probably have been screened for vocabulary difficulty and sentence structure complexity, and it would have formed part of a sequence of materials for helping to build knowledge and skill in the child. This transition in the curriculum was made possible through the development of a body of knowledge related to learning. Other aspects of the work of the child in the school have shown as dramatic changes as those involved in the choice of reading materials.

The term *research* is used in this volume to cover a wide range of activities. The empirical approaches of Horace Mann, Henry Barnard and William Torrey Harris of the last century are viewed as primitive forms of research, and forms that provided the background for more modern methods. These primitive forms of research share with their modern counterparts a solid empirical base. Modern educational research has its foundation in the fact finding techniques of the great educational organizers and administrators of the last century. Those individuals brought about the change from education administered in terms of tradition, to education administered in terms of knowledge. They created an atmosphere in education, accepting of new ideas and encouraging innovation based on knowledge. That transition had to take place before the emerging new sciences, related to learning and development, could have their impact. The volume traces that transition.

The volume cannot escape from being a study in the sociology of knowledge. The ideas derived from academic research that have influenced education have been inevitably those acceptable in terms of the values of the age in which they thrived. The impact of knowledge on education is far from being a cold, logical, application of useful knowledge to the solution of practical problems. All too often meager knowledge from the academic world has been hastily applied in education, because it provided a means of promoting a prevailing social philosophy. The volume attempts to trace this relationship between research, education, and social values.

Although the book emphasizes research involving empirical methods of inquiry, the author could not neglect the impact of other forms of inquiry. In the field of mathematics education, particularly, school practices have been substantially influenced by the type of analytic research in which mathematicians engage.

When the author began to study the history of educational research some years ago, he shared the view of perhaps most professional educators that research has had little impact on education. As the work progressed, an entirely different picture emerged. Research has had an immense impact, though, one should add, not always for the good. The author hopes that he can take the reader along the path that he explored over several years, and demonstrate the impressive way in which research has given new form to school practices.

Reviewers of drafts of the manuscript asked why so little emphasis had been given to the empirical research of sociologists, economists, anthropologists, and other social scientists. The answer is that empirically oriented research workers in the latter fields have, only recently, become interested in problems of education. Theoretical sociologists, who followed in the footsteps of Herbert Spencer, wrote many treatises on education. These documents were lacking in any empirical basis, and they faded into history without leaving any trace of impact on education. Sociology, as an empirical science, contributing to the understanding of education, is of too recent origin to be given any emphasis in this book. Of course, sociology existed long ago as an empirical science, but the problems studied had little relationship to education. The educational economist, and the educational anthropologist have been extreme rarities, and still are. The relative absence of these disciplines from the volume does not represent bias on the part of the author in favor of psychology, but reflects a lack of presence of these other disciplines in the field of educational research during much of the period covered.

Readers will also note that the emphasis on the modern era is slight.

The first draft of the manuscript excluded any mention of research beyond the year 1950, because the author believed that modern times cannot be viewed with any objectivity. Critics of the original draft asked that a chapter be added covering the last quarter of a century and, thus, a short chapter was added, but with some reluctance.

The author is particularly indebted to the Trustees and Administration of Western Michigan University for providing him with an appointment through which full time could be devoted to the preparation of this volume. The support and encouragement of Dean John Sandberg is also especially appreciated.

The substantial help of research assistants, and others, is gratefully acknowledged. Particular appreciation is expressed to Sandra Howe, who provided expert help on mathematics education, and Karen Schaper, Velda Iverson, and Janet Dillaman, who read and criticized early drafts of the manuscript.

I am also particularly indebted to Mrs. Ruth Kavanaugh for her meticulous help in the final phases of the production of the book. Finally, I must express appreciation to my wife, Norma, for her assistance in the long and tedious task of proofreading.

Robert M. W. Travers

Table of Contents

Table of Illustrations

PART I

The Foundation for Research in Education

The first part of this volume is concerned with a time in American education when the schools were swept forward on a tide of new ideas. During the first 50 years of the American republic, schools had made slow and halting changes from the Puritan tradition from which they had emerged. They had lacked the leadership that would make them the special instruments for maintaining a democratic society. Then, towards the middle of the nineteenth century, leaders emerged, who were to change American schools for all time.

Three of those leaders, Horace Mann, Henry Barnard, and William Torrey Harris, exerted an influence on schools that is of extraordinary importance for understanding how research came to play a role in American education. They influenced education profoundly in other ways too, but our interest in them here lies in the fact that they introduced, into the administration and management of education, procedures involving the collection and analysis of data. They demonstrated that the collection of facts was a vital requirement for establishing sound educational policies, and that problems could be solved effectively only after all the relevant information had been systematically collected.

The pioneer educators discussed in the first chapter developed an atmosphere in schools favorable to the systematic study and solution of educational problems, an atmosphere that was essential for the acceptance of educational research. Later generations of educational research workers were to bring to education far more than data collection techniques for solving problems. They were to bring a whole range of scientific ideas that were emerging from laboratories across the world.

The second chapter looks at some of the influential scientific ideas of the nineteenth century that had a profound, though indirect, influence on American education. Research workers were to be the first to use these ideas in relation to educational problems. Scientists in the nineteenth century were beginning to turn their attention to the study of the human as an organism engaged in adaptation to a complex environment. They came to understand that the human could be viewed as an object for scientific study, and could be investigated as an organism, just as other organisms had been investigated and studied.

The new ideas that the research workers were to bring to education represented a complete revolution in the conception of the nature of the child. Such a new conception represented a vast change from the Puritan's notion that the child was a soul entrusted to the teacher, who might help him, or her, achieve salvation through learning to read the Bible. Humans had now become objects for scientific inquiry, and events in the classroom could be studied just as any other set of events might be studied.

This first part of the book discusses the internal revolution that had to take place in education, before educational research could even begin. This is followed by a discussion of some features of the scientific revolution of the nineteenth century that had particular significance for the development of educational research.

HORACE MANN

Photograph courtesy of the Massachusetts Historical Society

CHAPTER 1

American Builders of the Foundation for Educational Research

Educational research did not come into being through the sudden appearance of a human mutant called the educational researcher. It finds its roots in attempts to collect facts that could be used for planning education and for providing support for schools. Systematic fact-finding as a basis for legislation related to schools goes back to the period of American education known as the period of the revival of the common school. The discovery that the systematic collection of facts could be used to build education was an important discovery that is still extensively applied. Over the century and a half that followed the revival of the common school in New England, the fact-finding process was gradually expanded as technology and the sciences of human behavior developed their techniques. We are not saying here that fact-finding should be the central activity of a mature educational research program, but it is a foundation on which a scientific approach to education was built. Fact-finding is an empirical approach to the solution of problems, but a scientific approach involves far more than mere fact-finding.

The Common School Revival of the 1840's had been preceded by 200 years of Puritan influence on education, for the Puritans had first introduced the idea of a common school. The Puritans were highly educated for their period of history and lost no time, after their arrival on the North American continent, in establishing schools. In 1635 the celebrated Latin School was established in Boston. In the years 1636 and 1637, Harvard College was established. Just a few years later the first legislation making education compulsory was passed through an act of the General Court of the Massachusetts Bay Colony that had far-reaching powers in regulating Puritan life.

The General Court functioned as a legislative body and was the ancestor of the New England state legislatures. The Act of the General Court of 1642 made education compulsory for all children, but it did not establish schools. The Act implied that parents, employers, and in fact the whole community were to be responsible for the education of children. The selectmen in each community were to be responsible for seeing that each child received an education, especially in reading, understanding the Bible and religion, and understanding the laws of the Colonies. Anyone found guilty of neglecting the training of children was to be fined.

The Act of 1642 does not seem to have worked well. The Puritans probably did what they could to give some instruction to their children, but life must have been hard and the pressing problems of providing housing, food, and clothing must have left little time for much else. The General Court soon recognized that more was needed than informal education, so in 1647 the General Court enacted the first school law that incorporated the requirement that communities had to establish schools. The General Court declared that one of the ways of Satan was to keep men and women from reading the Scriptures. The General Court ordered that Satan be defeated in achieving this goal by the establishment of schools in which children should learn to read and study the Scriptures. Every township with 50 householders or more should designate one of their number to teach the children reading and writing. The designated teacher was to be paid by the other members of the township. A township that had more than 100 families was also required to have a grammar school so that the youth might be fitted for attendance at a university. Be it noted that the Act recognized three levels of education--elementary, secondary, and university -- a system of levels that was first put forth by Comenius. The schools were to be supported either by those who lived in the township or by those who attended the schools. Parents were to be fined if they did not make provision for the education of their children.

How far the enactments of the General Court with respect to education were met is hardly known. One can say that many learned to read and write and study the Scriptures, which seems to have been the limit of the curriculum. A few went on to Latin School and a still smaller number to Harvard, where they received the kind of higher education that had been provided at Oxford and Cambridge for the training of ministers for the Reformed Church of England. The schools rapidly moved towards free tuition, because wherever pupils were required to pay for an education, the poor did not become educated, and the distinction between poor and rich was an abomination to the Puritan. No new school laws were enacted by the General Court with respect to the support of schools, but the free school supported by the township had been born. The General Court did levy fines on townships which failed to provide the schools required by law.

In those early days there was little supervision of schools and no appointed administrative officers. Whatever supervision there was, was undertaken by the selectmen of the township and the minister. As townships grew, the parts of townships in which schools were located began to demand a greater voice in the running of the school and school districts came into being.

The early enthusiasm of the Puritans for the development of education seems to have been followed by a declining interest during the eighteenth century. When the Constitution of the State of Massachusetts was formulated in 1780, it gave recognition to the free school system that the Puritans had developed, but added little. It was not long before the state legislature began to take away the great gains that had already been made. In 1789 the legislature wrote a school law which reduced the time of schooling to 6 months in the year and required communities to support a Latin school, but only if they had at least 200 families, instead of the 100 set by the Puritans. This law was the beginning of a 50-year period of decline of public education in Massachusetts.

Hinsdale (1898) has well documented the decline of education in New England during the eighteenth century. He describes how even the children of the well-to-do were often not able to read or write. This is evident from the fact that they were not able to sign legal documents kept in the records, but merely made their mark. From such records one can estimate that fewer than 40 percent of women with property were able to sign the deeds.

The Revolutionary War at the end of the century accelerated the downturn of education, for it left the country exhausted. In addition, the growth of private academies, which the wealthy attended, made it difficult to obtain money for publicly operated schools. This led to a differentiation of the education provided for the rich and the education provided for the poor, a differentiation which eroded the democratic ideals that had deep roots throughout New England. Despite this tradition, in the eighteenth century in New England there were schools for the poor, often run on the basis of a pittance handed out by the state and with little supplementary local support, and relatively well-financed schools for the affluent. Connecticut had also set aside the income from its western lands for use in public education, and this gave the local townships opportunity to take the position that education should be funded by the state rather than by the local community. This state aid, given unconditionally and requiring no accountability, turned out to be one of the major barriers to the development of public education.

The great revival of the common school did not take place until the late 1830's and 1840's. It was not just a revival of a democratic tradition of education, but a revolution in the manner in which schools were supervised. It involved, for the first time in history, planning on the basis of systematically collected data. It involved an examination of the ideas on which education was based, an intellectual crystallization of the function of education in a democracy, and the development of a literature on education that attempted to make available to teachers and educators important new ideas related to education that had emerged in various countries. Two men were responsible for this, more than any others. These were Henry Barnard and Horace Mann. A third, William Torrey Harris, showed how the ideas of Barnard and Mann could be translated into a large school system. These men, more than any others, are like three pillars on which the structure of twentieth-century education in the United States was built.

HENRY BARNARD: FACT FINDER, REFORMER, PROVIDER OF A NEW EDUCATIONAL LITERATURE

In the nineteenth century academicians in Western Europe, and to some extent in the United States, were slowly developing some of the scientific skills that led to sophisticated educational research; the leadership in American education, intelligently receptive to new ideas, was developing an intellectual climate that would permit educational research to flourish.

From the vantage point of the late twentieth century, the nineteenth century was an era of great leadership in almost all areas of education. The names of Barnard, Mann, and Harris are associated with the revival of the common school and what today would be termed educational administration, but equally distinguished names can be found in such other areas as higher education and the education of the deaf and the handicapped.

There have been times in history when leaders of distinction have not emerged, and whatever change was brought about was a result of forces other than personal leadership. American education was not in such an age. The impact of the leaders that emerged, evident even at the time, is now even more clear because of the long-term impact of that leadership.

Henry Barnard was born in Hartford, Connecticut, in 1811, and he died in the 90th year of his life in the same room in which he had been born. His family may be described as representing the cultivated and scholarly class of New England, and the young Henry seems to have had an inclination to succeed in academic work. He entered Yale sometime near his 16th birthday and graduated when he was still only 19. The Yale curriculum at that time was the kind that had long been used for the training of ministers, emphasizing the classics, humanities, and literary pursuits. The young Henry Barnard was probably exposed little to the sciences. On graduating from Yale, he seems to have spent a period reading classical literature and studying law for about 2 hours a day.

Then he spent a year teaching in an academy at Wilkesbarre, Pennsylvania. This experience whetted his appetite for learning more about education. He read everything he could find in the area of pedagogy. Despite his explorations of education, he was able to pick up enough knowledge about law to pass the bar examinations in 1835 at the age of 24.

The following 2 years were spent in Europe, and surely his travels must have been initiated by his knowledge of the educational reform movements that existed there. Joseph Neef had already brought the ideas of Pestalozzi to the United States in a book published in 1808. Neef had then gone on to found schools run along Pestalozzi lines in Pennsylvania. The Moravian Brethren of Pennsylvania had introduced into their schools the teaching methods advocated by their great bishop, Comenius. Joseph Lancaster had developed so-called Lancastrian schools in the United States and eventually died there. Henry Barnard must surely have been aware of these ideas and their European origins, and his European trip must have been a means of exploring these ideas further.

We know for a fact that Barnard's trip to Europe brought him into close contact with the intellectual life of that continent, and he came to know such distinguished figures as Thomas Carlyle, William Wordsworth, and Thomas DeQuincey. His affable personality made it easy for him to relate to others, and by the time he was 30 he had met and come to know many of the outstanding scholars, literary figures, and political figures on both sides of the Atlantic. When he returned to the United States, he served for three terms in the Connecticut State Legislature. As a state legislator, he became interested immediately in legislation related to the development of the common school. Connecticut had a long history of developing common schools, but following the establishment of the Government of the United States the schools had been in a state of decline. The colonial schools had been overseen by a meeting of the entire community, but in the early part of the nineteenth century this control was taken over by what was referred to as the "social society," but which in fact was the Congregational Church. The allowances for such schools were miserably small, and even early in the last century the sum of $1.25 per pupil per year provided little education at all.

Henry Barnard devoted considerable energy in the legislature to reforming education in the common schools in Connecticut. A committee of the legislature, of which he was a part, began to collect data related to the schools of the state. One startling fact that was revealed was that of all children aged 4-16 in the state less than 50 percent were in regular attendance. In addition, of the 1,200 schoolhouses in the state, only 300 were declared as suitable for use as schools and more than half were considered as unfit for occupation. Sanitary arrangements were typically an outrage. The teachers represented more a group of transient job holders than a professional body. The teaching positions of the state were held largely by men in winter, but in summer by women when the men were working in the fields. Fewer than one fourth of the teachers stayed in the same school for more than a year. Fewer than one percent of the schools had libraries. Although the state provided some support for each pupil in the school, the state established no requirements that had to be met and the school was not required to submit an annual report. The State of Connecticut was found to have slipped from the most advanced in education to that in which educational conditions were deplorable in terms of the standards of other states.

The work of the committee of the Legislature of the State of Connecticut is of importance because it introduced new methods for studying and controlling education. Data were collected from the schools all over the state, and the results were tabulated and studied. Nobody called it educational research, but it was far more significant as research than most dissertations and theses produced today, and far more original. The procedure introduced the notion that the state of education in the schools of any state should be monitored through the collection of appropriate data and that government needed to have machinery for collecting such data so that steps could be taken to improve the quality of education. The data thus collected in Connecticut not only demonstrated the general inadequacy of the common school in the state at that time, but also that the control of schools by a single religious denomination produced problems related to the financing of the school, for the denomination could not tax in order to support education. The deplorable condition of education in Connecticut seems to have been due to the latter with the result that, in the absence of local taxes, the schools survived on the pittance handed out for educational purpose by the state.

An important outcome of the legislature inquiry was the appointment of a state school officer. Henry Barnard himself played a prominent role in these activities of the legislature, making a stirring speech on the floor of the House when the school bill was debated. He ended his speech with the words:

> Here, in America, at last no man can live for himself alone. Individual happiness is here bound up with the greatest good of the greatest number. Every man must at once make himself as good and as influential as he can and help, at the same time, to make everybody about him and all whom he can reach better and happier. The common school should no longer be regarded as common because it is cheap, inferior, and attended only by the poor and those who are indifferent to the education of the children, but common as the light and the air, because its blessings are open to all and enjoyed by all. That day will come. For me, I mean to enjoy the satisfaction of the labor, let who will enter into the harvest. (Mayo, 1898, p. 777)

The person most qualified to fill the position of chief school officer for the state was Henry Barnard. His appointment was no surprise. His title was that of Secretary of the State Board of School Commissioners, but the modern equivalent would be that of state superintendent. Indeed, the function he performed came to define the role of the state superintendent in other states.

The problems Barnard faced were far more difficult than those faced by Horace Mann in Massachusetts where the common school had already come under public control. The weakness of the Connecticut system was the lack of control of the school by the school society with its limited parochial interests. In contrast, each Massachusetts community elected at a town meeting its own committee to oversee education. All was not well in the schools of Massachusetts, but a public administrative structure existed favorable for school development. That in Connecticut was most unfavorable.

Henry Barnard realized this problem, but during the 4 years he spent as secretary to the Board of Commissioners he made no effort to change the social structure of education. His method was more that of producing change by collecting and disseminating data. He traveled extensively, visiting as many schools as he could and offering constructive help to the teacher in charge. Throughout his work, he attempted to bring the new European concepts of education to those in charge of the common school. These techniques designed to promote educational change were those that he used throughout his life. His work was viewed by others not as propagandistic, but as a true labor of love. He believed in the enormous power of the common school in fulfilling the ideals of the American Revolution. He believed that no one could sacrifice too much to provide education for all.

As a part of his effort, Barnard initiated the *Connecticut School Journal*, through which important facts about education in the state could be disseminated and through which teachers could learn of new ideas. This also reflected one of Barnard's basic techniques of bringing about reform, namely, that of providing a literature through which ideas could be disseminated.

Henry Barnard's work was not always appreciated. It was attacked by the opposition party in the legislature, and when that party came to power in 1842, the party set out to destroy everything that Barnard had accomplished, including the repeal of the school legislation of 1837 which had made his work of reform possible. Barnard left for Rhode Island, where he was commissioned to make a study of the schools. He had been one of the inventors of the idea that schools could be improved by systematic data collection. Even though he was no longer appreciated in Connecticut, there were others who recognized the power of the new techniques of management and planning that he had introduced.

In Rhode Island, as commissioner for education, his first step was to find out about conditions in the schools. In his first written report of his activities, he stated that he had visited every town in the state and had visited 200 schools. There were probably few schools, if any, that he did not visit. He had made personal contacts with 400 teachers and had frequent contacts with parents and children as well as those adults particularly concerned with education. He was then prepared to inform the people of the state, and the legislature, what they needed to know in order to build a better common school. He pointed out that outside of Providence, and just a few other towns, the school year was less than 3 months in duration. There were only three towns that imposed a school tax. No attempt had been made to provide professional training for teachers, and there was no method of examining those who applied for positions. Of the 280 schoolhouses examined, 86 were viewed as unfit for human habitation and 200 had no source of ventilation. There were no blackboards, clocks, or thermometers in 270 of the schools, and boys outnumbered girls 4 or 5 to 1. Of the 35,000 children in the state aged 4-16, only 5,000 attended during the entire school year. Only 2,000 children received 9 months of schooling. Henry Barnard was entrusted by the legislature with drawing up a new school statute. The new law was passed and copies of it, together with a lengthy explanation written by Barnard himself, were sent to every school in the state. A system of local taxation was adopted to supplement the amount provided by the state for each pupil in school.

An important result of the publicity given to both the new school law and the facts and figures of Commissioner Barnard was an aroused public interest in the problems of education. Even the almanacs published in Rhode Island carried messages related to the development of public education in almost every town in the state, and an extensive literature in the form of pamphlets was distributed through the Office of the Commissioner. In the year 1847, Rhode Island had the largest per capita expenditure per pupil per year of any state, in the amount of $5.41. In comparison, the corresponding amount for Massachusetts was $4.06; for Connecticut, $3.25; and for New York, $2.49.

He was not forgotten in Connecticut. Two years after he left, in 1844, Governor Baldwin began once again to call attention to the unsatisfactory state of the schools and spoke of the fine work that Henry Barnard had accomplished. The legislature responded by appointing a committee and by providing the committee with the funds necessary for undertaking a thorough inquiry. The committee found that the supervision of the schools established through the work of Henry Barnard had dwindled to ineffective levels. There was still the same low level of public interest, and the chief weakness of the system lay in the control exercised by the school society. Data on the schools had become scarce and, in fact, most schools never provided the state with the data requested of them.

The report emphasized the need for a permanent state official to supervise the schools, and the need for each board of visitors to have an elected chairman who would see that the schools met the legal requirements. In addition, the committee recommended the establishment of a state normal school for the training of teachers. The report emphasized the importance of boards of visitors amassing the necessary facts and figures so that the legislature would have data on which legislation could be based. Henry Barnard's idea of the need of a permanent data base for the planning of education had won, and had now become firmly established. Much of educational research over the last century has been an attempt to broaden that data base.

In 1849 the Legislature of the State of Connecticut voted an appropriation of $2,500 for the establishment of a state normal school, and Henry Barnard was recalled from Rhode Island first as superintendent and then as principal of the normal school. During this period in Connecticut, Barnard worked hard to restore the control of the schools to the towns, and to the people of the towns. He also worked for the introduction of the graded system, originally derived from Prussia, which was widely regarded as a model for American schools.

Henry Barnard left Connecticut in 1855, and he did not hold any particular position until 1859 when he became president of the University of Wisconsin. During the years between positions, Barnard produced one of his most important contributions to education. He conceived of a national journal of education. There had been one previous attempt to produce this kind of periodical. A journal called the *Academician* had been published in 1820, but it lasted for only a year. In the last issue, the editor of the *Academician* stated that the journal had to come to an end because not enough of its subscribers had renewed their subscriptions. The *Academician* had the following full title:

The

Academician

containing

The Elements of Scholastic Science

and the outlines of

Philosophic Education

predicated

On the Analysis of the Human Mind

and

Exhibiting the Improved Methods of Instruction

The contents of the journal were as verbose as the full title. Much of the material published dealt with the teaching of grammar along traditional and pedantic lines. Small wonder was it that the *Academician* expired after only a year.

Barnard's *American Journal of Education* was entirely differently conceived. It was to do what the *Connecticut School Journal* had done, but on a national scale. The *American Journal of Education* was successful in just the way in which he must have wanted it to be. It became the most influential publication in the field of education in his century. Issued periodically, on no fixed schedule, it constituted a series of 32 volumes published between the years of 1855 and 1882.

The *American Journal of Education* has been called the Encyclopedia of American Education, since it summarized and presented ideas from all over the world as well as facts and figures related to contemporary education. It reflected all of Henry Barnard's skills in presenting facts and then using the facts to shape policies. It also incorporated his technique of changing education through exposing educators to ideas that were both new and worthwhile. Barnard's reputation and style were such that those who were exposed to the new ideas did not seem threatened by them, perhaps because the ideas carried with them Barnard's own personal enthusiasm for change in education. Barnard never ran into the kind of opposition that Horace Mann encountered.

A single issue of the *American Journal of Education* might include articles on such varied topics as a survey of schools for the deaf, an account of the development of the graded school in Prussia, a translation of a recent article by Froebel, and the reproduction of a sixteenth article on education. By any modern standard, the quality of the contributions was high. A considerable amount of space was devoted to Pestalozzi and attempts to apply his methods in different countries. Barnard recognized that educators had to profit from the important lessons that the great teachers of the past had learned. There was nothing in the *Journal* that reflected the more modern view that whatever is newest must be best, but there was respect for the knowledge to be derived from the history of education as well as the knowledge to be gleaned from the study of education in other countries. Barnard was the first to fully understand the importance of comparative education, which was to flourish for the next half-century and then decline to the point where most graduate schools of education did not even provide a course in the subject. Barnard was a man of broad vision.

During the early years after leaving Connecticut, he began to think about the need for a federal school officer, much like the state school officer who had been so influential in changing education in so many states. What he was beginning to conceptualize was a United States Commissioner of Education. He had already made a visit to Washington, D.C., in 1838, to obtain what school statistics existed in the Library of

Congress and other offices. He also contacted the officials in charge of the census and made suggestions concerning the data that should be collected in the forthcoming 1840 census. The data were subsequently collected and transmitted to Henry Barnard and Horace Mann before they were published for general distribution.

Ten years later, in August 1850, Henry Barnard addressed the American Institute for Instruction and called attention to the need for a federal agent who would monitor the state of education on a national level. The institute made some moves directed towards the appointment of a national agent within the framework of the institute, but financial support was not forthcoming from outside sources. Four years later, in 1854, Barnard proposed the idea again to another association, this time to the National Convention of the Friends of Education. This was the fourth and last meeting of the convention.

The plan proposed by Barnard was that of a central agent, with permanent headquarters which would function as an official depository of documents related to public education and a source of facts and figures. The agent should also edit publications and help to produce a literature on education of value to the local school and the local planners. This central agency should also have a library of plans for model schools, designs for furniture, and what would be called today visual materials. The central agent should also submit a report of progress related to the activities of each state. What he was proposing was the idea of a United States Commissioner of Education.

The association gave little more than a nod of approval to Henry Barnard's ambitious plans. The standing committee that examined the proposal responded favorably, but could see no source of funds. The association had no money except for that derived from a small entrance fee. Assessments and annual dues were not the way of running associations in those days. The thought that the Congress might finance the enterprise must surely have arisen, for even in those days there was a tendency to turn to Congress for funds for the support of every good idea that could not be financed locally, but it seemed unlikely that Congress would provide funds for any new project when the country was on the eve of a civil war. Far more important matters were occupying the time of congressional committees. There the matter rested for a decade. It was not until after the Civil War that a new effort was to be made to establish a national bureau of education, this time through the leadership of the National Teachers Association.

The post-Civil War situation provided conditions favorable for the establishment of a national education agency. Before the war, such a proposition would never have received the necessary support inCongress, for concern for the common school had existed only in the industrial East and the new West. The southern states had opposed any such form of education and had written laws prohibiting Negroes from being educated.

Private education had been the custom of the South.

As a result of pressure from the National Teachers Association, Congress established the position of Commissioner of Education in a new Department of Education. Henry Barnard, who had been president of St. John's College in Maryland since March 1867, was called upon by President Andrew Johnson to fill the new federal office.

The new Department of Education was the smallest department within the federal government. The total appropriation for it was $9,400, which provided the commissioner with a salary of $4,000, and three assistants with salaries of $2,000, $1,800, and $1,600. There seems to have been no money for clerks. The commissioner and his assistants wrote their own letters and undertook their own clerical work. Yet the office must have been involved in extensive correspondence with schools and state school officials all over the country.

The function of the new department was described in the statutes as existing for

> the purpose of collecting such statistics and facts as shall show the condition and progress of education in the several States and Territories, and of diffusing such information *** as shall aid the people of the United States in the establishment and maintenance of efficient school systems and otherwise promote the cause of education throughout the country. (Harris, 1903, p. 898)

The statute ordered further that the new department should report accurately concerning the use made by the states of the school land grants of Congress, and to give a reliable account of the state of education in the District of Columbia. The department was certainly not budgeted to carry out the extensive collection of data called for by the statute. The collection of data in the schools of Connecticut, that Barnard had used to such great political advantage in the revival of the common school in that state, was an easy matter compared with the collection of data from remote sources across the nation. Barnard could achieve little in the latter respect, for not only was the mail slow, but Barnard did not even know in most cases who the state agent was with whom he should be corresponding. For this reason, the statistical collection activity was limited to the conduct of two studies during his 3 years of office. One was a study of education in the District of Columbia, which he was able to carry out in much the same way as he had carried out the Connecticut and Rhode Island studies, and the other was a report on technical instruction.

Barnard did envision that a central educational agency should have an important role in disseminating general information about education. He took steps towards doing this by including discussion of interesting educational materials in the annual reports of his office. These reports attracted widespread interest, and far more interest than any statistical analyses that he ever produced. He had expected Congress to pass resolutions calling for reports on particular aspects of education and educational improvement, perhaps expecting requests for reports of the kind that Horace Mann had produced while he was secretary to the Board of Education of Massachusetts, but such requests never came. After only 3 years in office, Barnard tendered his resignation. One suspects that he was a disappointed man. The techniques of social change that he had used so successfully in Connecticut and Rhode Island were simply not effective at the federal level. His great legacy to what was first called the Department of Education, and which rapidly acquired the name of the Bureau of Education, was to set an intellectual standard for the reports of the bureau which was steadfastly maintained for the following 50 years. These annual reports of the commissioners, except for the statistical sections, represent some of the finest educational literature of their time. Insofar as one goal of Barnard was to produce a professional literature of education, his influence on the subsequent activities of the Bureau of Education was one way in which he achieved that goal. Of course, the *American Journal of Education* was another.

The statistical collection of data which Barnard also believed to be of vital importance for the development of the common school was later incorporated into the activities of the Bureau by his successor, John Eaton, though the statistics thus collected never had the dramatic effect on both legislation and on public opinion that they had had in Connecticut or, for that matter, in Massachusetts during the period of influence of Horace Mann.

HORACE MANN AND THE NEW ERA OF EDUCATIONAL MANAGEMENT

For every American who knows the name of Henry Barnard there are probably 10, or even 100, who know the name of Horace Mann. Both men were equally well known in the educational circles of their day and were viewed as making very similar and comparable contributions, but the name of Horace Mann stands out clearly in the pages of history while that of Henry Barnard remains embedded in the matrix of historical events. Both men, perhaps, deserve equal recognition, but Horace Mann was able to do one thing that few can do which will keep his name long alive. He was able to produce a new and outstanding literature on education that bears his name. That literature is filled with elegant, and often beautiful, statements that are widely quoted and which often have the quality of a rallying cry to a great cause. Generations of the future will continue to find inspiration in some of his famous words. Who is not stirred by the thought he expressed in his Commencement Address to Antioch College in 1859, "Be ashamed to die until you have won some victory for humanity." Mann was to die a few months later. He must surely have recognized that he had already won a great victory for humanity.

The legacy of Mann's ideas, embodied in an elegant literature of education that bears his name, has made him the most famous of all American educators. Even in his day he was known throughout Europe, and particularly in France where there was a continuing comparison between the ideas underlying the American and French revolutions. There is even a biography of Horace Mann written by a Frenchman (Compayré, 1907) in French and quite widely known among French students. Horace Mann was seen in Europe not only as the great educational reformer of his age, but as the embodiment of the ideas that formed the foundation of the American Revolution.

Horace Mann had a career that closely paralleled Barnard's both in circumstances and time, though Horace Mann was the junior by 15 years. They were most similar in the middle years of their careers when both became the champion of the common school. Mann did not have the advantages of an easy youth and an educated home as Barnard had. He was born on a farm in Franklin, Massachusetts, in 1796. He often spoke in later life of the harsh physical conditions of farm work in his boyhood and with gladness that the days of his youth were gone. There was no joy of living in his work on the farm, and even less in his leisure when he was exposed for long hours to the preachings of the local minister. In church he heard Calvinistic threats that eternal torment was to be the lot of most of those in the congregation who failed to live up to the stern Puritan standards. The later humanistic views of Mann are in such contrast with extreme Calvinism that one wonders how he managed to shake off the fear of eternal damnation that he heard from the pulpit week after week. Perhaps the picture of eternal damnation was so overwhelmingly sickening that this led him to construct a picture in which all humans were to be perfected through education. It took him years of his early maturity to shake off the paralyzing pall of Calvinism, and in many ways he never did completely succeed in doing this.

Mann entered school at a time when the schools of New England were at their lowest ebb. The public support given the schools by the Puritans had long waned. The so-called school year was rarely as long as 3 months. Books were few. The *New England Primer* was widely used. Few children ever learned to write easily with the awkward quill pen, and the slate was the common piece of equipment. Mann was fortunate, though, in another respect. The town of Franklin, where Mann was raised, had been named after Benjamin Franklin, and in return for the honor Benjamin Franklin had provided the town with a library of 116 books. The collection left much to be desired, perhaps because Franklin himself had not participated in the choice. Nevertheless, the young Mann waded through the odd collection of sermons, laws, and biographies. His education would have finished at 16 had it not been for the fact that one of the villagers, generally considered a ne'er-do-well, found time to teach young Horace Greek and Latin, and a Baptist minister who lived several miles away taught him arithmetic and geometry. These were essential subjects for entering Brown University.

Instruction in Brown University at that time was much the same as instruction had been in universities throughout the medieval era. The important task of the student was to memorize the text and to be able to recite it with precision. This was the system of instruction that had been first initiated in the University of Paris in the tenth century. However, the one area in which Mann did receive useful training was in writing and oratory. Even if the program was not the most stimulating, at least it provided a way of escape from the dismal, routine toil of the farm.

At Brown University in the early 1800's, the president of the institution knew each student personally, often inviting students over to his house. President Messer came to know Mann well and was impressed with him to the point that, on graduation, Messer offered Mann a position as tutor in the university. Mann accepted the position with some misgivings. He was not sure that his calling was that of a teacher, and yet in the classroom he must have been an impressive figure, tall and elegant and with a remarkable command of the English language. But the satisfactions of teaching were not enough for him, and after 2 years he abandoned teaching for law. He was not to become immersed in the problems of teaching for another 15 years.

Mann attended the first American law school at Litchfield, Connecticut. What today we would call a simulated courtroom was a central part of the training of young lawyers at Litchfield, and Mann found that pleading cases in the courtroom was a life that he loved. In later years, when Mann chose to leave the courtroom and a very profitable law practice for his work on the reform of schools, many wondered how he could ever have made that decision. It must have been a difficult decision for him to make. In 1824 he was admitted to the bar.

The study of the law is an entree to many fields, and Mann used it accordingly. In 1827 he was elected to the Massachusetts House of Representatives, where he remained in office for 6 years, and then in 1833 was elected to a 4-year term in the senate, where he served as president of the senate for his last 2 years. In those days, sessions of the state legislatures were short and occupied only a few weeks, so most of his time was devoted to the development of a successful law practice.

The decade following his admission to the bar was one which saw the development of the humanitarian strain in Mann's personality that was the central force behind his great contribution to society. Although his early contact with religion in Franklin had led him to see religion as providing an ugly picture of the nature of the human, a picture that Mann would not accept, his later contact with the growing movement of

Unitarianism made him realize that some religious views concerning the nature of the human were compatible with his own. He saw in humanity the seeds of goodness that had to be brought to full fruit. His own goodness seems to have been projected onto the rest of the world.

In the state legislature, Mann's first contribution was as a lawyer. The house of representatives was concerned with rewriting the statutes of the state which were in a condition of chaos. Laws had been revised, changed, modified, and amended so often that a state of such chaos existed that even the lawyers could not agree among themselves as to what the law was on a particular issue. Mann wanted to give the laws back to the people and to have a set of statutes that the common man could understand. One of the great goals of the common school and public education in Massachusetts had been the understanding of the law. The actions of the legislature had made it impossible for the citizen to achieve this objective. Mann did suceed in bringing clear and precise language to the new code, but the codes of law have remained, to the present day, such that they can hardly be understood even by lawyers. The direction of writing clear laws initiated by Mann was not followed by his successors, but he was rightly proud of the small step he had taken to make the laws more understandable to the people.

A second important activity of Mann in the legislature was to improve the lot of the insane. In those days, persons whose mental illness led to wild behavior were typically incarcerated in prisons, which were miserable, unsanitary, and badly run establishments. Except for the few who came from wealthy families and who could be taken care of privately, there was no place in which such individuals could receive care. Mann headed a committee in the state legislature that proposed to set aside money for the development of an institution for such hapless souls. The committee even went further and proposed that, within the new institutions, provision be made for the medical treatment of the insane. The latter was a radical move, for the prevailing opinion still was that the insane were possessed by the devil. Mann persuaded the legislature to provide the money for the building of such a hospital for 130 patients. His hope that the disturbed behavior of the patients would yield to medical treatment was beyond anything that could be achieved in his time, but it required the spirit of hopefulness embodied in the work of Mann that ultimately led to the reality of effective treatment of the insane.

Most memorable of all Mann's accomplishments in the eyes of posterity was the introduction of an act described as *An Act Relating to Common Schools*, which was passed in 1837. This act was passed 2 years before the Connecticut legislature, under the guidance of Henry Barnard, passed a similar law. Barnard must surely have been aware of Mann's legislation. Certainly Mann must have been influenced by his memories of the miserable days in his brief schooling in Franklin. The act included a number of important provisions. One was the establishment of a school board for the state. The board was required to appoint a secretary. The secretary, under the direction of the board, was to *collect information concerning the efficiency of the schools, and should diffuse information on the most successful methods of instruction to all those interested in education in the state.* The board was also required to prepare an annual report concerning ways in which the common schools of the state could be improved.

What the act proposed was a new management system for the schools of Massachusetts, but it was not a management system that was to be in any way dictatorial. The approach was to be rational and empirical. This was a vast step forward from the previous informal and unprofessional manner of supervising the schools, which involved no more than an occasional visit from the local minister who would make comments on such matters as whether the creed was being properly taught. Ministers rarely commented much on matters other than the theological. Certainly ministerial supervision had done nothing to raise the standards of school buildings above those of slums. The new act called for the collection of information on *all* aspects of the school.

When Mann was offered the secretaryship of the board of education, he was reluctant to accept the offer. Already in his early 40's, he had had little contact with education except through his own schooling. At this point in his life he does not seem to have been aware of the literature that existed related to educational reform. Apart from his own ignorance of education, of which he seems to have been aware, he felt some reluctance in giving up a successful career both as a lawyer and a state senator, for in both of these he had established an outstanding reputation. We do not know quite what reasons led Mann to finally accept the secretaryship, but surely his own sad experiences in school in Franklin must have been an important factor. The deep urge that had developed in him to perform some act that would contribute to the good of humanity must surely have led him to see that the reform of the common school was a place where "a victory for humanity" could be achieved.

After his decision was publicly announced, most of his friends described it as a foolish one. Only the great Unitarian minister William Ellery Channing rejoiced that Mann had decided to give his life to education, at great personal sacrifice. One suspects that personal sacrifice was no more appreciated in those days than it is today. The satisfaction of the humanitarian reformer is not understood by those who seek success in very material terms, and particularly one who sets out to provide for the next generation and not the contemporary one.

As a first step towards preparing himself for his new career, Mann went back to Franklin and read everything he could on education. We do not know what he read, but he surely must have encountered Joseph Neef's description of Pestalozzi's school in Switzerland. He spent most of the summer in Franklin preparing for his new career, and then set out for a trip across the state to visit schools and to talk with those in the communities interested in education. Such a trip is hard to visualize today since it must have been undertaken partly by coach, partly on horseback, and partly on any boat with a crew willing to take a passenger on board.

Mann must have made some provision for his office to collect data, for when he returned in mid-November, to Boston, he found a mass of material awaiting his analysis. The schools had been asked to submit information on attendance, budgets, and qualifications and numbers of teachers. Though Mann had understood rationally that such data were essential for the reform of the common school, he still hated the task of compiling statistics, which he had to do himself, and by hand. He was much more at ease with ideas about education than with tables of numbers. Yet he learned to use statistics to good advantage. In later years, when he sought to establish school libraries, he found statistics invaluable for obtaining support for his plans. School statistics were political necessities which would tell the politicians and the public facts that Mann knew to be true from personal experience. In his most famous of all contributions, the 12 annual reports of the Secretary of the Board of Education, statistics are used, but sparsely throughout. Mann may well have thought that the matters to be considered in the 12 annual reports were vastly more important than any facts that could be reduced to statistical tables. He was right.

In his 12 annual reports, Mann identified for the first time, and in a comprehensive fashion, all of the central problems of education. Generations of research workers have focused their attention on the problems that Mann identified. Mann recognized that all of the problems he raised would be difficult to solve, and he understood that all one could expect was progress towards their solution and that even a small amount of progress could make an enormous difference to the well-being of the next generation. The reports also embodied the vital new idea that education was valuable not because it opened up avenues for the salvation for the soul, but because it enabled humanity to achieve a whole new standard of living in the present world. Later on in his career, Mann attempted to collect data to show that education had a pragmatic value and that its success could be measured in economic terms. This was an advanced thought in an age when economics had not yet been conceived as a science and in which the only measurements made of psychological dimensions were undertaken by quite obscure people in German laboratories.

Although Horace Mann is remembered as a great humanitarian influence on education and as the champion of the common school, his impact was also great in the development of an empirical approach to education. He shares with Barnard the origination of the idea of collecting information systematically about what was going on in education and then using that information in educational planning. In this respect,

Horace Mann was the co-founder of educational research. There is a wide gap between the approach of the empiricist and that of the modern research worker, but a modern scientific approach to the solution to educational problems grows out of the simpler empirical approach.

The famous annual reports of Horace Mann as Secretary to the Board of Education of the Commonwealth of Massachusetts demonstrate his understanding of the need for an empirical approach to many educational problems. Some of his reports even describe actual experiments that were undertaken in the schools. Of course, the empirical approach does not have the sophistication of a modern experiment and the presentation of the findings often calls for an act of faith on the part of the reader, for they are often incomplete, but the approach of Horace Mann was a giant step towards the development of a research approach to education. He can also be considered as the founder of the comparative approach to educational research, obtaining facts and information about education in different countries and attempting to compare outcomes with procedures. Although such research lacks modern statistical sophistication, one cannot help wondering whether Mann, with his primitive methods but brilliant powers of observation, may have been able to extract more useful information from his comparative studies than some of his successors who have conducted many international studies of education with advanced statistical methods.

Let us now take a look at Mann's annual reports. A brief summary of each of the first 6 of these reports will show the empirical approach that runs through his work with schools. Interspersed with his empirical approach is also an analytic approach to educational problems. It is sufficient for us to provide brief summaries of only the first 6 of the 12 annual reports to illustrate the radical thinking that Mann brought to education and what was essentially a research approach to problems.

First Annual Report, 1 January 1838

In the report, Mann outlined what he believed to be the main problem areas of education in Massachusetts. The first important problem was the distribution of schoolhouses and the architectural designs of these buildings. The second problem was that of having committeemen who would supervise the schools properly. These individuals had the function of selecting teachers and of supervising the school program. Mann believed that committees needed to do much more than they actually did. In particular, he thought that committees should protect the schools from unscrupulous book peddlers who tried to push worthless books.

Committeemen were also supposed to see that the children of the poor should be provided with books without charge, but Mann noted that they had been neglectful of this duty. Also, although committeemen were required by law to ensure that all children attended school, Mann presented data showing that of 177,000 children eligible to attend school in the 294 towns studied, only 111,000 attended school in winter and 94,000 in summer. In addition, committeemen were scolded by Mann for taking little interest in schools, and rarely visiting any classrooms. He suggested that they adopt the practice of making regular visits and pay special attention to meritorious work undertaken by pupils. Children, Mann argued, could not be expected to show much interest in education unless the adults in the community demonstrated that they held education in high esteem. Mann described the attitude of committeemen as reflecting "dormancy and deadness" (p. 43).

Thirdly, Mann believed that excellence in a school required that the parents and other members of the community become interested in their schools and visit them frequently. Mann reflected on the fact that the well-to-do often sent their children to private schools and showed no interest in public education and that this left a great gap in the school program. The poor, lacking any concept of a standard of excellence, might have no source from which to acquire that concept. This led Mann into a discussion of the financing of schools, with him commenting regretfully that the wealthy, because they sent their children to private schools, were not willing to finance schools adequately. Mann's one argument in favor of private schools was that they were preparing students who would grow up to be superior teachers in the common schools.

The fourth problem discussed by Mann was that of raising the level of competency of teachers. The law in the Commonwealth of Massachusetts required that teachers manifest a whole range of virtues which were believed basic to the preservation of a republican form of government. Mann believed that the teacher should have these traits in order to be able to pursue a profession which involved "the most difficult of all arts, and the profoundest of all sciences" (p. 58). Mann added to the list of important qualifications of the teacher that of understanding the development of the child, surely an idea in advance of his time.

Second Annual Report, 26 December 1838

The second report returns again to the problem of poor school buildings and the effect of the buildings on the health of pupils. Mann cited an experiment undertaken by a physician who kept health records on the pupils from two schools in similar neighborhoods. One of the school buildings was dry and well-ventilated, and the other was damp and stuffy. In the inadequate building, four times as many children were sick and there was "seven times the amount of sickness" (p. 32) as in the good building. Mann was cautious in drawing conclusions, but suggested that the experiment be repeated elsewhere.

Teacher training is a central issue in this report. In large cities such as Boston, weekly lectures were given to teachers, but Mann was interested in the establishment of normal schools for the training of teachers.

In this report, Mann began to address himself to problems of curriculum. He urged teachers to differentiate between children who, in reading, manage only to say the words and children who both read and understand. He blamed what he called "unintelligent reading" partly on teachers but more on the selection of the materials read. Mann stressed that intelligent reading is much more important than fluent reading. Although Mann deplored the inability of the younger generation to spell, he did not view it as the same calamity as being unable to read intelligently.

In this report, Mann expounded a theory of learning which is not too far from a modern theory. He pointed out that the early years are those in which the child masters fundamental conceptions of the world. He stated that knowledge is not impressed on the passive mind of a child, but is reached for by an active learner. Knowledge is not annexed, but is "assimilated." Development is by growth and organization and "not by accretion" (p. 44). Thus, all teaching has to be related in some way to the effort of the learner. Then Mann said, "The first requisite is the existence in his mind of a desire to learn" (p. 45).

Mann proposed a complete theory of language acquisition which includes reading. Mann proposed that reading be started with word recognition rather than with letter recognition. In addition, Mann questioned whether the learning of letter names does anything except confuse, but he believed that the letter sounds should be learned. Mann suggested how phonetics should be taught as a part of reading instruction. Mann discussed at length the use of the dictionary, and deplored the memorization of dictionary definitions and even the use of dictionaries, but noted that words should be learned through their use. Words can be used to build representations of perfect worlds to inspire the pupil.

The second report is an extraordinary analysis of the problems involved in constructing and teaching particular curricula. Most of the problems raised in the report have been investigated, but there are definite answers to few of them. Much of modern educational research finds its origins in the second report of Horace Mann.

Third Annual Report, 26 December 1839

This report is a discussion of the whole problem of storing information in libraries, disseminating information, and the development of school libraries. Mann pointed out that New England had well-stocked libraries in concentrated population areas, but that this meant that most of the population had no access to libraries. Although the public library was of great service, it could not be of service to the widely scattered public schools. With his usual thoroughness, Mann included in his report a survey of the location and size of libraries in Massachusetts. Mann proposed that the problem be solved by the establishment of school libraries with well-selected books, though the selection of books presented a real problem. Mann suggested that what were needed were encyclopedic works, but that these were not available. Mann deplored the fact that itinerant booksellers flooded the small towns with cheap literature of fiction, some of it dealing with fortune-telling and dreams. In the case of one itinerant bookseller, Mann found only two or three volumes that he would put in the hands of a child. The rest would be described today as trash, and some also as obscene. The books in the public libraries, even if they had become widely available, would not have satisfied the needs of pupils.

Mann argued that in a developing country (he did not use the term), knowledge was vital to all if the resources of the country were to be utilized, and without books suitable for children there would be no building of knowledge. Mann viewed a productive community as one in which the individuals would be guided by knowledge.

Mann believed that children should have access to literature related to the controversies involved in the American Revolution and the ideas underlying the Republic. He saw a place for the study of the lives of great men, but he deplored the emphasis on military heroes. He thought all children should have access to natural history, physiology, and anatomy.

Mann argued that state money should support school libraries; otherwise, the wealthy districts would have libraries and the others would not. He asked the board of education to draw up a list of books suitable for a school library. One should add that Mann had in mind a list of perhaps 50-100 books and not the thousands that would occupy a modern school library. The State of Massachusetts had already endowed two college libraries, but Mann argued that libraries in the colleges benefited few but the common school libraries would benefit all.

Fourth Annual Report, 13 January 1841

This is a profound document covering a great range of topics. It is of particular importance in that it includes the first systematic study of the organization of education. Mann collected data on the size and distribution of schools and attempted to show that there were roughly 50 percent more schools than were needed, because the schools were not distributed across the state in an efficient manner. Also, Mann claimed that the data showed that there were too many small schools. Mann believed that there should be rather large classes and he deplored the existence of schools in which a teacher taught only a few pupils. Mann used the terms "inefficiency" and "unproductiveness" (p. 32) and, indeed, the report has a modern atmosphere to it in terms of the concepts used.

In addition, Mann included an analysis of public expenditures on education showing that the allocation of funds was such that the maximum good was not achieved for the people of the state. The school fund was divided into a portion tagged for private schools and another portion tagged for the public common schools. The private school funds were demonstrated to be inefficiently spent in that the average size of such schools was only 22 pupils. The section on the analysis of expenditures is filled with data reflecting Mann's entire new approach to the governance of schools.

The next section of the report is less research-oriented, and it could not be otherwise because it relates to the training and selection of teachers. Mann's analysis has much that is modern in its ideas. However, the teacher had to function differently in the early Commonwealth of Massachusetts' schools than the teacher has to today; because of the lack of books and libraries, the teacher was a source of knowledge. Mann listed what he believed to be the necessary qualifiations of teachers. These included knowledge of the common school subjects. In addition, Mann made an excellent analysis of what he called aptness to teach or the art of teaching. Embedded in the art of teaching is the art of diagnosing the source of a pupil's difficulty. Also within the concept of aptness for teaching is the art of explaining and the techniques of arranging subject matter in an effective order. High aptness for teaching requires a large repertoire of ideas and approaches. A third part of the report involves the management, government, and discipline of the school. Mann included in this category such obvious matters as discipline and the maintenance of control over the school. Earlier in the same report, Mann cited some cases of unbelievably bad forms of administration. In one classroom he visited, the ages of the pupils ranged from 2½ to 25 years, but they were all expected to follow the same rules. Mann saw a great need for a system of flexible rules in running such a school, a statement that is obvious but needed to be said. The fourth section discusses the teacher as a model of courtesy and good personal habits. The fifth section of the report deals with books and the problem of selecting them, and the sixth section with libraries and school apparatus.

A further section of the report deals with a quite complex analysis of data on attendance. Mann deduced from the data that the average child who could attend school for the 12-year period from age 4 to 16 managed to be absent from school for about 5 years. Mann aso reflected that those parents who sent their children least often to school were most likely to complain about poor progress. Mann had advice to offer teachers on how to maintain attendance. In this connection, he discussed the problem of disruptive pupils whose behavior resulted in the closing of many schools.

The latter is a topic to which Mann returned in a later report, armed with considerable statistical data. At this point in his career, he was inclined to pin the blame on the adult community, which placed too little value on school learning and whose influence led scholars to feel contempt for the school.

Fifth Annual Report, 1 January 1842

This report is of particular significance in that it attempted to demonstrate, through research, that the education provided by the common school had great economic value to the community. Mann attempted to collect data to support this hypothesis by writing to business men who had many employees, asking them to compare the productivity and quality of the most educated compared with the least educated. Modern research workers could criticize the way in which Mann collected data and also the relation of the conclusions to the data, but the study represents a notable beginning of research by one who managed to find problems of the greatest significance and then approach them by empirical means. Mann argued that good schooling produces, above all, intelligent and disciplined behavior and that such behavior is essential for working effectively on almost any job. Mann also presented the arguments that intelligent workers can slowly improve equipment over generations and that these slow improvements gradually increase economic productivity. He pointed out that the printing press, the power loom, and the steam engine did not come into existence at one point in time, but took many generations of intelligent workers to evolve. An intelligent and educated work force was necessary for the economic development of the United States.

This report, like the others, covers many topics which cannot be examined in detail here. There is a long section on the training of teachers, and another important section on the inequality of education in the different towns.

Sixth Annual Report, 3 January 1843

This report, perhaps more than any of the others, reflects Mann's research orientation. The early part of the report presents data on death rates in different groups, from which the inference is made that the high death rate of the less educated groups is due to their lack of education. The argument is then presented that a knowledge of physiology and a program of physical education would ward off much of the disease and malaise that afflicts individuals. Mann found support for his thesis in a series of letters from physicians. He then presented a curriculum in the area of physiology and health, worked out in considerable detail. The document is remarkable in that physiology had barely become established as a science, but was nearer to being a body of folklore handed down from one generation of physicians to the next. The report was written only 10 years after William Beaumont had published his classic and original work entitled *Experiments and Observations on the Gastric Juice and the Physiology of Digestion.* Mann must surely have known of Beaumont's extraordinary work in order to write what was then an up-to-date curriculum in the area of nutrition and digestion. The section on the physiology of the nervous system brings out the emerging knowledge of sensory and motor nerves and the dependence of knowledge on the inputs and outputs through these systems. Broca had not yet undertaken his classic work on the cerebral cortex, so little is said about the brain itself. Mixed in with the physiology of the human body is a considerable body of folklore of the time, which was only slowly removed from books on the subject. One may reflect that the mixture of knowledge and folklore that Mann presented may be like the mixture of folklore and knowledge presented today in books on psychology for educators, and we cannot yet tell what is knowledge and what is folklore.

The reports that followed covered a great variety of problems. They cover, among other topics, a discussion of the schools Mann visited abroad. Particularly impressive were the schools in Scotland in which the children seemed filled with enthusiasm for education. He found the curriculum of the Prussian schools carefully planned in terms of ideas similar to those that he had expressed.

The Later School Reports

Later reports dealt with problems of school funding and problems related to the staffing of schools. Mann deplored the inferior role assigned to women in society and took steps to introduce more women as teachers in schools. He believed that women were a particularly fine moral influence on children. From an administrative standpoint, women were an advantage over men as teachers, in that the men were likely to drop their teaching jobs as soon as the spring weather improved enough for them to go out and work the fields. Throughout the later reports, Mann provides data, year by year, on the increased number of women teachers.

A short section of the eighth report provides and discusses data on the reasons for schools being closed down, or "breaking up" to use his term, because of disruption. Teacher incompetency seems to have been the main factor, but rebellious behavior on the part of pupils was also sometimes the cause. At the time of his first annual report, between 300 and 400 schools had been closed down in a single year, and at least half of these closings were the result of insubordination of scholars. The number of closings was large and had involved about 10 percent of the common schools in the Commonwealth. By the time of the eighth annual report, the number of closings in the school year had declined to near 50, an enormous improvement, and few of these were due to pupil rebellion. Mann urged that the qualifications of teachers be improved so that incompetency of teachers would cease to be a cause of school closings.

The later reports in the series provide considerable data on the development of school libraries, and the distribution of funds provided by the Commonwealth for that purpose. Mann had his own ideas about what such libraries should contain, and envisioned them as sources of encyclopedic knowledge. In actual fact the typical school library, of less than 200 books, contained little in the way of general sources of knowledge, and much that was suitable only for adults.

The eleventh annual report is of particular interest here in that it presents one of the first opinion surveys on record. Mann sent out a letter to a number of people asking them how the moral influence of the school could be extended. The letter was long and expanded at length on how the school could impart virtue. He asked a number of specific questions to which he sought answers from the learned men to whom it was sent. The replies of the recipients of the letter were published in full and were almost unanimous in their recommendations, that children could acquire virtue if they would attend school regularly and if they had as teachers the kind of people who could be of moral influence. One should note that Mann distinguished morality from religion. Morality led to responsible behavior. Religion led to understanding doctrine and the formal steps to be taken to achieve salvation.

This discussion of the famous annual reports brings out the extraordinary range of data collection in which Mann engaged. What this brief discussion cannot bring out is the skillful way in which he used the data as a foundation for the formulation of policies.

Other Publications

The annual reports were widely distributed. Several thousand copies of each were printed and circulated free of charge. In addition, Horace Mann founded *The Common School Journal*, in which the first 10 annual reports were reproduced in serialized form. *The Common School Journal* was described as a depository of state laws and state papers related to education, but it was much more. In addition to publishing the data around which Mann wrote most of his annual reports, the *Journal* also provided some quite remarkable discussions of teaching methods and also materials that teachers could use. There are articles in it concerning the best way to teach handwriting, and how to handle the transition from writing on a slate to writing on paper with a quill. Other articles provided lists of mispronounced words, and lists of words that are often misused. Particularly interesting are the articles on conversation as an auxiliary to education and on efficient ways to conduct recitation.

The Common School Journal was the only publication that in its day survived for any time, but it survived continuously for only 2 years after Mann relinquished its editorship when he resigned from the secretaryship. Its total life was 14 years. *The Connecticut School Journal*, the sole related publication in the field, had a longer but broken existence, from 1838 to 1866. In 1840 the latter journal was for a time declared out of existence, but resources were brought to resusitate it and it survived for another 14 years.

The Horace Mann Legacy

Most essays on Horace Mann stress his philosophy of education as his main gift to posterity, as shown in his writings and in his impact on the schools of Massachusetts. But there was another legacy that this chapter has stressed, namely, his empirical approach to the solution of educational problems. Although Horace Mann was a person of philosophical and literary disposition, he understood better than any of his predecessors the importance of solving problems through the collection of facts. In this transformation of the management of education into a fact-based enterprise, he led American education into a new age.

Horace Mann also understood the importance of collecting facts and using them, within a philosophical framework. For example, he collected facts about the causes of disruption and closing of schools not to lay blame, but to find out where the solution to the problem should be sought so that his ideal school could come into being. He was not interested in developing schools where harsh discipline prevailed, but schools in which there was an orderly progression of learning managed by well-trained teachers who could fascinate the pupils with what they were learning. Philosophy gave direction to his program for the schools, but the collection of empirical facts provided a way to achieve the goals set up by his philosophy.

Mann may not always have had the patience with statistics that the dedicated empiricist should have, but one can easily excuse him for this, for he had to conduct all of his empirical studies entirely by himself, even to the point of having to tabulate the data. He must have viewed the time spent in dull tabulating work as time taken away from his literary and philosophical pursuits. Yet he believed that his empirical studies of education were of importance, and he never abandoned the empirical approach.

There is, of course, a very long step from simple empirical studies to the scientific study of behavior in educational situations. Nevertheless, some of the seeds of educational research are found in the work of Horace Mann. From such beginnings, empirical research on educational problems slowly developed.

WILLIAM TORREY HARRIS--A LINK BETWEEN THE RESEARCHER AND EDUCATOR

William Torrey Harris (1835-1907), though living into the present century, made his most notable contributions in the nineteenth century. Although his active life places him in the last century, he was sufficiently junior in age to Henry Barnard and Horace Mann for him to have had access to the new emerging sciences of sociology and psychology. When Henry Barnard and Horace Mann were struggling to revive the common school in New England, the era of psychological research had hardly dawned, but when William Torrey Harris became United States Commissioner of Education in 1889, he was fully aware of the new emerging sciences in the social and behavioral areas, and set about to introduce these to both professional educators and teachers and to those intellectuals who were interested in the problems of education. Harris not only had the knowledge necessary to do this, but he also had a medium through which this knowledge could be disseminated. The Annual Reports of the Commissioner of Education, which had been established by Henry Barnard as among the most valuable documents in education, continued to maintain their prestige throughout the administrations of Commissioners John Eaton and Nathaniel H. R. Dawson. Harris had a well-designed system for disseminating ideas that he used to great advantage throughout his term as commissioner.

The early life of William Torrey Harris would make him an unlikely candidate for the position of one of the most influential men of his century in the field of education. He was born in 1835, a generation later than Henry Barnard and Horace Mann, and represents a transition from the thinking of Barnard and Mann to the thinking that was generated by the new emerging experimental and empirical psychology. Harris' time in history made it possible for him to make a unique contribution, which he might not have been able to make if he had lived earlier or later.

Harris was born on a farm in Connecticut and spent his early years toiling in the fields and in the farm buildings. He attended the village school at about the time when Henry Barnard was attempting to bring reform to public education, but the schools as yet had not felt the impact o Barnard's work. The school year was just a few months long, and more emphasis was placed on punctuality and conformity than on intellectual development. Although the Harris family recognized young William as a scholar, the school, apparently, did not. Later he went to an urban school where conditions were even worse. Then, beginning in 1848, he started the round of New England academies, spending some time at five different academies in 5 years. This was not an unusual academic career at the time. Harris' biographer, Kurt Leidecker (1946), described how Harris had little use for the set curriculum of each academy but managed to obtain an education by undertaking studies on his own. His initiative in this respect took him too far on one occasion. He was experimenting with a percussion cap of a firecracker which exploded and resulted in the loss of an eye.

The academies gave him the knowledge of Latin and Greek necessary for admission to college, and in due time he entered Yale. There he spent 2 years studying the standard curriculum of the college of that period, consisting of Greek, Latin, a smattering of mathematics, and a little history. He struggled through a third year of similar offerings and then left without graduating. He stated as his reason for leaving that Yale had already taught him all it had to offer. In this he was correct, for in his final year he began to branch out for himself, exploring areas for which the college had no offerings. Later, after Harris had won some national recognition, Yale magnanimously bestowed upon him an honorary master's degree. Then in 1888 he was given the equivalent of a bachelor's degree and, still later, in 1895 at the height of Harris' career, he was awarded by Yale an honorary LL.D. An extraordinary turn of events for a college dropout.

As a dropout, Harris had to find some occupation that would earn him a living. In his last year at Yale he had become interested in phrenology, a set of ideas which had also fascinated Horace Mann. Phrenology was an attempt to read the character of the individual from the bumps on the surface of the skull. Phrenology towards the middle of the nineteenth century was not viewed as it is today. It had a certain scientific respectability, largely because of the indirect support offered by the work of physicians such as Paul Broca. Nobody questioned the soundness of the general theory, though there was controversy concerning which particular area of the brain corresponded to which faculty. Harris was quite convinced that phrenology offered a genuine means of determining the strengths and weaknesses of the individual and saw it as a way of earning a livelihood. He founded a phrenological institute which offered services and consultation, but from the financial standpoint the institute was a complete failure.

Then he became interested in what was at that time known as phonographic writing -- today known as shorthand. Harris was intellectually intrigued by the whole idea, and entered into a partnership with a Robert S. Moore to establish an institute for the teaching of shorthand. His partner turned out to be a doubtful asset, and had a penchant for not keeping his commitments. The bad partnership may have made no difference, for not a single student enrolled for instruction. The business was another failure.

The year of failure in business in St. Louis was not a year lost, for Harris, perhaps while waiting for the clients that never arrived, managed to read enormous quantities of literary and philosophical works. He read Shakespeare, Goethe, and Carlyle, sometimes deriving pleasure from their works as literature but often using them as starting points for philosophical inquiry. He also gained his first contact with such philosophers as Hegel and Fichte, about whom he was to become the world's leading authority of his time. He became active in the *Literary and Philosophical Society* of St. Louis, and be it noted that the term *philosophical* in that day referred to a great diversity of realms of knowledge including the scientific. Equipment in schools for undertaking basic experiments in physics was referred to as philosophical apparatus and advertised for sale under that name. The term *philosophy* still carried its Greek connotation, meaning "a love of knowledge." The *Literary and Philosophical Society* discussed every current topic from phrenology to anthropology. The age was one in which a true lover of knowledge could master all there was and hope to discuss it intelligently. The genuine savant was a generalist rather than a specialist, and Harris loved the role of the generalist. His personal scholarship, developed under his own direction, was as broad as his formal training in academies and colleges had been narrow. He understood this contrast and, when he came to work in schools, he sought to make learning in schools the same kind of learning he had achieved through his own initiative.

It was almost by accident of fate that Harris came to work with schools. During his first year in St. Louis, he had taken a competitive examination to qualify him to teach. The examination was oral and given by the school board, as was customary in those days. He did not approach the idea of teaching with any relish. Leidecker, in his biography of Harris, stated that he found an entry in Harris' journal to the effect that he wished there were some other occupation he could pursue. Harris needed money and had no other choice. He was fortunate, though, that the school system he entered was one in advance of its day, even though it was a quite rigid and highly disciplined system. It did have the policy of promoting those teachers who managed to conduct their classes without the use of corporal punishment. Whatever misgivings he may have had about his capacity or disposition to teach must have been rapidly dispelled, for he soon acquired an outstanding reputation as a teacher, and a year and a half after his appointment he was promoted to principal. His quiet and genuine manner must have contributed to his success. Among the records available of Harris' career as a teacher are a number of letters written him by grateful pupils.

Harris kept a scrapbook related to his work as principal which shows that much of his work in the job inolved what were then considered to be the main tasks of a principal. He was much concerned with what today would be called *pupil evaluation*. He gave examinations, some of which were held publicly, and the whole community was invited for the occasion. Record-keeping in those days was also complicated, for only a relatively small percentage of children attended public school and these would come and go during the school year. The curriculum consisted of arithmetic, geography, history, reading, and writing. The problem he attacked first as a principal was the one which he himself as a pupil had once seen to be the main barrier to pupil learning, namely, the rigid discipline system which emphasized obedience to rules rather than self-development and learning. His impact seems to have been limited by the overwhelming amount of administrative detail that he was required to handle. Nevertheless, he did manage to go out and visit other schools and bring back information about innovations he observed.

While Harris was principal, he heard of an attempt to revise the English orthography, in order to make it a phonetic system. He was able to introduce the revised system of orthography into his school for the purpose of teaching reading. When he later became superintendent of schools in St. Louis, the use of the system was extended to the entire school system where it was used for nearly a decade. The reasons why the system was abandoned are not clear. There were no very useful ways of evaluating the system in those days, except through the collection of the judgments of teachers.

In 1867, at the age of 31, Harris was appointed to the position of assistant superintendent, a position in which he was first able to demonstrate his social skills and his ability to bring together the parties in disputes. Superintendent of Schools Ira Dvioll was a sick man and left to his subordinate many of the thorny situations that had to be negotiated with the school board. He initiated a study of the conditions related to the teaching of reading, pleaded for making history a living and exciting enterprise, and proposed that geography be developed through the use of object lessons, and then he attempted to emphasize that education was not a matter of doing things to pupils, but rather a matter of encouraging the pupils to do things for themselves. Harris knew that this was the only way in which he had received an education, and he wanted all children to have the opportunity of learning for themselves. His skill in moving the educational system forward through positive leadership and positive ideas led to his being appointed as superintendent at the age of 35.

In this new position he changed the whole concept of school management, by permitting each school to innovate. Although the principals were held strictly accountable for the achievement of the pupils in their schools, the superintendent did not prescribe ways of achieving results. The central office was a tightly run hierarchy that worked closely with the board of education, which supported Harris. The public was not always as supportive, and Harris had to work hard to explain to the taxpayers why they should support what he believed to be the finest educational system in the country. Although he recognized the truth of the criticism that many who went through school could neither spell nor calculate, the many who had mastered these skills represented a great achievement. He could show, with statistics, that the actual proportion of children attending the public schools had increased during his administration, a sure recommendation for the meaningfulness of the school program. Like Barnard and Mann, he believed that the school was making a fundamental contribution to the development of democracy and, even further, to the development of humankind.

Like Mann, he believed that the collection of statistics and facts was of vital importance to the improvement of a school system. He collected a great deal of information informally through his frequent visits to schools, but he initiated a systematic method of data collection throughout the system. Unlike Mann, who found school statistics dreary necessities, Harris loved compilations of figures. Simple duplicating machines had just been invented, called *heliographing machines*, and these Harris harnessed for use in collecting and distributing statistics.

Unlike a modern superintendent, Harris also spent some of his vast energy on the development of curricula. He himself developed a curriculum in physiology. He also wrote numerous short messages to teachers suggesting ways in which teaching could be improved. He held special programs for those teachers who had become apathetic and had lost interest in their work. He understood that the personal dedication and vigor of the teacher was a vital factor in sustaining the work and initiative of the pupils. During the depression of 1878, he admonished the teachers to watch for children who showed what today we would call *states of anxiety* and to do what they could to help these children. Such a relationship of teacher to child would have been unthinkable at the time when Harris himself had attended common school.

Harris' innovations in the schools included the introduction of courses in science which had generally been reserved in the past for colleges and universities. He also introduced art and instruction in drawing, to which many objected on the grounds that the activities were recreations. He justified these subjects on the grounds that school was not just preparation for the world of work, but preparation for life. Harris also sought to design education so that it made maximum use of pupil initiative, a component of responsibility. Harris opposed parents who wanted to give children a great amount of help with their homework, for he believed that this took responsibility away from the child. Like Horace Mann, he believed that the school was the very foundation of democracy, and that a democratic society must consist of individuals who showed initiative and took responsibility for their own behavior. Later in this book, we shall see how this view of the school and the pupil has been slowly eroded through the dissemination of a scientific concept of the human that allows no place for personal responsibility.

During the period when Harris was assistant superintendent and later superintendent, he began to write prolifically and to devote time to the study of philosophy. He was not alone in this pursuit in St. Louis. He gathered around him a small discussion group which, through his initiation, founded the St. Louis Philosophical Society. Once the society had been established, Harris proposed that it publish the *Journal of Speculative Philosophy*. The journal did appear, but only because Harris was willing to pay for the publication. The formation of the society and the publication of the journal did more than just stir up interest in philosophy in St. Louis, which it did, but it gave the United States stature as a culture that fostered philosophical thought. This was a new development in that the orientation of the early settlers had been theological and had made philosophical exploration a virtual taboo.

The Philosophical Society gave Harris a sounding board for his ideas, and the *Journal of Speculative Philosophy* provided him with a channel through which he could publish and reach a wider circle of philosophers. During the years 1867-1869, he published 14 articles in the journal, including some important analyses of the work of Hegel, on which he became a recognized authority. Hegel had a particular fascination for him as an administrator, for he could see in Hegel's dialectic a model of how administrative problems should be solved. Conflicting solutions had to be brought together and fused into new and effective solutions that would satisfy all the different points of view.

A list of the Harris publications during the first 5 years of his life as a writer reflect the enormous diversity of his interests and competencies. Apart from the publications related to Hegel, he published papers on textbooks, their uses and abuses, which today would be described as papers on the design of the curriculum; articles on Pestalozzianism; and a contribution to physics which provided the first mathematical account of the behavior of the gyroscope. As one goes through his list of writings, one notes that each new year seems to bring a new interest as well as an expansion of previous interests. Thus, in 1870 he began to write on libraries and book classification. Then, in 1871, he published an article on the prevention of crime. Thus, his list of publications each year became longer as he added new topics and still made contributions related to the old.

His educational writings helped to identify many of the persistent problems of education that have been the topics for research for as long as a century. He wrote, for example, on the phonetic system for teaching reading. He wrote on the supervision of teaching in the schools, on the reasons for the listlessness of school children, on the reasons for the early withdrawal from school, on the promotion and classification of pupils, on the relation of the public schools to the American colleges, on suspension rather than corporal punishment, on culture and discipline, on teaching history, on educational psychology, on moral education, on the functions of Latin and Greek in education, and on methods of pedagogical inquiry which was one of the first works on educational research. In addition, he wrote textbooks for children including a set of readers which must have had to compete with the McGuffey readers. Undoubtedly, his readers were a product of the most careful analysis of how the books were to function, for every piece of Harris' work showed this same meticulous analysis, but he probably did not proceed by the empirical method of McGuffey, which involved trying out the materials with groups of children.

Many of Harris' educational articles were addresses given to teachers, teacher organizations, and organizations of administrators. He was a frequent visitor to the annual conventions of the National Education Association, where he gave some memorable addresses.

Harris had an enormous appetite for knowledge, and this appetite had to be satisfied through libraries. Harris made sure that the public library that came under the board of education was well stocked. Money was not always available for books, but Harris managed to find donors of collections of books, and admission fees to public lectures helped make up for a lack of funds. Harris himself accumulated books in his own personal library. When he died, his collection had over 12,000 volumes.

By the year 1880, Harris had become known as the leading philosopher in the United States. He was, of course, the leading authority on public education, too, but his role as a philosopher had given him international eminence. He felt a need to expand further his influence as a philosopher and in 1880 wrote a letter of resignation to the board of education. The City of St. Louis recognized the extraordinary nature of the man who was about to leave them and gave him farewell receptions and speeches. More unusual recognition was a gift from his friends of a letter of credit for $1,000. This was a large sum, not far off 6 months of pay for a superintendent. In addition, a fund was raised to erect a sculpture of Harris in the public library. Due to some rather inept handling of the latter enterprise, the sculpture never came into existence, but a portrait was painted and installed. One can hardly imagine a modern superintendent receiving similar honors. None probably compares with Harris, but one wonders whether a school system today would recognize a Harris if one happened to be employed.

On leaving the school system, Harris first toured Europe, and then he returned to find a new role as a professional philosopher. In order to accomplish the latter, he aligned himself with the Concord Summer School of Philosophy which thrived for a 9-year period beginning in 1879. The school attracted individuals of philosophical disposition from all over the country. It also attracted ministers from many denominations and particularly from those denominations that were liberal enough to encourage philosophical explorations. The Concord School of Philosophy had a reputation far above that of any college or university in the country as a center for philosophical thought. Fortunately, the credit system had not been invented yet, so students flocked to partake of its offerings without bothering much about whether they would or would not receive academic credit for their work. The school had the organization of a college, with a dean and a director and an academic staff. Although most of the important series of lectures were given by the older men, the younger philosophers were also given a chance to be heard. The lectures of Harris were noted for their elegance and beauty as well as for the clarity with which ideas were presented. Leidecker relates that even those newspapers that sneered at all forms of intellectualism were always willing to publish any materials of Harris that he would let them publish. This did not mean that he was not criticized by the press, for philosophy in nineteenth-century America was widely viewed as a form of dilettantism. The people of that age, without knowing it, embraced pragmatism as a philosophy of life but, at the same time, rejected philosophy as an academic discipline.

A writer whose topic is William Torrey Harris is tempted to expand on his role as America's first internationally distinguished philosopher, but in the present context that is not the contribution which gives him a special place in the history of education. For this reason, we will skip lightly over his career as a philosopher and draw the reader's attention back to the further contribution that Harris made to the developing concept of public education. The final phase of Harris' career as an educator came when President Harrison was inaugurated in 1889. It was customary then, as it is today, for a new president to exercise his own choice of a commissioner of education and, of course, for all other high-level government offices. Nicholas Murray Butler, then professor of philosophy at Columbia University, suggested to the President that Harris be considered for the commissionership. Some weeks later, Francis W. Parker also urged the appointment of Harris. When Harris was interviewed by President Harrison, he confessed that he had little sympathy with Republican policies and that he had, in fact, not only voted for Grover Cleveland in the previous election, but had written articles supporting Cleveland's candidacy. After some thought and consultation, President Harrison magnanimously appointed Harris to the commissionership, believing, correctly, that the teachers and educational administrators of the country wanted him there. Harris was probably one of the few commissioners ever appointed who was widely known throughout the American educational world, and who was not only widely respected but had every right to be respected, for he was both an intellectual giant and a man of great skill in practical affairs.

In order to understand the special contribution that Harris made to the development of the Bureau of Education, one must begin by understanding the development of the Bureau from its inception to the time when Harris took office. From its beginning the Office of the Commissionership had been one of prestige.

The appointment of Henry Barnard to the Commissionership brought to the position one of the most distinguished figures in education of the time. His immediate plan for the Bureau was to develop an organization that would make available the best that had been thought and said about education and also provide statistics on the state of education. Although some have said that Henry Barnard was a failure as a commissioner in that he waited for Congress to act, and Congress never did, the professional climate of the office was well established by his commissionership, and the Bureau of Education became a great influence in raising the level of professional thought in education. The annual reports of the bureau, which were some of the most widely read and influential educational documents of their age, are a monument to Barnard's vision. One is tempted to compare these reports with those of more recent vintage, which must be placed among the most innocuous and trivial of government publications.

The work started by Barnard, with a staff of fewer than 10, was continued by his successor John Eaton, generally known as General Eaton. Eaton's military rank had been bestowed upon him as an honor for his work on behalf of the Negroes in Tennessee. His only real military service had been as a chaplain during a short period in the Civil War. He served for 2 years as a State Superintendent of Schools in Tennessee. Then, during Henry Barnard's last year as Commissioner of Education, in 1869, Eaton became Assistant Commissioner for Education in Washington. During that year he must have absorbed much of Barnard's philosophy of education, and he must have needed this grooming, for his previous contacts with education had been only with the State of Tennessee during the abnormal years of Reconstruction. Whatever deficiencies in knowledge he may have had when he arrived in Washington, he must have been a good student of Barnard, for when Barnard retired and Eaton took over the commissionership, he ran the office for 16 years much as Barnard would have liked to see it run.

An important contribution of Eaton was the development of the Bureau of Education as a center for the collection of statistics related to education. Eaton had an intuitive understanding of the significance of particular forms of data. The policies of data collection that he established continued to be used for decades after he left. Eaton was also able to expand the staff of the bureau to handle these data-collection functions which had to be undertaken without computers and without even simple calculators.

The work of Eaton in establishing the Bureau of Education as a central collection point for data, to help the Congress develop legislation related to education, was an extension of the idea of both Barnard and Mann that policies should be guided by empirical information. Eaton undertook on a national scale what Barnard and Mann had undertaken at the state level. This empirical approach was not replaced at all during the nineteenth century by the pragmatic approach. The difference between the two approaches should be noted. The empirical approach calls for the collection of facts before a policy decision is made. The pragmatic approach emphasizes the determination of whether policies work satisfactorily, after they are established. Eaton emphasized empiricism and careful planning, but machinery was not established for determining whether the new policies or laws were effective. The pragmatic approach to improvement in education came much later, after policy-makers came to realize that often what appeared to be well-designed policies had quite unexpected results. The need for evaluating policies in terms of their consequences then became apparent. One might, perhaps, also add that the pragmatic evaluation of policies, procedures, and practices also ran into difficulties later and failed to provide the guide to practice that it was expected to provide.

Eaton was a man of considerable distinction. His successor, Nathaniel Dawson, was not. Dawson's term lasted only 3 years, being brought to an end by the election of Harrison as President. Harris had the advantage of following a wholly undistinguished predecessor, and yet the office still carried some of the glory given it by its first and second officeholders.

Harris continued the activities of the Bureau related to the collection of statistics that Barnard had begun, and probably used the data collected to better advantage than any of his predecessors. Harris also expanded the activities of the Bureau into new areas. He recognized that knowledge was now emerging from the centers of learning of the Western world that had potential for changing educational practice, and he saw the Bureau as the bridge over which that knowledge could be carried to educators.

Harris had been well schooled in the classic works of Johann Friederich Herbart and was not willing to abandon the products of Herbart's keen intellectual analysis of what was involved in the learning of concepts, but he wanted to see this knowledge linked to that which was coming from the laboratories of the new generation of psychologists. In doing this, he paved the way for education to be influenced by the findings of the new emerging empirical science. Harris studied the modern literature in enormous quantities, and his reflections on it were both constructive and critical.

In his Commissioner's Report for the Year Ending June 30, 1894, Harris wrote a section of the report entitled "The Old Psychology and the New." In this article, Harris reflected on the contribution of what he called "the old psychology." Some of his descriptions of the old psychology are quite modern in that he takes the position that the philosophical discipline of logic describes the rational nature of the human. Harris understood that his generation must be indebted to those who had so ably described the rational nature of the human in antiquity. Furthermore,

Harris recognized the great significance of Kantian categories of experience. Harris understood, as some psychologists have not, that the analyses of philosophers of the past have provided an essential foundation for experimental psychology. Harris went on to argue that nature produces an animal and not a civilized human, but that the new sciences of physiology and experimental psychology would be able to help us understand that transition and, ultimately, exercise some control over it. Above all, these sciences must help us understand how the child develops from one who has a mechanical view of the world to one who has an ethical view, and one who moves from a condition of subservience in relation to others to a condition of self-activation. Laws of growth derived from empirical data were to be of the utmost importance in understanding these transitions.

The other articles that accompany the Commissioner's in the same annual report reflect the elements that Harris attempted to bring together. The Harris article was immediately followed by one by Hugo Münsterberg, who had just been brought to Harvard by William James to develop experimental psychology at that institution. Münsterberg later showed himself to be much more involved in the implications of psychology for teaching than in experimental psychology, so his comments are interesting. An important part of his article deals with the future role of psychology in relation to teaching. Münsterberg deplored, in strong terms, the "high tide of confusion and dilettan" (p. 438) produced by psychology in elementary school teachers. Münsterberg even went so far as to suggest that tact, sympathy, and interest in children were far more important attributes in teaching than an interest in psychology. He deplored the attempt to popularize the new experimental psychology for teachers, even suggesting that Aristotle had much more to offer. He understood, as Harris understood, that traditional psychology, whether in the form of associationism or logic or the more recent rational psychology of Herbart, had much to offer teachers in helping them conceptualize learning and knowledge.

Münsterberg did see three major contributions of the new psychology to teachers. First, he believed that the new experimental methods produced an important new area of knowledge with which teachers should be familiar as a part of their general education. He believed that teachers should be broadly educated individuals, capable of interacting with children on a wide variety of topics. Second, he believed that psychology should become a content area in the school curriculum and that teachers should be able to teach psychology. He proposed that children be encouraged to undertake important psychological experiments on themselves in areas such as perception, where experiments are easily undertaken without the use of expensive apparatus. Thirdly, he believed that the classroom should become an important laboratory for the psychologist, using the teacher as the experimenter. He pointed out in the latter connection that G. Stanley Hall had encouraged his students to do just that. What Münsterberg proposed was that the classroom be used not for experimental purposes, but as a situation in which behavior under natural conditions could be studied. Today the approach advocated would be described as an ethological approach. He conceived of studies in such new areas as those of imitation, language, and personality, as well as the more traditional areas of will and emotion. Münsterberg admitted that the advances produced by the study of reaction times, the leading experimental technique, had been small and should not be viewed as providing a basis for action on the part of teachers.

Münsterberg's article was followed by one by G. Stanley Hall, who wrote in his characteristically expansive style about the entire field of the new psychology. G. Stanley Hall felt less obligation to emphasize what psychology could do for education, and what he did in his article was to summarize the scope of the new psychology. Though commenting briefly on the new experimental psychology, Hall moved quickly to a discussion of the emerging field of comparative psychology and the new study of instinctive behavior. This was an area of considerable interest to teachers in that the view had been widely held that the understanding of the instinctive behavior of children was important for teaching them. Although educators do not use the term *instinctive* any more, they still are interested in studies that relate to such nativistic behavior as exploratory behavior, and comparative psychology has shed considerable light on the area since Hall wrote his article.

Hall also saw anthropology as an emerging discipline that had important implications for education. Hall would have been surprised if he had been able to foresee the future and to learn that anthropology would have little to say, related to education, for another 75 years. Hall thought that in his time anthropology might throw light on how the conditions necessary for civilization are acquired anew by each successive generation, and by so doing would permit the planning of education so that particular developments in civilization could be fostered.

The final area of psychology discussed by Hall was that which he called the study of decadents. He included within the scope of this area the study of the mentally handicapped, the insane, the epileptic, and even those with sensory defects. He pointed out that research in this area was a great step forward from the earlier practice of referring to all deviations as either sinful or the result of sin. Hall remarked that the category *sin* is not a useful one and that as understanding of the "degeneracies" is achieved the concept of health and mental health will become the substitute for that of sin.

Hall made no specific recommendations concerning the way in which the new psychology, and possibly the old, might be of value to education. The implication is that these emerging sciences provide hope that the difficulties the educator encounters may ultimately be overcome through the new knowledge that had been and was being achieved.

Some years later, William Torrey Harris wrote a book entitled *Psychologic Foundations of Education* (1904), in which he attempted to show the genesis of the higher mental functions. In this volume he struggled to describe the origins and nature of logical thought. Although he tried to integrate the old psychology with the new, there was too little new that could be said about rational thinking to make the work an important one. Yet Harris did understand, as previous philosophers had not understood, that in order to comprehend mature thought one has to first understand the behavior of the infant. The development of imitation and language in infancy and childhood have to be understood before one can begin to understand the reflective thinking of the adult. The book was before its time. How much Harris would have enjoyed the work of later psychologists with their extraordinary integration of philosophy and empirical research! That integration was what Harris sought to achieve.

Harris' love of searching far and wide for ideas that had some implications for education is well illustrated by a "circular" produced by the Bureau of Education early in Harris' commissionership. The circular is a large book entitled *Abnormal Man, being Essays on Education and Crime Related Subjects* (1893). This volume was a well-documented summary of what was known about the causes of criminality, insanity, alcoholism, and distortions of ethical values. Harris, in his letter transmitting the report to the Department of the Interior, stated that education should have a role in preventing crime and insanity, but before it could develop such a role, the nature of crime and insanity had to be understood. The purpose of the report was to review the current knowledge that had to be understood before educational policies could be formulated. Further on in the letter of transmittal, Harris presented views that reflect the prejudices of his age. He referred to criminals, paupers, and the insane as the "three weakling classes" which tend to gather together and form slums.

Although the interest that Harris had in the expanding frontiers of science was commendable, attempts to apply the new knowledge to education were often nothing short of disasters. Although the report presented what was considered to be knowledge at that time, much of it, by modern standards, is not much better than folklore. For example, the report includes a lengthy translation from Cesare Lombroso's *L'homme criminel; étude anthropologique et médico-legale* (1887). Lombroso was an Italian anthropologist who held the theory that there was a criminal physical type that could be identified through inspection. The criminal was said to be characterized by a number of stigmata, many of which had to be present in order for a person to be identified as a criminal. The stigmata listed by Lombroso included such features as a small cranial capacity, lefthandedness, a scanty beard but abundant hair, a crooked or flat nose, muscular weakness, a difficulty in blushing, and many others. The theory was, even in 1893, somewhat controversial yet probably widely held. The stigmata theory did much to reinforce the idea that criminality was a result of genetic defects. That in itself was a harmful enough set of beliefs, but there the matter did not rest. Teachers, through the magazines they read, were instructed to look out for criminal types in their classes and to be wary in their relations with the children thus identified. Such theories of anthropology, derived from reputable academicians, must have had some deplorable consequences when they came to be applied by the naive teacher. One cannot blame Harris for these immature applications of what was alleged to be science, but one can learn from them, and view with suspicion at least some of the more modern attempts to apply to education what is alleged to be knowledge.

Harris, as Commissioner of Education, managed to bring into the mainstream of education research workers with ideas that had potential significance for education. For example, he asked Franz Boas, a leading developer of anthropometric measurement, to engage in studies of the growth of school children. The Reports of the Commissioner for the year ending 30 June 1897 and the year ending 30 June 1904 describe studies undertaken by Franz Boas on growth. It may be noted that Franz Boas later became America's leading anthropologist, under whose guidance Ruth Benedict and Margaret Mead blossomed. It would take at least another 75 years before an outstanding anthropologist would be invited by the federal education office to take part in an educational inquiry. The bringing together of the world of research and the world of practical educators was perhaps the greatest achievement of Harris.

Harris retired from the commissionership in 1906, after 15 years of service. He was a tired man. He had managed to be a powerhouse of energy throughout his career despite the fact that the years in St. Louis -- when he had not only built an exemplary school system for the day, but also had had a career as a major philosopher -- had sapped his strength. His years in the Bureau of Education showed him once again to have an immense reservoir of energy. But when he retired from the Bureau, there was to be no regaining of the losses. He planned books to write, and although he knew what he wanted to write, he did not have the strength to commit most of his ideas to paper. He could not come to terms with the fact that personal planning is realistic only when it is within the resources available. He died shortly after moving himself and his 12,000-volume library to Providence. He could not conceive of living without his 12,000 volumes of inspiration, but the move was too much for him.

The career of William Torrey Harris as Commissioner of Education has had no equal in terms of its long-term impact on education. Although he was no more distinguished, as a thinker, than his predecessor Henry Barnard, he had vastly more success in demonstrating that the Bureau of Education could exercise intellectual leadership. Barnard seemed unable to function effectively within the federal government, but Harris was able to use the full power of his intellect to exercise a long-term effect on education. No educational administrator before Harris had been able to bring to the attention of educators an understanding of the power of the new academic disciplines that were emerging in the developing human sciences. The Commissioner's Reports, under Harris, were converted from rather dull compilations of statistics into a medium for disseminating the new scientific ideas that might have important implications for education. Indeed, the Commissioner's Reports became the most widely circulated books in the educational field and, even more important, the most widely read. Probably the only other federal publications that have ever attracted a similar widespread interest in the present century have been the Department of Agriculture yearbooks.

William Torrey Harris was able to show the educational world that the new breed of scientist developing psychology, sociology, and the other new sciences had important matters to say to teachers and educational administrators. Harris was attempting to bring together the scientist and educator a full decade before Thorndike began to bring his new experimental psychology to bear on the problems of education and two decades before Judd began to develop a psychology of school subjects. Harris laid the groundwork for the cooperation between the research worker and the schools. Without the groundwork so carefully laid by Harris, the researcher-educator cooperation, seen in the early part of the century, might not have taken place.

However, one must also note that Harris would have been shocked by the lack of appreciation of philosophy manifested by many of the scientists who were to have an impact on education. The antiphilosophical views of the new generation of American psychologists would have shaken Harris. He would have understood the need for experimental psychology, but he would not have understood the lack of appreciation of the debt that the new psychology owed to its philosophical tradition. Although the philosophical psychology of Johann Friedrich Herbart was to become almost unknown to most twentieth-century psychologists, the impact of Herbart is clearly there in such areas as the flourishing research on concepts, and that research is based on the analysis made of concepts nearly 200 years earlier by Herbart. Again, modern mathematical psychology owes some debt to its founder, Johann Friedrich Herbart, but these debts are hardly recognized, though William Torrey Harris would have fully recognized them. Much of modern psychology was possible because of the analytic thought that preceded it. The present trend towards identifying the philosophical position implicit in particular lines of psychological work would have been much to Harris' liking, and compatible with the breadth of vision he manifested.

THEY LAID THE FOUNDATION

The foundation for an era of high impact for research was laid before the turn of the century and Barnard, Mann, and Harris played crucial roles in the laying of that foundation. This may seem like a great-man theory of history against which some historians have raised warnings, but in the field of the development of important ideas, great minds play a crucial role. The great minds are always dependent upon the thoughts of their predecessors, but they nevertheless move thinking along with a new acceleration. Isaac Newton was dependent upon the massive amounts of astronomical observation of previous centuries, for otherwise he would not have had the material out of which a physics could be created. The great leaders in education have also been dependent upon the entire body of thought that preceded them. Mann and Barnard were enormously impressed with the ideas that had radiated from Pestalozzi and also the ideas that had emerged from the Puritan concept of the common school. Much of what they said, and wrote, represented a formulation of the ideas that were current. Much of their creativity was in developing ways of bringing those ideas nearer to a reality, sometimes through the development of administrative procedures that might begin to convert the ideas into realities, and sometimes through the dissemination of those ideas. Both Barnard and Mann must be credited with the social invention of using empirical data for the management and development of the schools. This social invention could be usefully applied because it was backed by important ideas concerning the direction in which the schools should move. It could have been used, in the case of lesser men, for the purpose of strangling school progress.

Simple empirical methods of data collection could demonstrate to the policy makers in Connecticut and Massachusetts what needed to be done to improve the schools. The ideas available for improving education were many in the last century. The new idea that schools could also change society led to extensive informal experimentation with the curriculum.

The body of knowledge available to the school planner in the middle of the last century was about to become greatly enriched by the expansion of the work of scientists into areas related to human behavior. Mann's life was cut short before he could have become aware of this expanding body of knowledge that could produce radical changes in education. Barnard lived long enough to begin to see the emergence of this new enlightenment. Henry Barnard's *American Journal of Education* gave space here and there to this emerging body of knowledge. Barnard's scholarly literature on education that he sought to create had firm roots in the past, but it was ever reaching out towards the future. The *American Journal of Education* gave little space to the new developing sciences, which is hardly surprising since the last volume was published in 1882. The initial bringing together of the new developing sciences of human behavior and educational practice was a special task performed by Harris, who had both the knowledge needed to recognize what the new sciences could contribute, and the prestige in education to allow his proposals to be taken seriously.

THE NINETEENTH-CENTURY AMERICAN UNIVERSITY AND THE FOUNDATION OF EDUCATIONAL RESEARCH

William Torrey Harris and Henry Barnard turned as often as not to Europe for the sources of new ideas, and Mann was sent there by the Commonwealth of Massachusetts to search for innovations. Why did they look to Europe? Why did educational innovators behave as though the source of new ideas must be outside of the country, a fact which raises questions about what American universities were doing during much of the nineteenth century? During most of the last century, American institutions of higher learning were largely teaching institutions. Academicians were encouraged to write, but most of the writing that did take place was in the classics and humanities. The latter is hardly surprising, for the curriculum of the typical institution of higher learning in the United States in the nineteenth century was modeled after a curriculum designed primarily for the training of ministers. Even Harvard College in the early part of the nineteenth century not only had a curriculum that emphasized Latin and Greek, but most of its graduates went on to enter the ministry. Harvard did not even begin to show any breadth of program until Charles Elliot became president in 1869 and introduced the radical idea of developing programs of graduate work.

Columbia University did not exist as a university in a modern sense until 1897. The Leland Stanford University, though founded with great visions of scholarship, was little more than an undergraduate teaching institution until the turn of the century. The knowledge to be communicated to the American student was to be that which had emerged in institutions in other lands. The men and women of the emerging American civilization were slow in assimilating the idea that universities had to be places which created the knowlege they taught, for professors just taught whatever knowledge was available. The assimilation of the concept of a university as a place where knowledge was created, and then made available to the student, was to be a slow one in America, and even today it has not been fully embraced. The last of all areas to conceive of the role of the academician as a creator of knowledge has been pedagogy. Most departments of pedagogy still conceive of themselves as the disseminators of knowledge created elsewhere or derived by analytic thought. Few such departments make any effort to create a body of knowledge of value in developing education.

Professors of pedagogy existed in a few institutions in the last century, but these were not to be the means through which scientific methods were to be brought to bear on educational problems. Indeed, these professors had rather low status and, together with much of the educational establishment, represented a pattern of inertia.

The psychology that was taught in departments of pedagogy was not taught as a discipline distinct from pedagogy or philosophy. What psychology there was showed a domination by the ideas of Herbart of a century earlier. Indeed, translations of the works of Herbart were widely sold to students even as late as the beginning of the present century, a hundred years after they were written. This does not mean that students who expected to become teachers did not benefit from exposure to Herbart. At least they acquired some understanding of the nature of knowledge, how concepts were formed and how they were interrelated. The heritage of Herbart included much wisdom that has become assimilated in modern theories of instruction. What was bad was that the complete preoccupation with the ideas of Herbart prevented exposure to some of the newer ideas that were emerging from experimental approaches to human behavior.

There were a few American scholars who visited Europe and who came back fired with enthusiasm for the new ideas that were emerging, but even these had little impact on education. One may note that the new trend in experimental empirical psychology which plays such an important part in Commissioner Harris' reports includes few American names. Franz Boas and G. Stanley Hall made contributions, but few other Americans had their writings published in the reports.

In order to understand much that later transpired in American education, and particularly changes that were produced by educational research, let us now consider the emerging sciences related to human behavior as they began to emerge in Europe in the nineteenth century.

CHAPTER 2

New Lines of Scientific Discovery and Their Implications for Education

The nineteenth century showed an enormous expansion of scientific knowledge into new areas, which had been considered previously to be outside the scope of scientific experimentation and thought. The success of the physical sciences in their application to practical enterprises had brought an entirely new conception of how humanity could control its destiny. The educated public came to view science as an instrument for achieving new and better levels of civilization. Those areas of knowledge that had been considered subject to advance only through the collection of observations now became subject to experimental inquiry. Biology, for example, except for such work as that of William Harvey, had been advanced only through observation until the middle of the nineteenth century, but then biology and physiology became experimental sciences with a large accretion of knowledge. The century also showed an expansion of experimental methods into the field of human behavior, an area in which taboo had decreed that experimentation could never be applied. Indeed, the learned men of Europe had written on the subject. Johann Friedrich Herbart, the distinguished successor to Immaneul Kant in the Chair of Philosophy at Königsberg, had firmly held the position that psychology could not possibly become an experimental science. Herbart expected that psychology would become mathematical and wrote the first treatise on mathematical psychology before the end of the eighteenth century, but Herbart considered the possibility of an experimental science of behavior as just a wild dream.

Nevertheless, even the ideas of the prestigious Herbart came to be questioned and a genuine experimental science of human behavior began to develop.

While the American university was emerging from its conception and birth as a colonial college, universities in the German-speaking provinces of Europe were displaying a remarkable productivity of original work. French universities, devastated intellectually in the Napoleonic era, did not revive intellectually until near the turn of the nineteenth century, but English universities showed a rejuvenation of scholarship during that century, producing such extraordinary men as J. J. Thompson, the founder of electronics, and Ernest Rutherford, the most famous model builder of atoms of his generation. However, the British universities gave little impetus to the development of a science of psychology. Such a development could not take place because the institutions were still largely dominated by theologians of the Church of England placed there during the Reformation. Nevertheless, the British Isles did make contributions to the development of the new science of behavior, mainly through the activity of a leisured class that produced such notables as Charles Darwin and Francis Galton.

The revival of all institutions of higher learning in Europe as the creators of original knowledge was simply a return to a much earlier tradition. The European university had long been a place where great thinkers were able to organize and create knowledge and disseminate knowledge to whoever wished to acquire it. Teaching was almost incidental to the acquisition of knowledge. In fact, the holder of a chair at a great European university might not teach at all, for often the teaching of students was undertaken by underlings whose salaries were paid directly by the students. The revival of an atmosphere of free inquiry that had long constituted the very essence of the European university resulted in the nineteenth century in the expansion of knowledge into new areas, such as physiology, psychology, sociology, and economics, that had either been previously considered to be beyond the scope of human inquiry or had not been investigated because of lack of the necessary scientific techniques.

Certain distinct lines of sholarly inquiry in Europe had a deep and enduring influence on the development of education and educational ideas in the United States, though the chain of influence was not always a direct and simple one.

A first major influence on education came from Germany, where the concept of pedagogy as a distinct and expanding branch of knowledge first developed. This German influence permeated the programs of teacher training institutions as they developed in the United States in the last half of the nineteenth century. Ideas related to instruction, developed in Germany, also formed the foundation for much of American educational research, as it developed in the early part of the present century.

A second important European influence that had impact on both American educational research and on the literature and practice of education was the Russian development of conditioning theory. Modern

American behaviorism, with its repertoire of techniques for programming learning, and its emphasis on reinforcement, is a direct descendant of the emerging Russian psychology of the last century.

A third important European influence, that was to provide a new foundation for our conception of learning, is found in the development of the theory of evolution. When American psychologists began to embrace evolutionary theory, they saw a continuity between animal and human behavior that they had not seen before. This apparent similarity quickly led to the conclusion that whatever insight one could acquire from the study of animal learning could be readily applied to the planning and control of human learning. The fallacy involved in this argument has only slowly come to light.

The new sciences of human behavior, as they emerged in Europe in the last century, will be discussed only briefly in this chapter. Later chapters will expand at considerable length on their influences, and the men and women who brought them to bear on the problems of American education.

THE GERMAN INFLUENCE

The Work of Herbart

Systematic and orderly thought about education in the nineteenth century was dominated by the intellectual influence of Johann Friedrich Herbart (1776-1841). Although his academic profession was that of a philosopher, Herbart had close contact with the great educational innovations of Pestalozzi at Burgdorf and even ran a demonstration school of his own for a short time. Herbart was able to organize and systematize the new ideas about education that were developing in the context of schools and to provide the foundations for a discipline of pedagogy.

Herbart was not the first philosopher who had attempted to systematize ideas about how education could be most effectively conducted, for Socrates and Plato had approached this task in antiquity. But Herbart represented an important break with the past. He did not preoccupy himself with the social and interactive aspects of the educational process as those who promoted the Socratic method had, and he largely ignored the age old issue, raised by Plato, of the innateness of knowledge. Herbart opened the doors to our modern conception of education by recognizing that information flows in through the senses and leads to the building of an organized body of knowledge in the individual. From his point of view, a discipline of education had to focus on the way in which knowledge was acquired through the senses, and how that knowledge became organized. Detailed understanding of how the senses functioned as transmitters of information could not come until experimental psychologists and physiologists had undertaken experimental work, but Herbart started a train of thought that led to experimentation with the sensory acquisition of knowledge, and ultimately to the program of sensory education initiated by Maria Montessori (1870-1952).

Herbart came from a well-to-do middle-class family in Oldenberg in North Germany. His father was a lawyer, and also was active in civic affairs as a councillor. His father seems to have been aloof from his son, but his mother, a woman of substantial intellect, gave careful thought to the child's tutoring and to his intellectual progress. She selected his tutors and monitored his extraordinary and precocious development. Latin and Greek were the basics in the upper-class education of the time, and Herbart's mother mastered Greek herself so that she could participate more fully in the education of her son.

The young Herbart showed the development typical of a child prodigy, becoming particularly proficient in mathematics and philosophy. He began the study of logic at the age of 11 and then moved on to metaphysics at the age of 12. At the age of 14 he made his first known original contribution in the form of an essay entitled "Human Freedom." At 18, he entered the University of Jena, the center of philosophic thought in Germany at that time. However, he did not enter Jena to study philosophy, for his father had in mind that the young man should study law. Despite the wishes of his father, Herbart came under the influence of what was then Germany's most influential philosopher, Johann Gottlieb Fichte. Fichte was at the height of his intellectual achievement during the years that Herbart was in Jena. Herbart could not have come under a more powerful influence, with Ficthe's contagious enthusiasm for various causes, coupled with a vigor and impetuosity which resulted in his demise at Jena for political reasons. Perhaps some of Fichte's own impetuosity may have rubbed off on his admirer, the young Herbart. Herbart never completed his course of study at Jena, but dropped out and became a private tutor to the sons of the Governor of Interlaken in Switzerland, a position he held for 2 years. Then, in 1799, he paid a visit to Pestalozzi's school before leaving Switzerland and going to Göttingen where he received his doctoral degree in 1802. His visit to Pestalozzi must have left a deep impression, for much of what Herbart later had to say about education represents a formalization of what Pestalozzi was trying to tell the world about education.

In 1809 Herbart was offered the chair of philosophy at Königsberg, the most prestigious position in philosophy in Germany, for the chair had been occupied by Immanuel Kant. There Herbart spent 22 wonderfully productive years. During these years he was recognized primarily as a philosopher and, even though he made notable contributions to education, these were not widely recognized for their significance until after he was dead. In order to further his work in education, he formed a pedagogical seminar for the training of teachers and also a school of about 20 pupils to provide demonstrations of good teaching. In the seminary, he himself taught the mathematics courses, and he also taught at times in the school, experimenting with new techniques and permitting the students in the seminary to critique what he was doing.

Before turning to the long-term contributions of Herbart to educational thought and practice, let us consider his conception of psychology. Edwin Boring, in his *History of Experimental Psychology* (1950), devoted an extraordinary amount of space to Herbart, despite the fact that Herbart never undertook an experiment. Boring described the psychology of Herbart as mathematical, mechanical, but not experimental. Let us consider the last first.

In discussing Herbart's conception of experimentation, we will depart considerably from what Boring has to say about the matter. When Herbart said that psychology cannot be experimental in the sense in which physics is experimental, he was not denying that knowledge of psychology must be based on empirical observation. Just what Herbart conceived to be the nature of experimentation is not clear, but he does not seem to have limited the idea of experimentation to the Galilean model. Indeed, much that was then described as experimental would be described today as a demonstration of a particular phenomenon. For example, the demonstration that burning is the combination of a substance with the oxygen of the atmosphere does not fit the Galilean model, but it would have been called experimentation in the time of Herbart. Simple demonstrations with magnets would also have been called experiments as, indeed, they sometimes are today in physics textbooks. Samuel Johnson's famous English dictionary of the period defines *experiment* as "trial of anything; something done in order to discover an uncertain or unknown effect." Perhaps only in modern psychology and sociology is the term *experimentation* restricted to the Galilean model. In Herbart's time, the term was used quite loosely to describe a wide range of observational techniques used by physicists and chemists. When Herbart was saying that psychology cannot be experimental, he was saying that the kinds of laboratory techniques that the physicist and chemist use cannot be applied to the study of the mind, for the latter has to do with the metaphysical, meaning that it goes beyond the physical. However, the metaphysical can be observed and studied, as can the physical, for mind provides direct experience of itself. One cannot take a concept, place it on the table, and experiment with it, as one can a mineral, but one can make observations on what happens to a concept. Herbart even suggested experiment-like observation.

Nevertheless, psychology was to be for Herbart a mathematical science

(*Wissenschaft*), though one must not be led astray by use of the term *science* in this connection. Throughout the nineteenth century, the term *science* was used, as the Greeks had used it, to embrace all branches of knowledge, including many that would not be thought of today as sciences. Herbart asserted that mathematical laws of psychology could be developed. These had to be based on empirical observation and had to be consistent with subsequent observations through which they could be verified. Today, one recognizes that a science, as for example, geology, can be mathematical without being experimental, though the development of geology is related quite indirectly to experimentally derived knowledge. Mathematical psychology involves the idea that something can be measured, and Herbart wrote of the measurement of attention and the idea that an idea may have sufficient *strength* for it to pass the *threshold* or *limen* into consciousness. The concept of a limen or threshold was to have immense impact on later German psychology. Herbart expanded on his notion of a mathematical psychology in a number of his works and in a single monograph written in Latin on the subject.

Boring has also pointed out that the psychology of Herbart is mechanical, though this is a term that has many meanings and the meaning with which it was used by Boring is not clear. Herbart himself used the term but, nevertheless, did not conceive of a metaphysical psychology as having the properties of a physical universe. Yet his elements of consciousness, namely, ideas or concepts, are given properties closely similar to those of elements in the physical world. These properties he called time, intensity, and quality. Through these properties ideas may interact, and one idea may suppress another, or rival with another for entry into consciousness. Inhibition is a central concept of Herbart's psychology. Boring was right when he said that the psychology of Herbart is mechanical in the sense that Herbartian ideas and concepts can be viewed as having some of the properties of the physical world.

The concepts or ideas (*Vorstellung*) of the Herbartian system are characterized by attributes, a notion derived from Aristotle's discussion of classes but greatly expanded upon by Herbart. Contemporary research on concept learning, beginning with Clark L. Hull's classic study, are strictly Herbartian in conceptualization. Concepts are also organized structures of knowledge. Though the idea of knowledge being organized was not new, Herbart's discussion of how sensory information was transformed, organized, and utilized was completely novel. Herbart borrowed from Leibnitz the term *apperception* to describe how new inputs through the senses were acted upon by previous knowledge and experience, and laid the foundation for a modern psychology of perception. Although Herbart himself, in his writing, made only rare reference to the apperceptive process and the organized body of knowledge as the apperceptive mass, the concept of an apperceptive process had a long and profound effect on thought related to education.

The third aspect of Herbart's psychology is that it is mathematical. Herbart was an excellent mathematician and even taught mathematics during his academic career. Herbart even went so far as to write a treatise on mathematical psychology, only a few copies of which have survived. He did introduce some mathematics into his general works, in which he discussed the actions of ideas or concepts on each other. Boring was not impressed with Herbart's attempt to produce a mathematical psychology, dismissing it as an attempt to provide an illusion of precision in an area of vague ideas. Indeed, Boring implied that that is what mathematical psychologists have typically done. Herbart's difficulty was that he lacked the kind of data that might have some real possibility of providing a foundation for a mathematical psychology. Nevertheless, Herbart had an important idea that bore fruit after his death.

Herbart's impact on education came through a series of works which were not highly thought of at the time they were first published in German, but which acquired a world-wide circulation in several languages after his death. Herbart conceived of education as constituting a *Wissenschaft*, literally translated as "science," but perhaps nearer in current usage to the term *academic discipline.*

This in itself was a new conception of the nature of education. It went beyond the concepts of Plato and Locke in many respects. Herbart took the position that there was knowledge available that should be used in the planning of education. That knowledge was essentially empirical, but it was not empirical in the sense in which Barnard's and Mann's surveys were empirical, but was to be derived by the academician through the methods available for the exploration of the mind.

The first work of Herbart related to education appeared shortly after his visit to the Pestalozzi school near Zurich. The work appeared in 1802 under the title *Pestalozzi's Idee eines ABC der Anschauung Untersucht und Wissenschaftlich Ausgefuhrt von J. F. Herbart* (Gottingen: J. F. Bower, 1802). The work has been translated under many titles as, for example, *Herbart's ABC of Sense-Perception* (tr. 1903). The translated titles do not do justice to the original, which states that Pestalozzi's system was examined and scientifically enlarged upon. Indeed, Herbart's presentation of Pestalozzi went far beyond a mere presentation of what the Swiss lawyer was doing in his model school. It attempted to provide a framework of ideas within which the system could be understood and, where Herbart thought necessary, criticized. Indeed, one of the main criticisms that Herbart had of Pestalozzi was that he lacked a logically ordered set of ideas on which a system of teaching could be based.

Herbart criticized Pestalozzi for emphasizing visual perception to the exclusion of the other senses. He also pointed out that the training of perception is not enough, for advantage must be taken of the laws through which information is utilized once it enters the mind. In the English translation cited of the *ABC*, there is an interesting reference to the mind as a "machine" for handling the sense-perception inputs (p. 57), though this was not a part of the original *ABC*, but was included in a lecture at the Bremen Museum in 1804. In much of the remainder of the treatise, Herbart emphasized that what is known about the mechanics of the mind can be used to provide a much more adequate account of the Pestalozzi method of education than Pestalozzi was able to provide.

One of the most interesting discussions in the entire volume is a proposed "experiment" (Herbart used the word!) in which an attempt is made to train infants from birth in visual perception by displaying shapes and forms on a board designed for that purpose. Herbart thought that Euclidean forms should be presented, not realizing that such geometrical presentations could not be understood by infants in their cribs. This simple experiments shows not only Herbart's interest in beginning mathematics education at an early age, but it also reflects his concern for the process of attention, a subject on which he later was to write a treatise, *De Attentionis Mensura Causisque Primaris*. Thus, although Herbart rejected the idea that psychology can become experimental, in the physical scientist's sense of the term, he was not adverse to the undertaking of what today would be called experiments. For Herbart, the latter do not look like the experiments of the physical sciences.

Herbart's second major contribution was a rather large work published later in English under the title of *Outlines of Educational Doctrine* (tr. 1904; originally published, 1835). In many respects the book is extraordinarily modern in character. The first chapter points out that education is based on ethics and psychology. The goals are determined by ethics, and the means to achieve those goals by psychology. Education, he pointed out, assumes the plasticity of the child and education involves a transition from the indeterminate to the determinate, a phrase which could almost have been written by John Dewey. Herbart provided an excellent discussion of the role of philosophy in establishing the assumptions on which education is based, pointing out that if one were to accept the assumptions of fatalism, then there could be no place for education. The assumption of unlimited plasticity is equally unacceptable. The chapter on ethics and education that follows points out that all education involves education in ethical ideas, for the mere assembly of a group of pupils involves the introduction of a set of "laws and rewards," which have to have an ethical basis.

The chapter on the psychological basis of education introduces some important ideas that had not been so clearly stated and emphasized before. Herbart emphasized the importance of understanding the developmental pattern of the child, and particularly the slow transition of the child from dealing with the concrete, when young, to dealing with the abstract as the child matures. That idea was new in that Pestalozzi had never grasped the significance of the transition, partly because he was interested mainly in the education of younger children.

Outlines goes on to describe Herbart's famous four steps in education. The first of these is *clearness* in the presentation of specific facts or whatever is to be mastered. This includes the Pestalozzian idea of presenting concrete materials for the pupil to study, but such objects must be well selected so that they provide excellent illustrations of the matters to be learned. Herbart emphasized that learning in this stage must involve the presentation of very small steps to be learned and, in fact, what Herbart had to say reminds one of some of the statements made by B. F. Skinner in recent times. The second stage of learning is the stage of *association.* In this stage, facts are to be associated with one another as well as with knowledge previously acquired. In modern terms, one would say that this is the stage of the assimilation of new knowledge, and Herbart used essentially the same term, and he also used the term *apperception,* though he gave it none of the preponderance given it by later Herbartians.

The third and fourth stages of learning are somewhat different in that they emphasize long-term processes of learning. The third stage involves the later systematic *ordering* of the facts, ideas, concepts, and principles already acquired. This is an activity that takes place when one achieves some insight concerning events of the past. A contemporary example would be that of a 7-year-old child who has been collecting objects for years, but who suddenly begins to evolve classification systems for those objects. This kind of learning is a continuous process, for Herbart, throughout life. Knowledge does not just stay in place in the apperceptive mass where it is originally placed, but undergoes a continuous evolution as thought proceeds, if thought does proceed.

The fourth stage of learning involves *application* of what has been learned to new situations. Herbart maintained that permanent learning does not take place until the learner has had considerable experience in applying what he has learned. The stage of application calls particularly for vigorous self-activity on the part of the pupil.

Attention is necessary for pupil learning, and Herbart had much to say about it. He recognized that attention may involve either native tendencies or tendencies related to learning. The child attends to strong stimuli, because that is the child's nature. Herbart noted that, as a part of the native attention process, monotony produces weariness and lack of attention. Thus, sameness of presentation should be avoided. The individual also has a high probability of attending to objects with which there is some relationship in the past. Thus familiarity sometimes facilitates attention and sometimes inhibits it. Herbart referred to this process as apperceiving, or assimilating, attention. However, Herbart conceded that the teacher cannot always rely upon either native attention or apperceiving attention to take place, and sometimes the pupil must hold his attention on that which he is learning through his own resolution. When attention is maintained through the pupil's own resolution, then the teacher must be sure to give the pupil frequent information about his progress.

Herbart expanded on the problem of efficient memorizing, and what he had to say agreed with what modern research has demonstrated. For example, he recognized that what might be called frequent review is important for permanent retention, but suggested that the review be undertaken in the form of making new applications. He also stressed that many pupils lack efficient ways of memorizing. He also suggested that pupils memorizing material should be permitted to use whatever techniques they find useful, such as reciting the material aloud or writing it out. Herbart vigorously protested the technique of some teachers that involved immobilizing the pupil and forbidding any vocalization during efforts to memorize. Herbart emphasized that there is little point in memorizing material as an activity undertaken for its own sake. He stated clearly that only that should be memorized which has future utility. Also, not everything included in instruction should be memorized, for some of the materials of instruction may be there only to stimulate interest.

The remainder of the volume is filled with fascinating ideas, many of which are similar to those that have been rediscovered in more recent years. Herbart distinguished between what he called *analytic* and *synthetic* teaching. The former refers to thought and action initiated by the pupil, and the latter to thought and action initiated by the teacher. The terms are actually used in a less simplistic sense, the details of which cannot be discussed here.

The final part of the volume deals with what the Judd school of psychologists at the University of Chicago later would have called the psychology of school subjects. Separate sections discuss the nature of learning religion, history, mathematics, nature study, geography, the mother tongue, Greek, and Latin. His discussion of the teaching of geography reflects much of what later writers, including Horace Mann, had to say on the subject. He suggested that the teaching of geography should begin with the analytic, namely, the pupil's understanding of his neighborhood. The task of the teacher is synthetic and involves the introduction of knowledge of the globe beyond that of the immediate experience of the child. Herbart stated that the teacher must learn the art of narration in order to teach geography, and must give accounts of distant places as though he were a traveler. Such narrations must use a few fixed positions in space such as one or more towns and lines connecting them. Herbart recognized, as Horace Mann did, that a knowledge of geography presupposes a knowledge of the geometry of space. Another point made is that geography can help to integrate other knowledge. For example, geography integrates the events of history with mathematics, for the differences separating historical events in space and in time may be of crucial importance.

Herbart's discussion of school subjects focuses on how the pupil learns the content, in terms of what Herbart considered to be the findings of empirical psychology of his time. It focuses only indirectly on how the subject should be taught. This approach to the understanding of learning was not understood by Herbart's contemporaries, and was not understood by many even in the present century.

Although the discussion here has been limited to Herbart's two major works on education, he also lectured prolifically on the subject and wrote numerous letters on education that have been preserved. Several collections of these letters have been published. Some were written when he was still a young man as, for example, those written to his employer, the governor of Interlaken, whose sons he was tutoring. Others were written later during his career. The letters are of much less interest than the two main works we have considered, which provide highly organized presentations of his ideas.

The writings of Herbart had little impact on education during his lifetime, but they reached the height of their impact near the end of the century, when the rise of teacher training institutions in the United States needed scholarly materials on pedagogy to which they could expose their students. Even if teacher training institutions had existed in the early part of the last century, the idea of basing instruction on an empirical and mechanical psychology would hardly have been acceptable. It would have been too remote from anything that even education people understood for it to have been acceptable. Much had to happen before such radical ideas were to become acceptable, even to academicians. Herbart's ideas on education became acceptable only as a genuine empirical psychology was developed by new generations.

Herbart was able to produce a theory of how knowledge is acquired and organized by children. The theory was quite sophisticated, even by modern standards, and gave full recognition to the fact that organized knowledge was not acquired by rote learning or by memorizing particular passages from textbooks. Since the very core of education is the acquisition of organized knowledge, a theory of how knowledge is acquired and organized must lie at the very heart of a theory of education. Such a theory of knowledge, modified, expanded, and developed by John Dewey, was to lie at the very heart of the reform movements of American education in the early part of the present century. This was the kind of movement in education that Herbart had envisaged, and for which he laid the foundation, but which he never saw in his lifetime.

Herbart was a remarkable genius. His important contributions are not properly recognized today, partly because they have all become assimilated into the work of major psychologists who followed him. Much of modern cognitive psychology is built upon his work.

The Experimental Study of the Senses

Herbart was right in his emphasis on the role of the senses in the acquisition of knowledge, even though there was almost no scientific knowledge at that time of how the senses functioned. But before Herbart died new scientific techniques were beginning to open up avenues through which the functioning of the senses could be explored. In 1834 a professor of anatomy and physiology at the University of Leipsig, Ernest Heinrich Weber (1795-1878) published a classic set of studies on the sense of touch. Weber was able to demonstrate the extraordinary complexity of the sense of touch and the separate identity of warmth, cold, pain, and pressure. All this may seem to be quite academic until one walks through a Montessori school, run strictly along Montessori lines, and observes blindfolded children learning to explore the world through contact with their finger tips.

The sense of touch was an obvious place to begin the study of the senses and how they functioned in the acquisition of knowledge. Many of the sense organs related to touch lie near the surface, and can even be easily surgically excised for examination. The receptors of the eye or the ear lie deep within the body and can be neither easily studied nor precisely stimulated, one at a time.

Weber was not the only academician of his generation interested in the study of the senses. His contemporary, Gustav Theodor Fechner (1802-1887) spent a small, but important, part of his life in developing knowledge related to the making of sensory discriminations. Fechner hoped that, through the study of how the strength of stimulation is related to the intensity of experience, he could develop an exact science of the relationship of body and mind. He developed this idea in his classic work *Elemente der Psychophysik*, which he published in 1860. Although Fechner's main and lofty objective could not be achieved, by him or by anybody else, he was able to open the way to the study of the very fundamental process of discriminating one object from another. In doing this he provided educators with ideas about how the training of the senses might be undertaken in the classroom. The lesson was not lost on educators.

The century also saw an explosive expansion of knowledge about the functioning of the other senses. It required an intellect of the caliber of that of Herman Ludwig Ferdinand von Helmholz (1821-1894) to explore the auditory and visual mechanisms. The great Helmholz work on vision, *Optik*, appeared first in 1856 and stimulated research across the world. When the last edition of *Optik* appeared in 1896, it included an annoted bibliography of 7,833 titles. Helmholz also produced a corresponding work on hearing.

The extensive work on the nature of the senses and sensory learning of the nineteenth century left a rich legacy for those concerned with educational change. Mention has already been made of the influence that this new line of research had on the thinking of Maria Montessori, but the influence was slow in coming to other educators. Montessori had the advantage over her contemporaries of having had a scientific training. Also, her prestige as the first woman in Italy to ever graduate from a medical school gave her access to the halls of learning of Europe where the new physiology of the senses was one of the great developments of her age.

The emphasis of Herbart on sensory education and the work of the great research workers such as Weber, Fechner, and Helmholz that followed him, have left a permanent mark on education today. One can hardly find a textbook today on early education, or for that matter elementary education, that does not stress systematic instruction in sensory discriminations. Educating and using the senses of touch, hearing and vision, enter all kinds of school activities, and particularly those that involve art and music. The education of the senses has become almost a standard part of the school curriculum.

Memory and Learning

For scientists like Weber and Fechner, the study of learning and memory seemed far beyond anything that could be investigated in the laboratory. Not until a generation later did anyone have the boldness and imagination to embark on experimental investigations of these areas.

The man who was to develop the experimental psychology of memory was Hermann Ebbinghaus (1850-1909). Ebbinghaus lived a rather short life, but his span of years overlapped those of Weber, Fechner, Wundt, and Helmholtz. Ebbinghaus was aware that the new experimental psychology had been unable to develop experimental techniques for studying what were then called the higher mental processes, and he sought to develop the area experimentally. Boring has told how the stimulus for his work was the finding in a secondhand bookstore in Paris of a copy of Fechner's *Elemente der Psychophysik* which led him to apply the new methods of experimental psychology to the study of memory. Ebbinghaus at that time was in his late twenties, earning a living by tutoring the children of the rich, and it was in such a setting that he began his famous series of investigations. The work of his famous studies was published in his classic volume *Über das Gedächtnis.* The work brings together in a highly original style the associationistic tradition of learning and the new notion of psychological measurement developed by Fechner, and every psychologist knows that it introduced for the first time the idea of using nonsense syllables to provide uniform materials for learning. The work of developing his research took about 10 years from the finding of the copy of Fechner's work. His great work on memory was published in

1885. It was not until after the work had been published that he was given a professorship, having earned his living for the previous 5 years as a *docent*, or what one might call in American terms an instructor, who had little status and not much pay.

The discoveries of Ebbinghaus had such obvious implications for education that one is surprised to discover that he is not even mentioned in books on pedagogy early in the century. A part of the reason for this is that such works were often reprints of books that had been written much earlier. For example, one of the most common texts used in teacher training institutions was Herbart's *A Textbook in Psychology* (tr. 1896; originally published, 1816), which had been written almost a century earlier. When Thorndike wrote his massive educational psychology around the year 1910, he made bare mention of Ebbinghaus. Some use was being made of the concepts developed by Ebbinghaus at about the same time by research workers who were attempting to study how children learned arithmetic, and many Ebbinghaus-type hypotheses were tested using mathematical materials rather than nonsense syllables; but, despite these positive signs of impact, the impact on educational thought and education was extremely slight. Notable writers for students of education early in the century such as James, Sully, and Munsterberg wrote without ever recognizing that Ebbinhaus ever existed, though they did recognize the existence of a new experimental psychology. The new experimental psychology was slow in having impact on the thinking of educators. Indeed, it was to have impact on education only after a generation of American psychologists had been trained in Europe under the tutelage of the great master of experimental psychology, Wilhelm Wundt.

Wundt's New Laboratory Approach

The work of Herbart, Weber and Fechner had a clear and identifyable relationship to education, but the work of Wundt, that must now be discussed, had an indirect relationship.

Wilhelm Max Wundt (1832-1920) had a span of life that extended from Herbart's attempt to develop an analytic and mathematical psychology to much of psychology as it is conceived today. His indirect influence on American education came from the fact that he had contact with and influenced the training of several psychologists who were to leave their mark on American education. Cattell initiated research on the psychology of reading in Wundt's laboratory. Judd took his doctoral work in psychology with Wundt. Stanley Hall had a rather short contact with Wundt and then went back to found the psychological laboratory at the Johns Hopkins University. Münsterberg, who later wrote a psychology for teachers, was a student of Wundt. Everyone, across the world, who had asperations of becoming a psychologist and the money to spend a year in Europe, came to work with Wundt. Yet of those who worked with him, and who became American psychologists, only Edward Bradford Titchener (1867-1927) remained true to the line of thought and experimentation that Wundt had started. The others went on to develop their own special American approach to the development of psychology.

Only brief mention will be made of Wundt in this volume, despite his extraordinary stature in the founding of a science of psychology. He was not the first to undertake laboratory experiments in what is now called the field of psychology, for Weber and Fechner had done so before him, but they had viewed their work as a part of physiology. Wundt viewed his laboratory work in a different way from any of his predecessors. He saw the work as providing a foundation for a new science of psychology, which would encompass, not only sensory phenomena, but every aspect of human experience, including that involved in social and cultural events.

Like so many academicians of his generation, Wundt began his career by training as a physician, but decided to enter the rapidly expanding field of physiological research. Hardly surprising is it that, throughout his career, he emphasized physiological aspects of psychology, and wrote the first comprehensive physiological psychology. His first major research was on the physiology of the muscles. He then went on to publish a major work on the physiology of the sense organs. Wundt, like his predecessors, saw the study of the sense organs as the direct path to the study of the mind.

The study of the sense organs led Wundt to the exploration of the experiences that accompanied sensory stimulation, and to work which, today, would be referred to as the study of perception. This slowly led him to thinking through what he believed to be the very core of a science of psychology, namely, the laws that governed experience. Wundt tried to provide an experimental basis for the psychology that Herbart had attempted to formulate half a century earlier. Yet despite the emphasis of Wundt on mental states, the underlying physiological phenomena were always given a central role in the total functioning of the human organism.

The central core of Wundt's science of psychology was the identification of elements of consciousness and the discovery of the laws that related to the elements. The elements were not static, but were dynamic mental processes. Thus a sensation is not static, but is always a developing experience, as it interacts with knowledge already accumulated.

The conversion of psychology to an experimental science opened up the possibility that the psychology of school subjects, begun by Herbart, could be advanced as an experimental science. Two American students of Wundt were to do that, namely, James McKeen Cattell and Charles Hubbard Judd. Such notions of applying psychology to the solution of practical problems were far outside of anything in which Wundt was interested.

This new European psychology, with its emphasis on the physiology of the senses, the processes of perception, and the laws of experience, was to provide the mold into which a whole new literature for teachers in both America and Europe would be cast. Before this new literature can be discussed, we must turn to the other great European influences that helped to shape it.

THE RUSSIAN SCHOOL OF PSYCHOLOGY: THE FOUNDATION OF AMERICAN BEHAVIORISM

American behaviorism, with its powerful attempts to influence education, finds its roots in a scientific movement in Russia in the last century.

Psychology in Russia, as in Germany, had its roots in the work of physiologists, but it developed along rather different lines. In the nineteenth century in Russia physiological studies related to behavior showed an extraordinary expansion, but never developed into the kind of psychology that Wundt envisaged. To some extent, the development of a behavioral physiology was tied in Russia to the swelling movement to oppose the religious doctrines of the Greek Orthodox Church, and in the present century the development of a physiology of behavior became the official view of behavior of the Marxist state. Yet an important progeny of that movement was American behaviorism, with its philosophical ties to a capitalist society in which behavior is assumed to be controlled by rewards.

The basic conceptualization of psychology as a branch of physiology, and specifically neurology, is generally attributed to Ivan Mikhailovich Sechenov (1829-1905). The brief comments here on the life of Sechenov are based on a 1952 biography by K. S. Koshtoyants in Ivan Sechenov's *Selected Physiological and Psychological Works* (tr. 1965). Sechenov was born in a small village about 300 miles west of Moscow, of an upper-class family. The village is now named Sechenova after him. He attended the Military Engineering School in Petrograd, where he acquired a strong taste for physics and mathematics but little taste for engineering. He was able, somehow, to avoid the 20 years of service in the military that was the requirement of his times and began training as a physician at the University of Moscow. There, he was fortunate in studying under outstanding physiologists and biologists. When he graduated, he was sent abroad for 3½ years where he came under the tutelage of both Hermann von Helmholtz and Johannes Müller as well as some of the other outstanding German physiologists of his age. He also worked in the laboratory of the famous French physiologist, Claude Bernard. Few men had as illustrious teachers as Ivan Sechenov, and these teachers must surely have recognized what a remarkable student they had. Sechenov was one of the new generation of physiologists which viewed physiology as an extension of physics and chemistry and not an attempt to explore mysterious vital forces. Physiology was waging a battle to be recognized as a science, much as psychology had to wage a similar battle in the twentieth century.

In the days of Sechenov, even many of those who had studied such basic physiological functions as digestion, respiration, and metabolism still held to the view that the nervous system was the seat of vital forces that could not be studied through the chemical techniques that had been so successful in the investigation of other aspects of physiology. Sechenov took the opposite point of view. In his doctoral dissertation, completed in 1860, he took the philosophical position that all the phenomena of the universe were physical phenomena that could be investigated and understood through the methods of the natural sciences, and that even consciousness could be understood ultimately in terms of scientific concepts. Sechenov also believed that there was a certain unity between the organism and the environment, and that to understand an organism one had to understand also the environment of that organism.

In 1863, when Sechenov was only 34, he published an article developing the thesis that all acts of conscious and unconscious life were systems of reflexes. These reflexes formed the basis of all activity, whether that of the muscles or that of the brain or nervous system. Thought was viewed as a set of reflexes. This was, of course, a philosophical position that could not possibly be tested by collecting empirical data. Sechenov had some difficulties in publishing his article because of the philosophical position it presented. One should also note that the article was an attempt to divorce the understanding of the nervous system from philosophy, but in attempting to do this established a new philosophy. The paper aroused much controversy, but received some support from the Russian intelligentsia searching for a new conceptualization of the nature of society.

The philosophical position of Sechenov was strictly that of a monist, with material substance being the only substance in the universe. This position has encouraged contemporary Russians, with their monist and Marxist viewpoints, to revive his memory with warm feelings.

Although the science of psychology for Sechenov is a branch of physiology, it is not just a science of objectively observable behavior. Sechenov talked freely about consciousness and the internal events of which one is conscious. His thesis was that these must be understood ultimately in terms of what he called the *reflexes of the nervous system.* The latter would also explain thought, though for Sechenov at least some of thought could be regarded as muscular activity. He came near to stating what was later called a *muscle-twitch* theory of thinking. All this theorizing extends vastly beyond what the facts of his day warranted, but he attempted to make a convincing case that his conception of thought was still better than that which involves the notion of a spirit, or vital force.

Sechenov was also a reductionist, a position that was commonly held by scientists of his generation. Physical activity was to be reduced to the physiological, and the physiological was to be reduced to chemistry and physics. Sechenov also drew on the widely publicized work of Charles Darwin, who had not only emphasized the essential relationship between the organism and its environment, but had also stressed the relationship of all species. Sechenov took this to mean that the study of lower organisms could lead to an understanding of the components of the behavior of the human organism. Thus, Sechenov believed that comparative physiology could lead to an understanding of human behavior. Sechenov saw complete continuity between the irritability of the simplest organism and the complex behavior of the human.

Further elaborations of his theory seemed possible to Sechenov as knowledge developed during his century. In a paper on "The Elements of Thought," he attempted to reduce abstract ideas to the elaboration of elements derived from sensory perception. He foreshadowed many later ideas of psychologists in his idea that muscular activity and muscle sense formed the basis of understanding space and time and their measurement. He also attempted to show how human logic could be reduced to elementary physiological processes.

Sechenov held a number of academic appointments. From 1860 to 1870, he taught at the Military Medical Academy at St. Petersburg. Then, after a number of other appointments, he achieved the distinction of being offered the chair of physiology at the University of Moscow in 1891, where he remained for 10 years. These academic appointments made it possible for him to carry out a number of important researches. His best known discovery is that of an inhibitory center in the frog's brain that suppresses spinal reflexes. He also discovered that reflexes can be inhibited through the stimulation of particular sensory nerves. In addition, he made the important discovery of the summation of stimuli. In his laboratory, some of the first experiments on the direct stimulation of the frog's brain were undertaken. He also found evidence for biorhythmic activity.

Sechenov is important as the initiator of a strictly physiological and mechanical theory of behavior. The idea had, of course, been toyed with before. Thomas Aquinas had long ago suggested that most behavior was automatic, but Aquinas also allowed for the very occasional intervention of free will, upsetting the normal mechanical course of events. Sechenov's system was completely mechanical, with the reflex, a highly observable phenomenon, providing the model for all behavioral events. He was, of course, wrong in implying that consciousness could be *explained* as being merely a product of physical complexity, for such a theory is no explanation at all. Nevertheless, half a century later, this was to become the official Soviet view of the nature of consciousness. Sechenov's ideas achieved some popularity among the intelligentsia, but they were to have their longest impact through the impression they made on his student, Ivan Pavlov.

Although Sechenov was the founder of the Russian school of psychology that still flourishes today, American students are more likely to think of Pavlov as the founder, because Pavlov developed a model of the functioning of the nervous system that had profound influence on the development of psychology in the United States. Ivan Petrovich Pavlov (1849-1936) has written a short autobiography which says much about him as a person but little about his scientific work. His father was a Greek Orthodox priest who raised his son for the priesthood. The elder Pavlov was a man of considerable means as is evident from a picture of the Pavlov home, which would be described today as a stately mansion. The young Pavlov attended first the local theological seminary where he received his basic education and where, he said, the pupil could follow his own intellectual inclinations. Pavlov wrote with gratitude about receiving this kind of a freewheeling education, which he contrasted with the education then provided in the so-called Tolstoy Gymnasiums, named after D. Tolstoy, a disciplinarian minister of education, who had molded education along the stern barrack-room concepts of education of the czarist regime. Pavlov's interests turned to science at an early age. When he entered St. Petersburg University in 1860 he embarked on a course of study that emphasized natural history, physics, and mathematics. Later he took animal physiology as his main course of study, with chemistry as the minor. Pavlov graduated in 1875 and then proceeded to complete a medical degree since the latter provided an entrée into the academic world and the ultimate possibility of a professorship, a goal that seemed quite unattainable to the young Pavlov in his mid-twenties. He became the assistant to a professor of physiology, who was unexpectedly expelled for political reasons, an event which seems to have left a deep impression on Pavlov. He was able to obtain work lecturing and other assistantships, which Pavlov described as excellent experiences even though they did not seem to result in any notable scientific contributions of his own. The experience also helped him to acquire competence in laboratory techniques, an era for which he was famed throughout his life. Pavlov wrote his thesis on the cardiac nerves and then spent 2 years abroad. During this trip, he worked with the famous physiologists Karl Ludwig and Rudolf Heidenhain. On his return, he began his research on the digestive system which eventually brought him the Nobel prize.

In 1890 he obtained his first appointment to a chair. He was then 41. He actually held two chairs, one as professor of pharmacology at the Military Medical Academy at St. Petersburg, and the other as head of physiology at the Institute of Experimental Medicine. He was now relatively free to develop his own research and his own laboratory. His initial work involved studies of the nervous control of the pancreas, which led to a broad series of studies on the control of the digestive glands. He was awarded the Nobel prize in the field of physiology in 1904.

A part of Pavlov's extraordinary success in developing the physiology of digestion derives from his remarkable skill in operating on animals. One of the techniques developed by him was to partition the stomach of an animal into two components, one of which could be entered easily from the outside through an artificial fistula. In this way, he could study digestion directly without disturbing the animal's ordinary biological functions. Later, he used the same skill in changing the path of a salivary gland so that it dropped saliva to the outside and permitted the measurement of the amount secreted. Pavlov gave public demonstrations of his surgical techniques even when he was over 80 years of age. Without these techniques, he would not have been able to carry out his later work on conditioning.

In the late 1890's, Pavlov became interested in what he referred to as "the physical secretions." These were exemplified by the secretions of digestive glands that were produced by the sight of food. Pavlov was already familiar with the work of Sechenov, and had been particularly impressed with Sechenov's first important paper on the reflexes and the idea that reflexes might be the foundation of all behavior. The idea of reflexes had had a long history, for Descartes had written about them. Nevertheless, the work of Sechenov and Pavlov was undertaken within a completely new context, in that they sought to relate reflexes to specific pathways in the nervous system. In addition, Pavlov was exploring the idea that an important role was played in the coordination of reflexes by particular nuclei in the brain and that connections between these nuclei might be the means through which such reflexes were coordinated, inhibited, and conditioned.

Pavlov stated in later life that his interest in the nervous system was first aroused by Sechenov's 1863 paper on "The Reflexes of the Brain." He must surely have been aware of this important paper when he was still a young man, but its implications do not seem to have become a driving force in his work until he was nearly 50 years of age and began his work on conditioning. In accepting the idea that all conscious experience was a result of physical activity in brain, nervous system, and muscles, Pavlov accepted the idea that the study of neurophysiology would lead to an understanding of conscious experience and, in a sense, a science of conscious experience. The last paragraph of his speech made on receiving the Nobel prize for physiology reflects this viewpoint:

> In point of fact only one thing in life is of actual interest for us--our psychical experience. But its mechanism has been and still remains wrapped in mystery. All human resources -- art, religion, literature, philosophy and historical science -- have combined to throw light on this darkness. Man has at his disposal yet another powerful resource -- natural science with its strictly objective methods. This science, as we all know, is making big headway every day. The facts and considerations which I have placed before you are one of the numerous attempts to employ -- in studying the mechanism of the highest vital manifestations in the dog, the representative of the animal kingdom which is man's best friend -- a **consistent**, purely scientific method of thinking.

During the late 1890's, Pavlov and his students concentrated their attention on the response of the salivary glands. They showed that the salivary responses could be produced not just by placing food in the mouth, but by a number of stimuli associated with food. The quantity of saliva produced depended upon the relationship of the object shown to the actual consumption of food. They further demonstrated that a stimulus not ordinarily associated with food, and which would not produce the salivary reaction, could produce the salivary reaction under certain conditions of learning. During the next 30 years, a vast amount was learned in Pavlov's laboratory about this conditioning phenomenon.

Pavlov linked the concept of conditioning with the knowledge available about the nervous system. When Descartes had originally described reflexes, he had thought of them as responses of the total body. By the time that Pavlov had started his studies, specific tracts had been identified in the nervous system and related to specific functions. Pavlov had extended this work through his studies of the nervous mechanism involved in digestive functions and had been able to identify some of the nerves involved. With this background he came to regard reflexes and conditioned reflexes as the manifestation of the activity of particular paths and nuclei in the nervous system. Pavlov also extended his work to the study of the cerebral cortex, undertaking a large number of experiments involving the extirpation of particular parts of the cortex. Pavlov became fascinated with the idea that the cortex was at least partly a system for the analysis of information, and a part of his research involved exploring the location of the analyzers in relation to the senses. What he seems to have been groping for was a theory which would explain how the conditioned responses took place. He was moving in the direction of developing a physiological theory of behavior which, in turn, would explain the nature of experience.

Pavlov recognized that human learning was more complex than that found in lower animals. He attributed the difference to the presence of language in the human, which he described as a *secondary signaling system.* Like other psychologists who were later to attempt to describe human learning in terms of conditioning, he had difficulty in fitting language into his conception of learning and, apart from some brief discussion of the subject, did not try.

Pavlov was a man of remarkably wide interests. One only has to look through any collection of his papers to recognize that fact. He wrote criticisms of Gestalt psychology, reflected on the implications of his work on conditioning for understanding psychopathology, discussed the relationship of hysteria to conditoning, explored what he called *hypnotic states,* and so forth. He raised many questions concerning the utility of the conditioned reflex concept for understanding behavior in the human.

Boring's *History of Experimental Psychology* (p. 637) states that Pavlov was encouraged in his early work by reading the published version of E. L. Thorndike's dissertation, for he saw in that research new possibilities of studying behavior objectively. Pavlov's own work opened up new ways of exploring events that had hitherto been considered matters that could be explored only through subjective reports of human subjects and which could not be explored at all in animals. For example, through the use of conditioning procedures he explored the capacity of animals to make visual discriminations. Thus, a dog might be conditioned to salivate in the presence of a large circle, but not in the presence of a small one. Then, a further series of experiments could be undertaken to determine the extent to which the circles could be made equal in size and still permit the animal to make the discrimination. Pavlov believed that the new techniques would make it possible to explore what Pavlov referred to as the "psychical" processes of animals.

Although Pavlov, in keeping with the customs of his age, made frequent reference to psychical processes, this did not involve, necessarily, any conception of a vital force of a kind that had been traditionally invoked or which was then used by Pavlov's contemporary Henri Bergson in his formal system of philosophy. Sechenov much earlier had taken the position that learning and processes related to intelligence could take place without the intervention of consciousness. Such an idea paved the way for the idea, that was to develop later in the twentieth century, that learning was strictly a mechanical process and that an understanding of learning did not require an understanding of what Herbart referred to as the *mechanics of conscious experience.*

In the early part of the century, and particularly after the Russian revolution, Pavlov developed his philosophical position along Marxist lines. The new concept of psychology as a branch of physiology, that had been emerging, since Sechenov began to write on the subject, fitted well the Marxist view concerning the nature of consciousness and the biomechanical nature of behavior. He wrote in strong terms, rejecting the dualist position which he saw reflected in the new and developing Gestalt psychology that had evolved from the work of Max Wertheimer. Although he wrote extensive criticisms of Gestalt psychology, and seems to have been fully cognizant of the literature developing in the English language, he had virtually nothing to say about the development of behaviorism by John B. Watson in America.

The impact of the Russian model of learning was slow in coming to America, though it was ultimately to have substantial impact on American education and educational thought. Writers of materials for teachers and students of education hardly seem to have been aware of this new line of thought in the early part of the century. English versions of Pavlov's work were slow in becoming available. Thorndike seems hardly to have been aware of it until John B. Watson began to provide a popularized version of the Russian position. It was not until conditioning theories became in vogue among American psychologists that they came to have a hard impact on American educational thought and practice.

DARWIN, DARWINISM AND THEORY OF EVOLUTION

We must now turn to the third great scientific influence on educational thought, namely, the influence of evolutionary theory. The influence of the concept of evolution on educational thought and theory is today pervasive and is evident in every phase of education from the textbooks to which students of education are exposed to the way in which the learning of the pupil is conceptualized. Not all of this influence has been healthy.

Although evolutionary theory was not new with Charles Darwin, the particular form in which Darwin molded the theory was, and the massive evidence he provided, forced it on the attention of both his scientific colleagues and the public. The earlier theory of evolution of Jean-Baptiste Lamarck (1744-1829) had been laid to rest in scientific archives, but Darwin's theory could not be. His forceful presentation, written in a popular style that any educated person could read and understand, brought evolutionary theory to the front pages of the daily newspapers. The opposition to the theory of evolution by the churches of the day made it into a *cause célèbre*, which still has its advocates and opponents.

The influence of evolutionary theory on education came through its impact on psychology and sociology. Psychology of the early part of the nineteenth century was based upon the assumption that the human was basically different from the organisms lower on the evolutionary scale. The widely held view of scientists in Western Europe, derived from the theory of Rene Descartes (1596-1650), was that the lower organisms were strictly mechanical in nature, since they did not have souls, or consciousness. Only the human was believed to have a mind. Serious scientists, like Fechner, developed research which, they believed, began to establish the relationship between bodily events and the experiences of the soul.

Evolutionary theory forced the abandonement of this separation of the human from other living creatures. It postulated a continuity, through ancestry, of all living creatures. The theory gave support to the idea that the functioning of the human could be understood through the study of lower organisms. The latter idea was not entirely new, for a few scientists had long assumed that this was possible. The superficial resemblance of the interior organs of the human and other higher animals had led easily to the conclusion that one could learn about human physiology from the study of other mammals. The Russian neurophysiologists assumed that the nervous systems of all higher organisms were sufficiently similar and that what was learned about behavior from one organism could be applied to the understanding of the behavior of other organisms. The generalizations of the Russian scientists were from the behavior of lower organisms to the human. Evolutionary theory legitimatized that form of generalization.

The behavioral sciences, emerging in the limelight of evolutionary theory, embraced the position that human behavior could be understood through the study of the behavior of much simpler organisms. This approach also seemed to fit the scientific tradition of studying simple phenomena in the laboratory under highly controlled conditions. In time, this approach was to lead to the development of school materials and recommendations concerning how teachers should conduct their classrooms.

Darwinian evolutionary theory embodied the central theme that the mechanism of evolution was the survival of the fittest. This concept became a cornerstone of much theorizing in both sociology and psychology. Herbert Spencer, the founder of much of modern sociology and respected savant of his age, urged that the principle of the survival of the fittest should be applied to the development of societies. He proposed that the unfortunates in any society, unable to provide adequately for themselves, should *not* be helped by the state, but should be allowed to die out. The theory was that this was the way in which the human species could be improved, just as it had been improved over millions of years. Spencer believed that those whom he considered to be inadequate organisms should not be encouraged to survive and to propagate themselves. Spencer's proposal for the evolution of human society was applauded by the wealthy and well-to-do, but the poor were never even aware of Spencer's name. In this way evolutionary theory came to have considerable impact on public policy both in Western Europe and in the United States.

The sociological theory of the evolution of society through the survival of the fittest soon found allies. One ally was the newly developing theory of genetic inheritance. The leaders of the emerging field of genetics proposed that the improvement of society did not have to wait for the slow elimination of the less fit members. The less fit members of society could be sterilized and the most adequate members encouraged to proliferate. The affluent were generally considered to be the fit who should survive and the poor were those who should be marked for slow elimination. This genetic theory rapidly became linked to the theories of those who began to develop tests of intelligence, and the intelligence test was seen as the means of identifying those who should survive. The affluent expressed satisfaction with the fact that their children tended to score higher on intelligence tests than did the poor. This kind of theorizing by sociologists and psychologists near the turn of the century led to educational policies that provided a different education for the children of the poor and the children of the rich. Tracking systems in education had their roots in evolutionary theory.

Evolutionary theory led scientists to take a philosophical position which, in turn, influenced education. Once one accepts the continuity of life, from the human down to the simplest unicellular organism, one must also accept the idea that the linkage involves similarities in the way in which living things function. Evolutionary theory cannot tolerate the complete break, proposed by Descartes, between conscious humans that had souls and subhuman organisms that were postulated to be mechanical and lacking in consciousness. Either all organisms shared consciousness, to some degree, or, to take the ridiculous position, none were conscious. Probably, few had ever been willing to adopt the position of Descartes, and most humans, who had any contact at all with animals, viewed animals as conscious entities.

On the other hand, many behavioral scientists were at home with the idea that living organisms were mechanical entities. The Russians had adopted this view and produced brilliant developments. They had found it easy to conceptualize behavior as being based on a set of simple mechanical principles of the nervous system. Consciousness was easily disposed of as a mere byproduct of physical activity, with no particular consequences. Scientists found it much easier to view the evolutionary scale of living organisms as representing a scale of mechanical complexity, than to think of it as involving a gradation in levels of consciousness. Thus evolutionary theory became tied to a theory of the evolution of mechanical complexity in the eyes of many behavioral scientists.

The mechanical view of behavior, together with the view that behavior could be explained in similar terms at all levels of evolutionary complexity, formed the basic philosophy of the movement known as American behaviorism. By the midtwentieth century, behaviorism was to have some impact on schools, partly through introducing a language to describe pupil learning that included such terms as *reinforcement* and *shaping*. Implicit in the use of the language was the idea that the behavior of children could be controlled and modified by suitable actions on the part of the teacher. What children wanted to do, or what they experienced, was irrelevant to the control of learning by the teacher, for the orthodox scientific view of the child was that he, or she, was a mechanical system, like the rest of the animal kingdom. Psychologists might make the convenient assumption that behavior was based on a mechanical system, and it was not entirely their fault that the assumption should be taken by others to be fact. Some avant garde educators, and even a few teachers, began to preach the new philosophy of the mechanical nature of the pupil as though it were a scientific discovery. No longer could human thought and behavior be studied in isolation from the context in which it occurred. Evolutionary theory led to the asking of questions about how the human copes with the problems posed by the environment and how the human learns to cope. Education began to be viewed as the process whereby young humans learn to adjust to a very complex environment. Through this line of thought education came to be understood as a process of adjustment. The influence of this idea on American education was deep.

During the 1930s the publications of the United States Office of Education promoted the idea that education involved the adjustment of the child to the environment. Indeed, this became the central theme of the Federal agency. Although the concept of education as environmental adjustment had merit, the idea soon became distorted when some influential educators began to interpret environmental adjustment as meaning emotional adjustment. This led to bitter controversy and the adjustment education movement foundered in confusion. Yet the evolutionary concept of education as learning to adjust to the environment, both physically and intellectually, was a powerful one that continued to influence education, in subtle forms, down to the present.

FURTHER COMMENTS ON THE INFLUENCE OF NINETEENTH CENTURY SCIENTIFIC IDEAS ON EDUCATION

At various places throughout this chapter the relationship of the ideas of nineteenth century scientists to the development of education has been discussed. Now let us try and bring these ideas together.

The most direct impact of all of nineteenth century ideas on education is found in the work of Maria Montessori. Her own scientific training led her to search the scientific literature of her age for ideas that would help her in designing a curriculum. Although she spoke of this search, she said little about what she had found, naming only Fechner as a major influence. This absence of documentation for her ideas is hardly surprising in view of the fact that she did not write down the material published in her books, but let her students and admirers take down her lectures. These lectures were not taken in shorthand, but probably in note form, and later expanded into prose. In the process, many references to Fechner remained, and the discrimination tasks developed by Montessori might well have come straight out of the laboratory of Weber and Fechner. Montessori found in the work of the latter the analysis of sensory functioning that she needed as a basis for her curriculum.

Montessori's medical studies must have brought her into contact with the entire range of studies of the senses, including the work of Helmholz on hearing and vision. Her books include virtually no suggestion that she had any familiarity with the work of Herbart. Her materials do not include the kind of concept learning tasks that the educational theory of Herbart imply.

Montessori may well have been unaware of the nature of the Herbartian literature on which many teachers of her age were trained. With some of that literature she would have been in complete agreement, but her contribution included an originality that most of the literature did not have.

The new European psychology, with its emphasis on perception and the physiology of the senses, had its first and indirect impact on education through the changes it produced in the textbooks that were written for teachers. One of the most notable of these in the late nineteenth century was James Sully's *Teacher's Handbook of Psychology* (1886). Sully (1842-1923) spent much of his life as professor of psychology at the University of Aberdeen, Scotland. He had studied in Germany and had had some contact with Helmholtz, from whom he had acquired what would then have been considered a thorough knowledge of the senses, a knowledge which left an impression on his writings, which also show a deep respect for the work of Herbart. In a way, Sully's *Handbook* represents the first of the new vintage of books that were to be written for teachers. The book represents a break with the Herbartian tradition, which treated the soul as being quite independent of the body, for the newly developed science of physiology is given a central role in Sully's writings.

Sully's *Handbook* was important in many respects. First of all, it presented one of the first thorough discussions of the role of a science of psychology in the work of the teacher. Sully took the position that teaching was an art but that an art can be aided by technology and science. Sully believed that education should seek "by social stimulus, guidance, and control, to develop the natural powers of the child, so as to render him able and disposed to lead a healthy, happy, and morally worthy life" (p. 5). The picture of the aim of education is an artistic creation in itself, and it is to be achieved through the *art* of teaching. He believed that for the art of teaching to be performed successfully, the teacher must have "a body of well-ascertained truths respecting the fundamental properties of the human being, from which the right and sound methods of training the young may be seen to follow as conclusions" (p. 8). Sully saw this body of knowledge as consisting of facts and laws and not just a patchwork of pieces of empirical knowledge. Sully recommended that teachers should become aware of the general nature of psychological laws and principles, and become able to apply them intelligently to practical situations. Sully realized that good teaching does not involve a set of tricks that the teacher can use to produce learning, but that teaching always involves the thoughtful application of psychological principles. Sully provided a rather good account of what was known about the nervous system and the fact that lower centers might acquire the functions of carrying out quite complicated acts with little or no intervention by the higher centers.

Sully, like all who write for teachers, also extended his conclusions onto uncertain grounds, often drawing implications that today would be recognized as false. His attempt to describe mental fatigue as fatigue of the brain is just that. Sully used the term *individual differences* and speculated that each brain may have a physical limit of learning imposed upon it by its structure. He referred to this as the *coefficient of brain power.*

Sully, like many moderns, wrote about intellectual operations. He recognized such operations as the identification of objects, and the discrimination among objects. He also recognized that inference is an important operation and understood that all scientific thought and discovery involved the making of logical inferences. He gave to reasoning a role in education comparable only to that given it much later. Sully also saw that a knowledge of logic is necessary for understanding human behavior, because human behavior is to some degree logical.

The senses were well treated by Sully in terms of the knowledge available to him. Enormous advances had been made in the field of the physiology of sensation in the decades that preceded the publication of Sully's book. Sully was also able to show the relationship between the physiology of the senses and a general theory of the nature of knowledge and the nature of education. The object method of teaching of John Amos Comenius seems to lie at the background of Sully's thoughts on teaching through sensory experience. Sully also had a great deal to say about the training of perception, which, despite the lack then of an experimental base, has turned out through later research to be largely correct.

Although Sully attempted to use available scientific knowledge, he does not seem to have been aware of the work of Herman Ebbinghaus, which was slow to have impact on educational literature in the

English-speaking world, and even slower to have impact on education. Yet Sully was able to state and apply some of the same ideas that Ebbinghaus derived from his research, though Sully derived them from the common wisdom of teachers. For example, he advocated short learning periods interspersed with physical activity, an idea closely similar to the idea of distributing learning rather than massing learning. His discussion of concepts is quite Herbartian, but most of it would be acceptable to modern psychologists. Sully related concepts to classification and understood the important role of classification operations in logical thought.

Sully was at the forefront of the new way of training teachers and looking at children. The new way emphasized the physiological basis of behavior. Much as Wundt may have emphasized that psychology should be an experimental science based upon but independent of physiology, the trend in thought was to emphasize the physiology of behavior as Wundt had done in his early writings.

The new concept of behavior generated by the Darwin position began to influence the technical literature to which teacher trainees were exposed before the turn of the century. Not all books on psychology for teachers were influenced in this way.

What is probably the most notable example of the new generation of textbooks based upon the new biological concepts was James Mark Baldwin's *Mental Development in the Child and the Race* (1895). The book went through three editions during 20 years and several printings of each edition, and was one of the influential books of its day. The introduction to the first edition stated explicitly that the book was based on the concept of biological evolution and the evolution of the mind. The book attempted to provide a synthesis of what knowledge was available on the development of the infant and child with knowledge of evolution. The book placed emphasis on the idea that child development reflects the same kind of mental development that the human species must have undergone during its evolutionary history. Although Baldwin had been a student of Wundt, he seems to have been much more impressed with the development of biology than he was with the kind of psychology that Wundt was attempting to evolve. Baldwin's background and training was mainly in philosophy, a training which, in his day, suited him superbly to undertaking the task of synthesizing knowledge in different areas, for that was one of the tasks that philosophers of his generation undertook. Baldwin's synthesis of evolutionary theory, child study, psychophysics, and developmental psychology was superb. The very large number of printings of his book suggests that it must have been widely used in teacher training establishments, for the number of students of psychology was extremely small.

Not all books of the age showed the influence of physiology and evolutionary theory. William James's *Talks to Teachers* did not and, most surprisingly of all, the book by Lloyd Morgan entitled *Psychology for Teachers* (1906) showed a total lack of emphasis on the new biologically oriented view of the human.

Although the James book was probably the one most widely read by prospective teachers well into the present century, it did not represent the new trend in teacher education literature. The new generation of textbooks was heavily weighted with materials that reflected the Darwin tradition. Even a philosophically oriented psychologist such as Hugo Münsterberg, when he wrote his *Psychology of the Teacher* (1910), included a section on the biology of education. Münsterberg also seems to have been well aware of the work of Ivan Pavlov and Charles Sherrington in those parts of the book in which he viewed the human organism as a system of inputs and outputs. In the section on reading, Munsterberg also showed that he was aware of the research that had been done in that area, though he provided virtually no documentation either there or in other parts of the book. Münsterberg's book was about the last book of its kind for teachers that could be published without referencing research sources.

The influence of the German school of experimental psychology on education did not come only through its impact on textbooks. Its most dramatic impact came through the influence of two American students of Wundt who extended aspects of his work into areas of great significance for education. One of these was James McKeen Cattell (1860-1944), who spent the years 1883-1886 working with Wundt as his first assistant. While still with Wundt, Cattell began to explore the perceptual processes involved in reading. When he returned to the United States, he continued his work on the psychology of reading but also initiated work on the measurement of individual differences in the psychological processes studied in Wundt's laboratory. Cattell also played a notable part in the development of psychology in the United States through the exercise of his extraordinary talents as an organizer.

A second individual who brought the influence of the German experimental psychologists to the United States, and particularly to education, was Charles Hubbard Judd (1873-1946), who worked in Wundt's laboratory in the years 1894-1896. Judd brought Wundt and Wundtian psychology to the United States in several ways. One was through his translation of Wundt's great work entitled *Grundriss der Psychologie*. Another important source of impact was through Judd's development of the psychology of school subjects, an old Herbartian idea that Judd now attacked with experimental procedures. An entire chapter later in this book will be devoted to Judd and his conception of the psychology of school subjects.

The reader should not be left with the impression that the scientific developments of the nineteenth century found their way rapidly into educational literature. Influence on educational theory and practice was, in fact, slow. As a very rough and general rule one can say that it took 30 to 40 years for scientific ideas to influence professors of pedagogy. Sometimes the lag was even greater. The typical diffusion of ideas from the scientific world to education involves great inertia. As will be evident in later chapters of this volume, scientific ideas influence education rapidly only when the scientist involved is directly interested in education and educational problems. Without such a direct link, ideas diffuse only very slowly from one field to another.

PART II

The Emerging Role of Measurement in the Conduct of Education

In the new atmosphere that prevailed in school administration in the middle of the last century, adventuresome individuals were beginning to invent new ways of finding out what pupils were learning. Then, as now, there were doubts in the minds of many that schools were accomplishing all they were expected to accomplish. Clever individuals, concerned with the administration of schools, began to create methods of finding out just what pupils were actually learning.

Although examinations had been given in schools back to the time of antiquity, these had generally been recitations performed in front of an examiner. The great invention in education in the middle of the last century was the printed test administered under a set of standard conditions. This was a very important development, that permitted teachers, administrators, and parents to learn more than they had ever known before about the accomplishments of children in schools. At the time when this invention was made, it was acclaimed to be an important new administrative device, for, at last, the administrator could determine objectively whether a school was achieving the goals expected of it.

The measurement of pupil learning was to develop and expand as a technology for the next hundred years from the time of its invention. But a technology is not a science, though it may provide the basis of a science. The technology of measuring achievement was to become an important tool in the hands of educational research workers, even though it was only a practical technology based on common sense. Chapter 3 outlines that technology and the questions it was designed to answer.

Measurement also came to education in the last century through the attempts of psychologists to measure what they believed to be the basic human abilities. This work found its roots in the new laboratories of Europe where work had been initiated on what academicians believed to be the fundamental intellectual capacities for learning. This work began with the measurement of sensory functions, but the strongest thrust of the enterprise came with attempts to measure what was called intelligence.

The development of the concept that there were differences in intelligence, that could be measured, was quickly embraced by those in education concerned with the measurement of achievement. They quickly jumped to the conclusion that differences in achievement, among pupils of the same age, was surely a result of differences in intelligence. The explanation looked simple and obvious. Unfortunately, educational research workers had not yet learned that, what appear to be simple solutions to complex problems, are often only illusions of solutions -- not real solutions. That story is told in later sections of this part of the book.

CHAPTER 3

Assessment and Evaluation

In the Puritan schools, and in many of the schools of the last century, most learning had to take place through independent study. Horace Mann described schools in which as many as 50 pupils were assembled in one room under the tutelage of one teacher. The children could not be grouped in terms of level, because they often ranged in age from toddlers to grown men and women. Under such conditions the teacher could do little more than assign work to each pupil and to spend a few minutes each day checking the work accomplished. The typical means of checking the work of a pupil involved recitation, that is to say either asking a child to repeat back to the teacher the lesson he had learned or to answer questions based upon it. This recitation technique for evaluating pupil progress later became a standard teaching technique in graded classes.

THE GREAT BOSTON SURVEY

Recitation in the one-room New England school served three purposes. First, it provided an incentive for the pupil to learn. Second, it demonstrated to both pupil and teacher the extent to which the pupil's efforts had been successful. Third, it provided a rehearsal for the examinations conducted by the School Committee, which was the official body that supervised the conduct of the school. Be it noted that the examinations of the School Committee were often perfunctory or even absent, but those schools that had alert School Committees did have days of oral examinations conducted at least once each year. At those examinations the teacher as well as the pupils were under scrutiny. A teacher, who had thoughts for his future, did well to see not only that his pupils learned effectively, but that they were also experienced in being examined.

Otis W. Caldwell and Stuart A. Courtis (1924) have provided an excellent summary of the state of affairs in education in the Boston schools in the mid-1840's and the conditions that led to the first systematic school survey using printed tests in 1845. They were able to bring to light the records of the Boston School Committee that developed the idea of a survey. Caldwell and Courtis imply that the survey came into being after Horace Mann and the 30 Boston schoolmasters had had a brush, for the Committee was then under pressure to demonstrate that the schools of Boston were all that the Boston schoolmasters believed them to be, and that Boston needed no supervision by the State Board of Education. A subcommittee of the School Committee was appointed to consider the problem of how to conduct an effective inspection of the schools. The subcommittee discussed the problem of examining over 7,000 children and concluded that this could not be done through the usual oral examination. A sampling procedure was proposed whereby only the first (eldest) class in each school might be examined, but this proposal was abandoned in favor of examining all of the children in the Writing and Grammar Schools of the City of Boston by means of printed tests. Horace Mann hailed the enterprise as the dawn of a new era, for Horace Mann believed that the collection of facts should be one of the foundations on which school policy should rest.

The Writing and Grammar Schools of Boston included children about 7 to 14 years of age. Each school was organized into two departments, each presided over by a master who supervised the work of the assistants and ushers. One teacher was provided for about 60 children. The grammar department typically had charge of instruction in orthography, reading, geography, grammar, and history, and the writing department had charge of arithmetic, handwriting, and sometimes some algebra and geometry. In those days the term orthography referred largely to spelling. Spelling and grammar were taught separately from actual writing.

Children were generally divided into about four groups, roughly in terms of age, but the schools of Boston were nothing like modern schools. Many schools provided large open spaces where as many as 250 children might be assembled in a single room. Some schools had little more than two large floors with no partitions, and simple benches for the pupils and tables on which children could place a book or a sheet of paper. Most writing was undertaken on slates, though every child learned to use the awkward quill pen, the steel pen when available, and the scarce commodity paper. Textbooks of that day would be described by modern critics as dull, formal, and perplexing, reflecting a philosophy established by the Puritans and education should not be fun for it involved the serious matter of the development of the soul. Textbooks were also quite abstract and included a moral element in teaching largely absent today. Children as young as 7 or 8 might be required to read sermons written for adults and by scholars of the classics.

The committee in charge of the survey faced many of the problems faced by those today running large testing programs. Precautions had to be taken to avoid cheating so that a true assessment could be made of pupil achievement. However, their efforts in this direction, like the efforts of those in modern times, were often frustrated by the teachers themselves who hoped that the tests would provide a good account of the teaching in the school. The report of the survey committee points out that teachers were very aware of the fact that the tests reflected on their competence and felt threatened by the administration of the tests. Teachers in those days were probably not as sophisticated as modern teachers in moving scores upward through various tricks of the trade, but the results of the survey probably overestimated the achievement of the children as do the results of modern surveys.

Precautions were also taken to ensure that the information about the examinations was not passed from one school to another. The examination was conducted by members of the committees on a single day. The examination was first given in one of the schools and then, immediately, the committee member moved to another school, and then to another. By the end of the day all of the 19 schools involved in the survey had been visited and the pupils examined. Nevertheless, despite these precautions and the close supervision of the committee members, there seems to have been some cheating, both through the action of teachers and pupils. The Boston Survey was conducted separately by two different committees in the Grammar Schools and the Writing Schools. The reports of these committees have been reproduced in the Caldwell and Courtis book. Original copies are located in the Boston Board of Education.

The original intention was that every pupil in the 19 schools was to be examined, but the tables of data appended to the report show that only about 20 to 30 scholars were examined in each school and that these were the older children. In most subjects about 500 children were examined, with an average age of about 13 years and 6 months.

The Survey Committees did not have a set of objectives to use as a basis for the development of an examination. What they had were the textbooks used in the schools, and the objectives of instruction were assumed to be defined by the content of the textbooks. This was a common assumption of teachers, and recitation sessions were commonly conducted in order to determine whether a child had mastered the content of the book. Recitation had not yet become a teaching technique, but was strictly an examination procedure. Objectives and learning were so closely tied together that children commonly learned, by heart, large sections of the books to which they were exposed.

The following extract from the report of the survey committee describes the nature of the examination (reproduced by Caldwell and Courtis, pp. 26-28):

> It is our wish to have as fair an examination as possible; to give the same advantages to all; to prevent leading questions; to carry away, not loose notes, or vague remembrances of the examination, but positive information, in black and white; to ascertain with certainty what the scholars did not know, as well as what they did know; to test their readiness at expressing their ideas upon paper; to have positive and undeniable evidence of their ability or inability to construct sentences grammatically, to punctuate them, and to spell the words. One of the papers prepared was a list of words to be defined, all of them taken from the reading book and used in the class; another was a set of questions upon Geography; another upon Grammar; one upon Civil History; one upon Natural Philosophy; one upon Astronomy; one upon Whately's Rhetoric, and one upon Smellic's Philosophy.
>
> In Geography, there were 31 questions, some very simple, some rather difficult, but not one which well taught children of fourteen years of age should not answer.
>
> In History, a list containing 30 questions was submitted and certainly there is hardly a question which a child of thirteen who had studied history should not answer.
>
> In Definitions, there were 28 words selected from the reading book, which the classes have probably read through during the year, and some probably more than once. Some of the words are the very titles and headings of reading lessons; some of them occur several times in the book. It is true that some of the words are not in common use, and are what are called "hard words," but these are the very words which should be explained in our upper classes; -- as for the easy words, they learn them in conversation. We admit that Thanatopsis (like some other words selected) is a rare and difficult one, and it would not have been chosen, were it not the heading of one of the lessons in the Reader, and the name prefixed to one of the most beautiful gems in the whole collection of American poetry.
>
> In Natural Philosophy, we gave printed papers containing 20 very simple questions and required answers to as many of them as could be written in an hour.
>
> In Astronomy, 21 questions were put varying from those of the simplest nature, such as, what is the radius of a circle, up to questions about tides, change of seasons, etc.
>
> The whole number of questions in Grammar was 14; -- some being merely requisitions to write a simple sentence containing an active transitive verb and an objective case, and others being sentences which contain false syntax to be corrected.

> In forming an estimate of the relative rank of the several schools in Writing, the Committee confined themselves wholly to the specimens offered by the first class.
>
> The written examination in Arithmetic was adopted in all the schools except the Smith. It was limited to the first division of the first class, which varied in numbers from four to twenty-six. The committee prepared ten questions for solution on a variety of subjects, and caused them to be printed on a single sheet, leaving between each a sufficient blank space to enable the pupil to record the process of solution. It was not expected any considerable number could work out all the sums in so short a time (1 hour and 10 minutes) but it was thought expedient to propose such questions that even those who had made the greatest advancement might find employment during the allotted period. It was intended to have these questions embrace such a variety of subjects as to require a pretty thorough knowledge of the whole science of arithmetic to give the right answers to all of them."

Although the books used in the schools were the basis for the tests, the Survey Committees realized that the questions should go beyond the books, and should explore the ability of the students to apply what they had learned to other situations. An effort was also made to begin each test with simple questions and to grade the questions in difficulty throughout the examination.

Each test was an hour in length and, in each school, three hours a day for two days was devoted to examinations. The committeemen themselves administered every test. Short answers were required and these seem to have been entered directly on the examination sheets in the space provided between each question. In addition, some samples were taken of the handwriting of the children on work they had undertaken in their regular classes.

The examiners, like their modern counterparts, listed rules for the scoring of papers. The same examiners who defined the scoring rules also undertook the tedious task of scoring the papers. The following paragraphs from the Survey Committee Report (reproduced in Caldwell and Courtis, p. 33) show the extraordinary careful thought that was given to the scoring procedure:

> The results would have been more surprising had we rigidly adhered to the rules of criticism, and set down every answer as incorrect which was not faultless; but we have put the most lenient construction upon the answers, and whenever it appeared that the scholar had any tolerable idea of the subject, we have recorded his answer as correct. If we had put down as correct only those answers which were perfect in regard to sense, to grammatical constructions, to spelling and to punctuation, the record would have been very short.

> These tables have been prepared with very great labor and care. It was necessary, however, to have them printed in haste, and a work which should have occupied several months, has been done in a few weeks. It may be, therefore, that there are some errors in them; but it is believed that they will generally be found in favor of the schools. For instance, in looking for errors in definitions, the rule has been, that when the scholar expressed himself obscurely, but seemed to have an idea of the meaning of the word, he should be considered as having answered correctly. So in geography, history, philosophy, etc., though the answers were ungrammatical, and contained errors in spelling and punctuation, still they have been recorded in the column of correct answers, if the scholar seemed to have a correct idea of the subject.
>
> As to the columns containing the errors in spelling, grammar and punctuation, they probably fall short of the real number, because while none would be found that were not in the scholars' answers, hundreds may have been overlooked in such a mass of papers. The number of errors in punctuation seems so enormous, that the Committee may be suspected of hypercriticsm; it may be said that punctuation is a mere matter of taste, and that any man may point out hundreds of errors in the works of the best authors. But in looking over the answers written by our scholars, care has been taken to record only the most palpable errors in punctuation. The list has been swelled mainly by the omission of commas and periods where the sense absolutely required them.
>
> Sometimes errors will be found set down in the columns of errors in punctuation and spelling, against a question which is recorded as not having been answered; and this is the explanation: A boy writes against the question: "I dont know never studied the subject." Here the question would be recorded as unanswered, and yet one error in spelling and two errors in punctuation would be recorded against him.

The results of the survey were presented in a number of different forms. The main presentation was in tables showing the number of correct and incorrect responses to each question, and also the number of times the question was not attempted. Each response to each question was also scored for errors in spelling, punctuation, and grammar. The results show that the examiners were unduly optimistic in what they expected to be the level of the achievement of the pupils. On the history tests, only 26 percent of the answers were correct. The corresponding percentage for geography was 24; for grammar, 39; for words to be defined, 27; for natural philosophy, 24; and for astronomy, 30. What was referred to as *natural philosophy* would be described today as general science. Astronomy included geometry and the main features of the solar system.

The reports of the Survey Committees painted a discouraging picture. The following is an extract from the Report of the Grammar School

Committee (reproduced in Caldwell and Courtis, pp. 179-181):

> There is one painful reflection forced upon the mind by the answers generally; and this is that while in some Schools the scholars seem to be conscientious, and do not answer questions about which they are ignorant; in others they appear to be perfectly reckless, and put down answers quite at hazard, in the hope of hitting upon something that may pass for an answer. This shows an habitual carelessness in giving answers, or a want of that nicely-trained conscientiousness, which deters from trying to appear what one is not.
>
> There is another sad reflection suggested by these answers. They show beyond all doubt, that a large proportion of the scholars of our first classes, boys and girls of fourteen or fifteen years of age, when called upon to write simple sentences, to express their thoughts on common subjects, without the aid of a dictionary or a master, cannot write, without such errors in grammar, in spelling, and in punctuation, as we should blush to see in a letter from a son or daughter of their age. And most of these children are about finishing their School career; they are going out into life; some to learn trades; some to assist their mothers in the house; the larger part never to receive any supplementary education; and how, we ask, are they, by and by, to write a letter that they would not be ashamed to exhibit?
>
> But there is a still more melancholy consideration, which is, that, if the first class, -- if the children who have, during a year, enjoyed that special care and attention which our teachers give to the upper classes, go out imperfectly instructed, what must be the case with the hundreds and thousands of the children of our less-favored citizens, whom necessity forces to leave the schools without even reaching the first class! We know that the value of the services of most of our ushers would be underrated by proportioning it to their salaries; and that great injustice would be done to the many excellent instructresses, by supposing their work, as assistants, to be worth to the scholars only one-sixth the work of the masters, -- but, if there be anything like justice in the low rate at which the City remunerates their services, those who receive their instruction alone, must go out from the schools but very poorly taught.
>
> There is, however, in the papers which we lay before the Committee, evidence that such a state of things needs not continue for ever. That evidence is to be found in the papers written by the first classes in our best schools, and especially in those written in some of the neighboring schools, -- schools kept at much less expense than our own, -- kept by masters not superior to our best ones, and which produce better results, because they have a better organization, and a more effective supervision.
>
> We do not recommend the table of rank which we have prepared, and which is annexed to the appendix, as affording a precise estimate of the merits of the Schools. It is based upon the comparative amount of correct answers given to our questions;

> and even if it were a perfect demonstration, instead of an approximate estimate of the comparative intellectual acquirement of the scholars, still we would not have it considered as an absolute test of the merits of the schools. Far be it from us to consider intellectual activity and intellectual acquirement as alone worthy of consideration. Since the world will have it so, let such rewards as medals, prizes, parts, etc., be bestowed upon intellectual strength, as the wreath in olden, and the championship in modern times, have been awarded to mere physical strength; but let us look to the cultivation of the religious sense, the supremacy of conscience, the duty of self-culture, the love of knowledge, the respect for order, -- let the presence or absence and measure of these be taken into account, before we say which school is first or which is last. Upon this we shall not decide, but simply remark that, tried by these standards, some Schools that now stand high would stand low, and some that are not conspicuous would be in the foremost ranks."

These depressing comments were followed by a brief evaluative statement concerning each school. The comment on the Adams School begins with the words, "This school seemed to us somewhat characterized by a want of energy and activity. The reading was indifferent and lifeless." These statements were followed by remarks to the effect that the school seemed to have some redeeming features. Many of the comments on the schools refer to the moral tone of the classroom, meaning the personal relationship between the teacher and the taught. The most derogatory comments were reserved for the Smith school that served a population of black and West Indian students. The committee concluded that the master in charge of the Smith School lacked faith in the ability of the children to learn. It seemed that they were taught almost nothing because the master believed that they could not learn. The Survey Committee thought otherwise and could see no reason why the children in the Smith School should not learn as well as the children in other schools.

Printed tests were given again throughout the City of Boston schools in 1846, but they were not given in 1847. The Report of the School Committee, dated 2 May, 1849, explains why. The 1849 Report stated that no use had been made of the results of the tests given in 1845 and 1846, and the further giving of tests was clearly a waste of time. The School Committee continued to "examine" the schools, but mainly by oral techniques. The Report of the School Committee of 5 November, 1850 mentions that some written examinations were given, but the reference implies that these were informally administered and did not involve the use of printed tests. This may not have been all of the story. The School Committees of later years may not have had the energy of the committee that undertook the 1845 testing. Indeed, in 1847, the City of Boston set up a committee to investigate the inadequacy of the operation of the school committee, and the school committee was proposing that some of its work be undertaken by a new appointee, called a superintendent.

Caldwell and Courtis, after reviewing the results of the 1845 survey, concluded that the schools of Boston were very inefficient at that time. That conclusion may not be fully justified. When one reviews all of the questions that were given to the children, one cannot but be impressed with the difficulty of so many of them. How many 13-year-olds today would know the difference between gravitational attraction, cohesion, and chemical affinity? How many would know how often the moon revolves around the sun or how many satellites has Jupiter? The questions asked strike one as being extremely hard, though it is difficult to judge them without having access to the textbooks that were in use at the time. Modern writers of tests know that they are all too prone to ask questions that are too difficult. The Survey Committees were not aware of this tendency.

Horace Mann voiced his enthusiasm for the new method of inspecting schools introduced by the Survey Committee. He wrote lavish praise for what the School Committee of Boston was attempting to do in several pages of the Common School Journal, which was written largely by Mann. In those pages (*Common School Journal*, 1845, 7, 330-335), Mann outlined the advantages of the system of using printed tests and written answers and even went so far as to say that this invention "will constitute a new era in the history of our schools" (p. 330). He states in his discussion of the subject that he had heard of this method of inspecting schools being used in European countries, but the present writer has not been able to trace the source of Mann's information. Point by point, Mann outlined the advantages of the new method.

1. *The new method appeared to be impartial.* Mann viewed the written examination as a device which would make it possible to compare fairly the different scholars in a school and to compare schools. The problems produced by comparing one scholar with another were not yet understood, and Mann like other experts did not recognize that there were factors other than the effectiveness of teaching that produced differences between schools. The common school of New England had been founded on the premise that all children were equally capable of learning, if only they were given the chance. The common school was an institution promoted by those who truly believed that all were created equal. Mann even states that "all scholars are born free and equal" (p. 330).

Mann also recognized that the written examination eliminated the unreliability of the single oral question commonly used for assessment. He states that many questions have to be asked of a child in order to determine what a child has learned. He compares the use of a single question to the throwing of a die. Mann was clearly aware of the problem of reliability of measurement.

2. *The method is more just than any other to the pupils themselves.* Mann points out that in the typical oral examination an hour was assigned to a class of 30 pupils. That meant that each pupil might expect to be examined for only 2 minutes. Yet some pupils require time in order to collect and organize their thoughts, and 2 minutes is not enough for that. In the oral examination a pupil might fail because a question surprised him and he did not have enough time to recover from his surprise.

3. *The method is the most thorough.* Here again Mann returns to the matter of what today would be called reliability and validity. He says that the quality of a house cannot be judged by looking at a single brick, and neither can the performance of a child be judged by hearing his answer to a single question or to one or two questions. A wise examiner, like a wise house purchaser, must examine many different things before arriving at a conclusion. Apparently Mann had in mind a short answer form of test rather than the modern form of the essay tests, which does not permit a wide sampling of the pupil's knowledge.

4. *The new method "prevents the officious interference of the teacher"* (p. 331). One difficulty of the oral examination was that teachers, waiting in suspense for the pupil to give a correct answer to a question, would blurt out a prompt to the pupil. Although Mann writes that he understands a teacher who spoils an examination in this way, he does believe that, nevertheless, pupils should be examined without such prompting. The written examination is able to do this.

5. *The new examinations permit the assessment of what pupils have been "faithfully and competently taught"* (p. 332). Here again he emphasized the idea that the objectives of the school can be achieved in all pupils if they are properly instructed. Mann has some interesting statements to make about textbooks. He points out that textbooks are referred to by that name because they provide *texts* from which teachers teach, much as a preacher selects a text as a starting point of a sermon. The textbooks of the day did little to expound on applications of knowledge, and Mann believed that should be the task of the teacher. Mann emphasized that hearing recitations from textbooks is not teaching, but teaching should show the connection of the printed material "with life, with action, with duty" (p. 332). A pupil who commits a textbook to memory may virtually know nothing and may be as ignorant as a parrot.

Mann saw the possibility that printed examinations might open the way to inquire into the pupil's ability to apply the knowledge he had acquired. Such examinations can call for both explanations and applications and these are the criteria by which Mann would want to judge teaching. Mann believed that the instructor should be held responsible for the examination results of the pupils, except in the case of those pupils who attend school irregularly. Mann mentions the latter exception, in passing, almost glossing over the fact that only about half of those who should have been in school were actually there, and a very large fraction of those who attended were there on an irregular basis.

6. *The use of printed tests would eliminate all suspicion of favoritism.* Mann states that examiners were commonly accused of favoritism, even though the charge was often probably false. Some examiners were accused of giving easy questions to good students in order to make a teacher appear effective, or the reverse might take place. The advantage of giving the same questions to all pupils was effective in eliminating any suspicion of unfairness.

7. *The printed examination makes it possible for several independent individuals to judge the competence of pupils.* The oral examination had a major and central weakness. In most cases the results depended upon the judgment of a single individual who conducted the examination. After leaving the classroom where he had conducted an examination, the examiner would attempt to provide a general description of his impressions. Nobody else could take issue with the judgments thus written down, for only he, the examiner, had been present at the examination. The new examinations with printed tests provided what Mann called "a sort of Daguerrotype" (p. 334) of the pupil's mind, available for anybody to see. An examination would no longer be a matter of private judgment, but a public matter where anybody could examine the performance of the pupil.

Then Horace Mann adds some words of timely wisdom. Not all the blame for faulty performance on the examinations should be placed on the teacher, for the pupil is responsible for mastering the content of the textbooks. The teacher is responsible for applications of the text and for explanations, but the pupil is responsible for the text itself.

Caldwell and Courtis state that the Boston Survey initiated a wave of similar examination projects throughout the United States, but little is known about this. One suspects that the pupils in most schools continued to be examined annually by the traditional oral examination, if they were examined at all. School Committees may well have liked to perform this function for it was their sole contact with pupils and it did permit them to have some contact with classrooms and to be able to assess the relationship between teacher and students.

The concept of an end-of-semester examination did not appear as a common feature of schools until the end of the nineteenth century in elementary and secondary establishments, although written examinations have been used, here and there, for at least two thousand years. Formal written examinations were known in Chinese schools as early as the second century B.C., and these were used for selecting candidates for the civil service. Similar examinations do not seem to have been used for the evaluation of Chinese education or of schools, but were used to determine whether the candidates for government jobs had sufficient proficiency in literature and history. In addition, candidates were given performance tests in writing poetry, in music, and in archery. These abilities were considered to be of the greatest importance, so much so that the successful candidates were required to retake the examinations every 9 years in order to retain their positions. The highest ranking official, the prime minister, was also required to take the examination and was expected to retain first place in the results.

The Jesuits also had introduced written examinations into their schools in the sixteenth century. They even prepared a code of rules for the conduct of such examinations entitled *Ratio atque institutio studiorum.* The examinations were held at the end of each year and were used to promote, or hold back, students. Despite these early efforts at developing written examinations, they were rare until about a hundred years ago. Most teachers in the last century would have said that they knew the level of progress of each student and did not need examinations of a formal character.

WRITING MATERIALS AND EXAMINATIONS

The development of written examinations was retarded by the lack of materials that permitted the student to record his answers easily. Early in the last century, and through much of that century, the slate was the main medium for writing, but it was a medium unsuitable for examinations that were administered and scored later. The slate was heavy, and could not be readily taken away from the school and stored. As well, pupils needed their slates for daily work. Furthermore, the slate was an awkward medium for writing. The high friction between the special slate pencil and the slate surface made writing slow and clumsy. The chief advantage of the slate was that it was cheap and reusable.

The pencil had been developed long before the Puritans developed common schools and provided slates. The earliest pencils were essentially painters' brushes that used graphite to leave an impression on the paper. The term *pencil* is derived from an old word, *penicillum,* meaning an artist's brush, which was similar to the brush-like formation of molds. The great development in the pencil came at the end of the eighteenth century, when a method was evolved for mixing graphite and clay into a consistency that permitted the material to be drawn out into sticks. These sticks could be placed in wood containers. Pencils were manufactured in Europe in the early part of the nineteenth century, but were not manufactured in the United States until 1812 when the war cut off supplies from Europe. Pencils were not cheap instruments for writing and were far outside of the reach of school budgets during much of the nineteenth century. The production of a cheap pencil could not take place until high-speed machinery had been developed for this purpose.

The pen was widely used in schools, long before the pencil achieved widespread use. The pen has also had a much longer history than the pencil. The pen was probably preceded by the stylus in antiquity, and the earliest writing was produced by a stylus that engraved itself on clay or other soft material. The Greeks used a stylus of bone or ivory. Later this was displaced by tubes of grass filled with pigment, that are the true ancestors of the modern pen. The Orientals have long used similar pens made of reeds and bamboo canes, and there are still parts of the world where such pens are in use today. The Romans attempted to make metal pens, but the arts related to the working of metal were too crude to control the features of a pen point that have to be controlled, such as that the metal must have enough spring to it.

The quill pen was first mentioned in the writings of Saint Isodore of Seville in the seventh century, but the instrument may well have had a long history before Isodore's comment. The quill seems to have been by far the best writing instrument invented in its time for it displaced all other forms. It became the main instrument used in schools, apart from the slate. The span of its history of use may well be more than 2,000 years. Even in the late 1800's, the quill pen was still the most widely used instrument for writing. Quills were most commonly derived from the wings of geese, but swan quills were also highly valued. For fine work, the quills of crows were sometimes used.

In 1809, an inventor, Joseph Bramah, developed a machine for cutting quills into lengths, and the short lengths were then inserted into a wooden holder. This made it possible to change the point quickly. The separation of the point and the holder led to many inventions, and one of these was to make the point of such different materials as horn, or ivory, or tortoise shell. Then an attempt was made to harden the points of pens by pressing into them small pieces of hard material such as diamond or ruby. Then the Roman metal pen of classical times began to come back, enhanced in value by the advances that had been made in metallurgy in the intervening centuries.

Although the metal pen point was in use in Europe by the middle of the nineteenth century, it seems to have been quite an expensive luxury and did not find its way into schools in the United States until 30 or 40 years later. The first factory for the mass production of the steel pen was established in New Jersey in 1870, but it must have taken many years before the products of that factory were commonly found in schools. The steel pen must have had difficulty in competing with a quill which could be obtained free from any market where geese were plucked.

When the steel pen entered education, a revolution in school practice was produced. Writing with the quill had been a slow and unhurried art. The nature of the quill made it that way, for the writer had to stop frequently in order to reshape and sharpen the quill. Since writing was a slow art, pride was taken in it and children must have vied with each other to produce the most elegant page. The steel pen changed that. The steel pen made it possible to write continuously over long periods. There was ever increasing pressure on the pupil to produce written material in quantity. The new medium for written work then became used for examinations, which became substitutes for the form of oral examination provided by the recitation. In fact, although some of the activities of classwork continued to be designated by the term *recitation*, these no longer served the purpose of checking on the progress of the pupil, for they became what today would be called class discussions. In a modern classroom a teacher may present a group of pupils with a question, but the teacher is unlikely to record who gives a correct answer and who gives an incorrect one. The recitation is not primarily evaluative, but serves other important functions. The cheap manufacture of the steel pen produced this transition, and it also destroyed writing as an art. By 1890, students had become so used to the steel pen that examinations were commonly administered using this writing instrument as a tool to produce rapidly written answers. Thus the essay examination came into being.

RICE'S EVANGELISTIC EDUCATIONAL RESEARCH

Although empirical methods for improving education had been in existence for at least 50 years before Joseph Mayer Rice (1857-1934) entered the field of educational reform, he has been commonly and mistakenly regarded as the father of educational research. He undertook nothing as radical as the Boston Survey, and neither did he bequeath the field of education with rich literature interspersed with empirical studies as Henry Barnard had done, but his attempts to produce educational reform were driven by an evangelistic zeal that has given him color as an historical character. He cannot be given credit for any particular innovation in the field of education or educational research. Yet, he did promote the idea that some problems of education could be attacked by empirical means.

Information about the personal life of Rice is hard to find, a fact reflecting the judgment of his contemporaries that he was little more than a crank. When he died there was no obituary published in the New York Times, nor anywhere else as far as one can determine. His entry in *Who's Who in America* was brief and noninformative. His short biography in *The National Cyclopaedia of American Biography* (1904, Volume 12, 203-204) is exceptionally short. One suspects that he was regarded by his contemporaries more as a muckraker than as a serious research worker or educational reformer.

His brief biography tells us that he was the son of German immigrants, who settled in Philadelphia in 1855. In 1870, the family moved to New York City where he completed high school and then entered the College of Physicians and Surgeons. He graduated as a physician in 1881 and practiced medicine for 3 years in the New York hospitals, and then developed a successful private practice. He became interested in preventive medicine and this led him to the study of childhood. He believed that the best way to produce a healthy adult was to strengthen the constitution of the child. This led him to the study of child training. His studies must have brought him into contact with the new ideas on child development that were emerging in Germany. Apparently these new ideas fascinated him, for after practicing medicine for only 7 years, he left for Europe in 1888, determined to explore the new psychology of childhood emerging there. He spent 2 years in Jena and Leipzig. At Jena he attended the Herbartian seminar, which apparently impressed him, but he must also surely have encountered the thinking of Froebel, which had a place in academic thought even though it had been politically discredited as a threat to Prussia. Rice also had opportunities to study the various school systems of Europe. He must have been impressed with the new freedom that children in Germany experienced in educational settings, but he did not bring back the disillusionment of William Torrey Harris who complained that even though German children learned to think freely in school, they showed none of the same freedom as adults.

Rice returned from Europe fired with a zeal for educational reform. Immediately, he wrote an article entitled "Need School be a Blight to Child-Life?" (1891). In this article, he contrasted the educational methods used in an unnamed school in Germany with another in New York City. Rice contrasted dramatically the free expression of the children in the German school with the children in the New York school who were required to stare fixedly at the teacher who did all the talking. The German children were instructed "naturally" but the New York children were instructed "mechanically." In the one, school life for the children was a pleasure, and in the other, a burden. Perhaps as a result of this article he was able to persuade the *Forum*, a widely read periodical, to sponsor an investigation of the public school systems of the United States and set out on a 2-year venture to visit these schools. In successive issues of the *Forum* he wrote articles on the school systems of New York City, Baltimore, Buffalo, Cincinnati, St. Louis, Indianapolis, Boston, Philadelphia, Chicago, St. Paul, Minneapolis, LaPorte, and Cook County. Although Rice managed to say some favorable words about one or another particular school he had visited, his comments were mainly completely damning.

His observations were published in consecutive issues of the *Forum* in 1892 and 1893. The articles were brought together in book form in the following year (*The Public School System of the United States*, 1903). His attack on the New York City schools was quite typical of his attack on the schools of other cities. He singled out a school in which the work of the principal had been described as excellent over a period of 25 years. Rice believed from his observations that the educational philosophy of that particular principal pervaded the school. The central idea of that principal's philosophy was that the child came to school with a set of worthless ideas that had to be completely ignored. In school the child would be expected to learn to give answers automatically to questions that pertained to worthwhile ideas. Any thoughts the child might have on his own were considered worthless, but the verbatim answers of the child reflected his potential for acquiring worthy ideas.

The emphasis of the school was to conduct a program for the child to "immobilize him, automatize him, dehumanize him" (p. 31), and to do this efficiently in terms of time usage. The slightest movement of the child was prohibited in that it was a waste of time. When Rice asked the principal whether the children were allowed to move their heads, she answered, "Why should they look behind when the teacher is in front of them?" (p. 32). The children were required "to stare fixedly at the source whence the wisdom flows" (p. 33). Even when passing educational material along a row, the children were required to stare fixedly in front of them. Speed and efficiency were believed by the principal to be the very essence of a good instructional program. Every minute believed to be saved was a minute gained. Rice commented on the machinelike nature of the lessons in arithmetic. In one classroom he imagined that he was watching wound-up automata. Even the lesson in music was no more than the drilling of children in definitions. In writing, the children had to learn by heart principles of penmanship, which would not be recognized by experts in the art. A lesson in reading was dominated by drill in the recognition and spelling of new words.

Rice did concede that the typical New York City elementary school was not as bad as the one he described with so much detail. Nevertheless, he considered that the typical school was characterized by mechanical drudgery, severe discipline, mental passivity, unsympathetic harshness, and an enforced silence and immobility. Teachers secured what they believed to be results by drill and routine that surely must have antagonized the children towards learning.

There were at least some schools where things were not as bad as Rice made them out to be. There were immigrants, like Mary Antin, who entered the schools and who, only a few years later, wrote in glowing terms about the encouragement that she had received from sympathetic and understanding teachers. Some schools were like those that Rice described, but not all.

The most common criticism of the schools in the series of articles was that the schools were "unscientific." This comment reflected the growing idea that there was a body of scientific knowledge on which education could be based, but what was then considered to be scientific is not what would be called scientific today. Undoubtedly Rice had in mind, among other things, the kinds of principles of education that Herbart had expounded and the idea that knowledge had to be acquired in an organized form, but he must also have been thinking about the new psychology of perception that emphasized the real world as the fundamental source of all knowledge. Then, of course, there was the work of James McKeen Cattell at Columbia on reading. Rice must surely have known about that work. One suspects also that Rice included in his idea of a scientific conception of education the ideas that Froebel had developed, despite their religious source, and certainly the observations of Pestalozzi.

Rice must have expected that the articles he wrote would produce educational reform through aroused public indignation. He had seen the leaders of educational thought in Germany produce an extraordinary revolution in teaching methods in the schools of that country, and he had expected that a similar revolution would take place in the United States. His articles were widely disseminated through the *Forum*, a prestigious and widely read publication, but no public outcry resulted. Even the journals subscribed to by teachers failed to produce any noteworthy comment. How the public reacted, if the public reacted at all, is not clear. What is clear is that Rice quickly realized that his articles were not producing the impact he expected of them and he realized that further action was necessary if the schools of the United States were to be reformed. He realized that the central weakness of his writings, so far, was that they represented the opinions of a single individual, and that they could be written off as the comments of a prejudiced observer. What he needed were facts that others could verify if they wanted to. If his readers could not be persuaded by his opinions, then perhaps a set of impressive facts might do the persuasion. Rice set out to collect facts to back up the opinions he had so freely, and some said casually, expressed.

Rice waited for nearly 2 years for the public reaction which never came. Then, he embarked on what was at that time the most ambitious plan ever undertaken to collect data on education. The broad purpose of the testing enterprise was to demonstrate that children were not learning as much as they should and that the poor practices of schools were interfering with pupil progress. He was particularly eager to demonstrate the falsity of the idea, then current, that the more time spent on a subject the more was learned. He also wanted to show that how the time in class was used was of the most vital importance. Rice began his new testing enterprise in February 1895, and he continued with it for nearly 10 years.

He learned much about how to conduct such an enterprise as he went along. The first set of data collected was virtually worthless, but he published them in order to avoid the accusation that he was hiding facts. In this first effort, he sent out his spelling test to superintendents, asking them to have the test administered to pupils in particular grades. Twenty superintendents agreed to have the test given. The test material consisted of 50 words selected by Rice and these were to be read to the pupils, who were to write down the words on a strip of paper. In addition, the kit of materials sent to each superintendent included a questionnaire pertaining to the methods of teaching and any special problems presented by the children such as recency of immigration, poor home conditions, and so forth. Altogether 16,000 children were tested.

The results of the study were reported in the *Forum* in two articles that carried one of Rice's typically provocative titles, namely, "The Futility of the Spelling Grind" (1897). The articles present extensive summaries of the data, together with the data on additional improved experiments that will be discussed in subsequent paragraphs.

The results of the testing showed enormous variation in performance from school to school as well as from pupil to pupil. Some fourth-year classes averaged as high as 95.3 percent correct, while other classes at the same level achieved only 33 percent. Rice's first impulse was to go out and study the high-scoring classes to find out what brilliant teaching methods had been used, but he did not have to extend his inquiry very far to discover that the high scores were artifacts. He interviewed teachers and discovered that the crucial factor was the way in which the tests had been administered. Many of the words read by the teachers could be read in such a way that the enunciation might inform the student about how the word was to be spelled. For example, if the word "cabbage" were read as "cab-bage," the student would have no difficulty in deciding whether the consonant in the middle was single or double. The spelling of other words could be aided by placing the emphasis on a particular syllable. Rice had discovered only a few of the ways in which teachers can help children improve their scores on tests. Future generations of teachers would find other ways, which today seem to be so well developed that most state-wide testing programs produce results that are relatively worthless. Rice at least sought ways to circumvent the difficulties he encountered.

Rice decided that his initial results were worthless. What he then planned to do was to develop a new test and to administer it under his direction. He and his assistants set out across the country and administered a new spelling test to 13,000 children. Every test was administered either by Rice or by one of his assistants. The tests were first scored by the pupils and then checked by Rice's helpers. This time his testing was also more sophisticated. The test words were embedded in sentences as, for example, the word *weather* in the sentence "The weather is changeable." In the latter sentence, both of the long words were test words. Rice also used a second test in which children were read a short and simple story and were then asked to write down what they remembered. The results were scored for spelling and not for the degree to which the story was remembered.

In the analysis of the results, Rice classified schools into those described as mechanical and those described as progressive. He does not describe the criteria that entered into his judgments in the matter. In the first study that he had attempted to conduct by mail, he had asked the superintendents to answer some questions about how the schools were conducted, but the replies he received were regarded as worthless. In his subsequent studies of spelling, in which he visited classrooms, he made judgments about classrooms with respect to the mechanical-progressive continuum. Undoubtedly Rice believed that the distinction was clear and self-evident and that his ratings in this respect could not be questioned.

Rice's most surprising finding was that there were only small differences between schools. Schools that served upper-class families did no better than those that served the families of quite poor immigrants. Even more surprising to Rice was the fact that those schools rated progressive did no better than those rated as mechanical. The main differences presented by his data were differences between age level, from which Rice concluded that the main factor in spelling achievement was level of maturity.

Perhaps the most important finding was that the amount of time spent on spelling each day had little relationship to achievement in the subject. He stated that the results obtained with 40 or 50 minutes of instruction each day were no better than when 10 or 15 minutes were devoted to the subject. One should note that these results are in contrast to the present flood of experimental results that are claimed to demonstrate that *time on task* is the crucial variable in determining level of achievement.

Rice concluded the presentation of his study with some advice on the teaching of spelling. His advice showed considerable wisdom, but did not become incorporated into practice for many years to come. His first point of advice was that spelling should be taught by a variety of techniques and that teachers should vary their procedures and avoid falling into a rut. Second, the amount of time spent daily on the teaching of spelling should never exceed 15 minutes. Third, words should be carefully graded for spelling instruction. Fourth, emphasis should be placed on the teaching of the spelling of common words. Unusual and technical words might be taught as they arose, but they should not be emphasized. Fifth, words that spell themselves should be excluded. Rice estimated that there were between 6,000 and 7,000 common words that should be included in spelling lists because the spelling of them is not quite obvious. Finally, Rice comes back to a point that he raises at numerous points in his writing. He emphasizes that the most important factor in pupil learning is the "personal power" (p. 419) of the particular teacher. He expands elsewhere on what he means by this and his factors in teaching success include the charisma of the teacher and the ability of the teacher to relate to the child. He admits that some teachers are born with the necessary qualities, but he believed that those who are not thus born can develop the qualities essential for promoting classroom learning.

Rice's experience with his test in spelling seems to have had a marked influence on the trend of his thought. He no longer was interested in remaking over American schools into the pattern he had observed in Prussia. He had come to view research as a mere device for the presentation of facts which would then win over the public to his way of thinking, but perhaps the lack of success it had had in this respect suggested that a new approach was in order. His goals of educational reform had become more modest. Also, he had become an editor of the *Forum* in charge of their Department of Educational Research, and this new responsibility may well have added caution to his approach. The first of two articles on the subject of his inquiry into the teaching of arithmetic carried the sober title of "Educational Research: A Test in Arithmetic" (1902). The second article on the topic had the equally sober heading "Educational Research: Causes of Success and Failure in Arithmetic" (1903).

The first of the articles states that the questions to be answered have to do with what results "shall" be accomplished in arithmetic, and how much time "shall" be devoted to the topic. The topics imply the new interests of Rice which were to become the debated issues of his age. The first issue relates to the establishment of standards that schools should be expected to achieve. There was already considerable interest in this topic. The second deals with an issue of the age related to the emerging interest in what were to be called scientific management techniques which, at an early stage in their development, focused on the matter of exactly how the time of the worker should be used. Rice was rapidly restating his problems related to education in terms of the management concepts of the day. He seems to have set aside much that he had learned in Germany.

Rice prepared an arithmetic test that provided eight questions at each grade. Some of the questions were repeated at two or more grade levels. The tests were designed to be given at the fourth, fifth, sixth, seventh, and eighth school year. These tests were given altogether to 6,000 children.

The results of the tests were in striking contrast to those in spelling. The differences between classes were as large in arithmetic as they had been small in spelling. The possibility did not seem to occur to Rice that small differences in spelling and the large differences in arithmetic might well have been a product of the way in which the tests were constructed. Most of his differences seem to have been a result of differences between city systems. Some cities produced fairly uniform good results on the test and some uniformly poor. These differences could not be accounted for in terms of the socioeconomic levels of the cities involved. Schools in aristocratic neighborhoods seemed to do no better than schools that served poor immigrants. Rice also noticed that size of class seemed to have little to do with the level of achievement, for the smallest class had the poorest record.

Rice did not have much to say on the matter of establishing standards. He suggests that, on his test, a score of 60 percent right for the eighth year of school might be considered a minimum acceptable score, but he is vague and notes that this percentage has value as a standard only if it can be applied to tests of comparable difficulty. One can hardly be surprised that Rice found he had run into difficulties in the matter of setting standards for the matter was to be debated well into the century.

The matter of the effect of the time devoted to arithmetic on achievement could not easily be studied with Rice's data, because differences in time were small. Rice does not report the actual times devoted to the subject, but implies that these varied from around 40 minutes per day to a little over 50. Such differences were unlikely to have an effect, and they did not.

The second article, written in 1903, explores further the reason for the differences among schools in arithmetic achievement. Rice believed he had disposed of the criticism that the main source of difference might be in the amount of homework assigned. He stated that he had collected data on this point and had found that the school with the worst arithmetic performance assigned the largest amount of homework. In the schools that Rice judged to be successful in terms of performance on the arithmetic test, the teachers tended to frown on homework. Although Rice thought that he had proved "conclusively" that homework had little to do with achievement, his data were not convincing.

In the second article on arithmetic, he makes the surprising statement that he believed that the teaching methods employed were "modern," which implies that Rice approved of them. This statement is a change from those he had made 10 years earlier. There had been changes in the schools in the intervening years, but Rice had changed too. He claimed at this point in his career that differences in the methods used by teachers could not account for the differences in the achievement of the different schools.

Rice then makes an important point. He began to realize that the structure of arithmetic was different from that of any other subject, and that a pupil who was moved on, without understanding a particular operation, might never be able to master the rest of the subject matter. Rice suspected that those schools that produced high achievement in arithmetic were those which made sure that each pupil mastered each step, and did not allow pupils to proceed until all previous steps had been thoroughly mastered.

After considerable argument suggesting that there is little within the immediate control of the teacher that can account for differences in academic achievement, Rice is led to the conclusion that the major influence is in the nature of the supervision provided by the school system. This conclusion is arrived at by elimination, rather than by finding evidence to support it. A single item of information supports this conclusion. That item is the finding that schools tended to be fairly uniform in performance on the arithmetic test across all sections of the same grade within a school. Differences were between schools. Rice interpreted this finding to reflect the uniformity of supervision within any particular school. Rice declared that, under an ideal system, the superintendent should be responsible for the preparation of courses of study, the establishment of time schedules for the study of each subject, the helping of teachers to develop effective methods of instruction, the establishment of standards to be met, and the testing of children to see whether the standards were being met. This was a far cry from the pedagogical ideas that Rice had studied in Jena and Leipzig. What had happened to the idea that children should be free to explore? The classrooms now proposed by Rice would be strictly under the control of the teacher, and the teacher would be under the control of the superintendent.

The system was to be monitored by a series of examinations. Rice's proposal is puzzling, particularly in view of the fact that he must have surely been aware of the problems encountered by an examination-controlled system, for the Board of Regents examination of New York State had long been a controlling factor in the curriculum of the New York City schools, and some had protested its use. Rice had apparently discussed his new ideas on education with others, for he wrote about the criticism that he heard, namely, that emphasis on achieving results will crush the spirit and is incompatible with a "delightful classroom atmosphere" (p. 452). He stated that he did not think that this was so, and yet one must surely conclude, in the light of history, that he was naive in thinking that a system in which the superintendent puts pressure on the teachers and the teachers put pressure on the pupils could provide that delightful atmosphere.

Rice's final study in the series was reported in an article entitled "Educational Research: The Results of a Test in Language" (1903). What he called "a test in language" (p. 269) was administered to 8,300 students in the spring of 1903. The test consisted of a short story that was read to the pupils. The pupils were then asked to reproduce the story. The story was probably of much greater interest to Rice than to the children to whom it was read, for it was an account of how Pestalozzi ran his school in Switzerland.

Rice developed a very complicated system for grading the papers. Scoring for the details of mechanics was a simple matter, but Rice was interested in the literary quality of the products. He developed a quite elaborate system for doing the latter, and provided examples of pupil products scored at each of the five levels of proficiency, which occupied most of the space in the journal assigned to the paper. A discussion of the results were reserved for a second paper, "English (continued): The Need of a New Basis in Education" (1904). Rice investigated various conditions that might influence the level of performance of children on his language test. He concluded that "heredity, nationality, and home environment" (p. 445) played insignificant parts. He attempted to relate performance to class size and found, as many later generations found, a complete lack of relationship. Also, teachers with similar qualifications produced very differing results. Teaching method also seemed to make no difference. Rice came to the odd conclusion that good results might be achieved despite the use of what he called unscientific methods, and yet he concluded with the admonishment that "the methods used should be of the most scientific order" (p. 446). The factor which seemed to him to be at work was what he called "teaching power." The reader of Rice has a hard time in determining what is meant by this expression, but he seems to have had in mind some kind of drive on the part of the teacher. He abandoned the idea that teachers with "teaching power" are born and not made, noting that teachers in the same building tend to produce rather uniform results. By this stage in his career, Rice had come to believe that supervision was the crucial element in producing "teaching power."

Rice then wrote an interesting paragraph stating that teachers should not be judged by how they behave in the classroom, but by the results they produced, as demonstrated by examinations. This is a startling change from his earlier writing which had suggested that a mere observation of how the teacher behaved was a sufficient basis for deciding the effectiveness of the teacher. He expanded on this point by relating that he had sometimes found that pupils to whom high grades had been assigned by teachers would perform miserably on his tests. For that reason, teachers should be judged in terms of the performance of pupils on standardized tests. Rice was apparently not aware of the fact that this had long been the practice in England and had brought disaster.

Rice criticized the "radical" educators who have advocated abandoning the use of tests, stating that the only results worth having in education are those that are measurable. The implication of this section of the paper is that he is disagreeing with Dewey, for his comments on "learning by doing" seem to be directed against Dewey's rising star.

A final article in the series brings together Rice's later ideas on education. The article carries the sober title "The Need for a New Basis in Supervision" (1904). He starts out the article by noting that readers have asked him to explain what he meant by "teaching power." His answer was that this power was a mystery. He provided the analogy that the genuine painter possesses power that the bungling amateur does not have. He attempted to redefine it as the power to achieve success in the classroom, presumably, as measured by the products of the pupils. Rice had become what today would be called a behaviorist. He had moved to the position that states that the outcomes of education should be uniform for all children. There was nothing in his ideas that included the notion of individual differences. His data had persuaded him that what he considered to be the important objectives of education could be achieved in all children, a fact reflected in his idea that uniform examinations should be administered by higher authority. His position was not quite as rigid as it seems in much of the article for, although he admits to placing the three R's on a pedestal, and would set minimum standards to be achieved, he still believed that, with efficient teaching, these could be achieved in a small fraction of the school day, leaving time for other studies. He never said what those other studies should be.

The new basis for supervision was to be the administration of a set of uniform tests, but the tests should neither be administered, nor scored, by teachers. Rice noted that a few teachers may use undesirable methods to help pupils achieve good scores. He believed that most teachers would be too conscientious to do so, a belief hardly borne out by educational practice. The tests should be directed towards the measurement of the higher faculties and should not reflect the effects of mechanical drill. The tests would move to action those teachers who "will not move without a spur" (p. 604).

A department in the school district would keep records. Then Rice stated "the activities of a department of results would serve, in due course of time, to establish minimum standards is scarcely open to doubt" (p. 605). Teachers would be shown the examination papers of pupils who had achieved acceptable standards, so that the teachers would know the quality of work that they should expect from their pupils. The names of schools, teachers, and pupils would not be made public, but a small committee of citizens should have access to the full information on the schools. In 1907, Rice was quietly dropped from the editorship of the *Forum,* without note or comment on the part of the new editor. One suspects that the owners recognized that Rice no longer had influence and that his last araticle, cited in this paragraph, had shown that he had no new ideas with which to excite the public imagination.

Rice too seems to have recognized that his career in education had come to an end. The spirit of the reformer was still within him and still needed an outlet. He turned to political reform. He published a book on the subject, and the title, if not the content, reflected something of his old evangelistic zeal. What could have been a more appealing title in those days than *The People's Government: Efficient, Bossless, Graftless* (1915)? The book did not match up to its racy title for the volume is rather dull. His thesis is that on every major issue of policy within the executive branch of government, matters should be settled by bringing together all relevant facts and presenting them to what was essentially a judge and jury. Rice was impressed with the effectiveness of the judicial system and proposed that the manner of the judiciary in solving disputes should be extended to executive government. Under Rice's system, a minor bureaucrat might be able to challenge the decision of a superior and have a hearing on the matter before a panel. Rice hoped that, by this means, the efficiency of government would be increased. He claimed that graft and involuntary waste would disappear if his system were introduced.

Rice then faded into obscurity. There seems little record of what he did in his later years. He seems to have lived quietly in Philadelphia. His death in 1934 took place without note from the *New York Times*.

Did he make a difference? It is hard to say. He did attempt to sort out some of the variables related to educational achievement, but his statistical techniques for doing this were far too simple for the complex problems involved. As a reformer he lacked any central and all-pervading idea that a reformer generally has to have. As a thinker he lacked the knowledge and analytic ability of contemporaries such as William Torrey Harris or John Dewey. As a research worker he had little of the kind of competence found in Edward L. Thorndike and Charles Hubbard Judd. Yet, as a romantic figure in the history of educational research, he has considerable appeal.

THE GARY CONTROVERSY AND THE NEW RESEARCH APPROACH

The School System and the Controversy

By the turn of the century, surveys had become an established means of collecting data about educational problems. The Boston Survey and the Rice Surveys had impressed educators with the value of these techniques, though the threat to teachers implied by the techniques prevented any rush to apply them. Survey techniques, then as now, came to be used in attempts to settle public controversies.

In the early part of the century, no set of educational innovations produced as much controversy as the situation that developed in the new steel town of Gary, Indiana. The United States Steel Corporation had founded the town in 1906 by building the first large steel plant west of Pittsburgh. Gary developed along the same lines as most company towns of the era. Houses had to be built to attract the population that was to run the plant, but the housing was of typical minimum standards, just adequate enough to attract immigrants arriving in the Eastern seaports. The Corporation did nothing much in the way of planning to ensure that Gary would become a fine community, but left this responsibility to the inhabitants. The site of the new plant was a landscape of rolling sanddunes, spotted with clumps of scrub oak. Houses were built within walking distance of the nearly mile-square steel plant and the community mushroomed outwards in an organized manner. The steel plant was designed to employ ultimately as many as 140,000 workers. Already by 1909 the town had 12,000 inhabitants. When Randolph Bourne visited the city in 1915, he found it to be a modern city with gas and electric facilities, banks, churches, hotels, and three newspapers. The community had mushroomed, and it had managed to provide all the important accouterments of a modern city. These had come into being despite a typical history of municipal government with its endless turmoil of election frauds, graft, and corruption in high places. Those who seized power in such communities had concern for matters other than the welfare of the people.

The schools had to meet the needs of the typical American community of the era. Roughly half of the population in 1912 was native-born, but these first-generation native-born shared many common problems with the newer immigrant, including that of the difference in language in the home and community. The development of a school system was the responsibility of the community and not the Steel Corporation and, indeed, the steel corporation did all in its power to keep down its contribution to the community resources. The Corporation was able to arrange to have its property grossly underassessed, probably through payoffs to municipal officials. In addition, the lag between the time at which city property was assessed and the time when taxes were paid provided a very low tax base in a community that was expanding so rapidly.

The story of the development of the Gary schools has been best described by Randolph S. Bourne (1916). This is only one of many accounts of the unique system of education that was developed in Gary. The *Journal of Education*, that must have been read by almost the entire educational establishment, carried numerous articles, comments, and critiques related to educational innovation in Gary. John Dewey became interested in the Gary development and sent his daughter there to observe the system directly. Then John Dewey and Evelyn Dewey wrote a book together that included a description, and endorsement, of the events in Gary. The book appeared under the evangelistic banner of *Schools for Tomorrow* (1915). The tone of the Dewey volume shows that both John and Evelyn Dewey were thoroughly excited at what was taking place in the Gary schools, and in some other schools too. These were held up as models of what Dewey and his daughter believed all schools would be like in the near future.

A key move in the development of the Gary school system was the appointment of William Wirt as superintendent. Whatever merits the school system may have had were a direct result of Wirt's initiative, ingenuity, and enormous energy. The Gary school board brought Wirt from the small town of Bluffton, Indiana, where he had already worked out what came to be known later as the Gary Plan. Apparently the Mayor and School Board had examined the school system that Wirt was attempting to create in Bluffton and saw it as a model of what Gary needed. One must give the City officials some credit for recognizing that the extraordinary abilities of William Wirt might compensate for what Gary lacked in financial resources.

The plan of schooling in Gary has been described as a Work-Study-Play plan. The underlying philosophy was reflected in the fact that the first three school buildings of the new program were named Emerson, Froebel, and Pestalozzi. The new school buildings were developed on the basis of the belief that the school should educate the child physically, manually, artistically, scientifically, and intellectually. Although the philosophy was that the *whole child* was to be developed, Wirt was quite specific about the different facets of the whole child that had to be educated. For every facet of the child, there had to be facilities in the building that would develop that facet. In addition to ordinary classrooms, there had to be facilities that could be used as playgrounds, gardens, music studios, scientific laboratories, machine shops, cooking facilities, merchandising facilities, and so forth. The school served not only the function of providing intellectual stimulation and recreation, but it also had to bring the child into contact with the activities of the real world such as are involved in food preparation, health maintenance, commerce, manufacturing, and the rest. Every day the child should have contact with a wide range of activities related to these community functions, and through these contacts should also develop intellectually, though traditional classwork was not excluded.

In the Gary plan the whole school plant was to be used by all age levels. Thus, a single building would include both elementary and secondary grades. Wirt believed that the complete school should include all age levels from birth to death. In such a school the older children would help the younger and all would participate in the housekeeping chores necessary for keeping the school in order. As a further integration of school and community, Wirt looked forward to the day when the school playgrounds would also function as public parks so that they could be used by as wide a public as possible and during the longest hours. The playground of the Emerson school was not only a general playground, but it included areas where children could grow gardens, and then there were tennis courts, an area for skating in winter, and an area for keeping animals. Furthermore, Wirt believed that the schools should become art galleries and museums and libraries. Wirt also wanted to give up the usual school desks, but some pressure from parents limited what he could do in this respect.

The Gary school day was extended to 8 hours. The argument for this was persuasive. Wirt argued that, before the industrialization of America, children found the home and farm or small-town environment to be a rich source of learning. Indeed, such children spent as much time in active learning pursuits outside of school as they spent in school. In contrast, in Gary early in the century children would spend 5 hours a day hanging around the cheap amusements of the city and on the streets, where what they learned was counterproductive to the development of a good society. Of course, children are little better off today with their regime of 5 hours of television. Wirt believed that, with radical changes in the school program, much of the time wasted by children could be used to good advantage. The Gary program was designed to replace the absent role of the home in providing education. The richness of the program is illustrated by the arrangement of the rooms along a corridor of the Froebel school. The rooms in order were designed for pottery, laundry, freehand drawing, two regular-type classrooms, a physics laboratory, music studios, a conservatory, two more classrooms, a botany laboratory, and then four more classrooms. Every attempt was made to make the school a self-sustaining community. The manual training and industrial shops of the school were the shops for maintaining the school itself. The vocational training program worked on enhancing the facilities of the school and the school grounds. In the shop program artisans were employed, not to do the work itself of maintaining and improving the schools, but as teachers helping the children undertake the actual work. The children worked very much like apprentices in these classes. Reports about the school by the Deweys, and others, noted the responsible way in which children behaved in relation to their work and the enthusiasm with which they went about their tasks.

The form of manual work provided by the Gary schools was immensely different from that found in other schools of the day, where manual training had become the fashion through the influence of Nicholas Murray Butler and others. What one would commonly see in classes for manual training in most schools throughout the country were trivial tasks, manufactured to meet the formal requirements of a program. Thus, a child might spend a few weeks on the quite meaningless task of squaring up a board, for no other pupose than to ensure that the board was square. Gary did away with all such formal training. If a door frame had to be fixed, then the child working on it learned the importance of having a frame that was square. He learned also the value of having corners that were square on the door, for otherwise the door would not close properly. Every manual task was a meaningful one, and every child in the school engaged in such practical manual training. The caring for the school grounds was not just a matter of engaging in work that was drudgery, for the work came under the direction of teachers in botany and zoology, who converted every work hour into a lesson in biology. What was then called *domestic science*, and today home economics, was centered on the management of the school lunchroom. The children planned the meals within a budget and then prepared and served the food. In addition, the domestic science department had a laundry and sewing room. These enterprises were self-sustaining financially except for the salaries of the two teachers.

The work of the shops and other enterprises required systems of accounting that provided experience for the children studying commercial subjects, who also took care of much of the secretarial work of the schools.

The school auditorium played a special role in the Gary plan. Children spent an hour each day in the auditorium where a program was presented related to some aspect of the work of the school. There might be instrumental or choral presentations, or talks by teachers about special aspects of their area of knowledge and work. There might be dramatic presentations of plays written by the children themselves and through which some of history took on a more meaningful form.

The lavish educational program may have appeared on the surface to be expensive, but the fact was it was not. Such a program was possible within the confines of a modest budget because much of the school was used for a very large fraction of the day. This was possible because the school was run on the basis of what was called a platoon system, whereby groups of children were moved around from facility to facility. This plan was possible in view of the fact that every child, at every level, participated in all kinds of activity. Manual activity was not reserved for the slow learner, but was considered to be a significant part of the education of every child. No child had exclusive use of a desk, but each child used a desk when the activity required the use of that piece of furniture. The same was true of laboratory and shop equipment and books. Maximum utilization of whatever was purchased with public money was attempted. The buildings were even used in the evenings, by adults who wished to obtain an education that they had not had in their youth. Bourne reported that in 1914-15, 4,300 adults were enrolled in evening classes in Gary.

Another important feature of the Gary plan was to include all grades of schooling within a single building. This had many advantages, according to Wirt. One was that the shops and laboratories, ordinarily provided only for secondary level students, could be used by children at the elementary grade level. Another advantage was that the older children could help the younger children.

The time assigned to various areas of education was as follows: 2 hours were devoted to academics; 2 hours to manual work and the arts; 2 hours to play, physical training, dramatics, and what was called application; 1 hour was spent in the auditorium; and the remaining hour and a quarter was for lunch. The use of the term *application* is of interest in the play category. The Wirt program involved the idea that play should involve the application of academic knowledge. Thus, dramatics should involve the application of what had been learned in English and many games involve mathematics. One may note that learning mathematics through games has had a revival in recent years, but Wirt developed and applied this idea. Applications of classroom work in biology were made in physical work on the school grounds. Much of the application work was that which contributed to the school community.

The schools in Gary had a 10-month attendance and 2 months of vacation. Wirt planned ultimately to make even better use of the school plant by having an all-year school in which pupils would attend for 4 semesters of 12 weeks each.

The content of the academic curriculum was not too different from that found in more typical schools of the era, but the introduction of applications probably made the materials much more meaningful to the children. A child who learned elocution in a formal setting would surely have a different attitude towards his learning than one who learned elocution so that he could participate effectively in a dramatic performance. Knowledge and skills were taught in all departments, not in isolation from the world, but as an essential instrument for living in a real world. Children were encouraged to develop their own materials, and thus the history room was filled with maps and charts and materials that the children had made. At one point in the history of the Gary schools, the children campaigned for the development of a waterside park along the lake frontage. In history classes, when some important contemporary political event developed, the teacher and the children were encouraged to stop all other studies in order to study the event. The purposes of the school were continuously held up before the children so that they understood why they were given particular assignments. Although ancient history was taught, the children understood that the purpose of the study was to make them better American citizens by having the greatness of the human past on which to draw.

At the turn of the century, a science curriculum was an innovation. Whatever there was of it was concentrated largely in the secondary schools, though nature study had been introduced in the elementary grades. In the Gary schools, an attempt was made to teach genuine science at the lower levels, and laboratory work was provided as low as the third grade. The younger children did not do experiments by themselves, but were assigned as helpers to the children in the older classes working in the laboratories of chemistry, physics, botany, and zoology. The underlying theory was that children are natural scientists, a theory which reminds one of what Jean Piaget was to say 50 years later. The purpose of such work was not to give them a taste of what the professional scientist does, but to help them to understand the world around them. The care of the gardens that surrounded the school, and the care of the animals in the school's diminutive zoo, extended this experience. An especially fine experience for the physics class was the study of the boiler and heating system and the manner in which heat is transmitted through a school. In the shops the study of machines was made an integral part of the study of physics. Pupils were also encouraged to investigate any aspect of the community that struck their interest from a scientific point of view. The water and sewage problems would be examples of areas in which such work might be undertaken.

In Bourne's seventh chapter, he wrote about discipline in the Gary schools. This was to become a controversial issue with many different opinions being widely expressed. Bourne and Evelyn Dewey had very favorable impressions of the manner in which the children conducted themselves. Other visitors reported that all they could observe was chaos. Such contrasting opinions are found today in the description of open schools. One suspects those who think that, in school, children should be fixed to their desks, as the desks should be fixed to the floor, are those who cannot tolerate the free and easy movement of the children in such a program. What they see runs so counter to their conception of a well-run school that they see nothing but chaos. Nevertheless, there may be an underlying order. A view of a busy day on the New York Stock Exchange also looks like chaos, but there is an order there quite apparent to the individual who understands how business is conducted on the Exchange.

The Gary schools had attempted various forms of student government, but these had been regarded as failures except at the upper grades. The policy when Bourne made his visit was for the teacher to have nominal authority which was to be exercised to only a limited extent. Bourne's impression was that, although there was great freedom of movement, and much spontaneous activity on the part of the children, most of the activities in which children engaged were goal-directed and worthwhile. At least there seemed to be few serious disciplinary problems. Certainly, one would expect that in a school in which the children were responsible for maintaining the facilities, there would be few problems of vandalism. In such a school there would be few frustrations against which children would react with aggression.

The widespread appeal of the Gary schools did not derive from its program nor from its novelty. The main interest shown in the system by outsiders was a result of the fact that it provided a rich program at a minimum cost. Some outsiders also saw it as the model of the new education that would surely sweep the country, but the main appeal to superintendents and politicians elsewhere was due to the fact that it represented a superior use of the money and resources provided by the public.

The account of the Gary schools provided by the Deweys is not too different from that written by Bourne. The fact is that their contact with the schools was little more than perfunctory, for Evelyn spent only 3 days in Gary before going home to write over 25 pages on the subject. It is said that John Dewey was under pressure to meet a publisher's deadline, but a more likely story is that John Dewey was under pressure to meet John Dewey's deadline. Evelyn was impressed with the freedom of movement of the pupils, a freedom that other visitors condemned. She was also impressed with the degree to which the students participated in the actual work of running the school by participating in the maintenance, the clerical and bookkeeping work, and the operation of the cafeteria. Evelyn Dewey noted the close relations that existed between the school and the community, including that of providing adult education. She indicated that the schools served more adults than children, though the adults were in school a much shorter time each week. She reported that each teacher was assigned the task of knowing the parents of the children in certain blocks and with calling on them at home, in order to understand the conditions that might be influencing a child's development.

Evelyn Dewey, like most visitors to the Gary schools in the first few years of their existence, does not seem to have looked at samples of the work of the children. She did not ask questions about whether a bookkeeping system run largely by children would actually check out. She does not seem to have eaten in the cafeteria. She has nothing to say about the books used by the children. Her observations were very general and, some would say, of relatively little value. This is hardly surprising for John Dewey was hardly the kind of person who ever collected data. He left that to others and generally ignored what they did.

The Evaluation and the Verdict

No system of education created as much interest nationwide as did the Gary system in its time. The main attraction was the supposed economic saving that resulted from the platoon system. The tendency across the nation was to mimic the platoon system, without mimicking some of the more important features of it, such as the close relationship of school and community, and the breadth of experience provided by the curriculum. The platoon feature of the school lingered in fame long after the Gary school system was forgotten by all except the City of Gary. As late as 1927, the journal *The Platoon School* was started, which continued publication for nearly a decade. The journal was published by an organization known as the National Association for the Study of the Platoon or Work-Study-Play School Organization. In its time, though, the Gary school system was held up by some as a model for the future, but by others it was regarded as a mere whim of Superintendent Wirt.

In earlier times, the debate could have continued indefinitely, but the new technology of psychological measurement supplied a means of resolving the issues. In 1915, Superintendent Wirt asked the General Education Board to provide sufficient funds for a responsible group of individuals to undertake a thorough study of the Gary system. It is of particular interest to note that the move to undertake a comprehensive evaluation of the system came from Wirt himself, who was completely convinced that his schools were better than any others in the country. Indeed, Wirt is credited with stating that he would resign if the study did not result in full support for him and his system. The General Education Board responded positively to the proposal and approached Abraham Flexner to organize such a study.

In order to understand the resulting study and its conclusions, one has to understand the background of Abraham Flexner (1886-1957), who is still famous today for his survey of medical schools and his report that laid the foundations for present-day medical training.

Flexner had had an interesting background in education, which he has described in his autobiography *I Remember: Autobiography of Abraham Flexner* (1940). After graduating from The Johns Hopkins University, Flexner taught school for a few years and then founded his own school. His description of his school shows that it was run along quite traditional lines and was very much like a typical New England academy. However, every effort was made to give positive encouragement to learning and to avoid compulsion. The school was operated without rules or examinations, but there was a highly competitive atmosphere organized around the pursuit of excellence. The school was innovative in its day even though the curriculum was largely classical, but Flexner would not have tolerated the breadth of education sought after by Wirt at Gary. The school became well known for its ability to qualify youngsters for Ivy League colleges at an early age. The school, and its reputation, gave Flexner the opportunity to make important contacts in the educational world, which led him to obtaining an important position with the General Education Board, a philanthropic organization funded by Rockefeller. Later, Flexner became interested in obtaining funds to develop the Lincoln School in New York City, presumably along lines similar to the ones that had made Flexner's school famous for educational acceleration.

Thus, Flexner came to be appointed to conduct the study into the schools of Gary. He chose as his chief assistant in the enterprise Frank P. Bachman (1871-1934), a former assistant superintendent of schools in Cleveland, who had written extensively on educational administration. Bachman was a conservative and traditional schoolman who despised what was being undertaken in Gary. Apparently, Flexner knew of Bachman's views, which must have been quite in keeping with his own. The evaluation of the Gary system was biased from the start.

At the time when the issue of the evaluation of the Gary program arose, Bachman was functioning as a consultant to the New York City Board of Estimate and Apportionment. From that he moved to become an employee of the General Education Board, where he remained for 14 years.

The inquiry into the Gary schools was to be one of the most ambitious educational investigations that had ever been undertaken. It still dwarfs most other inquiries in the present century. The General Education Board published the findings in a series of eight volumes in 1918, three years after the inquiry was begun. Each section of the report was a book in itself, and one was over 400 pages in length. Flexner and Bachman wrote the introductory volume of 265 pages entitled *The Gary Schools: A General Account* (1918). The following seven volumes provided accounts of seven distinct investigations into different aspects of the program. The titles of the volumes, together with the names of their authors, reflect the breadth of the inquiry and the competence of the investigators and are listed below:

Organization and Administration, by George D. Strayer and Frank P. Bachman
Costs, by Frank P. Bachman and Ralph Bowman
Industrial Work, by Charles R. Richards
Household Arts, by Eva W. White
Physical Training and Play, by Lee F. Hammer
Science Teaching, by Otis W. Caldwell
Measurement of Classroom Products, by Stuart A. Courtis

Thus, the staff of the study included some of the best-established figures in the country, even though they would also have been described as conservative rather than progressive in educational philosophy.

The evaluation of the Gary schools was, perhaps, the first large enterprise in which objective tests of achievement were used to throw light on an issue of national public controversy. Tests that could be scored with some degree of objectivity were available for measuring achievement in spelling, arithmetic, and reading, and rather less satisfactory scales were available for the measurement of handwriting and composition. The project employed Stuart A. Courtis to undertake the testing. Courtis owned a consulting firm that also published tests of achievement and had become a recognized authority in the area.

Let us first consider the results as they were presented in the Flexner and Bachman summary of findings, because the interpretation of the findings given in this latter report seems to have been the interpretation that was widely accepted, undoubtedly because of the enormous prestige of Flexner.

With respect to handwriting, the conclusion was that the children in Gary had an inferior quality of handwriting compared with another sample from 56 American cities. The children were reported to write more freely than was typical, but they did not pay too much attention to quality. As the Gary children grew older, they gained in speed of writing, but not in quality. In reviewing these results, one must recognize that America was just emerging from the era in which handwriting was of critical importance in that most documents had been handwritten. The typewriter was moving rapidly into the business world and making handwriting an obsolete art. One suspects that the program of Gary emphasized more the production of written products rather than the quality of the orthography, and the test results reflected this fact.

Spelling tests, that used word lists, showed that when all children at all levels were considered, the children of Gary were considerably below the national norm. A point that Flexner and Bachman do not emphasize is that the spelling performance improved from grade to grade and surpassed the national norm by the eleventh grade. Flexner and Bachman brushed this fact aside by saying that, after the eighth grade, the data are not of interest in that the data cover only those who remained in school. However, in Gary the retention rate in the higher grades was unusually high. Another important fact is also that on spelling in compositions, the eighth-grade children of Gary made errors in only about 0.5 percent of the words. This fact suggests that even though the children at that level may have done poorly on the words included in spelling lists, they could spell quite adequately those words that they actually used in compositions. Since the emphasis in the Gary schools was on the functional use of language, one can hardly be surprised that the children were able to spell in a functional context even though they did not do as well in the artificial spelling-bee situation.

The tests in arithmetic were confined strictly to the mechanics of arithmetic and avoided the reasoning type of word problem. In arithmetic mechanics, the children of Gary attempted fewer problems and were less accurate than the norm group from 56 small cities.

The composition test, which required the pupil to reproduce a short story read to him, was so difficult to score that the results were virtually meaningless. One should note that the task was one to which the children in Gary were not accustomed. Indeed, the task would have been viewed by Wirt as a caricature of education.

The Gary children were administered both the Kansas Silent Reading Test and the Gray Oral Reading Test. The Kansas test was one of the few administered in the survey that involved thinking skills. The children did about as well on that test as the children in 19 Kansas cities. On the other hand, on the Gray test the children in Gary tended to read more slowly and made more errors than the children in a norm group consisting of 23 cities in Illinois. The latter difference was small. One wonders whether the Gary children, because of their informal schooling, were not used to reading aloud. In the early part of the century, reading aloud was part of the routine of every regimented classroom. The oral reading test favored children exposed to that kind of regimentation. The Kansas Silent Reading test, on the other hand, might favor children who were accustomed to look up material in books.

Flexner and Bachman did not comment on the results of the Trabue Language Scales. The Trabue scales involved entering a word in a blank in a sentence. This was an untimed test. The Gary children on this test did just about as well as the children in the norm group.

Flexner and Bachman came to the overall conclusion that the Gary children were academically inferior to children in the norm groups, derived mainly from small cities. However, they did point out in some elusive comments that the schools of Gary that did not follow the complete Gary plan did not do better than the schools that did. If this conclusion of the report had been underlined, the entire impact of the report would have been changed.

Our position here is that the summary of Flexner and Bachman was highly biased. The report did not point out that on the two tests that called for some thought, the Gary children did as well as those in the norm group. They were penalized on the kind of tests that reflected the kind of learning produced by drill. Such results would be later duplicated in studies comparing what were called progressive schools with what were designed as traditional schools. In such studies, tests of spelling and the mechanics of arithmetic favored the traditional schools.

A second matter that was not raised by any of those conducting the evaluation was the matter of finding a comparison group. Gary was not a typical midwestern community, and yet the scores of the children in Gary were compared with those in other cities that presented a more typical picture of midwestern Americana. A large percentage of the adult population of Gary was foreign-born and were non-English speaking. Thus, the children were bilingual and, like most bilingual children, would be expected to be a little behind in development with respect to English, the language of the school. In view of this fact, the children of Gary performed remarkably well on tests that called for a knowledge of English. The suspicion is that they may well have performed better than the children of other immigrant populations.

The manner in which the data from the Gary schools were interpreted raises questions about why those involved made the interpretations that they did. Would a modern group of evaluators have arrived at different conclusions, under the circumstances? One suspects that they would not, for the circumstances of the evaluation had far-reaching political implications, which have been studied by Adeline and Murray Levine in a very perceptive article which explores the topic designated in the title of their 1977 article, "The Social Context of Evaluative Research" (1977). This article takes the case of the Gary evaluation as an illustration of the way in which politics may bias and influence evaluation studies.

The Levine and Levine article points out that a more important factor in the evaluation than the widespread interest in the Gary plan was the fact that Flexner had become involved in New York City politics. The Republican Mayor Mitchell had proposed that the entire New York City school system be ultimately converted to the Gary plan because of the economies it afforded in the construction of school plants. The mayor defended the plan vigorously, but in 1917 the plan was opposed with equal vigor by the Democratic candidate for the office, John F. Hylan. The Mitchell administration had gone as far as experimenting with the plan in a number of schools in the Bronx, but there had been public demonstration against the plan by parents who believed that the plan was too vocationally oriented. Flexner was on the school board and publicly supported the introduction of the Gary plan. Flexner was a politician and, as a politician, he had no choice. Whether Flexner was intellectually behind the plan is hard to say, but what one knows about him suggests that his main basis for supporting the plan was his loyalty to the incumbent mayor. The Gary plan hardly fitted the elitist philosophy of education for which he was known. Flexner's political involvement is also suggested by the fact that he delayed the publication of the very derogatory report on the evaluation of the Gary schools until after the 1917 mayoral elections. The report must have been ready for distribution much earlier in the year, but the publication of the material would have had a disastrous effect on the election, at least so it was believed.

Even without the publication of the report, the election was a disaster for the pro-Gary forces. the incumbent mayor was turned out of office by about a 2-to-1 majority, but the results may have been influenced by the fact that the findings of the evaluation study were, somehow, leaked to the public before the election. The leaks may have been no more than the comments of subordinates who had seen the data.

There is an interesting epilogue to the entire episode. Flexner included in his 1940 autobiography a 2-page discussion of the Gary episode. Although the 2 pages include some bland praise for Gary and its school system, the punch line to the entire discussion is found in a strong statement to the effect that the report of the evaluation study dealt a disastrous blow "to the exploitation of the Gary system" (p. 255). The paragraph went on to state that once the report was published, the Gary system ceased to be an object of excitement. Then there follows a paragraph in which educators are assailed for failing to keep in touch with the real world. The material leaves little doubt that Flexner had little sympathy for what Superintendent Wirt had attempted to do, and that Flexner was pleased that the nonsense had been put to an end through the publication of his report. If this interpretation of the material is correct, then Flexner's stand as a proponent of the Gary system, as a member of the New York City Board of Education, must be regarded as purely a political ploy. One is also led to the conclusion that the evaluation study was loaded against the system from the start, as other evidence indicates it was. There is also no doubt that Flexner wanted to forget the entire episode, for when a new version of his autobiography was published, posthumously, in 1960, every reference to the Gary episode was eradicated from it. The forgetting or omission of such a major episode in a man's life happens only when there are very strong reasons for forgetting it. Flexner had good reasons to forget all about Gary.

On the positive side, the evaluation study resulted in attempts by Superintendent Wirt to remedy some of the defects in the system. He took seriously the comments by George Strayer and others that the teachers in the schools lacked adequate supervision and he attempted to improve the supervisory situation. Wirt had some doubts as to whether the tests had been properly administered and began to conduct a retesting. The effect of the report on the teaching and administrative staff was devastating and many resigned.

The style of the Gary evaluation set the style for future evaluations of school programs. Such surveys are typically conducted, as they were at Gary, by a highly conservative element in education that has little use for innovations. Measurements are made in terms of tests designed to fit the programs and experiences of schools run along traditional lines. Stuart Courtis, though an established expert on measurement, had produced and distributed through his consulting firm tests that were well tuned to very traditional curricula. He was a systematic and methodical man who saw the new testing movement as a means of removing some of the inadequacies of traditional forms of education, without producing any fundamental change in the ideas upon which that education rested. Thus, the traditionalists were able to undermine and hamper a set of astonishingly new and interesting educational ideas. Their interpretation of the data was as biased as their own educational philosophy. Since the conservatives and traditionalists were then, as they are now, well entrenched in power, one can hardly be surprised that their ideas would prevail.

EDUCATIONAL RESEARCH BEGINS TO SHOW ORGANIZATION

On 14 February 1903, a meeting was held at the Murray Hill Hotel, in New York City, for the purpose of organizing a Society of Educational Research. The term *educational research* had been well popularized through the pages of the widely circulated *Forum*. Indeed, though the term may have been used before Rice, it was he who made it a term in general circulation. In the previous century superintendents would not have known what the term meant, but by the time the society was formed every superintendent must have known its meaning.

The initial meeting at the Murray Hill Hotel resulted from an invitation extended by Rice to 24 individuals of whom 19 were superintendents. At the meeting, officers were elected and the society was established. The *Forum* provided some money so that the new society could carry out its initial work. The primary purpose of the society was to maintain a Bureau of Research whose main function was to desseminate information about the effectiveness of new methods of teaching. The Bureau was to concern itself with evidence that had to do with tangible results, and to collect data pertaining to the best way of achieving quite specific outcomes. In addition, the organization was to set standards, by taking as a standard the level of achievement found in the better schools. The Bureau also was to work out the optimum time to be spent on each of the three R's. Much of what Rice wrote in this connection seems akin to the thinking found among those developing the new industrial psychology and industrial efficiency systems.

Other problems to be studied by the Bureau were such matters as the grade at which a particular course of study should be begun, the amount of drill that can be effectively used, and the optimum order in which particular components of subject matter should be taught.

The reports of the Society were to be published in the *Forum*, but a review panel was to be established to ensure that the reports did not propagandize any particular viewpoint. The review panel would be asked to check each article and to certify that the conclusions followed from the data.

The plan was not very different from that of a modern Regional Research and Development Center. It was far ahead of its time. Yet it could not succeed because it had no backing from the new generation of educational research workers emerging on the scene. James Earl Russell, Dean at Teachers College, had already moved towards developing research in education as a discipline of its own and there were many on the academic scene who talked about the need for the development of a science of education. Rice was not able to muster the support of the academicians, for he was too much tainted with the image of a mudslinger and wild reformer.

The last reference to the *Society of Educational Research* is found in Rice's final contribution to the Forum, "Why Our Improved Educational Machinery Fails to Yield a Better Product" (1904). The last paragraph of this article notes that the newly formed *Society for Educational Research* should do much to develop standards for education, but it never seems to have reached the point where it could accomplish anything.

During the next two decades educational research was recognized by many as manifesting a chaotic development. The National Education Association recommended the establishment of a national clearing house for research, but this proposal received no support from Congress. Then the Association established a Commission on the Coordination of Research Agencies to work on the problem, but the result of the work of the Commission seems to have been the establishment of a Research Division within the National Education Association itself. This division was established in 1922, but never became a national clearing house. It is of interest to note that the one moderately successful attempt to establish such a clearing house was undertaken by the J. J. Rousseau Institute, in Geneva, Switzerland, which established an International Bureau of Education in 1926 that was to function as a clearing house for information and scientific research related to education. The International Bureau continued to function for some years.

The development of research enterprises in universities and schools was paralleled by a move on the part of foundations to set aside some of their money for educational research. As early as 1910, the Russell Sage Foundation established a department concerned with educational research, under the direction of Leonard P. Ayres (1879-1946), a remarkable man who had had considerable personal experience in developing educational measuring instruments. The resulting Russell Sage series of publications on education represent a quite notable contribution to the educational literature of the period. Ayres was not primarily an educator, but a wealthy railroad magnate, with a sharp intellect, who liked to explore whatever happened to fascinate him. His obituary in the *New York Times* (30 October 1946, p. 27) describes him as primarily an economist who had had unusual success at making economic predictions. He was one of the few who had predicted the 1929 crash of the stock market and the subsequent depression. He wrote several books on economics that were viewed as works of distinction. The misfortune for education was that Ayres spent only a few years of his busy life in that field, for he was one of the most brilliant men that the field had attracted during his era. His impact on the work of the Russell Sage Foundation was of great importance to the development of educational research.

The General Education Board was one of the larger financial supporters of educational research during the first quarter of the present century. The support was mainly for projects related to testing. The Board worked to develop State bureaus of testing which, in turn, tended to be the sponsors of large testing programs. The Carnegie Foundation and the Commonwealth Fund also made substantial contributions to the developing field of educational inquiry.

Local educational research associations also seem to have flourished during the era, usually as subdivisions of teacher organizations. Some were independent, as was the New York Society for the Study of Experimental Education, founded in 1918 for the purpose of encouraging teachers to undertake research in their classrooms. The society does not seem to have actually undertaken research, but meetings were scheduled once a month for the purpose of discussing research that had been undertaken elsewhere, and to desseminate the results. Similar research-oriented groups were formed in other cities.

The first educational association ever to set aside funds for the development of research seems to have been the Upper Peninsula Education Association of Michigan. In 1912, the Association set aside the sum of $200 to establish a Bureau of Research to make a survey of education in the Upper Peninsula. The survey was undertaken and two reports were published, but the Bureau had only a temporary existance.

What the school and university bureaus lacked in technical competence, they made up for in their enthusiasm for the idea that all major school problems would soon be solved through the application of scientific techniques. Faith in research and the scientific approach to problems has never been greater among school administrators. Many believed that within a few years research would have solved all the important problems that confronted the schools.

From the atmosphere of enthusiasm for the new scientific approach to education there emerged the first successful organization of research workers. In 1915, seven directors of research in school systems formed themselves into the National Association of Directors of Educational Research. The first meeting of the group was initiated by Stuart A. Courtis. The manner in which the organization was formed shows the source of the impetus for educational change. The directors of research must have viewed themselves as standing at the very frontier of the new education, and must have believed that through their efforts education would become more efficient in terms of achieving goals in a shorter time. These individuals did not constitute a body that had any kind of vision of progressive education, such as John Dewey was discussing in his then recently published book entitled *The Child and the Curriculum.* Indeed, research in schools, as it was viewed in the early part of the century, was an intensely conservative activity focused on improving traditional education rather than on making radical changes in it. The new educational research was to be the instrument of the conservative leader, and not the tool through which education would be radically transformed. One suspects that educational research has retained its same conservative values down to the present time.

The National Association of Directors of Educational Research remained a means of communication among those who worked in school bureaus of research for at least the next 20 years, but in 1930 the organization became a department of the National Education Association with a resulting change in the source of its membership. Although academicians had never wielded much power within the Association, the incorporation of the research organization into the Association led to a slow takeover by the academic research workers and supervisors of research. The name was also changed to the American Educational Research Association. These changes resulted in a considerable expansion of membership, which reached about 1,000 by 1940. In the 1930's, membership requirements were relatively stringent and it was considered to be at least a small honor to be asked to join, but after World War II membership requirements were relaxed and membership mushroomed. In 1968, in a belated effort to convert the organization into an association of scholars, the ties of the organization with the National

Education Association were served, and the organization began an independent existence. This was the final move in severing the relationship of the organization with the schools. Although begun as an organization of people attached to the schools, it has become, in half a century, an organization controlled completely by individuals outside of the schools. Whether this transition has been beneficial or not remains controversial. Yet, despite all of these changes, certain emphases in the Association and in its predecessor remain unchanged. Emphasis is still placed on statistics and measurement today, as it was when the organization was an Association of Directors of Educational Research in 1915.

EFFICIENCY AND STANDARDIZATION: THE NEW GOALS OF EDUCATIONAL ADMINISTRATION

The case history of the events at Gary reflect certain widespread trends in American education early in the century. The evaluation of the Gary schools, because of the political undertones of the events related to it, was much publicized, but much less publicized were the other attempts to apply the concepts of efficiency and standardization to the schools of the United States. Frederick Taylor (1856-1915) had already led the way in applying these concepts to the operation of businesses, and particularly those that involved manufacturing. His ideas on this subject had been well developed and tried out in the steel industry before the turn of the century, and were sufficiently well accepted that he was able to found the Society to Promote the Science of Management in 1911. Taylor himself wrote a widely read book on the subject, which laid a foundation for all later books in the area (*The Principles of Scientific Management,* 1911).

The immense success achieved by Taylor in the field of industrial management inevitably led school administrators to examine the same formula for running schools. By 1908, the Report of the Commissioner of Education was beginning to highlight the concept of efficiency and its related concept, standardization, in his annual reports. The concept of efficiency in an educational setting could hardly be discussed except with reference to an educational program in which there had been some standardization. Efficiency in manufacturing was always in terms of producing a particular product. Those who wished to apply the concept of efficiency to education realized that they could do this only insofar as education involved, also, a well-defined product.

The typical view of the schools held by administrators early in the century was that there was agreement as to what the objectives of education should be. The common school was the great equalizer, particularly for immigrants. The typical eight grades of schooling had as their major objectives the teaching of children to read fluently, to spell, to write an elegant hand, to perform common calculations, and to acquire a smattering of knowledge in geography and history. There was little debate about what was meant by the mastery of the three R's, but there was some about other content in the curriculum. The development of standardized tests in the three R's gave the educational world the impression that educators at last knew exactly what the schools were to achieve in the basic areas of instruction.

The first 20 years of the present century was a period when there was a proliferation of more or less objectively scorable measures of school achievement. Much of this work was stimulated by the ideas of Edward L. Thorndike at Teachers College. Earlier batteries of tests, such as that developed by James McKeen Cattell, had been aptitude tests that were designed to measure basic psychological characteristics of the young adult. The new tests, in the new century, were focused on educational achievement and the measurement of the products of elementary education. Stuart A. Courtis, who was to play a central role in the selling of objective tests to schools, produced an arithmetic test in 1909, a year before Thorndike came out with his handwriting scale. At about the same time, the Kansas Silent Reading Test became available, and Gray's *Oral Reading Test* appeared a little later. From then on, the publication of tests proliferated, extending the concept into every phase of the elementary school curriculum.

The development of more-or-less standardized tests were prompted by the idea that they could be used to check on the effectiveness of education and thereby lead to more efficient education. How this was to be accomplished was not clear. The classroom teacher, already overburdened by the presence of about 40 children in a typical class, was in no position to conduct studies of the efficiency of teaching. School administrators recognized that the development of well-constructed tests would permit them to undertake studies of the efficiency of teaching parallel to those that Frederick Taylor had conducted in industry, and some administrators took steps to develop machinery through which such studies could be undertaken. The machinery that was commonly proposed was a bureau of research within the school system. The manning of such a bureau presented a difficult problem in itself, for there were no trained research workers available for employment. The best that could be done would be to appoint some person who had managed to read some of the new literature on measurement, and that is what was most often done. For example, late in 1913 the City of Detroit became interested in the establishment of a school research bureau. The administration of the school system was aware of the fact that Stuart A. Courtis, a teacher in a private school for girls, the *Home and Day School of Detroit,* had undertaken extensive work on constructing tests in arithmetic and reading. Since Courtis was the best expert in the area, he was appointed as Director of the new Bureau of School Efficiency. His function was to examine children and to conduct studies of teaching efficiency.

Detroit's action was not the first, but it is cited to show the relationship between testing and the efficiency movement in education early in the century. The first school bureau of research in a city system was established in Baltimore in 1912. It was called the *Bureau of Statistics* and the person appointed to head the Bureau was the statistician for the school system. The function of the Bureau was to undertake what were called administrative studies, but these soon became involved in the compilation of test data related to achievement. Some 10 years later, the Bureau had become so involved in testing that a test expert, John L. Stenquist, was appointed to head the Bureau.

Harold B. Chapman has provided an excellent account of the development of research bureaus up to about 1925 (*Organized Research in Education*, 1927). He describes how in 1913 Schenectady established a *Bureau of Reference and Research* which devoted most of its energies to achievement testing. Oakland, Cleveland, Newark, and Indianapolis followed suit. The Paul Monroe *Encyclopedia of Educational Research* (1941) reports that by 1918 there were 18 bureaus of research established in school systems.

According to Chapman, these bureaus often served purposes other than those which would be described today by the word *research.* Chapman reports, for example, that the Bureau of Research, Reference, and Statistics of New York City answered more than 100,000 inquiries during the period from 1921 to 1924. The queries came from the teaching staff and the general public. Many of the bureaus were heavily involved in survey activities and were created for that purpose.

The movement to establish research bureaus in schools was paralleled by a similar development of educational research bureaus in universities. The first of these was established at the University of Oklahoma in 1913. Indiana quickly followed by a similar development in 1914. By 1917 there were at least 10 such bureaus in existence, according to an article by Harold O. Rugg ("How I Keep in Touch with Quantitative Literature in Education," 1917-18). Rugg listed the names of the directors of these research bureaus, but the only names recognizable as contributors to educational research are those of M. E. Haggerty and Walter S. Monroe. Many unknowns entered the field of educational research in the early part of the century, but few ever made recognizable contributions. Perhaps this fact merely reflects the difficulty experienced by these early bureaus of recruiting trained staff, but the situation may be no different today.

The United States Bureau of Education eventually jumped in to promote the development of educational research bureaus in universities.

The Commissioner sought to establish what were called *research stations* at major universities. These were established at the universities of California, Cornell, Illinois, Iowa, Kansas, Michigan, Minnesota, Mississippi, Missouri, North Carolina, Texas, Utah, Virginia, Washington, Wisconsin, and at the Oregon Agricultural College. The enterprise was short-lived, for within a year the entire project was abandoned. Incompetence on the part of the Bureau of Education seems to have been to blame. Although the stations were established with the understanding that each project developed by the research stations had to be approved by the Commissioner before the project was begun, there was nobody assigned within the Bureau of Education to coordinate the activity. The result was that the enterprise ended in chaos.

Although the efficiency movement was strong on hopes, solid accomplishments were hard to identify. The 1916 *Yearbook of the National Society for the Study of Education* was an attempt to bring together such material. The work of doing this had been undertaken by a committee connected with the National Education Association, designated as the Committee on Standards and Tests of Efficiency. The committee included most of the academic luminaries in the field of education, chaired by George D. Strayer, a top authority on educational administration. The names of committee members still known today would include those of Ellwood P. Cubberley, Charles H. Judd, and Edward L. Thorndike. Part I of the book explored some areas of measurement including those of physical growth, arithmetic, language skills, and the quality of school buildings. Part II of the book, about 100 pages in length, described the activities of various school systems with respect to the use of tests to increase efficiency.

The second part of this volume reflects the state of the art of producing efficiency through tests as the art existed in 1916. The first chapter in the section, quite a typical chapter, described how the Department of Educational Investigation of the Boston school system had administered tests in arithmetic, spelling, English, and geography to grades 4 through 8. The results of the arithmetic test led the investigators to conclude that the procedures for teaching arithmetic were rather ineffective. The section of the chapter on the English test concludes only that the test results could be used for comparison with later test scores to determine whether improved instruction had taken place. The chapter suggested that the use of tests could sharpen the purposes of teaching, and lead to the definition of objectives in more precise terms. Related to this was the development of a set of minimal standards that all pupils should achieve. Subsequent chapters reflected similar themes. The opinion was widely voiced that the regular administration of tests would make it possible to plot changes in the efficiency of a school system, or even of the practices of a particular teacher. The belief was also voiced that administrators should use test scores to identify teachers who needed better supervision.

These beliefs were backed up by little evidence. They represented hopes rather than accomplishments. Indeed, educators had not yet come to realize that tests and test scores could not be used productively within any such simplistic plan.

THE PROLIFERATION OF SCHOOL SURVEYS

The first two decades of the present century showed a proliferation of the practice of having school systems surveyed by outside authorities. The survey was the focus among school people of the idea that education could be improved in efficiency by the study of the "facts" related to education. The idea that all one had to have were "facts" to improve education was, of course, derived from Thorndike, who used this expression himself in his own writings and who identified a scientific approach with the collection of facts and figures.

At the center of the new survey movement was the Federal Bureau of Education which, since the retirement of William Torrey Harris as Commissioner, had ceased to exercise leadership and had adopted a policy of tagging along with whatever idea seemed to be popular at the time. The popular idea in the 1910-20 period was the survey, and the Bureau of Education made the survey the center of its activities. The Report of the Commissioner for the year ending June 30, 1916, describes at length the massive effort undertaken by the Bureau of Education to promote and use the survey at all levels of education. During the 1916-17 year alone, the Bureau undertook educational surveys on a statewide basis in Wyoming, Arizona, Colorado, Delaware, and Tennessee, while completing surveys in the states of Washington, Iowa, and North Dakota. In addition, surveys were conducted for cities including San Francisco and Elyria. Other surveys were conducted on a county basis in such diverse places as Appalachia and Texas. Surveys were also conducted of institutions of higher learning. The Bureau argued that the original mandate of the Bureau to collect whatever statistics were necessary to maintain efficient school systems was a clear mandate to engage in the making of surveys.

The advantage of a Bureau survey was claimed to be that the Bureau represented an impartial outsider. No one recognized at that time that every survey involves the hidden values of the surveyor, and there was a faith in the idea that what were believed to be objective facts would solve all problems.

The costs of surveys was not great by modern standards. Among the archival papers of Charles Hubbard Judd are several letters from school systems requesting that he conduct a survey. The estimated cost given by Judd was generally between $2,000 and $3,000, provided that the school system was not too far away. For $5,000 a very elaborate survey could be conducted. Such amounts represented a professional salary for a year of a senior professor. Today a school survey could not be conducted for the cost of a professional's yearly salary.

The Commissioner's Report concerning the Bureau's function in conducting surveys describes enthusiastically, but not specifically, the outcomes of the enterprise. The report describes vaguely that new laws were enacted as a result of the findings of surveys. The claim is made that the surveys had resulted in "constructive recommendations" (p. 20), but one really does not know just what was accomplished.

Enthusiasm for the survey was not confined to the Bureau of Education and some educational administrators, for the academic world also saw it as the way to implement a program of efficiency studies in schools. Professors participated widely in these surveys, often supplementing their incomes by substantial amounts. The journals that represented the voice of academia wrote descriptions of every major survey that was initiated. Such journals as the *Elementary School Teacher* and the *Educational Review* editorialized on the survey movement and announced the initiation and completion of each in their editorial columns. Here again, the emphasis was on the activity, and not on the results.

Impetus for the survey movement was provided by the new forms of educational and social measurement that had been provided through the work of statistically minded psychologists. Most surveys of the time collected some data on the achievement of students. Quality of education was often judged in terms of the results.

Another idea underlying the school survey of this era was the notion that there should be national standards of education. Ever since tests had become widely used in schools, the idea had been discussed that the Bureau of Education should establish national standards that all children, except the handicapped, should meet. The reports of many surveys conveyed the idea that there were implicit standards for school systems. For example, the criticism that too many children at the fourth grade were still not at the mean of the second grade implies that there are standards at the fourth grade that most children should meet. The Bureau of Education must have wrestled with this problem of setting standards, much as in recent times the U.S. Office of Education has wrestled with the problem of setting minimum standards for graduation from high school, but no attempt was made to set standards. The Bureau of Education escaped from this problem by approaching the problem from another angle. The new proposal was to establish not standards for the achievement of children, but standards related to the content of the curriculum, the amount of time spent in particular areas, the range of offerings, and so forth.

The *Report of the Commissioner of Education* for the year ending June

30, 1910, had discussed various aspects of the standardization of education at some length, even though the matter had been under consideration by the Bureau for several previous years. The first topic dealt with in the report was the certification of teachers and the steps that had been taken in Illinois and Ohio to ensure that teachers would be of uniform quality. A Conference of Chief State Education Officers had taken place in which the participants had endorsed the use of standardized tests for teacher certification. The Conference also recommended that mere graduation from a 4-year institution be a basis for certification, provided the institution had appropriate training facilities including that of a school for observation and practice. The concept of established standards was already becoming watered down.

Further sections of the Commissioner's report dealt with other aspects of the attempt to standardize education. One page discusses the efforts of the *American Philological Association* to standardize the Latin requirements for college entrance. Then there was a long discussion of the College Entrance Examination Board that had been established 10 years previously in an effort to standardize college admission tests. Further on in the report there is a brief announcement that the National Education Association, Department of Secondary Education, had adopted a standard unit of secondary school work for college entrance credit. Still further is a discussion of an attempt by the *North Central Association of Schools and Colleges* to establish standards of training for college instructors. The same association had also established standards for college admission. The emphasis was obviously on the establishment of standards for the facilities in educational institutions, and almost nothing was said about the standards that should be expected of products of those institutions. There was surely much wisdom in the pursuit of this policy, for the issue of standards of student achievement is still discussed quite unproductively over half a century later.

THE SCIENTIFIC MANAGEMENT OF EDUCATION THAT FORGOT TO MAKE IT A SCIENCE

In this chapter we have described how the development of techniques of measurement opened up new ways of studying education. These new approaches to educational problems were widely described as scientific approaches, just as the corresponding approaches in industry were referred to as the new scientific management. The methods were more orderly and methodical than any that had preceded them, and they had the potential for providing knowledge about education of a kind that had never been available before, but they were hardly scientific.

The new approaches to education were called scientific partly because they derived from the new discipline that Edward L. Thorndike was developing at Teachers College. The scientific standing of Thorndike was beyond question, and yet what his followers in school systems were doing was of an entirely different character. The misunderstanding of workers in the field concerning the nature of science must be attributed partly to Thorndike himself, whose comments on the subject were highly misleading. Thorndike stated again and again that one of the first tasks involved in the exploration of any new area was that of establishing what the *facts* were. Once the *facts* were established, then one had in one's grasp a body of knowledge. Thorndike spoke as though the gathering of facts was the essential core of scientific inquiry. He loved to use the word *facts* in this connection, but never provided his readers with a statement of what he meant by a fact. If facts were the essence of science, then, as Noam Chomsky has so often pointed out, the task of the physicist would be merely that of reading meters, for meter readings are the facts of physics. Physical science is vastly more than a collection of meter readings, and behavioral science is much more than a collection of facts.

One must note that for Thorndike, and for the other outstanding educational psychologists of the age, the development of knowledge in the area of education was far more than the mere collection of facts -- despite what Thorndike may have written on the subject. When Thorndike constructed his puzzle boxes from which animals escaped, he quite obviously had a theory of what learning involved. He must surely have realized that hunger leads to activity and activity would lead, through chance, to the moving of the lever that opened the door. He must also have realized, long before he conducted one of his experiments, that escape involved the strengthening of the correct response and the weakening of the incorrect ones. In fact, he must have had a theory of learning before he ever experimented. The experiments merely confirmed what he already believed to be true. This has been the classical approach to the conduct of scientific inquiry. Galileo had a complete theory of falling bodies before he ever conducted an experiment, and he may well have never conducted some experiments ascribed to him. He probably never dropped weights from the Tower of Pisa. His writings are not clear on this point, but what is clear is that he had a theory of the acceleration of falling bodies and, in terms of the theory which on rational grounds he believed to be correct, he was confident what the results of experiment would be. Thorndike, like Galileo, must surely have had a theory before he even started collecting experimental facts, for without a theory he would surely never have been led to collect the kinds of facts that he actually did collect. Despite Thorndike's statements concerning the importance of the collection of facts, the truth seems to be that the simple collection of facts has never resulted in the development of a science, unless it has been preceded or accompanied by the development of a theory.

Yet those who attempted to develop what they called a scientific approach to education in the early 1900's were convinced that science was a matter of fact-finding, for was not the world then impressed with the power provided by what were called the "facts of science"? Leaders in education, at that time, had a complete misunderstanding of the nature of science. This does not mean that the collection of facts about education has no value, for it obviously does. There is value in finding out that the children in certain schools are not learning to read, despite experienced teachers with good records and excellent materials and opportunities. This may lead to a search for the difficulties outside of the school. Fact-finding is a useful enterprise in the management of any organization. However, to confuse the collection of facts for administrative purposes with the development of a science is an absurdity. Yet this absurdity was created early in the century and still exists.

The early developers of what they believed to be a scientific approach to education had aspirations which went far beyond that of merely collecting facts for management purposes. They genuinely hoped that they would be able to develop principles, resembling scientific principles, that would have sufficient generality to be applicable to the solution of a wide range of problem situations. Optimism in this respect was so high early in the century that the belief was often voiced that most of the problems of education would be solved within a few years. The problems were to be attacked directly, by practical men, who surely could not fail to find solutions and then apply them. These practical men never understood that the important principles of science had rarely evolved in practical situations, but in situations that appeared to have no practical implications whatsoever. They would have been astounded to realize that a science of physics, with all of its implications for construction and transportation, evolved from thoughts about dropping weights and rolling balls.

Thus, the search for the development of a science of events in educational situations, through the direct study of those situations, was doomed from the start. Disillusionment among the practical men who started the movement in the schools was inevitable. The enthusiasm of school administrators for educational research was perhaps at its peak around 1920. It never again reached the same peak.

THE MOVE TO DEVELOP CONTENT TESTS

The early development of tests of achievement focused on the three

R's. This was a policy of first things first. The primary goal of the grade schools of the early part of the century was to provide the immigrant with the basic language and computational skills needed to succeed in American society. Whatever else was taught was secondary. Also, there was no question that the three R's should be taught as identifiable and separate subjects, but there was considerable controversy concerning what other subjects should be introduced into schools and how much time should be spent on them. Nature study was introduced as a subject, later to be replaced by a broad conception of science. The concept of a children's literature designed specifically for children had hardly emerged. The concept of social studies and civics as a subject matter area was being explored and debated, with communities such as Gary arguing that these subjects should be taught through the study of the local community and the school community. Manual training had appeared, and then almost disappeared. In such an atmosphere of turmoil within the curriculum, one can understand that testing should have concentrated on the three R's about which there was no controversy.

The curriculum did continue to expand in scope, as it had continued to expand throughout the last century. In addition, concern about questions of content had increased because of the expanding number of students attending secondary schools. This led to interests on the part of educational researchers and those with commercial interests in the development of achievement tests in content areas. Publishers had come to recognize that testing provided a new and lucrative market which developed rapidly during the 1930's, not just in the three R's but in the knowledge areas of the curriculum.

The new achievement tests expanded the horizons of educational research workers. The efficiency of schooling that researchers believed could be achieved through the use of tests in the three R's, they believed also could be achieved in content areas through corresponding tests. The belief was widely expressed that the first task of research workers was to assess the knowledge of students at all ages, to provide a baseline in terms of which improvements could be judged. Out of this viewpoint there emerged numerous statewide testing programs for schools, and a number of surveys of the knowledge possessed by students. The studies are of much greater interest than the statewide testing programs which developed later and thus will be considered first.

The most ambitious surveys of the knowledge of students were conducted as a part of an enterprise known as the Pennsylvania Study. These studies came about through the recommendations of a commission appointed by the Pennsylvania State Department of Public Instruction in 1925 to consider relations between secondary schools and colleges and the relationship of the secondary school curriculum to the college curriculum. The Commission eventually advanced proposals, which were presented to the Carnegie Foundation, to the effect that studies be undertaken on such issues as the responsibility of the school in orienting pupils with respect to the aims of college, and how the colleges might better build on the previous achievements of students. Frederick P. Keppel, a personal friend of Edward L. Thorndike and president of the Carnegie Foundation, had long had an interest in studies related to the measurement of talent and achievement, and had endorsed the support of many previous such enterprises to the tune of several million dollars. The new proposal appealed to him. A point to note is that, in all these preliminary activities, the initiative came from the State school authorities and not from the academic research establishment.

The task of undertaking the study went to the two New Yorkers most qualified to explore the knowledge of students. These were William S. Learned (1876-1949), a staff member of the Carnegie Foundation for the Advancement of Teaching, an organization completely independent of the Carnegie Foundation; and Benjamin D. Wood (1894-), who was Director of Collegiate Research at Columbia College, the male undergraduate college of Columbia University. Learned had achieved eminence in the academic field through the usual path taken by American scholars in his time. After graduating from Brown University in 1897, he spent several years teaching and then left for Germany to learn about the newest ideas that Europe had to offer. He spent 2 years at the Universities of Leipzig and Berlin, where he must surely have had contact with the new philosophy of pedagogy which was having impact on the rest of the world. He then returned to the United States and completed a doctoral degree at Harvard in 1912, and was almost immediately afterwards appointed to the staff of the Carnegie Foundation for the Advancement of Teaching. In the latter capacity he published works on the training of American teachers, the American library and its function in the diffusion of knowledge, and the quality of education in America and in Europe.

Less is known about the career of Benjamin D. Wood (1894-). He did not climb the academic ladder through study in Europe. He completed his doctoral degree in Columbia University with a dissertation on *Measurement in Higher Education.* This must have been a substantial work, for it was published in 1923 as a book by the World Book Company. James McKeen Cattell had started an interest in such measurement at Columbia, and the impact of Cattell's ideas were still felt there, even though he had been dismissed. Shortly after completing his doctoral work, Wood was employed to conduct a study of the law school at Columbia and this led him to a permanent appointment to conduct research on institutional problems for Columbia College. He remained there for the rest of his life conducting studies related to the new type of achievement test, the use of films in education, and various other matters related to education. His fame in history, like that of Learned, rests largely on his role in developing the Pennsylvania Study.

Learned was later instrumental in developing the Graduate Record Examination, and Wood became the initiator of the Cooperative Test Service. Both of these subsequent enterprises may be regarded as having emerged from the Pennsylvania Study. In the early part of the century, testing enterprises seem to have engendered an enthusiasm, in those that carried them out, that led to the development of new testing enterprises, even though tangible outcomes were hard to pinpoint.

Although the first actions related to the Pennsylvania Study were undertaken in 1925, the final published report did not appear until 1938, though many lectures were given on the subject during the intervening years. The final report of William S. Learned and Ben D. Wood carried the title of *The Student and His Knowledge* (1938). The report declared the purpose of the study to be "An Examination of the Results of Schooling" (p. 1). On the surface this may seem to be an overwhelmingly large purpose, but as one reads the report, one realizes that it is not. Learned and Wood took the position that the only sure outcomes of education were in the category of knowledge and that all other supposed outcomes either did not exist or could not be measured. For all practical purposes they considered knowledge to be *the* result of education. In an eloquent introduction, probably written by the philosophically inclined Learned, the report states that education involves the perception of meanings and relationships among ideas and the evaluation of those ideas for their truth and importance. Knowledge is regarded as the product of thought and not merely memorized factual detail. The report recognizes that schools and colleges all too often set course requirements that call for only the memorization of detail; nevertheless, the accepted aims of education called for much more than this. Learned and Wood stated that their plan was to measure knowledge as a product of thought rather than as a product of mere memory. Furthermore, Learned and Wood were interested in the knowledge of the student insofar as it represented a quite permanent repertoire over which the individual had immediate command. In order to be useful, knowledge had to be "permanent and available" (p. 8).

In a further paragraph in the introduction to the final report, Learned and Wood state that a major purpose of the Pennsylvania Study was to demonstrate to teachers just how much knowledge students had. Without such information, surely teachers would not know where to begin their instruction. The Study had the broad purpose of trying to demonstrate, at various levels, just what students knew and did not know.

In comparison with previous large-scale testing enterprises measuring achievement, the tests used in the Pennsylvania Study were carefully designed to ensure that they were reliable and, in some sense, valid. The tests were shown to be such that chance played little part in the scores of students and the tests were demonstrated to be related to the extent to which the student had been exposed to related course work. The latter was taken to indicate that the tests were valid measures of knowledge in particular fields.

The first series of tests were administered initially to graduating college seniors in 1928. The tests were truly an attempt to survey the academic knowledge of the student. The examinations were given in four sessions, with each session covering a broad area of knowledge. The breadth of the areas is shown by the following description of the general coverage of each session:

Session 1. This session covered the physical sciences, the earth sciences, and the biological sciences. The tests for this session were truly comprehensive, for they covered not only a knowledge of concepts, principles, and laws, but also methods and experimental procedures. The breadth of the examination was such that it must have shaken many college seniors into a feeling of being hopelessly ignorant.

Session 2. This session covered basic concepts and ideas in psychology, anthropology, and sociology, but it also covered what was known about statistical methods and historical methods. In addition, it called for a knowledge of two foreign languages, selected by the student, as essential tools for exploring knowledge in the social sciences. Furthermore, the examination covered primitive cultures, both prehistoric and modern, and a knowledge of Greek and Roman civilizations, including a knowledge of the philosophy, religions, and political ideas of antiquity.

Session 3. The tests for this session covered preindustrial civilization in the preindustrial period. It covered social and political institutions and their evolution, and also the evolution of religious, scientific, and philosophical thought. It also had sections on Western literature and art and music.

Session 4. The final session covered contemporary Western civilization. It covered economic and political theories, legal institutions, and recent political history. It also included sections on modern art and music and the trend in literature. A final section of the test covered Chinese, Japanese, Indian, and Moslem cultures.

One wonders how the students in the late 1920's responded to such a formidable array of questions. One suspects that the modern college senior would be overwhelmed by a similar examination. Learned and Wood say nothing about this problem. Perhaps the students of the 1920's were less overwhelmed than the modern student might be, because they were more highly selected than their modern counterparts. Also, requirements for graduation were such that the student was forced to study a great range of subject matter.

The tests were all designed along what were then considered to be new principles, that is to say, they involved objectively scorable test items. The forms of the item included the true-false, the matching, and the multiple-choice. The tests were widely criticized for the use of these forms of testing on the grounds that they tended to test quite trivial aspects of the student's knowledge. Learned and Wood responded to this criticism by saying that it reflected nothing more than prejudice and that all of their test questions called for some degree of thought.

The examination was administered first to 4,412 college seniors on the eve of their graduation at 49 Pennsylvania colleges. For much of their analysis, Learned and Wood used a total score representing the number of right answers on the four sections of the test taken as a whole.

The results were a shock to many, for differences between those who had a college education were so vast that the highest-scoring student in one college might have a lower score than the lowest-scoring student at another institution. A bachelor's degree obviously had no clear meaning, and certainly was no guarantee that the student had acquired a particular level of knowledge. The achievement of the students in the colleges were related to the reputation of the college. Those institutions with a high reputation turned out the more knowledgeable student, but one must recognize the fact that these high-reputation institutions were able to select not only gifted students, but students who were particularly competent academically in the first place. Learned and Wood encountered another surprising finding when the tests were administered again to graduating seniors in 1930. They found that some colleges showed a marked and significant shift in position when the tests were repeated. Some years were apparently better vintage years for competent students than were others. As a part of the 1930 testing, graduating seniors were administered a test of intelligence. The latter tests ranked colleges in almost the same order as the achievement test scores.

The differences between students within a particular college were also large, further indicating that college graduation was not a mark of having mastered a particular body of subject matter.

The tests were also given to 194 faculty who volunteered to undertake the task. The top professors on the test scored far above the best students, but about a quarter of the faculty volunteering had scores comparable to, or less than, the mediocre college graduate. The interesting finding also turned up that the scores of the professors were closely related to the scores of the students in the colleges where they taught.

Learned and Wood also found differences between particular groups of colleges. They were surprised to find that students in teachers' colleges scored lower than those in liberal arts colleges. The real surprise is that Learned and Wood were surprised, for teaching was the poorest paid of all the professions. Within liberal arts, differences between students in different curricula were small. Learned and Wood argued that differences between students was a result of differences in ability rather than of differences in any other factor. They also argued that the very bright student was held back rather than helped by the college courses. Indeed, their impression was that special provision needed to be made for the very bright student. They were particularly impressed with the group that entered college early. The woman scoring highest in the 1928 sample was a girl, graduating at the age of 18, who had entered college at 15½ and then finished college in 3½ years. Colleges claimed that such a person should not be rushed through a curriculum, but should be socialized; but Learned and Wood were not convinced by the argument.

The investigation provided a great amount of information about differences in total score of those majoring in particular fields, but the information is not of particular interest except insofar as it can be compared with modern data. Academic areas will attract the able or the less able, depending upon the demand for the knowledge and many other social factors. A field that might attract top students at one time might have to be content with mediocre students at another time.

In addition to the testing of college students, a broad battery of achievement tests was administered to about 70 percent of the high school seniors in Pennsylvania. The tests used for this purpose had been developed by Wood's Columbia Research Bureau and covered the areas of English, American history, ancient and European history, civics and government, mathematics, a foreign language, and natural science. Learned and Wood found that many of those who did not plan to go to college achieved high scores, and many of those who planned to attend college were low-scoring.

Prospective teachers graduating from teachers' colleges were tested so that comparisons could be made with the scores of other students and with the scores of the pupils they would be teaching. The first conclusion drawn was that the teachers were academically inferior to other graduating seniors in liberal arts colleges. This conclusion really was not justified. One suspects that if the liberal arts graduates had been given tests covering the curriculum of the teachers' colleges that the liberal arts students would have appeared to be academically inferior to the graduates of the teachers' colleges. The second conclusion was that many graduates of teachers' colleges were less knowledgeable than many seniors in high school. One has to bear in mind that the latter conclusion was based on an overall score in which the results of the tests in all areas were pooled together. The teachers may still have been vastly more knowledgeable than their prospective students in the areas in which they would teach. The Learned and Wood conclusion, that more able students should find their way into teaching, hardly seems to be justified in terms of their data, for the data also showed that what the student learned depended to a great extent on what he was exposed to.

The great error in the analysis of data of the Pennsylvania Study was in the use of an overall score, produced by pooling the scores from the separate tests. Just what such an overall score signifies is not clear at all.

Learned and Wood drew a number of interesting implications from their data that suggest needed changes in the way in which colleges are run. First, there is the conclusion, already discussed, that colleges do not select the most able students. Learned and Wood did not consider the possibility that the quite mediocre high school student might sometimes turn out to be excellent college material. They also did not recognize that college selection involves far more than matters of ability, for often colleges have to select prospective students who are poor risks just because they must keep their enrollments above a certain minimum in order to survive.

Among the more important recommendations are those that have to do with the individualization of the college program to meet the needs of each student. Learned and Wood believed that the very basis of a program of individualized instruction at the college level was an assessment of what the student knew. There is implicit in this view, as Learned and Wood developed it, the idea that there is a definite body of knowledge that all educated individuals should have mastered. The assessment of the student's knowledge would indicate to the college faculty just how much of that knowledge had been mastered at the time he was admitted. Learned and Wood stressed that the only path to education was self-education, and that self-education required a design for education very different from that found in the typical college. Students should be guided into those learning activities that would permit them to build on the knowledge they had previously acquired.

Learned and Wood also proposed that a system be established through which a cumulative record be kept of the knowledge of each young person. Presumably such a cumulative record would indicate the extent to which each had mastered the knowledge believed to be the mark of an educated individual.

The report of the Pennsylvania Study did not escape the impact of the view that intelligence tests measured innate ability. In this connection, Learned and Wood proposed that a registry of ability be established in each state which could be used for identifying college material. College admissions officers would have free access to the information stored in each registry. The aptitude assessments would also be used as a means for identifying those eligible for various aid programs. The plan for a registry of aptitude records anticipated the establishment of college aptitude testing programs, with their complicated systems for the distribution of test scores to admitting officers. Of course, this idea was not new with Learned and Wood, for the College Entrance Examination Board had already been in existence for a quarter of a century.

In a final section of the report, issue is taken with the idea of evaluating a college in terms of whether it meets such standards as having a faculty with particular preparation, whether it has adequate libraries and laboratories, and whether it meets certain standards in a multitude of matters. Learned and Wood take the position that all of these could be replaced with a simple single standard, namely, the knowledge acquired by the students measured by standardized tests. They argued that the only important characteristic of a college was the extent that it produced knowledgeable students.

This final proposal was to have zero impact on the course of higher education in America. The proposal suffered from the same shortcoming as most of the other proposals advanced by those who pressed for greater use of standardized tests. The main shortcoming of most of these proposals was the assumption that there was a well-identified body of knowledge that all should master in order to be designated as educated. The latter assumption was regarded as a fundamental truth related to education by many who lived in the early part of the century. Today we are no nearer than people were then in identifying such a body of knowledge. Indeed, most today would deny that one can identify such a body.

THE ACHIEVEMENT TEST SURVEY

The work that Learned and Wood accomplished in the late 1920's was a part of a general movement to measure achievement through the new objectively scored tests. Prime movers in this respect were the new bureaus of research in the schools, but no single individual did more to encourage the widespread use of standardized tests of achievement than Stuart A. Courtis. His path to fame began when he administered his test of arithmetic in the Detroit schools and, at once, was invited by New York City to administer the same test to 30,000 school children. The report of the New York City survey of arithmetic skills aroused widespread interest, and Courtis traveled up and down the country presenting lectures on the use of the standardized test. The tests developed by Courtis were also extensively advertised in teacher journals, and soon these tests were selling millions of copies a year.

Some of the programs mushroomed into large enterprises. In 1929, the State University of Iowa initiated a high school testing program on a statewide scale at the high school level and later extended this program to the upper elementary grades. The tests used carried the catchy name of Every Pupil Tests and soon the program mushroomed until it included most schools in the state. One should note, however, that this was not the first program of its kind, for the Board of Regents of the State of New York had experimented with new objective tests of achievement in 1927, but the Iowa tests came nearer to representing a statewide cooperative testing enterprise.

By the mid-1930's, over half the states had some kind of statewide testing program in operation. Materials were also by then easily available. The American Council on Education had facilitated the development of the new ways of measuring achievement by establishing in 1930 the Cooperative Test Service, largely through the promptings of Ben D. Wood, who provided space in an area near his office at Columbia University to house it. Commercial test builders had also entered the scene and the competition among them was intense. Sales of instruments soared to such high levels that publishers found that, during the early depression years, tests were the most profitable items they had to offer.

Most of the enterprises that consumed the huge quantities of achievement tests during the 1930's have left behind no record of what was done with the results. One suspects that little was done. A state such as Iowa, that seems to have given more tests to more children than perhaps any other state, does not seem to have produced a better school system as a result. In fact, the State of Iowa seems to have been remarkably lacking in innovation in education. The statewide testing program in Iowa was dominated by Everett Franklin Lindquist (1901-1978), an eminent statistician who made notable contributions to his field, yet did not publish a single paper in his lifetime describing specific benefits derived from the administration of his tests.

There were, of course, a few who voiced objections to the mushrooming of testing programs. Those who protested, protested loudly, even though they were not many. A majority of educators simply regarded tests as a necessary part of an educational program, and a part about which there could be no objections. Most of the criticism came from academicians in the field of pedagogy.

The professors of pedagogy saw that statewide testing programs had the effect of casting the curriculum into a rigid mold. The professors also realized that testing programs in England had had disastrous effects on teaching practices. In England, the State testing program in the last century had been tied to a payment-by-results system, and enormous pressure had been placed on teachers to obtain the best performances possible on the part of their students. Since the State examinations emphasized certain limited skills on the part of the pupil, teaching had become reduced to the development of those skills. The professors of pedagogy had good reason to believe that programs such as that in Iowa might sterilize educational innovation in that state. They were right, for it did. Furthermore, the criticism was voiced that the use of a statewide program would result in a standardization of the curriculum and prevent schools from developing programs that might cater to special local needs. Such testing programs do tend to define a set of quite narrow objectives for the school. The critics were obviously right, but what they said had little impact. Statewide programs have continued to flourish not because they have been particularly useful, but because they have had vigorous promoters such as the late Lindquist in Iowa. They seem to satisfy the needs of those who want to exercise powerful control over education, but their utility to education has not been demonstrated.

PROGRESSIVE EDUCATION AND THE ACHIEVEMENT TESTING MOVEMENT -- THE EIGHT-YEAR STUDY

In the years that followed World War I, there developed across the world an organized movement to reform education. In the United States this movement was organized under the banner of Progressive Education. Other countries had other designations for the movement. None of the ideas that the movement fostered were particularly novel, for they could be found 30 years earlier in the writings of John Dewey, and many of the ideas went far further back in history. Although the ideas were not new, the development of organizations to promote them was. These organizations had great catalytic power in that they provided platforms from which the ideas concerning educational reform could be disseminated, and meetings through which those developing the concepts of educational reform at the practical level could meet with others engaged in similar practices. In the United States the *Progressive Education Association* provided such a forum and a source of contacts for reform-minded educators.

Those engaged in the progressive education movement viewed the new emphasis on standardized achievement testing as a menace to everything they hoped to accomplish. They wanted to make radical changes in the curriculum, but the standardized test tended to encourage the retention of the established curriculum content. They wanted to emphasize the development of thinking skills, but the tests placed emphasis on the memorization of facts. They wanted to emphasize self-evaluation, with the child's own evaluation of himself as the point from which progress should be measured, but the achievement testers encouraged a competitive system in which a child was judged in terms of his position in a group. The use of criterion-referenced tests were minimal in the 1920's and 1930's, and although such tests would have answered this last criticism of the progressive educators, it would not have resolved even a small fraction of the misgivings that the progressives had about the new achievement testing movement.

There were many other criticisms of tests, but these seem to have had virtually no impact on the development of the achievement testing movement in its many forms. Despite these criticisms, the distribution of objective tests of achievement assumed massive proportions. Not only were the new tests promoted by commercial concerns, but influential individuals in the academic world became involved in the achievement testing enterprise. One cannot attribute the enormous development of the achievement testing movement in the 1920-40 period as merely a result of commercial pressure and advertising, for the schools were full partners in the enterprise. Many principals must have felt that, by participating in the new achievement testing enterprise, they placed themselves on the frontier of progress. Also, teachers and children did not seem to be bothered by the taking of standardized tests. They knew virtually nothing was ever done with the results. When the teacher spent the morning giving a test, it was an easy morning for him or her, and a not unpleasant one for most of the pupils. Such tests were much less threatening to the children than a test prepared by the teacher on which a grade might depend.

The Progressive Education Association was not opposed to tests, but the position was that most tests did not measure the important outcomes of education. The concept of education for life called for evaluation in terms of the individual's ability to cope with real life situations. The new achievement tests obviously did not do this, for their roots lay in the subject matter itself and not in life. Also, one could not argue strongly that the typical subject matter of the school was the best subject matter for preparing the individual for life. The Progressive Education Movement was active in seeking out new subject matter that would be more appropriate for life preparation than that most often found in school textbooks.

During the 1930's, some educators working on innovative programs made efforts to determine the effectiveness of these programs in the area of basic skills. The progressives agreed with the traditionalists that children should master the three R's. Differences of opinion lay not in whether the traditional basic skills should be achieved, but in how they should be achieved.

A few of those involved in innovation attempted to measure some of the outcomes of their new programs. For example, Carleton Washburne, who had introduced radical changes into the schools of Winnetka, made some attempt to demonstrate that the children in the program did at least acquire the basic skills as satisfactorily as children in other programs. Such attempts did not result in the acquisition of much useful knowledge. Typically, the studies were not well undertaken, and whatever differences were found between the new and the old programs were small. The knowledge acquired through such studies was also particularly meager in that the labels "traditional" and "progressive" did not carry any clear meaning. A school program that was viewed as a progressive program by one principal might be regarded as quite traditional by another. The several small studies that were undertaken involving the comparison of the so-called traditional and the so-called progressive programs were generally undertaken for political purposes. When

Carleton Washburne undertook his study, it was not for the purpose of discovering important facts about schooling, or for improving his program, but for the purpose of answering criticism from parents, anxious about the kind of schooling their children were receiving. Washburne was a master at handling criticism from parents. He was a large and impressive man with a booming voice and completely confident of his capacity to handle the parent, school board, the press, and everyone else. Whatever studies were undertaken by superintendents like Carleton Washburne were primarily for political purposes.

A single major effort was made during the 1930's to obtain some knowledge concerning the outcomes of progressive education. In April 1930, the Progressive Education Association established a Commission on the Relation of School and College. The primary purpose of the Commission was to reach an agreement between secondary schools and colleges that would permit the secondary schools to experiment with curricula without producing obstacles that would hinder the admission of their students to colleges. Wilford M. Aiken was selected to head the Commission. As a result of the work of this Commission an agreement was reached, to which most colleges subscribed, through which a select group of secondary schools were to be released from the usual subject and unit requirement for a period of 5 years, beginning with the class entering college in 1936. Students from the select group of schools would then be admitted to college on a basis other than the usual one of grades and units completed. Alternative college admission criteria were defined by the Commission. Altogether, 30 schools were selected in 1933 for participation in the plan and agreement was reached concerning the criteria to be adopted for admission to college.

Thus, the essence of the program developed by the Commission was to provide conditions under which the schools could freely experiment with their curricula, without prejudicing the chances of their students to enter college. Most of the schools already had highly innovative programs, and are still known for their historical contributions to the development of education. The schools began their work of curriculum development within the new framework of freedom in 1933.

The Commission was able to find support for its work through grants from the Carnegie Corporation and the General Education Board. During the 8 years of the project, the enterprise was probably the best-funded educational research project in the United States.

The Commission did not seem to have any clear ideas, initially, concerning how it should go about its business. Indeed, the philosophy seems to have been that, if one could just let schools experiment with curricula, then good must surely emerge. The enthusiasm of the Commission for innovation was matched in intensity only by naivete. Chaotic and uncontrolled innovation did result from the enterprise, but not in a manner that could possibly result in the orderly accumulation of knowledge. Generations of school people had engaged in similar attempts to innovate, but without any accumulation of knowledge. The staff of the study did at least recognize that more than massive innovation was needed if the study was to accomplish much.

In order to remedy the basic defect in the design of the study, and to make it possible to engage in an orderly development of knowledge, an Evaluation Staff was employed. Appointed to head the staff was Ralph Winfred Tyler (1902-   ), who was then associate professor of education at The Ohio State University. Tyler had graduated from a small college, Doan College, in Nebraska at the age of 19. He completed a master's degree at the University of Nebraska and in 1927 completed a doctoral degree at the University of Chicago. In his early adult years he taught science in secondary school and during the years 1922-27 was assistant supervisor in the sciences at the University of Nebraska. He was appointed to the faculty of The Ohio State University in 1929 where he shared appointments in the department of education and the educational research bureau.

Tyler was never a prolific writer, but at the age of 30 he authored a book with Douglas Waples, *Research Methods and Teacher Problems* (1930), which set the stage for many of his life activities.

The Waples and Tyler book is of interest in the present context in that it provides the setting for the work of the Evaluation Staff of the Eight-Year Study and all of the work derived from that study. Tyler had a genius for inventing what appeared to be highly plausible and simple solutions to very complex problems. Indeed, his entire impact on American education has been through this capacity. Others, who have also had impact, such as John B. Watson and B. Frederick Skinner, had similar capacities for inventing apparently simple, attractive solutions to complex problems. Of course, there are no simple solutions to the complex problems of education, but those who believe they have invented them do manage to exert influence.

The title of the Waples and Tyler book describes exactly what the book attempts to do. Teachers need to study carefully what is involved in teaching and need to make a careful analysis of the components of the classroom process. These components involve the definition of objectives, the construction of a course, selecting a text, adapting the materials to the particular class, and so forth. Waples and Tyler make the distinction between research and studies conducted by teachers. Teachers may conduct an orderly inquiry into instruction and the materials and equipment involved, but this would not be research; but it would be worth doing in its own right. One has to bear in mind in reading the book that the belief was widely held at that time that important studies could be conducted by teachers, and the *Society for the Experimental Study of Education* had been established for the purpose of helping teachers undertake such studies. Waples and Tyler proposed a simple plan through which such studies could be undertaken.

The formula found in the book is the one that has characterized Tyler's approach to education throughout his career. First, objectives must be operationally defined. The definition of objectives in terms of specific outcomes was not new, for journals in the early part of the century had filled many issues with attempts to define outcomes in terms of quite specific outcomes. Whether such attempts to define objectives precisely was worthwhile had long been a matter of controversy, but the writings of Percy Williams Bridgman (1882-1961) on operationalism in the early 1920's had made the task of defining objectives, in terms of identifiable specifics, a scientifically respectable activity. Waples and Tyler extended the methods of operationalism to the study of every phase of classroom activity. All terms had to be operationally defined to be useful; at least, that is what the theory preached.

Operationalism was heralded by many in education as the means of escape from the vague language that had plagued educational literature for so long. The theory was seductively attractive and seemed to provide a means of sharpening thought about educational problems. The fact that the theory had come from an eminent Harvard physicist, Bridgman, provided the illusion that this was the way in which the physical sciences had advanced. Of course, such was not the case at all, for the success of theory of physics had depended upon the postulation of conditions that were not directly observable. No science could develop along the lines of the physical sciences and confine itself to observable events. None of these weaknesses of operationalism were recognized by educators in the 1930's interested in the application of the theory to the problems of education.

The Waples and Tyler book was, in essence, an attempt to apply operationalism to the solution of educational problems at the classroom level. They may well never have heard of Bridgman, and do not reference his publications on operationalism in this book. The trend of thought of the times was towards operationalism and Bridgman may well have crystallized in words the thoughts that were on the minds of many. By 1940, operationalism had come to be a dominant idea in educational research.

When Tyler became Director of the Evaluation Staff of the Eight-Year Study, he brought to the enterprise the idea that variables had to be defined in terms of identifiable behaviors. The Eight-Year Study provided the challenge of doing what he had been telling teachers to do. The Staff of the enterprise, and the faculty of the schools too, had talked vaguely about the development of thinking. Tyler set out to define thinking in operational terms. Thinking was to be defined in terms of problems and their solutions. The idea that thinking involves transformations had not yet entered the scene.

Tyler wrote a series of papers on the subject of defining objectives.

These were later published in a small volume entitled *Constructing Achievement Tests* (Columbus: The Ohio State University, 1934).

The first task of the Evaluation Staff was to visit the 30 schools and to obtain a general picture of the educational objectives. This was done during the Fall of 1934 and the Winter of 1935. The lists of objectives formulated by the schools were then consolidated by classification into groups. A set of assumptions was drawn up to guide further work in a way that bears the clear stamp of Tyler thinking at that time. For example, one assumption was that the effectiveness of an educational program should be determined by finding out the extent to which the objectives of the program were actually realized. In other words, the assumption was made that the school as a system was a closed system, an assumption that was to dominate educational planning and evaluation for the next half-century. The set of assumptions as a whole was a powerful document that came to have great impact on educational thought and practice (see pp. 11-15 in Eugene R. Smith and Ralph W. Tyler, *Appraising and Recording Student Progress*, 1942). The same volume also contained an interesting discussion of the need to pin down objectives in terms of behavior. The general procedure for conducting an evaluation program, set out in the volume, provided a model which was to dominate the educational field for many decades to come. The model involved the steps of formulating objectives, classifying objectives into categories, defining objectives in terms of behavior, identifying situations in which the achievement of the objectives may be shown, selecting and trying promising evaluation methods, developing and improving appraisal methods, and interpreting the results. The introductory sections of the volume were written by Tyler himself and became an important medium for disseminating his ideas on how orderly progress in education might be made. Indeed, the first 29 pages of the volume represent a document that probably had more impact on education than any other product of the Eight-Year Study. This statement does not imply that the impact was necessarily good. An evaluation of the impact is difficult and complex.

The remainder of the Smith and Tyler volume describes the wide range of evaluation instruments that were developed. These fall into the following four categories:

- Aspects of thinking
- Social sensitivity
- Appreciations
- Personal and social adjustment

The instruments themselves were of considerable interest, and showed a talent and imagination rarely brought to bear on an evaluation problem. Those who worked on the project included Oscar K. Buros, Bruno Bettelheim, Louis E. Raths, Hilda Taba, Chester W. Harris, J. Wayne Wrightstone, and others who were later to become well known for their contributions to educational research. The potential of the Evaluation Staff for producing professionals of distinction was extraordinary. For this reason, the evaluation activities of the Eight-Year Study stand in sharp contrast to most other evaluation enterprises in terms of the imagination that was brought to bear on the problems of evaluation.

The tests developed in the area of thinking skills created more interest in their time than any other set of instruments produced by the entire program. Four aspects of thinking were operationally defined. These were the interpretation of data, the application of principles of science, the application of principles of logical reasoning, and the nature of proof. For each area, a test was produced following a Tyler-type analysis of the objective. The state of the art of test construction of that time was such that no recognition was given to the matter of how an assembly of test items came to identify a variable. The state of the art was also such that no attempt was made to determine whether the various tests constituted independent components of thinking ability that could be developed independently one from the other, or whether the tests measured largely a common factor. Such questions did not enter into the logic on which the tests were based.

A few comments seem appropriate on some of the other areas in which evaluation instruments were developed in the Eight-Year Study. Hilda Taba and her associates identified six major aspects of social sensitivity that seemed to be important objectives in the 30 schools. One must keep in mind that at that time the social development of education was stressed in schools and it represented the so-called progressive point of view. The objectives fell into the following six categories:

1. *Social thinking.* This was primarily an intellectual component and reflected the student's ability to apply knowledge to the solution of social problems and to view such applications critically.
2. *Social attitudes.* This included a large conglomerate, but the 30 schools seemed to be mainly interested in the development of democratic values.
3. *Social awareness.* This was the extent to which the student was aware of social issues and social problems.
4. *Social interest.* This was the extent to which the individual liked to engage in social activities.
5. *Social information.* This was the extent to which the individual was informed about social problems.
6. *Skill in social action.* This was the extent to which the individual had achieved social skill in his personal life.

The most notable instrument to come out of this analysis of objectives was the Social Problems Test. This device presented a series of social problems and the student was asked to select a course of action and to justify his action in terms of social science generalizations as well as in terms of his own beliefs.

One could write at great length on the instruments developed by the Evaluation Staff of the Eight-Year Study, but enough has been said to demonstrate that the project must be regarded as one of the extraordinary evaluation enterprises of its era.

Before leaving the Eight-Year Study, a second aspect of the evaluation of the 30 schools must be considered. The first group of students from the schools entered college, under the new school-college agreement, in 1936. The college follow-up study was conducted by a separate unit within the Evaluation Staff. The four members who prepared the final report on the study were Dean Chamberlin, Enid Chamberlin, Neal E. Drought, and William E. Scott. Their volume was entitled *Did They Succeed in College* (1942). The volume describes a comparison of the college careers of 1,475 students who entered college from the 30 schools with a similar number from conventional schools. The two groups were matched in pairs. The two groups were then compared on a large number of variables including traditional grades and also ratings by college faculty on traits that are not ordinarily assessed in college. Although the study found that those from the 30 schools performed slightly better in terms of grades than those from the control comparison group, except in foreign languages, the differences were small. Also, the two groups did not differ in terms of the choice of field of specialization. They did differ substantially in terms of social qualities in terms of both ratings and the degree to which they participated. However, the two groups did not differ significantly on ratings of adjustment. The conclusion was drawn that the students from the 30 schools were rather better prepared for college than were the students from the conventional schools. The conclusion was hardly justified in that those from the 30 schools also tended to come from homes that were superior in intellectual atmosphere, for that is why many of them were at those schools. The conclusion can be drawn with respect to socialization, but not in terms of overall preparation for college. An interesting comment in the final pages of the report states that, although the students from the 30 schools seem well prepared to participate in the running of the college, there was almost no opportunity for them to do this. Colleges, then as now, provide few chances for the student to participate in the planning work of colleges. Students have little opportunity to show initiative. The colleges did not make use of the qualities that the students from the 30 schools brought to higher learning.

Tyler left The Ohio State University in 1938 to become Chairman of the Department of Education and University Examiner at the University of Chicago. The reputation he had gained for organizing the Evaluation Staff resulted in his appointment to this important position. In 1938, Tyler was certainly the best known American educational research worker, and one whose thought was to have a continuing impact. According to *Who's Who in America* (1967), Tyler continued as Director of the Evaluation Staff until 1942, but few new ideas seem to have been developed in the project after he left Ohio. The five-volume work that described the Eight-Year Study still had to be written.

What was learned from the Eight-Year Study? When the study is viewed in its historical context, it provides, first and foremost, a lesson in method. It provided a model for most other studies to follow for perhaps as long as the next half-century. It provided a plan through which school programs and their outcomes could, it has been believed, be studied methodically. The study showed how the reduction of vague generalities in the area of objectives could be reduced to quite concrete elements of behavior. Studies that followed were to show a close adherence to the plan of reducing all objectives and outcomes to identifiable aspects of behavior, and tests would be built on the basis of this reduction. The final result would be a reduction of the outcomes of the elementary school curriculum to thousands of behavioral elements.

Tyler himself throughout his life has spent much of his own time meeting with groups and helping them apply the formula he developed. The simplicity of the formula, and its appearance of logicality, gave it instant appeal across the country. Those who questioned the Tyler formula were quite unable to provide an alternative as simple and as logically attractive. Most of the accountability models were derivatives of the Tyler formula. The Tyler formula remained unchallenged until the 1970's.

At the substantive level, the Eight-Year Study left a legacy of instruments, built with extraordinary ingenuity by very clever and creative people. The instruments should have become the basis for many studies, but they did not. The fault was not with the instruments. Progressive education was on a steep decline by the time World War II broke out and so also was interest in measuring the outcomes identified by the Evaluation Staff. Then, during the war, the entire study and its resources were forgotten. The instruments themselves were probably of greater interest and value than the methodology on which they were based, though the methodology became the main legacy of the project. The Eight-Year Study should have been the start of a series of studies that might well have produced an accumulation of knowledge. The Eight-Year Study itself produced a little, but uncertain, knowledge about how educational practices influenced outcomes. The evaluation instruments were never used in a design which would permit relating specific school practices to fairly specific behavioral outcomes, though the college follow-up comes near to being such a study. Some have commented that the Tyler type of evaluation procedure is like an experimental study that fails to incorporate a control group. The criticism seems to be quite valid. One cannot relate educational procedures to outcomes unless one includes a group in which the development of the same outcomes is studied in relation to the absence of the procedure. This is one of J. S. Mill's familiar canons.

State testing programs slowly came into line with the Tyler evaluation model, and were encouraged to do this through the influence of local academicians who taught the model in their courses in teacher education. Tyler's final promotion of the model came in his development of his National Assessment of Educational Progress. The latter enterprise is described as *his* in that it came into being through his influence in high political places, and the close guidance he gave to the project during its early development. The latter program, like its predecessors, has been the most expensive educational research program of its time. The assessment of National Assessment still has to be made, but the products have to justify the fact that the project has involved very large sums of money.

THE OUTCOMES OF STUDIES OF SCHOOL ACHIEVEMENT

The research and development described in this chapter is difficult to evaluate as a totality. Let us begin by considering the positive outcomes of this enterprise.

First, the experimentation with examinations in the early part of the century did much to improve the techniques of measuring educational achievement. The problems involved in the measurement of achievement were identified and teachers have become more aware than they were previously of the difficulties of developing good examinations. The development of the technology of achievement measurement has made it possible to produce useful measures of accomplishment of value to counselors, teachers, and others. The main significant outcomes of this technology have been in such areas as the development of advanced placement tests, high school certification by examination, credit by examination programs, and improvement in examinations for certification. Devices for the selection of those to be admitted to professional schools and graduate programs have also emerged from the technology, the most long-lived of which is the Graduate Record Examination. Whether these professional selection examinations resulted in improved performance on the part of those who graduate from these programs is not a matter that seems to be studied. One cannot guess what the outcomes of such studies would be.

Second, the efforts of Tyler have done much to help teachers realize the vagueness of many of their goals and to help them define these goals in more precise terms.

Third, studies of achievement have demonstrated what most teachers know, namely, that students achieve far less than teachers hope they will.

Almost every survey, from the survey of the Boston schools in 1845 down to modern times, has come up with a statement of disappointment concerning the products of education. This may merely take the form of a factual statement that many fifth graders are reading on the level of second grade, or the sweeping statement of the Boston Committee that the written work of the pupils in 1845 was nothing short of a disgrace. The conclusion is generally that the schools are at fault. Rarely is it suggested that the objectives set standards that are unreasonably high in terms of what can be accomplished. Some of the conclusions drawn by the staff of the National Assessment Program announce similar failures of students to become educated.

The shortcomings of the entire approach to educational research discussed in this chapter are considerably greater than the achievements. Indeed, of all the areas of educational research reviewed in this volume, that which has involved massive testing programs seems to have been the least productive, and also the most expensive. The first and foremost shortcoming of the approach is that it has absorbed very large sums of money without producing any particular improvements in education. There is no reason for believing that states which have a statewide testing program have shown any greater improvements in their educational program than those that have no such program. The states of the Midwest, in which such testing programs have thrived, have been notorious for their lack of innovation. The impact of a statewide testing program must lie somewhere between a point that represents a neutral or zero effect to a point that represents stultification.

A second negative impact is that large testing programs for measuring achievement tend to become institutionalized and self-perpetuating. The Iowa program is an example of such a program that has been perpetuated for about 40 years largely because there have been many hard-driving individuals, such as the late E. F. Lindquist, who kept it going. There seems to be no evidence that the testing program in Iowa, or the ones like it elsewhere, have ever resulted in any particular improvement, but still they continue.

The evaluation model, developed by Tyler, was an interesting innovation in itself in its day, but it has not yielded a body of knowledge about education as it originally seemed destined to do. The model has had a track record of failing to discover differences in the products of radically different forms of education. This failure to discover differences has generally resulted in the innovator becoming discouraged and the innovative program being dropped. All too often an innovative program is evaluated through a study conducted by educators who are highly conservative and out of sympathy with the innovation. This, in turn, introduces further bias and an increased likelihood that the results will be negative. The evaluation model of Tyler tends to be used in a way that is very unsupportive of innovation.

Third, although the Tyler model specifically implies that evaluation devices should be geared to the objectives of the curriculum, the reality is that the curriculum and the objectives tend to be geared to the tests. The tests create and stereotype the outcomes. Furthermore, administrators may place considerable pressure on teachers to match their efforts to whatever is required to produce high scores on the tests. Memoranda are sometimes even sent by administrators to teachers warning them about certain items that will appear in the next test and suggesting that the teachers give the children special training in that type of item. One such memorandum indicated that the forthcoming statewide test would include items on the use of encyclopedias and that the children should be given training in the use of such materials. Large-scale testing programs have introduced many forms of intellectual dishonesty into the classroom.

A fourth weakness of the programs discussed in this chapter is that evaluation techniques rarely have the power to accomplish what they set out to accomplish. Psychological measurement, through verbal devices, is at best crude, and does not measure the conglomerate that represents the important outcome of education. For example, one can measure reading skill in various ways, but it is the individual's compound of interest, drive, and skill that will determine whether he will turn to printed material to solve his problems of work and recreation. These human attributes, in addition, have to be combined with a knowledge of what printed materials exist that can be of use. The components of this conglomerate may develop simultaneously or successively, and over years. Thus, a test of reading skill may tell one little that has any prognostic value.

The problem under discussion has a parallel in engineering. Once a bridge has been built, tests can be run to determine some of the characteristics of the bridge as a structure, but these are of little value in determining whether the bridge will stay up or collapse, except in extreme cases. Bridge design has been improved not through the evaluation of brides already built, but through the development of new principles of bridge design. In a similar way, improvement in personal transportation was brought about not by the conduct of evaluation studies of the horse and buggy, but through the invention of the small, compact power plant that could be put on wheels. Changes in education have been brought about not through demonstrations of the inadequacies of the products, but through the invention of new ways of conceptualizing the learner. Faith in the value of evaluation studies today seems to be confined to the Federal government, which pours money into the enterprise.

A fifth limitation of the evaluation enterprise is that practical considerations limit it to short-term studies, but the real interest is in the long-term effect of education. There is reason to believe that short-term effects may be very different from long-term ones. One can readily see that a method of teaching reading, that produced rapid learning, might also antagonize the pupils to the degree that they would not want to read on their own. A less "efficient" method might have better long-term effects.

A sixth limitation of work in the area is related to the claim that achievement testing programs provide bench marks along the course of history against which the progress of education can be measured. The National Assessment enterprise embodied this notion, which is not a particularly new one. Several attempts have been made to compare the outcomes of education in different eras. The most unusual of these was the study by Otis W. Caldwell and Stuart A. Courtis (*Then and Now in Education*, 1924). This study is of interest here in that it illustrates the difficulties of using the tests of one generation to measure the achievement of a later generation. The Caldwell and Courtis study was an attempt to repeat the Boston Survey of 1845, described earlier in this chapter, and to administer the same tests to pupils in 1923. A first difficulty encountered by Caldwell and Courtis was that many of the questions had little meaning to children in 1923. City children in 1923 had little knowledge of acres, roods, and rods. They also had difficulty in answering the question "What is history?", but the Boston children in 1845 had less difficulty in that some had memorized the answer given in the textbook. The examination questions that are suitable for evaluating the knowledge and skills of one generation are not suitable for evaluating these in a later generation. The extreme case would be a comparison of the achievement of pupils in Puritan schools with the pupils in modern schools. Modern pupils simply could not answer the questions that the young Puritans could answer, for the questions asked the Puritan pupils had to do with the Bible and the common law.

A second major difficulty in making the comparison that Caldwell and Courtis attempted was that of finding comparable groups in the earlier and later period. Caldwell and Courtis compared the achievement of Boston children in 1845 with a sample of children from across the country. The Boston children of 1845 were mainly the children of immigrants with a large group speaking a foreign language in the home, and the later sample consisted largely of children of those who had migrated westward. Whether these two groups can be meaningfully compared is questionable. Caldwell and Courtis conclude, but with a weak case, that education in 1923 was better than in 1845, but the data do not bear close examination. Neither will more modern data making similar comparison bear close scrutiny.

Up to this time, the project known as National Assessment of Educational Progress had produced only rather obscure information concerning trends in educational progress. There do seem to be differences in the achievement of high school youngsters from decade to decade, and even for shorter periods; but, so far, the changes are obscure and largely uninterpretable. As the National Assessment program is extended over several decades, the difficulties encountered by Caldwell and Courtis will interfere progressively more with the interpretation of trends. The author's guess at the present time is that, despite the large sums that have been and will be spent on National Assessment, the data derived from it will not be very meaningful.

Seventh, one must ask why surveys of student knowledge, evaluation studies, and assessments of achievement, and related activities, have continued to be pursued on a large scale, despite their inability to produce educational change. The nearest that the author can come to an answer is that the giving and scoring of tests all too often provides only the illusion that scientific methods are being applied to the solution of problems of education. The activity reinforces the common sense idea that if one can just find out what students do not learn, then one can take steps to remedy the matter through changed teaching practices. The logic of the argument is plausible, but vastly underestimates the difficulty of developing improved teaching practices. Teaching has almost certainly improved over the last 500 years, but progress has been very slow and has had to be accompanied by a slow evolution in the concept that society as a whole has of the nature of the child and the nature of learning. The slow development of such ideas has been paralleled by a slow evolution of teaching as an art. So far, attempts to speed up that evolution have not been particularly successful.

Finally, there was an outcome of the movement described in this chapter that one cannot easily evaluate in straightforward positive or negative terms. That outcome was the establishment of measurement and statistics as the main focus of educational research. The largest single group in the American Educational Research Association represents these areas. Courses in measurement and statistics are commonly core courses in many graduate programs in colleges of education. These areas are important, but measurement and statistics cannot form the core of a vigorous educational research enterprise, any more than a course on the design of meters could constitute the core of engineering. The success of engineering derives from the ability of practical individuals to apply what has been learned in theoretical physics. Newtonian physics radically changed the design of bridges and other engineering structures, and nuclear physics brought about a revolution in the design of the products of electrical engineers, many of whom then became electronic engineers. Educational research workers and technologists have made little use of psychological theory, though some have flirted with various brands of behaviorism and, more recently, have embraced the theories of Piaget. Most educational research is undertaken outside of a framework of current psychological theory, perhaps because the training of educational research workers has emphasized measurement and statistics to the neglect of psychological theory.

One can, of course, argue that psychological theory is still in a primitive state in which it can have only the most primitive applicability. But even some quite primitive psychological theorizing may have utility in generating practical and useful ideas, as Edward L. Thorndike so clearly demonstrated. Psychological theory deserves to be examined and explored as a foundation for educational research, rather than neglected as it is at present.

CHAPTER 4

Intelligence Tests and Their Impact on American Schools

Research related to education has been immensely influenced by prevailing powerful political beliefs. One powerful belief that has had influence on education is that humans differ fundamentally and genetically from one another in their ability to handle life situations with competence. In the late nineteenth century, this belief in inequality emerged on the American scene and displaced the belief of the Puritans that all human beings had the same inherent capacities, though they might differ in the extent to which they felt moral obligation to use the capacities that God had given them.

The early phases of educational research in the United States were far more closely linked with the doctrine of elitism than with any concept of equality. In many ways this is a surprising linkage. The schools of the period of the great immigration were administered by men and women who believed that educational institutions should be the great equalizers. At least, to some degree, the schools managed to achieve this lofty goal, though perhaps for only a short period.

The hold on the common schools of the idea of equality was never a firm one, for private academies had existed even during colonial days when the elite could obtain an education widely believed to be appropriate to their social standing. Even the powerful political influence of Puritanism, with its emphasis on equality, had not prevented the New England academy from flourishing. While the common school was a social instrument for achieving equality, even back to colonial days, the academies fostered elitism and the conception that those born to exert influence, if not to rule, should be given an education worthy of their natural endowment.

Educational research in the United States was developed largely by men who embraced an elitist social philosophy. Later, we will discuss the philosophies of some of these men, but first we must consider some of the intellectual influences which led so many academicians to embrace an elitist social philosophy.

Elitist philosophy of the nineteenth century in the United States was provided with what appeared to be a scientific foundation in what has come to be known as social Darwinism. This was an outgrowth of the conception of the evolution of the species described by Darwin. Those who embraced this concept viewed the development of societies as following the same general lines as the development of species. The stronger and better adapted societies survived, and the weaker ones faded away. A similar attempt was made to apply evolutionary theory within complex societies. Thus, within industrialized societies, managerial and entrepreneur classes were viewed as emerging classes of superior individuals capable of making the high-level decisions that the corporate structures of such societies required. In this way societies became stratified, but the stratification was assumed to represent, also, levels of biological excellence. The idea is not at all a new one, except for its linkage with evolutionary theory. Plato held a similar view and based his Republic on it. Some were born to rule, and should rule, while others were born to undertake the menial work of the total society.

The champion of this doctrine of social evolution, with some variation, was Herbert Spencer, an English scholar, scientist, and philosopher. Herbert Spencer is of particular importance in relation to the development of social philosophy in America, because he spent considerable time here and exerted influence. Herbert Spencer wrote the first comprehensive *Principles of Sociology* (1876). His sociology was a part of a larger work entitled *System of Synthetic Philosophy.* Although the idea that the upper classes are genetically superior is associated with social Darwinism, Spencer did not embrace a Darwinian concept of evolution. He was, in fact, a Lamarckian evolutionist, who held that acquired characteristics were inherited. Thus, he held the view that whatever the upper classes learned during their successful entrepreneurship resulted in the development of traits of personality that were transmitted to their children. In this way the upper class slowly evolved, with each generation in the upper-economic strata becoming more capable than the previous one.

When Herbert Spencer visited the United States in 1882, his speeches met with strong approbation from wealthy audiences from Pennsylvania to New England. He developed a strong personal friendship with Andrew Carnegie, who saw in Spencer's views a rational basis for all of his prejudices about the working class. Carnegie viewed workers, Platonically, as masses of ignorant and stupid people who could not learn to do more than answer the call of the factory whistle and then do what they were told. If the working man's wage did little more than keep him alive so that he could work another day, his existence was justified in that it permitted others to live worthwhile lives. Carnegie understood nothing of the concepts being developed by Karl Marx across the Atlantic, which questioned whether the existence of Andrew Carnegie could be justified.

Andrew Carnegie was not the only great industrialist who saw Herbert Spencer as their prophet. Spencer was wined and dined throughout the Eastern states. When he returned to England, he was sent a substantial sum of money to support his work.

The wealthy found support for their ideas in the work of Herbert Spencer, and the academic world embraced his views. This is obvious from the fact that his books had a very large sale in America, and it was not just the great industrialists who bought them. They received free copies. Academicians and American intellectuals must have used his books extensively as assigned readings. This is hardly surprising, for American academicians, like others throughout the world, found sympathy for the idea that there was more than chance and luck involved in the emergence of an intellectual elite. Academicians tended to believe, and still tend to believe, that they are where they are because of intellectual genetic superiority. Spencer simply said what they believed to be true. The fact that most academicians came from an educated class that provided superior opportunities for their children was not considered to provide an alternative explanation. The elite of the American academic world believed that they had every right to be considered an elite, just as the aristocracies of Europe had held similar beliefs for 1,000 years until revolutions and social evolutions had shaken their status and led the masses to view them in entirely different terms. The elitism of the academic world, with its matrix of supporting beliefs, was to become the cradle of educational research and was to incorporate into educational research the same matrix of beliefs and prejudices.

The Spencer theory of the superiority of the upper classes found support from other sources. Studies of such families as the Jukes family showed how a single pair of humans might produce a whole family tree of individuals of low intelligence who became involved in all kinds of crime. *Jukes* was the name given to the family by Richard L. Dugdale, who conducted the study of the pedigree. The family tree begins with two sons of a backwoodsman who married two sisters. The two resulting lines of descent showed a large number of ne'er-do-wells in the one lineage and a high frequency of successful and substantial citizens in the other. On the bad Jukes side, Dugdale was able to trace 709 descendants, of whom 140 were imprisoned for crime and 280 were paupers, dependent upon public support.

The results of studies of such single families appeared to provide dramatic evidence that intelligence and other desirable attributes were strongly inherited. At the time when these studies were widely publicized, no one questioned whether the families represented typical patterns of the inheritance of intelligence. Indeed, the assumption was commonly made that just as the one Jukes lineage showed low intelligence, generation after generation, so too would the later generations of Carnegies and Rockefellers display industrial leadership throughout their family history. This was very much like a revival of the idea that royal blood carried with it desirable attributes not shared by the common people. The idea also carried with it a justification for the inheritance of wealth. The Puritan doctrine of the equality of all humans and the right of all to the same opportunity through schooling was crumbling. The concept of the inheritance of intellectual differences was sinking deep roots into American society, and the fruit that grew from these roots was to dominate American education for the next half-century.

The facts of the Jukes case slowly permeated the thinking of European and North American society. Accounts of the family were widely disseminated among teachers, and printed accounts of the case were advertised in journals directed towards teachers. The suggestion was that teachers should identify such children as those in the bad Jukes lineage, though what the teachers were supposed to do once the children were identified was not clear. One suspects that the implication for the teacher was that time should not be wasted on such children, for nothing could be done with them.

Teachers also received through their journals information on the identification of criminal types. A French criminologist of great repute Alphonse Bertillon, had developed a system for the identification of criminal types on the basis of physical features called *stigmata.* Bertillon incorporated into his theory most of the folklore that is associated with physical types and the identification of criminality. Such features as a low forehead and closely set eyes were viewed as damning features. Bertillon allowed for exceptions by stating that any single stigma was not enough to identify a criminal type, but claimed that a combination of stigmata did make a positive identification. Teachers were advised, through their literature, on how criminal types could be identified at an early age so that steps might be taken to control their inherent criminal behavior. The system was presented to the public as a scientific system, yet it did not involve the systematic collection of data. Bertillon himself was far more impressed by the cases he could find that fitted the system than with the many cases that did not.

Men like Bertillon were honest, but they did not have the necessary ideas and techniques for attacking the complex problems that interested them. Bertillon had no concept of the problem of sampling and the effect of discarding cases, which he did whenever a case did not fit his theory. Worthwhile studies could not be systematically undertaken until the concept of sampling had become part of the scientific repertoire.

Nevertheless, such work, conducted in the name of science and given a degree of scientific prestige, had enormous impact on the way in which people thought about the inheritance of characteristics and the physical basis for antisocial behavior.

THE NEW PSYCHOLOGICAL APPROACH TO THE APPRAISAL OF INTELLIGENCE AND ITS LINK WITH ELITISM

Herbert Spencer himself had little patience with the collection of data. He was a great synthesizer of knowledge and in some ways the greatest synthesizer of his century. His goal was to synthesize all scientific knowledge into a single coherent unity. The modern philosopher of science sees this as a fruitless pursuit, but it was the ideal of many men who lived in the last century. While Herbert Spencer was at work on the development of a theoretical basis for his Platonic conception of the good society, other scientists were developing methods of measurement which were to form what at first appeared to be a solid foundation for the emerging intellectual elitism that was to dominate much of educational research.

Those who initiated the mental measurement movement a hundred years ago were men motivated by strong scientific desires to explore the universe and to bring to that exploration the newest scientific techniques. They understood that the enormous achievements of physicists had been made possible through the initial quantification of physics by Isaac Newton. Chemistry could not have shown its dramatic development without the use of the quantitative methods of Antoine Lavoisier. For those who understood the significance of the work of Newton and Lavoisier, the way to develop the social and the psychological sciences was to develop quantitative methods through which knowledge could be systematically expanded. Herbart had much earlier had a vision of this kind, but was unable to conceptualize a science of psychology based on experimental knowledge. The generation of late Victorian scientists began to develop this idea. Notable among these was Francis Galton (1822-1911), who must be viewed as being outside the mainstream of psychological thought in his century, and yet as an extraordinary independent contributor. Galton was able to come to grips with the idea of measuring complex psychological functions.

The measurement movement included many individuals who today would be considered as historical scientific giants. The earliest of these was Francis Galton, but his work was consolidated later by the next generation that included Emil Kraeplin (1856-1926) and Alfred Binet

(1857-1911) who were to attempt to extend mental measurement to applications in the psychiatric and educational fields. Of more peripheral impact to the development of mental measurement was one of Galton's assistants, Karl Pearson. Just a little later came the influence of Cyril Burt (1888-1971). One has to understand these men, and the work that flowed from them, if one is to understand much of educational research in America in the present century.

Francis Galton came from a prosperous middle-class Quaker family that prized intellectual values and encouraged intellectual pursuits. Galton's mother's family carried the name of Darwin, and Charles Darwin was Francis Galton's cousin. Among the Darwins, Charles Darwin was not the only celebrated member of the family, for two of the brothers of Galton's mother, Erasmus and Robert Darwin, were elected to membership in the Royal Society of London. Galton would be described today as a child prodigy. He could read well before the age of 3 and was said to be able to read any book in English by the age of 5, but how much he understood of these books is an open question. He learned a considerable amount of French before he was 6. By that age he had also mastered much of arithmetic and showed the mathematical genius for which he was noted in adult life. There are on record brief poems written by the young Galton at the age of 6.

Although he showed enormous promise at an early age, schooling seems to have been an experience which dulled rather than stimulated his intellect, and may well account for the fact that he was slow as an adult in showing his ability. Galton attended a number of private schools, where he detested the education he received. He was given ample doses of Latin and Greek and English grammar, but what he wanted were mathematics, science, and training in the writing of the English language. After spending some time traveling in Europe in his later teens, he turned to the study of medicine, first at Cambridge and then in London. His pursuit of a medical career seems to have been more a choice made for him by his parents than a choice made by himself, for when Galton's father died when Galton was only 22, the young Francis quickly abandoned all thoughts of a career in medicine. Galton inherited enough money to enable him to live in comfort for the rest of his life. He lived a life of security in an age that gave those with wealth confidence that their future would be as good as the past, and that the world for them could only improve. The spirit of the Victorian and the Edwardian age was one of hope and great expectation, particularly for English gentlemen who saw their country not only as the outstanding political power, but also as one of the great centers of the sciences and the humanities.

When Galton left medical school without completing his work, he seems to have had little in the way of a plan for a career of any kind. In 1840 he published his first paper, about the invention of the Teletype, a device that would send a printed message over a wire without having to have a human coder at one end and a decoder at the other. Then, bored again, he set forth for South Africa in 1850. This trip became more than just another pleasant adventure for him, for he explored parts of South Africa that the white man had not yet explored and mapped.

The London Geographical Society awarded Galton a medal for his work, which gave him an immediate position of prestige in the scientific world. Yet, it seems that he had no yearnings to pursue the life of an explorer. Indeed, one cannot discern at this point in his life any long-term goals at all. He appears to his biographers at this stage as a romantic, content with the pursuit of one adventure after another. An important factor in helping him to settle down seems to have been a recurrent fever, originally picked up in Syria, which plagued him for many years and limited his activity. It was not until 1853, when Galton was 31 years of age, that he began to concentrate his interests on heredity, which occupied him for the remainder of his long life. The crystallization of Galton's interests was, nevertheless, quite slow, for his book entitled *Hereditary Genius: An Inquiry into Its Laws and Consequences* (1869) did not appear until he was 47 years of age. His slowness in producing a written work was not due entirely to his lack of discipline in placing his ideas on paper, for in 1866 he had a serious mental breakdown, the second in his life, that incapacitated him for more than a year.

The argument presented in *Hereditary Genius* was that all important abilities were inherited. The book was extraordinarily short on data, but Galton spent much of the rest of his life attempting to remedy this deficiency. The book ran against the prevailing view of the nature of the intellect. Galton's cousin, Charles Darwin, held the contrary view, commonly expressed, that all individuals were created equal in ability, but that some had more initiative and energy that brought them to the top. Darwin never tried to link differences in ability to environmental influences.

Galton attempted to make the link. He argued that those humans who lived in tropical forests that provided them with all their basic needs had not evolved high levels of ability. He saw Western civilization as slowly selecting individuals who possessed those faculties that had built that civilization. As that civilization swept across the world, Galton believed that it would eliminate those whom he referred to as belonging to inferior races, because he believed that they did not have the native abilities necessary for adapting to civilized life. Galton had some difficulty in explaining the rise and fall of civilizations in that the evolution of ability was assumed to be a very slow process and so too would be its decay. Galton attempted to overcome difficulty in his theory of hereditary ability by proposing that a civilization would last only if it included humans who were both intellectually superior and who also had hereditary moral qualities that would permit the civilization to survive. Athens, he argued, declined because the citizens lacked the necessary moral qualities for survival.

Galton took the position that any inherited quality was stable and could not be changed by environmental conditions. The idea that inherited traits were stable must have been a tempting one, when Galton considered such matters as the inheritance of color blindness and haemophilia. Galton's generation, and the generations that followed him, had difficulty in conceptualizing an inherited quality that could be modified by environmental conditions. One can hardly be surprised by this viewpoint, for striking examples of the way in which an inherited characteristic could be modified by environmental intervention had not yet come to light. No surgeon had yet converted an inherited club foot into a normal foot. The concept of the stability of inherited characteristics was a part of the thinking of Galton and many of his followers. In the discussion that follows of the work of Karl Pearson, Cyril Burt, Lewis Terman, and others, one must bear in mind that they were similarly influenced by the doctrine of the stability and immutability of inherited characteristics.

Later, Galton became interested in the development of eugenics, described as the improvement of the genetic stock of a nation through selective breeding. Galton saw around him the extraordinary results achieved in animals through pedigree selection. The English race horse was without equal in the world. Galton believed that the same could be done for the British through selective breeding. Galton did not propose to do this through any great coercion, though he did believe that, at the lower levels of his ability scales, steps should be taken to prevent reproduction. He did provide data showing that the poor had a much higher birth rate than the affluent. Since he believed that the affluent had all the hereditary qualities that should be conserved, he believed that the result of the differential birth rate would be a decline in the quality of the biological stock of British people. This was a theme which British scientists expounded for nearly another century and is found in the work of such eminent individuals as Karl Pearson, Cyril Burt, and some early writings of Raymond B. Cattell.

Galton's theory of heredity was short on data but long on speculation. He believed that all good qualities were inherited. Of course, Galton was quite biased in his views as to what were the qualities that were eugenically desirable for the future of the human species. In 1910, just a year before his death, Galton wrote of a Utopia that was organized around eugenic principles. The title of the manuscript was "The Eugenics College of Kantsaywhere," but it was never published and what is available consists of quotations in Karl Pearson's *The Life, Letters and Labours of Francis Galton* (1914-30), which is the most complete and thorough record of Galton's life.

In his Utopia, Galton described his experience as an emigrant to Kantsaywhere and the eugenic examination he must undergo in order to be admitted. The examination included a determination of such physical features as height, weight, span of arms, breathing capacity, swiftness of blow, ability to discriminate weights, ability to discriminate tones, color sense, auditory acuity, sensitivity to taste and touch, and other sensory characteristics. There seems to have been some kind of health inspection as a part of the imaginary examination, particularly of the teeth. Then there was an examination in aesthetics and literature, and tests were given that involved the writing of literary pieces. The person's pedigree involved an important part of the examination.

An interesting point to note is that the examination included mainly the measurement of characteristics on which Galton would have done well, with the exception of ancestry, for he knew little about his ancestors. The examination also did not include characteristics on which Galton might have fared badly. For example, no mention is made of whether the individual examined had ever had a nervous breakdown, yet surely one could have argued as strongly for using that characteristic as any that Galton included.

Galton's zeal for the measurement of human attributes was not surpassed until Edward L. Thorndike began to emerge as a scientist towards the end of Galton's life. Galton came to psychological measurement through a long and indirect route. His early travels brought him into contact with many unfamiliar cultures, and these contacts developed an interest in anthropology. This in turn led to an interest in anthropometry, which was already established as a scientific discipline. Galton must hve been familiar with the work of Lambert Adolphe Jacques Quetelet (1796-1874), who had examined measures of physical characteristics of various groups and had summarized data in terms of averages and dispersions. For Galton there was magic in measurement. Whatever could be measured seemed to have mystical powers to generate knowledge. So overwhelmed was Galton with the power of measurement that he seems to have been blind to the fact that measurement may often provide little more than a collection of trivia. In Galton's hands, measurement gave him a license to generalize often far beyond the facts, but Galton was a romantic and that is the way in which the romantic thinks and acts. Galton's studies involving measurement are scattered through many publications, but some of his better known investigations are assembled in his book entitled *Inquiries into Human Faculty and Its Development* (1883). This volume is still available in print at the time of writing, which testifies to its durability as a contribution to scientific literature.

Galton's *Inquiries* did not cover many of his important contributions. It did not cover, for example, his proposal to undertake follow-up studies of children in secondary schools. The latter was a completely novel suggestion, for nobody had ever previously proposed such follow-up studies of those who completed work in educational institutions. Galton's central interest in such studies was not to evaluate educational programs, though he did not exclude this possibility. He was more concerned with demonstrating what he believed to be the overwhelming influence of heredity on subsequent success, believing as he did that the best genetic qualities would bring success to whomsoever was fortunate enough to possess them, regardless of circumstances.

Among Galton's many ideas was one that there should be some kind of national center where an individual might go and obtain a certificate of genetic worth. Such a center would administer the kinds of tests and interviews described in Kantsaywhere. Galton attempted to provide a beginning for such a center in a booth at the *International Health Exhibition* at Earls Court, London, in 1884. In this booth, Galton had equipment for measuring the following human characteristics: (1) keenness of sight, (2) keenness of hearing, (3) color sense, (4) judgment of eye, (5) lung capacity, (6) reaction time, (7) strength of pull, (8) strength of grip, (9) force of blow, (10) span of arms, (11) standing height, (12) sitting height, and (13) weight.

Those who attended the exhibition could pay 3 pence for undergoing the tests and for which they obtained a record of their performance. Three pence was perhaps what a laborer earned for an hour's work, so the cost was not trivial, but Galton was able to collect data on several thousand individuals through such a means. Later, when the Health Exhibition closed, Galton transferred the testing laboratory to the South Kensington Museum of Natural History, where additional data were collected. In the later phases of the work, Galton also began to collect data on fingerprints, which he had proposed be used for criminal identification. Just what was accomplished by Galton's anthropometric laboratory is difficult to say. The idea was not entirely novel, but how many ideas are?

Quetelet had attempted to collect data of a similar nature and had seen the possible significance of calculating means and measures of dispersion as a basis for the development of norms. Galton's massive data, paid for by those who were the guinea pigs, stimulated in him thoughts about the statistical problems related to the use of data, and this led Galton to develop the method of calculating correlations, expanded later mathematically by Karl Pearson. Galton also seems to have been entranced with the idea of providing all the participants in the measurement laboratory with a set of scores indicating their eugenic worth to the future of society. Galton raised no questions about whether his judgment concerning the worth of the measures might be wrong. He had complete faith in the value of the measures for selecting the kinds of individuals who should hand on their inherited structures to a new generation. The magic involved in measurement gave the measures worth. At least Galton behaved as though that were so. Galton's own personal enthusiasm for his anthropometric laboratory was contagious, for similar laboratories were established at Oxford, Cambridge, Dublin, and Tokyo, which together raised the number of records collected to over 13,000.

In 1887, when James McKeen Cattell spent some time at Oxford, he dropped in to see Galton at Galton's laboratory at the South Kensington Museum and spent time there assisting with the project. When Cattell returned to America, he initiated work on individual differences after the pattern of research he had seen at South Kensington.

Galton himself did not do much of lasting importance with the massive amounts of data collected. The data fitted into his dream of a society in which great effort would be made to control the future evolution of the human species, and, as a romantic, he was more interested in bringing reality to his dream than in exploring the logical problems related to the justifiability of data. His data did provide subsequent investigators with a rich source of material for worthwhile analyses (see, for example, the analysis of Galton's data by Herry A. Ruger and Brencke Stoessinger in "On Growth Curves of Certain Characteristics in Man", 1927).

All of Galton's later work fitted into his grand scheme for a eugenic society, the romantic idea that came to dominate his life. For example, he had long been impressed with what he believed to be the inheritability of criminality. His main evidence for this was the study of the Jukes family. He was also impressed with general observation in society that criminals have children that are criminals. He does not seem to have even considered the alternative interpretation of the data, namely, that the criminal provides for his children an environment that is conducive to the raising of criminals. One suspects that his own personal prejudices confused his thinking on the matter. He must surely have been more satisfied with believing that he and his associates belonged to an intellectually superior class than with believing that they had just had superior opportunities.

Galton was the first to recognize the importance of twins in the study of heredity. He developed the first study of twins designed for the purpose of establishing the hereditability of characteristics. He came to the conclusion that nature played a far more important role than nurture in almost every aspect of development. Indeed, the only major impact of nurture seemed to him to be the effect of illness. In those days it was, for an attack of measles or scarlet fever or typhoid early in life might well have disastrous effects on development. Nevertheless, if the study were conducted today, one would probably criticize it as lacking adequate controls. The critic would certainly say that Galton's conclusions did not follow from his data. Perhaps because twin studies were so novel, the Galton work was not criticized in its time, though the work which sprang from it has been the center of raging controversy down to modern times.

Galton's work on individual differences set the stage for similar work for the next century. Galton's ideas, biased strongly in the direction of believing that nature was of vastly greater importance than nurture, introduced an element that had powerful impact on American thought related to education during at least the first quarter of the present century. Those who met him were content to listen to him and to probe his thoughts. None ever took issue with him. He was a man of kindly and loving disposition who wanted his ideas to benefit humanity. Also, he was not a critic of the work of others and did not participate in the great controversies of his age, many of which involved bitter feuds between well-known scientists, and between scientists and other public figures. He remained above those controversies in a world of romantic exploration.

No person ever did more to keep alive both the name and the ideas of Francis Galton than did Karl Pearson, who for a time worked as Galton's assistant. Galton and Pearson constituted the oddest mismatch of personalities, yet the young Pearson had an admiration for Galton that lasted long after Galton's death. Perhaps Pearson saw in Galton much of what he would like to have been, and yet was not. Galton was quiet and unassuming. Pearson was outgoing and presumptuous. Galton avoided all controversy, but Pearson was always ready to pick a fight in any academic forum. Perhaps many of their differences stemmed from the fact that Galton was a physically impressive man, but Pearson was small of stature and slight in build. Galton was gentle and thoughtful for others, but Pearson was aggressive and inconsiderate. Pearson fitted well the model described later by Alfred Adler of the individual who compensates for deep feelings of inferiority by an overwhelming need for power. Pearson could not even hold a conversation without wanting to dominate it. His contemporaries often thought of him as combining brilliance with cantankerousness.

Although Pearson is viewed today as the great developer of mathematical statistics, he was known in his day as much for his views on how to improve and develop society as for anything else. His classic work *The Grammar of Science* (1892) tells us that an individual can rid himself of prejudice and false ideas and biases through the pursuit of scientific ways of thinking, but the truth of that belief is hardly demonstrated in Pearson's own life, for today we view him not only as a great scientist but also as a dangerous bigot, tied to false ideas about heredity that he did not realize had no relationship to the data on which they were claimed to be based. One can excuse him for this, no doubt, for our own generation is tied to other false ideas, which we believe to be scientifically based but which are in fact figments of our prejudices.

The way in which Pearson seized hold of some of Galton's prejudices, and amplified them to an extraordinary degree, is illustrated in a lecture that Pearson gave entitled *National Life from the Standpoint of Science* (1901). In this lengthy lecture, Pearson argued strongly for the superiority of the Aryan stock and the inferiority of the black peoples of Africa. These arguments reflected Galton's views, but were presented in more vigorous terms. Pearson went on to say that the superior races will surely dominate the world, a typical Darwinian opinion. He asserted that the reason for the superiority of the Western European white man was the superiority of his genetic stock. Superior stocks, he claimed, were produced through natural selection and the suffering of those with less genetic virtue. The white man, he asserted, should not live amidst inferior races, but should drive them out as the early white man did in North America.

Pearson did not see a great future for the British at that time unless it would be possible to change the birth rates of the various classes. He argued that British biological stock was deteriorating because those classes least fit to produce the next generation were producing the largest part of it. Pearson did not think that education of the masses would achieve much, for what was needed, he said, was to bring into industry the brains that already existed. Pearson did advocate a form of education that involved problem-solving and intellectual discipline, but this should be for those who had brain power worth developing. Pearson believed that a nation should be viewed from what he called the viewpoint of a scientist. From that viewpoint it should be regarded as a total organism faced with a problem of developing means of adapting to an environment and competing successfully with other organisms. State aid should be given to the unfortunate, but not to the point at which such individuals would outbreed what Pearson believed to be the genetically superior stock found in the middle classes. This theme of Pearson and Galton, that the genetically inferior stock of the white peoples was displacing the best stock through the differential birth rate, did not fade away easily. It was again revived in the mid-1930's, when Raymond B. Cattell wrote a book on the same theme entitled *The Fight for Our National Intelligence* (1937).

In reading Pearson's lecture *National Life from the Standpoint of Science*, one sees clearly the line of thought developed by Herbert Spencer to the effect that the poor and inadequate should not be helped since this would interfere with natural selection and the promise of a better species, but Pearson never went that far. Nevertheless, Pearson was a powerful national and international figure who exercises enormous influence on thought. America had already been prepared by Herbert Spencer for the ideas on inheritance expanded upon by Francis Galton and Karl Pearson, but these ideas required the work of a Frenchman, Alfred Binet, before they could be directly applied to education.

BINET AND THE IMPACT ON EDUCATION OF THE NEW IDEAS ON MENTAL MEASUREMENT

Galton's interest in education was only incidental to his interest in the inheritance of ability. He did not think that schooling had much to do with success in life. Certainly his own life, and perhaps that of his cousin, Charles Darwin, testified to such a position. It was the work of Alfred Binet (1857-1911) that initiated what were to become massive studies that related measures of psychological abilities to what a person could or could not achieve in an educational program.

Binet was certainly familiar with Galton's attempt to assess the basic abilities of the human for the ultimate purpose of genetic control. In the tightly knit European community of scientists, everyone knew about the work of others, particularly when the work had a high degree of originality as Galton's work had. Binet must have been familiar also with the rising trend in European thought that assigned great weight to the role of nature and minimized the effect of nurture. Binet seems to have just accepted the then-prevailing view of the scientific community in the matter. Indeed, why should he have questioned it, for nobody else did. Certainly he did not question this view in any of his writings, but neither did other scientists. Binet was an original thinker, but the original thinker in any age is still likely to be to some degree a prisoner of the prevailing scientific paradigms and ideas, particularly in those areas where he is not completely expert. In order to understand Binet and his extraordinary impact on education, let us now view him in the setting of his age.

Alfred Binet was a generation later than Francis Galton, having been born in Nice, France, in 1857. His father was a physician, but his parents separated while he was still very young, and he was raised by his mother. He had an outstanding record as a scholar at the lycee, but when his school days were over he had trouble in finding a career. He first tried law, but did not go through with it. Then he began to study medicine, but dropped out of the program. He had some kind of mental breakdown, quite similar to what Galton had had while at Cambridge, and which interrupted his studies for a year. They called it *cerebral anaemia*, as was customary in those days. Then in the years 1879 and 1880 he began reading in the Bibliothèque Nationale, the large national library comparable to the Library of Congress. It was there that Binet found for himself a career. In the Bibliotheque he came into contact with the latest literature on psychology. These writings included those of Herbert Spencer, Francis Galton, John Stuart Mill, and Hermann von Helmholtz. Theta Wolf, in her remarkable biography *Alfred Binet* (1973), pointed out that he was particularly impressed with the associationism of John Stuart Mill, which became the cornerstone of Binet's thinking. Perhaps he may also have noted that the same associationism was the very cornerstone of the psychology of Francis Galton. Through these studies, Binet decided that psychology was the field which he would make his life work. It is of interest to note that both Binet and Galton developed careers through self-study and seemed to profit little from any formal training they may have had in higher education.

In France at that time there was no experimental psychology, and whatever psychology existed in the country was to be found in the clinical area. The center of psychiatric thought in Europe at that time was the great Paris hospital, the Salpêtrière, where the leading figure was the distinguished Jean Martin Charcot. It was there that the young Binet found a place where he could work further on the development of a career as a psychologist.

At the Salpêtrière he became involved in all of the ideas that were fashionable in clinical psychology in France in that era. Conversion hysteria was a common malady and a great mystery. Jean Charcot and Charles Feré had used hypnotism in treating it, and Binet began to experiment with the phenomenon. Hypnotism, or animal magnetism as it was then called, was a phenomenon of widespread interest both in the scientific world and in the wider world outside. Franz Anton Mesmer's (1724-1815) showmanship had been instrumental in developing this interest, and hypnotism was suggested as a means of curing all kinds of diseases.

Binet's first book, entitled *La Psychologie du Raisonnement,* was an attempt to reduce all behavioral phenomena, normal and abnormal, to an associationistic theory. As a work it lacks novelty, for this is a matter that has been argued for over 2,000 years. His second book, written in cooperation with Charles Feré, was entitled *Le Magnetism Animal* and expanded on the subject of hypnosis. He was only 29 when the latter work was published, and in the following year, 1887, he was awarded a prize by the Academy of Moral and Political Sciences for a paper of 511 handwritten pages which has not been preserved for us to read. The records of the academy declare that it was a distinguished contribution. He then went on to write articles on philosophical issues such as that of free will and personal responsibility.

In 1888 he began to undertake studies at the College de France. These studies would be described today as essentially biological, and they led him to prepare a doctoral thesis entitled *A Contribution to the Study of the Subintestinal Nervous System of Insects* (see Theta Wolf).

Wolf points out that Binet studied his two daughters in a manner very similar to the way in which Piaget later studied his own children. Three papers which Binet published in 1890 as a result of studies of his own infant daughters bear the following titles: *Researches on the Movements of Some Young Children, The Perception of Length and Number in Young Children,* and *Perceptions of Infants.* These titles could well have come from a list of the publications of Jean Piaget. Theta Wolf suggested that

Piaget may have been aware of this work of Binet when he started his own work on children.

Binet, like Galton, was a man of sufficient means that he did not have to have a job that paid a salary. He was not apparently paid for his work at the Sâlpetrière, and neither was he paid as associate director of the Laboratory of Physiological Psychology of the Sorbonne, to which he was appointed in 1892. Two years later he was appointed director. During his years with the laboratory he was a prolific publisher of both books and articles. His interests ranged widely during this period, as they did throughout his life, and he studied such varied phenomena as the Müller-Lyer illusion and the personalities of dramatic authors. During these years he also founded *L'Année Psychologique*, which became France's best known and, today, France's best established psychological journal. The journal survived in its initial stages only because of the enormous energy that Binet invested in his search for novel and publishable material. There were even times when Binet expected that the journal would collapse through lack of support, but somehow it just managed to avoid bankruptcy.

The laboratory itself seems to have been largely a one-man enterprise. Such laboratories were not supported in France the way they were in Germany. Wundt was able to find stipends for students who came to him from all over the world, but Binet lacked similar support. The fact that Binet did not have a paid academic appointment may also have been a disadvantage, for he had no access to the inner circles that made decisions about funds. Physiological psychology also had little support in the inner academic circles of France, which accounts for the fact that in his entire lifetime Binet was never honored with appointment to a chair or to a paid academic appointment. There were no paid positions for psychologists in France at that time, so psychological laboratories could not attract students preparing for jobs.

Theta Wolf, as a result of her careful inquiry into the life of Binet, has been able to describe how he came into contact with Théodore Simon, with whom he carried out his most famous studies. Simon was an intern, working in a colony for retarded children. He had read some of Binet's work, which he immediately recognized as being original and remarkable. He visited Binet in 1899 and asked to work under his direction. Binet had apparently been confronted before by those who had a sudden enthusiasm for his work and was skeptical about what Simon could do, but he accepted him on what one might call a probationary basis, assigning him the task of making a series of measurements on the 223 tots in the colony for the retarded. The work which Simon undertook with the retarded became his doctoral dissertation in medicine.

The closest intellectual association developed between the two men. The encounter also seems to have initiated the most important phase of Binet's work. In 1903 he published his most famous book, entitled *L'étude expérimentale de l'intelligence*, which included a considerable amount of data based on his two daughters. Then, in the autumn of 1904, he was appointed to a commission that was to report on the plight of the retarded in the schools of France. As a result of his work with the commission, Binet collaborated with Simon and produced the first crude scale for the measurement of intelligence. This scale appeared in 1905, but there were revisions both in 1908 and 1911.

Binet, working with the commission, sought to find a means of discriminating between children who were incapable of making progress in the French schools, and those children who were capable of undertaking the work, but who were unmotivated. Thus Binet sought to develop a measure of intelligence that would be uninfluenced by school achievement. In order to achieve that goal, he attempted to assemble a set of problems which could be solved in terms of the out-of-school experience of every child, if that child had the necessary ability to solve them. Implicit in this idea of measuring intelligence was the idea that native intelligence could be measured. Binet assumed that all children were exposed to a common core of experience, which could be used by all of them to solve problems. We now know that there are enormous differences in the out-of-school experiences of children in different sections of a culture. Binet's assumption was invalid.

Binet was treading on dangerous ground in France when his scale appeared and supposedly demonstrated large differences in the intelligence of French children. The French revolution had established the view that all children were born equal, and equally capable of learning, though it was conceded that some children were mentally handicapped just as some were physically handicapped. The French were not willing to abandon that philosophy.

Binet did not become involved in the nature-nurture controversy, though perhaps one should say that in his later years there was no real controversy. The big figures of the academic world, such as Francis Galton and Karl Pearson, were completely on the side that emphasized nature, and there was no opposition. Binet ignored the issue and was more concerned with understanding the way in which intelligence operated. For this purpose he welded together, for the first time, the biological concept of adaptation with the psychological concept of intelligence. Intelligence was, for him, adaptation. The concept of logic had no place in his description, a fact which is hardly surprising in view of the fact that Binet's theorizing was far more closely tied to associationism than to classical logic.

Binet became interested in education, in a broad way, only in the last 2 decades of his life. He had had an earlier interest in memory and had studied chess players and those who could perform high-speed mental calculations, but he had never focused the results on education. In 1898 he experienced the same dream that Henry Barnard had experienced, namely, that of producing a scholarly literature in the field of pedagogy. To this end he founded, with Victor Henri, *La bibliothèque psychologique et pédagogique*, which was to be a series of scholarly and scientific works on education with a bias in the direction of experimental literature. The initial publication was one which was to have widespread impact on education. Written by both Alfred Binet and Victor Henri, it was entitled *La fatigue intellectuelle* (1898). This was a subject of immense interest to educators at the turn of the century, and the book was cited in the extensive publications of the United States Bureau of Education. The Commissioner of Education at that time, William Harris, was himself interested in this new experimental literature and saw in it knowledge that needed to be applied in schools. One can understand today why there was such a widespread interest in the topic. The rigid regimentation in the schools must have produced a condition that pupils would have described as weariness, and the experts would have described as fatigue.

Then, in 1899, Binet became active in *The Free Society for the Study of Children.* This society was much like the child-study groups that had sprung up in various countries including Germany and the United States. Child study was not an area that had, as yet, been taken over by professionals. Most of the members of such groups were amateurs. The kinds of studies that G. Stanley Hall and his students had undertaken at Clark University provided models of what could be accomplished and these studies seemed to be within the capabilities of any educated citizen. Doctors, educators, directors of programs for the handicapped, criminologists, sociologists, social reformers, teachers and principals, and others were attracted to the area. Binet had considerable skepticism concerning the worth of the Free Society, sponsored by the Chair of the Science of Education of the Sorbonne. One can understand his skepticism, for he had almost a fanatical belief that knowledge of psychology and child behavior was to be derived only by experiment, and experiments could be undertaken competently only by the trained professional. Of course, Binet's conception of an experiment was considerably broader than the present American concept of an experiment, but within his concept there was little place for the amateur. Nevertheless, Binet gave support to the new society and featured its activities in *L'Année Psychologique.* His activity in this field led him, according to Theta Wolf, to become interested in training teachers in scientific methods and in improved methods of observing children. This was a movement that had already begun in America and was to play a considerable role in the development of American education. Binet eventually became absorbed in the affairs of the society, writing hundreds of letters to individuals inviting them to become members. In 1903 he became president of the society, and seems to have had a role of leadership in developing commissions to study various problems of education.

Yet, despite Binet's extraordinary productivity of ideas and his attempt to have direct impact on the French educational system, neither he nor his work was accepted in France. To some extent, this was probably a result of French intellectual snobbery. Binet did not belong to the accepted French academic establishment, the inner council of which consisted of the holders of chairs at the universities. Another important reason for his nonacceptance was the fact that the measurement of individual differences for which he became world-renowned was not a popular theme in France. The French educational system was dominated in every way at that time by the concept of the Perpetual French Revolution, with its emphasis on the equality of all individuals. There is little place for individual differences within such a schema of social thought. Even much of the curriculum of the French educational system was dominated by the concept of the school as the great leader in the eternal revolution that each generation could only partially fulfill. The French rejected intelligence-testing much as the Russians have since their revolution. Revolutions based on egalitarian ideas lead to educators focusing on ways of bringing out the essential humane potential of all. There is an accompanying tendency to overlook the obvious fact that there are differences, even when such differences are obvious and gross. Education was to be the means of achieving the French egalitarian society, and differences between individuals tended to be regarded as the result of moral failure to devote sufficient effort to the tasks involved in schooling.

Despite the distinguished contributions that France has made to the advancement of science, educational research has been notoriously lacking within France. There is here an odd contrast with Switzerland, where some of the most important ideas related to education have originated and where research that has had impact on education has flourished.

Before leaving European psychology and the emerging psychology of individual differences, mention must be made of the work of Emil Kraeplin (1856-1926). He was of the same generation as Alfred Binet and corresponded with him about problems of measurement, but his approach was entirely different. Kraeplin was trained as a physician in Leipzig and during a summer vacation took a course under Wilhelm Wundt in 1876. Wundt was at the peak of his fame and influence. Kraeplin then went on to specialize in psychiatry. In 1877 he won an award for a prize-winning paper on the effect of acute diseases on the development of mental illness. This paper was the first step in his lifelong attempt to develop a classification of mental illnesses. The prevailing view held about mental diseases, at the time when his paper was written, was that they were diseases, just like any other, and resulted from chemical malfunctions of the brain. When the brain had physical disease, then mental illness followed. Theories of conflict and guilt had not yet entered the scene.

Kraeplin and Binet present an important contrast in their approaches to measurement that have had important long-term implications for education. Binet attempted to assess the child's ability to adapt to various problem situations. This he called intelligence. Kraeplin, on the other hand, sought to assess the various components of human responses that were involved in the complete repertoire of behavior. These components could be assembled, in Wundtian theory, into complex behaviors. In the pursuit of this line of thought, the place to begin the assessment was with simple sensory functions, which Binet neglected as unimportant. For the next 100 years, one finds psychologists developing batteries of what are hypothesized to be simple components of complex behavior, while other psychologists have attempted to measure directly complex behavior forms.

JAMES McKEEN CATTELL -- AMERICA'S PIONEER

Among those who opened the way for the measurement of psychological human differences, James McKeen Cattell (1860-1944) represents America's most notable contributor. Historians have had some difficulty in assigning to Cattell a place in history, partly because his life encompassed such a great range of activity related to the development of psychology as a science in the United States, and partly because he consistently refused to write and publish an autobiography which might have indicated what he believed to be his most significant role. His scientific papers did not have the voluminousness of a Wilhelm Wundt or an Edward Thorndike and neither did they have the brilliance of a Helmholtz, but his life cannot be judged in terms of his publications alone. His influence far surpassed that of his publications.

Graduate programs had barely begun in American universities at the time when Cattell graduated from Lafayette College in 1880. He followed the custom of American students and went to Europe for graduate work. He studied first with the philosopher Rudolf Hermann Lotze at Gottingen and he heard Wilhelm Wundt lecture at Leipzig. Both men impressed Cattell. He wrote a paper on Lotze's philosophy which won him a fellowship at Johns Hopkins University for the year 1882-83, where he found John Dewey and Joseph Jastrow as fellow students. His interest in the measurement of individual differences seems to have begun at Johns Hopkins through his contact with G. Stanley Hall, who had established a psychological laboratory there. Then from 1883 to 1886, he spent three years in Wundt's laboratory, initially as Wundt's first assistant. Boring's *History of Experimental Psychology* tells the story of how Cattell arrived at Wundt's laboratory in 1883 and announced to Wundt that he, Wundt, needed an assistant and that he, Cattell, should be appointed. The story

JAMES McKEEN CATTELL

Photograph courtesy of Columbia University

may be apocryphal, but it does portray some of Cattell's boldness.

Cattell's views of how psychology should be developed were hardly in tune with those of Wundt. Cattell saw human variability as an enormously interesting matter, but for Wundt variability was referred to as experimental error. He demanded some freedom in the pursuit of his ideas, a freedom that a German student would never have thought of demanding. In the traditional German university, the graduate assistant did what he was told. Wundt regarded Cattell as an example of American idiosyncratic behavior, and Cattell was able to achieve some independence from Wundt by establishing laboratory equipment in his lodgings. Cattell found that he was allowed to work in Wundt's laboratory only at the hours prescribed by Wundt, for that was the way in which a German academic laboratory was run.

Cattell retained a warm personal affection for Wundt throughout his life, but the model for his own personal development seems to have been Francis Galton, whom he regarded as the greatest man he had ever known. He did not meet Galton until he had already embarked on a career of measuring individual differences, despite the frowning disapproval of Wilhelm Wundt. In Galton he found a sympathetic understanding of his ideas on the importance of individual differences, and a recognition that these constituted something more than just experimental error.

When he returned to the United States, Cattell spent a short time at the University of Pennsylvania where he administered a set of 10 tests to volunteer freshmen. Then he moved to Columbia University, where he stayed for 26 years. At Columbia he also introduced a testing battery, which was administered to 50 volunteer freshmen for several years.

One may note that his appointment at the University of Pennsylvania was as Professor of Psychology. This was the first professorship in psychology anywhere in the world. Earlier notables and notables of his time were all appointed as professors of philosophy. Cattell throughout his life took great pride in the fact that he was the first professor of psychology the world had ever known.

The tests given students at Columbia University were fundamentally different from those developed by Alfred Binet. They reflected two trends in measurement. First, there was an emphasis on the anthropometric type of measurement pursued by Cesare Lombroso and other contemporary anthropologists, and which had been applied extensively by Alphonse Bertillon in his system for identifying criminals. Thus, Cattell included observations on shape of nose, size of ears, complexion, and other observable physical features. The person measured was also required to fill out an extended questionnaire on his health. The tests themselves included a measure of breathing capacity, a test of color blindness and another of visual acuity, and then a test of auditory acuity. These were followed by tests of skin and muscular sensations, a measure of the strength of the right and left hands, and a reaction-time measure. Then there were tests of spatial perception such as is involved in drawing a line similar in length to a given line, and a similar test was provided for time perception. There were also tests of memory and imagery, very similar to those used by Galton.

The choice of tests shows a concept of behavior that comes right out of the laboratory of Wilhelm Wundt. Basic sensory processes are measured because it is from these basic sensory processes that complex behaviors are derived. There is nothing in the battery of tests that represents what have been called the higher mental processes, and very little that looks like the kind of tasks that Alfred Binet included in his set of tests. The Cattell tests are based on a reductionist theory of behavior, namely, that all complex processes can be reduced to a combination of simpler components. When there is inferiority of the higher mental processes, one is led to suspect some deficiency at a lower level. No consideration is given to the possibility that such a deficiency might be a deficiency in the higher mental processes themselves.

The general theory on which Cattell worked made indirect reference to higher mental processes. For example, the measurement of reaction times was used to measure far more than speed. Within Wundtian theory, reaction times could be used to measure the speed of higher mental processes. Thus, a simple speed of reaction to the turning on of a light would provide a base level of reaction time, but the reaction involved could be complicated by introducing the requirement that the subject make a choice before reacting. Thus, he might be asked to react if the light that went on were green, but not if it were red. By subtracting the time for a simple reaction from the time of reaction in the choice situation, the time required to make the choice was computed. In this way, speed of choice could be estimated for an individual. The assumption was commonly made that the more intellectually adequate the individual, the more rapid would be his choice.

Cattell made several attempts to develop a complete list of all the significant human attributes. The list used in the survey of the Columbia students was short. A much longer list is provided in a monograph edited by Robert S. Woodworth on "The Psychological Researches of James McKeen Cattell" (1914):

Physical health	Reasonableness
Mental balance	Clearness
Intellect	Independence
Emotions	Cooperativeness
Will	Unselfishness
Quickness	Kindliness
Intensity	Cheerfulness
Breadth	Refinement
Energy	Integrity
Judgment	Courage

Originality	Efficiency
Perseverance	Leadership

The man who presented the above list as a part of an article paying tribute to James McKeen Cattell in the *Archives* monograph was Edward L. Thorndike, who went on to comment that the attributes listed were probably not unitary in any sense of the term, and that a set of attributes, unitary in chracter, needed to be developed. Thorndike commented further that he had read somewhere in the writings of Cattell that there was a need to relate a list of attributes to "semi-Mendalian analysis" (p. 95). The comment was perhaps stimulated by the fact that Mendel's great paper had been rediscovered only 14 years previously and interest had developed in relating mental traits to Mendelian principles.

Cattell himself remained quite neutral most of his life on the matter of whether measures of psychological attributes could be considered as measures of inherited attributes. He did go so far as to say that the attributes considered in his survey could be regarded as the final outcome of the interaction of nature and nurture, but Cattell was too much of a pragmatist to become involved in nature-nurture controversies. Thorndike, on the other hand, had strong views on the relationship of measures of ability to genetic constitution.

The purposes of Cattell's surveys of human attributes were designed, much as Galton's were designed, to explore the range of human diversity. As the work progressed, Cattell became more interested in the relationship of these attributes to each other and to achievement. He seems to have been filled with anticipations that what he was measuring would indicate the individual's capacity to achieve, for he believed that he was measuring basic capacities to adapt. He collected a great quantity of data related to the achievement of the Columbia students. Surely, he must have been disappointed by the findings. Only very small relationships were found between the performance of the students on the battery of tests and their subsequent grades. Also, the relationship between the various measures were quite low, but Cattell did recognize that the low relationships *might* be a result of errors of measurement.

Nevertheless, Cattell remained optimistic about the future of testing. Long before counseling agencies and schools were giving tests as a part of their routine procedures, Cattell was advocating that they do just that. He suspected that the tests might have long-term predictive value even if they failed to predict immediate grades. In order to explore this further, he initiated a study involving a follow-up of 1,000 students at Columbia University who had been tested in the psychological laboratory. This was part of a much more extensive investigation that included a study also of 1,000 eminent men in history and 1,000 American men of science. In the course of the study, the Columbia graduates seem to have been forgotten and Cattell's efforts became concentrated on the study of the eminent scientists, a study which became for him a lifelong interest. He was impressed by the fact that American scientists tended to be derived from certain communities such as Boston, suggesting the important role of nurture in the development of the scientist. As a result of this work, Cattell founded the first directory of American scientists entitled *American Men of Science*, which is still published under a less sexist title.

Despite his attempt to remain neutral in relation to the nature-nurture controversy, the prejudices of his age show through in his later works related to scientists. For example, he studied the birth rate of scientists and discovered that it was much lower than the rest of the population. This suggested to him that the low birth rate might be preventing the evolution of a higher race, a theme that Karl Pearson belabored throughout his life. He toyed with the idea of limiting the size of family in certain classes, but rejected the idea on the grounds that it is dangerous to pit intelligence against the fundamental instincts. (See A. T. Poffenberger, Ed., *James McKeen Cattell, Man of Science*, 1947).

Cattell's publishing ventures not only added to his international fame, but also added substantially to the wealth he had inherited. In 1895 he acquired the near-bankrupt weekly periodical *Science*, and 5 years later he sold it as a thriving concern to the American Association for the Advancement of Science for an alleged $100,000. He also founded such directories as *Leaders in Education* and *The Directory of American Scholars*. He was also the editor of *School and Society* for many years.

Cattell's interest in educational matters was not limited to testing, for he produced the fundamental research on reading as a perceptual activity, work that will be considered in a later chapter.

By the turn of the century, Cattell had virtually completed his scientific work and turned to such enterprises as the development of journals and scientific organizations. He, together with John Dewey, was the founder of *The American Association of University Professors*. His work on founding the organization brings out another aspect of Cattell's personality that shows in a shadowy form in his work on mental tests. Underneath his scientific mask he had the soul of a reformer. Much of his interest in psychology, and particularly mental testing, seems to have sprung from his desire for science to have some practical impact. Later, when he played a leading role in founding the Psychological Corporation, he showed his interest in extending the impact of psychology to the industrial and commercial fields. He was one of the earliest to think of psychology and behavioral science in such terms, though Francis Galton had, and men as early as Horace Mann had recognized that social advance required that data be carefully collected and evaluated. Cattell understood Dewey's pragmatism even if he did not really understand Dewey as a philosopher, for Cattell was not a man of philosophical disposition.

Cattell should surely be regarded as one of the great pioneers of educational research, but his contribution was only a passing phase in a life that included many activities. He claimed to have invented the terms *individual differences* and *mental tests*. He was a leading figure in the founding of the American Psychological Association, and he also initiated two of the most distinguished psychological journals, *The Psychological Review* and *The American Journal of Psychology*. Perhaps his most notable contribution to education came indirectly, for it was he who nurtured at Columbia the young Edward L. Thorndike.

WHERE THE PRIME MOVERS LEFT THEIR ENTERPRISE

By the early 1900's, the initiators of the mental measurement movement had developed their enterprise to the point where the next generation of measurement experts could take over and apply the techniques to a host of problems. The concept of a scale of measurement had been developed. Galton and later statisticians had produced the concept of a measure of scatter of scores which could be used to supply a unit of measurement. The concept of a least noticeable difference, from the Weber-Fechner tradition, had also been used by Cattell as a unit of measurement. Psychologists had also come to recognize the limitations of psychological scales in that they lacked a true zero. The interest in the concept of an absolute zero of measurement had been highlighted in scientific circles by the development of the idea of an absolute zero of temperature in physics, and searches for zeros in the behavioral areas were still to be initiated.

Interest in individual differences shortly after the turn of the century seems to have been a preoccupation of English-speaking countries. In Germany the interest was limited to the few psychiatrists who were influenced by Emil Kraeplin. In France, the work of Alfred Binet remained extremely isolated and was not to have much impact there for another 50 years, and even then the impact would be minimal. In England and the United States, interest in the new science of mental measurement was considerable. It is always a guess to attribute causes to historical events, but one plausible guess is that the foundation for such an interest had already been laid through the acceptance of social Darwinism, brought about through the work of such figures as Herbert Spencer. England, as a feudal society, had an aristocracy and middle class that embraced such an idea warmly. The United States had an emerging class that controlled great wealth, that was equally receptive to the idea of a superior upper class. The new mental measurement movement fitted in with the concepts of the influential.

The new concepts of the mental measurement movement ran contrary to the mainstream of thought that had guided the development of the common school. From the time of the Puritans, such schools had been founded on the concept of the basic intellectual equality of all individuals. Horace Mann had worked for the education of all the children on the basis of the same concept. Whatever intellectual differences that were observed were to be regarded as the result of the advantages and disadvantages of the home environment.

Mental tests, and the genetic theory that came to be associated with them, ran contrary to much of the theory of education to which teachers were exposed in normal schools. Yet teachers embraced mental tests and the social philosophy implied in them. A teacher who struggled to help low-achieving students could now blame the difficulties not on the teacher's inadequacies, but on the lack of abilities of the student. The mental test movement offered an alibi for the failures of the school, and this alibi was to become firmly entrenched in the American educational system in the decades that were to follow. The ground had been well prepared for the fertilization of the ideas of Francis Galton, Karl Pearson, Alfred Binet, and others. The next generation that followed on the mental testing area was to find fertile soil in which to plant their own prejudices and to see them grow into vast crops of often profitless ideas.

THE AMERICAN DEVELOPERS OF THE NEW EUROPEAN IDEAS: GODDARD AND TERMAN

Francis Galton, Alfred Binet, and Emil Kraeplin were explorers, opening up new territory for scientific study. The explorers were followed by a generation of developers who found extensive uses for the instruments developed and who, to some degree, invented their own or modified those of the early masters. Among these developers, three names stand out in front of all the others. These are the names of Cyril Lodowic Burt (1883-1971), Henry Herbert Goddard (1866-1957), and Lewis Madison Terman (1877-1956). Two of these had important credentials as educators as well as psychologists. Notably, Burt was the first school psychologist appointed anywhere in the world, and Terman trained as a teacher in a normal school and later served as the principal of a high school in San Bernadino.

The political climate of the academic world in the United States at the turn of the century was entirely different from that in Europe. Each European country had its own small establishment of scholars in each academic discipline who controlled appointments and the development of the discipline. Those who did not belong to this academic power structure encountered the difficulties that Alfred Binet experienced in obtaining

LEWIS M. TERMAN

Photograph courtesy of Stanford University

recognition for his work. The power structure of a discipline in any European country tended to be inclusive of few and exclusive of many. Often it was a few excluded ones who, through sheer persistence, managed to have their views aired. Some, like Gregor Mendel, never managed to have their work recognized during their lifetime.

The United States, then and even now, has never had its academic life dominated by a few who managed to seize political control. A scientist who might be a great power within his institution might still have little say in matters related to national academic policies. Indeed, one of the great virtues of America is that the power of academicians tends to be very local and, thus, power over the control of inquiry is widely distributed. Many scientists could, within this atmosphere, have prestige within a particular academic area, and yet none might be in a position to control the direction of thought in the discipline. Some American academicians were also excluded from the academic community, as Alfred Binet was, merely because they worked in areas unpopular at that time. With just a few exceptions, the American academic community has been broad-minded in the kind of work it will support, and this was as true at the beginning of the century as it is today.

Within the favorable setting of the New World, the exploration and development of the new Binet-type test could take place in many centers, without political attempts of any particular academician to take political control of the enterprise. Very shortly after Alfred Binet had developed his test with Theodore Simon, adaptations of the test were explored in America. The test was known as the Binet test, as it was in France, for Binet had not included the name of his partner Simon in the designation of the final product. In America it caught the interest of Henry Herbert Goddard in the East and Lewis M. Terman in the West.

Henry Goddard was older than Terman, having been born in Maine in 1866. His background was that of a Quaker and academician. He graduated from Haverford College in 1887, and then completed a master's degree at the same institution. He was an assistant at Clark University during the years 1896-99, when G. Stanley Hall was president. He also studied in Germany and must have come under the influence of the new emerging experimental psychology. From 1891 to 1896, he was first assistant principal and then principal of the Oak Grove Seminary in Vassalboro, Maine, and later served as professor of psychology at the State Teachers College at West Chester, Pennsylvania, from 1899 to 1906. Then he accepted a staff appointment at *The Teaching School for Feeble-Minded Children* at Vineland, New Jersey, where he developed the first laboratory for the study of the feeble-minded, of which he was the director from 1906 to 1918. His Quaker background, with its emphasis on helping the less fortunate, must surely have been a factor in the development of his interest in what we would call today the mentally handicapped.

Goddard translated and adapted the Binet test for use in the children at Vineland, where he also gained considerable experience in matters related to the training of those in the lower categories of intelligence. His interest in the new tests was similar to that of Cyril Burt, namely, the identification of those who could not profit from the education provided children in the common schools. He was, however, particularly interested in separating those who were backward for strictly environmental reasons from those who were backward because of inadequate endowment. He considered that the genetically subnormal could be conveniently divided into the three following categories: morons, imbeciles, and idiots. It was he who coined the term *moron*, a fact which he thought was of sufficient importance to include in his *Who's Who in America* biography. He viewed the moron as an individual who had inherited an insufficient level of intelligence for him or her to profit from education provided by the common schools, but such individuals were viewed by him as educable to the point where they could become productive citizens. Imbeciles and idiots were viewed as categories that could not possibly profit from education as it was ordinarily conceived, though they might profit from training in institutions provided for them. In the last half of the last century, some states in the East had made efforts to develop institutions for the care of the severely retarded, but not until the turn of the century was consideration given to providing special classes for the retarded who, with a little patience and special care, could be viewed as educable. Goddard was particularly interested in the latter problem.

Goddard's work at Vineland came to the attention of the school authorities in New York City, who had already taken some steps to provide special education for the backward. The first classes for this purpose had been established in New York City in 1900. They were called ungraded classes at that time, though the term *special classes* was already in use.

In addition, New York City also had classes for other categories of pupils who presented problems. The school system had established *E* classes for those who were falling back in their schoolwork, but who were regarded as being otherwise normal children. The city also had established what they called *D* classes for students who were preparing to obtain a work certificate so that they could leave school at an early age. Still another set of classes were the *C* classes for those who had special language difficulties arising from the fact that they came from homes where English was not spoken. All of these various classes became dumping grounds for children who were in some way problems for teachers. If a teacher could not manage to transfer a child dubbed as undesirable to one of these classes, then an attempt was made to squeeze the child into one of the other categories of classes. Goddard soon announced that the situation was little other than chaotic, but the authorities were probably already acquainted with that fact.

Goddard undertook his work in New York City while he was still working at Vineland. Professionals in those days seem to have had much more freedom to undertake work outside of their jobs than they do today. Goddard must have devoted a great amount of time and effort to the enterprise, for he recorded having visited 125 special or ungraded classes out of a total of 131. This number represents many classes to visit, but fewer than one school in four had a special class for the mentally handicapped at that time. The results of his visits to the schools and the resulting recommendations were published in *School Training of Defective Children* (1914).

An interesting preface to Goddard's book on his experience with the New York schools, written by Paul H. Hanus, makes the comment that the most widely held view regarding the education of the mentally defective was that it should be handled by the regular classroom teacher. The latter view is very much like the view, revived in the 1970's, represented by the word *mainstreaming.* The view of the 1970's, that the regular classroom teacher should handle the main part of the education of all the handicapped, was widely held at the turn of the century. A central argument for the segregation of the handicapped was that this would permit more effective education of the normal child, and the benefit to the handicapped seemed to be secondary. One may note that Goddard's book was published as one in a series known as the School Efficiency Series, a title which reflects the view commonly held at that time that a school should be efficient in much the same way as a business should be efficient.

A first problem encountered by Goddard in his inquiry into ways of identifying the educable mentally handicapped was the attitude of the principals and teachers. The system in use at that time for the identification was the judgment of the principal who, in turn, relied upon the judgment of the teacher. The difficulty with the system lay in the fact that the teacher often did not want to admit that a pupil had been beyond the teacher's ability to teach. The principals did not like to admit that there were dull pupils in the school. An additional fact of great importance was that parents did not want to learn that they had dull children, and so principals did not want to be the ones who brought parents the bad news. In all, the pressures within the school and the community were such that few pupils were identified as needing special help with their schoolwork.

An additional problem encountered by Goddard was that the prevailing view in the schools was that mental handicap was accompanied by gross physical defects. Thus, children who were mentally handicapped, but who did not have such defects, were merely thought of as slow, while many with gross physical defects but who were intellectually normal were classified as mentally defective. Goddard found many children in the special ungraded classes who were there merely because of some obvious physical deformity, but who belonged intellectually in classes with normal children. One of Goddard's great contributions was in helping school people recognize the difference between physical deformity and intellectual handicap.

A still further problem identified by Goddard was that children who were so severely handicapped that they belonged in institutions were assigned to special classes. Such classes tended to become dumping grounds for children who were in some way labeled as undesirable or ineducable.

What Goddard tried to do was to introduce his version of what he named the Binet-Simon tests as a basis for assigning children to the ungraded and other special classes. He also gave the test to children in some of the *E*, *D*, and *C* classes, to find out something about the nature of the children who landed there. He found that in the *E* classes over one third of the children should have been in classes for the mentally handicapped. A majority of the children in the *D* classes were considered by Goddard to be seriously mentally handicapped. Goddard also found that a majority of the children in the special classes for children not speaking English were mentally handicapped. Many children who did not speak much were apparently commonly incorrectly assumed to be children who spoke another language at home. Goddard developed impressive evidence that the classification of children in the New York City schools was nothing short of chaotic.

Goddard's impression that intellectual level was determined by heredity must have been strongly reinforced by his famous study of *The Kallikak Family: A Study in the Heredity of Feeble-Mindedness* (1912). Goddard was familiar with the study of the Jukes family and, like Francis Galton and other contemporaries, was greatly impressed with this apparent demonstration of the inheritance of intelligence. Goddard's own parallel study of the Kallikak family history had some interesting variations on the Jukes theme, and the results must have impressed his generation as the Jukes study had impressed a previous generation.

Goddard's investigation of the Kallikaks began with a case study of a girl admitted to the Vineland institution. She had been born in an almshouse. The child had had a history of rejection, not only by her mother, but by both her father and the man with whom the mother lived. She made little progress at school and, at the age of 8, was admitted to Vineland. Goddard described her as a high-grade feeble-minded person, yet she learned to read and could perform quite well on what might be described as second-grade mathematics. She did nice handiwork in both carpentry and embroidery, examples of which have been preserved in photographs.

The custom at Vineland was to send out caseworkers to study the family background of the chidren, and the family of Deborah was closely studied. Goddard was particularly interested in the intellectual level of the relatives of those children went to Vineland for training. The caseworkers soon found that Deborah's relatives had been notorious for the number of defectives and delinquents they included. Caseworkers also came up against the puzzling fact that there were also groups of Kallikaks who had excellent reputations as citizens. As a result of this latter finding, the decision was made to trace the family back through the six generations that could be identified.

The story, as unraveled by Goddard and his staff, begins with a Martin Kallikak, Sr., a young man who joined a military company at the time of the Revolution. At a tavern he met a feeble-minded girl who bore him an illegitimate child who was given the Kallikak name. This boy, Martin Kallikak, Jr., was the ancestor of all the bad branches of the Kallikak family. Of the traced 480 descendants of Martin Kallikak, Jr., 143 were also feeble-minded, 46 were normal, and the rest were of unknown intellectual level. The descendants also included a quite large number of prostitutes and alcoholics.

Up to this point the story is similar to that of the Jukes family, but Goddard found out another very interesting fact about the senior Martin Kallikak. It seems that after Martin left the Revolutionary Army, he then married a respectable girl of good family, through whom another line of "good" Kallikaks developed. Goddard traced 496 of these good Kallikaks. All of these "good" Kallikaks were normal intellectually. There were only three that Goddard described as "degenerate," two being alcoholics and one "sexually loose."

Goddard made much of the fact that on the bad side of the family there were paupers, prostitutes, drunkards, and criminals, and his inference was that the social ills represented by such individuals were largely a result of inherited feeble-mindedness. He suggested, as Karl Pearson had suggested in England, that the civilized world seemed to have numerous families that spawned feeble-minded children at twice the rate of normal families and that this would result in a deterioration of the intellectual level of humanity. His data actually did not support that position, for the bad Kallikaks had 480 progeny and the good Kallikaks had 496. Nevertheless, Goddard was committed to a program of eugenic control of the population and the dream that the mentally handicapped could be eliminated from the population, together with most other social ills, through the sterilization of the unfit. Darwinian natural selection suggested that this could be done.

Goddard did not suggest other possible interpretations to his data. Indeed, his entire generation was blind to the possibility that the underprivileged might produce a new generation of underprivileged and perpetuate a poor environment of child-rearing and intellectual development. Such blindness is hardly surprising, for Americans of Goddard's day were committed to the belief that each individual, through his own efforts, could pull himself up in the world. If the immigrants could raise themselves in this way, then surely the reason that the Kallikaks could not must be the result of inferior heredity. Furthermore, Goddard thought he had a scientific explanation of the Kallikak phenomenon on the recent rediscovery of the work of Gregory Mendel. Goddard tried to explain the difference in the two branches of the family in terms of Mendelian inheritance. He did concede that feeble-mindedness could not be viewed as a simple Mendelian trait, and that it might depend on a group of such traits. His arguments, in their day, must have seemed plausible, and even persuasive.

Goddard proposed that the feeble-minded should be segregated and sterilized, admitting that much still had to be learned about the long-term effects of sterilization. He wanted to keep such individuals out of the ordinary schools and, despite his work at Vineland, seemed to propose minimum training for such individuals. The main purposes of segregation and sterilization were to keep such individuals out of the community and to prevent them from propagating the social ills which he attributed to them. So influential were these ideas that, by 1931, 31 states had passed laws requiring the sterilization of "defective" individuals, who in many states were defined to include criminals, the insane, as well as the feebleminded.

Another implication of Goddard's view was that just as the feeble-minded lack the capacity to think intellectually, so too do normal children inherit the capacity to engage in high-level thinking. Such thinking is implied to be inherited, and the implication is that thinking skills do not have to be taught in schools. The schools merely have to provide opportunity for the exercise of such skills.

Goddard's attempt to solve New York City's problem of classifying pupils was based entirely on his premise that the new tests of intelligence were capable of measuring innate intellectual ability. This position does not seem to have been challenged until much later. Practically all the major sources that Goddard could consult presented that point of view. Alfred Binet and Theodore Simon in France, and Cyril Burt and Alfred Frank Tredgold in England, supported the position. Tredgold, presenting this view through a Royal Commission, had taken the position that 80-90 percent of the mentally handicapped were thus indisposed for hereditary reasons. Goddard proposed, through the application of the new intelligence tests, to identify those children who needed some help to bring them up to the standards of other children and to separate them from those who could never reach those standards regardless of whatever help was given them.

However, Goddard found it difficult to explain the fact that children in the so-called *D* classes were, according to his test, nearly all innately feeble-minded, and yet many managed to pass the examination that would give them working papers. These were children placed in these classes at the age of 14 because they had not yet achieved the level of

4th-grade work, which was the level required for obtaining a permit to work. Goddard claimed that, despite inherent mental deficiency, these children were able to cram, by mechanical rote means, to pass tests that they did not understand. His description of this cramming is as follows: "It is not education; it is not making them any more efficient; it is simply evading the law" (*School Training of Defective Children,* p. 53). If Goddard had spent time in some of the classes for normal children, he would probably have found just as much cramming and just as much work that could hardly have been described as education. Goddard was not unusually prejudiced, for he reflected the widespread prejudices of his era.

Goddard disowned various plans for handling those who were identified as feeble-minded in terms of intelligence tests. What he would have liked to see was the segregation of these children into colonies where they could be sterilized. His only reason for not advocating such a program was that it would not have received the support of the parents. Goddard recognized that the children would have to be raised in the environment in which they were born. He deplored the fact that they would become parents and, he argued, as Francis Galton and Karl Pearson had said, they would spawn children as intellectually inadequate as themselves. Goddard thought that the problem of the proliferation of the feeble-minded would ultimately become so acute that strong action would be forced upon society. Such strong action would involve segretation and sterilization, with children taken forcibly away from their parents. In such colonies, children would be taught simple skills that they could use for earning some kind of a living within the segregated community.

Goddard believed that the schools would have to handle the problem of the care for the mentally handicapped until his ultimate solution could be introduced through the force of public pressure. He proposed that separate schools be established for such children and that these schools be placed under a separate authority so that the schools would not have to conform to any uniform school code. The programs of these schools would emphasize manual work and vocational training, and there would be an absence of anything that might be described as abstract work. A corps of special teachers would have to be trained for these schools, and the salaries were to be somewhat above those for teachers of normal children. Goddard envisaged the development of special training schools for teachers of the feeble-minded. He foresaw the difficulties of convincing parents that their retarded children should attend special schools, but believed that parents could be persuaded to see the advantages.

Goddard's plan was large and expensive. Of the 700,000 children in the New York City schools at that time, he considered that 15,000 belonged in the special schools, where classes should not have enrollments in excess of 15. The total cost would have added considerably to the school budget and was never fully put into effect. The mere cost of identifying 15,000 children by means of individual intelligence tests would have been large in itself. Had it not been for the cost, the plan would probably have had substantial public support.

Since Goddard's plan was the first of its kind, and involved a large and prestigious school system, it must have had considerable impact on the schools of the United States, all of which were faced with the problem of what to do with the backward child. The view was still widely held by teachers that the objectives of the common school could be achieved in nearly all pupils, and that the achievement of these objectives would make an egalitarian democracy possible. Only the backward child seemed to interfere with the achievement of this ideal. The concept of egalitarianism was to apply to all except those who supposedly were afflicted with some genetic defect. The majority were not so afflicted, and they would constitute the democratic society.

The doctrine that a small percentage of children, perhaps two percent, should be segregated and excluded from the American democracy was to survive for many generations. Looking back over the impact of Goddard's work, one must surely be impressed with the lack of any scientific basis for this doctrine. Yet it was put forward by Goddard, a man of integrity, as derived from the latest findings of science. The doctrine was in fact nothing more than an extension of the popularized ideas of social Darwinism that found its support in the aspirations of a moneyed class. This doctrine seemed to fit in with statements made by prestigious scientists who had entered and developed the field of intelligence testing. The basis for the entire doctrine and its political implications was at the best flimsy. In the years that followed, many were to be grievously harmed by such doctrines.

During World War I, Goddard played a part in the development of selection and classification procedures. He was a member of the National Committee on the Psychological Examination of Recruits of the National Army Cantonments. This committee did much to establish thought and attitudes towards the nature of ability that dominated education between the world wars. At the termination of World War I, he became professor at The Ohio State University. The designation of his appointment was that of professor of abnormal and clinical psychology. It must have been one of the first, if not the first, professorship to have been so designated. This was his first academic appointment, accepted at the age of 51. Few enter the academic world that late in life, but academia made possible an extraordinarily productive period in his life that terminated with his retirement in 1938.

One of his first publications as a professor was the book *Juvenile Delinquency* (1921). Goddard's approach to the problem of delinquency was rather different from that of Cyril Burt, who regarded delinquency as what he called an extension of childhood naughtiness. Burt looked upon the phenomenon as primarily a product of bad environmental influences and discarded the earlier theories that placed great stress on the influence of heredity. Goddard took what was essentially a middle position. He saw such a factor as low intelligence, which Goddard believed to be inherited, to be at the source of most delinquency. Hence he tied delinquency to inheritance, as earlier writers had done, but he also saw that the environment played a part. What he called a feeble-minded child might never become involved in delinquencies if the child were properly trained from an early age. He also believed that some children became delinquent because they were born of syphilitic mothers who transmitted the disease to their children, whose nervous systems were damaged by the disease. The immediate way of handling delinquency, according to Goddard, was that which involved training and treatment. He ruled out punishment, though Burt would not have. Goddard advocated keeping delinquents in institutions until they graduated, though they might never graduate because of a failure to rehabilitate them. Goddard said that assigning a child to an institution for the treatment of delinquency was as sensible as assigning a sick man to a hospital. Goddard's work initiated the era of the scientific treatment of delinquency. It was to take another 50 years to discover that therapy may have very little effect, even in the more advanced forms that were developed during the century.

Just as Cyril Burt was ultimately led to explore the problems of the schooling of the gifted, so too did Goddard engage in a brief exploration in the area. The opportunity to do this came through an invitation to assist in the establishment of classes for the gifted in the Cleveland Public Schools. This work is described in a book entitled *School Training of Gifted Children* (198). The gifted, like the mentally handicapped, supposedly owed their existence to the genes they had acquired from their parents. The work implied the need for what later was called *homogeneous grouping* and a multiple-track system of schooling for children of different levels of ability. The concept of the common school that equalized differences in background was on the way out. The impact of the new lines of psychological inquiry was undoubtedly of the greatest importance in the promotion of this new philosophy of education.

Goddard died at the age of 91 in 1957. Most of the early figures in the area of psychological measurement seem to have been long-lived. Those who lived to be at least octogenarians included Francis Galton, Cyril Burt, and James McKeen Cattell as well as Henry Goddard. Lewis Terman does not quite fit into this category, for he died at the young age of 79. Binet was the youngest of all, working himself to death at the age of 54. All of the long-lived members of the group became firmer in their beliefs as their years advanced, and none showed radical changes in the point of view with the passage of time. Perhaps, the psychological measurement area attracts people whose beliefs are extremely rigid and who feel secure in the beliefs they form early in their professional lives.

Goddard's work and views had great influence on American thought related to education. It forced a change from an egalitarian conception of the human, and education as an equalizing force, to a nonegalitarian conception of education in which differences in intellect were believed to be due to differences in endowment. Goddard's work provided a natural support for the emerging elitist view of the nature of human society. His work and influence illustrate the fact that the impact of the social scientist commonly arises from the fact that his reflections also mirror current views of society that are then in vogue. The reflections of the social scientist are then mistaken for scientific truths. Again and again one can see this pattern, and often with very damaging results.

Now let us turn to Lewis Madison Terman (1877-1956) who was also among the first followers of Alfred Binet who carried his work forward. He was the only one who had any credentials in relation to the public schools. Terman's parents believed that he was destined to become a teacher, so they sent him at the age of 15 to the Central Normal College. Unlike so many normal schools, Central Normal at Danville, Indiana, offered a course leading to a bachelor's degree. Terman told in his autobiography (C. E. Murchison, Ed., *A History of Psychology in Autobiography,* 1930) how he was able to combine a program of farm work, teaching in rural schools, and attendance at college to complete the work for the bachelor of science degree. Later he was principal of a township high school for 3 years. From his own account, he must have been desperately ill-prepared for either a teaching or administrative assignment. The college he attended was a private institution that was not far short of a degree mill. It asked no questions of those who applied for admission, and gave degrees generously to all who managed to stay for a few 10-week semesters. Teaching loads for faculty were as much as 25 to 30 hours, but Terman generously stated that, despite the teaching loads, instruction was surprisingly good.

Then Terman went to Indiana University, where he took all the psychology courses he could and also enough German and French to give him a considerable mastery of the languages. He also took a course in neurology, quite commonly offered in those days to students of psychology. After completing his master's degree at Indiana, he was offered an assistantship at Clark University which by then had become a mecca for the aspiring young American psychologist. G. Stanley Hall was not only professor of psychology at Clark, but had become president of the institution. Though the founder of Clark University had dreams of the institution becoming a world center for the study of geography, Hall had made it into a center for psychology.

Terman found at Clark University a freedom to study and pursue inquiry of a kind that is almost absent today. G. Stanley Hall, like most of his generation of psychologists, had studied in Germany where he had been impressed with the freedom of the student to pursue studies on his own responsibility. There was none of the stuffiness and the holding of the student to rigid requirements found at Yale and Harvard during the same period. Clark was moving in the direction of encouraging the graduate student to pursue work on his own. Even registration was informal and consisted of no other requirement than that of the student leaving his name with President Hall's secretary. Lecture courses were attended, but the student had to decide upon the readings for himself, and there were no course examinations though there were comprehensive examinations for advanced degrees. Terman thrived in that atmosphere. He had strong internal drives to achieve and required few external controls. His own drive to succeed academically is shown by the fact that when he graduated from Clark University, he was in debt to the tune of $2,500, an amount equivalent to the yearly salary of a full professor. This was an enormous debt for a young man to incur in those days.

The atmosphere at Clark was important for Terman's development. He said that he never functioned well under conditions involving rules and regulations. He said that at Clark there was *Lernfreiheit* (learning freedom) for the student and *Lehrfreiheit* (teacher freedom) for the professor. Professors lectured on whatever they felt like talking about, and the student studied whatever appealed to him. This atmosphere must have been of the greatest importance in the development of American psychology, for Clark, towards the end of the last century, was one of two centers for the training of psychologists in the new empirical approaches. One wonders how posterity will evaluate our regulated institutions of today.

Terman's memories of G. Stanley Hall are of interest in that they show the extraordinary impact that Hall had on his students and on the future of psychology in America. Hall was a physically impressive man who tended to overwhelm others with his social and scholarly competence. Indeed, his presence overwhelmed the entire university. Every Monday evening he held a seminar for students in psychology, sociology, philosophy, and education, and for whomever else wished to attend. The seminar was viewed as the highlight of the program at Clark. At the seminar, a student would present a written statement on the problem to be discussed. Terman noted that the presentation was always followed by some generous comments from Hall and the expression of just a few doubts regarding the conclusions. Then the seminar was opened up to the other participants. Hall would finally sum up the gist of the discussion with a brilliance which only he on the campus could manifest. Hall had a fertile imagination and an erudition which made his final remarks special jewels in the memories of his students. Then, after light refreshments, the seminar opened again with a second paper, followed by student discussion and another brilliant performance by Hall. Many of Hall's students became famous and their names, in addition to Terman, include that of Arnold L. Gesell. Hall's own brilliance was certainly matched by that of some of his most distinguished students. Terman talked about

Hall's *hypnotic sway* to describe the overwhelming influence that Hall had on the students, the institution, and the community of psychologists at large.

Terman's interest in individual differences developed while he was at Clark University. He read the works of Francis Galton and Alfred Binet. At Hall's suggestion he made a survey of the literature on precocity, and this led to his exploration of the literature on measurement as a basis for investigating both gifted children and children limited in capacity.

Terman's interest in individual differences was not to the liking of G. Stanley Hall, whose upbringing in the discipline of German psychology had led him to take the position that the only real science of psychology was that which sought general laws. The study of individual differences seemed to run contrary to the search for general laws. Nevertheless, Hall was as charitable towards the heresies of Terman as Wundt had been towards the heresies of Cattell. Scholars of the nineteenth century seem to have been more kindly disposed towards deviant views of their associates than have been twentieth-century scholars in the field of psychology.

Terman began experimental work on his doctoral thesis towards the end of 1904. The problem he chose was that of discovering differences in the abilities of a group of children selected as "bright" and a group selected as "dull." Very little previous work had been done, and theory of measurement was primitive. Thorndike's *An Introduction to the Theory of Mental and Social Measurements* (1904) had appeared just before Terman started his work, but he did not seem to feel that the volume helped him much. Also, he was taken aback by the way in which Thorndike expounded his position with complete cocksureness and with little regard for the opinions of Thorndike's elders (Thorndike was only in his 20's). Terman was a man of mild and gentle disposition, with a kindly regard towards all and particularly towards those he admired. His dissertation was supervised by Edmund Clark Sanford, who ran the laboratory that Hall had established.

At the end of his first year at Clark University, Terman suffered a pulmonary hemorrhage. Several years earlier he had had signs of lung disease, but this time there was no doubt that he had tuberculosis. In those days there was not much that was done about the disease, except for a brief period of rest until the fever had subsided and then a regimen of avoiding fatigue and a good diet. Terman must have had a strong constitution, though he was a young man of slight build, for he not only managed to recover from tuberculosis without special treatment but went on to live until the age of 79. The disease did have the effect of bringing him to California.

The jobs available to Terman when he graduated from Clark included the principalship of the high school at San Bernadino. The principalship was not exactly what he had prepared himself to enter, but the job was in

California in a climate that would help heal his lungs, so he went there. Terman was always able to make the most of things, and he described the year there as "a busy and happy one" (Murchison, 1930, p. 322). A year later he obtained, through the Albert Teachers Agency, a position of professor of child study and pedagogy at the Los Angeles State Normal College for Women where he spent 4 years. At the college he found his old fellow student from Clark, Arnold Gesell. Terman described the faculty as being difficult to match in any other normal school. He found the academic atmosphere stimulating, but he was afraid to push himself too hard lest his lung condition flare up. Once again, we see a man capable of making the most of whatever life happened to bring him. In discussing this period of his life there is no mention of any frustration caused by his physical limitations. He dared not push himself and become involved in research, so he erased for a time from his mind any thoughts of a research career.

Chance brought him to Stanford University in 1910. Elwood P. Cubberley, head of the Department of Education at Stanford University, had opened up a new position of professor of educational psychology and had offered the position to E. B. Huey, a long-time friend of Terman. Huey turned down the position because it did not fit his present interests and suggested to Cubberley that Terman might fill the position. Terman's credentials must have appealed to Cubberley with his background in school administration and his orientation towards helping the public schools improve themselves. Elwood Cubberley was a rather dry, practical administrator who wrote eminently practical books for American administrators. His books were useful, and very widely read, perhaps because they had no competitors, but they were devoid of any theoretical foundation or philosophical point of view. Cubberley's fortune from his books eventually ran into millions, even though he was not particularly interested in money. Nevertheless, Cubberley was a big enough man to realize that even though he was not a person concerned with developing psychological theory related to education, there were others attempting to do this. As a man who traveled, he must have realized that Thorndike's appointment at Columbia and Judd's appointment at Chicago were bringing education into a new world and that Stanford would have to introduce comparable developments if it were to remain among the outstanding institutions. The appointment of Terman was a step in this direction, and a major step.

It must have required a person of Terman's extraordinary adaptability to fit into the atmosphere provided by Elwood Cubberley at Stanford. Although Cubberley was described as a shy man, he managed to move in influential circles. He had been a former student of David Starr Jordan, president of Stanford, who had brought him to Stanford, and he was a close friend of Stanford's best known student, Herbert Hoover, who helped him convert a small income from the sale of textbooks into a fortune of many millions. Cubberley, though reserved, was a very practical man, practical even in the sense of having little interest in the things that typically interest academicians. His hiring of Terman was one of his few concessions to the idea that theoretically oriented men might be able to make some contribution to education. He did give Terman freedom to do whatever Terman wanted.

Terman started to work immediately on problems related to the measurement of intelligence. This probably appealed to Cubberley, for the work of Binet had been given considerable publicity in school journals and was presented as a potential solution to most of the problems that teachers encountered. The lack of learning of some children could no longer be considered as a failure on the part of the teacher. It could now be viewed as a genetic failure. The intelligence test provided an alibi for every failure on the part of the school. The measurement of intelligence was regarded as one of the most practical advances that the schools had yet encountered.

For 6 years, Terman and his graduate students worked on the revision of the Binet-Simon scales for American children. The results of this work appeared in a book entitled *The Measurement of Intelligence* (1916). This book made available, for the first time, Binet-type tests suitable for American children and properly standardized so that mental levels and intelligence quotients could be calculated. Goddard had not made his material available for public use, but the material had been published in bulletins issued by Vineland, and circulated mainly among academicians. Terman obviously had the Goddard materials and acknowledged their use in the development of his revision of the scales. Furthermore, Terman provided for the first time a set of extremely detailed directions on how each test should be administered. In this book, Terman claimed that training was needed to administer the scale, but in some of his later publications he took the position that teachers could train themselves.

Ellwood Cubberley's introduction to the volume is of considerable interest, for it reflects the view taken among those connected with public education concerning what they believed to be the value of the scales. Cubberley viewed the instruments as practical developments that could be of value to the classroom teacher. Cubberley stated that all teachers should know how to administer the new intelligence tests and perhaps should know the intelligence quotients of all the children in their classes. He did suggest that those teachers aspiring to be administrators should be given training in the handling of the tests. The suggestion seems to be that administrators would then be able to administer the tests to any children sent to the principal's office. Cubberley viewed the venture as eminently practical. The theoretical issues completely escaped him. He was a very practical man.

Terman's introductory chapter to the book stressed the inheritability of intelligence, and he cited the evidence that was typical in documents of the period. He also discussed the relation between criminality and intellectual defect. He suggested applications in the use of intelligence tests in brief but definite terms. He believed that such tests should be used for assigning children to particular grades and seemed to imply that a grade should contain children of similar mental ages rather than children of similar age. He also suggested that the tests be used to differentiate the trainable feeble-minded from what he thought were the non-trainable. He believed that intelligence tests could be used to discriminate between the delinquent whose delinquencies were a result of mental handicap from the delinquent who exercised thoughtful choice. In addition, he saw intelligence tests as a means of identifying the gifted so that they could be given appropriate education. He also had great hopes that intelligence tests could be administered to establish fitness for particular vocations. He thought that intelligence tests could be used to answer many important social questions that were widely discussed, such as whether "inferior races really are inferior" (p. 20), and whether the so-called lower classes in the social and industrial complex were lower because of inferior native endowment. Terman came out with the clear statement that "with the exception of moral character, there is nothing as significant for a child's future as his grade of intelligence" (p. 20). Intelligence, he believed, was the decisive factor in success in life, and thus success seemed to depend on native endowment.

The book describing the Stanford Revision of the Binet-Simon instrument was followed a year later by another volume that provided data related to the use of the device (Lewis M. Terman et al., *The Stanford Revision and Extension of the Binet-Simon Scale for Measuring Intelligence*, 1917). The volume provided considerable data of interest to school people, since it was derived from schools. The volume provided information about the intelligence quotients of children viewed as retarded and accelerated, and there were tables of distributions of intelligence quotients. The report also summarized studies relating intelligence quotients and mental ages to success in school. Although a modern reader might find the report rather dull because of familiarity with the findings, those who read the report at the time must have been impressed that an instrument had been produced which would predict which children would succeed and which would fail in school. Soon the myth developed in the subculture of teachers that some of the children in their classes were born failures and that there was little use in even trying to help them. The theme of the predictive power of the intelligence quotient was developed further in Terman's next book, *The Intelligence of School Children* (1919). Terman dedicated this volume to his graduate students during the years 1916-17 and 1917-18. These students conducted most of the studies reported in this volume, and their help is acknowledged in the preface. The book begins by providing data on the range of individual differences in intelligence at different school-grade levels. This is followed by further data on what were then called *school laggards.* This term had a certain moral tone to it and carried the implication that these were children who did not try hard enough, but Terman provided data believed to show that these children were feeble-minded.

In the third volume on intelligence testing that we are now considering, Terman provided data on what he called the constancy of the intelligence quotient. He claimed that the intelligence quotient remained constant throughout life, except for variations resulting from errors of measurement. He provided case histories to show that improvements in the environment of a child did little to change the intelligence quotient. The doctrine of the constancy of the intelligence quotient was to have great impact on the schools during the 1920's and 1930's. Even today, the implications of this doctrine are still apparent.

A final section on *Intelligence of School Children* is concerned with the administration of the intelligence scales by teachers. Although the chapter begins by suggesting that all such administration of tests should take place under the supervision of a psychologist, the position was soon abandoned. Terman suggested that teachers take a course in the administration of intelligence tests. Terman provided a brief outline of such a course. He then retreated still further from his initial position calling for trained supervision of the teacher administering intelligence tests, for he proposed that teachers who could not take appropriate course work learn to administer the tests themselves. He outlined a procedure through which a teacher could become proficient in the administration of intelligence tests. Terman cautioned the teacher not to jump to quick conclusions on the basis of an intelligence test, since the test should be the point where the teacher begins the study of a child and not the point where the study of the child is closed. Suggestions were made concerning how the study of the child may be expanded after an intelligence test has been given.

Terman implied that an intelligence test should be given to each child early in the year. If time is not available to give all the tests, then an abbreviated set of items could be given. If there is not time for that, then Terman suggested that the vocabulary test alone be given. Terman also expressed hope that the newly devised group tests would be available for children in the third grade and above.

As time passed, Terman's writing focused more on problems of education. In 1919 Terman was asked by Margaret S. McNaught, Chairman of the Commission on Revision of Elementary Education of the National Education Association, to form a subcommittee on the value of tests in school reorganization. Unfortunately, the subcommittee never received the funds that had been originally promised and had to limit itself to the study of certain experiments that were already in progress in several school systems. The final report consisted of a series of commentaries by different authors on these experiments, and an introductory chapter by Terman that provided direction to the total document. The Terman chapter provided a strong statement of his position on the use of intelligence tests in schools, and his emerging status as luminary must have led to his chapter being regarded as a source of leadership. The chapter, together with the rest of his writings, exercised substantial leadership, for almost every innovation implied in them became common practice in the schools within the next decade. The subcommittee report, edited by Terman, had the seductive title of *Intelligence Tests and School Reorganization* (1922).

Terman's introductory essay stated that thousands of teachers have been trained to administer the Binet and, at the time when Terman was writing, a quarter of a million children a year were being tested with the device. He also noted that, despite the widespread administration of the individually administered intelligence test, more children needed to be tested. The expansion of the testing capability of the schools was being facilitated, he noted, by the introduction of the group intelligence test, and in 1920-21 he expected that as many as 2 million children would be tested with the new group device. He predicted that within a few years the annual rate of testing would reach 5 million.

Terman had mentioned the possibility of group tests as early as 1916. A story which may well be apocryphal tells how the group test of intelligence was invented by one of Terman's graduate students. The student was Arthur S. Otis. The story handed down is that Otis attended Terman's course on the giving of the Stanford Revision of the Binet-Simon Scale, and, as a part of the course, was required to administer the scale to a considerable number of children. Otis found other, more interesting, pursuits to engage in, and when the end of the semester approached he was faced with the fact that he had not yet administered the test to a single child. But Otis was an ingenious and enterprising fellow who saw a quick way out of his difficulty. He went through the scale and selected those items that could be administered to a group of children, and then administered the items to a group of the required size. He scored the items as though they had been given to one pupil at a time and submitted his work to Terman. After the course was completed and the grades were safely in the office of the registrar, Otis went to Terman and confessed his shortcuts and misdeeds. Neither history nor legend records Terman's response, but shortly afterwards, when the United States Army became interested in testing the intelligence of recruits in groups, both Terman and Otis were asked to make contributions. Otis went on after the war to make a career of developing and selling tests of intelligence.

The war had hardly ended when efforts were made to adapt the Army tests for civilian use. The General Education Board of the Rockefeller Foundation set aside $25,000 for this enterprise, which was organized by a committee of psychologists under the auspices of the National Research Council. The result was a set of tests called the *National Intelligence Tests,* suitable for grades 3-8. These were not the only group tests available. Terman stated that by 1921 there were as many as 12 group intelligence tests on the market.

Terman saw two possible major uses of the tests. One was to group children, regardless of age, into classes that were quite homogeneous with respect to mental age. Thus, a first grade might include all children whose mental ages were between 6-6 and 7-5, regardless of age. He believed that this would permit uniformity of instruction. A second possibility was to include within a grade those of the same age but to handle the problem of differences in intelligence by the individualization of instruction. The latter solution did not appeal to Terman. His third possible solution was to develop what he called *homogeneous class groups.* Terman stated in his 1922 book that numerous experiments were in progress which involved the homogeneous grouping of students in terms of their intelligence tests scores. These were called multiple-track plans and had been used in some places for many years and had even preceded the use of intelligence tests for dividing children for this purpose. Although there were numerous experiments involving the homogeneous grouping of pupils, Terman conceded that the plan had not been widely adopted.

Terman proposed that children be separated into different tracks on the basis of intelligence quotients, within any particular age-grade group. He proposed a five-track system, an idea attributed to Karl Pearson. His suggestion was that within a school enrolling 2,000 pupils below the high school level, 50 pupils (2½ percent) be assigned to classes for the gifted. The next lower intelligence quotient group of 300 pupils, that is to say the next 15 percent, would constitute classes of what he termed *bright* pupils. The middle group of average pupils would include 1,300 pupils. These would be the middle 65 percent. Slow pupils would constitute the next 15 percent, or 300 pupils, and the "special" pupils would constitute the lowest 2½ percent. Small school systems might have only two or three tracks, but Terman insisted that even a village should have at least a two-track system. The track system was based largely on the idea that the intelligence quotient was constant throughout life, and thus one would expect that a child should remain in the same track throughout his schooling. The tracks would differ in the content and methods of teaching. The lowest track would teach the minimum essentials for survival in our society and the upper track would be greatly enriched. The slow group was to be taught only vocational skills above the eighth grade. Terman did comment, however, that the tracks between the systems should always be kept open, but he had little to say about the problems involved in switching tracks.

Terman's program was precisely that which Cyril Burt advocated in

England and which was introduced through Burt's influence in the London County Council Schools. There developed in the 1920's and 1930's a number of programs in which the gifted were placed in a special track, and the tracking of the very slow had already had a long history before Terman wrote on the subject. Massive tracking plans had to await the termination of World War II. It is of interest to note that these massive tracking plans, referred to later as programs of homogeneous grouping, generally seem to have broken down because of the difficulty of transferring from one track to another. The London County Council school system tracking program broke down for just that reason. Switching of tracks was difficult, and the difficulty of switching resulted in creating lifetime disadvantages for some pupils.

Terman proposed that intelligence tests be given to all children in school. Although Terman thought that psychologists should administer the tests, he thought that many of the new group tests could be easily administered and scored by any teacher. He did say that the scores should be interpreted together with other data. He had some qualms about scoring errors and errors involving the transcriptions of scores, which might do lasting harm, but the point was not pressed. The scores were to be treated as confidential material, and neither the parents nor the children should have access to them.

Terman's 1922 book introduced the public to the concept of the accomplishment ratio, a concept developed by Raymond Franzen. This was the ratio of a child's achievement predicted from his intelligence quotient to his actual achievement. If the child's intelligence quotient were average and his achievement were average, then the ratio would be equal to 100. A ratio of above 100 was viewed as overachievement, and that below 100 as underachievement. Terman predicted that the achievement ratio would become as well known as the intelligence quotient. Terman considered an ideal system of marking to be that in which grades were given in terms of achievement ratios.

In his 1922 book, Terman referred to measured intelligence as *innate* intelligence. There was no wavering or ambiguity on this point. The latter position together with the view that the intelligence quotient was constant, a necessary corollary of the idea of the innateness of the intelligence quotient, led Terman to take the position that guidance could be given to children at an early age concerning later occupation. Elementary school pupils could be sorted out in terms of future level of occupation and given corresponding levels of education. Terman was particularly concerned with discovering hidden talent in young children so that this talent could be used productively by society. He thought that the new tests could do this.

As a postscript to the history of the Stanford Revision of the Binet-Simon Scale, one should note that in 1937 Terman coauthored with Maud A. Merrill his final major contribution to the area of intelligence testing. The volume was entitled *Measuring Intelligence -- A Guide to the Administration of the New Revised Stanford-Binet Tests of Intelligence* (1937). This volume is totally devoid of any discussion of the school uses of the Binet scale, and confines itself to the description of the new extended scale and the introduction of the second form of the test. Individual tests of intelligence were no longer administered by teachers in schools, though the test was still administered by school psychologists in clinics and school district offices.

Although Terman is remembered by many as the man who introduced the intelligence quotient to America, his lasting effect on American education came from other sources, and notably his studies of gifted children. Just as Cyril Burt and Herbert Goddard turned their attention late in life to the gifted child, so too did Terman, whose research is summarized in a five-volume work with the collective title of *Genetic Studies of Genius* (1925, 1926, 1930, 1949, 1959). In these studies, Terman was not concerned with the kind of environment favorable to the development of giftedness, for he stated clearly that intellectual giftedness depends upon "original endowment rather than in environmental influences" (1925, p. 66).

One should note that Terman acknowledged his debt to Francis Galton in the initiation of his studies of genius. Galton had undertaken a study of eminent adults and their relatives and progeny in an attempt to demonstrate the hereditary nature of genius. The framework of Terman's study is very similar to that of Galton in that it has the inherent prejudice that genius is hereditary.

Terman's studies of gifted children grew out of an idea that it would be interesting to study the 1,000 most gifted children in the entire state of California. However, the testing and study of all the children in the state was an enterprise far larger than could possibly be undertaken. Terman had to reduce the original idea to workable dimensions. With the help of money from the Commonwealth Fund, Terman sought to identify gifted children of elementary school age in the major metropolitan areas of California. A majority of the children seem to have come from Los Angeles, San Francisco, and Oakland. The main group that was identified and then studied intensively over a long period consisted of 643 children.

The first step in the selection of the children was nomination by the teacher. Terman developed a form for this purpose which was distributed to teachers. On this form the teacher was asked to name the most intelligent pupil in the class, the next most intelligent, and the third most intelligent. In addition, the form asked the teacher to name the children who were the youngest in the grade.

Those pupils who were thus nominated in phase 1 of the selection procedure were then tested with the National Intelligence Test in phase 2 of the selection process. Those who tested in the top 5 percent of unselected children were retained for further study. In the third phase, those retained in the second stage were given abbreviated Stanford-Binet tests. Two different sets of items were used, the one set suitable for those from English-speaking homes, and the other for those from where another language was spoken. The children from the non-English-speaking homes were not tested on the vocabulary tests and on some other tests that involved linguistic skill.

The selection of the children involved the successive application of independent measures of intelligence, thus ensuring that a single chance high score would not admit a child to the gifted group.

Enormous amounts of data were collected on these children. They were administered the Stanford Achievement Test, tests of general information, science, hygiene, geography, language, literature, history and civics, and the arts. They also filled out interest inventories, inventories of occupational choice, and inventories of scholastic interests. They were investigated with respect to their hobbies, and a Home Blank asked the parents for numerous items of information. The children were asked to report on their leisure-time activities. Similar data were also collected on an "unselected" group of 474 children from two of the metropolitan areas studied.

Attempts were made to assess the reading interests of the children, and the parents were asked to estimate how much reading each child undertook. Social activities and social interests were also studied. A very ambitious attempt was made to assess certain aspects of character through performance-type tests developed by Paul Frederick Voelker. Terman described the tests as severe tests of actual trustworthiness. The battery also allegedly tested traits described as conscientiousness, willingness to accept undeserved credit, willingness to cheat, moral judgment, and other aspects of character that appeared to be important. The children were also rated by both teachers and parents on a long list of traits. A health record was obtained on each child together with a large amount of anthropometric data. Few studies have ever been undertaken in which so many children have been so intensively studied.

The main purpose of the study was to identify the characteristics of the gifted and to determine the validity of the ideas commonly held at that time concerning the concomitants of giftedness. Those who lived in the nineteenth century and the early part of the present century believed that genius was accompanied by many negative traits. The highly gifted were often believed to be psychotic, or near psychotic. At best, the talented were believed to be queer. They were also considered to be socially maladjusted and quite unable to relate to others in a normal way. They were considered to be physically inferior and prone to disease. The data collected by Terman were suitable for testing all of these hypotheses, and others.

Terman found that the gifted were above average in health, but the difference in this respect compared to the unselected children was small.

The gifted were certainly not undersized, weak, and nervous, as popular opinion described them.

The children did not show the same superiority of achievement that they showed on intelligence tests. They were superior to children in general, on the average, but not markedly so. Terman explained the lack of outstanding superior achievement by the fact that all children were exposed to the same schooling, and gifted children were not given work commensurate with their abilities. The gifted were not found to be one-sided in their development. A considerable proportion of all children showed one-sided development, and the gifted did not show an undue number of such cases.

With respect to interests, the gifted tended to like the school subjects that were considered difficult. Apparently, in such subjects the gifted found challenge. They also chose occupations which were intellectually challenging.

The gifted children were found to be much like most other children in their play activities. This finding again ran counter to the then-current prejudice. The gifted children spent fewer hours than other children in play, a finding that Terman explained as being a result of the fact that the gifted have very broad interests, hence many different activities competed for their attention. For example, the gifted excelled other children in both the quantity and quality of their reading. Terman found that the gifted child of 7 read more books than the unselected child of 15 years. The breadth and strength of the interests of the gifted were such that they tended to be carried into all kinds of intellectual and social pursuits.

The tests of character showed striking differences between the gifted and the unselected children. In every respect measured, the gifted were superior, showing greater honesty, trustworthiness, and superior performance related to other character traits. A test of "psychotic tendency," very similar to many modern personality inventories, showed that the gifted were better adjusted than were the unselected children. In terms of the prejudices of the age, the latter finding was viewed as particularly surprising.

Terman also found that teachers were not particularly skilled in identifying the child in a class who was brightest in terms of the criteria used in the study. Terman found that, at that time in the California schools, the brightest child in a class was more likely to be the youngest child than the one selected by the teacher.

The initial volume in the *Genetic Studies of Genius* series did much to dispel many of the prejudices related to the nature of the gifted child, but reinforced other prejudices. The volume dwelt at length on the finding that the gifted children came from families high up in the hierarchy of occupations. Terman argued that since the State of California provided equality of educational opportunity, the superiority of children from upper-class homes had to be a result of genetic superiority. Terman further argued that intellectual superiority is shown at a very early age and that this fact suggested the genetic basis of measured intelligence. His group of gifted children had shown precocity in reading, a high intellectual curiosity at an early age, and an extraordinary range of miscellaneous information. The views of Herbert Spencer, preached to Newport audiences 50 years previously, seemed now, to Terman, to have a genuine scientific basis.

Yet there are moments in his writing when one sees in Terman a degree of uncertainty about his dogmatically stated views. For example, he stated that an experiment should be conducted to determine whether a well-planned educational program could change the intelligence quotient. He noted that many educators believed that such a well-designed program could have such an effect.

The second volume in the series is presented as a further contribution to the hereditary study of genius. The study is an attempt to apply newer techniques to the kind of biographical data that Francis Galton had used in his work *Hereditary Genius: An Inquiry into Its Causes and Consequences* (1869, 1892). Terman's novel approach involved the estimation of the intelligence quotient from records of the childhood behavior and accomplishments of 300 selected "geniuses," and the data that James McKeen Cattell had used in his article entitled "A Statistical Study of Eminent Men" (1903).

Terman derived two intelligence quotients from the biographical records. One rating, referred to as the A-I rating, was the average judgment of the intelligence of the subject for the period up to his 17th birthday. The A-II rating was a similar average for the period up to the 26th birthday. The general thesis of the volume is that these geniuses had been children with high intelligence quotients and, since the intelligence quotient was assumed to reflect innate ability, the genius of these individuals reflected hereditary talent. Terman, like all the psychologists of his generation, showed tremendous bias in the interpretation of his data. Terman does not seem to have been disturbed by the fact that Antoine Lavoisier, who has often been described as the greatest scientific intelligence of his generation, had an estimated intelligence quotient before the age of 17 between 110 and 120. Terman and his associates were admirable, able people, but the prejudices of their age blinded them to alternative hypotheses in terms of which the data could be interpreted. The educational implication of the work was that the high intelligence-quotient child, because of superior endowment, was bound to come to the top even if his education was poor. The only argument for providing such a child with special schooling was that this would prevent him from suffering boredom. Within this viewpoint, teachers were quite powerless to alter the path established through endowment along which the child was inevitably driven. Much of what Terman had to offer the schools was a doctrine of despair.

Volume III of the series is a follow-up of the original California gifted group through about 7 years. The conclusions confirmed those outlined in Volume I. The follow-up reemphasized that the children came from predominantly gifted families and the fact was pointed out that these families were not reproducing themselves in terms of numbers. The gifted group were shown, again, to be superior in health and physique. These children lacked one-sidedness. They showed good intellectual stability. In social intelligence and play activities, the gifted were either normal or superior. On character traits, the gifted showed marked superiority. There was no doubt left that the gifted could no longer be regarded as a group of emotionally unstable and queer individuals, unable to have normal social lives.

The remaining two volumes in the series (Volume IV, 1949; Volume V, 1959) were follow-up studies of the original gifted group, the first after 25 years and the second when the members of the group were in mid-life. The materials covered by these volumes do not seem to have had the impact on education that the earlier volumes had. They were important contributions to our knowledge of development and have been followed by still later studies of the original group of gifted students. Some of these studies are still in progress.

Subsequent research workers had still to demonstrate that much of what Terman believed to be genetic endowment was nothing more than the result of a superior early home environment. This possibility had escaped Terman, perhaps because of the then-current belief that the preschool years had no great significance for the course of mental development, but rather that they were years waiting for maturation to take effect, the years required to bring the child to the point where he could learn effectively.

The studies of Terman had another indirect impact on education. Support by the Commonwealth Fund made it possible for him to employ a project staff of promising young men and women, some of whom became well-known psychologists. These included Truman L. Kelley, G. M. Ruch, Florence Goodenough, Catharine Cox, and Barbara S. Burks.

CYRIL BURT -- FIRST SCHOOL PSYCHOLOGIST

Although Cyril Burt (1883-1971) was an Englishman, and never even visited America, he nevertheless had considerable indirect impact on American education, by providing prestigious support for what Americans were doing in relation to schools, and by providing widely known examples of applications of psychology to education. Through

Burt's ideas and efforts, the first large-scale tracking system was introduced into a school system. The London County Council tracking system became a model that was copied all over the world. In addition, Burt's views on the genetic basis of measured intelligence, coupled with his enormous international prestige, did much to influence American thinking in the first half of the century.

Yet Burt is the mystery man of psychology and one of history's enigmas. Burt's own short autobiography in *A History of Psychology in Autobiography,* Volume IV (1930) tells much about his early childhood and education, and relatively little about his professional work and ideas.

Burt's life spanned considerable years in both centuries, since he was born in 1883 and died in 1971 at the age of 88. His father was a physician, but a keen classical scholar and an educated man in every sense of the term. His mother had a strong feeling for the street urchins and left Cyril Burt with a lurking curiosity about the nature of such children. His parents loved music and literature. Burt talked about the rare assortment of knowledge he collected at home which led him to obtain a scholarship for one of the better secondary schools. Universal secondary education had not yet reached England.

At school he acquired an even stronger taste for the classics than he had already acquired in the home, perhaps through the influence of a headmaster whom Burt admired. This led Burt to pursue classics as a career, a not uncommon goal in those days when the classics were the entree into such professions as teaching, law, and even medicine.

Burt eventually obtained a scholarship to Oxford, and although he toyed with the idea of studying medicine, the scholarship permitted him only to pursue knowledge in the classical areas. He was able to attend lectures in other areas and heard the great physiologist J. S. Haldane, and the equally eminent psychologist, William McDougall. Under the latter, he undertook a project that eventually launched him on a new career. The British Association for the Advancement of Science had established an anthropometric committee to standardize some tests for the purposes of undertaking a survey. The whole enterprise had been instigated by none other than Francis Galton. In connection with this work, Burt came into contact with Karl Pearson, who was working on the Bertillon system of anthropometric measurements and who had developed the solution to the problem of reducing a large number of measurements to a basic few. Burt saw how the same procedures could be used to reduce a battery of psychological measures. Through this activity, Burt undertook some of the early work on factor analysis. The influence of both Francis Galton and Karl Pearson was persistent throughout Burt's life. The problem that both of these believed to be of supreme social importance was the inheritance of psychological abilities. Burt developed the same belief.

In 1907, Cyril Burt went to Liverpool to work under the great physiologist Charles Sherrington, who, apparently, had a very broad conception of what professionals in his department should do. Burt taught psychology to medical students but also pursued his research on individual differences. He lived in one of the Liverpool slums for a time in order to become better acquainted with the full range of individual differences and to learn something about backward and delinquent children. Burt's interest, at this stage, seems to have been primarily in the factor problem in relation to tests and the search for the "highest common factor" as well as for specific abilities. He proposed that schools undertake surveys of mental and physical abilities, an idea that received the endorsement of Francis Galton.

Cyril Burt's theory-oriented approach to testing hardly made him a likely candidate to fill the position of first school psychologist. His life up to that point, and much of his subsequent life, fitted more the model of the academician than that of the practitioner. The appointment came about in an interesting way.

In 1893, James Sully, who was then Professor of Mental Philosophy at University College of the University of London, initiated the establishment of a child study society. The aim of the society, which was somewhat typical of its day, was to encourage teachers and other practitioners to study children along the line of identifying individual differences. Francis Galton had shown some interest in the enterprise, probably as a possible means of extending his own studies. An active member of the society was C. W. Kimmins, who was chief inspector of the public schools. Kimmins drew up a scheme for adding a psychologist to the office of inspectors. The matter was considered to be one of considerable importance and urgency in that there had been complaints about how the medical officers certified children as mentally defective. It seems that the medical officers relied upon what were called stigmata for certifying children and assigning them to special classes. Such stigmata included a low forehead, small cranial capacity, lack of symmetry of features, and protruding ears. Anatomists had prepared lists of such stigmata, and the same anatomists opposed the introduction of intelligence tests. Burt has described the common procedure as that of lining up the children in a school, by class, after which the physiognomist would read off the anatomical features that classified children as either defective or normal.

The appointment of a psychologist to the London County Council inspectorate was designed to change that procedure. Kimmins must surely have been aware of the new procedures developed by Alfred Binet and Francis Galton. There was only one young man in the entire British Isles who had any familiarity with the new techniques of intellectual assessment, and that young man was Cyril Burt.

Burt was thus appointed as the first school psychologist anywhere in the world. The situation in which he found himself was highly favorable.

He had a chief, Robert Blair, who was highly sympathetic to the kinds of things that Burt wanted to do, and a clientele of teachers who were glad to obtain some assistance in handling the many problem children in their classes. The appointment was only for half-time and for a probationary period of 3 years, to see how the new position would work out. Burt seems to have been pleased with the arrangement, for in this job, as in all the other jobs that Burt ever held, he had no fixed duties and was free to pursue whatever line of research he wanted to pursue. He had had that kind of job under Charles Sherrington at Liverpool, and would have a similar freedom in his later job as professor of psychology at University College, London.

Burt's own description of his job as school psychologist bears a remarkable resemblance to a similar job today. He organized testing in the schools and particularly with reference to the problem of identifying what were then called the mentally defective and the supernormal. He prepared reports on children referred to him by teachers, physicians, and the courts. He called his office the first child guidance center. In addition, he followed up a suggestion made many times by Francis Galton that the schools should become a laboratory for the study of many psychological and sociological problems. Burt made it possible for academic psychologists to undertake work in schools. His autobiography stated that during the first 15 years of his appointment as school psychologist, 30 investigations were conducted in the schools of the London County Council.

In order to understand further the kind of environment in which the typical London child was raised, Burt found a place to live in a settlement, near Euston Station, which was then a virtual slum, and spent at least some weekends living with poor families in various locations in the London area. One should not misunderstand Burt's motives for doing this. The interest was strictly intellectual. Those who knew Cyril Burt as an individual, as I did, are in fair agreement that Burt had little in the way of feeling for the unfortunate. His relations with students, even doctoral students, were cold and remote. He kept them in what he believed to be their place. All who were subjected to Burt's often demeaning attitude would agree that he was a man of enormous intellectual brilliance, but his own intellectual development and pursuits came first, and nothing could supersede them. He recognized his own intellectual brilliance, though he often felt that others did not. His cold, incisive intelligence had a way of striking at the very heart of a problem, but it was a cold intelligence. His decision to spend time in the slums must surely have been a strictly intellectual one, designed to provide him with the very best means of studying the subnormal and emotionally disturbed mind. Burt did have personal problems later in life that may well have clouded his capacity to act as a scientist, but, as a young man, there was no such clouding of his vision.

The other half of Burt's time, while he worked half time for the London County Council, soon became filled with another appointment, as assistant to the laboratory of experimental psychology that had been founded at Cambridge University by Charles S. Myers. The main benefit to be derived from that appointment was that it brought Burt into contact with Udny Yule, a student of Karl Pearson, and who, next to Pearson, was probably the outstanding statistician of his era. This was one of the links in the chain that tied educational psychology to the field of statistics.

Burt began to prepare an English version of the Binet tests about 1910. He engaged in correspondence with Alfred Binet, who died in 1911, and later corresponded with Theodore Simon. The English version of the test had to be standardized on English schoolchildren, and this was done with the help of a number of schoolteachers trained to administer the instrument. However, the project seems to have been interrupted by the onset of World War I, for the printed version did not appear until 1921, when it was published as a part of a book entitled *Mental and Scholastic Tests* (1921). The book is introduced by a preface written by Robert Blair, Burt's chief in the London County Council school inspectorate. Blair indicated that the book consists of three memoranda prepared by Cyril Burt for the London County Council. The first of the memoranda represented a translation of the Binet-Simon tests. The second memorandum provided evidence concerning their validity, particularly with respect to the usefulness of the tests for identifying the "mentally defective." The third memorandum provided a series of tests for measuring the achievement of children in the common school subjects. The tests covered the areas of reading, spelling, dictation, arithmetic, writing, drawing, handiwork, and composition.

Mental and Scholastic Tests is a typical document compiled by Burt. It is filled with tables of figures and incorporates a vast amount of data. Some of the data were collected by Burt and his associates, and some were derived from studies conducted by others. The tests had obviously been standardized on hundreds or even thousands of children. Even more important is the fact that the tone of the volume indicates that the test had become well established for the selection of children who were to be sent to what were referred to as M.D. schools, the letters standing for "mentally defective."

When I paged through *Mental and Scholastic Tests* for the purpose of writing this book, after not having looked at the volume for 45 years, certain features of the book impressed me. One was that there was no mention made of the issue of the inheritability of intelligence as measured by the Binet type of instrument. This struck me as odd in view of the fact that Cyril Burt is now well known historically for his position that nature plays an overwhelmingly important part in contrast to nurture in generating the intelligence quotient. Also, Burt, as an admirer and follower of Francis Galton and an associate of Karl Pearson, had surely embraced the position of these great men on the issue. There are cues in Burt's autobiography that he had. The author's interpretation of the absence of the discussion of the issue in his first major book is that he just assumed that what he called mental deficiency was inherited and that his English version of the Binet test measured this inherited factor. The volume implies that the low intelligence quotient group should be sent to special schools and that theirs was a permanent defect, though special education could help them to live with it. Burt did note that socioeconomic status was related to intelligence quotient, but he offered no interpretation of this relationship.

There may have been political reasons for not stressing what must surely have been Burt's position on the relation of nurture to the intelligence quotient. Burt worked for a public agency. He could not come out and say that the mentally handicapped, and the poor classes from which they were derived, were genetically inferior, even though he must surely have embraced that idea.

The years of World War I did not add to Burt's stature as a psychologist, for he was assigned most of the time to the Ministry of Munitions as a statistician. He admitted that his usual "exhaustive" style of reporting statistical data did not please those to whom he sent his reports. Winston Churchill returned one of Burt's reports with the comment, "The art of statistical reporting is that of picking out the plums" (See Burt's autobiography).

At the end of the war, Burt returned to his work at the London County Council, where he completed his book on tests. He also became involved in the new vocational guidance center at the National Institute of Industrial Psychology.

One should perhaps comment that the new vocational guidance center probably did not have either the empirical or the theoretical foundation needed for its work. There was no evidence that any of the tests and other instruments available predicted vocational success. There was a general theory that level of complexity of work should be related to level of intelligence, but this was only speculation. There were no interest tests available. Almost another decade would have to slip by before Clark L. Hull would write his general theory of vocational prediction in his remarkable book *Aptitude Testing* (1920). To some degree the art had to be developed in a practical situation.

Whatever scientific foundation the enterprise may have lacked, the Vocational Guidance Section of the institute prospered and clients were not lacking. Grant funds were obtained to discover the value of psychological vocational guidance, and the British Civil Service became interested in the use of psychological tests for selective purposes. However, one should note that no particularly significant publication emerged from this activity. One suspects that, like many other attempts to apply psychology, it survived on the enthusiasm of the proponents rather than on the impressiveness of the results. Burt did comment that the London County Council school people had considerable interest in the activity, so it was one more influence of Burt on the course of education.

Burt's work on the subnormal mind and the development of the English version of the Binet test was also accompanied by the slow accumulation of data on the delinquent. Burt was able to collect systematic data on delinquents because of the nature of his assignment with the London County Council school system. Cases were referred to him by teachers and the courts for what today would be called a diagnostic study. Burt systematized the entire matter of taking and recording case histories. His book reprinted the entire form used for the structured interview related to each case. In addition, Burt was able to administer to some of these children the intelligence tests that he had standardized on London children. He also obtained data on the home conditions of the child and the economic circumstances of the neighborhood. He established what he called the *poverty line*, a concept that he borrowed from Seebohm Rowntree. Indeed, the entire work on delinquency had a modern flavor to it, with a modern vocabulary and a modern set of methods of collecting data.

His general conclusion was that delinquency in youth was largely environmentally produced. This was a radical conclusion for his age. One must remember that the theory of the inheritance of criminality had been strongly reinforced in the early part of the century through the data published on the Jukes family, which supposedly demonstrated the tendency for criminality to run in families. Then, Henry H. Goddard published a similar case history on the Kallikak family. The case for the inheritance of what was referred to as moral deficiency was viewed as strong, for few ever questioned whether the Jukes and the Kallikaks were typical of families in which there was criminality.

Burt's position led to the conclusion that educational systems could do something about the young delinquent. The inheritance view of moral deficiency had taken the position that teachers could do little more than look out for the criminal type and be wary of those thus identified. The Burt position was that programs could be developed for handling the young delinquent. The Child Guidance Clinic was to play a central role in the management of the delinquent by setting up a program for each child that the school and other agencies would implement. The clinic was not expected to engage in therapy, for Burt did not see delinquency as involving basically a problem of psychiatric disturbance. Some delinquents needed to be treated for neurotic disturbance, but Burt believed that such treatment was more important for preventing the development of later psychotic behavior than in the treatment of the delinquency as such. Burt's beliefs accorded with the beliefs of the era of the 1920's. Burt believed in the value of psychotherapy and was a founder of the British Psychoanalytic Society, but he did not see psychoanalysis as a way of dealing with delinquency.

In 1926, Burt returned to the academic world when he was offered the professorship (the chair) of educational psychology at what was then called the London Day Training College. This was essentially a graduate-level teachers college run by the London County Council. A few years later the college was taken over by the University of London and became the major establishment in London for graduate training of teachers. It is now known as the Institute of Education. Burt moved his child guidance clinic to the college, where it became a part of the facilities for the training of teachers.

In 1937 he published the culmination of 30 years of work on the identification of what he called the subnormal child. The work was entitled *The Backward Child* (1937). This book ran into five editions, the last being published in 1961, when Burt was 78. The book explores the relationship of backwardness to an immense range of different variables. This exploration included such variables as height, weight, dentition, age of first eruption of a tooth, a large number of measures of physical condition, innumerable diseases, tests of motor capacity, left-handedness, measures of special intellectual abilities, tests of association, and so forth. Burt studied almost every conceivable condition that might possibly be related to intellectual functioning. Yet his thesis is very clear. In the first edition he concluded that over half the cases of backwardness in schools could be attributed to an inherited disability. In the fifth edition of the book he provided an even more encompassing statement of the influence of heredity, for there he stated quite clearly that between 60 and 70 percent belong in the category of those "innately dull." He concluded that "in the majority of cases the outstanding cause is a general inferiority of intellectual capacity, presumably inborn and frequently hereditary" (p. 572).

Burt's *Backward Child* (1937), and the work that led up to it, had great influence on education. The work established the use of special classes for the backward in the London County Council schools. This involved what Burt called "streaming." Burt tended to think of education as involving three streams of pupils, each with its own appropriate educational program. The three streams might be called, to use his terminology, the subnormal, the normal, and the supernormal. In the 1920's, just two streams were involved, but after World War II the London County Council put into effect Burt's entire program and introduced three streams, to correspond with Burt's three categories. American educators referred to this administrative practice as homogeneous grouping, but it was essentially the same plan and derived, in the first place, from Burt's theory of the nature of intelligence and the related concept of the constancy of the intelligence quotient. Burt seems to have been convinced, as were his American counterparts somewhat later, that the intelligence quotient was an immutable human characteristic, and streaming, or homogeneous grouping, was the way to handle individual differences in the intelligence quotient within an educational system. One must add as a footnote to the history of Burt's grand scheme for grouping pupils that in the London County Council schools it was a failure and was eventually abandoned. Intelligence, as it manifested itself within the educational system, was not the constant it was supposed to be. Great injustice was found to occur when pupils, at an early age, were assigned to a stream from which they could not easily escape. The streaming of the very backward children seems to have had more success, though even that has been called into question in recent years. In this area of applied psychology, as in so many other areas, premature applications can do an enormous amount of damage.

As Burt aged, he tended to attribute more and more of the causes of backwardness in the child to heredity. He also was equally adamant that superior ability was more a result of having the right genes than the right surroundings.

The idea that intelligence is basically an inherited characteristic, little influenced by variations in environmental conditions, became an idea as central to Burt's thinking as it had been to Francis Galton and Karl Pearson. Galton and Pearson had explored the implications in the area of genetics and eugenics. Burt explored the implications in relation to the school program, the development of special education facilities, and the certification of the mental defective, which was then undertaken by the British courts. He, like Galton and Pearson, outlined large social programs on the basis of only the most meager data concerning the inheritance of intellectual ability. Just how meager were Burt's data has been a source of considerable controversy, which will now be touched upon briefly.

In his later years Burt renewed his interest in data from twins which, he believed, were crucial for establishing the extent to which intelligence, as measured by tests, could be considered to be an inherited characteristic. The data were of world-wide interest to other psychologists and geneticists and were examined in the most minute detail. Burt published data as cases were alleged to be accumulated, and Burt acknowledged the help of two assistants, named in the articles, who were described as the persons responsible for the collection of the data. Although there are serious questions as to how the data should be interpreted, Burt took them to mean that inheritance played the central, major role in the determination of measured intelligence. Time and again in his writings, one finds the statement that special training may produce changes in scores on tests of achievement but that scores on intelligence tests remain remarkably constant.

A more detailed examination of the statistics provided by Burt has raised questions about the authenticity of the data themselves. There are odd facts as, for example, that after Burt added a substantial number of cases to his data, some of his correlations remained virtually unchanged -- a very unlikely happening. In order to resolve the doubts thus raised about the data, the assistants who were named as those involved in the collection of the data were sought, to see if they could provide explanations of the peculiarities. The search for the assistants had the strange outcome that the assistants could not be found. In a small country such as Great Britain, where affairs are conducted in an orderly way, people do not just disappear without questions being raised, and it was not just one assistant who had vanished, but two. The only person who could ever remember having seen one or the other of the assistants was the professor of psychology at Manchester, but the memory he believed he had was of a meeting of 30 years previous. Reporters from the press, who investigated the case, found that one of the assistants had written articles supporting Burt's position on the inheritance of intelligence and that these articles had been published in the *British Journal of Statistical Psychology.* At the time when the articles were published, the editor of the journal was Cyril Burt, and it was he who had made all decisions concerning the acceptability of the articles. The suspicion was further enhanced that the assistants had never existed, and this led to the even more serious suspicion that the data that Burt had stated to be the fruits of the labors of his assistants were a product of his imagination. There is no way of knowing for sure whether the latter conclusion is correct, but it is the most plausible conclusion at this time. This conclusion was arrived at not only by quite sober writers in the public press, but also by academicians who were very reluctant to come to that conclusion, because it raised questions about the integrity of their entire profession (see D. D. Dorfman, 1978).

Even if the damning conclusion is correct, Burt's early work stands as a great monument to how the psychologist can alter the course of education. Up to the time when he accepted the professorship at University College, no questions can be raised about the integrity of his work.

Burt's final publication was a volume entitled *The Gifted Child* (1975). This book was completed just before he died, but much of the material in it is derived from Burt's earlier publications. It represents a vigorous presentation of the position that he not only viewed backwardness to be an inherited condition, but that giftedness was also inherited. His position was essentially that of Francis Galton, suggesting that giftedness, like characteristics such as color blindness, ran in families and that particular combinations of genes predestined the individual to produce unusual accomplishments. In this last work he reviewed his data on twins, with some inexplicable inconsistencies in the table of correlations, inconsistencies which the editor pointed out could not be checked back against the original data since the data could not be found among Burt's papers.

In this small book, Burt proposed that special residential schools be developed for the gifted, who should not be bored with school materials provided for ordinary children. He cited some interesting anecdotes about the boredom of the gifted in ordinary classes in school and the remarkable effect of giving gifted children other, more challenging activities. Nevertheless, the book would not be a convincing one even if one did not suspect the authenticity of Burt's data. The book rehashes old and rather unconvincing data, and the strength of the argument is not enhanced by Burt's dogmatic conclusions. The book seems tied to a past era, but perhaps one can excuse an old man of 91 for wanting to reecho themes of his youthful career and to throw one final challenge at his growing number of critics. But Burt's era had passed and his message did not ring forth as a challenge, but as a voice crying weakly out of an earlier age, a message no longer of any great importance. A new age had dawned, in which it was recognized that the problems which Burt thought he had solved in such simple terms were known to be problems of great complexity which would take many future generations to solve.

THE DEBATE OF THE 1920's

The influence of Terman and Goddard on American schools was powerful and pervasive. Few questions were raised about the view that measured intelligence represented genetic endowment. The view that level of native intelligence endowed some to the extent that they could be leaders and others only to the extent that they could take orders and obey them on the factory assembly line was embraced by the affluent and the influential. Terman and Goddard seemed to give to those who wielded economic and political power a license to their positions and perhaps even a license to be ruthless. Plato had been used as a pillar to support this view through much of European history, but the new American civilization needed a scientific support. The new testing movement provided that support -- at least, many thought that it did.

Those who introduced intelligence tests into schools on both sides of the Atlantic were firm in the conviction that the tests measured native intelligence, and those who may have had doubts about such a position were hardly heard in the academic forum. Sooner or later, voices of protest and doubt were bound to be heard, for the concept of large native individual differences in intelligence was so contrary to traditional American thought that protest was bound to arise.

When the great wave of immigrants came to the United States towards the end of the last century and in the early part of the present one, the schools were viewed as the great equalizing institution. Whatever disadvantages a child might have suffered from being born of parents who did not even speak English, the school would erase these disadvantages so that all children might have equal opportunity in the land of opportunity. Within such a context, intellectual differences were viewed as transitory results of misfortunes of birth and not the result of differences in genetic endowment. The tradition of American education was solidly behind the position of basic intellectual equality of the majority of children in the schools.

In the early part of the century, the traditional doctrine of the common school had been challenged not just by an elitist group whose opinions could be brushed aside as so much prejudice, but by scientists in prestigious institutions. Furthermore, the views of the scientists seemed to be backed by voluminous quantities of data that most of the would-be critics did not even understand. The views of scientists were held in great prestige and tended to be accepted, because criticism of them was generally beyond the competence of the layman. Nevertheless, critics of the new doctrine of innate intellectual differences, and the implied doctrine of predestination, were to come.

The 1920's were marked by one notable attack on the new doctrine of the nature of measured intelligence. The main thrust of this attack came from the rising journalist Walter Lippmann, and was followed by a somewhat weaker confrontation by John Dewey. Lippmann wrote a series of six articles in the liberal publication *The New Republic*, which had an audience of intellectuals. Whatever impact the articles may have had, the impact was not on the schools, for *The New Republic* was hardly known among teachers and principals. Nevertheless, Lippmann's attack on the concepts underlying tests of intelligence must have had some long-term impact, for his articles are still read and cited 50 years later.

Lippmann began his attack on the growing intelligence-testing movement with an attack on a book by Lathrop Stoddard entitled *The Revolt Against Civilization: The Menace of the Under Man* (1922), in which Stoddard stated that the average mental age of Americans was only about 14 years. Lippmann pointed out that that was absurd, for the intelligence of an adult cannot be compared to that of a child. Lippmann stated that "the average adult intelligence cannot be less than the average adult intelligence" ("The Mental Age of Americans," 1922). Stoddard had used his conclusion to predict the downfall of civilization.

Lippmann pointed out that Binet had spent years wrestling with the problem of what constituted intelligence, and without too much success in pinning down the concept. Binet had then turned to the practical matter of developing puzzles that would differentiate the majority of children that Binet regarded as normal from a certain percentage that Binet regarded as backward. Lippmann was aware of the fact that the Binet tests not only had a weak theoretical foundation, but he also realized that the data on which the Binet scale was based were limited. Binet had used only 200 Paris schoolchildren as his standardization sample, and these had ranged from 3 to 15 years of age, and Binet had then died before continuing his work to a point where it would have had some solidity. Lippmann then pointed out that Terman had found the Binet materials unsuitable for California schoolchildren and had rearranged, edited, and supplemented the original Binet materials to produce his revision of the original Binet scale. Lippmann rejected the conclusion that the average American had a mental age of 14 was derived from a sample of 82 children tested 10 years previously, in 1913. He also pointed out that a larger sample of 400 adults had also been used, but that one could not tell how representative these adults were. A similar criticism was also raised concerning other samples. Lippmann then showed that although 1,700,000 men were tested in the army, these also were not representative of the adult population. In World War I, as in other wars, those who escaped the draft were different from those who were actually drafted. The most intelligent in terms of test scores as well as the most affluent are those who escape. Lippmann then considered the problem of converting the army scores into Binet scores, and presented devastating criticism of how this conversion was accomplished.

Although Lippmann conceded that Terman had developed a series of puzzles that differentiated one age group of children from another, Lippmann had doubts whether the guesses of the test-maker had any great validity. In the practical application of the Army Alpha test, validity was not a great issue ("The Mystery of the 'A' Men," 1922). The army wanted a device that would enable the authorities to identify 5 percent who could be put into Officer Training School. The test did this and seemed to have some scientific authority behind it. At the very least, the test selected those who could read, and the test eliminated both the illiterate and the severely mentally handicapped. The test was not designed to compare the intelligence of adults with that of children in various age groups, and to do that, as Stoddard had, was absurd.

The third article in the series, entitled "The Reliability of Intelligence Tests" (1922), was a discussion of the validity of the tests. The term *reliability* was commonly used in those days to refer to validity. In this article, Lippmann pointed out that virtually nothing was known at that time concerning the relationship between success in life and intelligence-test scores. Lippmann's own suspicion was that those who were good at intelligence tests were the individuals who had had experience in solving problems in the Sunday newspaper. He recognized that success on the tests was related to school success, but success in schoolwork was well recognized as having little relationship to success in life.

The fourth article in the series, "The Abuse of the Tests" (1922), is perhaps the most significant in the series. Lippmann expressed the fear that a child would be labeled, after an hour's testing, as a *C* child, or a *D* child, and would be treated accordingly for the rest of his school life. Lippmann referred to the literature on testing to show that this kind of thinking had already taken place. Certainly, the writings of Terman did seem to imply that an intelligence-test score indicated the role in life to which the individual was predestined. This led to the fifth article, "Tests of Hereditary Intelligence" (1922). As a first step, Lippmann disposed of the evidence provided by the Jukes family and the Kallikak family, which had been widely disseminated among educators as evidence that intelligence and degeneracy were inherited. Lippmann emphasized what is today obvious, that the apparent lack of intelligence and the degeneracy might well have been perpetuated in both families through the unfavorable circumstances in which the children of each new generation were reared. He made the significant suggestion that the early years of childhood might be of crucial importance to intellectual development, though Terman seems to have taken the opposite position, which was the popular position in his day.

The final article in the series, "A Future for the Tests" (1922), expressed the hope that psychologists would ultimately arrive at what Lippmann believed would be a more modest set of claims for the intelligence test. He correctly concluded that the test should be viewed as reflecting a mixture of native capacity, stored-up knowledge, and acquired habits, and that the intelligence examination was simply just another examination of what the individual could do at a particular time. Lippmann had doubts whether the test would ever be a useful means of classifying individuals, but he thought that tests measuring more specific abilities might have far greater value in occupational selection. The broad-spectrum intelligence test, he thought, should be abandoned in favor of instruments that measured more specific aspects of what an individual could do.

Terman must have been provided with advance copies of the Lippmann articles, for a month after the final article in the series was published, Terman's reply appeared in print ("The Great Conspiracy," 1922). Terman was a man of mild and quiet disposition, but the Lippmann articles must have engendered in him a deep and festering anger. He must have seen them as undermining the professional reputation that he had spent 20 or more years in building. He felt humiliated and, even worse, persecuted. In formulating a reply, he abandoned his usual calm, logical, and ever-inquiring disposition. He began his reply with a blast at Lippmann that was completely out of keeping with his usual quiet, academic approach to problems. Terman wrote that Lippmann was simply another William Jennings Bryan, unable to cope with the new scientific theories of a new age. In writing this blast, Terman was unconsciously comparing himself with Darwin, a comparison that was out of keeping with Terman's usual modesty. Terman wrote that the idea of intelligence testing had "hit the bull's-eye of one of Mr. Lippmann's emotional complexes" (p. 117), but it was Terman who was being emotional. Lippmann's criticisms were calm, inexorable, and persuasive; they lacked emotionality. Terman did not advance his case when he said contemptuously that "the validity of intelligence tests is hardly a question the psychologist would care to debate with Mr. Lippmann" (p. 117).

Terman's initial pages of vituperations were followed by an equal amount of space devoted to specific issues raised by Walter Lippmann. Terman defended the view that the average mental age of the draftee was about the 14-year level, implying that this conclusion was based on data other than those which Lippmann had cited. Terman did not answer the criticism that adult intelligence may not be at all comparable to intelligence in childhood. Terman firmly defended the position that measured intelligence represented inherited intelligence. Here again he accused Lippmann of being like William Jennings Bryan opposing evolutionary theory. Terman scorned the idea that teachers might misuse intelligence tests and dub a child as poor or mediocre on the basis of a 50-minute test. There was no such misuse of intelligence tests, he claimed. In this, Terman was undoubtedly wrong, for intelligence tests have been misused in that kind of way throughout their history, and still are. There are still, today, teachers who look at intelligence-test scores at the beginning of the year and then virtually decide what grade they are going to give a child at the end of the year. Terman ended his article with a discussion which had strong overtones of prejudice related to race and nationality. Terman stated that in California the Portuguese child carried "through school and into life" (p. 120) an intelligence quotient of only 80, despite a favorable nursery and kindergarten environment provided by the state. This intelligence quotient was compared with that of California children of Nordic descent and with Japanese children whose average intelligence quotient was 20 points higher. The implication was that the Portuguese were genetically inferior. Terman had apparently not taken seriously Lippmann's argument that the environment of the early childhood home was of crucial importance.

Lippmann replied in quite contemptuous terms both in a letter to *The New Republic* (1923) and in an article, "The Great Confusion" (1923). His replies added little to what had been said. Terman's position had been intellectually demolished.

The encounter failed to filter down into the schools. It received no mention in the major teacher publications of the age. The boom in the use of intelligence tests in schools expanded to mammoth proportions. Even after the great crash on Wall Street in 1929, the market for intelligence tests continued to grow despite a shrinkage in the publication of books. Devices that appeared to give almost instant answers to many questions that teachers raised were not to be dismissed by intellectual analysis, even though the analysis might come from one of the most remarkable minds of the era. Intelligence tests were now firmly rooted in the schools and were to remain so for several decades to come.

Lippmann's voice was not the only voice in the early 1920's that was to protest the ideas of the intelligence testers. John Dewey wrote two articles, presented in his difficult and often obscure philosophical style: "Mediocrity and Individuality" (1922), and "Individuality, Equality and Superiority" (1922). Dewey saw the work of intelligence testers as providing a pseudoscientific form of Aristotle's idea that some were born to be slaves and others, rulers. Intelligence testers added to this Greek notion that the differences discussed by Aristotle were innate. Dewey noted the claim made by some enthusiasts of the intelligence test movement, that only 15 percent of the population could profit from college and that this 15 percent constituted an intellectual aristocracy. Dewey saw these views as leading to a new caste system which, if widely embraced, would destroy our democratic system. Dewey argued that perhaps with new and improved teaching methods, most of the population might be able to profit from a college education, and that nothing was known about the limits to which human intelligence might grow even if differences as measured by intelligence tests were innate.

Dewey raised strong objections to the use of intelligence tests for classifying individuals. The use of broad classes obscured for him the possibility of looking at each individual as a unique member of society. Dewey was afraid that individuality would be completely lost if the vast majority of individuals could be placed in a class denoted as average. Such a class of average individuals would then be given a uniform education, by the worst methods available and for the purpose of producing a uniform class of factory workers. Even the designation of a superior class would lead to a uniform curriculum for the gifted. Dewey saw the goal of mental testing to be scientific rather than practical. He could not see intelligence tests as having any implications for the practical matter of schooling. He seemed to concede that in a distant future the testers might develop a very complex system of assessment which would treat each individual as an individual, but that goal could not be achieved through the use of a test of general intelligence. Dewey urged that educators devote themselves to producing changes in education within their control, that it was profitless for them to spend time contemplating innate differences over which they had no control. Although innate differences might set limits on what a person could achieve, those limits could not possibly be discovered until new educational opportunities were explored. The limits set by heredity might be far beyond anything so far contemplated.

The second article by Dewey began by stating that an industrial civilization subordinates education to gross social stratifications. The broad classifications of leaders and followers, management and labor, dominate industrial thinking. Dewey pointed out that even the concept of a leader cannot be reduced to a simple category. What the academician views as a leader is quite different from what the industrialist views as a leader. The standards applied in deciding whether a person belongs in the class of leaders depends upon who is making the decision. Judgments of the superiority of one race over another also depend upon the particular viewpoint of the person making the judgment.

Dewey protested the idea of an abstract, uniform standard of superiority, for superiority was always a concrete matter, an ability to perform some particular task with excellence. A dynamic society would be one which would continuously invent new tasks to be done and call for new combinations of ability. The alternative to such a society would be a static one, characterized by a caste system. A democratic system is far more than a society committed to universal suffrage, for it must also have a certain moral meaning denoted by the word *individuality.* Dewey described this as "aristocracy carried to its limit" (p. 26), in which each individual may be the one best suited to achieve some particular goal. The idea of uniform broad classes of individuals, within which each person is equal to every other, cannot be a part of a democratic society which has to recognize the great range of differences among human beings. Democracy should have as its chief concern the release of the distinctive contribution that each person can make.

Although Dewey was often cited in educational journals during the 1920's, his views on intelligence tests do not seem to have had much impact. His main influence in this respect seems to have been on the small but growing group of teachers, administrators, and academicians who became identified as a movement under the banner of *Progressive Education* in the United States and other banners in other countries. The ideas that Dewey had explored in these articles and in his other writings developed among the progressives an abhorrence of tests of intelligence, and often a similar abhorrence of testing in general. In the public schools at large, the conditions that Lippmann had feared were fast becoming a reality. Simplistic ideas, such as are involved in intelligence testing by the unsophisticated, were rapidly assimilated by the educational establishment, for such ideas seemed to provide easy solutions to very complicated problems.

Even after Lippmann had terminated his controversy with Terman, his interest in the use of intelligence tests continued. A year later he encountered Cyril Burt's *Mental and Scholastic Tests.* Lippmann mistakenly concluded that Burt was a moderate in his views of intelligence tests, and believed that he had found a testing expert whose views corresponded with his own. Lippmann probably looked over the Burt volume and found criticism of the Binet-Simon scale and jumped to the conclusion that Burt was critical of all general applications of intelligence tests. Burt was critical of the Binet-Simon scales, but because the materials included in them did not seem suitable for English children. In addition, Burt was no doubt interested in promoting his own tests. Burt was an egotistical man who was convinced that what he had to offer was superior to anything else available.

Lippmann devoted two articles to the Burt volume: "Mr. Burt and the Intelligence Tests" (1923), and "A Judgment of the Tests" (1923). The first of the two articles dealt with some of Burt's criticism of available intelligence tests, and particularly Burt's point that an intelligence test has to be designed with a particular locality in mind. Lippmann also cited a long quotation from Burt which said that scholastic attainment contributed to intelligence test scores. However, the quotation of Burt also emphasized that innate intellectual differences seem to be the main source of variation in intelligence test scores. Somehow, Lippmann overlooked the latter point, perhaps because he was overwhelmed by his happiness at finding a psychologist who admitted that intelligence tests were partly measures of scholastic attainment. A later quotation from Burt did suggest, however, that scholastic attainment may account for more of the variation in scores than innate intelligence. At that stage of his life, Cyril Burt was vacillating in his position. One wonders if Lippmann ever knew that Burt's final position was virtually identical with that of Terman.

The second article provides further suggestions that the view of Burt was moderate, and it may well have been at that stage of his career. Burt, rightly, did plead for the use of very comprehensive assessment procedures in evaluating any child, and this pleased Lippmann.

A final contribution to the series of articles came a month later in the form of an article by Edwin G. Boring, later to become famous as a chronicler of the history of psychology ("Intelligence as the Tests Test It," 1923). Boring must have been influenced by what was then the new trend in the use of operational definitions, stimulated by the work of the well-known physicist Percy Bridgman. Boring proposed that tests provided an operational definition of the term *intelligence* and that an operational definition was better than no definition at all. Boring proposed that the concept of intelligence was analogous to that of *power* in physics, which is defined as the amount of work that can be done in a given time. Boring did not expand on this analogy, which is probably a poor one. He accepted the idea that intelligence seemed to be largely predetermined by the age of 5, but left the question open as to whether that predetermination was due to a favorable early childhood environment or whether it resulted from the genes. Boring ended his article by urging that psychologists concentrate on collecting further observations and withhold inferences until they knew much more.

DISSEMINATING THE SCIENCE -- AND THE FAITH

The new concept of intelligence testing of the early part of the century was disseminated by the channels through which academic ideas have always flowed. Professors wrote books which were assigned as readings for students, and the students carried the new ideas to the schools. The journals read by teachers played some part in this dissemination, but probably a minor part. The journals could not train school personnel in the techniques of administering and scoring the new instruments. They could do little more than describe situations in which the instruments had been used in schools.

The new literature on measurement had begun with Edward L. Thorndike's *An Introduction to the Theory of Mental and Social Measurement* (1904). This was a theoretical book, few copies of which ever came into the hands of teachers. It dealt with statistical problems related to measurement and seems to have been influenced by the English school of statisticians represented by Francis Galton and Karl Pearson. Probably the only measurement enterprises in the behavioral sciences to which Thorndike had access were those of Cattell and the few other Americans interested in similar problems. Thorndike was no linguist and had no knowledge of German which might have brought him into contact with Emil Kraeplin and William Stern. Yet the Thorndike book was important, for it set the stage for the academic tone of much educational research that was to come, with its emphasis on statistics and lack of emphasis on psychological theory.

The first decade of the century was also marked by a proliferation of testing devices. Although the published test was a rare enterprise, psychologists and psychiatrists invented tests for research purposes and for the purpose of producing diagnostic procedures. The number of devices invented during this period is demonstrated by the extraordinary volume produced by Guy M. Whipple, a professor at the University of Michigan who had a central interest in educational reform. The volume was entitled *A Manual of Mental and Physical Tests* (1910). This volume provided 534 pages of description of tests that had been used for some purpose. Whipple provided directions for the administration of these tests and proposed that they be administered to schoolchildren in the laboratory and in the classroom. One can search through the hundreds of tests described in this manual and discover almost every form of test used today and many that are forgotten relics of the past. Whipple's manual had a long life, for it was reprinted, unchanged, in 1924, and was still used by students of psychology in the 1930's. Whipple himself does not seem to have been the kind of psychologist who gave tests to schoolchildren. His main interest, other than that of compiling test materials, was in the area of the development and use of phonetic alphabets, which were also in vogue at that time. In addition to the manual, his only other publication was *Relative Efficiency of Phonetic Alphabets. An Experimental Investigation of the Comparative Merits of the Webster Key Alphabet and the Proposed Key Alphabet Submitted to the National Education Association* (1911).

Whipple also has some claim to fame as the translator into English of William Stern's *The Psychological Methods of Testing Intelligence* (1914). The Stern volume probably did more to familiarize American students with the growing movement to measure intelligence than any other publication in the pre-World War I years. Stern's interest in individual differences had long preceded the invention of the Binet-Simon scale, for as early as 1900 he had published a monograph on individual differences, which he rewrote completely for a new 1911 edition. His work on methods of testing intelligence appeared in German in 1910, only 5 years after Binet had first published the work he had undertaken with Simon.

Stern's book on testing intelligence was a cautious, critical, and scholarly work. He viewed intelligence testing as a new method of psychological inquiry. He deplored the efforts of some to apply the new methods, all too hastily, to attempt solutions of practical problems. He scorned the legislation that had been passed in the State of New Jersey which required that the educational authorities give intelligence tests to all pupils suspected of backwardness. He could not share with Charles Spearman the vision that the day was soon to come when every child would be administered an annual and official determination of his intelligence. Stern also took issue with military men who believed that soon all army recruits would be given intelligence tests by mechanical routines by low-ranking soldiers. On the contrary, Stern was cautious in his views, and his book represents a notable attempt to bring to the attention of academicians the great research possibilities that were inherent in the new method of appraising intelligence.

The book had none of the pioneering enthusiasm of a Lewis Terman and neither did it display Terman's tendency, derived from his enthusiasm, to advocate widespread application. Stern stated explicitly in his book that "psychological tests must not be overestimated" (p. 12). Stern dealt at length with the problem of the selection of test problems, recognizing what one would call today the problem of developing a reliable test. A lengthy chapter dealt with the use of age scales and his proposal that intelligence be measured by means of a ratio of the mental age to chronological age which Stern called the *mental quotient.* Terman took hold of Stern's idea of a mental quotient, but he multiplied it by 100 for convenience and referred to it as the intelligence quotient. Others had been impressed by the correlation between intelligence tests and school marks, but Stern was more impressed with what he saw to be the relatively low correlations. This lack of agreement between the tests and school marks gave Stern confidence in the new devices. He took issue with his contemporaries in finding no evidence to show a relationship between moral deficiency and intellectual deficiency.

Stern discussed at length the problem of validating intelligence tests and believed that an external criterion of validity should be developed. He believed that teachers could provide good estimates of the intelligence of pupils in the elementary grades, if the teachers were properly trained to do this task. He thought that teachers could come to distinguish intelligence from academic performance. Teachers in the elementary schools were to be preferred for making these estimates of intelligence, since these teachers remained in contact with the pupil for the entire school day throughout the year.

Stern's book was a classic which did not have the impact that the book merited. It was no match for the impetuous enthusiasm that was so typical of the American educational world. It should have been a sobering influence, but it was not, for by the time it had reached the American market the stage had already been set for a massive intelligence-testing movement.

Although the growing literature on testing may have manifested some of the sobering thoughts of William Stern, the flood of new textbooks that appeared after World War I generally advocated the widespread use of tests in schools. Rudolf Pintner wrote what became a well-known text, *The Mental Survey* (1918). Sidney L. Pressey and Luella C. Pressey wrote *Introduction to Standardized Tests: A Brief Manual in the Use of Tests of Both Ability and Achievement in the School Subjects* (1922), and by the mid-1920's one could list at least another half-dozen texts in the area that had considerable impact on the new generation of teachers. The authors included such well-known academicians as William A. McCall (*How to Measure in Education*, 1922), and Walter S. Monroe (*Educational Tests and Measurements*, 1917). These books probably did not reach into schools in the way in which Terman's had, for they were designed for use in the training of teachers, and the expansion of teacher-training facilities within a college milieu had called for a new technical literature that the academicians were quick to produce.

Even compilations on the subject of intelligence testing promoted Terman's prevailing view. When the National Society for the Study of Education published its 21st yearbook in 1923, the yearbook stated clearly and explicitly that general intelligence was an "innate capacity measured by intelligence tests" (*The Twenty-First Yearbook: The Nature, History, and General Principles of Intelligence Testing*). The authors of the yearbook gave prestige to this view, for they were prestigious academicians. Their names included those of Edward L. Thorndike, Harold Rugg, Guy M. Whipple, and Henry W. Holmes. The yearbook explored the application of intelligence testing at all levels of education within the framework of a philosophy of predestination. The lengthy list of group intelligence tests prepared by Whipple for the volume indicates the magnitude to which the intelligence-testing movement had grown.

A literature also developed for the sophisticated academician interested in following development in the field of testing. The most notable publication in this field in the years just before and after World War I was the *Journal of Educational Psychology.* The story of this publication is a tale in itself. It was published by a Baltimore newspaper man, H. E. Buchholz, who had much to do with the founding of the journal and who kept a tight hand controlling it as long as he lived. Buchholz had started a small publishing firm named Warwick and York, which established a distinguished record for producing notable publications relevant to education. In this chapter we have already discussed Whipple's manual and Stern's classic work on intelligence testing, both of which were published by Warwick and York. The author once asked Buchholz, who were Warwick and York? He told me there were no such people but that he had taken the names for his publishing company because they looked so dignified on his letterhead.

Despite Buchholz's tight hold over the *Journal of Educational Psychology,* he did bow to the judgments of a distinguished editorial board. The original editors were William C. Bagley, who was then at the University of Illinois; J. Carleton Bell, well known in his day but today unknown; Carl Seashore, famous for his studies of musical talent; and Guy M. Whipple, whose other contributions have already been noted. From the beginning of the journal, and for the first 20 years of its existence, a major emphasis in the contributions published was on testing, and particularly intelligence testing. The journal was not particularly theory-oriented, for the early developers of tests were not as concerned with theory of measurement as are their present-day counterparts. The articles in the journal up to 1930 generally supported the idea that intelligence tests measured inherited ability. This is hardly surprising, for the most notable and distinguished contributors to the journal, including Edward L. Thorndike and Lewis Terman, took the nature side of the nature-nurture argument. The *Journal of Educational Psychology,* like most other journals, tended to present the popular scientific paradigms of the era and devoted little space to the critique of those paradigms or to alternative paradigms. Thomas S. Kuhn has discussed this feature of scientific literature in his volume, *The Nature of Scientific Revolutions* (1970). Thus, the establishment of the new emerging science of psychology spoke to itself, and to others, in terms which the establishment approved. There was little room for dissent in the most prestigious publication channels.

THE NEW SCIENTIFIC ESTABLISHMENT AND THE NEW RACISM

When the results of testing recruits in the United States Army in World War I were published, they were seized upon by many to bolster longstanding racial and nationalistic prejudices. The fact that what were then classified as Negroes scored lower than whites was taken to indicate that a dark skin was a sign of inferior native intelligence. Indeed, in the early part of the century a white person who proposed that the black was equal in intelligence to the white would have been viewed not just as unorthodox, but as one who could not see what to others was obvious. The fact that the Negroes in the army scored lower than the whites, on the average, came as no surprise. It was not even treated as a scientific finding, but was viewed as a demonstration of the obvious.

The prestige of the army tests was backed by the most eminent scientists in the field of psychology of the time. The *Committee on the Psychological Examining of Recruits* within the medical department of the army included such well-known names as Robert M. Yerkes, Walter V. Bingham, Henry H. Goddard, Lewis M. Terman, Guy M. Whipple, and the lesser known T. H. Haines and F. L. Wells. Other names connected with the enterprise were those of Robert S. Woodworth, Arthur S. Otis, and Edward L. Thorndike. Almost every person destined to become a luminary of the American psychological establishment in the 1920's was connected with the army testing program. Those among these luminaries who took sides on the nurture-nature issue related to the interpretation of intelligence tests were all on the side that emphasized the importance of inheritance. Hardly surprising was it that the army testing program was simply assumed to be the scientific basis for the view that the white was intellectually superior to the black. The findings were also taken to mean that certain national groups were intellectually superior to certain other national groups. Specifically, the army data bolstered the notion that the Anglo-Saxon stock was superior to that of most other nations, and particularly superior to members of Eastern and Southern European nations. The seeds of prejudice were deeply embedded in American culture, though they never bore such poisonous fruits as they did in Germany or Japan, but they were there and the new science of testing seemed to provide them a medium within which they could grow.

The detailed findings of the army psychological examining program were published as Volume 15 of *Memoirs of the National Academy of Sciences*. The volume was edited by Robert M. Yerkes and was designated by the title of *Psychological Examining in the United States Army* (1921). The volume is a massive historical document providing an immense amount of detail regarding the army program. The early part of the volume covers the history of the program and the administrative framework within which it was established. The last 350 pages represent an extraordinary compilation of tables of data with rather short statements of conclusions. The third section of the report summarizes the results of actual measurement. Apparently, even the trivial were not excluded, for there are massive summaries of differences in the measured intelligence of recruits in different camps. The report was as comprehensive as could possibly be produced in the age that preceded the high-speed computer, but the rather slow Hollerith machines from which the findings were ground out were vastly more rapid than the hand methods of earlier times. Such machines were able to generate vast quantities of tabulations, and they did.

The first interesting chapter in the results section of the report is the chapter on differences in measured intelligence of immigrants of different national origin. Differences were striking. The groups of immigrants with the highest measured intelligence were those from England, Holland, Denmark, and Scotland, all countries where most of the population speaks English either as a first or a second language. Lowest were the immigrants from Russia, Italy, and Poland, all countries where at that time English was rarely spoken and almost never was a second language. The report does not attempt to provide any interpretation of these data, but the English-speaking American reader in the 1920's would surely have jumped to the conclusion that the differences were a result of differences in native intelligence. Such a reader would have been prejudiced not only by the prevailing views of academicians, such as Lewis Terman, but he probably would have been raised in the tradition that the Anglo-Saxon was more competent than anyone else. When Congress came to write the *Emergency Quota Act* of 1921 and the *Immigration Act* of 1924, the data were persuasive in arranging immigration quotas so that they favored the Northern and Western nations of Europe and permitted only 20 percent of immigrants to come from the Eastern and Southern countries. The quotas were not set up in terms of the army data, but in terms of a complicated formula which produced exactly the same results. One psychologist who gave advice in connection with these acts was Edward L. Thorndike, who remained convinced for the rest of his life that the army data reflected basic and native intellectual differences in the various immigrant groups.

The chapter on "Intelligence of the Negro" is the longest in the entire report. Apparently, not only the army, but also the investigators were interested in the data. That the Negro tested far below the white is hardly surprising in view of the fact that at that time, of those Negroes drafted, a very high percentage were classified as illiterate. Schooling for the Negro in the South had often been for only 3 hours a day for less than 6 months in the year. Hardly surprising, in some examination centers, examiners complained that they could not persuade the Negro draftees to even attend to the test. Sleeping during the test sessions was common.

Attempts were made to give black recruits individual Stanford-Binet tests to check on whether the individuals should be regarded as genuinely of low intelligence. The results were interpreted to confirm the prevailing prejudices.

The army studies were of importance and had impact in that they were the first major studies of racial differences and were undertaken on a massive scale. Although the Yerkes report was cautious in the interpretation of the differences presented by the data, others who interpreted them were not. The results simply became integrated into the prevailing set of beliefs held by the Whites, and even held by many Blacks of the day, that the White race was the superior race. The effect on education was also pronounced, for those who argued for improving the education of the Black, and particularly the Southern Black, were met with the argument that the data showed that these could benefit little from schooling. When this was countered by the fact that the Northerners and better-educated Blacks had scores nearer to those of the Whites, the idea was advanced that the Blacks who immigrated to the North were of superior stock to those they left behind. The latter argument was not disposed of by scientific data until another 15 years had passed. More important an effect on education, and on the advancement of the Black people, was the fact that a generation of teachers were taught that they could not expect much of Black children, and did not.

Nevertheless, the academic community has a basic integrity. Although new discoveries may be hastily assimilated to current prejudices, sooner or later the academic community begins to question whether such an assimulation is justifiable. Slowly, very slowly, questions were asked. Does a bad early environment depress intelligence quotients? Do Eastern Europeans in their native lands also test lower than other nationals on intelligence tests? Does it make a difference, in taking a test, whether the test is given in one's home language or one's schoolroom language? These and other related questions began to be raised during the 1930's, but not until a generation of teachers had treated the Black as a person of inferior intelligence and had learned to classify children in terms of their national origins as equal to or lower than the Anglo-Saxon. It is hard to assess the damage and injustice that were done through the perpetration of these science-linked prejudices, but it must have been great since it involved ideas that permeated the training of teachers. Some children must have been classed as stupid just because they were Black, or Rumanian, or Sicilian. The prejudgment of children in schools has always been a problem. The new intelligence-testing movement accentuated that problem.

Not until the 1930's was there any notable challenge to the view that differences in intelligence test scores, whether for individuals or groups, reflected differences in innate ability. Those who came to question that position represented a small minority who were not taken seriously by the majority of psychologists. The author was then a young man who attended scientific meetings and listened to what the elder statesmen of the research profession in the behavioral sciences were saying. His impression was that the critics of what was considered the orthodox position were generally viewed with ridicule. At least, they were not taken seriously.

Sociologists, rather than psychologists, seem to have been the main challengers of the belief that racial differences in intelligence quotients reflected innate differences. The Department of Sociology at the University of Chicago was particularly active in this challenge, but leadership in the field seems to have been largely centered on Otto Klineberg (1899-), who spent much of a lifetime working on the issue. The details of these studies cannot be presented here, but they have been well summarized in a volume edited by Klineberg entitled *Characteristics of the American Negro* (1944). The significance of this volume, which cited mainly research conducted in the 1930's, is reflected in the fact that the book was reprinted in 1969, 25 years after the appearance of the original edition. More than a third of the book was written by Klineberg himself. He showed in his writing that he was particularly impressed with the mounting evidence that differences in the education received accounted for a large part of the differences in intelligence quotients of Blacks and Whites.

Klineberg, in one of the earliest studies of the problem, had shown that Black children migrating from the South to New York City tended to show increases in intelligence quotients as they remained in the New York City schools, which were vastly superior to any to which they had been exposed in the South. The intelligence quotients of these children tended to approach those of Whites, increasing by about a point in intelligence quotient for each year of Northern schooling, but the intelligence quotients of these children still did not reach those of white children. The remaining discrepancy could well be accounted for in terms of differences in home conditions and also in the lack of emphasis placed in the Black culture on speed of work. Speed was an important factor in most tests of intelligence of that era. Klineberg came to the obvious conclusion that most of the differences in measured intelligence between Whites and Blacks seemed to be derived from differences in educational opportunity and cultural conditions that gave Whites an advantage on speeded tests.

Later attempts were made to develop so-called culture-free tests. The idea of a culture-free test never became accepted, though that is what Alfred Binet had attempted to produce. Many thought that the idea of a culture-free test of intelligence was a nonsense idea, for how can one possibly measure intelligence except through the cultural setting that permits the exercise of intelligence? Are there experiences common to all children that provide universally familiar situations through which intelligence can be tested? These are issues that remain sources of controversy. Whether they can ever be resolved is an open question. Even less general questions seem to defy answers. For example, is a black child penalized when he is given an intelligence test in what is called standard English when the child speaks a dialect called black English?

Although the data collected in the 1930's seemed to provide logically persuasive evidence that differences between races in their performance on intelligence tests were a product of differences in experience, the evidence did much less to persuade than did political events of World War II. The Germans and Japanese both justified their actions in terms of doctrines of racial superiority, a doctrine which has been long established in their respective cultures. The wars forced on the American people a picture of the disastrous consequences of such doctrines. The world saw the picture of millions held subject, virtually as slaves, both in Europe and the Orient, and the slavery was justified by a doctrine of a master race. Once history had painted this vivid picture of inhumanity for all the world to see, there were few left willing to toy with the idea that some races, or some nations, were superior to others. The picture presented by Nazi Germany and Imperial Japan made the picture of racial differences painted by Francis Galton and Karl Pearson absolutely unacceptable to civilized peoples. Although, before the war, a majority of psychologists might have taken the position that whites were superior to blacks, the majority had abandoned that position by the time the war was over, not so much persuaded by the carefully collected evidence of sociologists and psychologists but by the persuasive power of history.

The book that Klineberg edited on the subject continued to have a distribution and an impact. New books on the subject rehashed the old evidence and had a strangely familiar flavor, but they now represented the majority opinion of academicians. When a psychologist appeared on the scene who argued that his data showed evidence of one race being superior to another, he tended to be treated as an outcast. Furthermore, Supreme Court decisions took the position that the apparent inferiority of the black was a result of unequal opportunity both in the schools and in the job market. The law required the people to think in terms of equalities.

Now let us return to consider the foundation on which the doctrine of racial inequality was based. This foundation was the idea that the intelligence quotient was based on the original nature of the germ plasm which predestined the individual to operate at a certain intellectual level throughout his life. During the 1930's, attempts were made to attack this foundation. The point of departure for these new studies was the fact that children had been tested and retested with intelligence tests and the data had tended to support the theory of the constancy of the intelligence quotient. Not that it was always completely constant. Terman's sample of gifted children, when retested, had tended to move closer to the mean.

This was, of course, the phenomenon of regression, which was hardly recognized during the 1920's, let alone understood. The critics of the doctrine of the constancy of the intelligence quotient took the position that the intelligence quotient would not be expected to change if the social and cultural circumstances did not change. The critics sought situations in which the effect of special educational and cultural advantages could be studied.

Beth L. Wellman (1895-1952), of the Iowa Child Welfare Research Station of the University of Iowa, conducted one of the most impressive attacks on this problem. Wellman had access to the children in the pre-school conducted by the Iowa Child Welfare Research Station and also to the children in the demonstration school conducted by the College of Education. The data showed that substantial gains were made in these relatively superior students while they were in the university school, but when they transferred out no further gains were made, even though the original gains were largely maintained. Wellman argued that the conditions for intellectual development provided by the university schools were exceptionally fine. She argued that typical schools did not permit children to raise the intellectual level at which they functioned, and were responsible for producing the data used to support the doctrine of the constancy of the intelligence quotient. Wellman argued that the intelligence quotient represented the intellectual level at which a person was functioning and that the level of functioning could be improved by exposure to a good learning environment.

Beth Wellman's lengthy paper, "Growth in Intelligence Under Differing School Environments" (1934), summarizes the series of studies undertaken over a period of more than a decade starting in about 1925. The research represents one of the most impressive series of studies of that era, but how were they received?

The elders of the profession discussed the studies at professional meetings and in classes and seminars. The typical response was one of incredulity. Critics said that there must be something wrong with the research. The suggestion was commonly heard that the results must surely be the result of either the regression-to-the-mean phenomenon or some other source of artifacts. The latter suggestion came particularly from those who had not actually read the studies, for a reading of them would show that regression towards the mean could not possibly have generated the data. The suspicion was sometimes voiced that the university school must surely have been training the children to pass specific items on the tests of intelligence by which they were assessed. Wellman was probably much too capable an investigator to have let such a possibility slip by. Wellman was a person of integrity, for whom scientific honesty was of the greatest importance. The criticism of the work of Wellman generally failed to hit the studies themselves, but hit at the research worker herself. The line of thinking of Beth Wellman was outside the accepted paradigm of her times, and she died without her work ever receiving proper scientific recognition though it did create waves on what had previously been a very still ocean.

Although the testing establishment placed little emphasis on the studies of Wellman, professors of education and some individuals more closely connected with schools did begin to wonder whether the doctrine of the constancy of the intelligence quotient could be maintained. The studies did sow seeds which slowly grew and led to a great amount of skepticism concerning the idea that the basic intelligence of a child could not be changed, but it was not until several decades later that the idea of the trainability of intelligence found a real champion.

BEYOND THE PUBLIC DEBATE -- NEW ATTEMPTS TO EVOLVE A SCIENTIFIC CONCEPTION OF INTELLIGENCE

The public debate on the nature of the intelligence quotient was to continue far into the present century, but one should note that it had little impact on the use of intelligence tests in schools. The tests seemed to provide easy solutions to complex problems, and school people were little impressed with arguments about whether the tests really did provide the solutions their proponents claimed them to have. The schools were also little influenced by the questions raised by academicians concerning whether intelligence could be represented usefully by a single score or whether intelligence was multifaceted and called for tests which measured separate aspects of intelligence. Those raising these important new issues were academicians who worked in ivory towers remote from the schools. Among them there was no Terman, equally at home with academicians and with schoolteachers and principals.

The first psychologist to raise serious questions about whether intelligence should be considered a unitary adaptive capacity was Charles Edward Spearman (1863-1945), who was professor of psychology at University College, London, from 1911 to 1931. Spearman has an interesting place in the history of the measurement of intelligence in that he spent the first 14 years of his adult life as an army officer. He retired from the army in 1893 and then, for the next 10 years, spent intermittent periods working with Wilhelm Wundt. He completed his doctoral degree at Leipzig.

Spearman adopted a typically Wundtian approach to his study of intelligence. He sought to establish general laws that would account for intelligent human behavior. Alfred Binet had tried to do this in work undertaken long before he attempted to produce a test of intelligence.

Spearman had considerable mathematical knowledge and began to apply mathematical, and specifically correlation methods, to the study of the interrelationship among measured intellectual abilities. He saw that if two variables were intercorrelated, then the degree to which they were correlated represented a common factor, but that each of the two tests also represented a factor that was specific to each test alone. Spearman concluded from his study of the intercorrelation of test scores that there was a common factor *G* that ran through all tests of intelligence. Thus, intelligence consisted of an overall general factor *G* and a large number of specific factors. The relative influence of the specific and the general factor varied from task to task.

One should note that Spearman had to be quite selective in what he included in his test battery to be able to show that it involved a single general factor *G*, and specific factors, one of which characterized each test. Not all batteries of tests permitted this interpretation. He justified his selection of tests on the basis that the tests all fitted his psychological theory of the nature of intelligence. He appeared to feel no need to demonstrate that *G* represented the capacity of the individual to cope intelligently with life's daily problems, once he had proclaimed *G* as the sovereign factor of intellectual life. The coronation of *G* as the sovereign of the intellect seemed to remove any further need to demonstrate its power.

Those who knew of Spearman's military background said the model of the *G* factor with a large number of *S* factors was built after the image of a general and his troops. Be that as it may, one should note that a much clearer influence on Spearman's work was that of Wundt. Just as James McKeen Cattell built his tests in terms of many of the ideas that he had acquired from Wundt, so too did Spearman. His test items represented the kind of simple thought operations that might have been studied in Wundt's laboratory, based on either simple geometrical forms or word relations. Spearman was highly cognizant of the history of the psychology of thought and what had been said about the nature of intelligence and problem-solving. Spearman attempted to identify the *G* factor in intelligence with certain forms of mental operations.

What Spearman had to say about *G* and *S*'s was not taken to have any particular implications for education. Those who were measuring general intelligence in schools identified what they were measuring as *G*.

The next major development in the area came through the work of Louis Leon Thurstone (1887-1955), originally trained as an engineer at Cornell University. Thurstone served for a short time as assistant to Thomas Edison, and then completed a doctoral degree in psychology at the University of Chicago, where he spent most of his time from 1924 until he retired in 1952. His work focused on mathematical theories of learning and abilities, and showed the dominant effect of his engineering background. He was not interested in developing the kind of theory of the nature of intelligence that Spearman had attempted, but his emphasis was on mathematical analysis. This led him to view intelligence not as consisting of an overall *G* factor energizing specific *S*'s, but rather as consisting of a set of independent components. Thurstone set himself the task of identifying what he referred to as the primary mental abilities, and he produced a set of aptitude tests based on this analysis. The primary mental abilities included such factors as verbal meaning, space, reasoning, number, word fluency, and perceptual speed.

Thurstone viewed the "factors" he had discovered as quite basic elements in behavior and on several occasions expressed the opinion that he anticipated these elements ultimately would be shown to be determined by particular genes and inherited along Mendelian lines. There was, of course, absolutely no evidence to support that point of view, but it fitted Thurstone's conservative view of society and his upper-middle-class values.

Thurstone was not particularly interested in demonstrating how the "factors" thus discovered functioned in the life of the individual, and thus his tests included little information with respect to practical validity. He felt no more obligation to show that the factors were important components of intelligence in a real world than the chemists of his age felt an obligation to demonstrate that new elements discovered were important elements. The factors, like the chemist's elements, were believed to be real components of a real world, and whatever constituted the real world was important.

The Primary Mental Abilities Test battery was never a success in schools and had only limited use. School guidance workers, counselors, and administrators assumed a pragmatic position that Thurstone and his tests lacked. School people wanted to know what the tests predicted and would not accept the tests as just measuring basic components of the intellect. Although the schools were not willing to accept the tests, the ideas on which they were based had far-reaching impact on aptitude-testing programs in the armed services. Elementary schools in particular remained tied to the concept of the intelligence quotient and to the notion that intelligence could be designated by a single measure.

Towards the end of the period covered by this volume, secondary school guidance workers began to have doubts about the value of a single global measure of intelligence, though they were unwilling to embrace Thurstone's approach to the development of a theory of intelligence. An approach that was much more impressive to them was that of assembling groups of aptitude tests which had had a history of predicting academic success and, to some much smaller degree, success in other activities. In the late 1940's, the Psychological Corporation began to assemble such a battery for use with high school adolescents and adults. The resulting battery, the Differential Aptitude Tests, gained widespread acceptance with high school students. The pragmatic approach appealed to high school personnel, who liked the practical approach. The Differential Aptitude Tests were strictly American in design. The pragmatism underlying their design assured their acceptance.

We cannot fully review here the various models of intelligence produced by psychologists in the first half of the century, but mention must be made of the model of Joy Paul Guilford, based on a factor structure, in view of the fact that it was seen as a basis for curriculum design. At least his model was mentioned in books on curriculum design, even though the Thurstone model was not. The appeal of Guilford's model seems to have been the fact that it made some provision for creative aspects of intelligence, aspects of intelligence to which educators have long been attached. However, a model of intelligence that involved 120 components was too complicated to survive long in the educational arena of controversy, for practical people need quite simple models as guides to their activities.

While attempts to partition intelligence were in progress, and with varying degrees of impact on the schools, a strictly nonpragmatic approach was being developed by Jean Piaget. The nature of Piaget's approach to psychology was such that it ensured that it would not be readily understood by practically oriented Americans. Nevertheless, we have to note here that Piaget's views on the nature of intelligence were virtually fully formed by the late 1940's, as is evident from his book *The Psychology of Intelligence* (tr. 1950). Only later, when practical implications of his work had become evident, was attention paid to his work by educators.

LESSONS FROM THE PAST AND THE FUTURE

The story outlined in this chapter provides lessons for the future. Indeed, few chapters in the history of educational research provide so many lessons that can be used to guide future enterprises.

The judgment of the author is that a century of work on the development of tests of intelligence and related devices had made, on the whole, a positive contribution to education. The problem of making an overall evaluation of such devices presents the same difficulties that are involved in making an overall evaluation of the impact of the products of pharmacology. Most would agree that we are better off today with the medicines that have been developed than we would have been without them. One can point to the millions of lives that have been saved through the use of antibiotics, but questions may be raised as to whether such benefits are not negated by the long-term disastrous effects of other drugs, such as the carcinogenic effect of estrogen compounds. Medical opinion and even those outside the medical profession seem to be agreed that the good that has been achieved far outweighs the harm that has been done. There also seems to be agreement that there is no way of fully testing a new drug before it is put on the market. Technological advance in medicine, as in other areas, involves taking a certain amount of risk, and there is no way of eliminating that risk.

The introduction of tests, like the introduction of medicines, involves some risks that could not have been evaluated in advance. The development of intelligence tests provided means of measuring the intellectual level at which a child is functioning at a particular time. This has been a useful thing to do. Misuses of intelligence tests came about largely through linking their development to the view that the social class structure of society was a result of genetic stratification. The concept of the innate superiority of the upper crust of society has had a long history, going back several thousand years, at least to ancient Egypt where the belief developed that only royalty could produce in progeny the characteristics required of royalty. This doctrine was later expanded to the aristocratic classes who, for the same reasons, did not permit marriage outside the caste, lest the stock become adulterated with less worthy traits. Social Darwinism expanded this genetic view of class structure to the bourgeoisie and emerging middle class. The development of intelligence tests appeared within this late-nineteenth-century philosophical framework and had great difficulty in extricating itself from that framework.

Over the century of work that has been undertaken on the psychological measurement of intelligence, great progress has been made in moving from a position in which test scores were interpreted in terms of an elitist philosophy to a position where verified empirically based theories would be the basis for interpretation. The latter are not yet in sight, but there is now a healthy willingness to keep an open mind on the major issues.

The scientific problems related to the nature-nurture controversy are not likely to be solved easily. There are no easy solutions, and theory related to those solutions is still in its infancy. We are still far from even identifying the conditions under which the human intellect functions effectively. We do not know, for example, why only rare periods of human history have been periods of great intellectual progress. Although the human brain seems to have existed in its present form for at least a half-million years, we do not understand why it was not used to maximum effectiveness in producing civilizations until after the end of the last ice age. Some hold the opinion that it required a half-million years of cultural development to lay the groundwork for the early civilizations of the Euphrates valley, a very unlikely theory. Others believe that only under certain environmental conditions will the human intellect flourish, and that those conditions did not exist before the last ice age. Then, again, we even know little about how poverty can depress the functioning of the intellect not through poverty as such, but the concomitants of poverty.

New work on theory of evolution also has important implications for our understanding of the modifiability of intelligence. The evidence that the human brain has not changed in the last half-million years comes from studies of reconstructed cranial cavities based on fragments that have survived and which now can be properly dated. The function of the brain may have changed radically, even though its form remained uniform. Until recently the latter was considered to be unlikely because scientists believed evolution was a very slow process, hence brain function probably has not changed in the last half-million years. We now know that major evolutionary changes can take place within relatively short periods of time and perhaps no more than the time needed for 10 generations to reproduce. New theories of evolution, such as has emerged through the work of such scientists as P. A. Weiss and C. H. Waddington, emphasize the dramatic genetic changes that can take place in quite short time spans. Such research raises questions about the way in which our schools and other institutions may be contributing to the evolution of human intelligence. Although we have completely abandoned the differential birth rate, across classes, as a cause of slow genetic changes in the population, there are new possibilities that have to be explored. But as we explore, we must exercise a caution in promoting our ideas, a caution absent from past generations, until our ideas have a far more solid basis than they have today. In the meantime, intelligence tests can be used effectively in schools, provided they are used cautiously and not tied to any particular genetic or social theory.

PART III

The American Science of Behavior and Its Focus on Teaching and Learning

The events covered in Part II of this book show the development of a technology of measurement to assist in quite practical problems related to teaching. The emerging technology had a minimal contact with the work of established scientists, and must be viewed as largely the work of practical men, concerned with the solution of practical problems. There were, of course, exceptions. The work of Alfred Binet on intelligence went far beyond the mere development of a technology, and so too did the work of Lewis Terman, but the work on aptitude measurement in the schools was more closely tied to the philosophy of social Darwinism than to any scientific theory of behavior.

In contrast, Part III of this book describes work firmly rooted in scientific research, and based on attempts to develop a scientific theory of how children learn. The end of the last century was a time ripe for this development. Harris, as Commissioner of Education, had publicized through his *Annual Reports* scientific work that seemed to have implications for education. The *American Journal of Education* during its long years of publication 1855-1882 had set new standards of scholarship in educational literature, and had emphasized the importance of empirical inquiry. During the same period, American teachers began to receive some professional training that made them receptive of new ideas. Some may even have come to understand that the work of Maria Montessori had a scientific foundation. As the nineteenth century approached its closing decade, powerful forces had produced a high degree of receptivity on the part of educators to new ideas, and particularly scientific ideas.

Receptivity of educators to scientific ideas at the turn of the century, must also have been a reflection of the widely held view that scientists would soon solve all the problems that humanity encountered. Those who lived in the nineteenth century viewed science as the means of transforming the World into a paradise. Only a very few had reservations concerning the limits of what science could accomplish. When the work of scientists began to be extended to the study of the individual and society, the expectation among educators was that some of the fruits of that work would transform and revitalize the educational system. Just as physiology, chemistry and physics had provided a scientific basis for medicine, so now would the new sciences of human nature provide a scientific basis for education. Optimism concerning what these new sciences could accomplish reached its peak in the first quarter of the present century. Expectations were far beyond any that today would seem reasonable, and later disillusionment was inevitable.

The chapters in this part of the book describe and discuss a period of educational research that today looks like a golden age. They cover a period when scientists, school administrators and teachers alike, were all energized by the greatest enthusiasm for what they believed research, related to education, could accomplish. The chapters cover some of the most important years in the history of educational research, and years of great achievement as well as great expectations.

EDWARD L. THORNDIKE

Photograph courtesy of Columbia University

CHAPTER 5

The Thorndike Sphere of Influence

Perhaps no psychologist has ever had greater impact on education than Edward L. Thorndike (1874-1949), but to understand that impact, one has to understand the particular circumstances under which Thorndike lived and worked. The impact of Thorndike on American education is closely associated with the rise to fame of Teachers College, Columbia University. If Thorndike had not been caught in the light of the rising star of Teachers College, he might have had only indirect impact on education, and his fame might have been primarily as an experimental psychologist who worked with animals. The evangelistic role of the then newly founded Teachers College exercised a special power over the professional future of the young Thorndike.

THE NEW SPIRIT AT TEACHERS COLLEGE

The history of the early days of Teachers College has been written in vivid and colorful terms by Lawrence Cremin and his associates, *A History of Teachers College, Columbia University* (1954). These authors identify three individuals who have to be considered as the creators of Teachers College as an institution. These were Grace Hoadley Dodge, Nicholas Murray Butler, and James Earl Russell. These founders gave Teachers College its distinctive character and a special position of renown on the American educational scene.

Although Cremin *et al.* paint first a portrait of Grace Dodge, our point of departure here is Nicholas Murray Butler whose link with thought about education is much more clearly defined than that of Grace Dodge.

Nicholas Murray Butler (1862-1947) came from an educated family and received his college education from Columbia College. He later earned a doctorate in philosophy from Columbia in 1884. Like many young undergraduates of his day, Butler came into contact with the president of Columbia, Frederick A. P. Barnard. It was not uncommon in those days for the president of a college to know personally the students in his college and, in many colleges, the president interviewed each student for admission. Barnard introduced the young Butler to some of the standard works on pedagogy of the time. He also made him familiar with the work of Henry Barnard and Horace Mann. Even before Butler had graduated from Columbia College, he saw before him a career that embraced both philosophy and education. President Barnard had long sought to establish a chair of pedagogy at Columbia but had been opposed both by the trustees and by the faculty. After graduation, Butler spent a year in Europe studying in the Universities of Paris and Berlin. Such a year abroad was common for American students since graduate programs had hardly begun to develop in American universities. He returned to Columbia as a teaching assistant in philosophy. There he immediately distinguished himself by giving Saturday morning lectures on education to packed audiences of teachers. The success of the lectures encouraged President Barnard to once again propose to the trustees that a chair of pedagogy be established, but once again the trustees turned him down. Two main arguments were used to quash the proposal. One was that there was no local interest in the subject matter, though the lectures of Butler had shown that there was, and the other argument was that the teaching of courses on pedagogy would bring women into the college.

The rejection by the trustees seems to have goaded Butler into searching for other means of developing a professional school of education. Butler had been active in an organization known as the Industrial Education Association and, when he was elected to the presidency of the organization, he saw this as an opportunity to align the Association and its resources behind a plan to develop a program for the training of teachers. The Industrial Education Association was dedicated to the preparation of teachers in manual and industrial work. The Association was the focus of a movement that sought to make education more practical and to guide it away from the formal discipline that was the aim of the subject matter that had been brought into education during the last half of the nineteenth century. The making of education more practical was an interest of Butler, yet his interest in education was far broader and far more profound.

The objective of the Association became that of developing the New York College for the Trainig of Teachers. The Industrial Education Association seems to have merged into the College when it was founded in 1887. Two years later the College received its provisional charter as a professional school. Cremin *et al.*, describe the charter as giving the college the right to give instruction in (p. 22) "the history, philosophy, and science of education, psychology, in the science and art of teaching, and also in manual training and the methods of teaching the various subjects included under that head." The emphasis on manual training gave the Industrial Education Association a firm foothold in the enterprise.

One should note the odd paradox that a professional philosopher, such as Nicholas Murray Butler, should have been so interested in promoting manual training. He was not just interested in the Association because of the opportunity it provided for the development of a program for the training of teachers, but his interest in manual training was a genuine one. He wrote articles on the subject and was one of the leaders of those who believed that the school should teach children practical arts related to earning a living. Some moderns would interpret Butler's interest in the manual arts as bourgeois, that is to say the kind of interest that the middle class person has in ensuring that others will be trained in the less intellectually exacting work of the world. There may well have been a tinge of this in his behavior, but Butler saw that education involved far more than the mere acquisition of a trade. Butler was at heart a scholar and familiar with the ideas of Comenius, Pestalozzi, Herbart and Froebel. His time spent in Europe had given him a vision of a new emerging education, and when he came to design an American program for the education of teachers, the basis of that program was going to be the best thinking that could be found in German pedagogical literature, (see Richard Whittemore, *Nicholas Murray Butler and Public Education*, 1970).

Nevertheless, Butler's primary tie to the Industrial Education Association was through this interest in manual training. As a conservative young man he found in the Association those who shared his conservative views. Oddly enough when Butler came to write his autobiography, *Across the Busy Years* (1935), he does not mention this early preoccupation with manual training and the training of workers for factory jobs, in which he invested much of his youthful energy. With Butler, as with so many other academicians of his generation who sought to reform education, the reforms were closely tied to personal social philosophy.

The efforts of Nicholas Murray Butler would have achieved little had it not been for the presence of a lady of immense influence, Grace Hoadley Dodge, who shared the vision of a professional school for the training of teachers. Cremin *et al.*, describe Grace Dodge (p. 10) as a "gracious example of Christian philanthropy and social humanitarianism." She had been raised in a wealthy New York family that had for several generations cherished an interest in human welfare. Grace Dodge must have learned at a young age that family wealth, and later her wealth, was to be considered as a trusteeship. She proved herself to be a worthy trustee. We must here gloss over her work in connection with settlement houses and organizations for working girls, and turn to her work connected with education. There came a stage in her life when she no longer felt comfortable in the development of working-class organizations, for those with which she had become most closely associated had become tied to the emerging labor movement and these new ties made Grace Dodge an unlikely sponsor.

Her first excursion into educational development was through a tie with the Kitchen Garden Association, an oddly named organization that promoted the idea that the early education of children could be assisted through the development of materials that children could use similar to those which their parents used. The Kitchen Garden movement was a revolt against the abstract materials that had been developed by the Prussian Kindergarten movement. The Kitchen Garden movement was also a revolt against the idea-oriented education of the last century that shunned the manipulation of meaningful materials. Grace Dodge gave herself to the promotion of this movement for educational reform. When the Kitchen Garden Association had its purposes expanded and changed its name to the Industrial Education Association, Grace Dodge was there playing a central and important role.

Grace Dodge was able to raise the money necessary for the Association to obtain substantial space in which it could locate its activities and promote practical activities in educational programs. Her greatest achievement in the development of the Association was in raising money so that a full-time president of the Association could be employed on a salaried basis. Such an individual today would be described as an executive secretary rather than as a president. Such an executive is responsible for running the affairs of the organization and promoting its causes. Grace Dodge understood the importance of employing such an individual for she was a person of considerable competence in affairs of management and if she had lived in modern times would have been a business executive. She also realized that the executive officer of the Association would have to be thoroughly competent both as a manager and a developer of ideas. She was able to persuade her friend, George W. Vanderbilt, to supply money for the salary of such an executive and even more important, identified Nicholas Murray Butler as the man to fill the job.

Butler was then Associate Professor of Philosophy at Columbia College. He was only 25. The opportunity must have aroused his spirit of adventure. Perhaps the thought of spending a life teaching philosophy at Columbia lacked appeal. Whatever the attraction of the new position may have been, it offered Butler a chance to try his hand at creating an institution, an activity for which he had a rare talent.

The professional school that Butler sought to create was initially said to be represented by three *M*'s, which stood for "Moral, Mental, Manual," but despite the fact that he had published at length on the importance of manual training, he sought to make the new school a thoroughly professional enterprise. The new school, named the New York College for the Training of Teachers, was created in 1887 with a faculty of three, but rapidly expanded. Butler was almost a compulsive writer of articles about everything he did, and the first few years of the college saw him write numerous articles which stressed the need for teachers to understand educational theory and to learn to apply it in the classroom with the help of a qualified supervisor. The new institution soon was granted a charter to confer the degrees of Bachelor of Pedagogy, Master of Pedagogy, and Doctor of Pedagogy.

The New York College for the Training of Teachers was a completely independent institution, but Butler maintained his connection with Columbia College and in 1890 was selected as Dean of the new Faculty of Philosophy at Columbia. Butler also played a significant role in the transformation of Columbia College into Columbia University. Only the enormous energy of Nicholas Murray Butler made it possible for him to be both President of the teacher training college and, at the same time, hold a key position on the Columbia campus, but the time came when he had to choose between the two positions. He chose Columbia, a decision that turned out to be of vital value to the future of the New York College for the Training of Teachers. From his vantage point at Columbia University, Butler was able to influence the development of ties between Columbia and the new teachers college. By 1892 plans were well on the way for the association of the two institutions. The trustees of the Training College bought land on 120th street in New York City at the same time that Columbia University was buying the 22 acres on the other side of the street. The two purchases, made roughly within the same time span, were no coincidence.

The new building for what was to become Teachers College was opened in the Fall of 1893, but was not ready for use until a year later. The appearance of a new building on a beautiful site, and fully paid for through the energetic fund-raising efforts of Grace Dodge, seems to have persuaded Columbia that a tie to the new institution would be profitable for both institutions. An agreement was reached between the two Boards of Trustees by means of which Columbia came to grant the degrees offered by Teachers College (the new name it had acquired under its new charter).

The next few years were years of struggle for Teachers College, and years through which it would not have survived except for the capacity of Grace Dodge to find money at crucial times. The school had grown out of the Industrial Education Association that had had widespread support from industrialists, but, as Teachers College sought to become a graduate school of education, the industrialists began to voice their suspicion of the academicians who ran the new programs. Graduate courses on pedagogy were a far cry from the emphasis on manual training that the industrialists had been so willing to support. At the height of the crisis, the president, Walter L. Harvey, resigned, leaving a vacancy which could not be filled without struggle and controversy. The story of the struggle has been well documented in the papers of Nicholas Murray Butler and other sources. It is sufficient to say here that the upshot of the search and conflict was the appointment of a staff member of Teachers College to fill the presidency. That staff member was James Earl Russell (1864-1945). However, before looking at the Russell era let us consider further the intellectual climate that Nicholas Murray Butler had created in the field of professional education for teachers.

Nicholas Murray Butler, during his years with the New York College for the Training of Teachers, had made a considerable effort to encourage the development of a professional literature in the field of teaching. His travels in Germany had exposed him to the German literature in the field. He was also aware of Henry Barnard's magnificent publication, the *American Journal of Education.* In 1890 Butler founded the *Educational Review,* which he continued to edit until 1919. The *Educational Review* was born of the tradition established by Henry Barnard. Henry Barnard's journal had expired in 1882, and no publication had filled the gap that its expiration had left. Butler's new journal filled that gap and it became the medium through which he expressed his views on educational policy. The tone of Butler's journal was close to that of Barnard's. While Barnard might have published an article on the recent developments of the kindergarten in Prussia, Butler might have had an article on the then new Prussian educational system. Both journals attempted to bring to their readers the innovations in education that were taking place across the industrialized world. Each presented, in its own way, the new lines of thought related to pedagogy that were emerging. In the first few volumes of the *Educational Review* one can find articles by such well-known contributors as John Dewey, Josiah Royce, James Mark Baldwin, William Torrey Harris, Joseph Jastrow, and James Sully. The galaxy of authors with dazzling reputations gave the impression that the problems of education were, at last, being studied by the finest minds, and, indeed, they were. The extraordinary success of the journal, together with the prestige of its young and already distinguished editor, must have encouraged many in the academic world to take note of the new and emerging discipline of pedagogics, and to encourage some to make a contribution to this new field.

The *Educational Review* also took note of the developing research in the behavioral sciences, although the early issues tended to emphasize the psychology of Herbart, which still exercised an immense influence on education. There was some recognition of the new experimental psychological science.

NICHOLAS MURRAY BUTLER

Photograph courtesy of Columbia University

Although most of the material in Butler's *Educational Review* was analytical and historical, there were also articles that gave recognition to the growing body of research relevant to education. Thus, one can find articles on the new scientific interest in heredity, child study, perception and the physiology of the senses, experimental studies of memory, the use of tests and even the new sociology of education found a place. The publication was a long step forward from the journals of pedagogics found in Germany, with their strong emphasis on the old analytical psychology and philosophical issues. Butler's journal gave recognition to the place that the new scientific approaches to education were acquiring. The publication was avant grade and beckoned the rest of the educational world to follow.

One may note that Butler's views on the relationship of research to education would be quite in keeping with the views of research workers in the 1970's. Among the Butler papers that are stored at Columbia University is the outline of a course on pedagogy given by Butler in 1898. In that course Butler took the position that knowledge of the new sciences of physiology, psychology, and sociology was fundamental to the planning of education and the conduct of teaching. He had moved far beyond the point where the main guide to education was the analytic psychology of Herbart, and yet he understood the important contribution that the philosophically oriented psychologists of earlier generations had made.

James Earl Russell had much in common with Nicholas Murray Butler. Russell had graduated from college with honors in philosophy. Later he had gone to Europe, as one had to do in those days if one wished to make a name in the academic world. Although Butler had been influenced largely by German philosophers, Russell came under the spell of the new German experimental psychology, and particularly the work of Wilhelm Wundt and Oswald Külpe. Between his undergraduate degree and his European adventure he spent six years teaching Latin and Greek and administering a private academy in Ithaca, New York. The latter experience left him quite disillusioned about what a teacher could accomplish within educational institutions as they existed. With borrowed money he set out for Europe, which was viewed at that time as the center of educational reform in the world. In 1894 he completed his work on a doctoral degree at the University of Leipzig and returned to the United States. What he saw of education in Germany did not entirely please him, for the liberal thought regarding education seemed to have accomplished nothing to change an authoritarian Prussian social system and a public subservient to it. Much more was needed to transform a society than mere excellence in pedagogy; and yet, Russell believed that the teacher could perform a vital role in the development of an enlightened society and in the maintenance of a society that could be so described.

On his return from Germany, Russell worked for three years at the University of Colorado, a forward looking institution that recognized the

JAMES E. RUSSELL

Photograph courtesy of Columbia University

title of professor of pedagogy, a title that Columbia University had not wanted to recognize. Russell's title was that of *Professor of Philosophy and Pedagogy,* a title that recognized the close link that still existed between these areas. The link today may seem strange until one reflects that the great philosophers were those who first produced a literature on education.

Russell came to Teachers College in 1897 as head of the Department of Psychology and General Method. Within three months he became Dean of the college. The college was in the throes of searching for a new president. Russell came to the top position in Teachers College by proposing that the College did not need a president, since it was a part of the Columbia University complex, and colleges in the complex required only a Dean as a senior executive. The proposal was accepted and Russell became Dean of Teachers College, a position he held with great distinction for 29 years.

Russell set to work to create an entirely new type of institution. Over the years that followed he succeeded in bringing to the College an extraordinary range of new talent which included individuals that were to be among the most notable in education.

A particularly notable appointment made by Russell was that of Edward L. Thorndike in 1899. There had been a number of contacts between Russell and Thorndike for over a year, with the initiative coming from Thorndike, who had recently completed his doctoral work at Columbia University under James McKeen Cattell. Cremin *et al.*, write of Russell visiting Thorndike in his classroom at Western Reserve University. Geraldine Joncich, Thorndike's main biographer, does not mention such a visit. Thorndike, himself, later said that the appointment at Teachers College was engineered by James McKeen Cattell, who had now emerged as a man of great influence. Cattell was noted for his capacity for placing his protégés in significant positions. There is no doubt that James McKeen Cattell was regarded as a very special person by Thorndike. The author can recall an occasion in the late 1930's, when he was in Thorndike's office, and a call came through from the doorman at Teachers College saying that a Mr. Cattell was downstairs waiting to see Thorndike. Thorndike jumped from his chair and ran down the stairs to greet Cattell, despite the fact that he, Thorndike, had a bad heart and was forbidden to engage in strenuous exercise.

The Thorndike appointment was a part of Russell's general strategy of bringing bright young men and women to Teachers College. Russell was not sure what Thorndike could do within an educational setting, but he felt intuitively that the kinds of approaches that Thorndike had introduced into the study of animal learning could surely be applied to the study of human learning. Russell's intuition had a way of being right.

THORNDIKE AND THE CREATION OF A NEW ERA

Edward L. Thorndike's home background has been well described by Geraldine Joncich in *The Sane Positivist: A biography of Edward L. Thorndike* (1968). This source is useful as a description of Thorndike's early life. The author's own personal contact with Thorndike over the year 1938-39 and a close knowledge of his research has been of greater value as a basis for discussing his research and its impact on education.

Edward L. Thorndike was born in a parsonage in Williamsburg, Massachusetts, in 1874. Thorndike's father was a Methodist minister, and belonged to a denomination which required that the minister be moved to a new parish every few years. The result was that Thorndike was raised in eight different New England localities. Thorndike's father was successful as a minister and earned a substantial salary for the times. Thorndike was raised in an environment in which all the necessities were available, even though there were few luxuries. Education was valued in the home as is evident from the fact that all three sons of the minister and his wife ultimately became professors at Columbia University and the daughter became a high school teacher. Indeed, Edward L. Thorndike's brothers were almost as noted in their fields as he was in his. The emphasis on scholarship in the home is hardly surprising because New England ministers of that era were the main bearers of the tradition of scholarship.

Thorndike entered Wesleyan University in 1891 where his education was largely classical. The progressive colleges of that day had introduced courses in the sciences, but these were often poorly taught because of a lack of competent instructors. Laboratory work was limited, and in some institutions of higher learning the students were permitted only to look at scientific apparatus displayed in locked glass cases. The science courses at Wesleyan were probably better than those in most institutions of the time, but Thorndike did not take advantage of them. Thorndike did take a course in psychology in his junior year which must have been typical of its vintage, and one which retained a respect for the analytic approach of Johann Friederich Herbart, but which acknowledged the existence of the emerging new experimental psychology of Europe. Thorndike had no interest in philosophy and never developed one. Thorndike was equally unimpressed with the writing of William James and James Ward, now considered classic contributions to the development of psychology. Thorndike seems to have been empirically oriented from his first contacts with psychology to his last contributions. He would say in conversation, as he wrote many times, that the important thing to do was always to establish what the facts were. He was not always clear about where facts ended and theory began and, indeed, sometimes seemed to confuse facts with theories, as so many other psychologists have done.

Thorndike's performance in college was outstanding and he graduated with the highest average of any student in more than half a century. He had already demonstrated himself to be the compulsive worker that he continued to be throughout his life. His plan of living included no place for play. For Thorndike, the essence of living was work and study. He didn't know how to play and never even tried. The author recalls one of the few occasions on which he had a social interaction with him. He had invited a few of his assistants and others to his house for supper. After supper, he pulled out some tests which the guests worked on, as games, for the rest of the evening. That was as near as Thorndike came to a social evening of fun. Another incident in his life reflects his inability to play. On one of his trips to Europe, he was not seen by anyone on board ship except at meals. When he was asked how he spent his time on the ship, he said that he had been busy in his cabin writing test items for a series of intelligence tests. That was typical Thorndike behavior. One could not imagine seeing Thorndike participating in the ship's bingo game or in the usual horse racing in the lounge. Work and study were the very essence of his life, almost up to the end of his long career.

On graduation from Wesleyan University, Thorndike applied for admission to Harvard. He had other plans if he were not admitted or if he were not able to finance his graduate work. Those other plans were to teach English in a secondary school. In order to qualify for admission to the graduate program, Thorndike was required to take a year's work at the undergraduate level which gave him a Harvard bachelor's degree. In those days Harvard admitted to its graduate program only those who had already a Harvard undergraduate degree. Thorndike enrolled in three courses in English literature, but was promoted to attend two series of lectures in the Department of Philosophy, one by Josiah Royce and the other by William James. The philosophizing of Josiah Royce must have irritated Thorndike beyond all measure. He had no patience with the kinds of conceptual manipulations that delighted Royce. His response to James was different, and was the beginning of a relationship that involved admiration on Thorndike's part that lasted a lifetime. James had a respect for empirical methods and presented a pragmatic view to which Thorndike must have warmed. James was also a loveable figure, without an enemy in the world, whom students worshipped as a scholar-gentleman-father figure. Thorndike perhaps recognized in James many of the attributes that he would like to possess but never would. James also had aspirations to develop the new European psychology on the Harvard campus, and although no experimentalist himself, he recognized the importance of experimentation. Later he tried to introduce experimental psychology to Harvard by bringing over Hugo Münsterberg from Europe. Thorndike developed a warm relationship with James, who must have seen in the young Thorndike a patience for systematic experimentation that he, James, completely lacked. When the authorities at Harvard first turned down Thorndike's request to experiment with children, and then turned down his request for space to experiment with chickens, James came to his rescue and allowed him to use the James basement for his animal research. James and Thorndike were an admirable combination, for each respected the other for possessing what each lacked.

Thorndike completed a Masters degree at Harvard. The earned Doctor of Philosophy degree had not become widely adopted yet in the United States. The Ph.D. was a German degree and there was much controversy as to whether it was a suitable degree for American universities. For Thorndike to obtain a doctoral degree in experimental psychology, he had to move from Harvard, but there was not much choice. Indeed, the only Universities in the country that provided opportunities for young experimental psychologists were Cornell University and Columbia University. Cornell would have been quite unsuitable for Thorndike because of the views of Edward Bradford Titchener (1867-1927), but James McKeen Cattell at Columbia was a man with whom Thorndike could work. There was, of course, a new psychology developing at Clark University under the guidance of G. Stanley Hall, but that new psychology was totally out of tune with the thinking of the young Thorndike. Through the help of James McKeen Cattell, Thorndike was able to obtain what today would be called an assistantship, which provided him not only with exemption from the fees of Columbia University but also provided a generous living allowance. Columbia was also able to provide him with housing for his animals in the attic of what is still called Schemerhorn Hall. There he experimented with chickens and kittens on problems of escape from puzzle boxes. He received almost no help from Cattell, his supervisor, since Cattell was no longer interested in experimental psychology and had moved on to work as the great entrepreneur in the behavioral sciences through promotion and development of scientific organizations. Cattell had also started to work on the geneology of scientists, following Francis Galton's line of work on hereditary genius. Nevertheless Thorndike and Cattell developed a warm relationship with each other which lasted for the remainder of their lives. Thorndike also met Frederick K. Keppel, a fellow student, who later became immensely important to Thorndike's work, for Keppel, in 1923, became President of the Carnegie Corporation. Another fellow student at Columbia University was Robert S. Woodworth, whom Thorndike had already known at Harvard. Later the two were to collaborate on a number of projects. Although all of these relationships may have had value to Thorndike for their companionship and support, Thorndike was a loner in the way in which he worked. His products were always uniquely his, as was the dissertation that he submitted to Columbia University for his doctoral degree.

The title that Thorndike finally selected for his dissertation was *Animal Intelligence* (1898). Although Thorndike regarded it in its time as just a dissertation, no manuscript of the same period in psychology has achieved comparable fame. The book is still available in a modern reprint series and has a considerable circulation. Its interest to us here lies in the fact that it set the stage for all of Thorndike's later work, and indeed of much of the work of B. F. Skinner who has stated that his work grew out of Thorndike's work on puzzle boxes.

In order to understand how radically new Thorndike's *Animal Intelligence* was, one must understand the kind of controversy on which the volume threw some light. Whatever data had been available to students of the psychology of animal behavior prior to Thorndike had been data collected in naturalistic settings, data that Thorndike had every reason to mistrust. This naturalistic data had led some, such as Descartes, to take the position that the behavior of animals was strictly mechanical. Animals were automata. This view was expanded upon by the 19th century biologist Jacques Loeb, who proposed that behavior reflected above all a set of tropisms. Animals moved towards light, or dark, or warm places, or whatever else, as a result of laws built into their behavior that had survival value. Such mechanical models of animal behavior were tempting models to apply to human behavior, for did not the human go out into the sunshine, seek the warmth of his home at night, and so forth. Lloyd Morgan had also made observations on animal behavior in natural habitats, and had been concerned mainly with instinctive behaviors which were viewed as quite mechanical and automatic. An alternative interpretation of animal behavior was found in the work of George John Romanes, who read into animal behavior many human attributes and who believed that animals showed thinking processes similar to those of humans. Thorndike took the view that the nature of animal behavior could be understood only through systematic experimentation. His learning curves for cats showed learning to be a slow continuous process which Thorndike interpreted as a slowly building up of associations between situations and responses. A thinking model of learning, such as that proposed by Romanes, would show learning curves with sudden breaks to new levels of performance. Thorndike's learning curves were smooth and showed no sudden breaks.

Thorndike's associationism was different from that of his predecessors. The associationism of the British school of philosophers had involved a classical associationism in which links were developed between ideas, but Thorndike's associationism was primarily between situations and responses, much along the lines of the developing school of Russian physiologists and psychologists, whose line of thinking was virtually unknown in America at the time when Thorndike was engaged in his work on animals. The idea that all learning involved the development of links between situations and responses was later extended to include human learning. As Thorndike's system grew, it came to include human learning within a simple process learning. Most of Thorndike's later experiments on human subjects, of which there were hundreds, all tended to conform to a pattern in which the learner had to associate a particular situation with a particular response.

Even in those days the completion of a doctoral degree did not automatically lead to a job, particularly when the degree was in an academic area that had hardly yet received any recognition. Furthermore, Thorndike's position was penalized by the fact that American universities now sought to fill their positions in psychology with those that had received their degrees from the recognized European centers of experimental psychology. Thorndike might have hoped that the influence of Nicholas Murray Butler might have helped him find a job, but Butler supported psychology only in theory, and, when a position opened up at Teachers College, Butler submitted the names of candidates who were philosophically oriented. Thorndike was known to be antiphilosophical, which made his position even more difficult insofar as obtaining a job was concerned. The best that he could manage to find was a job as instructor in pedagogy in the College for Women at Western Reserve University. His qualifications for the job were probably completely minimal for he did not even have access to the German literature on the subject since he had never acquired any knowledge of that language, though he did have a knowledge of French in addition to Latin and Greek. Thorndike wrote later quite extensively on pedagogy, but as a psychologist, and at a much later date in his career. At the time of his appointment to Western Reserve, Thorndike's field of specialization was in animal behavior, and he regarded himself as an expert in that field.

His year at Western Reserve, 1888-89, must have been the most frustrating of his entire career. An obvious symptom of that frustration is that the year seems to have been quite unproductive. He virtually produced nothing, and yet his lifetime production of papers and publications was over 10 per year.

Towards the end of his year in Cleveland, an offer came from Teachers College for the appointment that Thorndike had long sought. His experience at Cleveland had not led him to think of himself as an educator, and James Earl Russell, who made the appointment, saw Thorndike as somebody who might turn to experimentation with human subjects and advance the cause of education. Without Russell's extraordinary vision the appointment might never have been made. Nonetheless, Russell did not view Thorndike as one who should devote his time to research. Thorndike's course load was to be 15 class hours of teaching a week and then, in his spare time, he was to advance the cause of education through research. This schedule did not seem to disturb Thorndike in the least. He had been productive before under strenuous and demanding conditions, and expected to be in the future. He had enormous energy, and a class load of 15 hours a week left long hours of the day still to be accounted for. None of those hours was to be wasted.

THE EARLY YEARS AT TEACHERS COLLEGE: THORNDIKE AND THE NEW PEDAGOGY

In his first few years at Teachers College, Thorndike engaged in work which surely would have been objectionable to him both in earlier phases of his career and in the later phases too. He had to design courses, and course design in the center of educational leadership in education was a much more demanding task than it is today, for course outlines not only had to be thorough, but they were typically published. The early issues of *Teachers College Record* made available to the whole world the content of the courses taught in the institution. Today one may not know what the professor next door teaches in his graduate course in education, but in 1900 every professor at Teachers College knew exactly what every other professor taught, and the whole world knew it too.

Teachers College Record (1901, Vol. 2 (3)) provides an outline written by Thorndike of a course entitled *Child Study.* The next issue of the *Teachers College Record* outlines two courses. One was entitled *Elements of Psychology,* which placed heavy emphasis on the reading required on William James' *Psychology, The Briefer Course* (1892). The other course called *Applications in Psychology* was also heavily loaded with the same reading materials, but it also carried one strong novel element. The outline proposed that students spend the last part of the course analyzing teaching materials in terms of the extent to which they conformed to the psychological principles discussed in the early class periods.

Thorndike developed materials for his course in child study. These materials for students were published under the title of *Notes on Child Study* (1901). The publication is of interest because it reflects Thorndike's growing conception of the nature of a science of psychology. Most of the material from which Thorndike could draw was that produced by the child study movement, which had concentrated on the collection of data through questionnaries. Thorndike generally rejected such techniques. In the chapter on attention, he suggests that the teacher should avoid attempting to identify the interests of children through asking children questions about what they like to do. Instead, the teacher should observe children and find out their preferences for particular activities. The proposal carries with it Thorndike's disdain for anything other than objective data. Nevertheless, he is not entirely consistent in this position, for he includes a chapter on imagery after the style of Francis Galton's essays and experiments on the topic. Other chapters on individual differences, memory, unlearned responses, and the active side of the child's life, stay close to the objective data available.

One wonders how G. Stanley Hall responded to the volume, because it ignores completely his work and the work of his students. G. Stanley Hall, who by then had become president of Clark University, did not like to be ignored for he had a quite inflated idea of his own importance. He must surely have seen the work and been extremely unhappy with the absence of any recognition of his accomplishments in the field. He may well have decided that the 27-year-old Thorndike was young and might even mend his ways as he grew older. Whether Hall liked the book or not, it was a real challenge to those engaged in the child study movement, which from then on had to move in the direction of becoming an objective science.

Each of these three courses became the basis of a book. Indeed, throughout his life Thorndike had the reputation of writing a book every time he gave a course of lectures, a reputation that was largely deserved. Then, too, he wrote books on subjects about which he never lectured.

A Literary Venture

There was little opportunity for Thorndike to undertake research during those first few years at Teachers College, but he tried his hand at other ventures. The first was a popular book on psychology entitled *The Human Nature Club, A Study of Mental Life* (1900). One cannot tell from the preface for whom the book is written. Perhaps Thorndike had in mind the naive education students he had encountered in Cleveland. In a way it can be viewed as Thorndike's first effort to present to a public of educators the new scientific conception of psychology based on data. Viewed in the latter light, it is different from any other book on psychology that was available at that time. The book is a tremendous break with the then current literature for teachers that included James' *Talks to Teachers* and Herbart's ponderous volumes that were still in use. The book presents what Thorndike considers to be the general content of modern psychology through a literary device that involved the creation of a Human Nature Club in a small town. The club met to discuss and study various topics of psychology and Thorndike presented the discussion at the meetings. In conformity with the new emerging concept of psychology, the book begins with a discussion of the nervous system. The doctor, who is a member of the club, provides much information about what is known about nerves and how they function. The discussion shows how Thorndike's later connectionist conception of the nervous system was already deeply rooted in his mind. A later chapter dealt with sensory inputs. In the chapters on learning, the members of the club discuss the problems they have in learning various competencies and interpretations are given of those difficulties. Later chapters treat attention, memory, habit, mental training and other current topics of the experimental psychologists of the day. The emphasis throughout the book is on the new empiricism of psychology. Every conclusion has to be based on observations that can be repeated. Mere opinion, or introspection is to be viewed as being of doubtful value. The book can be viewed as Thorndike's first attempt to produce from empirical sources an overall psychology of learning.

As a literary effort, the book was an obvious failure and Thorndike regarded it in that light. When one reads the book today, one can feel glad that Thorndike had abandoned his literary career at Harvard, but perhaps Thorndike still tried to explore his role of a man of letters, no doubt encouraged by James' brilliant literary career as an expository writer in psychology. Thorndike never completely gave up that quest, and it was one of his few failures. Nevertheless, despite its dismal literary features, the book sold. The first edition in 1900 was followed by a second edition in 1901 which was then reprinted in 1902.

The Landmark Studies of Transfer of Training

During his first two years at Teachers College he undertook research with Robert Woodworth on the problem of transfer of training which led to an empirical attack on the entire doctrine of formal discipline. Woodworth had been a fellow student of Thorndike's at Harvard, and, after Thorndike entered Columbia, he persuaded Woodworth to follow him there. Woodworth was not of the same stature as Thorndike as an experimentalist and, in fact, Woodworth's patience with experimentation and data gathering was limited, but he did participate with Thorndike in the classic studies of transfer of training and later wrote what was the classic text on psychology of the early part of the century. Woodworth remained a colleague of Thorndike at Columbia for his entire professional life. Woodworth's personal interests were also broader than those of Thorndike and he was much concerned with relating to people. He was as sociable as Thorndike was withdrawn. Despite these differences the two men worked well together, though one can be sure that Woodworth must have found it trying to keep pace with the fast running Thorndike.

The basic research of Thorndike and Woodworth on transfer of training followed a typical Thorndike style of investigation. A very simple situation was used for the study of transfer, namely, the extent to which practice in judging the area of one particular geometrical form resulted in improvement in judging the area of other geometrical forms. Thus, one group of individuals was trained to judge the area of rectangles of different sizes and size ratios. Then a determination was made of the extent to which this training produced improvement in judging the area of triangles on which no training had been given. They also studied the effect of training in the estimation of weights, and lengths, on the estimation of other weights and lengths. Another task involved learning to identify, in prose, words that included a pair of letters such as i and t, and then a determination was made of the improvement in locating words that had another combination of letters. The conclusions from the studies were that improvement in one function did not necessarily produce an improvement in functions that carried the same name. Thus training individuals to estimate the length of lines from 0.5 to 1.5 inches long did not result in an improvement in judging lines 6 to 12 inches long. Even when there was some improvement in a related function the amount of improvement was small compared with that on the function that had been trained. Then there was the best-known conclusion, namely, that the spread of practice occurs only where identical elements are concerned.

The studies were presented at a meeting of the American Psychological Association where they must have been viewed not only as an attack on the educational theory of formal discipline but also a blow at faculty psychology. Of course, faculty psychology was the theoretical psychological position that underpinned the educational doctrine of formal discipline. An attack on one was inevitably viewed as an attack on the other.

During the next ten years a great number of different studies of transfer were undertaken. These were summarized at length in Thorndike's 3-volume work *Educational Psychology* which will be discussed later in this chapter. The chapter on transfer of training provided a mass of rather confused evidence. The conclusion that Thorndike drew was that it seemed absolutely impossible to predict whether transfer of training will or will not occur. He found that it was a quite unpredictable phenomenon and rarely of any striking size. Thorndike continued to hammer out his original conclusion that transfer will take place only in so far as there are identical elements between the training situation and the transfer situation. Yet, the overall data do not confirm that conclusion. Thorndike did try and relate the idea of identical psychological elements to the idea of identical systems of connections in the brain between stimuli and responses, but that was theorizing way beyond the data. Nevertheless, despite the problem of relating his scientific conclusion to the scientific data, the idea of formal discipline had been killed as an educational doctrine. The research had undermined the theoretical basis on which formal discipline rested. The doctrine would show a revival in various forms in the decades that followed.

Thorndike's Model of the Intellect

Thorndike's view of the intellect dominated all of his work and, like some of his more modern counterparts, Thorndike took the position that his model of the intellect was the true and final model. The trend in philosophy of science in modern times is to view models of behavior as just convenient ways of viewing the organism for the purposes of research, and not to treat a model as though it represented ultimate truth. Even the modern nuclear physicist treats his models as though his model was little more than a set of game rules to be used in the conduct of research, and to be used only insofar as it is productive in leading to either control or prediction. Models are then abandoned as soon as they cease to be productive in this sense. In contrast, Thorndike grew out of the eighteenth century, a century in which models were viewed as representations of final truth, and in which there were even questions raised as to what scientists would do after they had discovered everything about the Universe. Thorndike believed that his model of human and animal intelligence was a correct construction of the nature of behavior and the nature of that part of the Universe that involved behavior. Since Thorndike felt sure that he had discovered ultimate truth about behavior, he set out to apply that truth in whatever areas intrigued him. The reform of the entire area of education was his goal.

The basic model of the intellect that Thorndike had evolved in the early years of his professional life was one in which learning consisted of establishing connections between situations and responses. The model was supposed to find support in the new work on the nervous system that had come out of laboratories such as that of Charles Sherrington. The model of the nervous system adopted by Thorndike was that of a telephone exchange in which incoming signals were connected to outputs. This model of the nervous system was a gross oversimplification of anything that Sherrington had to say, neglecting particularly the idea that the nervous system was hierachically organized in a way that permitted the organism to handle situations at different levels within the system. Thorndike's associationism required no such complexity. Any situation could become linked with any response. All that was required was some kind of central hook-up mechanism.

If one limits one's conception of the intellect to a set of bonds that connect situations with responses, one has a quite chaotic model of behavior. The model is chaotic because there is no relation between one situation-response link and another situation-response link. Every response to every situation is quite specific and isolated. If behavior were truly of this character, then behavior would lack any kind of organization. In actual fact, behavior is highly organized and the organization is complex. Also, the organization involves far more than just a set of internal links between behaviors, as was ultimately incorporated in the Thorndike model in order to account for behavioral organization.

The Thorndike model had one great virtue in that it provided a foundation on which a monument of research could be built. As a scientific model it was highly successful, and Thorndike adhered rigidly to the model in every experiment he designed. His entire vast program of experimental studies incorporated into every study the idea that at the core of all learning was a bond between a situation and a response and each study explored how to weaken or strengthen that bond. *The Law of Effect* provided a description of the main mechanism for strengthening or weakening that bond.

The model also had the dubious virtue of being readily grasped by teachers and nonacademicians. Thorndike could take his model to large gatherings and explain it to audiences that knew nothing of the developing science of behavior. Later, when Thorndike developed materials for teaching in schools, he could easily explain to teachers exactly what he believed learning to involve. His model, because of its simplicity, had an impact on a wide audience in his day because it was easily understood. Thorndike attempted to incorporate his model into an entire social philosophy. A strong feature of American intellectual life has been to embrace simple, and often absurdly over-simplified, models of the nature of behavior. There has been and still is a great public craving for knowledge in America, and a resulting populist literature on science. Simple models of behavior, such as that of Thorndike, satisfy that craving.

Thorndike's complete rejection of all philosophical ideas had led him to discard some of the valuable contributions that philosophers had made to the area of epistemology. There was much in the textbooks on psychology for teachers at the end of the last century that had merit and which ultimately had to be incorporated into a theory of knowledge that could provide a sound foundation for teaching. The ponderously written textbook of Johann Friederich Herbart had emphasized the fact that knowledge is organized into systems, a conception that goes back to Aristotle. The concept of knowledge as a hierarchy did not fit easily into the new emerging models of behavior of the kind that were appearing early in the century. Thorndike simply ignored problems of that kind.

Another major difficulty with the connectionist model was that of how to handle reasoning. Later, John B. Watson and B. F. Skinner came up against similar difficulties. The associationist philosophers had attempted to understand reasoning as a mere string of associations of a particular kind, but reasoning is obviously far more than that. Reasoning involves complicated rule structures concerning what responses are or are not permitted in particular situations.

Thorndike's New Psychology and Its Application to Education

The most notable book that Thorndike published in his youthful years, and perhaps the only early publication of real distinction, apart from his dissertation, was his short *Educational Psychology* (1903). This volume reflected the way in which Thorndike's work was to evolve in future years, every chapter being based on a foundation of empirical research. The book was his first attempt to produce a book for education students in this form. Its success led to a much more ambitious venture we must now consider.

By the end of Thorndike's first 10 years at Teachers College, he was not only America's leading experimental psychologist, he was the focus of American experimental psychology. His rise to fame was dramatic. Within 5 years of receiving his first appointment at Teachers College, he was a full professor. His work far overshadowed the work of the psychological laboratory of Columbia which had entered a quiet period after James McKeen Cattell became interested in organizational problems of science. Robert S. Woodworth had become interested in problems of mental health and inventories. This left Thorndike in a supreme position. Harvard had attempted to encourage the development of a psychological laboratory when William James had brought over Hugo Münsterberg (1863-1916) from Germany to run the psychological laboratory in 1892, but Münsterberg had become interested in other things. Münsterberg had the typical philosophical background of the German psychologist of his day and he also had a compulsion to write prolifically on whatever subject happened to interest him at the time.

There did exist albeit on the American continent a small but isolated empire of experimental psychology at Cornell University. That empire was presided over by Edward Bradford Titchener who had been imported by Cornell in 1892 to develop a psychological laboratory. Titchener had worked in the laboratory of Wilhelm Wundt at Leipzig and had studied the combination of psychology, physiology and philosophy that students customarily studied. He came to Cornell quite embittered by the fact that Oxford University had not established a chair of psychology and, incidentally, did not do so for nearly another half century. He also came to Cornell with the prospect of establishing a laboratory similar to that established by Wundt, where research workers would attempt to discover the laws of consciousness. The technique was mainly introspective, but it involved the use of subjects who had been trained to observe and report on events in their own phenomenal fields. Titchener's school of psychology, like that of Wundt's, was a structural psychology. Titchener, like Wundt, was absolutely uninterested in any activity that might be called applied psychology. His approach to all problems was that of the typical European ivory tower academician.

One would have a hard time in finding a greater contrast between two approaches to psychology than those of Titchener and Thorndike. Yet, there was one point in which they shared a common ground. Both were prolific writers. Both produced works of encyclopedic size. Titchener's 4-volume work, *Experimental Psychology*, is a massive assembly of knowledge in the Wundtian tradition, so massive that no person has probably ever read it from cover to cover. Thorndike's three volume work, *Educational Psychology,* is the largest work on the subject ever written.

Titchener would like to have been viewed as the central figure in American experimental psychology and, although famous, he never had a position of centrality in that he and his students worked in an atmosphere of isolation, and without influencing the rest of psychology on the continent. In a way, also, the star of structural psychology was setting. Thorndike was the luminary in the new era.

The new psychology of Thorndike was born when he wrote his dissertation on *Animal Intelligence,* but its mature development was not apparent until he published his three volume *Educational Psychology* (1913). The three volumes took 10 years to write and were far different from Thorndike's previous books which were virtually just expansions of his lecture notes. These expanded lecture notes were often poorly documented and often contained few references except to William James and the few other authors of books that the students were required to study. They did represent an expansion of the ideas expressed in *Animal Intelligence* and were characterized by a freshness of viewpoint and readability that made them widely used by instructors. These books were also, one suspects, attempts by Thorndike to explore ways of developing and expanding his ideas. There is a slow transition from his first attempt to produce in 1903 a simple *Educational Psychology* to the production 2 years later of his *Elements of Psychology* (1905), and from there to the production of his magnum opus *Educational Psychology* in 3 volumes.

His *Elements of Psychology* explored the application of connectionism to a great many phases of life and experience. It is surprisingly devoid of empirical data for an author who had become known as the man who always demanded to know exactly what the facts were. Nevertheless, as an exploration, it was a foundation for Thorndike's later experimental studies. Titchener did not like the *Elements* which made virtually only footnote reference to Titchener. Titchener reviewed the *Elements* in *Mind* (1905). The review was devastating. Not only does Titchener voice the oft heard criticism that Thorndike writes a book simply because he has had to teach a class on the topic, but Titchener also accuses him of being concerned more with making money out of his enterprises than in contributing to science. Titchener also criticized the book in terms of its content. He failed to see in it the kind of precise analysis of phenomena for which Titchener and his students were famous. This criticism was directed particularly at the first part of the book devoted to what was called *descriptive psychology,* which Titchener identified as his own area of specialty. In many ways, his criticism of the *Elements* was right, for the book dies not show Thorndike at his best. Thorndike was always at his best when faced with a table of empirical data that he himself had collected. He was least adequate when he attempted to make an analysis of common experience. An additional point to note about Titchener's review was that Titchener was extremely irritated by the fact that William James had written an introduction to the book. James' introduction does read very much like a modern Madison Avenue commercial for the book. It recommends the book "to all those who are interested in spreading the knowledge of our science."

Titchener's admonitions may have had a profound effect on the young Thorndike. Thorndike had always managed to criticize and needle the elders of his profession in a way that shocked his contemporaries and Thorndike had received little criticism in return. Now he had been reprimanded by Titchener. Whether the reprimand had an effect or not, the fact remains that his later works were far more carefully prepared than was the *Elements.*

Thorndike's three volume work *Educational Psychology* (1913-1914) was in the process of being written from 1903 to 1913. It was the first really significant book for Thorndike to produce since his dissertation. If his reputation had depended upon the books that he had published in the intervening years, he would have been viewed by history as just another writer of his age. But the 1913 *Educational Psychology* was a landmark publication and reflects Thorndike absolutely at his best, and Thorndike at his best was brilliant. The volumes demonstrated that books on the application of psychology to some practical area could no longer present just a mass of speculations, but must be soundly rooted in what Thorndike liked to term facts.

In order to understand how radical was the contribution of Thorndike in his 3-volume work, one may contrast it with two other volumes written by eminent scientists on educational psychology in the same era. The two scientists, contemporary to Thorndike who wrote books on psychology for an educational audience were Conway Lloyd Morgan (1852-1936) and Hugo Münsterberg. Both were considered to be scientists with impeccable credentials. Lloyd Morgan had been elected to membership in the Royal Society of London for his work on instinctive behavior that led to his concept of emergent evolution and is still today famous for his canon stating that explanations of behavior should be sought at the simplest levels. At the time when he wrote his *Psychology for Teachers* (1911) he was Vice-Chancellor of Bristol University where he later became Professor of Psychology and Ethics. His training for his distinguished career had begun when he was a student at The Royal College of Science and came under the influence of Thomas Henry Huxley.

Despite his impressive qualifications as a scientist, Morgan's book has only a scientific flavor. It does place considerable emphasis on the physiological basis of behavior and the related idea of levels of behavior, and there is some discussion of the structure of the nervous system, but there the impact of science ends. Morgan was apparently quite unfamiliar with Thorndike's *Animal Intelligence*, or he did not realize the important implications it had for a psychology of learning. He makes no mention of the work of Hermann Ebbinghaus on memory, and neither is there any recognition of the important new work on individual differences taking place in France, Germany, the United States, and in his native land, England. Even the scientific work on the structure of the senses and perception remained unnoticed. Studies of perception in relation to reading had already explored fundamental aspects of the psychology of reading, but these remain unmentioned.

Hugo Munsterberg's book *Psychology and the Teacher* (1914) shows a slightly greater relationship of research to the topic of the book. Lengthy sections of the volume discuss what should be the relationship between the new experimental psychology and education, without trying to apply the new experimental psychology. Münsterberg liked to explore potentials for application, and was often much more interested in them than in actual applications. The book is in many ways a collection of such essays on potential applications. It is full of ideas that are never fully explored and references to research are never documented. In many ways it reads like so many of the early works of Thorndike, and gives the appearance of being a collection of interesting thoughts tossed out in the classroom.

But Thorndike had grown beyond the point of producing books that were just expansions of the reflections of a classroom teacher. His new *Educational Psychology*, and the new Thorndike, recognized that there had to be a proper balance between the theoretical and speculative on the one hand and the empirical on the other. As the chief proponent of the view that the psychologist had to first establish the *facts*, he had been taken to task for not doing this, but his new magnum opus, and it was a magnum opus, was completely exemplary as a model of what he advocated.

The first volume of the *Educational Psychology* attempts to bring together what is known about what Thorndike calls the original nature of man. It was firmly rooted in knowledge about the nature of the human as a biological organism. It draws heavily on the large body of knowledge that was emerging related to what was called instinctive behavior, and developed by such notable scientists as C. Lloyd Morgan and William McDougall. Unlike any other book of its era on the topic, the work is heavily documented, particularly with sources of empirical research. It is to Thorndike's credit that he included references to work by men, such as G. Stanley Hall, whom Thorndike detested and even despised. The volume is an enormous effort to provide a single overall picture of the original nature of the human organism and to explore the implications that original nature has for teaching and instruction. The volume is a complete break with Thorndike's previous books. It shows none of the haste and rather dull sentence construction and drab metaphor of some of his speedily written volumes of the past. The writing is often elegant and shows a poetic quality that one had hardly expected to find. Consider the following paragraph (*Original Nature of Man*, p. 311):

> The impersonal wants, the cravings for truth, beauty and justice, the zeal for competence in workmanship, and the spirit of good will toward men which are the highest objects of life for man seem far removed from his original proclivities. They are remote in the sense that the forces in their favor have to work diligently and ingeniously in order to make them even partial aims for even a minority of men. But, in a deeper sense, they reside within man himself; and, apart from supernatural aids, the forces in their favor are simply all the good in all men.

The second volume in the 3-volume series is entitled *The Psychology of Learning*. It is a 452 page treatise presenting the state of knowledge in the field in the first decade of the century. It is a work in which Thorndike is at his best for the presentation is highly tied to massive amounts of data available to him. In the years that had passed since he had published his dissertation, a very large number of researches had been conducted in the field of learning, influenced to some degree by the dissertation itself. Some of the data presented preceded Thorndike's dissertation, for learning curves had been plotted back to the time of Hermann Ebbinghaus. Nevertheless, much was new.

A reader of the volume notes that Thorndike did not separate off educational psychology from the rest of psychology. The psychology of learning, with all of its ramifications, was conceived to be the core of educational psychology. There was no division for him between experimental psychology and educational psychology and how could there be, for Thorndike, the most eminent experimental psychologist of his age, was also the most eminent educational psychologist. Experimental psychology and educational psychology had a unity to them at that time that they do not have today. Thorndike could not conceive of a study of learning that did not have some implications for education. If there was to be a science of education, it was to be a science of learning.

The introductory chapter, entitled *Associative Learning in Man*, presents Thorndike's form of associationism. Learning involves the selective association of responses to situations. Thorndike does admit to the existence of something other than the mere connections of situations with responses as when he wrote of selective thinking and reasoning, and analysis and abstraction, but he expanded little on these topics because they do not fit easily into his particular paradigm. He expanded on the thesis that learning is essentially a process of trial and error, or what he sometimes calls the "try and try again" method. Schools exist to make sure that the right connections are made in learners. There are laws that determine the way in which connections are made and the most important of these is the Law of Effect, but there are also subsidiary laws. Attitudes are viewed as important but these are conceived to be tendencies for certain responses to occur in the presence of certain situations. Thorndike wrote of satisfyingness and annoyingness as important conditions related to the operation of the Law of Effect. In later works he was able to relieve these words of their subjective quality by defining satisfiers and annoyers in objective terms, much as B. F. Skinner later defined positive and negative reinforcers, but at this stage Thorndike has not yet developed a fully-fledged behaviorism and never did.

The chapter following that on associative learning is one on the selection of responses. Bonds or connections that occur within the brain are referred to as mental functions. Thorndike used the term *mental* quite frequently to refer to inner process but had absolutely no use for introspection as a scientific technique. Mental functions were introduced because connections between external situations and responses are not enough to account for behavior, and thus internal bonds and connections have to be introduced, but he never seems very comfortable with these. The efficiency of mental functions can be measured, and Thorndike gives examples of the measurement of efficiency in the fields of handwriting and representational drawing.

The chapter on practice effects is a rich source of facts on rate of learning. The data cover all of the classical studies of practice from Hermann Ebbinghaus to the time when the chapter went to press. Some of the material on which learning is demonstrated involves strictly laboratory tasks, such as are involved in the use of nonsense syllables. Other tasks come from the fields of work and school. For example, there are several graphs demonstrating learning in typewriting under different conditions, and then there are also data on children learning mental arithmetic.

The remainder of the volume is an extraordinary compendium of data covering a great range of experiments. The final chapter covers the transfer of training problem to which reference was made earlier in this chapter. In looking through the volume 65 years after it was published, one cannot but help be impressed with how much was known about learning at such an early stage of the development of a science of psychology. Indeed, if an author today were to prepare a book on educational psychology and were to limit himself to the data available to Thorndike, the book would be quite up-to-date. Such a modern author would be able to describe the form of the learning curve, point to the importance of feedback, and what today is called reinforcement; he would be able to demonstrate the results of massed versus distributed learning, and could describe many of the important phenomena related to forgetting. In addition, he would have quite a large quantity of useful information about transfer of training, some of which is still cited in the literature. A book based only on the data available to 1913 would not be a bad book. At least it would be a book from which teachers could still profit.

The first part of the third volume covered what was known about work curves. The interest in such curves had come out of industrial settings where a new breed of industrial research was beginning to study means of improving the output of the factory worker. Thorndike saw the implications of such research for teaching. He was not the only one interested in this type of inquiry for there had been widespread interest in what was described as the problem of fatigue in schools. The belief was widely held in the early part of the century that mental fatigue was a serious problem in schools and that mental fatigue not only reduced the efficiency of learning but also might have serious long-term consequences. The interest in this matter in the schools is reflected in the fact that the Federal Bureau of Education published Bulletins on the topic of fatigue. Most of the material in the Bulletins was based on a false conception of fatigue, for the belief was held that the nervous system could be fatigued through use of the brain, much as muscle could be fatigued through prolonged exercise. This idea was a part of the general conception of the nervous system of the time. The view included the notion that brain power could be improved by exercising the brain with any kind of hard mental exercise, and the form of the exercise did not matter.

Thorndike found little evidence to support the idea that fatigue interfered with school learning, but his data were quite remote from the school. Thorndike conceded that excessive work may deprive a person of some of the joys of life and lead to an unhealthy schedule of living. Certainly, Thorndike's own schedule was such that it resulted ultimately in a breakdown in his health. His discussion of the means of preventing injury from overwork provides exactly the regime that he should have followed. Rest is not included in the remedy, but the pursuit of activities involving pleasant exercise and social activities are.

The second part of the volume dealt with individual differences and conditions that influence them. When this section of the book was written, Thorndike's thinking had come under the spell of Francis Galton and Galton's belief that ancestry was all important in determining intellectual capability. In the pursuit of Galton's ideas Thorndike had begun some work with twins, though twin research never became a major line of inquiry for him as it did for Cyril Burt. Thorndike examined Galton's data and related data to determine whether he could see any traces of simple Mendelian inheritance. It was natural that he should do this for Gregor Mendel's work had only recently been rediscovered and was widely discussed in scientific circles. Thorndike concluded that imbecility could not be regarded as a simple Mendelian trait, even though some of his contemporaries believed that it was. Nevertheless, Thorndike took a position similar to that of Lewis Terman, namely, that the basic human capacities were determined largely by inheritance.

The chapter on *Relations Between Mental Traits* anticipated much of the psychometric work that was to dominate psychology for the next quarter century. Thorndike's examination of mental traits included not only the new measures of intelligence but also the kind of characteristics that James McKeen Cattell had introduced into his work. Thorndike drew no rigid line between paper and pencil tests and the measures used in psychophysics. His conclusion that all good traits tended to be positively correlated has stood the test of time. He was familiar with the new work of Spearman and the hierarchial model which the work seemed to imply and his discussion anticipated the kind of work that later focused on factor analysis.

The final chapter in the volume pertains to the nature of individuality. His position was that, despite the fact that all learning involves only the making of connections, individuals can differ enormously one from another, partly because of the differences in the many inborn capacities and traits, but also in the nature of the connections made. Thorndike's system provided vast sources of individual differences.

A notable absence in the entire 3-volume work is any reference to the work of the Russian physiologists whose work had culminated in the discoveries of Ivan Pavlov. Thorndike probably did not have access to this literature and American psychologists did not become acquainted with work on conditioning until nearly 1920.

Pavlov's work represents an extension of the doctrine of associationism that would surely have been quite congenial to Thorndike's way of thinking. Pavlov was, we know, acquainted with Thorndike's work *Animal Intelligence*, since like most of the Russians of his generation he was fluent in French and had a reading knowledge of English. The language barrier worked only one way. Translation of those aspects of Pavlov's work which had significance for psychology did not become available to English readers until the 1920's.

The 3-volume *Educational Psychology* thus provided one of the great milestones in the history of education. The work presented the most compelling evidence that educational policy had to be established, not on the basis of opinion, but on the basis of what Thorndike called "the facts." Many heard his message. It became the point of focus of the educational research movement which Thorndike's followers were to build and foster. Many of the most enthusiastic supporters of the point of view came to believe that all educational problems could be solved through the application of empirical methods. This excessive and unreasonable enthusiasm ultimately led to the development of skepticism concerning the claims of educational researchers as a whole.

The 3-volume work not only changed educational psychology, but it changed Thorndike. The works that he published after the appearance of his major opus were at a higher scholarly level than most of those he had published before. Of course, his dissertation was a fine example of good scholarship, but his numerous books that represented expanded class notes were not. They were all too often undocumented and lacked the kind of factual base that he advocated. The latter type of work was now in the past. The 3-volume *Educational Psychology* had set a standard for himself that he now had to live up to. He now wore the mantle of leadership and the mantle was a powerful influence in determining what he could or what he could not do. He was never sure that he wore that mantle even through many honors were given him in the form of honorary degrees, special awards and honorary memberships in foreign societies.

THE MIDDLE YEARS AT TEACHERS COLLEGE

The middle years at Teachers College for Thorndike are viewed here as the years from the publication of the large *Educational Psychology* to the mid 1920's. Certainly the publication of the latter set of volumes was a landmark in Thorndike's life and a great transition followed. Looking back over Thorndike's list of publications for the years preceding 1913, one is struck by the lack of much research despite an extraordinary proliferation of writing and the exploration of numerous ideas on a wide front. His main experimental contributions up to that time had been his studies of associative learning in animals and his studies of transfer of training in humans, both of which became classics in the field. Much of the material published had been an application of Thorndike's form of associative learnig to a great variety of fields including those of teaching, classroom management, and educational administration. Thorndike's pattern of intellectual development had been one commonly found in American life, namely, that of finding a simple formula and then applying that formula to every situation that happened to be encountered. This simple formula gave many who encountered it the illusion that behavior was not really very complicated at all and that schooling could easily be arranged to maximize learning with little difficulty. Thorndike himself believed that he had a highly useful model of learning with universal applicability to the solution of practical problems everywhere.

The middle years at Teachers College were characterized by three developments in the intellectual life of Thorndike. One was a growing emphasis on the production of materials for schools based on his conception of learning; another was a renewed emphasis on research on learning, particularly on human learning; and a third was an interest in measuring what he believed to be the native capacities of the individual.

Thorndike had had a long interest in the application of his ideas to school learning. During the early years at Teachers College he had been concerned with the development of devices for rating handwriting, English composition and children's drawing. This particular approach to education was in conformity with his idea that action should always be preceded by the collection of facts. The measurement scales were provided so that teachers and educational administrators could find out how well children were doing in these areas and, where deficiencies were found, then steps could be taken to correct them. The Thorndike instruments were not the only devices on the market available to teachers and administrators, but the Thorndike instruments were probably better designed than their competitors. Thorndike had been a pioneer in bringing to America the new statistical techniques that were being developed in Great Britain and he had published the first work of its kind on the Continent entitled *An Introduction to the Theory of Mental and Social Measurements* (1904). This volume brought to the attention of psychologists not only the new field of statistics as it has been developed by Francis Galton and his student Karl Pearson, but it also emphasized for the first time the problems involved in reducing errors of measurement. Thorndike, unlike many others who produced early instruments for the assessment of pupil skill, was very much aware of the technical problems of producing a reliable and valid measure, even though these terms had not yet become established in the field.

The measures of handwriting, composition, and drawing were widely mentioned, and advertised, in journals written for teachers, but one does not know how extensively they were used. They were the kinds of devices that a teacher might use, if pushed by the principal. One must remember that in the very early part of the century most teachers had had only a normal school education and many had not even had that. The whole concept of precise measurement that Thorndike attempted to promote was a quite unfamiliar one to the majority of the teaching professions, who had not been exposed to books on the measurement of achievement, for there were no books on the subject as yet. Thorndike himself had a faith in the use of scales of measurement that involved the use of typical samples of pupil products and expected that there would be a great future for them, but history has not shown him to be correct.

Contributions to the Teaching of Mathematics

A contribution that had a far greater impact on the schools than the measuring scales, was the work he undertook in the area of teaching arithmetic. As early as 1909 Thorndike had attempted to produce some materials for the teaching of arithmetic which carried the odd title of *Exercises in Arithmetic, Graded and Arranged to Meet the*

Requirements of the Hygiene of the Eye and Neuromuscular Apparatus (1909). Apparently the exercises failed to be a success. One suspects that the title itself was not particularly attractive and savored of fadism. For eight years Thorndike must have thought about the problem of teaching arithmetic before he came out with a new effort at providing teaching materials in the area. Then, in 1917, he published a three book series named *The Thorndike Arithmetics* (1917). This series of books probably had a wider circulation than any book that Thorndike ever wrote. At the peak of their use in the United States they were selling over a million copies a year. Although the books sold for less than a dollar a copy, the size of the royalties were such that they made Thorndike a wealthy man, a wealth he hardly needed since he was already the top paid professor on the Columbia campus.

Let us now turn to consider two topics; first, the reason for the success of the arithmetics and second, Thorndike's interest in promoting the materials. The preface to each book, written for teachers and for those involved in the purchase of the books, states that: "These books apply the principles discovered by the psychology of learning, by experimental education, and by the observation of successful school practice, to the teaching of arithmetic."

"Nothing is included merely for mental gymnastics. Training is obtained through content that is of intrinsic value."

"The preparation given is not for the verbally described problems of examination papers, but for the actual problems of life."

The claim that the arithmetic books were based on scientific knowledge of learning carried enormous weight in 1917, for the idea had taken strong hold that research would soon solve all the problems of education including the day-to-day problems of the classroom teacher. The books claimed to be based on this new foundation and came from the pen of the man most famous for promoting the idea of advancing education through research. Regardless of the merits of the books, the prestige of the author must have marked them for instant success.

Thorndike was also interested in the success of the books for reasons far beyond those that involved royalties. Thorndike, in his own field, had an evangelistic trend in his personality. He saw himself as a reformer in education, and the success of his ability to produce reform was a measure of how far he could consider himself to be a success. When he traveled to give lectures related to the use of his new arithmetic materials, he was traveling not as a salesman bent on obtaining a commission but as a preacher heralding the new order in education. He was never a fiery evangelist, being generally a quite dull speaker, but in his soul there was the goal of changing the world and making it a better place. His arithmetic books were one means of achieving that goal.

Now let us return to a consideration of the arithmetic books. A notable feature of them is that they were designed to produce what today is called mastery learning. Thorndike states clearly and unequivocally in his preface that "The demand here is that pupils shall approximate 100 per cent efficiency." He could see no reason why children should not be able to follow a clear explanation and then work every example correctly. The preface also says that the task of teaching arithmetic is to teach correct habits. Elsewhere, Thorndike defines correct habits as useful bonds between situations and responses. Every task included in the arithmetic series was claimed to be a task from daily life and one which the children should master if they were to live successfully.

A very important factor in producing the enormous success that the books achieved was the trend in educational philosophy of the time. The turn of the century showed a move towards a curriculum for public education emphasizing the practical. An important part of the Americanization of the immigrant was to give him a command of the English language and to introduce him to the practical arts of writing and calculating so that he could take his place in society. Although the doctrine of formal discipline of the last century had tended to make education oriented towards the abstract and the historical, the new trend was the acquisition of the practical arts. Thorndike's arithmetic series illustrated this new philosophy of education. Nothing was included which could not be included for reasons of practical value. Nothing was included merely to provide the child with an opportunity of exercising the intellect. A child who worked through the series of three books, and who understood his work, could be said to have mastered every aspect of the mathematics of arithmetic found in the transactions of daily life.

A surprising fact emerges when one peruses the list of Thorndike's publications. That fact is that much of his research related to the psychology of arithmetic seems to have been undertaken after, and not before, the publication of his arithmetic books. What this means is that the books were published as applications of his general theory of learning. Thorndike, like most psychologists who have developed systems, believed implicitly in the worth of his system for planning practical activities. He moved ahead to apply his ideas, without testing whether the ideas were genuinely applicable.

Thorndike never showed any doubts that his fundamental principles of science could be wrong, that they were even rough approximations, or that they applied only under particular circumstances. Despite the research on the teaching of arithmetic conducted in the early 1920's by Thorndike himself, and later by him and his students, there was no trace of any attempt to evaluate the teaching materials directly. There is no publication of Thorndike or any study that attempted to compare the new materials with the old. One suspects that Thorndike would have thought that such a study would be a silly one to conduct.

Thorndike was interested in promoting his teaching materials in arithmetic, and in 1921 published a book for teachers explaining how the materials should be used. The book, *The New Methods in Arithmetic* (1921), was designed to help the working teacher. The book explained what Thorndike believed to be the advantages of his materials over other materials, not only with respect to the way in which mathematical principles were taught, but also with regard to the inherent interest that the materials were claimed to have had for the children. The emphasis in the book was on the development of well-established habits through drill. The *Law of Exercise* and the *Law of Effect* are discussed at length, but always in relation to the teaching of mathematics. There is also extensive discussion in the book of a new interest of Thorndike, namely, the simplification of the vocabulary used in teaching. Thorndike found that the vocabulary of technical terms used in most arithmetic textbooks was unnecessarily complicated, and he believed that mathematics should be taught with a minimum use of technical jargon. Thorndike had a shrewd eye for identifying the conditions in learning situations that hampered the learner.

A year later, in 1922, Thorndike published a much more technical work on the psychology of arithmetic. This new book (*The Psychology of Arithmetic*, 1922) represented a published version of the course that Thorndike had been giving to teachers in the elementary grades. Thorndike describes the book as an application of what he called the "newer dynamic psychology." He claimed that he had been urged to publish his lectures by former students who were now in supervisory positions. Undoubtedly, there were many such students for those who had been exposed to Thorndike were scattered, not only across the United States, but across the world. To be a follower of Thorndike in the schools was to identify with the new scientifically based leadership. Here again one must remember that the age was one which regarded educational research with great favor, and anticipations were widely expressed that research would soon solve all the great educational problems and the minor ones too.

The volume on the psychology of arithmetic presented and exploited the Thorndike theory of learning and behavior. The book begins with a presentation of the theory of bonds, later called connectionism. There is an attempt in it to describe a theory of the nature of number, but it is a primitive theory. Thorndike does not seem to have been aware of the work of Bertrand Russell and Alfred North Whitehead. Thorndike's theory of numbers is a common sense one, and it probably had more appeal to his audience than the Russell and Whitehead theory would have had.

Thorndike includes in his *Psychology of Arithmetic* a chapter on interest in the subject. He presents data from several sources showing that arithmetic in his day was a very popular subject for children to study. The only school activities that generally came above arithmetic in popularity for boys was handiwork and shopwork, and for girls, household work. Arithmetic was generally at the top of the academic subjects. One doubts whether the same would be true today. Thorndike explains the high interest in the field providing an explanation given by his colleague David Eugene Smith, who suggested that arithmetic was looked upon as a game by children, and a game which everyone could play and do well. Thorndike suggested that the immediate knowledge of accomplishment found in arithmetical work made the work a real source of satisfaction. Thorndike claimed that satisfaction with accomplishment was crucial for effective learning. What today would be called positive reinforcers were referred to by him as satisfiers, reflecting a state of satisfyingness. The use of these terms did not imply that the scientific aspects of Thorndike's work involved subjectivity, for he was able to define satisfiers in a way that involved only objectively defined conditions. Yet despite the fact that Thorndike's system included only objectively defined terms, he was apt in his popular writings to identify some of these terms with subjective states. The degree to which he did this depended upon the level of sophistication of his audience. The more that his audience was unsophisticated, the more he introduced subjective elements. Thorndike wanted the school to be a pleasant place, despite his emphasis on drill. Later he became deeply involved with the enjoyment factor in learning.

These theoretical works on the teaching of arithmetic probably did much to maintain an interest in his books on arithmetic in the schools. Certainly sales of the books continued in substantial amounts. The books underwent minor revisions in 1924 which carried them on into the 1930's as texts that continued to be used. Their death was slow, brought about by an emerging new philosophy of education and teaching mathematics that centered on the Progressive Education Movement. No set of schoolbooks in this century are likely to survive for more than a decade. Teachers like to have some variety in the materials they use to keep them, the teachers, from dying from boredom.

Thorndike moved from his interest in arithmetic to one in algebra. The two areas were viewed at that time as being distinct disciplines. Teachers taught algebra following the mastery of some arithmetic. Arithmetic equations were never used as an introduction to algebra. Indeed, algebra was rather late in being introduced into schools, and only a small percentage of students were exposed to this branch of mathematics.

Thorndike's *Psychology of Algebra* (1923) was written partly by several other members of his staff, but it is still Thorndikeian throughout. Indeed, the style is so much that of Thorndike that one suspects that the other authors listed must have contributed some of the data discussed but little of the writing. The whole approach of the book is typical of Thorndike's pragmatism. A first step in designing a course in algebra is to find out who needs algebra and for what purposes. His general answer to such questions was that very few students needed algebra, just those who were preparing for a scientific career or who wanted to take courses in physics and chemistry. A brief study of the Army Alpha scores of those who took algebra suggested to him that the subject had appeal only to the brighter students. Then, too, he found a correlation between Alpha scores and passing or failing in algebra, suggesting again to him, that considerable native capacity was required in order to succeed in algebra.

Thorndike made an analysis of the requirements of various scientific fields for particular algebraic operations, and this was to be used as a basis for developing a high-school curriculum in algebra.

One of the longest chapters in the book is a discussion of drill. Thorndike, unlike those later who worked in the progressive education movement, believed that drill was of the utmost importance. His basis for this was what he called the *law of exercise*. Bonds could be strengthened by exercise, and should be strengthened to the point where they were permanent. Drill was necessary in order to produce permanent bonds. Thorndike takes the interesting point of view that the final stages of learning require very little time. A child who is learning factoring may slowly stumble through the first problems. Then, as the child acquires some skill, the examples are worked more and more rapidly. A type of problem that first required 2 minutes to work might soon be worked in 8 seconds. What this means is that the overlearning, that is necessary for permanent retention, requires only a small amount of additional time. This seems to be a very important point that has hardly yet been recognized in schools.

Although Thorndike believed in drill in such subjects as mathematics, he was opposed to drill as drudgery. He believed that every problem presented to the pupil should have some inherent interest for the pupil. He also believed that the adult could judge which problems would be of interest, though this is questionable. He identified practicality with interest, but practicality for some adults is probably a poor criterion of childhood interests.

Thorndike also argued for a system of distributed learning. Practice sessions, with respect to the development of any bond, should be such that they were progressively more and more spaced. This was an application of the work of Hermann Ebbinghaus conducted a half century earlier, but still not applied to school learning.

What Thorndike had to say about the teaching of algebra was limited by his very inadequate epistemology. This limitation has been a recurrent limitation of psychological theories of behavior, and it is one of the limitations of operant psychology today. Knowledge is much more than a chaotic system of bonds or conditioned operants. Academic learning is much more than the learning of a set of specific responses.

Thorndike's book on algebra emphasizes a theme that had begun to emerge through other writings. That is the theme that the use of a simple vocabulary is important in the design of materials for schools. He gives a long list of words that clutter up the typical algebra book and that could be eliminated. As examples of unnecessary vocabulary he cites such terms as *abacus, aequalis, commutative law,* and *antecedent.* Thorndike believed in the building of vocabulary but not through the teaching of algebra which seemed to him to provide more than enough challenge in itself. He attempted to develop a list of essential vocabulary for the teaching of mathematics by asking some mathematicians, psychologists, and graduate students teaching mathematics in secondary schools to rate several hundred terms for their usefulness in the teaching of algebra. He then produced a combined rating for each of the words in the list. His recommendation was that only terms that were rated high in value should be included in an algebra for children. The unnecessary learning of vocabulary was described as the wasteful formation of unnecessary bonds. The formation of superfluous bonds should be avoided wherever possible since the formation of such bonds constitutes a source of inefficiency in education.

Word Counts and Controlled Vocabulary

Thorndike had been interested since about 1910 in the frequency with which words occurred. He saw clearly that the choice of vocabulary in writing textbooks for children was closely related to comprehensibility of material. He also saw that the comprehensibility of a word should be related to the frequency with which it was encountered in daily life. The frequency of words in conversation could not be easily estimated, particularly in the days before tape recorders, but word frequency in written and printed materials could be determined. Such frequencies, he believed, could provide measures of word difficulty. The idea was not new, as he acknowledges in his article "Word knowledge in the elementary school" (1921). Word counts had already been made of words in correspondence, words in newspapers, and words used in business, all for the purpose of providing a basis for the development of instructional materials. These earlier lists had also been used for the development of spelling lists, a matter of considerable interest to educators who lived in the earlier part of the century.

Thorndike's word counts were different from those of his predecessors in the field. First, they were far more comprehensive. During the period of 10 years, beginning in 1910, Thorndike slowly accumulated counts of word frequencies on about 4,000,000 words of printed material. He recorded word frequencies for every word in such children's classics as *Black Beauty, Treasure Island,* and *Sleepy Hollow.* He counted words in school readers, in samples of the Bible, in volumes of poetry, newspapers, and school textbooks. The work must have been a Herculean task for it corresponds roughly to tabulating all the words in at least three volumes of the Encyclopaedia Brittanica. Only a Thorndike would have ever thought of undertaking such an enterprise.

Even more extraordinary was the fact that he did the work himself. A modern entrepreneur might have thought of employing some cheap labor to do the work, with the thought that a small investment might produce a great return, but such an idea never occurred to Thorndike, for the task itself intrigued him. Much of the work that Thorndike ever produced in his entire career, he produced himself. He firmly believed that the only way to understand data was to work with it. He always worked up his own data and, for much of his career, even performed the necessary calculations himself. The author recalls hearing him give advice to some younger research workers and urge them always to work on their data themselves. He did say that there was nothing wrong in having a punched card machine check the work, or sometimes even to do a portion of the calculations, but there was only one way to understand data and that was to work with it.

The end product of Thorndike's 10 years of work on words was *The Teachers Word Book* (1921). This book is a list of the most commonly occurring 10,000 words. Later books expanded this work to include 20,000 words and finally 30,000 words. The first book in the series also provided a list of the 500 most common words, the next 500 and so forth up to 2,500 words.

The Teachers Word Book is, as its title denotes, addressed to teachers. The book is provided so that teachers can determine what words to teach. Experienced teachers, Thorndike said, know a great amount about what words children know and do not know; hence the book should be particularly useful to the beginning teacher who lacks experience.

Thorndike also hinted that the word lists might later be used in the design of educational materials. He stated that at least one third grade reader he examined used 9,000 different words and that was far too many for the particular grade level.

For a long time the Thorndike word lists were the only ones widely used for the purposes of textbook design. The utility of the lists was also expanded by the fact that many reading difficulty formulae used them to determine vocabulary level as a component of readability. The lists probably never became widely used by teachers, though they did become a basis for selecting materials for teachers to use. There were also many other byproducts for schools that grew out of the word lists that became the focus of much of Thorndike's activity in his later years at Teachers College.

Before leaving this discussion of the middle years at Teachers College, let us consider briefly an aspect of Thorndike's personality that played a part in his enormous productivity. Thorndike probably died with a greater accumulated wealth than any psychologist of his time. Indeed, probably nobody has ever turned psychology into gold in the way that

Thorndike did. There were contemporaries of Thorndike who accumulated small fortunes, but they were small compared with that of Thorndike. James McKeen Cattell had a scotsman's aptitude for making money and salting it away, and most of his enterprises became extremely profitable, but Thorndike's ability to produce materials for which there was a vast market excelled that of Cattell many times over. One is bound to ask the question whether Thorndike turned to those activities that made money or whether, through chance, the activities in which he was interested became lucrative. The author's personal opinion is that money was symbolically important for Thorndike. He didn't need money to satisfy lavish tastes for his entire style of living was modest. His house in Montrose was no mansion, though he was able to obtain enough land so that he could sell parcels of it to those he liked. Later, when he lived in an apartment near to his office, the apartment was furnished in the simplest style. His clothing matched the stereotype of the professor's. The author remembers once hearing him discuss the use of time and he commented that there was just so much time available in life to accomplish useful ends. Then he glanced down at his unpressed pants and said "If one spends time thinking about clothing, then one does not have time to think about other things."

Thorndike's entire life style was modest and his salary at Teachers College was far more than he ever needed to maintain his standard of living. He was not interested in luxuries, and had no time to indulge in them. Yet, that money was very important to him and it was important to have that money in the bank or in good investments. He was no supporter of particular charities, and the author can remember him answering one such plea for funds over the phone. He told the person on the line, who obviously was asking for money to support some cause, that he was just a poor professor. Somehow he believed that statement when he made it. That was the kind of way in which he thought about himself. Even if he had salted away many times as much as he did, he probably would have still thought of himself as a poor professor.

Money was of deep symbolic value to Thorndike as a symbol of success. Somehow the money that rolled in in such massive amounts told him that he really was America's outstanding psychologist. He did little with the money, but the money told him what he wanted to believe.

Thorndike's Excursion into the Measurement of Intelligence in the Twenties and then Vocational Guidance

Thorndike's work in connection with the development of the Army Alpha Test sparked an interest in the measurement of intelligence that occupied a considerable amount of his time for many years, and particularly the years following World War I. Money was available to hire a staff to handle the mechanics of collecting and analyzing data and the enterprise blossomed into one of the largest in his office. Despite its size, this entire project became perhaps the least significant of Thorndike's entire career, and achieves barely footnote status in most modern textbooks on measurement. Perhaps this has to be the fate of a large project run by an undistinguished staff. Of those who worked on the project only Herbert A. Toops achieved any professional reputation in his lifetime, a reputation which was diminished by the fact that Toops was wholly unable to be a productive writer when he was on his own. During the time when he worked for Thorndike he did produce a few monographs, but when he left the Institute to spend the rest of his life at The Ohio State University he virtually ceased to publish.

Thorndike's efforts to develop work in the field of what was then called mental measurement revolved around three main enterprises. First, there was the matter of the development of a general theory of the nature of intelligence and its measurement. Second, a very large enterprise involved the development of a scale for the measurement of intelligence. Third, an attempt was made to explore the use of measures of intelligence for vocational guidance. Although these three enterprises can be presented here as though they formed a logical sequence, they were all explored simultaneously. The scientist's work, that appears to form a logical sequence when viewed in retrospect, is often not produced in that sequence. Explorations in many different directions are commonly pursued by a scientist in order to generate in the final product a logical structure.

The rationale for the development of a measure of intelligence appeared first in a volume entitled *The Measurement of Intelligence* (undated but published circa 1926). This is a massive work and, despite the multiple authorship, the work is obviously written by Thorndike himself. Stradivarius may let his assistants make the crude cuts of wood, but the final cuts and the finish are his. In Thorndike's case this was inevitably so because of the choice of his collaborators.

Thorndike's work on the measurement of intelligence pays little attention to the history of the topic. Indeed, it is an attempt to make a fresh start. The first chapter voices concern that not all is well with the measures of intelligence that had already been developed by Alfred Binet, Lewis Terman and the Committee that produced the Army Alpha. The implication is clear that these previous instruments lacked the theoretical basis necessary for the design of a good instrument. Thorndike set out to remedy that deficiency by attempting to provide a theoretical basis for the development of intelligence tests.

The initial chapter of the book attempts to provide a theoretical analysis of the nature of intelligence, and yet it is, to a great extent a summary of what (p. 22) "sensible people in general" believe to be the core of intelligence. Thorndike summarizes his position in three statements to the effect that, other things being equal,

(p. 22) "the harder the tasks a person can master, the greater is his intelligence."

(p. 24) "the greater the number of tasks of equal difficulty that a person masters, the greater is his intelligence."

(p. 24) "the more quickly a person produces the correct response, the greater is his intelligence."

These three aspects of intelligence are related to *level*, *extent*, and *speed*. In most tests of intelligence these are combined in unknown amounts.

The criterion of intelligence is the agreement of sensible individuals concerning those in history or contemporary life who can be considered to have the highest intelligence. A valid intelligence test should be able to identify such individuals.

Although level, extent, and speed are all factors in intelligence, Thorndike decided that level was the most important of the three to an overwhelming extent. At this point in his discussion he renames *level*, and calls it intellectual *altitude*. This aspect he regarded as (p. 33) "indispensable, irreplaceable by anything else." Thorndike appeals again to common sense in defending altitude as the central aspect of intelligence that should be measured. Thorndike argues that nobody would ever ask how quickly Pasteur was able to invent his ideas, but the important thing was that he had them. Then Thorndike adds the odd comment that an intellect so superior that it could prevent war would be worth employing at a million dollars a day. For Thorndike, intellectual worth and economic worth were closely tied together. This remark is followed by a long discussion of the tasks to be included in a scale of intelligence for application to individuals (p. 64) "bred in the United States and aged twelve or over." His eventual choice of tasks were designated by the letters CAVD and the resulting scale of intelligence was called Intellect CAVD. In broad terms the letters referred to comprehension, arithmetic, vocabulary, and understanding directions. The latter also included reading comprehension. Thorndike has much more complete and precise definitions of these categories which need not be reproduced here.

Thorndike then proceeded to develop tasks in each of the CAVD components of the intellect at 17 levels of difficulty. These levels were designated by the letters of the alphabet from A to Q.

At intervals throughout the book there is mention of a connectionist theory of learning in relation to the measurement of intelligence. Thorndike had difficulty in developing the relationship. The measure of vocabulary can be viewed as a straightforward measure of the number of connections that had been made between situations and responses, and Thorndike had already, in previous works, attempted to show that mastery of arithmetic was merely a matter of developing the correct connections in the nervous system, but the arguments had never been convincing. A connectionist viewpoint has not been successful in explaining relational thinking, and Thorndike was convinced that relational thinking was at the very core of intelligence. Thorndike implies that if one were able to map out and study the relations of nerve cells in the nervous system, then one might be able to count the number of possible connections and that this number might be a basis for estimating intelligence, but he concedes that this would seem to be an impossible task. The connectionist position is not pursued at any length in his volume on intelligence. Thorndike had the wisdom not to pursue profitless lines of thought.

One of the most interesting features of Thorndike's work is a discussion of the establishment of an absolute zero of intelligence. He points out that, unless an absolute zero were established, a measure of intelligence could not be used as a ratio scale, and thus one could not say that one person was so many times more intelligent than another. The establishment of a zero would open the way for the making of such statements. Thorndike suggests that a problem that an earthworm could master could be considered as near to an absolute zero, but he says that pressure of other work did not permit him to identify such a problem. Since the book on intelligence was written, the learning of earthworms has been investigated and these simple creatures have been shown capable of learning very simple tasks. Thorndike named two tasks which, he believed represented positions just above the zero of intelligence. These two tasks were the following (p. 348);

"Responds to his best and kindest friend, for example, mother or nurse, differently from his response to strangers."

"Will not try and pull off his own fingers."

The attempt to do what Thorndike was trying to do has not been pursued further by later generations of psychologists, for the task of developing true ratio scales of intelligence has not seemed to be important. Nevertheless, the problem of establishing an absolute zero is one that has a certain fascination attached to it. Thorndike pursued further the concept of an absolute zero of intelligence and tied his new measure of intelligence to that concept. After making numerous assumptions and undertaking a long line of reasoning he concluded that the test items in level A of the CAVD tests were 23 units above the absolute zero and the items at the top level, level Q, were 43 units above the absolute zero. This would imply that a person who passed level Q would be considered to be twice as intelligent as one who only passed the level A items. Thorndike agreed that it may seem preposterous that the intellects of the top one per cent of Americans should be only twice as great as the intellect of those imbeciles confined to institutions, or that a child of 3 should have attained two thirds of his mature level of intellect. He tries to overcome this implied criticism by pointing out that the altitude of the intellect is different from the total intellect which must also include the results of experience.

Thorndike was attempting to provide an alternative to the intelligence quotient and mental age systems for designating intelligence. He was sure that his conceptual system would displace that which was being promoted by Lewis Terman in California, but it never did. His own faith in his instrument was firm and the scale was administered routinely to applicants for nonprofessional jobs in the institute. The main practical use of the CAVD scale was for measuring the ability of graduate students, for no other scale available had as much capability of discriminating among individuals at high levels. The scale was used for the selection of graduate students in some institutions, including Harvard University and, of course, Teachers College, but the instrument was never widely used. The concept of the intelligence quotient, because of its great simplicity, was already too well established in the minds of teachers, school administrators and others, to allow a new concept of the measurement of intelligence to find a place.

Before leaving this topic, a few comments must be made concerning Thorndike's position on the extent to which his scale measured native intelligence. The statements he makes in the book on the subject are cautious. He was always cautious whenever he placed an idea in print. His private ideas on the subject were much less cautious. Indeed, he seems to have believed that scales such as the CAVD would ultimately be shown to provide quite good measures of native intelligence. It would have been hard for him to have escaped from such an idea for it was a dominant idea of his age. Terman was willing to express such an idea in print, but Thorndike was not.

In addition to his theoretically oriented work on the measurement of intelligence, Thorndike also undertook some research related to vocational guidance. He typically moved from a theoretical base to a practical application. Work on vocational guidance was initiated quite early when Herbert A. Toops came to him as a doctoral student in 1920 and then stayed on in Teachers College for 4 years. Toops was interested primarily in statistical aspects of psychology, but he was also a man with considerable imagination. Indeed, many would have said that his imagination was wild and uncontrolled.

Toops administered tests to 2,225 children in the public schools of New York City and then amassed, in addition, a great amount of information pertaining to each child. The information included as much as could be found in academic records including such matters as the number of times that the child was not promoted, and also other details about the child's background and what today would be called socioeconomic level. Toops' main interest was in relating the scores on the tests to the other measures included in the study. At that time, such an endeavour was not the commonplace enterprise it might seem to be today, for almost nothing was known about the extent to which tests scores predicted academic achievement and were related to other aspects of behavior. The study also provided the basic data for a subsequent study, undertaken by Thorndike and his associates in 1931 and 1932, in which an attempt was made to determine the extent to which the tests administered by Toops predicted occupational success. Thorndike shared the view with other psychologists of his time that test scores would provide good predictors of occupational success. In fact, Thorndike held the position to the end of his days that life was basically just and that people were generally rewarded for the competencies that they had to offer society. The good came to the top and the inadequate sank to the bottom of the economic system. That was probably the thought that underlay the work.

The follow-up study of those who had been tested by Toops was an elaborate enterprise, and it could not have been undertaken had not Thorndike's friend Frederick Keppel of the Carnegie Foundation provided lavish support. The sample originally tested had to be located in the world of work and then contacted. How this was done is described in the volume *Prediction of Vocational Success* (1934). Lorge was in charge of much of the work related to the identification of the present whereabouts of the original sample and he also played a part in collecting data from them. The task of identifying a school population eight years after testing was not as formidable as it might appear to be. New Yorkers tend to stay within the City and can be located through telephone directories, marriage bureau records and motor vehicle license bureaus files. Neither the social security system nor the credit bureau system were available to provide this service as they would be today. Losses were relatively small in the follow-up samples. Of the original sample of 2,225 children tested in 1921 and 1922, 1807 were traced to the age of 22. Cases were lost through death, moving out of the city, and the inability of the investigator to obtain information. The information derived from the group contacted included age on leaving school, grade reached, grades for scholarship in school, and then a series of measures related to vocational success. The latter included average annual earnings, level of work, percentage of time employed, and the number of changes of employer. In addition, the nature of the work engaged in was recorded. Thorndike was particularly interested in the differential prediction of clerical versus mechanical occupations.

The findings were disappointing. The most notable positive finding was that a person's total *educational* career can be accurately predicted from his performance in school before the age of 14. Small correlations were found between performance in clerical occupations and scores on what was called a clerical intelligence test. Predictions of success in mechanical work from mechanical aptitude tests were low to the point of being completely worthless. Tests showed almost no capacity to predict earnings or any measure of job success, such as the number of times a person changed jobs. Thorndike was surprised by the finding that the data provided no support for the idea that education had an economic value.

Thorndike's study of the prediction of vocational success set the pattern for a large number of studies that were to be undertaken in the decades that followed. His findings were a preview of those to come. However, the negative findings of Thorndike did little to limit the use of tests as a part of the vocational guidance undertakings that were to flourish during the 1940s and 1950s.

Thorndike's undertakings in the field of measurement, despite the fact that they were novel and ingenious, do not represent that part of his work that had the most impact on education, although they showed the same spark of brilliance that made so much of his work shine.

THE LATER YEARS AT TEACHERS COLLEGE

If one examines the year-to-year production of Thorndike's pen, one cannot help noticing an extraordinary uniformity in the quantity of publications each year during the entire 40 years at Teachers College. There were a few years of low production, such as 1930, when he published only 4 articles and these were articles of little consequence, and in 1902 he also published only 4 articles. Then there were years of enormous productivity, such as 1913 when he produced 17 publications, including substantial books. Despite these ups and downs the production of publishable materials is extraordinarily uniform throughout his career. One would never suspect that in 1921 Thorndike's small office was converted into an institute for the alleged purpose of increasing Thorndike's capacity to produce and to influence education.

The move to transform Thorndike from a one-man institution into a director of a research institute came from the Dean, James Earl Russell. Geraldine Joncich suggests that this was a move to help Thorndike to be more productive, but that is a most unlikely story. Whatever was said in conversations between Russell and Thorndike may well have had little to do with the facts of the situation. Thorndike was already one of the most productive scientists in the United States, if not the most productive, and the whole idea of increasing his productivity looks absurd. Russell probably had other matters on his mind when he made the proposal.

Although Russell was in many ways a retiring and thoughtful man, he was, nevertheless, a man who was extremely sensitive to trends in his contemporary world of education. Russell must have been fully aware of the trend towards the institutionalization of research on education in every phase of the system. Russell had observed the emergence of research departments in school system, and several schools of education in universities had now well-established research departments including the University of Illinois and the University of California at Los Angeles. The year 1921 saw Teachers College on the brink of losing its position of leadership in this respect. In order to maintain the position of leadership that Teachers College had held in the past, Russell saw that some action needed to be taken.

Action probably was not difficult to take. The Commonwealth Fund had set aside funds for the development of educational research and Russell was able to collect some of this money. Other sources of funding were also open to Russell from the General Education Board financed with Rockefeller money. Russell undoubtedly had other motives in wanting to establish an institute. Teachers College, when it became a component of the Columbia University system, had become an affiliated institution which did not share in any of the income that Columbia derived from its mushrooming endowment. Nicholas Murray Butler had been able to persuade wealthy industrialists and merchants to give vast sums to the University and, before he retired from the presidency of the institution, he had made Columbia one of the richest institutions in the country. Teachers College obtained no support from this massive wealth. Indeed, the only advantage that Teachers College gained from its affiliation with Columbia University was that students at Teachers College were given Columbia Degrees. This was no small advantage but it did not solve any of the College's financial problems.

The teaching of students had been quite lucrative, particularly in the summer sessions when Teachers College had attracted students from not only every state in the Union but from the entire world. Nevertheless, a teaching institution had then as such institutions have today, difficulty in maintaining a research program, particularly when the institution was a private one. State institutions that were starting to establish bureaus of research were able to go to the state legislatures and to suggest that a bureau of research in education could perform functions analogous to the successful agricultural research stations, and the argument was a persuasive one. Teachers College had to find funds for research from new sources. Such funds could then relieve some professors of teaching loads since their salaries would no longer have to be paid out of student fees. Dean Russell undoubtedly saw that Thorndike's salary, claimed by Thorndike to be the highest of any professor in the United States, could well be paid partly out of funds from other sources now that funds were available. The formation of an institute would then make it possible to reduce Thorndike's teaching load to 3 hours. A similar situation exists in some universities today where teaching loads are reduced when professors obtain research contracts to which they can be assigned for a part of their time.

The traditional means by which a professor expands his research is through having doctoral students who will undertake a part of the professor's research as a dissertation. Thorndike had long had access to such students at Teachers College, though the College had not generally attracted students interested in basic research. After the formation of the institute, Thorndike still continued to have such access to students but he was able to pay those who otherwise would have come to him financed from their own resources. This alone accounts for the fact that the founding of the institute made surprisingly little difference to Thorndike's work. The Institute provided opportunities for the making of long term appointments for promising young men and women to be kept on, even on permanent appointments. The new sources of funds provided some opportunity for Thorndike to establish a school of devoted followers who would carry on his line of work after he departed.

The accomplishment of all the potential goals of an institute required a different executive than Edward L. Thorndike. He was a man who was so engrossed in his own work that he had little inclination to undertake the kinds of tasks that an executive has to undertake. He also lacked the extraordinary capacity to select individuals with long term potential that Russell had and used to build Teachers College. Thorndike was a shy retiring man who wanted to do his very best on his own work, so he paid minimum attention to the details of the Institute. Whatever time he gave to the institute detracted from the time available for the development of his own work. In the case of a few projects one can see that Thorndike may have been able to obtain data that might have been difficult to collect except for the existence of an institute, but the new organization seems hardly to have been an asset.

The Staff of the Institute

The most important activities of the Institute, during the 19 years that Thorndike was the director, were the personal pursuits of Thorndike himself. Next in importance were the contributions of some of his temporary staff, consisting of individuals who were there only a year or two. This staff carried the titles of research assistant or research associate and appointments were rarely for more than 2 years. Much of the work of these individuals was quite unrelated to Thorndike's own work and did nothing to extend his theories. Most of the staff completed a study and then moved on to a more permanent position elsewhere. Perhaps the most notable contributions of all were made by Mark A. May and Hugh Hartshorne who spent 3 years undertaking their classic Character Education Inquiry. As a result of this study three volumes appeared.

These three volumes became the most widely cited works in their field. Yet most who read them at the time they were published and those who read them today, do not associate them at all with the work of Thorndike.

They bear none of the marks of Thorndike's touch. One suspects that, once Hartshorne and May were at the Institute, Thorndike recognized their competence and left them alone to work on their studies. The research was undertaken with brilliant imagination. The results disposed of many of the prejudices on which much Sunday School teaching at that time was based. The volumes had impact more on the thinking and attitudes of those involved in religious education than on practices, for they did not suggest how the obviously ineffective educational practices related to character education could be improved. One would surely expect that if Thorndike had had any close contact with the studies that he would have published a set of materials related to character education that would be designed to remedy deficiencies. That was how he proceeded in nearly every area that he touched.

Hartshorne and May published over 30 journal articles on their studies and then seem to have given up research. May moved on to Yale, his reputation having been established. Hartshorne returned to the University of Southern California.

A large inquiry conducted by the Institute for the American Classical League was nearer to the mainstream of Thorndike's work. The purpose of that study was to explore the value of teaching Latin for the support it allegedly gave to mastering the English language. As a component of this research, a study was made of the derivations of the words found in 5,000 book pages of commonly read material. A by-product of this study was a word count of the 1.7 million words in the 5,000 pages. This enabled Thorndike to extend his word-count lists from the original 10,000 to 20,000. Thorndike was probably more interested in this feature of the investigation than in any other. Nevertheless, the study of the transfer study of Latin as a school subject did extend the work on transfer that Thorndike and Woodworth had started a quarter of a century earlier. The results also confirmed the findings of the earlier studies. Latin was shown to be an inefficient way of teaching English as Thorndike's theory of learning had predicted. The theory of transfer was, of course, not a particularly sound one; and yet it had considerable power of predicting when transfer effects could not be expected.

The results of the study can hardly have been what the American Classical League expected. The League was faced with the problem of declining enrollments in courses in Latin in high school. There was hope that research would show that the study of Latin would have transfer value and assist in the learning of other school subjects, but the evidence was to the contrary. The results doomed the study of Latin which, perhaps, had been taught with stress placed on the wrong objectives. In the twenty years that followed, the study of Latin would disappear as a school subject in most high schools of the country.

The institute was generally approached to sponsor studies on topics of particular interest at the time. This practice reminds one of the present

Federal practice of commissioning research on topics that are either politically hot or in which the public has become interested. An example of such studies was the series conducted within the Institute on problems related to the education of the gifted. These were conducted by Leta S. Hollingworth who had worked with Lewis Terman in the early 1920s on problems related to the measurement of the intelligence quotient and the identification of gifted children. These studies appeared during the period of 1924 to 1936. As a group of studies they are inconsequential. They dealt with such trivial topics as the tapping rate of children whose intelligence quotients exceeded 135, and the size and strength of gifted children. Such matters had already been investigated by Terman, not as isolated studies, but as a part of a broad and systematic attempt to assess the overall nature of the gifted. The output of the Institute on the gifted appears from the vantage point of the present to be conceptually weak. The project did have interesting aspects which must be mentioned if one is to find any redeeming features whatsoever. The City of New York placed at the disposal of the Institute, Public School 165, which was given the task of developing a program for the gifted. Some of the later and more interesting work of Leta Hollingworth involved evaluation studies of this program.

When one looks over the products of the program for the gifted, one comes away with the impression that Thorndike exercised little supervision over what went on in his Institute. The age was one when almost anything could be published, and journals did little to review manuscripts. The manuscripts that were published provide a rather good picture of the inadequacy of some of the research that was undertaken, on a quite large scale, by the Institute during the late 1920s and early 1930s. Such research today would have remained hidden for it would never have reached a stage of publication in journals.

The quality of research produced by the Institute seems to have depended entirely on the particular person who undertook the work. The Hartshorne and May studies were of the highest caliber. Also excellent were the studies of Herbert A. Toops.

The work of the Institute in the Thorndike years will probably be remembered most for Thorndike's personal work and for the work of a few of the distinguished research associates such as Hartshorne, May, Gates, and Maslow. Thorndike had difficulty in building a permanent staff that would create new extensions to this theory of learning. The small staff whom he had organized for the collection of data related to Thorndike projects was notoriously unable to create any new ideas of their own.

The number of long-term staff members of the Institute who had permanent positions were few. The most notable of these was Irving Lorge who became a research assistant at the Institute in 1925, a year before he graduated from the College of the City of New York. Lorge completed his masters degree at Teachers College in 1927 and his doctoral degree in 1930. From the start, he had a close personal relationship with Thorndike who admired the young man's extraordinary analytic intelligence. Many who worked in the Institute would have regarded Lorge as the outstanding intellect among the staff, though not the most creative. Lorge had an extraordinary capacity for making an analysis of problems and for setting up procedures through which they could be studied, though the procedures were typically those that had been used in previous studies. Lorge was also a competent organizer and could handle effectively the mechanics of large projects, and some of the projects that he managed for Thorndike in later years were of a very large magnitude, involving several hundred workers.

Lorge's personal relationship with Thorndike was also unique. The young Lorge, who was an ambitious Jewish boy, realized that the academic world was largely closed to him because of rife antisemitism. He found in Thorndike a great man who was willing to accept him for what he was, a brilliant and growing intelligence. Lorge had every reason not to expect that kind of acceptance in academic circles, which in the early part of the century had virtually excluded those of the Jewish faith. Not only had a professor accepted him, but he, Lorge, had been accepted by one of the most distinguished professors in the United States. Lorge was forever grateful for this acceptance, and far more grateful than for any intellectual stimulation that Thorndike had given him. Lorge found through this acceptance a means of partly overcoming the most deep-seated feelings of inferiority that often played havoc with his life, and which caused him to behave in ways that antagonized so many of his colleagues.

Although the initial role of Lorge in the Institute was that of a very bright student, who needed and received encouragement, as he acquired maturity he was able to give back to Thorndike a role of support and help in Thorndike's declining years. Thorndike's physical decline began early. After a few years of poor health, he had a heart attack in 1933 at the age of 59 a short time before his brother Ashley died of a heart attack, falling on the street, and passed over by hundreds of pedestrians who thought that they were watching a drunk. Thorndike was a changed man as a result of both the heart attack and Ashley's sudden demise, and particularly the circumstances under which it had occurred. For the rest of his life he had recurrent attacks of angina pectoris which left him terrified. Lorge played an extraordinary role in helping Thorndike adapt to these new circumstances in his life. Thorndike was so afraid that he would die alone as Ashley had done, but he was able to prevent this fear from overcoming him by taking Lorge with him on every trip when he had to leave town to give a lecture. Lorge was told exactly what to do if Thorndike were to collapse and carried the medication in his, Lorge's, pocket. When they took a trip together, it was usually by Pullman and

Thorndike would have the lower bunk and Lorge the upper. Lorge said he never slept much on these trips for he would listen for any unusual stirring in the lower bunk.

Lorge would share a hotel room with Thorndike, sit in the front row while Thorndike gave his lecture, and then take him back to New York, not just to the railroad terminal but to the door of his apartment where he would deliver him to Bess, Thorndike's wife.

On one such trip, Thorndike and Lorge were strolling back to the hotel after the lecture and Thorndike suddenly said to Lorge, "Irving, I am just so grateful for the way in which you have come with me on all these trips. I want to do something for you to show my appreciation." Lorge didn't know how to respond and wondered what was coming next. Then Thorndike said anticlimactically, "Irving, I've never done this before, but I want to buy you a coke." Thorndike probably had never gone out and had a coke with anybody before in his life. He would have regarded it as a waste of time. He had paid Lorge a great compliment by inviting him for a coke and implying that to have a coke with him was not a waste of time. The mutually supportive behavior of Lorge and Thorndike was of vital importance to both of them and sustained each through the most difficult years of their lives.

Lorge and Thorndike communicated easily about professional matters. They both had comparably sharp intellects, and shared some professional prejudices. Both believed that intelligence quotients reflected the most important characteristic of any person and that little could be done to change the intelligence quotient. Lorge was comfortable with a connectionist model of learning and could discuss such a theory with Thorndike without being critical. Lorge was exactly the kind of helper that Thorndike needed in the later years of his life and some of his later productivity was a result of the support that Lorge gave him.

Lorge's role in relation to Thorndike was a special and personal one, but it never resulted in Lorge applying the work of Thorndike to new frontiers after Thorndike retired. Throughout physics one finds that the students of a great man carried on the work of the master extending it into new frontiers. J. J. Thomson's student Ernest Rutherford carried on the work on atomic structure that Thomson had started, and Rutherford's model of the atom was extended by his student Niels Bohr. Thus a great man produces another great man who produces still another, and each expands upon the work of his master. Such a building by succeeding generations has not happened in psychology. Thorndike left no star performer to build on his work as Rutherford had built on the work of Thomson. Thorndike may well have hoped that Lorge would do this, but Lorge never did. Lorge did succeed Thorndike as Director of the Institute, but he published little and there was no originality to his work. Lorge complained to his friends that he had such difficulty writing, and he did have difficulty writing, often undertaking research and never publishing it. Sometimes he even tried to convert this difficulty into an asset by boasting that he did not publish every study he undertook. His central difficulty was not just in writing but in finding some central theme that he could explore over a period of time. What research he did is a patchwork of unrelated ideas. Much of it was work undertaken by his graduate students with whom he authored publications. Lorge was in many ways at his best in working with graduate students, and surprisingly enough, with the less brilliant students who needed so much help. A very large number of those who hold doctoral degrees from Teachers College owe their degrees to the fact that they were helped by Irving Lorge. Their accomplishments are his real monument. Thorndike had no successor.

The largest single undertaking of Lorge was a semantic word count of 4.5 million words undertaken in the late 1930s as a project of the Works Progress Administration. This enterprise involved the employment of nearly 300 workers who were placed on a very meagre government payroll in order to undertake the task. This was perhaps the largest word count enterprise ever undertaken and it provided material for later editions of the *Teachers Word Book.*

Thorndike's only other long term major staff member was Ella Woodyard, about whom history has little to say. The author could find no entry in any biographical source concerning Ella Woodyard and neither could find an obituary in the New York Times. Yet Ella played a major role in the Institute. She was a Kansas school teacher who came to Teachers College in the early 1920s and stayed there to complete a doctoral degree. Her intellect was in many ways much like that of Lorge. She had a brilliant analytic mind that appealed to Thorndike, and, yet, she lacked any spark of creative ability. She was an excellent project organizer and functioned much as an office manager. She worshipped Thorndike even to the point where some said that she was deeply in love with him. She may well have been, for he was a very lovable man. She stood ready to do whatever he needed to have done. She had fewer personal ambitions than Lorge, and was not particularly concerned about the choice of projects to which she was assigned, and these varied from studies of human learning to research on the degree mills of the United States. She had something of Lorge's forthright manner and for this was sometimes dubbed as a typical Kansas farm woman.

Ella Woodyard had almost no publications of her own, a fact suggestive of the way in which the staff of the Institute operated. She published her doctoral dissertation through Teachers College in 1926, but this was a requirement for awarding the doctoral degree. She did publish a report on her own in 1940 covering a study undertaken on correspondence schools that awarded higher degrees (*Culture at a Price; a Study of Private Correspondence School Offerings*, 1940). She was designated as a joint author on Thorndike's work on *Adult Learning* and *The Psychology of Algebra*, presumably for her participation in the research related to the books, but the writing of these books was unmistakably that of Thorndike.

One wonders whether the intellects of both Lorge and Woodyard would have shone more brightly if they had not been overwhelmed by the brilliance of the light of their intellectual master. A candle shines brightly in the dark, but is hardly noticeable in the light of the sun.

Woodyard could not have carried on the work of Thorndike for she retired at about the same time as he did, and on retirement she also retired intellectually from psychology, directing her efforts towards helping the Frontier Nursing Service in which she had had a deep interest while in Kansas.

Thorndike's Work in His Later Years

The existence of the Institute did little to change the work of Thorndike in his later years. Once he had a measure of word difficulty through word counts, he sought to develop materials for schools in which the vocabulary would be appropriate for children of particular ages. With this in mind he began to revise children's classics, such as *Black Beauty*, in order to bring the vocabulary into line with the words he thought children knew at particular ages. The result was a series, known as the *Thorndike Library*, published by Appleton-Century in 1935. An enormous amount of work was involved in the development of this series. Much of this work was undertaken by Thorndike, in bed, and in the hour before going to sleep. He claimed that he found the work relaxing. The work was actually quite strenuous in that all difficult words had to be marked, and then he had to find, from the word list, a word at a lower level of difficulty. The work was hardly bedtime reading. Thorndike once admitted that when he had finished the work he had assigned to himself for the night, he sometimes found it necessary to relax. He also added that when he had the time to relax, he would spend 15 minutes reading a detective story. On the other hand, when the hour was such that he could not afford the time to relax with a detective story, then he would take a sleeping pill and relax in that way. Such was the life of a man who had a bad heart, and who probably needed relaxation and systematic exercise, but the discipline in his life was all related to his work. None of it pertained to keeping his body in good order.

The readers were not a success, probably not because of the work of Thorndike, but because the old time classics were beginning to move out of the classroom and to be displaced by other more modern materials.

Thorndike's work on vocabulary and word counts led him in the early thirties to begin to consider the matter of making dictionaries. The problem of designing dictionaries in a particular language is a relatively new one, for the early forms of dictionaries were of the polyglot variety and were designed for translating one language into another. The first English dictionaries appeared in the early 1600s and were derived from earlier lists of words prepared for teachers who might want to ensure that children developed a vocabulary. The early word lists were strictly word lists and no attempts were made to define the words. The lists were based on somebody's judgment of what words were important. Richard Mulcaster had developed such a list in 1852 and used it as a basis for his instruction in the Merchant Taylor's school. The word list seems to have been used as a basis for word recognition, pronunciation, and writing. Only a short step was needed to move from the word list to the word list with definitions. The development of dictionaries was followed by dictionaries expanded to include archaic words that the person might come across in documents, and then hard words which were so rarely used that many who encountered them would need to have a means of identifying their meaning. The pronouncing dictionary seems to have been a product of the early 1700's and a particularly difficult enterprise in that local dialects probably differed then more than they do today.

The early 1700's also saw a movement in the direction of developing dictionaries for the purpose of standardizing the English language. This need for standardization seems to have reflected a need for convenience. Reading was difficult in a day when a common word could be spelled in a dozen different ways. Indeed, rapid reading is possible only after uniform spelling has been adopted. At the center of this movement to provide an authoritative source on the best English usage was Samuel Johnson who contracted with five leading booksellers in 1746 to develop a dictionary of English usage. Samuel Johnson, perhaps the most extraordinary scholar of his age, made the work into something far more than a mere set of definitions. Illustrated with 118,000 quotations it became truly the first attempt to define words in terms of usage by the most educated persons of the age. The work, which took 7 years to produce, included about 43,500 words, not many more than were included in the final *Teachers Word List* produced by Thorndike.

Dictionaries came to be used in schools in the American colonies, and several dictionaries were prepared for this purpose before the Revolutionary War. These dictionaries included American words and American usage that had already begun to drift away from the usage of the mother country. Samuel Johnson himself had recognized that the standardization of a language was possible only to a limited degree and that language, as a human creation, was bound to have considerable flexibility. Noah Webster was, of course, the individual who played the largest role in providing an authoritative source of American usage. Of some interest is the fact that Webster began his career as a political essayist and as a compiler of spelling lists which had as their main purpose the establishment of a uniform spelling system for the American colonies.

Thorndike was aware of the problems that dictionary makers had faced in the past. He realized that dictionaries had to be based on word lists, and that the word lists of the past were arbitrarily assembled by single individuals who exercised what best judgment they could. Word counts now provided an empirical basis for the development of dictionaries at particular levels. In addition, definitions could be written in terms of words with which pupils of a particular age were familiar. Thorndike set out to develop a dictionary for the Middle School level that would be based on the new foundation provided by research. The first product was the *Thorndike-Century Junior Dictionary* (1935). This dictionary was a personal product of Thorndike's own hand. When he was not sitting up evenings editing the classics for children, he was writing definitions for his new dictionary. The result was a splendid and successful product. It could add nothing to the fame and prestige of Thorndike for these were at a zenith, but it brought him a small fortune. Royalties from New York State alone during the year 1938 were close to 10,000 dollars, and the dollar in those days had a high purchasing power, but Thorndike's satisfaction was far more than any derived from the wealth it brought him. He was deeply satisfied to know that he had brought to children a teaching device that might help them all of their lives. Thorndike thought in such terms and far more along such humanitarian lines than along monetary lines.

The success of the *Junior Dictionary* led him to develop a dictionary at a higher level that was published in 1940 (*Thorndike-Century Dictionary*, 1940). This dictionary did not receive the tremendous reception that the *Junior Dictionary* had received, probably because it had to compete against other excellent dictionaries.

The Later Expansion of Connectionist Theory

Thorndike's major development of learning theory was in his dissertation which brought him more fame than any other study he ever published. Then, nearly 15 years later the publication of his 3-volume *Educational Psychology* extended the application of his initial theoretical position to much of psychology, for Thorndike viewed all of psychology as being educational psychology. His contributions during the war years and the years shortly after the war were occupied in other endeavors, mainly enterprises of application, but the late 1920's brought him back to a consideration of theoretical issues related to learning. He now had more doctoral students at his disposal and also funds from the Carnegie Corporation, where his old school friend Frederick Keppel was now president and made sure that Thorndike had all the funds he needed for his work.

Most of Thorndike's work on learning in the late 1920's was brought together in a volume *Human Learning* (1931). The work in this volume presents a series of lectures given at Cornell University in the academic year 1928-29. Ironically, it was not Titchener, but Thorndike, who had the last word on the Cornell Campus. The first two chapters of the book provide research related to a problem which came to intrigue psychologists for another 30 years, namely, whether mere exposure to a situation, or the mere repetition of the connection between a situation and a response, could produce learning. This became known later as the latent learning issue, and still later the issue of whether learning could occur without reinforcement. Thorndike could find no evidence that repeated exposure to a situation or a repeated response to a situation could produce learning. He conceded that if learning was produced, it was in a very small amount indeed. We now know that he had not chosen situations in which there was learning by mere exposure, but his evidence was convincing at the time when it was produced.

Several chapters in the book deal with the problem of how after-effects function. In his earlier works he had taken the position that animal learning and human learning were essentially the same, but Thorndike was slowly coming to the conclusion that there were important differences. He then suggested that human learning involves information processing of a kind that could not possibly take place in animals. Ivan Pavlov, who, at the time Thorndike was doing his work on human learning, was considering the idea that human learning involved a "second signalling system" of a verbal nature. Thorndike was now playing with the same idea. Thorndike pointed out that in human learning, long delays in rewards might not reduce their effectiveness because of the operation of verbal mediators. One can learn by being rewarded tomorrow for what one has done today, because one can rehearse verbally the response that is rewarded even if it took place sometime earlier.

Further chapters in the book discuss the work of Ivan Pavlov that had been by then popularized in America through the extravagant writings of John B. Watson. Thorndike had difficulty in fitting the facts of classical conditioning into his system, although others viewed classical conditioning and connectionism as completely compatible. Both belonged to the family of psychological theories known as associationist theories, and were later to form the background of a new type of associationist theory known as operant psychology.

Of some interest is the fact that Thorndike's attack was not on John B. Watson who had popularized conditioning theory in America, but on Ivan Pavlov and his work. Thorndike respected Pavlov, but he detested Watson whom he regarded as nothing more than a charlatan. Watson had been a visiting professor at Teachers College in 1915 and had left a negative impression on Thorndike.

Thorndike used the concept of response probability frequently in his book on *Human Learning*. This was a new usage in the 1920's, but what he wrote using the terms has quite a modern ring to it. Indeed, there are sections of the volume that are so much like the later writings of B. F. Skinner that one can see in them the foundation on which Skinner built his system.

Thorndike's treatment of the new emerging Gestalt theory of learning was brushed aside rather quickly. The issue of whether psychology should remain strictly reductionist had not been fully aired. Thorndike's discussion of Gestalt psychology is rather surprising in that he typically completely ignored those who criticized his point of view.

In a final chapter Thorndike dreamed about the future, a dream that carried him through the final years of his professional career. He speculated that in the future the human will learn more, and what he learns will be nearer to being true and wise. In addition, what he learns will be learned more easily and pleasantly. Furthermore, learning in the population will be better organized and distributed to permit society to operate more smoothly. He hoped that eugenics would result in a more intelligent population, a fact which brings out Thorndike's basic view that intelligence is the one characteristic that has to be developed. Presumably, a more intelligent population simply means one in which individuals can make more connections, though he had begun to talk about the *organization* of connections, a term suggesting that Gestalt psychology had begun to have some impact on his thinking.

The book *Human Learning* had none of the impact that Thorndike's previous great works had had, perhaps because there was not much that was new in it. The volume reflects the fact that Thorndike recognized that his work was emerging from the state in which it was the only experimentally based theory of learning to a state where it had to be evaluated against many competitors. In the past he had been able to ignore criticism, but now it could no longer be ignored.

Thorndike's two final major contributions to theory of learning were probably more significant than his *Human Learning*, because of the new ground they broke. These two major contributions were his *Adult Learning* (New York: Macmillan, 1928) and his *Psychology of Wants, Interests and Attitudes* (1935).

The volume on *Adult Learning* presented important new experiments on the learning of adults. The emergence of adult education programs, during the depression years, had raised questions about whether adults could learn effectively. The then current view was that the younger one was, the better one was able to learn, and that the elderly were virtually unable to learn. The volume on adult learning presented studies that challenged these assumptions. The conclusions from systematic studies of the learning of adults in academic learning situations was that age had only the smallest effect on learning. There was a very slight decline after the mid-twenties, but so slight that it was of no practical significance.

Nevertheless, adults expected to learn too much too quickly and tended to be disappointed with their achievements. The problem of adult learning was one of motivation.

The *Adult Learning* volume was a technical work designed for the consumption of the psychologist and professor of education. Yet the work had important implications for the growing adult education movement. Thorndike inevitably saw the need for a subsequent volume in which the implications for the adult movement could be discussed, and in terms that those involved in the movement would understand. The book that followed, *Adult Interests* (1935), pursued the view that the basic problem in adult education is one of motivation. The book is a treatise on the motivation of the adult, and particularly the older adult. There are some new data presented in this book, and considerable advice on how programs of adult education should be run.

The data in the volume are mainly responses to questionnaires. In conducting studies through the interview and the questionnaire, Thorndike did not take the advice he had handed out to teachers in his classes, who were advised to pay little attention to what children said interested them, but rather to watch and see what activities children chose, for activities were the real expression of interest. Thorndike had, perhaps, changed his mind on that issue and had forgotten the admonitions he had extended to G. Stanley Hall for doing just what he, Thorndike, was doing.

The most interesting part of the book is on the organization of adult education for it reflects Thorndike's social philosophy, antiphilosophical though he was. He argued strongly that adult education should not be compensatory education for those who had made little use of their time in the common school. Adult education, thus, was not viewed as an equalizing force, for he did not believe that individuals were ever equal either in intellectual level or competency. Adult education should be for those who could profit most from it, those who had already shown their ability in educational settings.

Thorndike did not believe that children should be kept in school after they had ceased to be interested in learning. He deplored the continuing increase in the school leaving age and believed that many children who could not profit from it were kept there against their will. Adult education should be for those who wanted to master some skill and who had a need for it. It should always be tied to interest and need. He did not view aging to be a factor in this respect because interests could be acquired at any age.

Thorndike's last major contribution to the psychology of learning was his book *The Psychology of Wants, Interests and Attitudes* (1935). Few scientists produce highly original works when they are past 50 years of age, but this work is one of remarkable originality. Thorndike had long been concerned with motivational aspects of learning. His concept of satisfiers and annoyers were conditions that involved the energizing of behavior and were objectively defined. Thus a satisfier was a condition that the organism tended to perpetuate, and an annoyer was one that the organism sought to avoid or to escape. Thorndike also noted that the original nature of a living organism made it seek out certain situations rather than other situations. Thorndike had even proposed a mechanism to account for the acquisition of new energizing factors being produced by learning. The main mechanism proposed was that of associative shifting. A condition present when a satisfier was operating could also acquire satisfying properties through this association, or through the operation of an associative shift.

A quite typical Thorndikeian experiment was his study of valued versus valueless facts. The hypothesis tested was whether valued facts were learned more rapidly than valueless facts. In order to study this problem, Thorndike had prepared a number of lists in which a person would have to learn the birthdates of celebrities and the birthdates of nonentities. Thorndike hypothesized that the birthdates of celebrities would be more easily learned than those of nonentities. In another experiment individuals learned useful and harmful facts. Harmful facts were the dates when celebrities were *not* born. Individuals, presumably, *want* to learn useful facts. Wants and needs were closely tied to a search for truth and a desire to know that which is useful.

Thorndike's conclusions from a very large number of experiments were that the intrinsic wants, attitudes and interests of the individual were powerful forces in learning, and far more powerful than the extrinsic motives produced by the manipulation of satisfiers and annoyers. He believed that schools should harness the intrinsic wants and needs of the individual and should rely much less heavily on the control of pupil behavior through external means. In this connection he makes a rare reference to John Dewey who had hammered at this theme for half a century before Thorndike came to experiment and write on the subject.

The experiments cited above were just two of many experiments. The experiments discussed in the book are all numbered, the highest number being 66, but not all 66 experiments are described in detail. Thorndike is probably the only psychologist in the history of experimental psychology who conducted so many experiments that he had to number them. During his lifetime his experiments must have run into the thousands.

Many of the experiments in the book dealt with theoretical issues that were not central to the topic of the volume. The book was just a convenient place in which to report the results. For example, extensive research was presented demonstrating the spread of the effect of reward and the spread of the effect of punishment. The data showed how the rewarding of a response also had a weak effect on the responses that took place shortly before or shortly after the rewarded response. The same kind of effect was demonstrated in the case of punished responses.

Thorndike was not surprised by these findings in that rewards and punishments functioned with complete automaticity.

Human Nature and the Social Order

The last 5 years of Thorndike's career at Teachers College were largely devoted to a project that carried the label of *Human Nature and the Social Order*. The project was sponsored by the Carnegie Foundation, and that sponsorship had much to do with the fact that Thorndike's old friend Frederick Paul Keppel was president. The sum of $100,000 provided by the Carnegie Corporation undoubtedly went largely to purchase Thorndike's time from Teachers College and to make it possible for him to work without a teaching load or committee work. A small amount was available to employ graduate assistants and associates. The overall purpose of the project was to explore the implication of Thorndike's position as a connectionist for the organization and improvement of society.

Although Thorndike was described by his contemporaries as antiphilosophical, he had a deep rooted personal social philosophy. This was evident in all the materials that he had prepared for use in schools. These materials all reflected the belief that the task of the school was to prepare the child for the world of work in American society. The child was to grow up to fit the system. Arithmetic was taught because it was a basic tool for solving immediate and practical problems within the system, and the teaching of arithmetic did not presume to teach children to handle new problems that might occur because of changes in the system. Thorndike believed that the schools should develop those connections between situations and responses that the practical world of America required. There was nothing in Thorndike's vision of the future that included such ideas as those of George Counts who was proposing that the school should be a primary instrument for social change. For Thorndike, the schools were there to maintain the system, not to change it. His view was a strictly conservative one.

Thorndike presented a common mix of characteristics. On the one hand, he displayed extraordinary kindness and gentleness in all of his personal relationships. On the other hand, he believed that individuals should help themselves and should not be overly helped either by others or by the state. He believed that to extend much help to others was to do them harm by depriving them of opportunities to show initiative and resourcefulness. That was the way in which he handled his own fortune. The money was his, and rarely did he use any of it for favorite causes. Yet, those who worked for him believed that, in an emergency, one could always count on him.

Thorndike believed in the virtue of work, and work was for him a driving passion. In his writings he protested the idea that work was dull and should be reduced to the minimum number of hours necessary. He held the view that almost any activity called work was an activity that somebody, somewhere, pursued for leisure. This was a view concerning work that was based on ignorance of what people did. He would have had a hard time convincing anybody that what men and women did on assembly lines was ever done for pleasure. Nobody ever did for pleasure the kinds of tasks that fill the daily lives of coalminers. Thorndike's conception of work was more related to what he had seen in small towns in New England and in the suburbs of Boston. In such places much of what is called work is performed by others for pleasure. He had no conception of the conditions in sweatshops and mines that unions were fighting against, which was why he thought that unions should concentrate more on raising the general quality of life than on wages and conditions of work.

Thorndike was also politically ignorant. He never participated in any political battle and would not have known how to act. When his dear friend James McKeen Cattell was summarily fired by Columbia University, for advocating military exemption for conscientious objectors in World War I, Thorndike was deeply disturbed by the incident, but he didn't know of any action he could take. Any politically knowledgeable adult could have told him that he, as one of the most prestigious professors in America, could have taken vigorous action to support Cattell, as James Beard and others did, but Thorndike seems to have been almost paralyzed by the experience. As an organizer, he was naive as his work in organizing the Institute showed him to be. He was so thoroughly absorbed in his own work that he was quite cut off from people, even to the extent that he hardly knew there was a depression in the 1930's, except for the fact that some of his stocks stopped paying dividends. He was not a callous man, but a caring person. Nevertheless, his way of life cut him off so much from the rest of humanity that there were few towards whom he could express this caring relationship. He certainly could feel no caring relationship for the millions of unemployed, or for those working for such desperately low rates that they emerged from work each day with just enough money to hold body and soul together to bring them to another day's work.

One can understand a Machiavelli writing about the techniques that rulers should adopt in order to produce happiness and prosperity, for Machiavelli had spent years in the highest courts and knew every political trick that had ever been invented. The understanding of Thorndike's desire to produce social reform is much more difficult. One cannot understand it in terms of his political qualifications for the task, but one can understand it in other terms. He lived in an age when the behavioral and social sciences had begun to conceptualize themselves as having a special role to play in social change. The Technocrats had popularized the idea that societies should be built through a new kind of social engineering. Frederick Taylor and others had begun to show how methods, called scientific methods, could be applied to improve industrial efficiency. Many believed that similar approaches could be applied to improving the functioning of other aspects of society. Thorndike was convinced that his work had resulted in improved efficiency in schools, and to a considerable degree it had, and all that improvement occurred without Thorndike ever visiting a school. He must surely have been led to believe that there was no more gap between him and adult society than there was between him and the schools. Surely, by the same kind of process through which he had brought enlightenment to school practices, enlightenment could be brought to other aspects of society. His project *Human Nature and the Social Order* was the vehicle through which this was to be achieved.

Some of the work in this new enterprise involved digesting a literature with which Thorndike had had very little previous contact. He had learned in the writing of his 3-volume *Educational Psychology* that a scholar had to be fully informed about every previous piece of work of any importance, if his work was to bear the mark of scholarship. Thorndike began to delve into the literature of economics, and, to a lesser extent, sociology. His writing during this period shows that he acquired more than superficial knowledge of research in these areas. He was always a very thoughtful reader. His attempts to have graduate students delve in the areas for him were not successful, for the younger generation of graduate students was far more liberal than he, and he had difficulty in assimilating what the younger generation wrote. His excursions into economics were always for the purpose of attempting to synthesize the ideas he found there with his own ideas on human nature derived from laboratory studies. This synthesis was difficult because the human, as a laboratory animal, is very different from the human as a political animal.

The project resulted in two main products. The first was a volume that carried the popular title of *Your City* (1939), but it was quite a complicated sociological study of American cities and what makes them good or poor places in which to live. Thorndike had a criterion of what makes a city good, much the same as the concept of what makes a school good. He identified 37 statistical indices which he thought that good people would agree to be criteria of a good city. These criteria included infant death rate, the general death rate, deaths from diseases of childhood and death from Typhoid. Then there were eight criteria based upon education. Most of the latter had to do with expenditures and pupil attendance. Two items concerned public provision for recreation. This latter small number is in keeping with Thorndike's evaluation of recreation. Then eight items had to do with economic welfare, and five items were concerned with creature comforts such as ownership of automobiles, and availability of electricity and other facilities. In addition, there were measures of literacy and readership of good magazines and, finally, a miscellaneous group of six items. These items taken together provided a measure of goodness of life for good people in each one of the 300 American cities studied.

The final section of the report was on how to improve your city, and it was an essay on Thorndike's personal philosophy. He stated at the beginning of this final section (p. 157) that "at least four fifths of the differences of cities in goodness is caused by the personal qualities of the citizens and the amount of their incomes." In order to improve a city it must attract good people to it who will earn more money. Perhaps Thorndike was telling us in this section why money was important to him. It is the mark of a good and successful citizen. The discussion of the role of education in improving a city is particularly interesting. He argues that a city can be improved through good educational facilities, but not by forcing education on people who do not want it. Those who strive to have an education should be handsomely rewarded, but there should never be coercion in inducting individuals into educational programs.

Thorndike displayed his political naiviete when he suggested that all matters pertaining to education, public health, recreation, crime prevention, and poverty, should be kept outside of political partisanship. Most of these are highly sensitive political issues, but Thorndike believed that scientists and other people of wisdom should recommend the decisions to be made. In this connection, Thorndike pointed out that schools had been improved by just such a process, and not through self-government of pupils or through various pressure groups. He also believed in the autocracy of the teacher and, one suspects, the autocracy of the wise and influential citizen who, Thorndike believed, would surely come to the top.

A final section of the report comes back to an issue that Thorndike had raised since his earliest writings at Teachers College. A good society can be good so far as it includes many citizens with superior genetic endowment. He anticipated advances in the science of human breeding that would produce new generations with greatly enhanced potentiality for good.

The finale to the project was the volume entitled *Human Nature and the Social Order* (1940). This is a ponderous and massive volume, the largest book that Thorndike ever wrote, and more than twice as long as any other. He felt great pride in the work and was constantly worried during its preparation that a fire or accident might destroy a part of the manuscript. He also had some fear that he might not live to see the work through to completion. He regarded the work as the crowning achievement of his career.

The volume begins, as one would expect, with a brief summary of his connectionist theory of behavior. This introduction begins with an exposition of the idea of response probability and the effect of environmental conditions on changes in the probability of a particular response. It would take only a few minor changes in vocabulary to make it read like an authentic discussion of operant psychology. To do this one would have to substitute a term such as *after-effects* by the term *reinforcers*. Such changes are hardly drastic. Thorndike even made a firm distinction between classical conditioning and the strengthening of connections between situations and responses which is very much the same as the distinction made later by B. F. Skinner between instrumental and classical conditioning.

Two subsequent chapters on human abilities present Thorndike's position on the nature of individual differences. Although he recognizes that abilities may be improved through training, he still placed solid emphasis on the theory that there are important genetic differences. Although the volume was written in 1940, it still shows the influence of the work of Francis Galton on hereditary genius of a half century earlier. Thorndike was particularly interested in the source of high level ability, since individuals with such ability constitute the source of leadership and advancement in our society. He pointed out that high level ability occurs much more frequently than is apparent from common observation, and that special conditions are needed for it to flourish. However, Thorndike suspected that those who have very high ability indeed may be very rare, and perhaps may occur with a frequency of only one in 500 million. Such individuals may perform services that perhaps none other in the same generation can perform. The examples he gave of individuals with such high abilities are odd from today's viewpoint. They are those of Enrico Caruso, Andrew Carnegie, and Theodore Roosevelt. He argued that a scientific personnel manager for the world should keep track of those born of parents of high ability and who show promise of excelling. He believed that the profit from such a venture involving the monitoring of the young would pay for itself many times over. He also believed that even a small rise in the level of the ability of world leadership would result in enormous gains for humanity.

His outlook was like that of Plato who envisioned a ruling class of the wise. Meritocracies have always been favorite political systems for academicians, and from Plato on have been criticized for being fascistic in outlook. The criticism is not entirely warranted in the case of Plato for he did make provision in his *Republic* for the consent of the governed. Thorndike did not deal with this issue but argued that there is a correlation of at least 0.5 between ability and virtue and that the able should also make the virtuous decisions. His example of Carnegie hardly seemed to support his case.

The testing movement, in which Thorndike had played a role, would provide the basis for identifying talent and ensure that the meritocracy would function effectively. However, Thorndike would want to be sure that those who came to the top of the system would exercise judgment, and presumably leadership, in only those areas in which they were expert. His studies of transfer of training had told him that expertise in one area did not imply expertise in another area.

Thorndike had an interesting discussion of salaries paid for high ability. He argued, but not persuasively, that executives of large corporations are underpaid. He based this argument on the assumption that these executives represent extremely rare and irreplaceable abilities. He also argued that great ability is more likely to come to the top in a free society than in a planned type of communistic society. The argument for the latter is not persuasive for the main instruments proposed for filtering ability to the top is the bureaucratic machinery of testing, guidance, and education, which presumably, could operate as effectively in a communistic society as in a free society.

The good society has to use the abilities of the people to satisfy their wants and needs. So it was appropriate that Thorndike should give consideration to this topic. The consideration is necessarily weak in that the amount of data available at that time was very small indeed. Thorndike attempts to provide a list of desires and aversions based on original nature, but argues that rewards and punishments may alter wants just as they may alter any other response.

Thorndike then proceeds with a long series of chapters which attempt to apply what is known about human nature to the various facets of human government. He discusses such a diversity of topics as the formation and use of capital, buying and selling, the selection of rulers, ownership, money and credit, improvement in the law, and a great diversity of other topics. The reader is not always clear about what Thorndike's position is. In the chapter on rulers, various ways of selecting rulers are discussed, and one comes to the end of the chapter with the impression that Thorndike does not have much faith in the election process but looks to a Platonic form of meritocracy. Thorndike does suggest how trustees might be selected from among the individuals of distinction to function as the trustees of a community. He even states that his ideas on the subject might shock many, and they did.

A final chapter brings together his ideas for the reform and improvement of society. His first proposal was to improve the genes of the human race through encouraging the breeding of the able and good. The proposal was probably less controversial then than it is today. Thorndike could see no real problems in implementing this idea. The second suggestion, much like that of later operant psychologists, is to use rewards more effectively in every phase of human life for developing desirable behaviors. The third involves what Thorndike called the *law of exercise*. If one can cause humans to do good things, then one can work on establishing good behaviors in all phases of life. A fourth proposal is that the social sciences can help to determine what changes are within the realm of possibilities, and the fifth is a need for better guidance by scientists of the process of change. A sixth suggestion is that government and peoples must learn to respect the truth. A seventh proposal is that able individuals should acquire power, though how this is to be done is far from clear. There are several recommendations concerning the use of able individuals in government and the suggestion that the able and good should constitute a national overseeing body to ensure that government served the people. This again is an example of Thorndike's Platonic political philosophy. The hope is also expressed that a shortened work week will enable all to spend time acquiring wisdom.

One can hardly be surprised that the work attracted little attention. A typical response was that the work said nothing new. None wanted to criticize the last major work of a man who had achieved so much and who had made so many positive contributions to education. There was also a widespread warmth and affection felt for Thorndike as a man, which inhibited the criticism which would have been raised if he had written it in his younger years. The work was his swansong and his academic colleagues left it at that. Whether Thorndike himself was disappointed with the reception is hard to say, for he had long ceased to be concerned with what reviewers might write.

THE DECLINING YEARS

Thorndike retired from Teachers College in 1939 at the age of 65. He gave up his apartment on 120th Street and Amsterdam Avenue and moved to the house he had long owned at Montrose. At one time he had commuted from Montrose to Teachers College, but when his health began to decline an apartment in New York City seemed in order. Also he had fewer troubles in the City with allergies than he had in Montrose. In Montrose he was surrounded by friends. Since the beginning of the century, he had held a large piece of property there that he had slowly sold to friends including Frederick Keppel and Leta Hollingworth.

He continued to publish 10 or more papers a year. Many papers were based on a reworking of data that he had accumulated over the years. It was very characteristic of Thorndike not to throw away anything and data were often used and analyzed 20 or more years after they were collected. Much of it was quite repetitive of what he had written earlier, and he, himself, recognized that this was inevitably so. A publisher who visited him in the mid 1940s found him propped up in bed reading a detective story. A pile of other detective stories were stacked on the table beside the bed. The publisher was horrified. "Ned," he said, "How can you waste your time in this way. You have done more to influence education than any other man, and here you are, reading cheap fiction."

Thorndike answered his critic quite sadly. "I have had every idea I am ever going to have," he said, "Every idea I have ever had I have written about. What is there left for me to do?"

He did love to read detective stories. Reading them was his one small recreation. Outside of work he had never enjoyed anything else very much. That was all that he had left to do. Nearly all of his old friends had also gone. He was a tired, and lonely, and rather sad old man.

On 9 August 1949 Thorndike died of a massive cerebral hemorrhage.

THE THORNDIKE LEGACY AND THE LEGATEES

Thorndike made a permanent difference to education, but not through everything he did. Let us review those aspects of his work that have had the greatest impact. His permanent impact on education comes not through his theoretical posture but through the results of his empirical research. Although his theoretical creations were the very foundation of everything he did, they do not represent the main point of impact. His *Animal Intelligence*, the very foundation of his search for ways of improving education, came to have impact on the thought of experimental psychologists across the world, but not on educators.

Thorndike's first source of major impact on education was the series of studies of transfer that he conducted with Robert S. Woodworth. The series forcefully demolished the doctrine of formal education of the last century and changed the curriculum and educational materials for all time. One should note that the theory of transfer on which the studies were based has long ceased to be of significance, and the empirical findings are now known to apply to only a very limited aspect of education. Nevertheless, the components of educational practice that they attacked were appropriately attacked by them. Transfer does take place in education in a way that Thorndike never envisaged, but it is transfer within the domain of logical operations, an area where Thorndike had very little useful to say. As theory of transfer has developed, psychologists have been able to identify sources of transfer and to apply the knowledge to the design of educational programs. Thorndike's work began an era that has resulted in enormous impact of psychological research on educational practice.

The second great landmark provided by the work of Thorndike comes in the publication of his 3-volume work *Educational Psychology*. This is a landmark in that it provided a standard of scientific writing in relation to education that all subsequent writers had to try and live by. It set a new standard for educational literature and demonstrated a recognition that education had to advance through the systematic application of organized scientific knowledge. His smaller *Educational Psychology* of 1903 had done this to some degree, but not with the same scope of his 3-volume work.

The 3-volume *Educational Psychology* was the first massive attempt to bring scientific thinking to bear on problems of education. Many had tried to do this before Thorndike, but in a quite casual way. For example, Maria Montessori made casual references in her works to recent medical, physiological, and psychological research, but there was nothing systematic about the way in which such material was drawn upon. William Torrey Harris, as Commissioner of Education, liked to draw the attention of educators to recent scientific advances, but even Harris did not conceive of education as being changed by bringing to bear on its problems massive amounts of scientific findings. Thorndike had that vision and spent his life bringing it nearer to realization.

The next most influential piece of work of Thorndike was that which involved word counts, and such spinoffs from word counts as are found in his compilation of dictionaries for children. This enterprise, like the production of his large *Educational Psychology* required an initial 10 years of work. Thorndike's projects that were most successful in influencing the long term course of education were those in which he invested long years of his own time. The work on word-counts also had other consequences, namely the development of controlled vocabulary readers. Still another was the development of formulae for measuring the difficulty of reading materials.

The materials that Thorndike developed rather rapidly often brought him great financial gain, but little lasting fame, and the long-term effect of the materials on education was typically slight. The *Thorndike Arithmetics* fall into this category. Only a few individuals today would even know of their existence, despite the fact that they sold over 5 million copies. The lack of long-term impact of these materials is probably a result of the fact that they were developed in an area about which connectionist theory has least utility, namely, the area of reasoning. Modern attempts to build mathematics curricula draw upon an entirely different tradition and way of thinking.

Thorndike's attempt to develop a social philosophy in which science became the central technique for social change had no impact at the time nor since. On the other hand, his philosophy of education, which was not his original creation, has returned to fashion periodically. There is appeal to many in the idea that the schools should teach only that which is of direct practical use in adult life.

The legacy of Thorndike was widely distributed which is why one cannot discern any tightly knit groups of Thorndike followers. His general theory of behavior blossomed into operant psychology, as Joncich points out in her biography of Thorndike, in citing a letter from Skinner to Thorndike. When Skinner published his *Behavior of Organisms* (1938), he was admonished by some for failing to credit Thorndike for the source of his ideas. Joncich cites a letter from Skinner to Thorndike in which he was apologetic for this omission, and stating that his work was simply an extension of Thorndike's work on cats escaping from puzzle boxes. The tie of Skinner to Thorndike is extremely close, and operant psychologists are the main legatees of the Thorndike legacy.

Those who design any kind of curricula materials today are also legatees of the Thorndike heirloom of knowledge. Few textbooks for schools today are ever published without some steps being taken to check for vocabulary level and reading level. His work led to the development of whole families of reading difficulty formulae and methods of measuring word difficulty.

The legacy of Thorndike often remains quite unnoticed, because students of psychology and education are typically lacking in any historical knowledge.

CHARLES H. JUDD

Photograph courtesy of the University of Chicago

CHAPTER 6

Judd and His Dream of a Psychology of School Subjects

JUDD'S ACADEMIC PREPARATION

The Early Years

Two previous chapters discussed the influence of two important figures in research related to education in the early part of the century, namely, Edward L. Thorndike and Lewis M. Terman. One must also recognize a third important figure, if one is to recognize all of the key figures of the period who brought the findings of research to bear on education. That third figure was Charles Hubbard Judd (1873-1946). Judd's lifespan corresponded closely to that of Thorndike and that of Terman. All three belonged to the same age and each influenced his age in his own unique way.

Judd was born in India of missionary parents. The health of both parents seems to have been failing during their years in India, and they may well have been suffering from tropical diseases about which little was known. They returned to the United States in 1879, but his father died in 1880 and his mother in 1884, so the 11-year-old Charles Judd was left to be raised by an older sister. Judd wrote a short autobiography for the volume edited by Carl Murchison (*A History of Psychology in Autobiography, Volume 11,* 1936). In this autobiography he emphasized the strong impression left on his mind at an early age by the fundamentalist religious views of his parents. In high school he encountered a book on evolution, which brought him face-to-face with the conflict between the fundamentalist religious position and the scientific position. He seems to have resolved this conflict by modifying his religious position, but without abandoning religious beliefs. When he entered Wesleyan University, he had plans to become a Methodist minister, a goal that he seems to have abandoned while an undergraduate. His contact with evolutionary theory during high school had led him to study biology and anthropology, which slowly led him to develop a life-long interest in the biology, psychology, and sociology of the human. These interests displaced the interests he had had in the ministry.

Judd's comments on his schooling in Binghamton, New York, are interesting. He related that he started high school with no great enthusiasm for academic work, but that a clergyman, who had befriended him, one day took his aside and told him that the teachers in the school thought that Judd was just stupid and that it was time Judd showed his teachers they were all wrong. Judd related that from that time on he began to work with vigor. Indeed, he became a man of enormous energy, noted for the drive with which he attacked every problem.

Young Charles Judd also had a science teacher who became a significant person in his life. The science teacher permitted him to work in the science laboratory before school opened and after it closed. Judd wrote later of his lasting enthusiasm for scientific apparatus.

In 1890 he went to Wesleyan University. He must surely have had a scholarship, since his elder sister could hardly earn enough to support the two younger siblings let alone pay for a college education. Judd must have been at Wesleyan at the same time as Thorndike, but neither one ever commented on the fact. They may well not have known each other, for Thorndike, with his intense dislike for handling apparatus and equipment, followed a humanities curriculum, while Judd plunged into the study of the sciences. Judd's brief autobiography relates that he learned from Professor E. B. Rosa that science was not just a collection of facts, but a system of thinking. Thorndike never really appreciated that point of view, for he preached throughout his life that the first task of the scientist was to ascertain the facts. If Thorndike had studied physics and chemistry, as Judd had, his views concerning the nature of science might have been quite different from what they actually were. Few psychologists have ever had the broad scientific training that Judd had at Wesleyan.

Judd's studies at Wesleyan expanded into neurology and then into physiological psychology and experimental psychology. Judd was particularly influenced by A. C. Armstrong, who taught the courses in psychology and who also first interested Thorndike in the study of psychology. There was no laboratory in experimental psychology at Wesleyan in those days, and A. C. Armstrong was nearer to being a philosopher than a psychologist. Nevertheless, Armstrong took the inquiring Judd over to the physics laboratory where they were able to try out some of the new experiments on the physiology of the senses.

Armstrong appears to have been a remarkable man in being able to interest students in psychology. Judd relates that Armstrong, in 1893, took him to a meeting of the American Psychological Association at Columbia University. There he not only met James and Dewey, but he saw Cattell's laboratory and some of the experiments that Cattell was undertaking. The young Charles Judd was overwhelmed with the experience and set himself the goal of becoming a psychologist.

Armstrong also seems to have been responsible for the development in Charles Judd of many of the important characteristics that dominated his approach to psychology. Judd recognized that Armstrong taught him to be wary of the captivating quality of James's writing, which can easily lead a reader to embrace the James point of view without adequate critical assessment. Armstrong also taught him to avoid accepting one viewpoint without first considering all the alternative points of view. Armstrong wanted his students to have a broad view of the entire field of psychology and exposed them to such varied writers as Herbert Spencer, Lloyd Morgan, Francis Galton, and Wilhelm Wundt, as well as the writers of popular textbooks of the day such as William James and Alexander Bain.

The German Experience

After Judd graduated from Wesleyan University, he followed the customary path of the budding academician of his age, and went to Europe for graduate work. He was able to do this without any money of his own, because his old friend the minister, who had originally shamed him into working harder, offered to lend him money to finance his studies. Judd, with the boldness of youth and with few thoughts about how long it would take to repay the loan, jumped at the offer. He went to Germany in July 1894 and, after 3 months at a Berlitz school, managed to acquire enough German to benefit from lectures at the University of Leipzig, where Wilhelm Wundt gave his daily lecture at 4 o'clock. Ernst Meumann was in charge of the laboratory. The young Charles Judd was thrilled with the intellectual experience that Leipzig provided, though angered by the regimented and autocratic organization of German society.

Judd was not the first American psychologist to enroll in the University of Leipzig. His predecessors had included men destined to lead American psychology into the new era. They included G. Stanley Hall and James McKeen Cattell. G. M. Stratton studied in Leipzig at the same time as Judd. The enrollment at Leipzig also included Europeans destined to become leaders in American psychology, such as Edward Bradford Titchener and Hugo Münsterberg. No school has ever produced a comparable galaxy of luminaries in the field of psychology as did Leipzig in the last quarter of the last century.

In his autobiography, Judd comments on the personal influence that the model provided by Wundt had on his life. One suspects that Judd deliberately modeled himself after Wundt in many ways. Wundt was methodical in every aspect of his regular life. Every day of his life, he collected and organized knowledge related to whatever ponderous tome he was in the process of producing. He critiqued, in detail, every dissertation that came from his laboratory, and later edited the dissertation down to the last comma and period. Wundt was a prodigious writer, producing an average of two and one-half printed pages for each day of his professional life.

Though Charles Judd never had the influence that Wilhelm Wundt had on the overall development of psychology, his way of life was very much like that of Wundt. He also was a prodigious writer, with a lifetime list of publications of 685 items. Some of the items listed were dual publications of the same article, but even if one eliminates such duplications, the list of publications is extraordinary by almost any standard. He was able to produce such a large number of publications because of his orderly way of living, modeled very largely after Wundt. His manner of running a department, as we will see shortly, paralleled closely the style of Wundt.

The education provided in Wundt's laboratory was broad, for every student was required to study also in two minor fields. For Judd, these were comparative anatomy and pedagogy. The breadth of training thus provided influenced him the rest of his life. The narrowness of training of so many modern American psychologists is to be contrasted with the training provided by the University of Leipzig. This breadth must have contributed to the extraordinary quality of the men produced by the institution.

Judd believed that his training under Wundt freed him from ever becoming a slave to Watsonian behaviorism which was to flourish during the heyday of Judd's career. Wundt taught him, very much as Piaget was to teach half a century later, that there was no way of reducing complex behavior to a collection of simpler behaviors, but that complex behavior had its own laws, which could not be understood in terms of a set of components. Judd came to look upon behaviorism in his later years as a mere trap for the gullible and for those searching not for scientific understanding, but for simple applicable formulae. Judd comments in his autobiography that if American psychologists had bothered to study Wundt, they would never have fallen for the simplistic notions of the later behaviorists.

The neglect of Americans of Wundt, except for those who went and studied him, is understandable particularly in view of Wundt's unwillingness to have his works translated. Wundt's writings might have remained available only in German for much longer than they actually were, had it not been that the persuasive young Judd was able to persuade Wundt to permit him to translate the *Grundriss der Psychologie*. The translation of the *Grundriss* was an extraordinary experience in self-discipline for Judd, who attempted to emulate the standards of excellence of his master. Judd related that he made a complete translation of the volume, and then threw it away and started again. The pressure on Judd was immense, for Wundt insisted on reviewing every word of the translation and demanded an explanation of why particular English words had been chosen rather than others. Wundt wanted to ensure that his concise, compact style had been strictly followed in the English version.

Of particular influence on Judd's future was his contact with Wundt's new social psychology that appeared in his volume *Völkerpsychologie*. This was the first tome on social psychology written by a psychologist rather than a sociologist. The volume was also a demonstration of how historical inquiry could be incorporated into psychological research. When Judd wrote 35 years later a work entitled *The Psychology of Social Institutions* (1931), he acknowledged his debt to Wundt for having first brought him to the study of social institutions and social problems. Judd's admiration for Wundt remained strong throughout his entire life.

Judd returned from Leipzig in the summer of 1896. On his return he applied for a position of instructor in psychology at Wesleyan. The other candidate for the position was Edward L. Thorndike who, despite his academic record at Wesleyan, had little chance against Judd. Universities sought instructors who had had the benefit of graduate training in Europe, and not only had Judd had that training, but he had received it in one of the most distinguished centers of learning in Europe. The new psychology was European in birthright, and Wesleyan sought to embrace that new psychology. The American-born psychology of Thorndike had not yet appeared on the scene.

Academic Career

Almost as soon as Judd entered the academic world as an instructor, he began to publish prolifically. His work in Germany had already set him on this road, for the *Grundriss* translation was in publication before he left Leipzig. Later, when Wundt produced his fourth edition of the *Grundriss*, Judd would produce a new translation of it. During the early years of Judd's writing, he showed a continued production of experimental studies, most of which were an extension of his doctoral dissertation on space perception and binocular and monocular vision, but he also began to write on educational topics such as the application of psychology to teaching, conditions that were favorable for instruction, and the role of teaching in the maintenance of government. He showed an enormous range of interests, comparable to the range shown by Wundt, and also the capacity to write with precision and scholarship, sometimes at the expense of extinguishing imagination. The pedantic precision of Wundt, that had been partly responsible for the lack of enthusiasm of his American readers, was incorporated in the writings of Judd, and often with the result that these writings were not recognized for the works of scholarship that they were.

Judd stayed 2 years at Wesleyan before accepting a full professorship in the field of pedagogy at New York University in 1898. His first few lectures to teachers convinced him that he knew nothing of pedagogy, and that his audience of teachers was there only because attendance brought an increase in salary. Quite suddenly Judd became aware of the fact that a great gulf existed between the psychology of the laboratory of Wilhelm Wundt and the knowledge needed to conduct a class in the New York City schools. This led Judd to develop studies of school children. First, he experimented unsuccessfully with voice recordings, and then pursued with more success the study of motor behavior of school children.

Judd was far from happy with the kinds of studies that were being pursued with children in the child study movement, that focused in America on the work of G. Stanley Hall and his associates. Judd thought that the work was nothing short of amateurish and violated the canons of good research that he had learned under Wundt. The child study movement preached that any well-intentioned person could arrive at significant knowledge about children merely by observing them. In contrast, the thesis of Wundt's life was that worthwhile knowledge of human behavior could be achieved only by those who were well versed in the knowledge already available and were also well trained in the techniques of laboratory experimentation.

Judd's emphasis on high academic standards was not appreciated by New York University. During his second year at New York University, Judd conducted a vigorous campaign to raise the standards of work in the area of pedagogy. He considered that what was taught and what was required of students was nothing short of a disgrace in the area of pedagogy. The administration handled the matter in a manner quite typical of university administrations. Judd was asked to resign and had no choice in the matter. This did not cure him of emphasizing academic standards, but he had learned something about how to achieve the goal of academic improvement.

Judd's demise as an academic reformer at New York University was followed by an uneventful year at the University of Cincinnati. Fortunately, there was a span of 2 months before the new appointment began, and he used this time to study the history of education, an area in which he was assigned to teach a course. He was able to keep a few paces ahead of his class when he came to teach it, but only by abandoning his writing and research work. This he could not continue to do for very long, and when Yale University offered him a position in psychology, though only as an instructor, he did not have to be persuaded to make the move to New Haven.

At Yale, Judd found a well-equipped laboratory and well-trained graduate students working there. This permitted him to return to research on visual perception and the understanding of spatial relationships. Judd must have had several graduate students working for him in the laboratory, since over the next few years he was able to publish a number of papers and monographs in his field of research. The research was of good quality and was conducted with diligence. In its day, psychologists thought so well of the work that in 1909 he was elected to the presidency of the American Psychological Association. The Association, founded in 1892, had had such distinguished presidents as G. Stanley Hall, William James, James McKeen Cattell, Hugo Münsterberg, and Josiah Royce. Judd's election to the presidency of the Association demonstrated that he had achieved eminence as a psychologist. Yet, Judd will not be remembered for his work as a laboratory psychologist or by his research on perception. He will be remembered for his contributions to education.

During the 7 years he spent at Yale, he continued to pursue his work on education. He wrote a book entitled *Genetic Psychology for Teachers* (1903). Judd admitted later that his efforts to produce a literature for teachers, based on psychology, was probably premature, and that there was not enough material available for writing a monograph, let alone a textbook. Nevertheless, Judd's *Genetic Psychology for Teachers* is a remarkable volume, and worth reading today. It is heavily Darwinian in outlook, and attempts to trace events back to their origins. The teacher's experiences in the classroom and the way in which the teacher views particular situations are viewed as a product of the nature of the teacher and the previous experiences to which the teacher has been exposed. What the teacher sees is always only an *interpretation* of what is there. Judd illustrates this by using visual illusions which demonstrate the interpretive aspect of all visual perception. Judd stresses that, in order to understand teaching, one has to understand how the teacher interprets the classroom. A later chapter discusses how the teacher is to some extent a victim of traditions handed down from generation to generation. Schools were not always rigidly disciplined, as they were early in the century. The rigidly disciplined school was a product of the monastic tradition, introduced into schools when the religious orders of the Middle Ages became the great educational institutions of the time. The classrooms were run with the discipline expected of monks. Teachers were viewed by Judd as victims of this tradition. Judd argued that new ideals, and new practices, must come from a new tradition, and he believed that this new tradition should be derived from the new scientific tradition in biology and psychology. This new tradition helps to understand that development reflects human capability for adaptation.

Adaptation, and the change that it implies, permits the human race to progress through invention and the social transmission of new knowledge acquired. In keeping with the ideas of his age, Judd stressed the importance of imitation in social transmission far beyond any stress given to it today.

Judd then went on to explore in his book the origins of writing, reading, and number concepts in the history of civilization, stressing the way in which these reflect the adaptation of the human to his social problems. The volume is thoroughly readable, and very little of it would have to be changed in the light of subsequent research.

In three years, Judd had risen from the rank of instructor in psychology to full professor and Director of the Psychological Laboratory at Yale. His star shone brightly in the academic world, and to a considerable degree because of his publications. His translation of Wundt's *Grundriss* had given him status in the academic world, and the publication of his own *Psychology: General Introduction* (1907) had done much to establish his reputation among a wide public. The latter textbook was at the forefront of the new literature on psychology. It began with a presentation of physiology of the senses, and then dealt with such fundamental aspects of experience as space and time and the unity of objects. Later chapters dealt with concept formation, language, the concept of the self, and choice. A final chapter discussed applications, but in quite modest terms. The *Psychology* was the physiologically based science of the German tradition. He did not mention the work of Thorndike, with whom he had strong disagreements, and neither did he mention the work of G. Stanley Hall and the child study movement. Despite these omissions of the new research emerging on the American scene, the book brought prestige to its author.

By the year 1907, Judd had emerged as the most prestigious psychologist on the educational scene, as well as being one of the most notable American psychologists of his age. Nobody could have been surprised, when the University of Chicago sought to regain the prestige it had originally had in education when Dewey was there, and enticed Judd to leave Yale. Judd's emerging interest in educational problems and his success in relating to school people were special qualifications that must have appealed to the administration of the University of Chicago. Furthermore, his academic qualifications were of just the kind that Chicago had emphasized in the building of the faculty of the new institution.

Judd was undoubtedly the most eligible candidate for the position at the University of Chicago in terms of his academic qualifications and academic productivity, but his personal qualities must also have set him apart from others of his generation. He was an impressive figure of a man, tall and physically strong, and every gesture seemed to convey the strength of his personality. His bright blue eyes would fixate a person to whom he was speaking and reflected the fact that his attention was riveted on them. If a student in one of his classes were to murmur a word to another while Judd was lecturing, a glance from his eyes would silence the interrupter. When he spoke, he assumed that he had something to say worth hearing, and he expected attention. But he extended the same courtesy to others when he was the audience. His voice was strong and clear and could reach out to large audiences in a time when public address systems had not yet been developed. Those who heard Judd speak noted the extraordinary quality of his voice and the use he made of inflection and variation in volume. In addition, he seemed to have instant access to the vast range of knowledge that he had mastered. He never hesitated or faltered in making reference to the source of an idea or to a piece of research that another had undertaken. This same command over his knowledge made him a formidable debater concerning contemporary issues in education. Though much of his public discussion of education was warm and constructive, he could be absolutely devastating to a protagonist who advocated, for example, that education should be converted into a play-like activity. Judd himself was a supreme example of how an effective education could produce a well-organized and disciplined mind.

Judd's intellectualism was often mistaken for a coldness with respect to personal relations, but he was not cold. His letters that relate to family matters reflect charm and personal warmth. Those who worked with him for a large part of a lifetime, such as Frank N. Freeman and William S. Gray, admired his deep feeling for the rest of humanity. His letters also reveal that when he had to choose between telling a doctoral student that the student's work was not good enough, and building a personal relationship with that student, academic standards always came first. He would have no reservations in telling a student that his work was not good enough to retain him in the program. Some of his letters written to doctoral students make a cold and precise analysis of the student's limitations. There was nothing he could tolerate less than a student who failed to enlist maximum effort into his studies.

After he went to Chicago, one of his important contributions was in his efforts to develop in others the same fine intellectual qualities that he had. Much of his correspondence involved letters and memoranda to graduate students making precise analyses of their research reports. These letters were typically constructive, but criticism was never held back. His was a helpful intellect and competent students felt free to discuss with him the intellectual problems involved in their research.

Judd's frankness and open honesty was recognized by all those who associated with him. These qualities were the ones that embroiled him in deep trouble at New York University. The administration of the latter institution was interested in enrolling teachers in courses, because the size of the enrollment determined the size of the budget. For Judd, such a view introduced hypocrisy into education. He believed that education should raise the intellectual level of the participants, and if it could not do that, then it should be abandoned.

The description of Judd as a personality parallels closely a description of his mentor, Wilhelm Wundt. They must have shared much in common before they ever met. Two years of close association must have made them into an even closer match.

JUDD IN CHICAGO

In 1909, Judd moved to the University of Chicago as head of what was then called the School of Education where he stayed for 29 years and made his most notable contributions to education. Later the School became a Department. Judd's national prestige brought him to Chicago and there must have been few, if any, competitors for the prestigious job. Thorndike's prestige in education was derived almost solely from his original work on puzzle boxes, and his works on education were not considered prestigious at that time. Judd also had the advantage over Thorndike of having spent 2 years at the Mecca of psychology in the nineteenth century, namely, the University of Leipzig.

The University of Chicago at the time of Judd's arrival had no status at all as a center of educational thought. Judd's task was that of transforming it into a rival of Teachers College as a place where advances in educational thought were created. Chicago still had the prestige left by the fact that John Dewey had spent some years there and had founded the experimental school that still survives, but at the time when Judd arrived in Chicago the University of Chicago as a center of educational thought was in a decline. Chicago was not unique in that respect, for in 1910 the *U.S. Educational Directory* listed 156 heads of departments or professors of pedagogy, nearly all of whom have never been cited in a footnote to a book on education. The field of education in the United States, taken as a whole, represented at that time a quite undistinguished academic area and with no established tradition of scholarship.

The School of Education at the University of Chicago had been founded in 1901 through the incorporation into the University the Chicago Institute that trained teachers. The first head of the School of Education was Francis W. Parker, whose auspicious appointment lasted for only a year. He was followed by the appointment of his distinguished colleague, John Dewey, but Dewey stayed for only 2 years. Then there followed a period of decline of several years during which no director was appointed.

The Board of Trustees finally took action in 1907. The School of Education was to have three sections. These were to be the College of

Education, the University Elementary School, and the University High School. The School of Education was to be the organization for the training of teachers and for the development of research related to the development of a science of education.

Judd immediately set about doing at Chicago what he had been unable to do at New York University. His first task was that of making the academic requirements for the graduation of teachers comparable to those for graduation in other fields. Judd also demanded that admission to the College of Education should also depend upon the same standards set for the rest of the University. Teachers continued to learn the practical aspects of their profession, but every practicum was closely tied to preparation in a body of related theory. In undertaking his reform of teacher education, Judd encountered all of the problems encountered by a modern dean of a college of education. The liberal arts specialists often wanted to be in complete control of teacher education and they had little respect for the body of educational theory that the instructors of pedagogy were assigned to teach. The conflict between those involved in instruction in pedagogy and those involved in instruction in the traditional academic disciplines continued through much of Judd's career at Chicago. Eventually, in 1930, in an attempt to resolve the conflicts involved, Judd proposed that the policies of the teacher education program be placed in the hands of an all-University Committee.

During his first few years at Chicago, Judd also brought about certain other administrative changes. A Department of Education became established, comparable to that of any other academic department and with an emphasis on graduate study. It was as head of such a department that Judd made his main contributions to education.

Judd had problems in staffing his new department in a way that would make possible the achievement of his ideals. At that time there were virtually no qualified applicants available and Judd had to develop his own. He had a remarkable way of identifying prospective academic talent in his selection of graduate students, and particularly those who were later to assume major roles in the department faculty. Among these students were William S. Gray, Guy T. Buswell, and Karl J. Holzinger. At the time of Judd's retirement, 10 of the 15 full professors in the Department had been trained by him.

Judd also set out to change the periodicals produced by the Department to make them reflect his new policies. These publications included *The Elementary School Journal*, *The School Review*, and *Supplementary Educational Monographs*. He took over the editorship of *The Elementary School Journal* and wrote an editorial in every issue until 1914. He did the same for *The School Review*. Many of the editorials are unsigned, but they bear the unmistakable marks of Judd's writing. Furthermore, the publications had been losing money and, when Judd arrived, the University was on the brink of abandoning them. Judd provided the University with a written personal guarantee that he would make good any financial losses and thereby was able to persuade the University to continue their publication. The achievement of academic goals and ideals was vastly more important to Judd than any mere matter of personal financial loss. Hardly surprising is it that he died a poor man. Once Judd had developed a faculty after his own liking, he was able to delegate to them many of the editorial tasks. At that point he became Chairman of the Joint Editorial Committee.

The transition in the Department of Education was paralleled by a transition in the content of the journals. They ceased to contain speculative material on the worth of new educational programs and included an increasing number of articles reporting the results of empirical research.

Special Features of Judd's Approach to Education

Judd's approach to education had certain unique features that made the Department of Education at the University of Chicago a special center of thought and research. These must now be considered.

Throughout his career, Judd emphasized the importance of understanding education as a social phenomenon. This was apparent in his *Genetic Psychology for Teachers* as well as in his *Educational Psychology* (1939) written over 30 years later. The learning of reading must be understood as a social process, and so too must every other subject matter area. The human is a biological organism, but also an organism with marked social characteristics. Without these characteristics, culture could not possibly have developed. Speech is viewed as the main means of transmitting the culture to new generations, and an understanding of the nature of language is vital to the understanding of education. Judd's lifetime emphasis on the necessity of understanding the human as a social organism found its roots in the work of Wilhelm Wundt, who was working on social psychology at the time when Judd was in Leipzig. Wundt's afternoon lectures at that time must have focused on his thoughts in the social-psychological area. Judd's emphasis, in that respect, in education was new to American psychology, though sociologists wrote extensively in the early part of the century on the application of sociology to the understanding of education. John Dewey had, of course, already written on the relation of school and society. Despite that emphasis on the social aspect of human learning, American psychology, at the time when Judd went to Chicago, virtually neglected the social basis of human learning. Edward L. Thorndike had embraced a connectionism that had little place for social factors. James McKeen Cattell had been interested in measuring fundamental aptitude for academic achievement, and had emphasized inherited factors as determinants of what individuals could accomplish. Lewis Terman was beginning to develop tests of intelligence. Judd alone emphasized schooling as a social-cultural phenomenon.

A second special emphasis of Judd is found in his effort to relate the learning of subject matter to basic psychological processes. His effort to develop what came to be called the *psychology of school subjects* was an effort to spell out that relationship. His attempts to do this are most completely illustrated by his book entitled *Psychology of School Subjects* (1915). The best worked out example in his book is related to the teaching of mathematics and particularly geometry. The psychology of mathematics is introduced by a discussion of the psychology of space, a field in which Judd was superbly expert. Judd brings to bear on our understanding of mathematics the knowledge that had been developed concerning understanding of space, and the role that experience plays in complex space perception. He introduced the idea, later to be discussed by Jean Piaget, that an understanding of space calls for movement and action. We know space because of the way in which we act on objects in a spatial environment. Perception and action are intimately related and the development of perception can only take place where there is movement. The conclusion drawn was that extensive practical experience with space is necessary before the child can be expected to understand geometry. The understanding of geometry not only requires that the pupil has had extensive experience with objects in space, but he must also have the ability to code some of that experience into words. Definitions and technical terms are also of help in indicating to the student what properties he should think about. Thus, the definition of a line as the shortest distance between two points implies that the student should not be concerned with such properties of the line as its thickness or color, but only its abstract property of representing a distance.

Geometry involves not only a foundation of space perception, but also a foundation of logic. Some aspects of geometry are given directly through space perception, but others are inferred. A student cannot be expected to understand geometry unless he also has command of the logic it requires.

Although Judd saw that the development of geometry depended upon a mastery of the spatial environment, he never embraced a reductionist viewpoint. Geometrical understanding was based on the understanding of space through action and movement, but it could not be reduced to mere action and movement. Higher levels of abstraction represent new learning and new forms of behavior.

Judd's objection to reductionism brought him up against Thorndike. His general policy was to ignore Thorndike, and only rarely does he ever refer to him in his published writings. There was occasional reference to Thorndike in Judd's personal correspondence in which he quite clearly thought of Thorndike as a second-rate scholar. In Judd's *Psychology of*

High School Subjects, he wrote one of the few public confrontations that he ever had with Thorndike and his ideas on the issue of transfer of training. Judd was clearly disturbed by Thorndike's position that little transfer could be expected from one task to another, and even more by Thorndike's effort to apply this concept to an understanding of education. Judd considered that Thorndike's attack on the doctrine of formal discipline was not justified in terms of data that Thorndike together with Woodworth had collected.

Judd's first point in his attack on Thorndike's theory of transfer was that transfer of training was a reality and that nobody doubts that transfer takes place. An engineer applies the concepts of elementary physics to the solution of numerous and very different problems, and he does this successfully. If the engineer could not transfer his knowledge and skills to new situations, he would never be able to solve the varied problems that he has to solve in his professional life. Transfer is a reality.

Judd argued that the absence of transfer from, say, the study of Latin to English composition was a trivial issue, for the main reason for the study of Latin and the classics should not be to improve English. Judd believed that the doctrine of formal discipline had never been widely held and had rarely been used for constructing curricula.

Judd proposed that the extent to which transfer could be expected to occur had little to do with the extent to which there were common elements, but depended more on the degree to which instruction resulted in generalizations. Only through the understanding of important generalizations does useful transfer occur. Good instruction results in the student understanding generalizations that have quite broad applicability. Thus, the study of Caesar's Gallic War may be a mere exercise in translation and Latin grammar, or it may help one to achieve a grasp of the territorial features of Europe which have influenced the course of all European wars down to modern times. The problems of pacification encountered by Caesar have parallels in modern times. The common elements between the study of Latin and the study of other subjects may go far beyond mere superficial similarities of Latin and English as languages, as Thorndike had supposed.

From Judd's point of view, the most significant aspects of learning could not be accounted for in terms of the strengthening or weakening of connections. He did not deny the existence of the connectionist form of learning and might have been willing to concede that some aspects of schooling, such as learning to spell, could be accounted for in terms of a connectionist model, but Judd had little interest in the development of such simple skills. One should note that Judd was, personally, mainly interested in secondary education.

Most modern educational research workers know the name of Judd in connection with the classic experiment which he undertook on transfer. The problem involved shooting at a target placed underwater. The results demonstrated that a person who had been taught the principle of refraction could shoot at the target more accurately, and was more adaptable when the depth of the target was changed than was a person who did not understand the principle. The results of the experiment were enormously influential in that they provided evidence for a principle that every educated person knows, namely, that if one knows a well-established principle, then one can use it to solve a whole range of problems.

That experiment has been repeated later with essentially the same results. The original experiment, as far as one can find out, was not well executed and the data would not be convincing to most modern experimental psychologists. Nevertheless, in its day the experiment was viewed as a convincing demonstration of a principle basic to education.

The views of Judd on transfer were, for a long time, not explored by American psychologists, who preferred to work within the Thorndike tradition and the allied associationistic framework. A later product of this work has been the transfer surface developed by Charles Osgood. Judd would not have been pleased with such developments. Recent developments that would have been much closer to Judd's views of what a worthwhile human psychology should be like are found in the work of Jean Piaget. Much as Judd was opposed to structuralism, Piaget's structures are similar to the kinds of generalizations that Judd believed to be the focus of significant learning.

Judd's Sociology of Education

Judd lived in an age when education was viewed as an almost exclusively intellectual activity. Educators recognized that social development was important, but that was to take place outside of the school. Principals and teachers had not yet come to the view that the classroom was a community, with all the problems that plague all communities.

Educational sociology existed, but in obscure corners of the academic world. The journals and magazines read by teachers in the early part of the century hardly mentioned the work of sociologists, though they featured the work of luminary psychologists. There were good reasons why the ideas of educational sociologists were largely ignored. These become evident when one examines the early sociological work related to education.

The *Review of Educational Research* published in February, 1937, was the first issue on *Educational Sociology.* The publication brought out, very clearly, the primitive state of the discipline. The issue had seven authors for the various chapters, but only three of those authors could claim any credentials as sociologists. Apparently, sociologists who could write on topics related to education were hard to find, and particularly scarce if they were expected to base their statements on research. Many discursive and speculative books had been written that carried the title of *Educational Sociology* and the *Review* issue listed seven of these, but they were volumes long on speculation and short on research. Some of the chapters in the issue of the *Review* discussed empirical research. One dealt with the advantages of working in groups versus working in isolation. Another dealt with problems related to delinquency, though the material was only indirectly related to education. The publication *Educational Sociology* could not have had any impact on education, but it brought out the tardy arrival of sociology on the educational scene. The time was overdue for the development of an educational sociology with important implications for education, but an identifiable discipline would not emerge for a few more decades.

Judd, in his *Psychology of Social Institutions*, had a new approach to the sociology of education. In that book, Judd explored the sociology and psychology underlying the important elements in the school curriculum. Those elements included the understanding of number, the comprehension of time and the related skill of punctuality, the use of written language, the development of spoken language, and other basic curricular elements. The implication was that an understanding of the social origin of each of these concepts and skills should be of value in developing effective teaching procedures. For example, if one understands that number systems developed from the need for measuring land and for exchanging goods, then one should be able to devise situations in which children could learn easily to use number systems in solving similar problems. Furthermore, concepts of number tie individuals together within a society. Numbers are necessary for all commercial and social transactions. One cannot even plan to meet a friend at a particular place and time without the use of numbers. Our society would fall apart if our comprehension of number were suddenly to fade. The school curriculum related to number comprehension is far more than just an intellectual exercise. It is also a part of the fabric that holds society together.

The Judd volume had an evolutionary tone. It reflected a concept, still popular, that ideas evolve just as species evolve and that growing children may recapitulate some of the evolution of significant ideas and concepts. That form of recapitulation was not the biological recapitulation proposed by G. Stanley Hall, but a recreation in the brain of the growing child, of the sequence of ideas that were vital for the development of civilization.

Judd viewed all the fundamental ideas and skills mastered in the elementary school as far more than a set of useful tools. He viewed them as a part of the structure that held society together. In doing this, he also failed to recognize that an even more important force in holding society together is the system of values shared by its members. That was why Judd, like others in his generation, placed little emphasis on the development of values as a goal of education.

Judd's Later Activities

Before considering in greater detail the psychology of school subjects as it emerged under the guidance of Judd and others, some mention must be made of other important activities in which Judd engaged.

He was a successful fund-raiser. He mentioned in a number of his letters in the late 1920's the extent to which work in his department was supported by foundations. He mentioned amounts on the order of $50,000 per year, which at that time was a very large amount of money. Most of the money went for the support of graduate students and those involved in the collection of data.

An even more ambitious money-raising venture involved finding funds for a building to house Judd's expanding enterprises. Judd managed to raise $1.5 million for the building of what came to be named the Charles Hubbard Judd Hall, built in the same elegant Gothic style of the other main buildings on the campus. The building symbolizes Judd in many ways, particularly in the elegance of its style, and it represents a fitting memorial to a man who built education on his campus as a discipline.

Judd spent a substantial amount of time engaged in survey work in schools. How he managed to do this in his tight schedule is difficult to understand, for he taught 8 hours a week, which was considered at that time a full teaching load. He also had many responsibilites on University committees. His better known surveys were those conducted in St. Louis, Missouri, and Grand Rapids, Michigan. He believed that the survey should be a scientific study of a school system. His faculty also worked with him on these surveys and used them as a means of conducting research within school systems.

Judd retired from the University of Chicago in 1938. Then he served for 2 years as a consultant to the National Youth Administration. He had worked on the development of the Civilian Conservation Corps in previous years, and had already acquired considerable knowledge in the area prior to his 1938 appointment.

One of Judd's last major contributions was a report entitled *Research in the United States Office of Education* (1939). The document was also printed and sold to the general public, for there seems to have been considerable interest in it. The report was the outcome of meetings of an Advisory Committee on Education appointed by President Roosevelt in 1936 under the chairmanship of Floyd R. Reeves, a fact which leaves one somewhat surprised to find that the authorship of the final report was that of Judd alone. The "Foreword" to the report, presumably written by the chairman, stated that Judd wrote the report and that all conclusions are his, rather than those of the committee. The "Foreword" indicated clearly that Judd simply took over the task of conducting the study. Judd was probably the most capable man on the committee, and not one with whom the other committee members cared to argue. Judd had such enormous prestige in the world of education that it would have been almost presumptuous for any other committee member to have suggested that he could write a better report. The "Foreword" also indicated that some on the committee were dismayed by Judd's assumption of full command, for the committee never voted to endorse the report. The committee must have voted to have the report submitted to the President, but without strong endorsement.

Although the Advisory Committee was established by President Roosevelt to study existing programs of Federal aid for vocational education, and the need for expanding such aid, the report was devoted to the broader issue of the effectiveness of research, investigation, and inquiry in the Office of Education. One suspects that Judd seized the opportunity and used the report as a sounding board for his ideas on what the Office of Education should do.

The initial pages of the report provide an excellent brief history of the Office of Education and its predecessor, the *Bureau.* The introduction is followed by a table showing the staff of the Office, and its enormous concentration on activities related to vocational education. In 1937, the Office of Education had 140 employees outside of the Commissioner's and the Assistant Commissioner's offices, plus some temporary employees and administrative employees related to the Civilian Conservation Corps camps. More than half of the staff were assigned to problems of vocational education.

The central activity of the office at that time was the conduct of studies and surveys. Judd listed the kinds of studies undertaken by the Office. These included surveys of city, county, and state school organizations, and surveys of higher education. The Office also conducted surveys of school equipment, libraries, curriculum materials, educational finance, and teacher education and certification practices. The Office had also moved recently into the field of radio education. Some of the research undertaken by the Office had moved beyond the scope of the survey designed to provide data useful for administrative purposes, and had involved child development studies. An example of such research is a study of the problem of parents of exceptional children. Another example is a study of the adjustment problems of school children.

Some of the surveys conducted by the Office of Education had involved very substantial funds. The Survey of the Land-Grant Colleges and Universities had cost $117,000. A National Survey of Secondary Education was undertaken at a total cost of $225,000. A Survey of the Education of Teachers cost $180,000. These were very large sums of money during the years of the Depression.

Judd's survey of the surveys of the Office of Education led to his conclusion that "no phase of investigational activity has yielded larger dividends in improved service than the various surveys" (p. 33). In order to justify that conclusion, Judd drew upon a follow-up of Office of Education surveys that had attempted to determine the degree to which survey recommendations had been carried out. The follow-up had been carried out by the Carnegie Foundation and had been limited to higher education. The Carnegie study had listed about 1,000 recommendations made in 15 surveys of higher educational institutions and then had obtained information from the institutions concerning the degree to which the recommendations had been carried out. The data were far from convincing, for many of the surveys had been made nearly 20 years before the Carnegie study was undertaken, and surely many of the recommended changes would have taken place even if there had been no survey. Also, one wonders what an investigator really learns when he asks an institution whether some quite deplorable situation has been remedied. He is probably going to be told that it has been. The data referred to by Judd did not really support his case at all, but one suspects that Judd had at the back of his mind his own experience in making school surveys. His personal experience told that the results of a survey were to change practice, and he was convinced that this happened.

Some support for Judd's enthusiastic support of surveys in the Office of Education comes from the fact that Judd found that the Office was overwhelmed with demands for survey work. The demand was so great that the activity tended to interfere with other activities of the Office and to preclude them. Most requests had to be turned down. Judd proposed that a division of the Office be established to conduct surveys, so that other divisions of the Office would be free to purchase other enterprises.

When one looks back over the life of Charles Judd, one cannot help but see him as a man of extraordinary breadth of viewpoint. Although he became almost obsessed with the value of the school survey as a means of achieving educational progress, he never abandoned the idea that the science underlying an understanding of education had to be an experimental science of psychology. The persistence of the latter point of view is quite evident in his *Educational Psychology*, published towards the end of his professional life. Despite his conviction, he never developed a laboratory within his department for acquiring such knowledge, apparently believing that such an enterprise belonged in the Department of Psychology. He was for a time head of the Department of Psychology at the University of Chicago, a fact reflecting his own undiminished prestige as an experimental psychologist. In contrast with the fundamental knowledge related to education produced by the psychological laboratory, the knowledge to be derived from the school survey dealt with matters of more immediate and practical importance.

Yet the survey never yielded data concerning the relationship between methods and approaches to teaching and outcomes. The survey never produced the kind of data that Judd hoped it would and, as the 1930's approached, most of his associates in the Department had abandoned the survey and had begun to undertake research that involved other sources of data.

During his busy life he held numerous appointments with all kinds of committees, professional organizations, government organizations, and foundations. His long entry in *Who's Who in America* gives the appearance that he was omnipresent throughout the educational world. He was. He loved that kind of life and realized that his presence had enormous impact.

Although Judd will be remembered for his catalytic role in the development of psychology of school subjects, he was a catalyst of ideas in other areas too. Whoever worked in his department seemed to develop new concepts. Franklin Bobbitt (1876-1956) produced his new conception of constructing curricula in the atmosphere produced by Judd. Henry Clinton Morrison (1871-1945) developed the concept of mastery learning which, as Morrison noted, was as old a concept as education. Morrison advocated 100 per cent mastery for the promotion of a pupil to the next grade. Morrison also developed the concept of a unit of learning and a pupil-contract system, later to be revived as the latest invention of behaviorism.

Unlike Thorndike, Judd did not develop an integrated research program of his own. He was not the central research worker in his enterprise, but his role was one that combined the teacher, the administrator, and the inspiring leader. The fact is obvious when one scans his list of publications. His method of developing his ideas was to train a staff, sympathetic to his goals, and then provide them with facilities for developing research. Judd viewed administration as the channel through which his ideas could be developed. He built the Department of the University of Chicago as a center for the study of the psychology of school subjects.

The idea of a psychology of school subjects was not new for Herbart had written extensively on the matter at least a century before Judd wrote on the topic. Judd must surely have been aware of Herbart's ideas, for all psychologists in his era were raised on an intellectual diet of Herbart who provided the analytic foundation for the new experimental psychology. Judd must surely have viewed as a part of his mission in life to be the one who converted Herbart's analytical ideas into an experimental science designed to explore the psychology of learning school subjects.

In that enterprise Judd differed from most of his contemporaries and, in that difference, lay Judd's unique contribution. The other giants of his age in psychology, including such figures as Cattell, Baldwin, Watson, and

Thorndike, all sought to establish general laws of psychology which could be applied to the practice of teaching. Presumably, such general laws, if they were really general, could be applied to the improvement of the teaching of any school subject.

Judd was interested in utilizing whatever was known about psychology, and, yet, he saw that the study of the psychology of school subjects must involve approaches that differed considerably from that of the typical laboratory psychologist of his time. The nature of subject matter had to be understood as well as the psychological problems related to learning it. General learning laws might have applications, but the particular circumstances related to the mastery of a particular school subject had to be understood. Thus, the key to the child's understanding of arithmetic was to be found in an understanding of how young children acquired number concepts and the logic related to their use. Judd began a program of research related to the latter problem, but it did not develop very successfully. He envisaged a laboratory program which would explore the development of the child's concept of time and space, a program which would surely be relevant to an understanding of aspects of the child's grasp of geography and history. He believed, too, that social psychology and sociology should provide the means for exploring other aspects of these subjects. The development of language and the language arts was also to be understood through social psychology, since language was conceived to be primarily a social instrument. Quite basic research related to such matters as space, time, and number were to provide the foundation on which educational research should proceed. Improved methods of teaching and improved materials for instruction could evolve only after a foundation of psychological research had been properly laid.

Judd was appalled by the lack of any research foundation for the teaching of subject matter. In his writings he made some attempt to illustrate what he had in mind, but the more he probed, the more he was impressed by the lack of such a foundation. Nevertheless, he did see an advance in this field during his lifetime, for when he came to write his last major work, entitled *Educational Psychology* (1939), much of the volume was devoted to bringing together the results of research undertaken during his lifetime that might provide a foundation for the teaching of subject matter.

Judd, like most American psychologists of his day, was hardly aware of the developing work of Jean Piaget in Geneva. Judd cites Pieaget in his *Educational Psychology*, but he mentions only Piaget's work on the early development of language in the child. He seems to have been quite unaware that Piaget was developing a line of thinking closely related to his own. A modern psychology of mathematics based on a conception of how the child acquires concepts of number, derived from the work of Piaget and later workers, would have been highly acceptable to Judd and, indeed, a vindication for his ideas. Such developments in the psychology of school subjects is just what Judd was seeking to promote in the early part of this century, but they will probably not be fully apparent until the last part. Nevertheless, the developments that are in progress have more than validated the conception of a science of education that Judd sought to promote. The developments that have already taken place in this respect have, as Judd predicted, gone far to displace the psychological approach of Thorndike and his successors. Time plays strange tricks in deciding whose ideas are the winners and losers. Those that seem to be the winners at one time may be the losers at a later time.

In the chapter that follows examples will be discussed of the development of the psychology of school subjects. The material is limited in examples of the development up to the middle of the nineteenth century. What was accomplished during the years 1900 to 1950 was built upon work that had already taken place, but during that half century the center for the development of the psychology of school subjects was the University of Chicago. One should not lose sight of that fact even though some of the material covered in the chapter comes from widely scattered geographical locations. Chicago became the coordinating center of that work, partly through the research undertaken by Chicago faculty, and partly through the extensive reviews of related research that came out under Judd's editorial supervision.

CHAPTER 7

The Psychology of School Subjects: The Revival of an Old Approach to Educational Reform

In this chapter some account will be given of the development of research in particular subject-matter fields. Not all subject-matter areas will be covered extensively, but only those in which there has been a long and substantial tradition of research. Reading and mathematics are the areas in which research comes nearest to meeting this criterion and in which a great deal has been learned. They will be presented as examples of how a psychology of school subjects can be developed. The matter of developing a psychology of school subjects is complicated by the fact that the way in which subject matter is divided up into school subjects changes from generation to generation. For example, in the early part of the century, arithmetic was taught as a distinct skill and was regarded more as a skill necessary for the pursuit of certain trades rather than as a discipline. Later, arithmetic came to be taught as a part of the broad field of mathematics and it became fused with geometry and algebra. Within this new setting a psychology of mathematics would have greater potential value than a psychology of arithmetic, though the latter would be valuable. Reading has also lost some of its distinctiveness as a subject-matter field, since it has become fused into a language arts conglomerate. There is some trend at the present time to reverse these changes in the structure of the curriculum.

For these reasons the concept of a psychology of school subjects has to be flexible, assembling knowledge related to the teaching of particular areas in different ways as subject matter fields change in structure. Despite changes in the structure of the curriculum, there are at least two fields in which research related to teaching has been pursued along consistent lines for a century or more. These are the areas of reading and mathematics. Research in these areas dominated the work at the University of Chicago in the 1910-1940 period, though it was not the first research. Nevertheless, it was the first large scale and continuing program.

Early in the century, the curriculum focused on reading, arithmetic, spelling, and handwriting. Despite the efforts of Horace Mann to broaden the curriculum and to give equal weight to other areas of subject matter, the focus was still on the development of the traditional skills. The research of academicians, then as now, tended to be focused on those aspects of the school that were stressed by teachers, administrators, and parents. For this reason, the program of research in subject matter areas developed by Judd at Chicago focused on areas of public interest, namely, reading, arithmetic, spelling, and handwriting. Judd himself was mainly interested in secondary school subjects and saw these as rich areas for research, but the time was not ripe for research on the teaching of social studies and history, a matter of great interest to him. The teaching of science was only beginning to find a role in the school curriculum, so research on the teaching and learning of science had to be left to later generations.

Research on handwriting had a short history because of changes in the role of handwriting in our society. When Edward L. Thorndike and Frank Freeman were initiating research on handwriting early in the century, the skill was already on the wane as an art, through the development of the typewriter. Before the latter device became widely used, records had to be kept in handwritten documents. These had to be highly legible and unambiguous, and the quality of written materials was made possible through the fostering of handwriting as an art. The art ceased to be of social consequence once mechanical means of writing had been invented, and research workers turned to studying ways of teaching typing skills.

THE PSYCHOLOGY OF SCHOOL SUBJECTS: READING

Mention has already been made of the efforts of McGuffey to determine the appropriate age level of materials to be introduced into his readers. In doing this, McGuffey introduced empirical methods into the design of school materials and, even though his methods were extremely primitive, he can be said to have initiated inquiry and research into the field of reading instruction.

McGuffey's approach to the development of his readers was a primitive research approach. He was one of the first to realize, if not the first, that a passage of literature might have appeal to one age group and not to another. So he realized that what he had to do was to determine the age level at which each passage selected was most enjoyed. He was able to do this, in a rough way, by inviting children to his yard after school, and there they heard him read selections for his readers. McGuffey watched carefully to see which of the children seemed to respond most to a passage. Then by judging the age of the responding children he felt he had data that would permit him to assign the passage to a particular age level. The grading of passages into age levels was certainly a concept ahead of his time. The procedure also permitted him to determine whether a passage aroused interest in children. One suspects that the success of the McGuffey readers must be attributed partly to the careful selection of the materials in terms of age level and interest value. Over 92 million copies were sold during the half century when the readers were in use. There were, of course, other factors that played a role in making the readers some of the best sellers of all time. One of these was McGuffey's capability of judging the tone of passages that would be approved by both parents and teachers. The moral tone of the passages was unmistakable, and unmistakably that of the age in which McGuffey lived. A story for children had to do more than tell a story. It had to provide also a lesson in ethical conduct. The readers did that.

Nevertheless, even after McGuffey had taken his radical step, little was done to build upon it for more than half a century. Another approach to the study of reading was initiated by James McKeen Cattell, who must be viewed as the real initiator of research in reading with a framework of scientific psychology. McGuffey was an empirically oriented developer of educational materials with little knowledge of the methods and approach of the scientist. Cattell, in contrast, was interested in the development of a body of knowledge that would lead to an understanding of the behavior known as reading.

When Cattell arrived in Leipzig in 1880, he confronted Wilhelm Wundt with his notion that he wanted to study the psychology of reading. The idea did not appeal to Wundt, who was nevertheless tolerant enough to permit the young Cattell to go ahead with his studies. Perhaps the redeeming factor in Cattell's research that prevented Wundt from rejecting it outright was that Cattell had ideas about measuring the various components of the reading process. The Wundt laboratory was concerned with the time taken for various mental processes to occur, and so the Cattell proposal offered some possibility of contributing to what Wundt believed to be a significant area of knowledge. The studies of the rapidity of mental processes that Wundt and his associates had undertaken had used mainly reaction times, comparing, for example, simple reaction times with reaction times involving choice. Through such experimental situations they had been able to measure the time occupied in the choice processes. Wundt and his students studied mental processes in artificial fabricated situations far from any practical activity. The argument for doing this was strong in that these fabricated situations were far simpler than those occurring in daily life and hence permitted a higher degree of experimental control. They generally did, and the approach of Wundt has been adopted by most experimental psychologists down to the present day. Nevertheless, Cattell was right in proposing that perceptual processes can sometimes be studied successfully within the context of a practical activity such as reading, for a long series of studies of the perception of letters and words produced significant knowledge over the next 100 years.

Cattell was interested in what today would be called the information processing time for recognizing letters of the alphabet. The letters were located on a revolving drum. As the drum revolved, each letter passed in front of a slit through which the subject could read the letter from the other side. The slit could be changed in width so that more than one letter might be presented to the subject at a time. Cattell showed that the time per letter decreased as several letters were presented simultaneously. Thus, it might take 1/3-second to recognize one letter, but two letters could be recognized in only a slightly longer time when the two letters appeared in the slit at the same time. Cattell interpreted his results in terms of the amount of information that could be held in consciousness at one time. In a further series of studies, Cattell showed that the grasp of consciousness could hold at one time three or four letters, two disconnected words, three or four words consisting of a sentence, and four numbers. What Cattell was demonstrating, using a modern vocabulary, is that visual information can be processed simultaneously as well as successively. A short sentence can be read by processing simultaneously each of the three or four words it contains. Cattell also showed that about twice as many words could be grasped if they made a sentence as when the words had no connection.

Cattell extended the Leipzig studies of reaction time to words. He determined the time required to recognize and read words. The rate of reading of disconnected words was about half as fast as the reading of prose. Cattell also experimented with the reading aloud of foreign languages. He found that the rate at which a person reads a foreign language is proportional to his familiarity with it. Of interest is the fact that the individual does not realize that he is reading a foreign language slowly, a finding that accounts for the fact that one has the impression that foreign languages, with which one is not familiar, are spoken at a very high speed.

Cattell also went on to investigate the time that a stimulus had to be present on the retina in order for it to be recognized in consciousness. This was not a productive line of work at the time when it was undertaken, because techniques of measuring light intensity were primitive, and the effect of a stimulus on the retina is a function of both duration and intensity. The work that Cattell undertook in this connection was an outgrowth of Wundt's emphasis on understanding the relationship between physiological processes and the nature of experience.

Still further studies were undertaken by Cattell on the legibility of particular letters of the alphabet and of printing types. Cattell's work on this problem initiated a long series of studies undertaken over the next century. The studies had implications both for understanding the cues to which individuals react in recognizing letters and for providing knowledge that might be of value in the design of type faces. Much later work was stimulated by Cattell's initial explorations in this field. The high readability of modern type faces was a product of this line of work.

Cattell wrote ten papers that focused on reaction time and reading. These were published in such prestigious journals as *Philosophische Studien, Mind, Brain,* and the *American Journal of Psychology.* An excellent summary of this research has been provided by another great early expert on reading, Walter Dearborn ("The Psychological Research of James McKeen Cattell," 1914).

Cattell's research established the basic facts related to the perception of letters and words in reading. Later research workers produced refinements in his results, but the broad outcomes of his research have never been seriously disputed, and they laid the foundation to our understanding of the reading process. The next major development in research related to reading came from a different direction and has been summarized by Edmund Burke Huey in his remarkable book *The Psychology and Pedagogy of Reading* (1908). The nature of this book is reflected in the fact that the original edition was reproduced in 1922 by Macmillan, and then the M.I.T. Press reproduced it again in 1968. A reader of Huey's book comes to realize that most of what is known today about the psychology of reading was known in 1908.

Huey began his book by pointing out that readers have the impression that reading involves the sweeping of the eyes across each line of print, but what actually happens is quite different. The movement of the eye along each line is discontinuous, a fact which seems to have been first observed by Emile Javal in 1879, just before Cattell began his classic work on perception. Javal noted that there were at least two pauses on each line, and sometimes more than two. Javal also noted that the pauses, or fixations as they are now called, were not successful because of their brevity and extreme irregularity, and also because the eye blinks and eye movements of the observer interfered with accurate observation. Javal estimated that there was a pause about every 10 letters. He also proposed that the eyes tended to follow the top half and middle of the letters, rather than the lower portion, since he was able to demonstrate that the upper parts of the letters provided the information by which they were identified. He demonstrated the latter by the simple procedure of showing that print was quite legible when only the upper halves were visible, but quite illegible if only the lower halves were exposed.

The work initiated by Javal was taken up by other academicians, who attempted to refine the technique of direct observation. Raymond Dodge and Bruno Erdmann found that the number of pauses did not vary much from line to line, but did vary with the difficulty of the material. More pauses were also made in the reading of a foreign language than in the native language. Erdmann and Dodge made one notable improvement in the observation procedure, which previously had involved viewing the reader's eyes in a mirror placed beside the reading material. The image in the mirror was viewed from behind the reader's back. Erdmann and Dodge introduced a telescope through which the movements of the eyes could be more readily observed. They claimed that, through the use of this technique, they discovered that fixations were on the middle of words, but it was doubtful whether they could have observed what they claimed.

Dodge also became interested in the speed and duration of eye movements, and developed an interesting technique for doing this. He flashed a small bright light at regular intervals in a fixed position. If the eye moved between successive flashes, then two after-images could be observed. Through quite a complex procedure involving this fact, Dodge was able to estimate the time occupied in eye movements.

One of Javal's students developed a technique for studying eye movements by recording the electrical changes in the eyelid produced by a movement of the eye. However, techniques of electrical recording were crude in those days and the resulting data added little to what was already known.

The next development in the recording of eye movement was attributed by Huey to a Professor Ahrens (first name unknown) of the University of Rostock, Germany, who fastened a small ivory cup, shaped like a modern contact lens, to the eye of the readers. He then attached a bristle to the ivory cup and used the bristle to record movement on a surface covered with lampblack. The technique did not produce usable data. Others also were unsuccessful in using this technique until it was developed further by Huey himself in 1897-98.

Huey substituted for the ivory disc a small cup of plaster of Paris moulded to the cornea. A hole was drilled through the center of the cup so that the wearer could see, and the eye was anesthetized to prevent discomfort. Huey then attached a fine thread to the plaster of Paris corneal cover, and the thread moved a recording lever. In this way Huey was able to obtain the first actual records of eye movements. One such record is reproduced in his book. It is remarkably clear, and quite as clear as the records produced by later photographic techniques. Through such recordings, Huey was first able to show that eye movements occasionally were reversed. The number of eye movements was also shown to be unrelated to the distance of the reading materials from the eye. Huey was also able to measure accurately the duration of each pause and the speed of eye movements. Huey could not determine whether information was taken in during the movement of the eye, but his suspicion was that information intake took place only when the eye was still.

Dodge experimented with photographic recording of eye movements and the technique was finally improved by Walter Dearborn at Columbia University. Dearborn developed the procedure that was to be used for the next half-century. Out of Dearborn's efforts emerged a practical way of studying the eye movements of individuals referred to clinics for reading problems. The photographic method also opened up the way for many research workers to undertake studies in the field. Yet one has to recognize that virtually all the important facts related to eye movements and reading had been discovered before Dearborn perfected photographic methods of recording. The facts discovered later, related to eye movements, were not particularly consequential.

Dearborn's development of a practical way of recording eye movements paved the way for making the eye camera a practical tool for the reading specialist. Yet the fact remains that, with the passage of time, the eye camera has fallen into disuse as a practical instrument for the diagnosis of the source of reading difficulties. Clinics have tended to relegate their eye cameras to the closet.

Research on eye movements and reading also opened up another productive line of research. Once eye movements had been recorded, apparatus was developed which could record not only eye movements and fixations, but also the position on the page on which the eye was centered. Through such devices, research could be undertaken on how individuals scan pages of material for information, and on how individuals examine illustrations. Such research made it possible to explore the significance to viewers of various parts of illustrations, demonstrating, for example, that boundaries of figures were the first components of an illustration to be examined, since these contained more information than any other features. The techniques were also extended for use in the study of advertising materials.

Modern educational research has done little to exploit the use of the techniques that can be used to study the manner in which the eye gathers information. Few schools and colleges of education even have faculty members who would know how to use the experimental equipment that is now available.

Huey's impressive description of what was known about the perceptual and motor aspects of reading is the most notable part of his book. Many of the later sections are speculative, though the chapter on rate of reading shows that there was an early interest in the matter. He brought out (p. 170) that the earliest attempt to measure reading speed was attributed to the great biologist George John Romanes (1848-1894), who was surprised at the enormous differences in rate of reading found among different individuals, for some read four times as fast as others. Romanes had limited data, and many of his conclusions were not just false, but actually misleading. For example, Romanes concluded that highly intelligent readers were commonly slow readers, but they took time to assimilate the knowledge presented. Huey also cited a study of Wellesley College girls who had been tested by Mary Calkins (who later became president of the American Psychological Association). Here, also, very large differences were found in rate of reading, with the fastest reading six times as fast as the slowest. One of the students was not only the most rapid, but was also the one who remembered the most, a result which seemed to question the conclusion of Romanes. The Romanes and Calkins studies were studies in silent reading. Further studies in the chapter report rates of silent reading and reading aloud. The data compare quite well with modern data. Maximum rates of silent reading reported by Huey are given at 732 words per minute. Presumably, this maximum was under the condition where the reader was pushed to read as fast as he could. Under conditions where the reader was not pushed, but was reading at his normal speed, the maximum was given at 528 words per minute, and the range of different readers was from 210 to 528 words per minute. The latter data were derived from students at the University of Wisconsin. Though collected nearly a century ago, they still have a modern ring.

Another important finding from the early studies of reading speed was that lip movements seemed to interfere with speed and comprehension. Slow readers were commonly characterized by lip movement. One notes that these early workers discussed lip movement rather than subvocal speech, a fact which demonstrates their emphasis on the recording of objective data and aversion to subjectivity. Huey himself repeated the experiments conducted at Wellesley College and the University of Wisconsin and arrived at very similar ranges of reading speeds.

The studies of reading rate were clever, but limited by the fact that little had been done to develop systematic ways of measuring this. The tests were given informally. Sometimes pressure was placed on the student to read as fast as he could, but sometimes the reading was undertaken without any such pressure and even without the student knowing that he was taking a test.

Huey reported that, previous to the publication of his book, work had already been extended to the identification of word features that result in word identification by the reader. The early research workers recognized that words were not read through the identification of each letter, but through the identification of particular letter features and general word features. The prevailing theory was that, although word identification by the reader was preceded by feature identification, the features were identified without respect to order. This conclusion was drawn from experiments in which words were presented briefly, by means of a tachistoscope, and the subject was asked to identify the words. A typical misidentification was when the German word *Farbe* was misread as the German word *Fabrik* (the subjects of the study were German). In this misidentification, the middle letters *r* and *b* are correctly identified, but their order is reversed in the word reported by the subject. If the letters had been identified in their correct positions, then the word could not have been identified as *Fabrik*.

The early research workers also recognized that not all letters, in all positions, within a word were recognized equally well. Letters in key positions, such as first and last letters, tended to be recognized most easily. Sometimes key groups of letters were recognized, such as a key syllable. Also, letters might not be recognized in their entirety, but the reader might identify certain features of a letter and, from those features, identify the letter either correctly or incorrectly. The letter features that were recognized appeared to involve those parts of letters that projected above the line. Features that projected below the line tended to be ignored. Thus, the letter *g* was often read as the letter *a*, because the subject attended to the upper half of the letter. For a similar reason, the letter *q* tended to be recognized as an *o*.

Early research workers, and particularly Oscar Messmer, also studied the way in which perception of a word evolves. They could do this by presenting the word for a very short interval of the order of a few thousandths of a second, and determining what the subject had seen. They then repeated the exposure and asked for a further report. In this way the slow development of a percept could be studied. The method of experimentation was sophisticated, even by modern standards.

The sophisticated methods of research developed made it possible even to explore the features of letters that resulted in letter identification. The main letter features that the perceiver used were the breadth of the letter, the height of the letter, and the geometrical configuration. The latter category was also broken down into letters involving mainly vertical strokes, and letters involving curved lines.

An additional characteristic of the word-recognition process was that the initial part of the word seemed to provide more cues than the later part. Indeed, the last part of a word might be completely disregarded in the reading process. Huey undertook a very simple experiment to demonstrate that the first half of a word provides more information for word identification than the last half. He simply sliced words in half and showed that words were more easily recognized from the initial half of each word than from the final half. Anyone can repeat this experiment for himself and verifying this finding.

Other studies by Huey showed that the time required to recognize a word was unrelated to its length. The conclusion in this case probably was incorrect, particularly since no effort was made to equate short and long words for frequency of occurrence.

A reader of Huey's book comes away from it impressed with the results of research and, perhaps, even astounded that so much was known about reading even before the turn of the century. Even more surprising than the amount of knowledge, that had been developed by 1908, is the fact that every promising line of research described in the Huey book was abandoned and then left untouched for another 50 years. If one had been living in the early part of the century, one would surely have predicted that the then flourishing research on the psychology of reading would have been greatly expanded, and with the production of a wealth of new knowledge. Yet the fact is that it was abandoned, and displaced by research of a much less useful and productive nature. It became displaced by research on the measurement of reading skill in children and the development of a great variety of tests of what were believed to be component skills. A few reflections on the abandonment of productive reading research in favor of the less productive is in order here, for a similar cutting-off of productive lines in favor of the unproductive has been a marked feature of the history of educational research. An understanding of what is involved may help prevent this from happening in the future.

First, those who undertook the early research on reading were individuals of extraordinary ability. These are rare in any age. Individuals of the same stature do not seem to have been attracted to the field until, in recent times, Eleanor Gibson undertook her remarkable work on the psychology of reading, taking up the work very much where Huey had left it in 1908 (see Eleanor J. Gibson and Harry Levin, *The Psychology of Reading,* 1975). The years that intervened between the appearance of Huey's publication and that of Gibson were remarkably barren except for a few studies of letter and word recognition and a quite pedantic series of investigations on problems of type design.

Perhaps a second reason for the absence of any continuity in the research on perception and reading is that those who became involved in educational research during the first half of the present century were individuals who had little familiarity with laboratory techniques. Research tended to be based on testing in the schools. Laboratory research workers in the field of perception were interested in other problems, and notably those problems that were studied so productively by the Gestalt psychologists. Schools of education, where most of the research on reading was conducted, were quite devoid of any equipment that could be used for conducting studies of perception and reading. Most schools of education had no facilities for research at all. This does not mean that the research conducted on reading through schools of education was worthless, for much useful research was undertaken. It means only that the research undertaken was limited to the use of paper-and-pencil devices which have no value for the study of the perceptual aspects of reading.

A third possible reason for the changed emphasis of research on reading is that the U.S. Bureau of Education became preoccupied early in the century with the efficiency movement. The obvious approach to the improved efficiency of schools was to determine what was being accomplished, and then to find ways to raise the level of accomplishment. The first step in doing this, in the case of reading, was to develop tests of reading. Once the latter had been done, the rest appeared to be easy, even though it was not. Once William Torrey Harris left the Commissionership in 1906, there was nobody in the Bureau who had any conception of what experimental psychology was, and could accomplish. Nothing experimental received any support from the Federal Bureau for another half-century.

Reading Tests and the Improvement of School Efficiency

One might have expected that Judd would have been the great promoter of the further development of research on perceptual processes in relation to reading, but he was not. By the time he reached the University of Chicago, he had long given up work in the laboratory and had become directly involved in the work of schools. Judd became completely absorbed in whatever he touched and work with the schools became the focus of his interests, even before he accepted the Chicago appointment. He still held at the back of his mind the thought that the laboratory would provide the essential knowledge needed by teachers, and he returned to this problem towards the end of his professional life, but in his middle life at Chicago, he turned to the immediate and pressing problems of schools.

Judd's new viewpoint is well illustrated in an article he wrote in 1913, when he was active as a member of the Committee on Standards of the National Council on Education (1913-14). In this article, Judd argued that standardized tests provided a means whereby the individual teacher can obtain objective evidence of what a pupil has accomplished. Judd recognized that all teachers judged children in terms of some vague subjective standard, and that the process of judgment could be improved by providing the teacher with an objective standard, such as the performance of the larger group of pupils. He argued that schools should be judged by their products, and products are judged by comparing one with another. In this paper, Judd promoted the idea that teaching efficiency should be measured in terms of the quality of the products of teaching.

Apparently, there had been much opposition by teachers to the expanding testing movement in schools. The proposal that achievement tests be used to help supervisors improve the practices of teachers was threatening enough, but the widespread interest in the establishment of national standards, an idea promoted by the U.S. Bureau of Education, had completed the antagonism of teachers toward the new testing movement. Judd recognized all of these problems and hoped to circumvent them by reasoning with teachers about the worthwhile uses of tests.

Judd continued his article by explaining to teachers what is involved in the development of a standardized instrument. He explained why materials have to be selected properly for reading tests and the need for uniform conditions of administration. He emphasized that the resulting standards are social rather than absolute. What today would be called a criterion-referenced test Judd would have regarded as one involving a social standard. He was right, for any standard of performance has to be evaluated in terms of a social standard before it is of much use. Merely demonstrating that a child can read simple material at 160 words per minute, with good comprehension, is not a very useful piece of information unless one knows that this is a socially useful or useless reading speed. Criteria have to be evaluated in terms of a social criterion at some stage.

Judd then made an interesting analysis of oral and silent reading, arguing that oral reading was an activity of childhood but that silent reading was an activity of the adult world. Judd held that both oral and silent reading should be measured in that they represented different skills, the one at a more mature level than the other.

Judd believed that the most basic aspect of reading that a test should appraise should be speed. He believed that the evidence was firm that speed of reading was a good measure of reading efficiency. He also expected that oral reading would be more rapid than silent reading in the lower grades, if silent reading were at all possible, and that silent reading would be more rapid than oral reading at the higher grades.

Judd outlined a plan for research on reading within the context of the classroom. The task for developing this plan of action was the life work of one of Judd's students, William S. Gray (1885-1960).

William S. Gray was probably the most influential man in the area of reading during much of his adult life. He had a quite typical preparation as a teacher at the Illinois State Normal University. After graduation he became an elementary school teacher during the years 1905-1908. Later he became principal of the training school at the Illinois State Normal University. He did graduate work at Columbia University, where he must surely have encountered the work of Edward L. Thorndike. Then he completed his doctoral degree at the University of Chicago under the direction of Judd. Although his biography in the *National Cyclopaedia of American Biography* (1965, 48, 106) does not mention his reading tests, indicating that he did not think them to be an important outcome of his career, he is probably remembered more by the *Gray Oral Reading Tests* than by any other of his publications.

Gray's famous tests used a series of standardized paragraphs arranged in order of increasing difficulty. The tests followed the plan laid down by Judd and involved both a silent reading section and an oral reading section. The materials were appropriate for testing children from the second to the sixth grade inclusive. Measures of speed of reading and comprehension could be derived from the tests. The oral reading test also permitted the study of the particular difficulties that the child encountered in reading. The tests were originally sold by Gray himself for the modest price of 50 cents per hundred during the World War I period. Later, when the demand for his tests became voluminous, he had the tests published by the Public School Publishing Company of Bloomington, Illinois.

Gray's career, outlined by himself in his brief autobiography, stressed matters other than reading tests. From his over 500 publications he selected for citation his books on the reading interests of adults, on the teaching of reading and writing, on the nature of reading problems in American education, and his summaries of investigations of reading. The latter were a series of journal articles that listed all of the research on reading during a particular time span. Thus, Gray viewed himself as being primarily a research worker.

Another chapter in this volume told how the achievement test movement mushroomed during the first and second decades of the present century. The Gray tests were not the only ones that had a major place in the test market during that period. The *Kansas Silent Reading Tests*, developed before Gray's tests appeared, were widely used, and had long been attractive to school administrators, since there were forms both for the primary grades and for the high school. The *Courtis Reading Tests* probably sold more than any other tests, perhaps because they were marketed through a commercial organization set up for that purpose named *Courtis Standard Research Tests.* The tests were advertised in the widely circulated journals of the day, together with facts about the enormous quantities that were used. Courtis himself also spent much time giving lectures on the new measurement movement to assemblies of teachers and school administrators. The Courtis tests were well designed, even in terms of modern standards, and were so arranged that separate measures for speed and comprehension of reading could be derived. Courtis also introduced an important innovation. The tests were in two forms that were also about equal in difficulty, though perhaps not as well matched as comparable modern parallel forms. The reason for the parallel forms was to provide a means of measuring pupil performance at the start and end of the school semester or year, so that the progress of each pupil could be gauged. This procedure suggested by Courtis seemed logical, particularly in view of the fact that research workers had not yet identified the fact that practice on one form of the test transfers to performance on the second form.

Research on reading, that was centered on tests of reading, is a little difficult to conceptualize today. The work was highly tied to the new efficiency movement in schools, and the expectation was that once the achievement of pupils had been measured, then there should be little difficulty in identifying the reasons for the poor performance of some pupils and the excellent performance of others. A series of articles by Gray entitled "Reading in the Elementary Schools of Indianapolis" (1918-1919) described the use of the Gray tests in a survey of the schools of Indianapolis and the kind of results that were achieved. One has to bear in mind that the survey was viewed as an instrument for conducting research.

The Indianapolis survey of 1917 was very much like what would be called today an evaluation study. Gray first spent time in Indianapolis attempting to determine the objectives of the teaching of reading. He was able to establish that the objectives of the teaching of reading were quite similar in many respects at all grades from 1 to 8. There were, of course, some differences. The objective *appreciation of literature* showed an increasing emphasis with grade level. Gray also studied the time devoted to both oral and silent reading, and the reverse was true at the higher grade levels.

Gray studied the time devoted to reading in the classrooms in Indianapolis. The amount was quite small. In the lower grades it averaged about an hour a day, but by the fourth and fifth grades this amount of time had declined to less than 30 minutes, and even less at the sixth, seventh, and eighth grades. Despite what teachers said about the importance of reading, it does not seem to have been emphasized in the schools of Indianapolis. The City of Cleveland, surveyed by Judd at almost the same time, showed that the children there spent 2½ times as much time reading as those in Indianapolis.

The second paper in the series dealt with the results of the oral reading tests. Compared with the results from surveys in Grand Rapids and Cleveland, the results of the Indianapolis survey were poor. Gray provided an extremely sophisticated analysis of the results. The scores were relatively low, but in view of the fact that the time spent on reading was rather small, perhaps the results were commendable. Also, the tests were given at the start of the school year and Gray was aware of the fact that test scores on reading tests tended to slip during the summer when children were not exposed to books. Despite the overall poor showing of the Indianapolis pupils on the test, a more detailed analysis shows that, in terms of rate of reading, the Indianapolis students tended to catch up with the students in Grand Rapids and Cleveland by the seventh grade. Since Gray believed that rate of reading was the most crucial single measure of reading competence, he must have been surprised at the finding, which suggested that the time spent on reading in the

Indianapolis schools produced as much reading competence over the grade school years as twice the amount of time spent elsewhere. Very similar results were provided by the silent reading tests, with the Indianapolis pupils behind at the lower grades, but slowly inching up as they moved through elementary school.

More important than any of the results considered up to this point was the finding of the great differences between schools. Gray could not explain such differences in terms of the instruction provided or the quality of the teaching. Other factors seemed to be at work, and the identification of some of these other factors was necessary in order to develop a theory of reading. Gray recognized that variables other than the skill of the teacher and time spent in reading were of importance in the acquisition of skills, particularly sociological variables.

The manner of conducting the survey in Indianapolis seems to have been the pattern set by Judd in a similar survey in Cleveland in 1915. Judd has described how he undertook the Cleveland survey in Chapter 10 of the *Fifteenth Yearbook of the National Society for the Study of Education.* The testing of the achievement of the pupils seems to have been at the very core of the survey. Efforts were made to determine the objectives of teachers and to ensure that the outcomes measured by the tests were related to the objectives. Yet, neither Judd nor Gray was very clear as to what was to be achieved through the survey procedures that were adopted. One has the impression that both believed that the schools would benefit, though it is not clear how. Both also believed that the survey of the school system would produce data that could be used in research. Both seem to have been unduly impressed with the potentialities of what they called exact measurement, perhaps seeing in such measurement the same potential that the physical sciences had achieved as they had gained in precision.

The Indianapolis survey was the first opportunity that Gray had to study sociological variables related to reading. His attack on this problem was through investigating the relationship between socioeconomic background of pupils and reading achievement. He did not have at his disposal the refined measures of socioeconomic status used today, but based his inquiry on classifying schools in terms of the economic level of the areas they served. On this basis he found a relationship between socioeconomic status and reading achievement. Joseph Mayer Rice had not found this relationship in his studies undertaken 20 years earlier, but he had not used anything as sophisticated as the Gray tests of reading. The relationship found by Gray may seem to be a commonplace finding today, but in the 1910-1920 period it was a matter of great interest, particularly since it fitted with the idea that the poor were genetically inferior. Gray did not exploit his finding in terms of the latter idea, but he followed the leadership of Judd who took the position that there was no solid evidence to support the position that intelligence as measured by tests was inherited. Judd preferred the view that intelligence tests reflected the immediate level of functioning of the individual. How much this level could be changed was an open question. Gray followed this line of thought, and he also recognized that the socioeconomic level was a complex mixture of elements, the effects on reading of which needed to be studied.

Gray was impressed with the influence of sociological variables on reading achievement. When he came to write his article on reading in the 1941 edition of the *Encyclopaedia of Educational Research*, he opened the article with a long discussion of reading as a sociological phenomenon. Not only does reading depend upon social transmission, but it is a basic instrument through which a society is held together. As Gray's work progressed, he became steadily more impressed with the significance of sociological variables in the reading achievement.

Although Gray, in the early part of his career, was caught in the whirlwind of interest in conducting surveys of schools through the medium of tests, he must have become disappointed in what this could achieve. The most important part of his work was undertaken during the period 1920-1940 and, although this work was centered on research, virtually none of the data came from school surveys. He was a great collector and collator of research studies and devoted substantial efforts at bringing together the knowledge acquired into a comprehensive theory of reading. The progress in Gray's thought in the direction of the development of a theory of reading is quite apparent when one examines and compares the two yearbooks of the National Society for the Study of Education (the 24th and 36th yearbooks), produced in 1925 and 1937. These two yearbooks were both prepared under a committee chaired by Gray, and substantial sections of each were written by him. Both yearbooks show throughout the unmistakable influence of Gray.

The first of the two yearbooks was centered on reading programs in the schools. The first chapter written by Gray was concerned with the overall role of reading in life and society. It reflected his own interest in the social setting of reading and the total function of reading in society. The Puritan child had learned to read in order to achieve salvation through the study of the Scriptures. Gray saw reading as a means of making the child into a useful member of a society that could not function without a widespread distribution of reading skill. Reading was not just a school subject, but a means of acquiring a role in society. Gray's initial chapter had a freshness to it that the rest of the volume does not have.

Whatever inspiration Gray may have tried to give to the rest of his committee, it did not permeate the entire volume. The two chapters that followed his own chapter presented a rather pedantic description of a reading program for all 12 grades of school. There was no vestige of a theory of the variables that are related to the acquisition of reading. The chapters described what are believed to be effective practices. There was no recognition of the important work on perception in relation to reading, described by Huey in his classic book. Inquiry into the reading process had moved away from the research-oriented phase of the turn of the century. Now the attempt was to identify effective teaching practices by means of a subjective analysis of what the teaching practices involved. This kind of analysis had come to the forefront as a result of the use of survey techniques, which attempted to appraise pupil achievement and thereby to identify deficiencies in teaching. The surveyors still had to learn that the problem of identifying effective teaching practices was a much more difficult and complicated one than they had conceived it to be. Two major chapters on phonetics and vocabulary development showed the slow identification of problems that were to be investigated later. Another chapter on materials of instruction discussed word lists and the ways in which they might be derived. The issues and problems discussed in the yearbook were those that were to be the basis of dissertations in the coming years. As yet there was little research that could be introduced into a discussion of them.

A long chapter on reading tests, both informal and standardized, was written by an author who showed little enthusiasm for the entire enterprise. It was written by Laura Zirbes, who was then attached to the Lincoln School of Teachers College. It does a commendable job of describing the tests that were available, but nowhere suggests that these might be used to develop knowledge of how children learn to read. The enthusiasm of the previous decade for giving tests in schools, with the hope of acquiring great knowledge about education, seemed to have been displaced by apathy towards tests. The enterprise had just not yielded the kind of knowledge that many had expected it would yield.

Theories of Reading

The transition in Gray's thinking from 1925 to 1937 was dramatic. His lengthy chapter in the *Thirty-Sixth Yearbook of the National Society for the Study of Education* provided what was essentially a theory of how reading develops. His chapter began with a statement of the broad purposes of reading instruction. He was concerned with matters that went far beyond the mere acquisition of the mechanics of reading. He wanted the schools to develop in pupils a deep interest in reading and the many joys that could be derived from the activity. In order to accomplish such broad goals, the pupil had to be able to master the mechanics of reading, but stress on the mechanics must not be allowed to interfere with the development of good feelings about the worth of reading. Gray was more aware than some modern writers of the possibility of developing very efficient methods for developing the mechanics of reading which might leave the student bereft of any good feelings about the worth of the activity.

By the time that Gray's theory of reading had been developed, a considerable number of investigations had been undertaken on the conditions prior to formal school instruction that made significant contributions to the acquisition of reading. Gray recognized that the child, through home experiences or preschool experiences, should learn about the significance and worth of reading. Gray had learned that children who learned to read easily in the first grade were those who had had worthwhile experiences with books, who had seen adults use books in ways that were profitable, and who had learned through having had stories read to them that books could be a source of great enjoyment. Unlike most previous discussions of reading, Gray's theory placed heavy emphasis on matters of motivation. He recognized some of the important factors involved in enjoying a story, such as that of being able to identify with the characters involved.

The theory of the development of reading was closely tied to the procedures for teaching that Gray recommended. The initial step, discussed in the previous paragraph in relation to motivation, involved the development of readiness to read, but much more is involved than motivation in the development of readiness.

Gray recognized an overall reading readiness factor, but he also recognized that reading readiness was multifaceted. The concept of reading readiness had already been widely discussed and does not seem to have originated in the work of Gray. The phenomenon had been subjected to extensive empirical investigation (see Arthur I. Gates and Guy L. Bond, 1935-36). The procedure for studying reading readiness was to obtain measures of pupils as they entered a reading program, and then these measures were compared with level of reading achievement at some later date. The results from the Gates and Bond study, and other studies, are far from being clear. Gray rightly concluded that the combination of factors was the crucial matter. This makes sense, for one can understand that a child who had had little experience in the readiness factor of letter recognition might still do well if he had very high motivation to read.

Gray tried to summarize a great mass of literature on reading readiness, coming up with a list of seven factors which he believed to be of crucial importance. The first factor was called *wide experience.* Without such a range of experience, Gray believed, the child would have difficulty in interpreting the content of most reading materials. The second factor was *facility in the use of ideas.* Gray meant by this the capacity to discuss in an organized, thoughtful way things that happen. Such thoughtful use of ideas seemed to be essential for the thoughtful use of the printed page. A third prerequisite was a *reasonable command of simple sentences.* A child who could not talk in simple but complete sentences surely would have difficulty reading and understanding sentences. Gray advocated training in this prerequisite with children being given opportunities to talk about the experiences they have had, as well as dramatization and storytelling.

A fourth factor was identified as a *relatively wide speaking vocabulary.* Quite obviously the child should have mastered the vocabulary of the words that he would encounter in reading. A fifth factor was *accuracy in enunciation and pronunciation.* This fifth factor was important since a child who enunciated incorrectly during reading would have to be corrected and the task would then become not only one of learning to read but also the task of learning to speak. Gray thought that the two tasks should be learned separately. A sixth factor was *reasonable accuracy in visual and auditory discrimination.* The reading task obviously involved the ability to discriminate visual and auditory forms and to associate the one with the other. Without previous experience at making quite fine visual discriminations, the child would surely see printed materials as just a uniform jumble of signs, much as most Americans see Chinese or Japanese as a random display of black marks. In recent years, Eleanor Gibson has explored the matter of the extent to which a child's familiarity with letters of the alphabet facilitates reading. Her research comes out with the clear answer that the ability to discriminate and recognize letters is of considerable importance.

The seventh factor was that which has been previously discussed, namely, *interest in learning to read.* Later work has generally shown this to be the most powerful of the factors considered.

William S. Gray made considerable efforts to implement this theory of the nature of reading readiness with suggestions to teachers concerning how the various facets of reading readiness might be developed. These are presented in a pamphlet he wrote with Marion Monroe entitled *Before We Read: Developmental Activities for the Pre-Reading Period* (1937). Marion Monroe had undertaken much of the important basic research on this problem.

The second stage of learning to read involved initial guidance on the part of the teacher. Gray listed three objectives at this stage. The first was a motivational factor referred to as an interest in reading. The second factor was a cultivation of a thoughtful attitude towards reading activities. The third, and last mentioned, factor was the development of what Gray calls the habits of reading. Gray was enormously impressed with the motivational factors in reading. Indeed, one gathers from his writing that, if motivation to read were sufficiently high, then the acquisition of the basic behaviors related to reading would be learned rapidly and easily. This theory is almost the reverse of some modern theories of teaching reading, developed by operant psychologists. Highly programmed methods of teaching reading assume that the initial focus has to be on the acquisition of the skill itself.

Gray already had considerable evidence to support his views

concerning the conditions that favored the acquisition of reading skill, and little subsequent research supports an alternative view. Gray also, unlike some modern operant psychologists, took a long-term view of the problem of teaching reading. The problem of the teacher was not just that of how to develop the perceptual skill of decoding words, but that of developing a lifelong desire to extract information from the pages of books. Gray recognized that the acquisition of the mechanics of the skill, or what he called the reading habits, was of little consequence if these were rarely put to practical use in the person's daily life. Gray wanted to produce a generation of children who would eagerly search the human heritage of knowledge stored in books, so that that knowledge could be put to use to improve the human condition. Gray realized that reading had to be made an enjoyable and worthwhile activity, right from the start.

Gray provided an interesting discussion of when reading should be initiated as a school activity, concluding that no simple answer could be given to the question. Although reading should generally be initiated in the first grade, if the pupil had not been as yet exposed to the prerequisite activities by the time he reached first grade, then these activities should be the starting point.

Gray stressed the need for having materials of high interest to children, but he did not say much about what such materials should be. He seemed to favor commercially published materials, in that these are generally better sequenced than are teacher-made materials. Gray stressed the importance of developing a sight vocabulary of words of high frequency in simple reading materials. He implied that a controlled vocabulary should be a most important feature of published reading materials, but did not acknowledge the contribution that Gates had made in developing readers with a controlled vocabulary. He stressed again here, as he does almost throughout the yearbook article, that the development of interest and favorable attitude was as important as the development of word recognition.

Gray enumerated a number of procedures that may be used to give the child cues to use in decoding particular words. These included picture cues. Gray believed that reading should be looked upon by the child as a fascinating puzzle to which answers had to be found, and the finding of the answers was viewed as an activity that developed the child's thinking skills. The development of thought in relation to the content was viewed as a most important objective related to basic reading experiences. A matter to note is that although the early research workers, near the turn of the century, regarded reading as being a perceptual process, the new view sponsored by Gray was that reading should be primarily an exercise of the reasoning and thinking capacities of the individual.

The problems of maintaining interest and a thoughtful attitude seemed to be most acute in the early stages of reading. Once the pupil engaged in continuous meaningful reading, the problem of maintaining interest was far less acute, since reading activities can then be adjusted in terms of the pupil's own interests. Nevertheless, even at the more advanced stage, socialized activities such as are involved in dramatizations and oral reading may be useful in developing thoughtful interpretations of what is read. Gray believed that the initial period of instruction should emphasize oral reading. This seemed easier than silent reading, and permitted correction by the listener.

The third stage of reading was reached when the child was able to read simple materials with ease and understanding. In the next stage, children began to read to satisfy curiosity, and as this was done, there was a great advance in their fundamental attitudes and skills. In the third stage, the children were weaned from being dependent on the supervision of an adult. By the end of this stage, the pupil should be a rapid and independent reader and also an effective oral reader. Although there are great individual differences, this stage was considered to be reached by the end of the third grade. Once this stage had been mastered, pupils should learn to read for a number of different purposes. Pupils must learn that some material needs only to be skimmed for major ideas, some material must be read and thought through in detail, and some is read so that it may be summarized or otherwise used. The increase in speed of reading is best achieved through the reading of simple, interesting material, but children should also be exposed to other types of reading materials that call for different skills.

Gray took the position that most reading difficulties can be corrected through the teacher observing the oral reading of the pupil and then introducing corrective measures. Extended clinical study of the poor reader is rarely thought to be worthwhile, since most problems can be readily identified. Gray recommended that a graphical record of progress in reading be kept in a form that the child understood, since he believed that this practice was motivating to the child.

The fourth phase of the acquisition of reading skill involved an increase in speed and efficiency and increased breadth in the use of reading skills. Gray pointed out that, in his judgment, schools in the 1930's were doing a good job of developing the fundamental reading skills in the first three grades of schooling, but that there was little emphasis on increasing and expanding these skills in the subsequent grades. It was almost as if reading skills were acquired and then not adequately used. Work in the upper elementary grades should involve an increasing use of the library and reference materials. Unless the work of the school were designed to use such materials, reading skills would not develop as they should.

In some final comments, Gray pointed out that oral reading skills tended to be neglected in the upper elementary grades. The reasons for this were many. First, children at the fourth-grade level tended to read silently at a faster rate than aloud and hence found the silent method best for the acquisition of information. Also, fourth-grade children tended to read aloud in a rather dull and uninteresting monotone. Gray thought that oral reading skills should be developed so that the children would be able to provide good oral interpretations of literary materials. Oral reading is far more than a mere skill, it is an art that should be developed for its own sake.

Gray discussed a fifth stage in the development of reading, but this fifth stage seems to be essentially an extension of the fourth stage into the high school. Gray believed that every teacher in high school should be keenly aware of the importance of giving assignments that called for the development of reading skills. Every teacher should be a teacher of reading. Gray did believe that there was a place for the specialized reading teacher, to provide help for those reaching high school but who were still reading at a rather low level of competence. Gray estimated that, in the 1930's, about 4 percent of the students in high school were reading at a level equivalent to that in the lower elementary grades.

The Gray theory of the development of reading, much of it solidly grounded in research, is not very different from a theory that might be formulated today. Gray, following the lead of Judd, was most careful to keep his knowledge of research up-to-date. Like most of his contemporaries in Judd's department, he devoted considerable time to the preparation of bibliographies of research contributions, and these were published in the publications of the department. Gray kept very close to the research literature, and his students authored a substantial fraction of it. As the volume of research increased, steps had to be taken to collate and summarize the findings. Occasional conferences were established for this purpose. At each conference, an effort was made to review the research on a particular topic related to reading. These conferences became regular features of Judd's department and Gray's work beginning in 1925. Reports of the conferences were published, many as special issues of the *Supplementary Educational Monographs.* Gray was the editor. After Gray retired from the University of Chicago, the task of running the conferences and editing the reports became the task of Helen M. Robinson.

Gray was always searching for ways in which to convert the results of research into practice. One of his first efforts to do this was in the form of the development of tests, but he soon put out a series of grade school readers based on the general theory of reading that he was slowly evolving. His first set of readers was developed together with William H. Elson and was known as the *Elson Basic Readers.* Presumably, most of the work was undertaken by Elson, and Gray played the role of a consultant. These readers were published in 1930. Gray produced his own series of *Basic Readers* in 1940. Both series were published by Scott Foresman. These were successful series, and hardly surprisingly so, for Gray was the most eminent authority on reading in his time. One suspects that they sold numbers of copies comparable to the millions of copies that

Thorndike's arithmetic books sold.

Gray followed the pattern of his contemporaries of turning theory into practice through the production of materials. Gray, like his contemporaries, recognized that the production of new materials represented the simplest and most straightforward way of influencing practice. Gray was an advocate of improved teaching methods, but the materials themselves were the avenues through which teaching methods could be influenced. This approach to transforming theory into practice is to be contrasted with parallel efforts of the Progressive Education Movement, which advocated new methods of teaching but had the greatest difficulty in introducing those methods into the classroom. The latter movement regarded the entire community and its resources as the materials out of which the curriculum should be constructed, but this concept of a curriculum and a community source of materials probably had much less influence on teaching method than that produced by the introduction of simple materials which have a direct effect in structuring what teachers do. Unfortunately, this concept of changing classroom practices has in recent years been greatly abused through the introduction of what have been termed "teacher-proof" materials, a term that is almost insulting to teachers and to the important functions they perform.

The results of administering reading tests as a part of school surveys did not produce the spectacular research results that many had hoped they would. Gray and others concerned with the acquisition of reading skills were already turning to other avenues for acquiring knowledge by the mid-1920's, for it was by then clear that the difficulties were insuperable of relating teaching method to achievement in a natural school setting. Alternative, and far more promising, approaches were available, as, for example, the collection of case histories of children who had serious difficulty in learning to read. Workers earlier in the century had written off such children as laggards, a derogatory term with moral implications. The assumption had been that such children were just lazy. A few may have been, but by the mid-1920's some academicians and school teachers had come to recognize that there was more to the problem than what the term *laggard* implied. The result was the appearance of numerous studies which presented the case histories of children who had difficulty in learning to read. The most impressive and influential of these was the set of case histories collected by Marion Monroe (*Children Who Cannot Read*, 1932). Monroe was a student of Gray. Although case history studies are not popular today, one should note that the findings from these case history studies in the late 1920's produced results that have stood the test of time. They showed, beyond a shadow of doubt, that reading difficulties are strongly related to the experiences the children have had, in relation to books, before they ever enter the schools. The results of the case history studies were later repeated using larger samples and better statistical techniques, and these later studies produced essentially the same results.

A second development in the area of reading has already been touched upon with reference to Thorndike, namely, the use of carefully selected vocabulary in readers. Arthur I. Gates became the main figure in the 1925-1940 period in relation to this matter. Gates had been a student of Thorndike at Teachers College and had stayed on as a faculty member and as the specialist in reading. His function at Teachers College was very much what Gray's was at Chicago. Gates was fully familiar with the work that Thorndike had undertaken on the development of word counts, and Gates was the first to use word-count data for the purpose of designing basic readers for the grades. Gates also attempted to adapt aspects of Thorndike's theory of learning to the design of readers. In the Thorndike paradigm of experimentation, learning took place as a result of multiple exposures to whatever was to be learned. A response was rarely well established after it had been made on a single occasion. Thus, the correct reading response to a new word should be made many times in order to ensure that the stimulus-response connection would be strong. A consequence of this fact for the design of readers was that new words introduced into a reader should be repeated many times in subsequent parts of the text in order for the reading response to the printed word to be thoroughly learned. This has become an almost standard practice in the design of readers. The rationale for the procedure seems sound, and yet it is hard to find a study that demonstrates that careful control of vocabulary produces better learning than a more casual approach. Such systematic repetition does have disadvantages in that it tends to produce material that is quite lifeless. Literature cannot use a controlled vocabulary in this way.

Revised Alphabets and the Spelling Problem

During the period from 1880 to 1930, when research on reading was developing rapidly and producing a wealth of significant findings, there was relatively little controversy concerning how reading should be taught. There was some mild discussion concerning the matter of whether reading should be taught before or after initial instruction had been given in writing, or whether reading and writing should be taught simultaneously, but there was no heated debate on the issue. Indeed, there was little heated debate on issues related to teaching. Even the flamboyant writings of Joseph Mayer Rice had raised little more than a murmur of discussion. Other issues related to reading may well have been discussed in the halls at meetings of educators, but they did not appear in prominent places in educational literature. One matter that must surely have been discussed occasionally in the background at such meetings was that of the use of special alphabets for the teaching of reading.

John A. Downing has reviewed attempts to provide special alphabets for the facilitation of reading (*Evaluating the Initial Teaching Alphabet*, 1967). Downing pointed out that the apparent irregularity of the way in which words are represented by letters in the English language has been a matter that has concerned scholars for a long time. Two approaches to simplifying the relationship between the printed word and the sound of the word have been proposed. One has been to augment the ordinary alphabet with additional symbols and the other has been to regularize English spelling. According to Downing, augmentation goes back to that proposed by John Hart in 1570. Later, in 1633, Charles Butler also proposed an augmented alphabet. The first attempt to regularize spelling in the English language has been attributed by Downing to Richard Hodges, who proposed a completely regularized system as far back as 1644.

In the last century, Edwin Leigh developed a system that could be used in the early stages of reading. He was able to bring it to the attention of William Torrey Harris, who was then principal of the Clay School in St. Louis. Harris introduced Leigh's system for teaching beginning reading in his school. Later, when Harris became superintendent of schools in St. Louis, he introduced the modified alphabet into all of the schools of St. Louis, and the system continued to be used there for about 10 years. Why it was eventually abandoned is not clear, but surely if the system had been an outstanding success it would have survived. The Leigh system was of course transitional, and, at some stage, the child would have to make the switch to the traditional system of spelling.

The development of the Initial Teaching Alphabet had no striking novelty to it, and it hardly seems to have been an improvement over earlier systems, but it was backed by the financial resources of Isaac Pitman's organization and also strong political backing from the British government. It is to the credit of Isaac Pitman, and those who developed the system, that they made no personal profits from their product but gave the system to the public for the public good. However, if the system had been all that some claimed it to be, then surely earlier systems, and notably that of Leigh, would have also demonstrated extraordinary results. That they did not do.

Downing has reviewed the findings of the early research on the use of the Initial Teaching Alphabet. The results are far from clear, though Downing comes down on the positive side, concluding that there are more advantages than disadvantages. The main difficulty in drawing conclusions stems from the fact that during the transition to traditional orthography, typically in the third grade, children who have learned reading through the Initial Teaching Alphabet suffer a setback, and the extent of the setback is a matter of controversy. One cannot be particularly surprised that children learn to read books in the Initial

Teaching Alphabet more easily than those who learn from the traditional orthography, for the one system presents a simpler task than the other. The real question is whether there is a saving over the long haul, which includes the transition to the traditional system.

The conclusions of Downing have also been drawn, in almost idential wording, by those who have undertaken later studies of the use of the Initial Teaching Alphabet. Shortly after Downing's book appeared, F. W. Warburton and Vera Southgate published the results of a very elaborate study in *i.t.a.: An Independent Evaluation* (1969). An equally elaborate study was also undertaken by D. V. Thackray and published in a monograph, *Readiness for Reading with i.t.a. and t.o.* (1971). The Thackray study drew precisely the same conclusions as the others that had been undertaken.

Modified alphabets have had periods of being in vogue over the last century, when they were received locally with unrestrained enthusiasm. There has not been a national movement to introduce children to reading through a transitional system. In contrast, in the early part of the century there was a strong movement, both within education and without, to change the entire spelling system of the English language. This effort was much publicized not only in educational journals, but in the press. The *Chicago Tribune* introduced a more or less phonetic system of spelling into the newspaper and used it for many years, and long after all public interest had been lost in the matter. The use of such a simplified system of spelling was debated at conferences of teachers, where its obvious advantages of early reading instruction were lauded. Those who promoted the plan realized that, without the introduction of additional characters, a new system of spelling could be only partially phonetic, but a partial system would still be easier to master than the present highly irregular system. The assumption underlying the spelling reform movement was that English spelling lacked any rational basis, and that was incorrect. The English spelling system is in actual fact an extremely sophisticated spelling system, in which the irregularities convey meanings about the sources of words. Thus, even though the words *know* and *no* are pronounced identically, the difference in spelling gives the reader meaning cues. The difficulty with the spelling system is that it is not designed to be understood by 6-year-olds because of its extreme sophistication.

In the early part of the century, the issue of the simplification of the spelling system was of great interest to those in education. In 1903 a special committee was appointed by the Department of Superintendence of the National Education Association to consider the issue. The committee proposed that a national committee be established to prepare a simplified spelling system, or at least to oversee its preparation. The proposal was that the committee consist of educated individuals from all walks of life. The proposal was approved by the Department of

Superintendence. In 1906 the proposed board was established and given the title of The Simplified Spelling Board. The Board rented an office at 1 Madison Avenue in New York City and performed the kinds of activities that characterize reform movements such as publishing pamphlets and the organizing of meetings and the giving of addresses. There was substantial opposition that had to be overcome if a simplified spelling system were to be adopted. The Board proposed that individuals should be free to use either the simplified or the traditional method of spelling.

The Board never seems to have acquired the prestige and backing necessary to make the change. Other countries have been faced with a similar problem at times in their history and have followed the dictates of a body established to make the change in the spelling system, but Americans do not like to be dictated to by the voice of authority. Also, the revision of the spelling of English involves a much more drastic change than the kinds of changes that have been produced in spelling in France and Germany at various times in their history. The Academie Francaise produced a major revision of the spelling of the French language in 1718. In 1762 the Academie published an even more drastic revision of the spelling system, changing the spelling of about 5,000 words, or about 28 percent of all the words in the dictionary that it prepared and published.

Teaching Methods and Classroom Experiments

Issues related to the introduction of new spelling systems and the related matter of the use of new alphabets were not matters that led to empirical research, even though they involved careful analytic thought. Throughout the early part of the century, they played no part in the development of empirical methods of studying reading, but it was these empirical methods that had impact on the way in which reading was taught.

Indeed, research on reading resulted in the development of what were termed methods of teaching reading. Since the results of research could be interpreted in many ways, different reviewers of research on reading produced rather different methods of teaching reading. From the year 1925 onward to the half-century, one finds the proliferation of methods of teaching reading, all of which claimed to have some footing in the results of research. In the earlier part of the century there had not been theories of education specifically related to the teaching of reading. There had, of course, been theories of overall education associated with such names as those of Froebel, Pestalozzi, Montessori, and others, but these had not provided specific recommendations concerning how reading should be taught. There was no question but that reading was learned by exposure, first to the alphabet, and then to the printed words of the primer. Research asked important questions about how reading should be learned.

The reading methods that evolved, though numerous, fell into two main groups. The one class of methods stressed the analysis of words and the development of rules for the decoding of particular words. The other class of methods emphasized the rapid development of actual meaningful reading, either by exposing the child to words in which the rules for decoding were as uniform as possible or by developing in the child immediate recognition for all the common words. Those who pushed word recognition methods still believed that later stages of learning should involve word analysis and the understanding of rules that would permit the decoding of particular words. Both conceptions of how the initial stages of reading should be managed could claim some support from research, even though the support was not strong. The early studies of perception in relation to reading had shown clearly that individuals did not read words letter by letter, but that they seemed to grasp the word as a whole from general cues related to its form and cues derived from the context. If the latter described how words were actually read, then children should learn to read words in exactly the same way, from the general contour of the words. Furthermore, research had shown that the reading errors made by children were commonly a result of mistaking words with similar spatial forms. The argument was quite persuasive, particularly when it could be demonstrated that children could rapidly learn to identify, as word wholes, enough words to be able to read the very simple narratives of first-grade readers.

But the arguments on the other side of the debate were also strong. Even though one conceded that children could rapidly build small sight-recognition vocabularies, the limits of these were rapidly reached. Even if reading materials confined their content to the most common 500 words, the first-grade child could not learn these words on a sight-recognition basis. Those on the other side of the debate argued that the results achieved in learning to read by building a sight-recognition vocabulary would be followed rapidly by a period of frustration when the limit of this method was achieved and means of decoding words had to be introduced. Those who emphasized phonics and decoding believed that these methods should be introduced from the start.

Jeanne S. Chall has reviewed much of the research undertaken up to 1965 on the comparison of methods of teaching reading (*Learning to Read: The Great Debate*, 1967). Chall found the data provided by the various studies difficult to interpret in that what happens in a classroom where reading is being taught is always complicated. A technique that emphasizes word-whole recognition and meaning may also involve the use of writing as a means of developing reading skill. Of course, it may also involve other techniques such as flash cards, games, and the use of printed material thoughout the classroom and through which children may acquire an incidental knowledge of reading. No teacher ever uses a word-recognition method without many other forms of teaching. The same is true of those who claim that they emphasize a decoding approach to reading.

Chall recognized all of these problems connected with the interpretation of the data and came to some cautious conclusions. The decoding approach seemed to have a very slight advantage over the word-recognition approach with a meaning emphasis. The more able children seemed to be less influenced by the method used than those who were slow learners. The abler pupils find ways of learning even if they are not specifically taught. Such children will develop their own phonetic rules, and thus learn to decode new words even though this is not emphasized as a part of the classroom routine. The less able children need direct instruction in the irregular decoding process.

One can hardly be surprised at the apparent weak effect of method on instruction in the acquisition of reading in view of the great importance of motivation and prereading experiences. The latter seem to have an overwhelmingly strong effect compared with the effect of differences in instructional procedure.

The Return to Traditional Lines of Research

The survey did not produce useful data relating teaching method to outcome, and neither did the new experimental studies of classroom practice. Both were failures in producing the kind of knowledge that the academicians hoped they would produce, though the survey had many important practical outcomes. Experimental studies of methods of teaching reading continued into the 1950's and then tended to fade from the educational research scene. The difficulties involved in the planning and conduct of such studies are considered in much greater detail in the chapter concerned with research on teaching methods and hence will not be considered further here.

Although the subsequent history of reading research falls outside the period covered by this volume, a comment on more recent trends has value in understanding what a worthwhile trend in reading research seems to involve. Since the time when classroom research on reading was virtually abandoned, those conducting research on reading have returned to the study of perceptual processes involved in reading, but with an emphasis on information analysis aspects of perception. This trend is shown in the extraordinary book *The Psychology of Reading* by Eleanor J. Gibson and Harry Levin (1975) and the book entitled *Understanding Reading* by Frank Smith (1971). The first of these volumes, written by one of the world's leading authorities on perception, appeared as a sequel to a long series of experiments on perception in relation to reading, but it does not confine itself to problems of perception and reading, covering most of the research that has ever been undertaken in the area. The only notable omission from the volume is any discussion of experimental classroom studies of reading. The omission suggests that Gibson and Levin considered that the studies undertaken of teaching methods were completely inconsequential.

The second volume, by Smith, focused on the psycholinguistic analysis of learning to read. The book drew on modern cognitive psychology, and particularly that aspect which has to do with information processing. The Smith book also made virtually no mention of teaching method.

The absence of discussions of teaching method studies in both of these volumes reflects the fact that methods of teaching reading were devised, and studied experimentally, before research had reached a point where enough was known to construct an effective teaching method. Research is far nearer today in providing the foundation needed for the construction of an effective teaching method than it was in the early part of the century. The research that appears able to provide this kind of a foundation is research from the psychological laboratory and not the field study. Judd's early intuitions on the matter seem to have been correct, even though his hopes for the survey were not realized. Research on reading shows that the hopes for a psychology of school subjects, envisaged in the early part of the century, can be realized through an adequate program of studies conducted by individuals who not only understand the approaches of laboratory psychology, but who also are familiar with the problems of education.

THE PSYCHOLOGY OF SCHOOL SUBJECTS: MATHEMATICS

Mathematics as a Trade Subject

Mathematics had had a fundamentally different place in the schools of past centuries than has reading. Reading was regarded as the central school subject in Puritan schools as it was in earlier monastic institutions, because reading was the key to studying the Bible and the Bible was the key to salvation. The teachers of mathematics could never claim that mathematics was necessary for eternal life, and so the subject entered the curriculum only slowly. Books for instruction in mathematics had been introduced into the continent by the Spanish invaders. As early as 1556, Juan Diez Freyle published a book in Mexico City on arithmetic calculation. The book was mainly about the conversion of the value of gold ore into various forms of coinage, but it was probably mainly used by merchants and may never have had any use as a book for schools. An interesting item in early mathematics instruction was the book by Pedro Paz, published in Mexico City in 1629. The title of the book shows clearly how mathematics was learned at that time. The title was *Arte para aprende todo el menor del Arithmetica sin maestro*. The item of special interest in the title is the *sin maestro*, meaning "without a teacher." The book was strictly a do-it-yourself instructional device.

There was little continuity between the books for teaching arithmetic, published in Spanish in Mexico, and the books that were ultimately used in the prerevolutionary schools in the colonies. What books were available to the colonists were brought from England. The most famous of these was John Hill's *The Young Secretary's Assistant*, first published in Boston in 1703. The English books, like the Spanish books, were strictly practical in aim and content. The Spanish books had emphasized problems of gold and coinage and also the use of mathematics in military matters and surveying. The English books were strictly commercial. Mathematics in the new world was to be regarded as a practical matter. This is hardly surprising, for mathematics had not yet become recognized as the very cornerstone of a science of the physical world. Although Galileo and Newton had clearly shown how important natural phenomena could be described in mathematical terms, the educated public had not become fully aware of this fact. Indeed, the education of the public had not been extended into the scientific areas.

Puritan schools did little to teach arithmetic, for the curriculum was limited to learning to read the Bible and the common laws, serving the purposes of achieving salvation in the next world and living the life of a law-abiding citizen in this. A detailed knowledge of the law was important in an age when a person could be hanged for minor theft. What arithmetic was learned seems to have been acquired through special instruction given outside of school. Arithmetic was regarded as primarily a trade subject that could achieve none of the purposes of the good ethical life that the schools attempted to achieve. It was not perhaps until a century later that the curriculum became broadened to include anything that one might call mathematics.

In the eighteenth century in New England, some mathematics was taught, but mainly in the Latin Schools that served the more prosperous classes. Arithmetic does not seem to have entered the common schools until the beginning of the nineteenth century. The typical method of instruction was for students to be provided with a book of blank sheets of paper, referred to as ciphering books. In these books the pupil entered rules and problems to be solved by means of the rules. In this way, as instruction progressed, the pupil was able to develop for himself an arithmetic book of his own in which he could find the means of solving all the common practical problems of arithmetic that he might encounter. The teacher usually had a book from which he dictated the rules and the problems to be solved. The best known of these was Thomas Dilworth's

The Schoolmaster's Assistant: Being a Compendium of Arithmetic Both Practical and Theoretical. This volume was first printed in America in 1773, after having had a long history of use in England.

One should also note that special *reckoning and writing schools* also existed in New England in the eighteenth century. In these schools children could, for a fee, learn to use arithmetic. The schools were regarded much as one would regard a trade school today, as a place where one might learn a skill useful for the pursuit of a particular occupation. Several American-written textbooks in mathematics appeared in the early part of the nineteenth century, the most notable of which was that by Nicholas Pike (*A New and Complete System of Arithmetic Composed for the Use of Citizens of the United States*, 1788).

The Pike book was not suitable for children in the elementary grades since it presented much of the mathematics that was needed for scientific study including algebra, trigonometry, geometry, and conics. Its main use was for teaching mathematics in the colleges, where it was commonly a required subject at the fourth-year level. Nevertheless, Pike's book presented a radical change in mathematics teaching, viewing it as a subject that went far beyond the needs of commerce. Pike recognized that mathematics was a necessary foundation for understanding the emerging scientific conception of the universe. Pike's pioneering work probably had considerable impact on the teaching of mathematics at the college level, but another century would have to pass before mathematics at the elementary school level would be considered to be much more than a commercial subject.

Mathematics Viewed as an Intellectual Discipline

The great advance in the teaching of mathematics to young children came with the publication of Warren S. Colburn's famous book, *First Lessons in Intellectual Arithmetic* (1821). Colburn's book represented a radical reform in the teaching of arithmetic to children.

Warren S. Colburn, an interesting figure in the history of American education, was born in Dedham, Massachusetts, in 1793, the son of a farmer. The family seems to have moved several times during his youth, but he managed to have some instruction in the common schools where the family happened to be. The boy showed aptitude for numbers and was able to obtain instruction from an old schoolmaster who lived with the family. Presumably, the tuition the boy received in his home from the old schoolmaster was necessary because of the absence of mathematics instruction in the schools. Private tutoring in arithmetic was the rule. Warren Colburn showed a considerable aptitude for understanding machinery, and the family moved to Pawtucket, Rhode Island, so that the boy would have opportunity to learn about machines. He worked in factories for 5 years, and then at the age of 22 began to prepare himself for college. This preparation was undertaken by himself and on his own initiative. He was able to complete the work in a year, and he entered Harvard College in 1816. As a student he was noted for his performance in mathematics, achieving some mastery of the calculus, a feat rearely undertaken by most of his contemporaries. He graduated in 1820.

While at Harvard he must have encountered the work of Pestalozzi on the teaching of children, for a year after his graduation he published his famous textbook on arithmetic, developed along the lines proposed by Pestalozzi. During the year while the book was being completed and prepared for publication, he taught in one of the Boston schools. His teaching career lasted only a year, for his interest in machinery drew him again into manufacturing, in which he obtained an executive position which he held until his death in 1833 at the young age of 40. Despite the fact that his job was that of a manufacturer, he continued to have some interest in education, serving on the School Committee in Lowell, giving and organizing popular lecture series on science, and serving as an examiner for Harvard in the field of mathematics.

Later he published a textbook on algebra and a series of readers. Walter S. Monroe has done more than anyone else to delve into the work of Warren Colburn and his theory of teaching arithmetic (see "Warren Colburn on the Teaching of Arithmetic Together with an Analysis of his Arithmetic Texts," *Elementary School Teacher,* 1911-1912 and 1912-1913). The second article in this series reproduced an address given by Warren Colburn before the American Institute for Instruction in Boston in August 1830. In this address, Colburn dwelt on the great progress that had been made in the teaching of arithmetic in the schools in previous years. He pointed out that, although in earlier times the teaching of arithmetic had been postponed until the scholars reached the age of 12 or 13, arithmetic was now taught to those entering school. He also claimed that scholars not only now knew how to perform an arithmetical operation, but were also able to explain why the operation was performed in the particular way in which it was performed. Colburn also advanced the view that arithmetic was far more than a subject of use in trades and commerce, but that it had value in disciplining the mind. Then Colburn elaborated on his method of teaching arithmetic derived from Pestalozzi. The new system, he explained, always starts with practical examples, and with numbers so small that the child can easily reason with them without being overwhelmed. Pupils must be encouraged to discover rules for themselves, rather than memorizing rules in books. Colburn's own book began with counting the fingers and with simple mathematical operations based on finger counting. Colburn exhorted the teacher to teach one idea at a time and to be sure that the one idea was properly mastered before the next idea was introduced. He did not use the term "mastery learning," but he comes close to it.

A further important principle was that the child should never be told directly how to perform any operation in arithmetic. If the learner encounters some difficulty, then the teacher may help him overcome that difficulty. In addition, all the examples studied should refer to common objects.

After the fingers ceased to provide a good base for calculations, then counters were introduced. The counting board, introduced by Colburn, was to be used throughout the rest of the century for the teaching of arithmetic to children.

The designing of a textbook in terms of a theory of instruction was a very important idea, though one that had been unproductively explored in earlier centuries by the designers of catechisms. Colburn broke new ground in designing his textbook in arithmetic in terms of a theory of instruction that was to dominate much of educational thought for at least the next century and a half, and would find such champions as John Dewey and Jean Piaget.

The late David Eugene Smith, the dean of scholars on the history of mathematics education, has traced the influence that Colburn's views had on other instructional materials in the field of arithmetic. For example, Smith cited the case of the *New Arithmetic* by Daniel Adams, first published in 1801. When Adams produced a new edition in 1827, he modeled if after the method of teaching arithmetic described by Colburn.

David Eugene Smith noted that the methods proposed by Colburn were also used in extreme forms by teachers driven by excessive enthusiasm for Colburn's ideas. There were those who latched onto Colburn's idea that arithmetic should be an intellectual as well as a practical experience, and who would use arithmetic instruction for pushing the children into attempts to solve excessively difficult problems. If the solving of problems easily within the capacity of the child was good, then the solution of much harder problems should be that much better. The use of the difficult mathematical problem for training the mind became one of the techniques promoted by those who clung to the doctrine of formal discipline. Smith concluded that the influence of Pestalozzi, through the work of Colburn, was a strong influence for the good and, at the same time, a strong influence for evil (see David Eugene Smith, "The Development of the American Arithmetic," 1916).

As the century advanced, the learning of arithmetic came to be regarded as a lesson in logic as well as a lesson in a practical art. Instructional materials seem to have been produced largely by practical men rather than by those with a philosophical disposition. As the century advanced, a few individuals interested in issues related to the nature of number turned their thoughts to the matter of how arithmetic should be taught. One of these was Charles Davies, who wrote a book on *The Logic and Utility of Mathematics, with the Best Methods of Instruction Explained and Illustrated* (1850). The need for the consideration of such matters as those taken up in the Davies book is evident if one looks over some of the textbooks available in schools. Some were written with complete naivete concerning the nature of mathematics. One can find, for example, books in which zero is not recognized as a number, teaching that there are only nine numbers, but zero represents an absence of number. Theory concerning the nature of number had to be brought together with the practical matter of the teaching of number. Of course, much theory still needed was lacking. For example, mathematicians in the nineteenth century had not yet developed very precise ideas on the nature of proof, and sophisticated ideas on the nature of number had to await the publication of the great work on the subject by Alfred North Whitehead and Bertrand Russell.

Charles Davies was a remarkable man. He was raised in the New York community of Black Lake where he attended public schools. When he was 14 years of age a General Swift visited the boy's father and was impressed with the talent and energy of the boy. The General was able to arrange for the boy to be admitted to West Point in 1814, when Charles was 16. His career at West Point was cut short by the pressures of war, and he was commissioned and graduated in 1815. He must have been a remarkable young man, for a year later, at the age of 18, he was offered an instructorship at West Point, and for the next 21 years continued his association with that institution, ultimately becoming professor of mathematics. During his time at West Point he produced a whole series of textbooks for the teaching of mathematics. These covered all branches of mathematics of the time, and covered every level from the lower grades of the common school to the fourth year of college. Some of his textbooks were in use for more than 50 years. The final 16 years of his professional life were spent at Columbia College, from which he retired with emeritus status in 1865.

Few professors of mathematics have made notable contributions to the teaching of mathematics in the elementary school, but Charles Davies did. Through this contribution, he also laid the groundwork for a future trend in research on mathematics teaching.

Davies' book *The Logic and Utility of Mathematics* was an extraordinary analysis of how mathematics should be taught to young children. He emphasized that mathematics is simply an extention of logic. Thus, what children have to learn in learning mathematics is the logic of using numbers. Davies deplored the fact that many children learned little more than a set of rules that they could parrot, when they learned mathematics. Davies wanted them to learn logic, and to learn to apply that logic to practical matters. Much of this view was implicit in the teaching methods proposed by Colburn who, although he was not a professional mathematician, was competent in mathematics.

The first section of Davies' book discussed logic and the relation of logic to mathematics. Davies, almost in Piagetian style, discussed the relation of the logic of classes and classification to the formal logic of Aristotle. The second book dealt with the nature of mathematics. Davies noted the dependency of the understanding of number on the comprehension of space. The manipulation of objects in space may involve iterative processes that form the basis of numeration. Davies discussed number systems and the use of scales in measurement. One cannot do justice in a brief paragraph to the sophistication of his discussion of mathematics. It is sufficient to point out here that Davies viewed his analysis of mathematics as being a fundamental step towards designing a sound method of teaching elementary arithmetic. The thesis was that the teaching of arithmetic should be pursued through the development of an understanding of units. Fractions and decimals are then taught by showing that a fraction involves merely the changing of the size of the unit. Thus, when a unit is divided into sixths, it is divided into six smaller units. The problem of the addition of fractions could be then introduced as a matter of finding common units that could be added. The multiplication of fractions was handled in a similar way. Davies attempted to develop Colburn's idea that the child should fully understand every principle that had to be applied, and along lines that could work well in practice.

Yet the Davies analysis of the nature of logic and mathematics and the way in which it should be taught had absolutely no impact on the design of elementary textbooks during the next half-century. The reasons for this lack of impact are obvious. First, the textbook writers were not mathematicians, as Davies and Colburn had been. Most of them were out to make money, and they wrote what the teachers wanted them to write. The teachers had little understanding of mathematics, and most of them had not been exposed to any algebra in either high school or normal school, if they had had a normal school education. Indeed, most of them had little more than a bare knowledge of how to perform certain routine arithmetic operations. They were in no position to teach arithmetic in terms of understanding the problems related to the use of particular systems of units. They taught the addition of fractions, for example, by the application of a simple rule. They could not teach the fundamental logic underlying the operation, for most of them did not understand the fundamental logic themselves. Then there was the matter of public expectation. Parents wanted children to be drilled in the kind of mathematics that the world of business needed. They expected to find the textbooks filled with examples derived from the business world. Many parents had had a sufficiently meager background in mathematics that they called on their children to help them with simple business arithmetic. They expected their children to be drilled in rules and cared little if the children did not understand why the rules worked.

So the writers of textbooks of mathematics continued to produce books that the teachers and parents demanded. These were books filled with rules for solving common commercial problems. Even the use of concrete objects, that Pestalozzi and Colburn had stressed, tended to be dropped in favor of more formal exercises. The trends that were apparent in the arithmetic textbooks of the late nineteenth century are still apparent in many of the mathematics books in use today.

Nevertheless, the trend in thought presented by Davies did eventually have impact on mathematics teaching, but it had to first pass through a long channel of intellectual development. Nearly half a century after the appearance of the Davies book, the theme of the book was once again explored by James A. McLellan and John Dewey in their book *The Psychology of Number* (1895). McLellan was the principal of the School of Pedagogy in Toronto, a normal school for the preparation of teachers, and John Dewey was about to develop his famous school at the University of Chicago. McLellan and Dewey do not seem to have been aware of the Davies book, but what Davies had written about the nature of number had probably already become assimilated in academic thought. McLellan and Dewey expanded considerably on the Davies conception of the psychological nature of number. They pointed out that units have meaning only insofar as they are viewed as parts of a whole. In counting a number of objects, the individual says "three," designating the third object. The saying of "three" has meaning only insofar as the counter knows that the number is part of an organization of number names, and that the word implies that "one" and "two" had already been counted. The objects counted must be viewed as a group to which the counting can be applied in any order. Furthermore, counting involves a special form of abstraction in that the person counting must ignore all the properties of the objects counted except their numerosity.

Although previous works on the teaching of mathematics had taken the position that mathematical knowledge starts with counting, this new contribution took the position that an understanding of numbers was rooted in other prerequisite learnings. The child's ability to relate parts to wholes was one such prerequisite, and this was derived from the child's experience with the environment. However, mere contact with the environment was not enough, for the child engaged in such a contact must discriminate each object as a separate unit, that is to say, he must abstract the oneness of each object, then he must group the objects together into a class. The book proposed further that the conception of number and quantity arises only when means and ends are to be considered. A very young child may play with some marbles and have no use for the concept of quantity, but when he is required sometime later to share the marbles with another child, then the notion of quantity has to be introduced. This idea of quantity may first appear in a primitive form, as when the child judges that he has more marbles or fewer marbles than the other child. Dewey and McLellan even go so far as to imply that an infant, who reaches only for that which is within his reach, has a primitive concept of distance and quantity. This analysis was coming close to laying the foundation for the kind of research on mathematics education that was to dominate the field in the last half of the present century. A psychology of mathematical understanding was on its way to being constructed.

Number was viewed as a product of attempts to engage in exact measurement and to establish limits. Thus, the frontiersman measures out his land and establishes a claim. By doing this he is establishing the limit of his land. Measurement always involves the prior idea of the establishment of limits. Measurement begins with vague estimates on weight, size, amount, and so forth, but soon the refinement has to be made of introducing a scale of measurement. Units had to be developed for comparing quantities of qualitatively different things. Thus, a scale of grams makes it possible to compare the quantities of apples and oranges. Children have to have experiences which lead them to recognize why scales of measurement have to be used. These authors make no distinction between measuring and counting, for little recognition was given at that time to the different forms of scale that might be involved.

McLellan and Dewey argued strongly against the two common methods of teaching number to children. One method taught number as merely a set of abstract symbols. This was clearly based on a misconception of the nature of number. The other method taught number as a property of objects, as though it had a completely objective character to it. Both these methods failed to recognize the way in which number concepts have been developed as means to ends. McLellan and Dewey developed the theme that number concepts ought to be developed in children through activities in which they are attempting to achieve goals, and in which the achievement of those goals requires the use of measurement and number. In discussing how number should be taught, there is an interesting statement: "There is no question here about the need of drill, of discipline, in all instruction" (p. 88). The book went on to explain the difference between what the authors call the discipline of the slave and the discipline of the free individual. The drill related to the acquisition of mathematics in which children should engage should be an activity in which the children recognize that they are achieving a mastery important to them.

A detailed description cannot be given here of the McLellan and Dewey analysis of how arithmetical operations should be taught, but the book provides a detailed analysis of the matter. The analysis would be quite acceptable to most of those who have written in recent years on the teaching of arithmetic. Even more important for our present purpose is the fact that the trend in thought that these authors presented reflects avenues along which research related to the psychology of number has been productively developed in the present century. However, one must reiterate here that many who engaged in the development of a psychology of number in the present century may not have been aware of

Dewey's writing on the subject, even though they seem to have been familiar with the ideas he expressed.

Despite this lack of direct contact, there has been, obviously, an indirect contact. Dewey influenced the writings of many. Dewey and his coauthor may also have expressed ideas which were in the air and which continued to have wide impact on the thoughts of other scholars of his time. The way in which ideas are handed down is complex. There is rarely a simple passing on of an idea of one writer to a writer in the next generation. What is passed on is a cultural tradition and the thoughts of a community of scholars. Ideas only rarely have a simple lineage of descent across the generations. Thus, over the last century one finds slow but persistent progress in the development of the concept of the nature of number and its psychological basis. Those who wrote on the subject may not have been the originators of all the ideas they presented, but they did provide benchmarks along the way showing the state of knowledge in the field. Davies and Dewey and McLellan provided such benchmarks.

The thinking reflected in the words of Davies, McLellan, and Dewey also began to appear in the writing of those concerned with establishing policies related to curricula. The National Education Association established in 1892 the famous Committee of Ten to report on secondary social studies. The committee appointed nine subcommittees in various subject matter areas. After rather brief deliberations, a report on secondary school education was produced entitled *Report of the Committee on Secondary School Studies* and was considered of enough significance to be printed by the Federal Government in 1893. The report of the subcommittee on mathematics is of interest to us here, particularly since it provided recommendations for the teaching of mathematics from the first grade through high school. The subcommittee on mathematics found it necessary to expand their activity into the elementary field in that they encountered the criticism that education in grade school did not prepare children for the mathematics provided in secondary education. The committee gave careful thought to the question of whether the elementary school curriculum should or should not have a commercial orientation. The committee concluded that most of the business arithmetic introduced into the elementary school curriculum was quite meaningless to most children. Problems related to the market value and par value of stock had obviously no significance to children who did not have 10 cents of their own. Problems concerning banking, insurance exchange, and customs house practices might be appropriate subjects for instruction in business colleges, but they had little place in the common school. The subcommittee deplored the fact that such subjects had tended to be introduced to an increasing extent by those who viewed the common school as the place where children learned skills that would make them employable as soon as their education was completed.

On the positive side, the subcommittee proposed that children should learn the fundamental logic of dealing with units and the partitioning of a unit, such as is represented by a line, into units of smaller size. The subcommittee stressed the importance of children understanding the logic of arithmetic. The report also stressed that the logic of arithmetic should not be taught by abstract procedures, but that it should be learned through simple experiences much like those that Pestalozzi had stressed in his school in Switzerland. The subcommittee also recognized that the understanding of units, and the partitioning of units into smaller units, lay at the very core of understanding arithmetic. The subcommittee seems to have assumed, as McLellan and Dewey had assumed, that an understanding of number finds its roots, from the psychological point of view, in the understanding of measurement. Practical problems of mensuration and physics should underlie the development of mathematical understanding at the grade-school level.

Although the Pestalozzi view of education represented an underlying theme of the work of the subcommittee, another underlying theme was that mathematics provided a means of disciplining the mind. The subcommittee could not have escaped from the latter idea in that the concept of formal discipline was then at its peak of popularity. The educational community had faith in the power of difficult and logical exercises to discipline the minds of young children, and mathematics offered just the tool for disciplining the mind that the doctrine demanded.

The matter of teaching algebra in the common school was considered, but the main recommendation was that algebra should not be taught until about the age of 14. Such a practice would be justified today on the grounds that younger children do not understand the formal operations involved. The subcommittee believed that, in terms of past experiences of teachers in the schools, algebra could not be justified in the elementary grades. The subcommittee conceded that grade school children should be introduced to the language of algebra, through the study of arithmetic, but that mathematical operations with algebraic symbols should be avoided.

The Focus of the New Emphasis on Research in Mathematics Teaching

Starting around the turn of the century, a new approach appeared for improving instruction in mathematics education, through the development of empirical research. This new approach could not have taken place had it not been for the long period of reflective and analytic thought that had already been undertaken. The idea that improvements in mathematics teaching could not take place until empirical research had been initiated is, of course, nonsense, for before empirical research can even be begun, an analysis must be made of what the problems are that have to be identified. All too often, empirical research has been undertaken with an inadequate foundation of thought. When such research starts with confusion, it inevitably ends with confusion.

By the year 1900, thought with respect to the nature of mathematics and mathematics teaching had reached the point where productive empirical research was possible. Much of this research centered in two places, namely, the University of Chicago and Teachers College. Within these centers, the research was related to the activities of just a few individuals. At Teachers College, Thorndike was engaged in the type of associationistic research already described in the chapter devoted to his work. A contemporary of Thorndike at Teachers College was David Eugene Smith (1860-1944), who espoused a completely antithetical position to that of Thorndike. David Eugene Smith must be regarded as one of the great scholars who have had an impact on mathematics education, and a few words in his praise and honor seem approprite even though he is largely forgotten by most of those who write on mathematics education today. David Eugene Smith was trained as a lawyer, but in 1884 he left the legal profession and accepted the chair of mathematics in the Normal School at Cortland. He must have been largely self-trained as a mathematician as so many were in his generation. He was later professor of mathematics in the Michigan State Normal College.

David Eugene Smith traveled extensively all over the world, visiting schools and becoming acquainted with teaching practices and instructional materials. On returning from his travels, he accepted the post of professor of mathematics at Teachers College where he remained until he retired in 1926. He was the most prolific publisher of mathematics textbooks in his time, but he was also a noted scholar in the field of the history of mathematics across the world. He published books on the history of Hindu and Japanese mathematics, and mathematics on the American continent. He wrote prolifically on almost every phase of both the history of mathematics and the history of the teaching of mathematics. He also amassed an extraordinary collection of documents and materials related to the history of mathematics. His collection included 3,000 portraits of mathematicians from every part of the world, 10,000 autographs, and 150 medals. He founded the History of Science Society, of which he was president in 1927. He was also president of the Mathematical Association of America during the academic year 1922-23.

Smith's most important innovation with respect to mathematics education was the introduction of courses on mathematics teaching. Such courses on pedagogy had not existed before. He must have found the views of Thorndike and the success of the Thorndike Arithmetics extremely trying, for he viewed mathematics as strictly an extension of logic to be mastered through an understanding of the logic involved. He also departed from the view that mathematics could be viewed primarily as a trade and commercial subject. Smith did not engage in the kind of empirical research which was coming into being while he was at Teachers College. He was a synthesizer of empirical research rather than a producer, and the major scholar of his age in the field of mathematics education and the history of mathematics. The field of mathematics education has probably never had a more distinguished member, and neither has it had one who had so much status within the field of mathematics itself.

One wonders what contacts Smith had with his colleague, Thorndike, during the 25 years they shared at Teachers College. One suspects that they could hardly have conversed. Smith emphasized mathematics as a discipline, but Thorndike seems to have viewed it as a practical art. Smith emphasized the logical basis of mathematics, but Thorndike saw it as a set of associations, and did not quite know how to fit logic into his system. Smith's approach to mathematics was historical and philosophical, but Thorndike's was empirical and practical. The two men could not have been more different.

At the University of Chicago, the focus of activity of mathematics research was Judd. His work in promoting the psychology of school subjects began with the development of work in reading by his student William S. Gray, but work on arithmetic was much slower to develop and was not in progress until the 1920's when his student Guy T. Buswell (1891-) completed his doctoral work with Judd and then went ahead to develop research on the psychology of mathematics as a school subject. Judd himself, together with Buswell, prepared what was probably the first comprehensive bibliography of research on the teaching of mathematics ("Summary of Investigations Related to Arithmetic," 1925). Then, in 1926, William A. Brownell (1895-) completed his doctoral degree with Buswell and worked in the area of mathematics education for much of his life.

The individuals mentioned in the previous paragraphs were but the focus of research on the teaching of mathematics, and there were many more who undertook interesting studies. Nevertheless, Judd and Buswell, and to a lesser extent Brownell, played key roles in the development of the area, and they were the ones who attempted to compile and synthesize the research that had been done.

The extensive thought that had gone into the matter of how to teach mathematics, and what to teach, that had occupied so many in the last century, resulted in the development of research in this area, led by people like Judd, Buswell, and Brownell. Let us now consider the nature of this research reviewed by Judd and Buswell.

Research on mathematics education related to social utility. By the year 1900, a foundation of thought had been established on which the research of the next half-century was to be based. Two structures of research appeared. The one structure built knowledge related to the social utility of mathematics in general, and specifically, arithmetic. The books on arithmetic during the last half of the eighteenth century had shown an ever increasing expansion of the business fields that were represented by the problems presented for solution, but these were largely problems that had been concocted by the writers of the texts, most of whom had had little contact with the business world. The new approach initiated through the development of research was to find problems that were actually solved by people in business. The result of this research was to remove from the texts many problems that had been there for several decades and to add problems that had not been there. Many different approaches were taken to the study of mathematics in terms of its social utility. There were studies made of the actual arithmetical operations claimed to be performed by business people in various fields. These studies, like the other studies in the social utility area, were undertaken with questionnaires. In those days, hardly anybody had any doubt about the validity of data collected through the use of a questionnaire. A few studies attempted to use more objective data, making an analysis of the arithmetical operations performed by clerks on sales slips, or on other materials on which a written record of the arithmetic was left behind. Another approach to the study of the social utility of mathematics involved the analysis of common reading materials for the presence of arithmetical problems. Thus, magazine articles might include articles that involved arithmetic in determining the quantities to be used in a recipe, or in the building of a simple piece of furniture.

The study of the social needs of the individual also extended into the new attempt to develop curricula on the basis of empirical findings. Activity analyses provided a common means early in the century for developing curricula. In the activity analysis approach, a common technique was to make counts of how often particular concepts or operations were called for in work or home activities, but the data were difficult to interpret. Guy T. Buswell, in his discussion of this early period of mathematics research, pointed out the difficulties of interpreting the activity analysis data ("A Critical Survey of Recent Research," in *The Twenty-Ninth Yearbook of the National Society for the Study of Education*, 1930). Buswell stated that research has shown that the fraction *one-half* is used far more frequently than any other fraction. Given this piece of information, how does one use it to design a curriculum in arithmetic for the elementary grades? Some might jump to the conclusion that the frequency of occurrence of the fraction suggests that the curriculum builder should be sure to emphasize this fraction in his curriculum. But surely that conclusion is not justified. The fact that the fraction is widely used results in the child learning something about what it means long before he enters school. The facts can be taken to imply that very little emphasis should be given to the fraction since the children have already been exposed to much learning related to it. Furthermore, the specific analysis as the basis for a curriculum implies that the child should go to school and learn a large number of specific habits related to the activities thus identified. This may not be a good assumption. A much sounder basis for the design of a curriculum might well be the discovery of important ideas that the child should master. One such important idea might be that any unit can be divided up in a number of ways, and that this division of the unit into subunits is what fractions are all about. Once the child understands how these subdivisions can be made, and the way of denoting them on paper, then the child has mastered fractions. Equally difficult to use are the data showing that one activity involves a greater use of numbers than another activity. How does one deal with data in curriculum development showing that 30 percent of all numerical activities included in a survey have to do with commercial transactions, but only 2 percent have to do with the calendar? Despite the fact that the calendar occupies so little adult time, it is still used as one of the ways of introducing number to children in kindergarten and first grade. Research on the mere counting of events yields data that cannot be used in any straightforward and simple way for the construction of curricula, but such research had to be undertaken in the early part of the century in order for this to be discovered. One should perhaps note that a dissertation is still undertaken from time to time that revives this idea of how a curriculum should be built in the field of mathematics.

Research on the development of mathematical concepts in children. An alternative approach to research on mathematics education is to study the development of mathematical concepts in the child. This concept of research has had a long history of development, emerging slowly towards the end of the last century out of the ideas that mathematicians and philosophers had evolved. One of the earliest of these studies was developed by D. E. Phillips, working under the direction of G. Stanley Hall ("Number and its Application Psychologically Considered," *Pedagogical Seminary*, 1897, 5, 221-281). One of the features of the article that makes it so interesting is that it summarized a large amount of research, mainly by German experimental psychologists, on the estimation of number in various situations. This estimation was generally with respect to a temporal series, the subject having to estimate the number of clicks or beats. Other research came from the field of psychophysics and investigated the ability of individuals to recognize the number of points that were pressing on the skin as a function of the separation of the points and the location on the body. Judd later extended this work to the study of the estimation of the number of flashes of light or sounds and wrote the monograph *Psychological Analysis of the Fundamentals of Arithmetic* (1927).

Although Judd would have been highly critical of the Phillips monograph, it represented an advance in many respects. First, it was a break with what had been the American tradition of viewing the matter of mathematics instruction as strictly a matter of making an analysis of the nature of mathematics. Phillips sought to find a basis for mathematics instruction in child development. His approach to the problem was typical of that of the G. Stanley Hall school. Hall's students always began by making an exhaustive and thoughtful search of the literature, and then followed with a questionnaire or interview study. The questionnaires were sent to 800 individuals, mostly teachers, in the first to ninth grades. The data show that there was a return of at least 616 questionnaires, in that Phillips reports that 616 answered the first part. Of those who returned the questionnaire, 72 percent were teachers. Just how the sample was selected is not clear. Research workers were not fussy about such matters in those days.

The range of questions asked was extraordinary. The first part of the questionnaire explored the development of number concepts. The first question asked for examples of animals displaying an understanding of number concepts in relation to such matters as recognizing the absence of one of their young. Further questions asked for examples, on the part of children, of behavior showing an awareness of counting before the children had learned the names of numbers. The questions were not clear as to whether the respondent should think of other children or confine his or her reflections to his own childhood.

Further questions in the first part of the instrument asked for information about the affective aspects of numbers, and whether the individual had any associations with particular numbers. Then there was a question on any observations the respondent had made on children who were particularly forward or backward in their development of number skills. The respondents were also asked to question children on what part of the year's mathematics they liked best and liked least. If the respondents had provided the data with any completeness, the resulting volume of material would have been immense.

The second section of the questionnaire dealt with pedagogy. The first item posed the comprehensive question: "Please state how you would teach beginners. Describe your special methods with any phase of the work. Special drills" (p. 246). One wonders whether the respondents were overwhelmed by such a question or whether they responded with stereotyped answers. Other questions asked for examples of errors made by children in mathematical thinking. A further section of the questionnaire dealt with what was called "higher arithmetic." This section dealt with such matters as the place in instruction of some of the more difficult concepts of arithmetic such as proportion, roots and powers, and the less well-known business practices. The final section asked about when geometry and algebra should be introduced to children.

The questionnaire dealt with every phase of mathematics learning, from infancy through high school. It was designed to provide a comprehensive picture of how mathematical knowledge accumulated, largely through the collection of anecdotal material.

The data from the study were handled with a casualness that would horrify modern research workers. No attempt was made to summarize the data in the form of statistical tables. There were no tests of significance provided. What was provided was a set of offhand comments and impressions of the data. Yet, despite these deficiencies, the article was accepted by *Pedagogical Seminary,* which was probably America's outstanding psychological journal of the age. The article would also have been acceptable to many of the European journals of the day. Although the article would not have been accepted by a modern psychological journal, it nevertheless was a valuable contribution to the literature in that the data suggested many ideas that needed further exploration. Whatever the analysis of the data lacked in orderliness, it made up for in the wealth of the ideas that were explored. All too often, modern articles show the reverse trend with an excessive orderliness and an impoverishment of ideas.

Some interesting data were provided that at least gave the illusion that some animals could count, as when a cat appears to search for a missing kitten. Phillis recognized the possibility that animals could count up to , say, three, suggesting an innate component of number operations. Phillips failed to recognize that there might be alternative explanations to counting in understanding animal behavior, and that the phenomenon described by observers of animal behavior might not be counting at all. Phillips also presented some anecdotes about very young children who tapped a foot or finger against the floor in unison with some rhythmical phenomenon such as the dripping of water or the striking of the hour by a clock. These phenomena do show a primitive form of a one-to-one relationship, and might well be a precursor of the understanding of number that also depends upon a one-to-one relationship. Phillips recognized, in sorting the data, that there was a real difference between counting, as a verbal ritual learned by rote, and true counting, which involves a one-to-one correspondence.

Some of the data must have been voluminous. One respondent sent back a 55-page account of the development of number ability in a child, beginning at the eighth month. The account provided a detailed record of a child learning to count, although it is not quite clear at what age she finally mastered the task. Nevertheless, the record is taken as evidence that one must distinguish between the saying of the numbers and saying the numbers in a task in which numbers are related to objects on a one-to-one basis. This distinction has been lost and periodically recovered in psychological literature through much of the century. There appeared also to be some interesting data on the relation of the development of counting to the use of body parts and movement. Phillips seems to have accepted a motor theory of thought, coming to the conclusion that the early stages of learning to count always involve some motor component.

This was a popular theory of thought at the time.

Judd and Buswell presented in their monograph a few other studies related to counting and number in children. Some of these were more systematicaly undertaken and reported than that of Phillips, but the more systematic studies also tended to be the more trivial. For example, there were studies in this early period of the rate at which children could count. Some of these rate-of-counting studies extended counting to counting by twos, threes, and so forth. Other studies concerned themselves with the matter of how far children could count in the number series.

What has been said has been presented to show a stage in the development of research on the teaching of mathematics. The early researches started at the point where the analysis of mathematicians and philosophers had ended, but it benefited tremendously from the work they had undertaken. The early research work helped to define further what the problems were and began to explore methods by which they could be systematically studied. One should not write off these early studies as simply the efforts of the incompetent to solve very difficult problems. They were not, but they were steps in the acquisition of research competence. Nobody can predict in advance which research techniques are going to produce interesting findings. Also, even after a research technique has been explored initially, much work has to be undertaken to refine it and to identify the errors that contaminate the technique. The early studies in an area often identify very interesting and worthwhile problems to explore, but fail to make headway because the techniques are still too primitive. In the present connection, the early researchers identified the idea that a good place to begin to study mathematics education was in the child's development of the concept of sequencing and one-to-one correspondence, but the research also demonstrated that little understanding of this aspect of development could take place through the collection of anecdotes. Another 40 years had to pass by before useful approaches to this problem were developed. This 40-year development showed a slow transition from the simple questionnaire technique to the use of experimental situation, in which the behavior of children was studied directly. The research workers at mid-century may have been no brighter than those at the start of the century, but they had behind them a long history of what earlier workers had learned about the problem.

Research on the age at which topics in arithmetic should be taught. The basic problem in this area was when arithmetic should first be studied. Child development studies had shown that children acquire a great amount of information about number before they ever enter school, but during the period covered there were no experimental attempts to introduce children to the topic at an earlier age than was usual, nor studies involving the postponement of training in number concepts. The use of textbooks in arithmetic had to be postponed until the second grade since they required some mastery of reading. Numerous studies were undertaken on the way in which various topics of arithmetic were distributed across the grades. These studies showed a great variation in practice, but Judd and Buswell pointed out that the level at which a topic can be successfully introduced depends upon the method of teaching adopted, and on how the curriculum is organized. Related studies were concerned with how much time should be devoted to a particular topic and how much time actually was. The studies of Joseph Mayer Rice suggested that more time was devoted to arithmetic than could be profitably used. Rice claimed to have shown that those pupils who spent long hours studying arithmetic in schools learned no more than those who spent much less time. Obviously, there was a lower limit of time below which learning could be reduced. Despite the fact that the children tended to be fatigued during the afternoon, time of day seemed to make little difference in the amount learned, but the evidence was far from adequate.

Research on textbooks and exercise materials. This was a common form of inquiry early in the century. Thorndike was very careful to study what other textbooks contained before he prepared his own arithmetics. Research of this kind represents a very simple form of inquiry of questionable value. At best, the information derived may tell one something about what the writers of the textbooks believe to be the best sequence of items. The objectives of instruction can also be inferred from the textbooks.

The most interesting material on the analysis of textbooks comes from studies that showed the social context of the problems provided in the books. The predominance of problems came from the area of trade, although only a small percentage of the population at that time would ever be engaged in trading activities. This emphasis represented the tradition of arithmetic being a trade subject to be mastered mainly by clerks. Such analyses of content showed that textbooks in mathematics dealt mainly with problems that were quite foreign to the world of not only the child, but also the world of parents.

Research related to tests and the standardization of the curriculum. The emergence of the standardized test of arithmetic skills has been discussed in Chapter 3. A major outcome of this development was the finding that children showed a great range of individual differences, and this finding was inevitably linked with the then current belief that most academic differences could be attributed to genetic differences in intelligence. The emergence of this view also led to the belief that mathematics was for the more able student. This was almost a reversal of the Puritan notion that arithmetic was just a trade subject hardly worthy of introduction into the common school.

The widespread use of the tests developed by Stuart A. Courtis in the early part of the century resulted in them being regarded as the means of setting standards. Courtis himself was largely responsible for the tests being regarded in that way. He promoted the idea by publishing and distributing to users of the tests annual reports of data showing how each school system performed in terms of level of achievement. The average performance of all the pupils on the tests tended to be accepted as the desirable standard that all should achieve, though the logic underlying that idea was never made clear, and is still not clear today. Courtis was able to show that school systems that used his test year after year showed a steady improvement in the scores achieved. He regarded this as a beneficial result of the test. The testers of the day did not recognize the ways in which teachers, and school administrators, can arrange conditions so that scores will rise. It was not understood then that children acquire skill in taking tests and that scores will rise year after year as the children acquire sophistication in the taking of tests. Then there is the fact that the curriculum may slowly become more and more test-oriented, even to the point of teaching the children to answer the particular test problems that they will encounter on the test. There are, of course, even more corrupt practices designed to ensure an apparent improvement of test scores from year to year.

The development of standardized tests was also hailed as a means of making it possible to compare one method of instruction with another. Interest in such comparisons was not to come until after World War I, when great issues related to method of instruction were debated.

A more positive contribution of the development of standardized tests in arithmetic was the emergence of the idea that they could be used for diagnostic purposes to determine areas in which the child needed further work. Courtis was impressed with the fact that a child might be good on addition but not on subtraction or the reverse. He proposed that tests should be used as the basis on which remedial work should be provided. This proposal involved many difficulties that were not fully recognized at the time and which still have not been solved. Nevertheless, some positive applications of this idea were being developed. Carleton Washburne, who was beginning to develop his individualized program of instruction, seized upon the idea of checking each child with tests at key points in the curriculum.

Research on the relative levels of difficulty of particular arithmetic operations. Considerable research at a very pedantic level involved investigations of the relative difficulty of the number combinations. The research came up with such findings as that the additions 8 + 5 and 7 + 9 were the most difficult and 0 + 0 and 5 + 5 the most easy. This particular finding comes from studies that determined the number of errors made. Another approach to the same problem is to determine what would today be called *latency,* and what was then called speed of response. The two approaches produced roughly the same results. Other methods were also used. One was that of determining the time taken to learn particular number operations or combinations; another, the extent to which particular number combinations or operations, once learned, were retained; and still another was to ask children about how difficult particular number combinations or operations were. The variety of methods used indicates the extraordinary amount of effort that was devoted to this rather trivial problem. Only one finding in this extensive series of studies seems to have any application. That was the finding that a combination presented in reverse, as, for example, 7 + 9 and 9 + 7, does not represent two combinations equal in difficulty. Thus, the data suggest that children should learn all 100 combinations rather than the 55 which omit all reversals.

More interesting studies were those that explored the way in which children add columns of figures. Many children attempt to find shortcuts through scanning the column looking for combinations that make 10, such as 2 + 3 + 5. Such shortcuts may add to speed but, in the inexperienced child, may add to the errors. The recommendation of the research workers was that children should be discouraged from taking such shortcuts and should discipline themselves to add the items seriatim. Studies of the errors of addition, other than those derived from abandoning a seriatim approach, were not particularly productive. Most errors seemed to be due to lack of adequate habits. As the habits became firmly established, both accuracy and speed showed great improvement. As one would expect, speed and accuracy were closely related. Studies of the difficulties in the carrying operation showed that this was a difficult operation for children, and that the main source of their difficulty was that they did not understand what it involved.

The prolificness of the research literature on each aspect of the learning of arithmetic is shown by the fact that Buswell and Judd listed 18 studies on the process of subtraction alone. As with addition, research workers determined the relative difficulty of number combinations involved in subtraction. In the early part of the century there was controversy concerning how subtraction should be taught, and research workers attempted to solve that controversy. The studies dealt with the minutia of arithmetic instruction rather than with understanding the logic of arithmetic, and the conclusions were of the order of minutia. Consider the following methods of subtracting 39 from 82:

Method 1: 9 from 12 equals 3 and 3 from 7 equals 4.

Method 2: 9 from 12 equals 3 and 4 from 8 equals 4.

The second of these two methods was shown uniformly to be better than the first, at least for young children. Such studies seem to avoid the real issue of finding out whether the children understood what they were doing. The studies did show that the main source of error in such subtractions was in the borrowing process, a fact which suggests that many children did not understand what they were doing.

There is little point in dwelling on the numerous other investigations that involved similar kinds of inquiry into the processes of multiplication, division, the use of fractions, and the use of decimals. They represent a line of thinking that is quite common today, that advocates the teaching of specific competencies of arithmetic, to the detriment of the development of an understanding of the underlying logic. Indeed, a perusal of some of the studies shows a complete neglect of the idea that an understanding of the underlying logic of all arithmetic is of any particular consequence. The emphasis, derived partly from the work of Thorndike, was on the development of correct habits. The same emphasis is still apparent in modern recommendations from operant psychologists.

Research on the relationship of reasoning to arithmetic skills. Although Buswell and Judd included some material related to this problem, the material is weak. Much of what they included was based on a summary of earlier work by S. Carolyn Fisher ("Arithmetic and Reasoning in Children" (1912). This earlier summary had concluded that the weight of evidence seemed to show that primary emphasis should be placed on the mechanics of arithmetic, since reasoning about arithmetical problems was not possible until the mechanics had been mastered. This conclusion was drawn from data showing that arithmetical abilities seemed related, more than anything, to the time devoted to the mastery of mechanics. Joseph Mayer Rice would not have agreed with that conclusion. Buswell and Judd mentioned a study, that the Fisher review had missed, by Willis L. Gard ("A Preliminary Study of the Psychology of Reasoning" (1907), which developed the interesting technique of asking children to work arithmetic problems and to explain what they were doing as they went along. Gard was able to identify a number of strategies by which children solved arithmetic problems. Such a study showed a beginning of the later attack on the problem of the nature of human reason and its relationship to specific competencies.

Research related to the use of drill. The early educational research workers did not miss such an easy topic on which to do research. Joseph Mayer Rice pursued this problem and, though he established that learning was unrelated to the amount of drill, it did not occur to him that there still might be a critical amount of drill that might be beneficial. An even simpler matter was that of establishing the amount of time devoted to drill. The early studies showed an immense range of teacher practices in this respect. Some teachers spent as much as 80 percent of the class time in drill activities, but in others the percentage approached zero. The data should be treated with some caution since they were all based on the reports of teachers, who might well have felt under pressure either to report that they spent much time or little time in drill activities. Analyses of textbooks were also undertaken to determine the amount of drill assigned to particular number combinations. Thorndike was one of the first to undertake such an analysis, and he came up with the conclusion that, in the case of number combinations, some were grossly overlearned, but others were given almost no practice at all. Just as readers required a controlled vocabulary, arithmetic books required a carefully controlled amount of practice with each number combination on all basic arithmetical operations. Rules were drawn up for developing practice materials for pupils.

Studies showed that drill, at least in small amounts, was beneficial. At least one study showed that the effects of daily 5-minute drill practices persisted even through the summer vacation. Drill, as it was advocated by the research workers, was in a form that John Dewey would have endorsed. Unfortunately, the resulting enthusiasm for drill that teachers manifested went far beyond what any research studies advocated, so much so that the Department of Educational Investigations and Measurement of the Boston Schools issued a strong caution to teachers on the time that could be wasted through the excessive use of drills ("The Courtis Tests in Boston, 1912-1915: An Appraisal." School Document Number 15, 1916).

The Hermann Ebbinghaus problem of the effect of distributed practice was familiar to the early educational research investigators. Though later research workers have produced data almost uniformly in favor of distributed drill, that is to say, distributed practice, the early studies related to arithmetic showed little uniformity of results. This failure to produce consistent results probably hindered the effective use of drill in the teaching of arithmetic.

Studies related to the diagnosis of the source of difficulties in arithmetic and remediation were common in the early part of the century. Buswell and Judd counted 31, distributed over the years 1909 to 1924. These were mainly studies of the errors made in computation. The research shows a clear trend towards the development of a diagnostic approach to instruction, an approach which seems to have been an invention of research workers of this period. In many respects, this invention of instrumented diagnosis was to have more influence on education than any other of the period.

Research relating pupil characteristics to achievement in arithmetic. Early studies showed relationships between scores on intelligence tests and every aspect of achievement, including that in mathematics. The interpretation given to intelligence test scores as measures of innate ability led to the belief that differences in mathematics achievement were also a result of genetic factors. In terms of this theory there were difficulties in explaining why it was that rural children showed lower achievement in arithmetic than urban children. Sociologists speculated that the genetically superior populations migrated to the cities, a speculation that was later shown to be false. Smaller differences in arithmetic skills were found between boys and girls. This difference was generally attributed to the fact that the problems given in arithmetic books were of a kind with which boys were familiar.

Research related to teaching methods. Research in this area was almost absent in the early part of the century in relation to mathematics teaching. The nearest that research workers came to it was in studies of method elements such as drill. Few attempts had been made to consider what mathematics teaching would be like within the framework of Pestalozzi or Montessori. Most of the educational establishment believed they knew what should be taught in the mathematics curriculum and how it should be taught. Differences were with respect to such minor issues of whether there should be 10 minutes or 30 minutes drill a day. In such a climate there were no great debates among the majority of teachers and administrators with respect to issues of teaching method.

Undoubtedly, Judd and Buswell must have seen their 1925 review as a prelude to a new era of research on the psychology of school subjects in which the University of Chicago would play a central role. In order to initiate the program, Judd himself, with characteristic energy, began some research of his own in the area. His approach to an understanding of mathematics instruction was also quite characteristic of him. In accordance with the style of thought he had learned to pursue under Wilhelm Wundt, he began to study the emergence of mathematical concepts in their simplest forms. His general technique was to present to his subjects either a series of flashes of light, or a sequence of sounds, and he then investigated how the subject perceived the number of flashes or sounds involved (see *Psychological Analysis of the Fundamentals of Arithmetic*, 1927). As the title implies, Judd was interested in exploring the very fundamental psychological processes involved in arithmetic. A similar study was undertaken by Judd's student, William A. Brownell, who published a lengthy monograph entitled "The Development of Children's Number Ideas in the Primary Grades" (1928). Brownell's approach involved the presentation of arrays of dots printed on cards and arranged in various geometric patterns. The idea was that the estimate of numerosity on the part of the children might be facilitated by certain patterns. Brownell found such a relationship and attempted to relate the child's ability to estimate number to the child's ability to understand number in the abstract. The study claimed to show that there was slow progression from the understanding of number in the concrete to number in the abstract. Brownell advanced the thesis that children should not be introduced early to the memorization of number combinations until they had a thorough understanding of the meaning of number in very concrete situations. This thesis is a return to the ideas of Warren Colburn of a century earlier.

Numerous reviews of research on mathematics teaching have appeared over the years since the 1925 review. Buswell provided annual reports on the research in the area for several years, but then the task of periodical review was assumed by the Review of Educational Research. None of these later articles had the impact of the 1925 article, partly because they covered a much shorter period of time, and partly because they seemed to be dealing with an enterprise in which there was a declining interest. Still later, in 1955, the U.S. Office of Education began to publish a series of wholly undistinguished reviews of the state of research in the field. These too came to an end, perhaps because of their inconsequential nature.

The great new era of development of mathematics instruction through the growth of a new psychology of school subjects did not occur, at least not within Judd's lifetime. Indeed, the 1930's showed a decline in the type of research that was to herald the new era. The easy problems had been investigated repetitively over the previous 30 years and the difficulties of breaking new ground were immense. The approach that Judd had hoped to develop was to be set aside and to remain in relative obscurity for almost 50 years. In the intervening years the central stage was to be occupied by large curriculum projects such as the University of Illinois Committee on School Mathematics, the School Mathematics Study Group, the Greater Cleveland Mathematics Program, the Madison Project, and others. These were well-funded projects that absorbed most of the money that might otherwise have been used for the development of research related to how children develop mathematical knowledge. In many respects, they attempted, with some would say disastrous results, to bypass the whole problem of the psychology of number. Indeed, the assumption underlying most of these projects was that there was no underlying problem at all. Another assumption often made was that the central problem of mathematics instruction, even down to the first grade, was to modernize it in terms of the thinking of mathematicians. Since set theory was popular among mathematicians at mid-century, later to be a matter of dwindling interest, set theory was introduced into the elementary mathematics program. If the interest of mathematicians had been in areas other than set theory, then that is where the school curriculum would have been led. The period was an experiment to determine whether the thinking of mathematicians about mathematics would be a good basis for designing an elementary school curriculum in mathematics. Since the projects were lavishly funded, those interested in developing educational research in the area of the development of mathematical understanding tended to jump on the bandwagon, and to abandon any attempt to develop a psychology of the development of mathematical ability.

Although the psychology of understanding number was successfully destroyed as an academic enterprise in the United States, interest in the problem survived elsewhere, to some extent in the work of Russians, but to a greater extent in the work of Jean Piaget, who was later to become the prime influence in the area of mathematics education. Let us consider briefly some of the research work of Jean Piaget, undertaken before the turn of the century, that was to remain unnoticed by American workers for 30 or more years, before it blossomed forth as a major influence on the entire field.

Piaget and the Psychology of Number

The work of both theoretical mathematicians and psychologists, during much of the 100 years covered by this book, led to a culminating enterprise at the very end of the period. That enterprise was to influence mathematics education in the elementary school more than any other event that preceded it. Reference is made here to the developing work of Jean Piaget at Geneva and the publication in 1940 of his book *La Genèse du Nombre chez L'Enfant* (1941). Although this book was understandably not entirely correct in what it had to say about the development of mathematical concepts in the child, it was an important step forward. Piaget attempted to do what Davies had done, and to fit mathematical thinking into the overall picture of logical and prelogical thinking of the child. Davies had viewed mathematical thinking as the extension of logical thinking to a field that involved special concepts and symbols, but it was still no different from any other field of logical thinking. The model of thinking of Davies was limited by the fact that he was not able to describe, and did not even consider, the development of logic in the child. Piaget was able to fit his understanding of the nature of mathematics, as a branch of logic, into the overall picture of the developing child from birth to maturity. Piaget had, of course, a vastly greater source of experimental material on which to draw than any of his predecessors, but this was only one of many factors in the success that Piaget achieved. His approach was essentially rationalistic and involved a most thorough analysis of what the prerequisites of a mature logic had to be. He recognized that in order to understand the logic of the child in general, and mathematical knowledge specifically, one had to understand the entire process through which knowledge of the world is developed. The operations of which mathematics consists are dependent upon the creation of what Piaget calls intellectual structures, but these structures cannot be created until the groundwork has been laid through experience in the early part of life.

Piaget also was able to identify certain aspects of behavior that are crucial for understanding mathematical ability. One of these is the one-to-one correspondence and to trace it from a perceptual phenomenon to its later emergence as a conceptual phenomenon. The early work of Piaget undertaken in the 1930's in this area did not provide a complete and accurate picture of the development of one-to-one behavior, for later inquiry has shown that the beginning of the idea emerges at a much younger age than Piaget ever dreamed that it did.

A second emphasis of the early work of Piaget on number was on seriation, which had not been emphasized by those who had previously discussed the psychology of number. Earlier writers had tended to view a number as a class of classes. Thus, classes such as 6 houses, 6 cows, 6 pencils, 6 trees, and 6 colors represent a class of classes characterized by sixness. The number 6 is thus a class of classes. Piaget imposes on this idea the idea that the psychological concept of seriation is also of crucial importance for the development of the concept of number.

Piaget's approach to the psychology of number is basically different from that of McLellan and Dewey. The latter emphasized measurement as the operation from which number eventually arises, but Piaget seems to regard measurement as following the development of the concept of number. Piaget had the advantage over McLellan and Dewey of having based his work on experimentation, after a lengthy reflection on the nature of mathematical behavior, but the ideas underlying his experimentation are philosophical. Indeed, some would say that Piaget's experiments are only attempts to demonstrate the truth of his philosophical ideas.

Piaget's conception of the nature and development of the child's concept of number has had considerable impact on education, at least partly because it is related to a larger and more comprehensive theory of the development of the entire intellect. The stages that the theory supposes provide some indication of the kind of curriculum that should be planned for children of different ages from the earliest stages of infancy through adolescence. Materials for the teaching of mathematics at the elementary school level have been developed, based on the Piaget theory of intellectual development. The most notable series published was that prepared by the Nuffield Foundation in England.

A second contribution of Piaget to the theory of how mathematics was learned came through his study of space outlined in the volume written by him and Barbel Inhelder, *La Représentation de l'Espace chez l'Enfant* (1948). This volume was a precursor of a volume on the development of understanding of geometry published in the same year (Jean Piaget, Barbel Inhelder, and Alina Szeminska, *La Géometrie Spontanée de l'Enfant* (1948). Space is treated as a Kantian category, with a primitive understanding of space as one of the givens of experiences. Piaget and Inhelder attempted to trace the child's development of his concept of space beginning with this primitive experience. Incidentally, Piaget treated numerosity in many ways as though it emerged from a primitive Kantian category, though Kant never considered it to be one of his categories. With respect to the development of the concept of space, Piaget and Inhelder proposed a theory that the early concepts of space are topological, that is to say, they involved such concepts as proximity, boundaries, and openness rather than Euclidean properties such as triangularity and circularity. The transition from a topological to a Euclidean concept of space seems to take place in the late preoperations period. This transition has very important consequences for the child's behavior in that it makes it possible for him to improve greatly the accuracy with which he can locate himself in space and find his way around a neighborhood.

Although later work gives much support to Piaget's general theory with respect to space and number, the newer evidence also indicates that he has greatly underestimated the capacity of the young child to develop in both of these areas. In this connection there has been a long controversy between the followers of Piaget and the Russian psychologists. The latter view the development of number concepts to be less a matter of distinct states, as Piaget has proposed, and more of a continuous process. At the time of writing, there is a considerable body of research showing that number concepts do develop at a much earlier age than Piaget has proposed, and even that a primitive notion of numerosity may be very much like a Kantian category of experience.

Despite this controversy, we are now in a vastly better position to understand the problems of teaching mathematics to children than were previous generations. We now know a great deal about what is meant by *understanding* mathematics compared with what previous generations knew. Yet the basic ideas of Warren Colburn concerning how mathematics should be learned are as true today as they were 150 years ago.

Some Thoughts on the History of Research on Mathematics Education

In many respects, research on mathematics education has been a more difficult enterprise to develop than research on the teaching of reading. Research on reading started with the investigation of the perceptual processes involved. In the hands of brilliant investigators such as James McKeen Cattell and Edmund Burke Huey, the main facts related to our understanding of the perceptual aspects of reading were quickly discovered, and these facts have never been seriously disputed. In contrast, research on mathematics learning had great difficulty in exploring the perception of numerosity of young children. Indeed, three-quarters of a century elapsed between the first identification of this problem and successful efforts to attack it. The reason may well be that the perception of the threeness of a group of three objects *may* involve behavior at a higher level of complexity than behavior related to the recognition of a particular letter. Regardless of whether this is correct or not, the fact is that the basic problems of understanding mathematical behavior have proven themselves to be vastly more difficult than those related to reading behavior.

Research on reading has moved, over the last century, from research related to basic perceptual processes to research on the way in which information derived from reading is assimilated, organized, and ultimately used. In contrast, research on the learning of mathematics has focused, almost from the start, on the logical thought needed to understand and solve mathematical problems. Such research unavoidably starts with very difficult problems about which there was virtually no knowledge early in the century, but an increasing body of related knowledge since mid-century. The difficulties of the experimental psychologist have not been eased by the fact that logic itself, as an academic area, is in a state of turmoil.

There is also another important difference between the two areas which has made research on mathematics learning far more difficult than that on reading. Reading is a practical art. On the other hand, although mathematics originally entered the school curriculum as a practical art, there was even before the present century a strong move to view mathematics as a means of training the mind in logical thinking. Although the latter view of mathematics was strongly attacked by the early American experimental psychologists such as Edward Lee Thorndike, it has had a strong revival in recent years through the work of Jean Piaget and his followers, who view mathematical thinking as an extension of logical thinking, and perhaps the ultimate extension of which the human is capable. In the latter view, mathematics education permits the individual to create in himself the logical structures of mathematics, which then permit the solution of a great range of problems. Charles Hubbard Judd would have been fully in accord with such a view of the nature of mathematics and the way in which it could be generalized to solve a great range of problems, but some psychologists, both past and present, hold the view that mathematics should be learned as a set of habits, and that habits have limited capacity for generalization. The latter view seems to run contrary to much that one can readily observe about human behavior.

Attempts to discover what is completely basic to all mathematics do not seem to have resulted in any great improvements in mathematics teaching. Bertrand Russell's belief, which he held for a short time, that all mathematics could be reduced to set theory, was used as a basis for much mathematics teaching in the 1960's. Unfortunately, Russell's belief in this respect does not seem to have been mathematically correct, let alone a sound basis for the development of mathematics instruction.

THE DEVELOPMENT OF THE PSYCHOLOGY OF SCHOOL SUBJECTS IN OTHER AREAS

Spelling and Handwriting

During the first quarter of the century, the main thrust related to the development of a psychology of school subjects was in the fields of reading and arithmetic. The third of the three R's, involving both writing and spelling, did not receive the same attention. Attempts had been made to develop spelling lists for several hundred years, and the new efforts in that direction were attempts to identify lists of words that children should know because they were used either in practical activities or in reading materials. More effort was devoted to the debate over the revision of English spelling than to actual research, perhaps because of the thought that, once a phonetic spelling system was introduced, then there would be no problems left in the teaching of spelling. The problems of phonics were recognized and the newer lists of words grouped together those that were decoded, or spelled, in terms of a common rule.

Handwriting also came under scrutiny, but did not emerge as a focus of research. Research workers were not able to do much with either understanding the development of handwriting as a motor skill or to improve handwriting as an art. The psychological understanding of motor skills was minimal at that stage of psychology, despite the fact that motor skill theories of thinking had had a history back to the middle of the last century. Handwriting was a matter of declining interest to research workers during the first quarter of this century.

Science

The development of research on the teaching of science and social studies was slow. Let us consider the frustratingly scanty research related to science education early in the century.

A first point to note is that science was slow to acquire a solid base in education. In the last century, the pupils in elementary and secondary schools were sometimes exposed to some concepts of physics as a part of their training in mathematics. The private academies may even have provided scientific equipment advertised for sale in educational journals as "Philosophic Apparatus." There was little systematic effort made to teach scientific disciplines, and even colleges were still dominated by the tradition of a classical education that came from the days when the primary purpose of higher education was that of preparing ministers. Towards the end of the last century, nature study was introduced into the schools. Horace Mann, while secretary of the Board of Education in

Massachusetts, had attempted to introduce physiology into the curriculum as a foundation for health education, but the subject does not seem to have been widely taught during the last century, perhaps because of the absence of suitable textbooks, and also the lack of knowledge on the part of teachers whose normal school training may not have included more than a superficial contact with biology.

The introduction of nature study into schools at the end of the last century seems to have been designed to serve two purposes. First, the educated public of the day seems to have been impressed with the role of observation in the development of science, and nature study gave the children the opportunity to observe. The idea that children should be trained in observation fitted the view of education as a means of training the mind in all of its fundamental processes, and few argued against the idea at that time that the power of observation was one of the fundamental faculties.

A second important purpose was that of bringing children into contact with what were believed to be the fundamental and eternal facts of science. The prevailing popular view of science at the turn of the century was that the facts were there, in the outside world, to be collected by whomever might be willing to use his eyes and ears to collect those facts. The view was, of course, Aristotelian, and highly acceptable to those who had had the typical college education in the classics and humanities, which had exposed them to Aristotle and other great thinkers of antiquity.

This conception of science, as the gathering of facts, found its proponents in the academic world. An earlier chapter of this book pointed out that Edward L. Thorndike took the view that the first task of the scientist was to establish the facts, and his students and followers wrote in similar terms. Thorndike's psychology and that of his followers was much more than a collection of facts, for it embraced a comprehensive philosophical position concerning the nature of human thinking, but this did not become incorporated in the pronouncements of Thorndike and his followers concerning the nature of science. Thus, even among the leaders of educational thought, the notion that science involved observation of facts was dominant, and this provided the essential structure used in introducing science into schools.

The role of experimentation in science was largely ignored by those who wished to develop a curriculum in science. Indeed, as late as 1880, the venerable institution Oxford University showed students of science chemical apparatus stored in glass showcases, to which the students had no access. The idea that children should do experiments is a relatively new one.

Science education during much of the first half of the present century lacked leadership. The National Society for the Study of Education, reflecting through its yearbooks the main developments of education, failed to produce a yearbook on science education until 1932, when the

Thirty-First Yearbook appeared entitled *A Program for Teaching Science.* There had been some bits and pieces related to science education in earlier volumes as when the teaching of physiology was discussed in relation to physical education, but the 1932 Yearbook was the first major publication of the society that focused on problems of science education.

A particularly notable feature of the Yearbook was a negative feature, and that is the total lack in it of any recognition of the existence of a body of knowledge and thought related to the nature of science. The area had produced nobody like Charles Davies, who had so successfully integrated ideas about the teaching of mathematics with the views of mathematicians on the nature of mathematics. Nobody of the stature of Charles Davies had emerged in the field of science education, though some of the work of Thomas Henry Huxley came close to this, even though it was restricted to the field of biology. Science education in 1932 seems to have been no more developed than mathematics education was in 1850, and in many ways less developed. The Yearbook made no mention of those who had attempted to conceptualize the nature of science, as William Whewell had attempted to do in his two-volume work *The Philosophy of the Inductive Sciences* (1847; revised, 1867). Whewell was a contemporary of Charles Davies and belonged to the small group of thinkers of their age who were asking important questions about the nature of science and mathematics. The writers of the 1932 Yearbook on science education seem to have been either ignorant of this body of thought, or did not believe it to be important. The Yearbook included much vague discussion about the facts of science, and even a reference to principles, but the basic issues related to the nature of science and the role of scientific knowledge in the cognitive development of the individual were not even recognized.

The Yearbook was developed under the chairmanship of Samuel Ralph Powers (1887-1970). Like many of his generation, Powers had taught school in the years 1905-1908, before he had had any formal training beyond high school. He then spent 2 years at the Illinois Normal University from which he graduated in 1910. Then he obtained a bachelor's degree from the University of Illinois in 1912. Then, while working in the University of Minnesota high school, he completed his work for a doctoral degree in education at the University of Minnesota. He filled at least two posts teaching education courses before being appointed as Associate Professor of Natural Sciences at Teachers College in 1923, remaining in that institution for the rest of his professional life. One wonders how a man with such minimum qualifications in the natural sciences could have been appointed to the major position in science education in his era. Whatever his limitations were, Powers, nevertheless, was regarded as whatever leadership there was in the area of science education early in the century. When the National Society for the Study of Education decided that the time had come to prepare a yearbook on the subject, Powers was appointed as chairman of the committee to undertake the project.

Powers was able to obtain some early status in the field of science education by promoting the use of objective tests for measuring achievement in science. Objective tests for measuring the outcomes of science education were quite late in development. In the 1920's, many individuals created status for themselves in various fields by doing that, and Powers seems to have been the only one who promoted tests in science areas to any extent.

Powers assembled the best committee that he could to undertake the Yearbook. The weaknesses in the resulting document were not entirely a result of the limitations of the committee members, for the entire area was at that time extraordinarily lacking in conceptual frameworks in terms of which science education in schools could be planned.

The two chapters in the Yearbook that were focused on research related to science teaching were written by Francis D. Curtis, Associate Professor of Secondary Education and the Teaching of Sciences at the University of Michigan. Curtis did a commendable job of reviewing the meager research that was available, even though most of it was peripheral to the central problems of science education. There were studies of such matters as the vocabularies of science textbooks, the relation of intelligence testscores to achievement in science, the value of study habits and techniques, and the value or lack of value of laboratory experiences. What had been learned by research hardly went beyond common sense.

One of Powers' own chapters reflected as much as anything the inadequacies of the field. The chapter in question was entitled "The Psychology of Science Teaching" (pp. 59-75). Powers must have heard that Judd at Chicago was attempting to develop the psychology of school subjects, and the chapter was an attempt to do for science teaching what Judd and his students were trying to do for reading and arithmetic. However, Powers interpreted the idea of a psychology of a school subject in a way that was more in accordance with the thinking of the previous century than with the thinking of the period in which he was writing. Powers viewed a psychology of science teaching as an attempt to apply psychology to science teaching. This view is to be contrasted with the view of Judd and his associates, who viewed a study of the pupil learning science, as a subject matter, as the psychology of the pupil attempting to master the field. The development of such a psychology probably was not possible at the time of the publication of the 1932 Yearbook for two reasons. First, the psychology of problem-solving, such as may take place in the laboratory, was still in an extremely primitive state. A second, and much more important reason was that there had been virtually no attempts among science educators to conceptualize the nature of science as a thinking activity and to relate such a conceptualization to education.

Thus, those engaged in the development of the teaching of science in schools had made no efforts, of the kind that mathematicians had made in the middle of the nineteenth century, to relate the processes involved in understanding mathematics to the thinking of the child.

The failure of Powers and his associates to develop a psychology of the child learning science, as others had begun to develop a psychology of the child learning mathematics, was quite excusable in terms of the difficulties involved. The task was made doubly difficult by the unfamiliarity that this group apparently had with the emerging conception of the nature of science and the parallel emerging conception of the nature of the child. The fact that none of those who wrote the handbook had any status in any of the recognized sciences set the stage for the takeover of curriculum design for schools by recognized scientists who, in turn, were limited by their ignorance of child development. Still another generation had to pass before curricula in science came to be designed by individuals who were not only scientists, but also knowledgeable in the area of child development.

After the Yearbook had been completed, Powers went on to write a number of reviews of research on science education for the newly created *American Educational Research Journal.* Powers could hardly have written interesting reviews, for the research in the entire area was at an extremely poor level. Research was undertaken mainly by graduate students, but was supervised all too often by professors who had little understanding of the nature and difficulty of research. The material was weak and inconsequential in content, and was not to improve for at least another 20 years. Powers himself attempted to develop a Bureau of Educational Research in Science during the years 1935-43, and although this enterprise was liberally supported by the General Education Board, it left no significant trace in the sands of time.

Social Studies

The development of research related to the social studies has had a rather different history from any other subject matter field reviewed here. The term *social studies* is a relatively new one, having become a recognized part of a pedagogical vocabulary early in the present century. The term *social studies* generally refers to those parts of the social sciences that have been selected for inclusion in the school curriculum. Since the social sciences cover such a wide range of subject matter as history, sociology, economics, political science, and other areas of knowledge, the fields from which the social studies may draw material were vast. From the time when public education was initiated in the colonial period, the material drawn has varied greatly. In the early Puritan schools, pupils were required to study the current laws, and that was as near as they came to anything in the social studies areas. Neither history nor geography was taught, and most of what we know as the social sciences did not exist. History did not begin to be included in the school curriculum until after the American revolution, and books on the subject were not available in New England. During most of the past century, most pupils in the common schools were not exposed to history, though a few states had introduced legal requirements that some history had to be taught at some grade level during schooling.

A major change in the emphasis given to history was produced by a series of reports by the American Historical Association, beginning with its *Study of History in Schools: Report to the American Historical Association by the Committee of Seven* (1899). In 1909, the American Historical Association produced a similar report on the teaching of history in the elementary schools and in 1911 produced a further report related to the teaching of history in the secondary schools. These reports moved history away from the traditional practice of teaching dates and facts about historical hero figures. The American Historical Association has had a record of exploring new content for school historical studies even though it has not been particularly concerned with educational research.

In the elementary grades, the teaching of history and particularly American history seems to have peaked during the years of the great immigration to the continent towards the end of the last century and in the early part of the present one. Since that time there has been a decline in the teaching of history in general at the elementary level. History has become displaced through the teaching of a melange of the other social sciences, sometimes under the title of civics, and sometimes under other titles. A new emphasis in recent years at the high school level has been on the introduction of the economics of capitalism into the schools. Sociology has also found a place from time to time in the curriculum, and psychology has also been a competitor for the time to be allotted to social studies.

Although the American Historical Association had attempted to expand the scope of its activities in relation to schools, those who sponsored the social studies movement eventually formed their own organization. This was the National Council for the Social Studies, which came into being shortly after the end of World War I. A decade later, in 1931, the Council published its first yearbook, and established a publication series still in existence today. The yearbooks showed only an occasional excursion into research materials, perhaps because the burning issues have pertained to issues of content and values. Individuals preparing materials for the social studies were concerned with the research that was being undertaken and the influence showed up in their products.

The indefinite nature of the boundaries of the social studies has made them a difficult area in which to develop research related to instruction.

The single unifying idea that underlies this aspect of the curriculum is that it has to do with the socialization of the individual. American history has been viewed as a means of developing in the American child, and particularly the immigrant, an understanding of the ideals on which the American civilization was built. Since there were some doubts about whether the teaching of history did this, attempts were made to introduce other subjects, to achieve this basic objective of handing on to each generation the traditions and values of the American culture. The problem is clearly a very important one.

The early researchers in the area engaged in activities related to the determination and clarification of objectives, much as researchers did in the physical and biological sciences. The area attracted the attention of some highly competent individuals, including Franklin Bobbitt, Carleton Washburne, Ernest Horn, and Harold Rugg. Most, but not all of the research in the area, was done under the supervision of such notable individuals, though not by the notables themselves, who functioned as supervisors and guides and summarizers. There was nobody in research related to the teaching of social studies as directly involved in research as William S. Gray was involved in reading research.

There is, perhaps, some interest in determining what citizens believe to be the mark of a good citizen, though probably not much merit in making analyses of textbooks to determine the implicit objectives of such materials. The determination of what are socially approved forms of behavior is of little consequence if one has no promising means of developing those behaviors. Indeed, the curricular studies of the period following World War I leave the impression today of being peculiarly inconsequential.

The post-World War I years were characterized in the area of curriculum research by attempts to determine objectively what were the useful ideas, techniques, and skills that the child should master. The growing emphasis in educational thought was on the adjustment of child to society. The concept was essentially a biological one. The human, like any other organism, had to adjust to its environment in order to live successfully. The studies related to objectives of instruction sought to determine just what a pupil should have to learn in order to adjust successfully. Within this context, the child was viewed in Darwinian terms as an organism relating to an environment. The study of the child's environment was assumed to provide an inventory of the conditions to which the child would have to adjust in order to live successfully. The early studies involved surveys of what were described as expert opinion on the conditions to which a child should adjust, but the more sophisticated research workers attempted to obtain more objective evidence of the conditions to which students had to learn to cope. Efforts of the latter kind involved surveys of newspapers, textbooks, and literature to determine the historical facts and references that were made and the facts which the student would have to understand if he were to comprehend the communication. The discovery of the basic facts that should be learned in history and geography even attracted the attention of such innovative administrators as Carleton Washburne, who sought to establish an objective basis for what was taught in these subjects in the Winnetka schools.

Interest in developing research in the area of social studies instruction preceded interest in research on science instruction by nearly a decade. In 1923, the second part of the *Twenty-Second Yearbook of the National Society for the Study of Education* was devoted to "The Social Studies in the Elementary and Secondary Schools." The material was prepared under the direction of Harold Ordway Rugg (1886-1960), who had assumed by that time the role of coordinator of knowledge in the area. His brother, Earle Underwood Rugg, was in charge of the social studies curriculum at the then recently developed Lincoln School, attached to Teachers College, and was a prolific summarizer of research in the area. Earle Rugg also chaired numerous theses in the area, but does not seem to have undertaken much research himself. The Yearbook reflects the influence of research on the construction of the social studies curriculum. Carleton W. Washburne, for example, wrote on the study he had undertaken of what were the important facts that should form the basis of a curriculum in history and geography. He used this research to construct a curriculum for the Winnetka school system, of which he was the superintendent. Unlike so many other fields, research related to the teaching of the social sciences had an intimate relationship to the development of teaching materials.

Ernest Horn (1882-1955), another contributor to the volume, wrote a chapter on the relationship of the findings of research to the design of courses in history. Then, together with Mabel Snedaker, a teacher in the University Elementary School of the State University of Iowa, he also wrote a chapter on the design of the course in history at that school.

Rugg's own introductory chapter was an interesting contribution. Much of it develops the thesis, on the basis of empirical studies, that the social studies textbooks used by children in schools had little to do with what historians and others believed to be the most important problems and issues related to American society. He deplored the teaching of history as the presentation of the lives of national heroes, and hoped that materials would evolve which would familiarize students with the great transformations that had occurred in the American society since its founding. He also deplored the absence of thought stimulation in much of the material, which had been designed for memorization only. Rugg called for a radical change in the nature of the materials included in social studies, a change for which he was preparing himself to participate.

Finally, the Yearbook included a chapter by Lean C. Marshall and Charles H. Judd. Marshall, a professor in the School of Commerce at the

University of Chicago, had been active in the Association of Collegiate Schools of Business, which organization had attempted to develop a social studies curriculum for secondary schools. Apparently, business schools were concerned about the inadequate knowledge their students had in the matter of how the American society functioned. Judd had apparently had some contact with the latter enterprise that led him to cooperate with Marshall on the chapter. The interesting feature of the chapter is that the social studies curriculum proposed is surprisingly like that developed nearly 50 years later by Jerome Bruner and his associates at Harvard University.

In order to understand the intellectual climate that prevailed in research on the social studies, let us consider a single case history of a leader in the field, namely, Harold Rugg (1886-1960). Rugg was one of the more interesting and colorful academicians of his age and a man with broad and impeccable academic qualifications. He completed a bachelor of science degree at Dartmouth in 1908, and a year later completed a degree in civil engineering at the Thayer School, which was a part of Dartmouth. He had a broad scientific education and was well trained in both the physical sciences and mathematics. He completed a doctoral degree at the University of Illinois in 1915, but during much of the time when he was working on his doctoral degree he was teaching in the engineering school. His doctoral work was in education, psychology, and sociology. Then he joined the Department of Education at Chicago. He must have been very much a man to Judd's liking, for the young Rugg was competent in research methods and, with his excellent mathematical background, found it easy to pick up the emerging discipline of statistics, an area in which he wrote a textbook. While at Chicago, Rugg became interested in the use of objective tests as did most of his generation. He also served on the Committee on Classification of Personnel of the U.S. Army in 1918. In 1920 he was brought to Teachers College by Earl James Russell, who was forever on the lookout for talent in the area of educational research.

Rugg's preoccupation with testing was short-lived, for before he had left the University of Chicago he had become interested in research related to social studies in schools. He may well have been influenced by his colleague on the Chicago faculty, Franklin Bobbitt, who had initiated research related to the design of curricula, and Judd became recognized at that time as one of the authorities on the teaching of social studies in the secondary school. Rugg must also have recognized that this was an area in which he could make a special contribution.

He became disillusioned with the value of research for improving the social studies curriculum and, almost immediately after leaving Chicago, began to write materials for schools. These came out as a series of pamphlets published over the years 1921-28. He also became involved in the work of the Progressive Education Association, but eventually abandoned the idea of a child-centered school in favor of a community-centered school. His engineering background also led him to participate in the technocrat movement of the early Roosevelt years, a movement that fostered the idea that all the problems of society could be solved if only engineers were given the chance to solve them.

Rugg stated that he was a radical, and by that he meant that he believed that one had to go to the roots of problems in order to solve them, and the solutions to many social problems might lie in making changes in our social system. His rather mild form of radicalism showed through at times in his social studies pamphlets, which were promptly and strongly attacked as being subversive. Although Rugg may have appeared publicly to have been angered by the attacks of the American Legion, the Hearst newspapers, and numerous other organizations, some of his friends thought that the attacks pleased him, for they told him that he really was the reformer that he wanted to be. Nevertheless, the public controversy was heated and bitter. Some schools banned his social studies materials, and at Bradner, Ohio, the materials were burned in the furnace.

Perhaps the most interesting feature of the case history of Rugg is that he abandoned research in order to devote his extraordinary talents to the development of very original materials. Rugg's plunge into the development of new study materials, after his initial ventures into research in the area, was rather typical of those who promoted research on the teaching of social studies early in the century. The temptation to plunge into the development of new materials was great, for the field encompassed is so great and the potential objectives so numerous that there are infinite possibilities of developing new materials. Teaching in the field did need to be shaken up, and the initial researches led to a revolution in the content of what was taught, even though the research would be regarded today as superficial and even amateurish.

One cannot leave a discussion of research related to the development of social studies without discussing the work of Franklin Bobbitt (1876-1956) and Werrett Wallace Charters (1875-1952). Bobbitt is significant in that he led what was acclaimed to be a new scientific approach to curriculum development. The essence of the approach was that the research worker should determine exactly what children needed to know to adapt to the world and then build the curriculum in terms of the knowledge that was thus identified. Charters advocated a similar approach. Bobbitt and Charters must have had close contact when they both worked in Judd's department at the University of Chicago from 1925 to 1928. Both had written books on curriculum which were published in 1924, the year before they became colleagues. Bobbitt is probably better recognized as the father of what was then the new approach to curriculum, because he mapped out, with some precision, the way in which the researcher should go about identifying the knowledge needed by pupils. The approach did attract much attention and doctoral students in education across the country produced dissertations that involved the plan for curriculum development that Bobbitt advocated. For example, the graduate student might make an analysis of newspapers to determine what the high school graduate had to know to interpret the materials in the papers. Graduate students in the field of the teaching of science made studies of what scientific knowledge was necessary to maintain health, to purchase food intelligently, to read magazines with understanding, and to engage effectively in numerous other adult activities. The approach was a gift to the graduate student of education, hard pressed to find a dissertation or thesis topic, even if it was somewhat lacking as a foundation for curriculum reform. However, it did have influence on the school curriculum, particularly in the social studies area.

One only has to look through the exhibits of social studies textbooks at present-day educational conventions to recognize that many academicians are still struggling to revitalize the social studies. But the truth has also become apparent that much more is needed than the research related to objectives and potential content that took place early in the century. Insofar as the objectives of social studies are those of socializing the individual and teaching productive ways of social change, much more needs to be known about how the child is socialized. Unfortunately, social psychologists and sociologists, who have learned much about this matter, have not been interested in developing a psychology of the social studies, which might provide an account of how the school and the curriculum can develop the kind of socially responsible adult that so many have envisioned to be the ideal product of the social studies. A psychology of the social studies of the kind that Judd must have envisioned would surely have to be developed by those expert in the sciences of social behavior. Although sociologists were intensely interested in education early in the century, their interest waned before educators became interested in research related to the teaching of the social sciences.

There were some studies of significant problems other than those already discussed that were well executed, but failed to have impact because they appeared at a time when few were interested in the issues involved. Among the latter were the studies of J. Wayne Wrightstone and the Evaluation Staff of the Eight-Year Study discussed elsewhere in this volume.

Other noninfluential research related to the social studies has been summarized in the lengthy articles on "Social Studies" in the 1941 *Encyclopedia of Educational Research,* edited by Walter S. Monroe.

Considerable research was undertaken by graduate students on such varied matters as child interest in social studies topics, the immediate and remote value of particular items of information, the difficulty level of particular social studies concepts such as democracy, patriotism, and political representation, the vocabulary level of social studies textbooks, the value of field trips, the best ways to utilize museums, and numerous others. Little of the research showed any consistent picture, perhaps because differences between experimental and control groups were typically very small. One of the few areas in which there were consistent findings was in the use of tangible teaching aids. The trend of such studies seems to show that the introduction of any aid improves learning. This finding fits the more recent discovery about classroom teaching to the effect that variability in procedure on the part of the teacher tends to produce better learning than a single rigid procedure. Another interesting finding was that, during the decades preceding the publication of the 1941 Monroe Encyclopedia, textbooks had increased in size, but the additions had been related to the findings of research. A somewhat dismal finding was that much of the literature on the teaching of social studies remained detached from the research literature, including the yearbooks of the National Council for the Social Studies. The main impact of research seems to have been on the materials available rather than on the teachers themselves.

PSYCHOLOGY OF SCHOOL SUBJECTS: WHERE NEXT?

The psychology of school subjects had a magnificent beginning. Its greatest achievement was the development of a psychology of reading which represents a model of how Judd conceived of the entire enterprise. The success of the work in reading, that led to the development of a quite remarkable theory of reading in 1925, must be attributed to some extent, but not entirely, to the extraordinary ability and drive of William S. Gray. Reading, as a form of behavior, has properties that made it possible to study essential components at an early stage in the development of psychology as a science. Much that goes on in reading is directly observable and can be recorded and studied with quite simple equipment. In contrast, there is little that can be studied directly about the pupil who is solving a problem in terms of the scientific principles he has learned. The psychology of perception was relatively well developed by the turn of the century, and could be applied to the development of a psychology of reading, in a way that the psychology of thinking was not. Of course, there are many aspects of reading that involve information-processing at high levels, and may call for reasoning and very complex processes. These aspects of reading are just now being successfully studied. They could not possible be investigated profitably in the days of James McKeen Cattell or William S. Gray.

The psychology of elementary mathematical operations was another area that offered considerable promise for the development of a psychology of school subjects. The essential logic of arithmetic was quite well understood by mathematicians, and had been formalized to the point where it could be considered to describe the behavior of pupils who were learning arithmetic within the framework of logical thought. Just why the psychology of arithmetic did not produce the same fruitful research as reading is difficult to say. Those who led the quest of the development of a psychology of arithmetic would seem to have had all the necessary qualities for doing just that, but a psychology of arithmetic hardly even began to emerge. Men like Judd, Buswell, and Brownell were not only brilliant, but also men of enormous energy and considerable ingenuity. A main difficulty seems to have been that the pupil solving problems of arithmetic does not generally provide much observable and recordable behavior. To solve this problem, Brownell and some of his associates asked children to solve problems aloud, but they did not pursue this line of research long enough for productive results to be achieved. The technique has been widely used by contemporary Russian investigators and with interesting results. The research related to the development of a psychology of arithmetic made progress in solving some of the more pedantic problems of the area, but failed to make headway in developing an understanding of arithmetic as reasoning and problem-solving. Such problems could not be attacked at that time because they were far beyond the state of knowledge.

Nevertheless, the Chicago University group made an interesting and worthwhile start in developing a psychology of arithmetic. Even though it could not possibly have fulfilled the hopes of Judd and his associates, it was a start, and almost everything the group began to do was later taken up and profitably explored by Russian and other European psychologists. The work at Chicago began an intellectually profitable and useful venture. Although work after mid-century is beyond the scope of this book, the author cannot help commenting that American work in this area was to be sidetracked by mathematicians, influenced by the then-fashionable set theory, who tried to impose patterns of mathematical thinking on children rather than exploring the mathematical ways in which children think. Unfortunately, this sidetracking of research was aided and abetted by educational researchers.

In no other areas were there any real attempts to develop a psychology of school subjects, though research, of a different nature, did have considerable impact on the development of materials in the social studies. Academicians interested in improvement in social studies teaching saw obvious deficiencies in social studies materials and jumped ahead to remedy those deficiencies, rather than develop research. One suspects that research in the 1920's and 1930's on the role of the school in the socialization of the individual could not have progressed very far at that time because of the limited knowledge that existed with respect to this problem either in social psychology or sociology. The expansion of knowledge in the latter two areas since mid-century makes the time now ripe for the development of a psychology of the teaching and learning of the social sciences based on what is known about the socialization of the individual. This should not be taken to belittle what was accomplished earlier in the century, for it represents the best example of how curriculum research can have enormous impact on what is taught in schools. Also, thought in the social sciences earlier in the century was dominated by people of substantial stature, and one doubts whether others, with perhaps different backgrounds, would have made more progress.

A psychology of how children learn a scientific conception of the nature of the world around them showed no signs of developing during the first half of the century. In the natural sciences there were few individuals of stature, if any, interested and knowledgeable in how children learn a scientific conception of the world. The extraordinary mediocrity of thought in the area is striking. Instruction in science was late in being taught in universities on this continent, still later in being taught in schools, and this tardiness seems to have been accompanied by a corresponding slow development in thought related to how children develop a scientific conception of the universe and how the subject should be taught. In contrast, the area today is one of vigorous development and seems to have outlived the incompetency of its infancy and adolescence.

This chapter has discussed only the birth of the psychology of school subjects. The area has, unfortunately, had a prolonged infancy and there have been times during the last 50 years when the infant seemed likely to die through neglect. This promising infant still survives, but there are now few who understand its needs. Confusion still exists between the application of psychology to the teaching of a discipline, and the psychology of the child mastering a discipline.

CHAPTER 8

Behaviorism and the Shadow of the Vienna Circle

This chapter will explore the impact of behaviorism on American education. We will not be concerned so much with an evaluation of that impact as the identification of the impact itself. We can expect some difficulty in separating the influence that derives from the strength of ideas and the influence that derives from the evangelistic zeal with which the ideas were promoted. Also difficult to separate are the ideas that derive from behaviorism and the ideas that derive from other movements in education with which behaviorism became allied.

American psychology, with its own unique approaches, had become well established by the time that John Broadus Watson (1878-1958) appeared on the academic scene. Although Watson had no use for any form of psychology except his own, the American psychology (as well as the European) that he attacked had been a success. By the year 1910, James McKeen Cattell had established the value of the psychological laboratory as the means of exploring the psychology of reading, and Edward Lee Thorndike was internationally famous for his studies of learning in animals. In addition, child psychology was becoming firmly established, largely through work at Clark University, and psychological problems related to measurement were being widely investigated. Watson had little good to say about any of them, and nothing good to say about European psychology, with the exception of the work of Pavlov and his associates. Watson saw himself as the man who would extricate psychology from the morass of theological and philosophical tradition in which it seemed, to him, to be mired. Just as Kepler and Newton had freed the physicist from a conception of the physics of the universe rooted in ancient theology, so did Watson expect that his ideas would free psychology from that same tradition. Some would say that psychology had already been liberated, before Watson promoted himself as the liberator.

WATSON AND HIS BEHAVIORISM

John Broadus Watson was one of the strangest characters who has ever had an impact on the development of psychology. He was born near Greenville, South Carolina, in 1878. Little is known about his early history. In his own autobiography (*A History of Psychology in Autobiography*, Vol. 3, 1931) he said nothing whatsoever about either his mother or his father. The omission is striking in that every other psychologist, who contributed to the same volume, said something about his family background. Watson also wrote about himself, as a child, in terms which, if written by another, would be regarded as libelous. He stated that he never made a passing grade in school, and that whenever the teacher left the room he spent the time boxing with a "friend" named Joe Leech until blood was drawn on one side or the other. He also said that his favorite pasttime on his way back from school was what he called "nigger fighting," for which he was at one time arrested. He described himself as "lazy" and "insubordinate." He entered Furman University at the age of 16, and one wonders how he managed to do that if he had the deplorable record he described. College bored him. He said he had only one real friend during his high school and college days, but he did join the Kappa Alpha fraternity, and one is left wondering why. Even in college, he still seems to have been a hostile and defiant individual. When a professor announced that he would flunk any student who handed in a paper "backwards," the young Watson took up the stupid challenge. When he handed in his paper backwards, he was promptly flunked. Watson wrote that his college experience had left him "bitter" and that he had come to view colleges as places where boys and girls were penned up until they achieved maturity.

Watson's portrait of himself as a child and youth was that of an angry, objectionable, and socially incompetent youth who had no idea how to make the most of his opportunities. Further light is thrown on Watson's early development through some research by Lucille T. Birnbaum, in her excellent study entitled *Behaviorism: John Broadus Watson and American Social Thought* (Doctoral dissertation, University of California at Berkeley, 1964). Birnbaum viewed the basic influence in Watson's life to be that of his maternal grandfather, John Albert Broadus, a Southern Baptist minister of some distinction. Broadus was particularly critical of philosophy, as his grandson John was later, but the grandfather had probably far more knowledge of philosophy than his grandson ever had. Birnbaum supplied some other information about John Watson's defiance of a philosophy professor at Furman. She said that the defiant episode with the paper was a climax to other encounters with the professor. In one of these encounters, John B. Watson had refused to read Kant, having learned from his grandfather that all rationalist philosophers should be suspected of inherent heresy. On the other hand, John's grandfather had considerable respect for the sciences and believed that psychology could provide considerable help to ministers.

John B. Watson, as a young man, was a believing Baptist. When he graduated from Furman University, he planned to become a minister. He applied for admission to the Princeton Theological Seminary, but was turned down because of inadequate preparation in the classical languages. Later in life, he became extremely critical of Latin and Greek as subjects for high school and college students. He had promised his mother that he would enter the ministry, but since his mother died before he had to make further decisions, he seems to have felt free to explore other areas of study. His first choice was to study medicine at the University of Chicago, but when he arrived on the campus he discovered that the $50 in his pocket would not get him far towards a medical career.

Watson's own account of how his plans developed after graduating from Furman University are confusing, but that is hardly surprising, for he seems to have been a confused young man. He was still very much interested in theology, and his thinking still seems to have been patterned along Baptist lines. He wrote to Mark Baldwin, who was the leading philosopher at Princeton, inquiring about the Greek and Latin requirement, but Baldwin's reply was that there was no way around the requirement. He then considered the University of Chicago, a choice that Birnbaum suggested may have been motivated by the fact that Rockefeller, the founder of the University of Chicago, was a Baptist. Watson himself said that he had heard of the name of John Dewey, and Dewey's reputation as a philosopher.

Birnbaum wondered whether Watson's thoughts of studying medicine may not have been motivated by a desire to become a medical missionary, but nobody knows. His entrance into psychology seems to have been produced by the combination of the offer of an assistantship in psychology and his admiration for the erudition and polemical skill of James Rowland Angell, the professor of psychology. Angell combined two qualities that must have had extraordinary impact on the young Watson. On the one hand, Angell was interested in identifying what should be the essence of a science of psychology, separating out the structural, the functional, and the genetic. On the other hand, Angell was also an experimentalist, engaging in the new form of reaction-time experiment that had come out of Wundt's laboratory. Angell set himself off from Titchener, the structural psychologist, by using his experimental data to develop a functional psychology.

Angell's attempt to formulate a philosophy within which a science of psychology could be developed profitably must have had great impact on the young Watson, but Angell was not the only one concerned with such matters at that time at the University of Chicago. John Dewey had been attacking the atomism of the concept of the reflex arc that formed the focus of Russian psychology and was beginning to influence the newly developing American psychology. Watson commented in his autobiography that he never knew what Dewey was talking about, hardly surprising since Watson and Dewey spoke entirely different languages.

Watson took several courses in philosophy at Chicago, including two from Dewey, but Watson wrote that philosophy "wouldn't take hold" (Murchison, 1931, p. 274). Just what he meant by the latter statement is hard to say. The philosophy of Kant was particular anathema to him, but he could see some worth in the philosophy of the British empiricists.

Watson became interested in neurology and physiology and also animal experimentation. His doctoral dissertation, completed under Angell, carried the title *Animal Education: An Experimental Study on the Physical Development of the White Rat, Correlated with the Growth of Its Nervous System* (1903). The dissertation was concerned with the relationship between the development of the medulla and learning in the white rat. The dissertation had to be published in those days, and Watson borrowed the large sum of $350 for that purpose. The published version of the document is now a rare collector's item. One should note that the title implies the philosophy of psychological science developed by the Russian school, which sought to explain the events of consciousness in terms of the underlying physiological processes. The title also embraces the Darwinian notion of consciousness in animals. Watson was very shortly to abandon both of these concepts.

Shortly after graduation, Watson had a severe nervous breakdown which he described in his autobiography as "a typical *Angst*," a term that referred to a Freudian anxiety neurosis. He had sleepless nights and would rise at 3 in the morning to go on long walks. His disability lasted weeks. Then, there was a sudden recovery.

The breakdown seems to have made a radical change in Watson and in his outlook on life. He referred to it as one of his "best experiences." He said that the breakdown taught him to accept a large part of Freud, a statement that is surprising today in view of the fact that later behaviorists held up Freud as a model of how psychology should not be developed as a science. A feature of the work of Freud that impressed Watson particularly was Freud's emphasis on the automaticity of much behavior. Thus, Freud saw the neurotic as engaging in much self-damaging behavior over which he had no control. The contact with Freud appears to have helped Watson develop a concept of behavior and learning as a strictly mechanical phenomenon. Sechenov and Pavlov had developed such a concept as a result of what was known about the physiology of the reflex, but Watson derived a mechanical theory of behavior on the basis of behavioral observations.

Watson's breakdown had other important effects on his style of thinking. His deep involvement in the Baptist Church became displaced by a complete antagonism to religion. His attitude to philosophy had long been ambivalent, with acceptance of the empiricist position and a rejection of the rationalist, but after his breakdown he became extraordinarily antagonistic to anything that had to do with philosophical thought. The system of ideas that he developed, and named *behaviorism*, had no place within it for anything philosophical, even though it was a philosophical system, but his new antagonism to philosophy was deep and emotional, and went far beyond the rational.

Despite his personal problems, his professors had faith in his ability. John Dewey was in charge of the Department of Psychology during the academic year 1903-04, in the absence of James Angell, and offered Watson a minor position in experimental psychology. Watson stayed in that position for two years and then was promoted to instructor. Although Watson did not understand Dewey, Dewey saw in young Watson a freshness in his approach to problems. Later, when Watson had developed his ideas on behaviorism quite fully, Dewey wrote in positive terms about behaviorism, not so much endorsing it as admitting its originality. During the four years that Watson spent at Chicago after completing his doctoral work, he seems to have concentrated on developing his skills in experimenting with animals, and particularly his operative techniques. During this time, he did produce one research that has stood the test of time, on the significance of the kinesthetic sense in maze-running in rats. Watson was able to separate out the effect of vision, smell, and kinesthesia in maze-running. To do this, he used rats that had been surgically operated upon.

In 1907, at the age of 29, Watson was offered the chair of psychology at Johns Hopkins. The offer came through Mark Baldwin, with whom he had had a long acquaintance. At Hopkins, Watson came into contact with some of the finest minds in psychology of the era, to whom he has expressed gratitude for the stimulation and ideas they gave him. There he met Herbert Spencer Jennings, noted for his studies of the behavior of protozoa, and he had as a student Karl Lashley, who exerted particular influence on him. Robert Yerkes was also working in the medical school at Hopkins, and Watson and Yerkes began some cooperative projects on vision in animals. Watson related that the first time he heard the term *conditioned emotional reflex* used was by Lashley in a seminar.

The association Watson had with psychologists of great distinction at Hopkins did much to develop what was to be his own unique point of view on the nature of a mature science of psychology. Some of the central ideas of this new point of view had already been formed in the laboratory at

Chicago, where he had developed the notion that experiments with human subjects should be conducted along precisely the lines that had been productive with animals. Watson recognized that one did not have to assume that animals were conscious, and one could not ask animals to introspect about their experiences in the experimental situation. Why assume that the human was conscious, and what possible purpose could be achieved by the questionable technique of introspection when much could be learned through objective observation alone?

Even with such insights, Watson needed the experience at Hopkins before he was ready to present to the public a complete version of his viewpoint. One suspects that the associations of mutual respect that he developed at Hopkins gave him something he had never had before in his life, namely, confidence in himself. A new Watson emerged at Hopkins, a Watson about whom colleagues were to write with considerable respect. This personal development seems to have taken place the first few years as a professor. His new development and new maturity became apparent in his famous paper entitled "Psychology as the Behaviorist Views It" (1913). This was followed by a textbook, *Behavior: An Introduction to Comparative Psychology* (New York: Holt, 1914). A large number of publications followed, developing further his theme, which will be discussed further in the next section on the nature of the system and the implications that Watson believed the system had for education.

Work related to the development of the idea of behaviorism ceased with the advent of the entry of the United States into World War I. Watson attempted to obtain a commission in the army, but was turned down on account of his vision. Then, like most other psychologists in his age group, he was called upon to work with the Committee on Personnel in the Army and was given the task of establishing examining boards for the selection of aviation cadets. There he came into conflict with politically oriented army officers, more concerned with their own advancement than with the course of the war. Later, he had the more interesting assignment of studying homing pigeons, but the introduction of radio communication made the project obsolete. And so the story continued throughout the war. Watson described his whole army experience as a "nightmare." He portrayed the officers with whom he had contact as a group of "overbearing" and "inferior" men. Watson was undoubtedly a great deal more intelligent than those assigned to supervise his work, and he had absolutely no toleration for anyone intellectually inferior to himself.

After two years of wasted time in the military, Watson returned to Baltimore and plunged into work on infants. His assistant in that work was Rosalie Raynor, a 19-year-old student and daughter of one of Baltimore's foremost families. Watson's relationship with Rosalie was to change his entire life.

Watson was at that stage of his career 42 years of age and married to

Mary with whom he had had what was called a "good marriage" since 1903. They had a son and a daughter and had lived a rather commonplace middle class life, but all that was to change. The events that followed Watson's association with Rosalie Raynor have been researched and described by David Cohen in his book, *J. B. Watson: The Founder of Behaviorism* (1979). Watson developed a passionate love affair with Rosalie, and made the mistake of writing her letters that reflected his passion. Watson's wife, Mary, suspected that such a relationship was developing, and came across a letter of love written to Watson by Rosalie. Mary also suspected that there must surely be correspondence from her husband to Rosalie, and managed to gain access to Rosalie's room in the Raynor mansion, which she searched, and where she found a dozen letters from John to Rosalie. A further complication in the situation arose when Mary's brother obtained copies of the letters and attempted to blackmail the Raynor family. Also, the president of The John Hopkins University seems to have been made aware, by someone, that Professor Watson had been having an affair with a student and sleeping with her. Watson was asked to resign, but the word dismissal provides a better description of his situation.

Watson left Baltimore for New York in the early Fall of 1920. He wrote in his autobiography that he was glad to leave Baltimore because the newspapers blazoned headlines about the scandal throughout the Fall, but a search of the Baltimore Sun during that time showed no headlines. One suspects that Watson would have liked the kind of publicity he imagined he was getting, but it was all a fantasy. Indeed, nothing much was evident in the press until the divorce proceedings began on November 24th when one of his passionate letters to Rosalie was read in court. Whatever publicity there was, it was short lived. He did marry Rosalie immediately following the divorce, but the total sequence of events left him not only emotionally shattered but economically on the verge of bankruptcy.

Watson married Rosalie Raynor the week the divorce became final. They had two children, both boys. The youngest, Billy, grew up to be a successful physician. The eldest, Jimmy, had no intellectual interests, became a drifter and committed suicide in his forties. The son from the first marriage was also rootless. Perhaps that was a coincidence. Rosalie died at the age of 36 from an attack of dysentry, and Watson was never the same again. He ceased to do any creative work, began drinking heavily, but still continued to accumulate a fortune as a successful business executive.

After Watson's forced resignation from The Johns Hopkins University, he was not without friends. After some months of unproductive idleness, he was able to obtain an interview with the president of the J. Walter Thompson Company, one of the largest advertising firms. He was offered a chance to try out for a permanent appointment and was sent to towns along the Mississippi to make a survey of the use of rubber boots. He achieved sufficient success at this to be given a permanent appointment on January 1, 1921. In the summer of 1921, he felt a need to know more about the consumer, if he were to be a success in the advertising business. To expand his knowledge of consumers, he took a 2-month job selling at Macy's. He came to view the curve showing the growth of sales in the same way as he had viewed the curve of learning in animals. The two curves were certainly similar in form, and had he not stressed in his writings the essential similarity of animal and human learning? The transfer from the academic world to the business world was not as hard as he had anticipated, for in 1924 he was made a vice president of the company.

Watson's writings show a progressive change both in character and quality, over time. His doctoral dissertation, *Animal Education*, is an impeccable example of behavioral research. Watson's landmark publication that laid out his conception of a behavioristic science was *"Psychology as the Behaviorist Views It."* This article established, once and for all, the notion of the psychologist as behaviorist. The article took the firm position that psychologists should be concerned with developing a science of observable behavior and that behavior and not consciousness should be the point of attack. Watson claimed that he wanted to produce the same revolution in psychology that Darwin had in biology. Yet Watson did not recognize that his position was in many ways contrary to that of Darwin, who had introduced the idea that continuity in evolution forced the scientist to take the position that animals were conscious as well as humans. The idea of consciousness in animals had influenced the work of students of animal behavior, such as Romanes. Watson was a Darwinian, but only insofar as it suited him intellectually.

Watson's first major book-length work was a fine example of scientific inquiry entitled *Behavior: An Introduction to Comparative Psychology.* The volume was a remarkable synthesis of what was known at that time of the behavior of animals. The introductory chapter to the volume implied that the value in collating what was known about animal behavior was that it provided a foundation for understanding human behavior. Throughout the book there was none of the rash generalization that characterized much of his later writings. Where he compared human and animal behavior, it was with respect to behavior that is comparable. Watson pointed out, for example, that there is not a problem in human vision that is not also a problem in animal vision. He also said emphatically that psychology does not need introspection any more than does physics or chemistry. However, he stated that consciousness is the instrument of all sciences, though that is a position from which he wavered in his later publications. His objection at this stage was only to studying states of consciousness, as Wundt and his students had. Watson was right in saying that, at that time, the study of states of consciousness had been an unproductive enterprise.

One should also note that the study of behavior of lower organisms was considered by Watson to be a worthwhile endeavor in itself, even if there were no obvious applications to improving the human condition.

The next major work was his *Psychology from the Standpoint of a Behaviorist* (1919). This work was also a sound scientific volume, with an introduction which spelled out the basic ideas of the new behaviorism. In this volume, he included verbal reports in the data that the psychologist was permitted to use. This was a withdrawal from his earlier position, for the difference between verbal reports and introspection is a difficult one to make, though Watson tried to make it. Some even criticized Watson for backing away from his original position which seemed to consider psychology to be a science of the overall, gross behavior of the individual. Behavior was claimed to be governed by habit, which involves a relationship between a particular stimulus and a particular response. Habits were claimed to be learned by a process of classical conditioning. Thus, all adult behavior represented a structure built through classical conditioning. Watson conceded that one cannot understand habit in terms of any simple cause-and-effect relationship, for the formation of a habit is an enormously complex affair. Language was viewed as a set of motor habits, and language spoken under the breath is still just a set of muscle twitches, but of diminished size.

The volume also engaged in the kind of polemics that characterized much of Watson's later writing. The word *polemic* is used here to mean an attempt to persuade by means of rhetoric or by the mere repetition, time and time again, of the same unsubstantiated statement. Although the work as a whole cannot be criticized on the latter basis, it nevertheless suffers from vast overgeneralization, a defect that characterizes much of the later work by those who describe themselves as behaviorists.

Watson's next major publication offered far-reaching suggestions for education, being based on his own studies of conditioning in infants. Before considering that publication in detail, let us turn briefly to Watson's *Behaviorism* (1924). The book was originally written as a set of lectures. It was extraordinarily short on data and long on polemics, as polemics have been defined here. The first chapter was entitled "What is Behaviorism?" and presented Watson's final attempt to state his position. He stated that there is no such *thing* as consciousness. This does not mean that Watson assumed the unbelievable position that people were not conscious. He meant only that consciousness was not an object comparable, in some way, to the other objects in the environment that scientists studied. Watson drew the unjustified inference that since consciousness was different from other objects that it could not become an object of rational inquiry. In this book, Watson also considered that consciousness is an epiphenomenon, that is to say, an artifact produced by material phenomena. The latter has been a popular theory among

Russians, but it is a theory that assumes the magical appearance of consciousness, under certain physical conditions. The theory invoked magic, for there are no casual concepts that can be called upon to explain such a concept.

The book also brought out Watson's extreme antireligious views that developed after his nervous breakdown. He blamed the existence of what was then the current state of psychology on its origins in religion and in doctrines that involved the invocation of a soul. Watson viewed the concept of mind as a mere substitute for the soul concept.

The book was filled with what are claimed to be practical applications of behaviorism. Mental disease was described as faulty conditioning, to be remedied by proper behavioral approaches. Feelings of inferiority were described as faulty habit systems developed at the mother's knee. Watson looked forward to the day when children would be raised not by mothers, but by properly trained personnel. Watson's overall program for a better society was well described in the last paragraph of *Behaviorism:*

> I think behaviorism does lay a foundation for saner living. It ought to be a science that prepares men and women for understanding the first principles of their own behavior. It ought to make men and women eager to rearrange their own lives, and especially eager to prepare themselves to bring up their own children in a healthy way. I wish I had time more fully to describe this, to picture to you the kind of rich and wonderful individual we should make of every healthy child if only we could let it shape itself properly and then provide for it a universe in which it could exercise that organization -- a universe unshackled by legendary folk lore of happenings thousands of years ago; unhampered by disgraceful political history; free of foolish customs and conventions which have no significance in themselves, yet which hem the individual in like taut steel bands. I am not asking here for revolution; I am not asking people to go out to some God-forsaken place, form a colony, go naked and live a communal life, nor am I asking for a change to a diet of roots and herbs. I am not asking for 'free love.' I am trying to dangle a stimulus in front of you, a verbal stimulus which, if acted upon, will gradually change this universe. For the universe will change if you bring up your children, not in the freedom of the libertine, but in behavioristic freedom -- a freedom which we cannot even picture in words, so little do we know of it. Will not these children in turn, with their better ways of living and thinking, replace us as society and in turn bring up their children in a still more scientific way, until the world finally becomes a place fit for human habitation?

Before turning to the educational impact of what Watson had to say, let us bring together the main ideas of Watson's system. First, the human was to be regarded, not as a conscious person, but as an object, that could be studied just as other objects were studied by the scientist. Second, consciousness was not regarded as a phenomenon to be studied. Watson assumed that consciousness somehow emerged from complex organizations of matter and did not control behavior. The theory assumed that consciousness appears, as if by magic, under certain material conditions. This is nearer to being a magical theory of consciousness than a scientific theory, and it is not a particularly defensible philosophical position. Third, behavior was considered to be composed of combinations of small units of behavior called reflexes and conditioned reflexes. Thus to understand a complex behavior means to understand the units of which it is composed and the relationship of those units to each other. This position is referred to today as the reductionist position. Fourth, behavior was assumed to be controlled by stimuli, and not by anything happening inside the person or organism. Thus the teacher does not have to be concerned with what the pupil is thinking, but with what the pupil is doing and with the selection of stimuli that will trigger the desired behavior or produce particular conditioned responses in the pupil.

It is no coincidence that Watson chose the term behaviorism, though, traditionally, scientific movements have not been referred to as *isms*. Most *isms*, like socialism, atheism, and agnosticism, are sets of beliefs that constitute doctrines. Watson apparently, perhaps unconsciously, wanted to give his new conception of a science of behavior something of the character of a doctrine to be preached. Perhaps, for him, it was a substitute for his discarded Baptist beliefs. He created an *ism* for that was what he needed.

THE IMPACT OF THE SYSTEM ON EDUCATION

The previously cited quotation of Watson from his book *Behaviorism* brings out his evangelistic zeal to use his new psychology to change human society and, as a part of that change, to reform education. Some of his zeal must have been derived from his own unhappiness with the world in which he lived. Watson was not a happy man, but neither is any reformer.

There are scattered references to what he believed would be improvements in child rearing practices in many of his writings, but his main influence on education came through a volume entitled *Psychological Care of Infant and Child* (1928). He was assisted in writing the book by his second wife, Rosalie Raynor Watson, with whom he had undertaken the famous experiment on Albert and the extinction of conditioned fear. Watson acknowledged that the book was an extension of L. Emmett Holt's book *The Care and Feeding of Children* (1894). Holt himself, though not an acknowledged behaviorist, was nevertheless one who emphasized the need for building psychology out of objective data. Holt's book had also had considerable influence on parents, for at the time when Watson wrote his own book, the Holt book had run into some 28 printings. Watson must have had at the back of his mind a book more completely behavioristic than that of Holt, and yet designed to reach mothers throughout the country. That is the implication of the introductory section.

One suspects that Watson was not so much interested in making money as in extending the influence of behaviorism. The book was written throughout in the polemic style of the preacher. The beliefs asserted in the book about the rearing of children are asserted with the confidence of the polemicist, even though based on the most flimsy evidence.

The book began with a description of some experiments conducted by Watson concerning the stimuli to which infants responded positively. Watson was interested in establishing the stimuli that produced native emotional responses in very young infants. He showed that infants did not show fear of fire, and neither did they show fear of furry animals. Even when the animal was a white rat, no fear of the furry animal was displayed. He was able to show that infants showed fear responses to the loud rasping sound when a steel bar was struck with a hammer, and to loss of support as when the blanket was jerked from under the infant. He then went on to describe what is now known as the famous Watson and Raynor experiment, in which they first showed that a 9-month-old infant manifested no fear of a rabbit. The pictures illustrating the experiment indicate that the rabbit was a live one and not a toy. After establishing this lack of fear, the infant was then shown the rabbit and, as he started to reach for it, a steel bar was banged behind the infant's head. The infant whimpered, cried, and "showed fear." The infant was then quieted by being allowed to play with blocks. He was then, again, shown the rabbit. The infant did not react eagerly this time, but gingerly reached out to touch it. Again the steel bar was struck, and again there was a "pronounced fear response" (p. 52). Then the infant was quieted down again, and once more, the rabbit was produced. This time the infant showed fear at the sight of the rabbit. He cried and turned away. Watson wrote that if the rabbit were shown a month later, the same response would be observed, but one cannot be sure from the text whether the follow-up experiment was ever carried out. Watson was also able to show that the fear conditioned to the rabbit also extended to a fur coat, a rug, and to a Santa Claus mask. Watson claimed, but probably did not demonstrate, that the fear also extended to other animals such as a dog, a cat, a rat, and a guinea pig. Here, as in other parts of Watson's writings, one has difficulty in separating the results of experiments from broad generalizations derived from Watson's imagination. One can understand his difficulty, for it is one that has plagued behaviorists and other writers in psychology down through modern times.

The demonstration was used as a basis for the claim that most fears were acquired in this way. The claim was that there were very few native fears and that most fears were acquired through simple conditioning. Watson indicted parents and teachers alike for conditioning children to fear all kinds of situations. Indeed, he suggested that parents should have their children taken from them and reared by technicians trained in child-rearing so that the world would not be filled with unhappy, fearful adults.

However, Watson held out hope that even if fears were conditioned in infants, they were still curable. He claimed that fears could be extinguished through a technique developed by Mary Cover Jones. In the case of a child conditioned to fear the rabbit, the fear could be extinguished by introducing the rabbit, at a distance, at the time when the child was happy having a meal. The next day the rabbit was introduced again as the child began to eat, and then was moved a little closer. The next day, the rabbit was introduced at the place where it was last seen on the previous day, and so the procedure was continued until the rabbit was on the child's lap.

Watson suggested how many fears of children may be thus eliminated. If a child fears the dark, then he may first be put to sleep in a lighted room, and each night the light is lowered in level of illumination.

Watson had much to say about negative, or withdrawal, reactions produced as a response to pain. He claimed that such withdrawal reactions were conditioned to a great number of objects, to which such a reaction should not have been conditioned. He claimed that the main instrument for such conditioning was the use of the word "don't" by the parent. He described the word *don't* as a "sledge hammer" (p. 57). He reprimanded parents for using that word, writing almost in a Rousseau style, and with strange inconsistency. Children should grow up free, he claimed, from both fears and negative reactions. This polemical discussion, written almost in the style of a sermon, was based on shockingly little data for a man who claimed that his new way of child-rearing was based upon research.

Watson described that there were only three inborn emotional responses. These were *fear*, already discussed; then there was *rage*, produced by restraining the activity of the infant. What Watson did not realize was that the response he called rage was not objectively distinguishable from fear. Then there was a response called *love*, which, despite the term used to denote it, was not a social response at all. The emotional response he called love was produced by stimulating the skin, and particularly the erogenous zones. Social behavior had absolutely no innate basis in the human, in terms of Watson's theory. The social aspect of the response was allegedly a response conditioned to skin stimulation.

Then, in an extraordinary *non sequitur*, Watson also concluded from his flimsy data that parents should avoid displays of loving their children and should not dote upon them as they typically did. His advice to parents in this respect was presented in concise form in the following paragraph, prefaced "Should the mother never kiss the baby?":

> There is a sensible way of treating children. Treat them as though they were young adults. Dress them, bathe them with care and circumspection. Let your behavior always be objective and kindly firm. Never hug and kiss them, never let them sit in your lap. If you must, kiss them once on the forehead when they say good night. Shake hands with them in the morning. Give them a pat on the head if they have made an extraordinarily good job of a difficult task. Try it out. In a week's time you will find how easy it is to be perfectly objective with your child and at the same time kindly. You will be utterly ashamed of the mawkish, sentimental way you have been handling it. (**Psychological Care**, pp. 81-82)

Since the paragraph follows in no way from the data, one must assume that it reflected some deep personal concern in Watson himself. One does not know enough about his childhood to know why he should have been so against parents showing love to children. Most of what Watson had to say in the matter has been shown by subsequent research to be fundamentally wrong.

The next chapter, "Rage and Temper Tantrums and How to Control Them," was based on the dubious premise that the rage/temper-tantrum syndrome derives entirely from the response of having movement restricted. The derivation, once again, of all rage and temper tantrums was assumed to be produced by conditioning of what Watson believed to be the basic and native rage response. He argued unconvincingly that the infant, restricted in movement while being dressed, showed rage, and the response was immediately conditioned to all the stimuli present. Watson obviously had not had much experience at bathing and dressing infants. His proposal for eliminating many of these supposed conditioned rage responses was to have clothes for infants redesigned so that dressing and undressing would not be a frustrating event. He also suggested that life would provide fewer frustrations for the young child if the adult would permit the child to do as much as he could by himself. The idea was hardly novel.

Watson finally asked whether tantrums can be "unconditioned." He came to a surprising conclusion with respect to this matter at the end of a chapter full of speculations, and that is that one would be unwise to speculate on a matter about which little was known. Apparently, Watson did not recognize that most of the rest of the same chapter was unwarranted speculation.

The last half of the book was quite data-free, and Watson, unhampered by data, felt free to provide advice on a multitude of aspects of child-rearing. Much of the advice he gave was certainly wrong in terms of what is now known. For example, he said that the habit of thumb-sucking should be cured in the first few days of infancy. His final paragraph in the book, summarizing what he had tried to do, began with a statement that is manifestly false. He started the paragraph by saying, "Above all, we have tried to create a problem-solving child." The fact is that the book has nothing to say about how to create a problem-solving child, for the central theme is that of controlling the emotional development of the child. Indeed, the book is quite anti-intellectualistic in its approach to child care and child development.

Watson's book on child care was widely discussed in its time and is still well-known among psychologists. Its fame stems from its extraordinary, if not outrageous, proposals. As a book, it compares very unfavorably with the other books on child development of the same era. Watson was not strong on either logic of scientific caution, as were Holt and Baldwin, and Watson's lack of understanding and caution in generalizing from limited data must have shocked them as it shocks contemporary readers. Yet, Watson's writings related to education began a movement that has had continued thrust over the years and has had a definite and prolonged impact on education.

This movement and its impetus derive from the fact that Watson offered very simple solutions to very complex problems. Whoever does this on the American scene wins wide support and even public acclamation. Tyler offered a simple solution to the problem of evaluating outcomes, and his solution, because of its simplicity and attractiveness, is still applied and endorsed 40 years later. Watson's solution to the problem of raising children had appeal, partly because it was simple and partly because there was no equally simple alternative offered.

Watson's basic ideas was simple and brilliant. He took the idea that had come down from Descartes, that animal behavior was strictly mechanical, and extended it to humans. Darwin had done the reverse, extending to animals the human attribute of conscious experience. Although Watson reversed Darwin's formula, Watson was still basically a Darwinian, otherwise he would not have believed that the study of animal learning could throw light on human learning.

A footnote should be added to Watson's excursion into giving advice to mothers. Watson's second wife, Rosalie Raynor Watson, whom he married at the end of 1920, a week after his divorce was finalized, bore him two boys who were raised more or less along Watsonian lines. In 1930, Rosalie wrote an article entitled "I Am the Mother of a Behaviorist's Children" (*Parents Magazine*, 1930). Rosalie described her attempt to raise children along behavioristic lines, with some compromises, Fortunately, she seems to have had a quality that Watson entirely lacked, namely, humor. The chief theme of the article was that the children were trained to be as independent of adults as possible. This meant no coddling or overt expressions of affection, but the article made it clear that Rosalie was a warm and loving person who gave much of herself to her children, despite the behavioristic prescription to do otherwise. The children were given many toys, but the parents, without knowing it, followed the Montessori prescription of allowing the child to play with only one toy at a time and to avoid a cluttered environment. Rosalie wrote of the "resentment" she felt at the children being excluded from the adults' part of the house and of having separate eating arrangements from the adults. Watson seems to have known very little about giving affection to a child and handled his own problem by excluding the children as far as possible from his life. The Watsons seem to have been surprised that the children showed athletic excellence, but little intellectual or academic excellence. They could hardly have shown the latter without being exposed to the intellectual stimulation of adults, a source of stimulation that may well have been excluded from them. Undoubtedly, Watson was not disturbed by this lack of academic excellence in view of the fact that he himself had distressed his teachers in this respect; but his children showed the quality that he admired most, and that was independence of spirit.

Rosalie Watson admitted that she was a poor behavioristic mother because, she said, she was too much on the side of the children. The latter would have been anathema to Watson, for it implied that Rosalie identified with what she believed to be the content of consciousness of the child. Worst of all, Rosalie admitted that she liked to make merry and giggle, a practice that Watson found to be juvenile. In one of her final comments, she stated that one of the things she was able to give her children was a sense of humor. Too bad that she could never give it to Watson himself.

Most of the page on which the Raynor article was completed was occupied by an advertisement for Watson's book on child care. The advertisement announced that 50,000 mothers had read the book, but did not say how many copies had been sold over a 10-year period. The advertisement claimed to quote the *New York Herald Tribune* as having said that the book was the most important book ever written. The mother who wanted to read more was referred to Watson's *Behaviorism.* The publishers claimed that the books brought happiness to parents.

THE IMPACT OF WATSON

This is a most difficult subject to discuss, because Watson's influence is hopelessly entangled with other influences of the time. One can begin the discussion by disposing of the myth that Watson founded experimental psychology, based on objective data, in America. Experimental psychology using objective data and requiring no introspection was already a flourishing enterprise in the United States before Watson had even completed his doctoral degree. By that time, Thorndike had undertaken his studies of animals escaping from puzzle boxes, which had already had world-wide influence. Cattell had undertaken his work on perception, work which, although it had been started in Wundt's laboratory, made no use of Wundtian introspection. Indeed, Cattell was highly doubtful that introspection of the kind that Wundt had advocated was of any value for the development of a science of psychology. The first psychological laboratory in the United States was founded by G. Stanley Hall at The Johns Hopkins University in 1883, and there a new generation of experimental psychologists were to be nurtured. Joseph Jastrow received his training there and went to the University of Wisconsin in 1888, where he founded a new psychological laboratory. Shortly after the turn of the century, Charles Hubbard Judd was developing a psychological laboratory at Yale. Edmund Clark Sanford, also a student of Hall's at Hopkins, wrote the first laboratory manual in experimental psychology, and was noted for his skill in the design of laboratory equipment. American psychology had certainly assumed its posture of emphasizing objective data long before John B. Watson appeared on the scene. On the entire continent, the only proponent of Wundtian psychology with its emphasis on introspective techniques was Edward Bradford Titchener, who wrote prolific materials to train students in the Wundtian approach, but who never was able to influence the mainstream of American psychology. Titchener's ponderous 4-volume *Experimental Psychology* was perhaps so dull that it could not have the influence exerted by the often polemic style of Watson.

Watson's influence on experimental psychology seems to have been that he was able to state the philosophy implicit in much of the new experimental work being developed on the American continent. He was able to put into words the philosophy underlying what the mature generation of American psychologists were doing. He told them what their philosophy of science was and provided the younger generation of psychologists with what amounted to a creed. Behaviorism was, as much as anything, a creed, that is to say, a set of beliefs related to what was claimed to be a productive way to develop psychological research. The creed was not established truths, but creeds have a way of becoming viewed as established truths, and Watson's creed was no exception. His pronouncements, often written in the style of his grandfather, the Baptist evangelist, had behind them an unmistakable religious fervor. To say that one was a behaviorist was to imply that one was avant-garde, and breaking with the tradition of philosophy that had dominated American psychology during the previous century.

The evangelism of behaviorists also had a negative effect. It tended to outlaw certain lines of research that later became productive lines of inquiry. For example, the study of imagery, a topic about which Watson was particularly negative, virtually disappeared from the American scene. In the 1960's, the topic was revived and became investigated with worthwhile outcomes. The development of models of memory systems also became taboo through Watson's influence, and work in the area was stultified for another 30 years.

The immediate impact of Watson's behaviorism on education was negligible, though the long-term impact, often through the work of others as intermediaries, was substantial as will be evident in later parts of the chapter. The 1930's were not a time when behaviorism could possibly have had an impact on education, for education was dominated throughout Western Europe and the United States by the new progressive movement. This movement in the United States was tied to the thinking of John Dewey, a line of thought that Watson absolutely did not understand. The progressive movement was equally unable to understand the new philosophy of behaviorism. There were few writers who attempted to write about the implications of behaviorism for education, though Percival M. Symonds wrote a book, *The Nature of Conduct* (1928), which was designed for educators. It was a book widely read by academicians in both psychology and education, but it probably had no impact on those closer to education. Symonds' flirtation with behaviorism was brief, for he later became preoccupied with clinical, and specifically Freudian, psychology. Nobody raised children in the way that Watson prescribed, except perhaps for a few of his devoted followers. That was fortunate, for most of what he had to say about child-rearing in his book on the subject was blatantly wrong.

Watson wanted teachers to view children as empty black boxes, such that the outputs could be controlled by the inputs. This was not an acceptable philosophical position in the 1930's, when educators were becoming concerned with the thoughts of children and how they viewed the educational experiences provided for them. It was an age in which education was centered on the child as a self-directed and self-energized system. The black-box conception of the pupil had no place within the prevailing educational philosophy.

The contemporaries of Watson in educational psychology, who might have sponsored his cause, viewed him only as a man of unreasonable excesses. He must have been well known to Judd at Chicago, but Judd's writings completely ignored the existence of Watson. Thorndike also ignored Watson, though one summer Watson lectured at Teachers College, but Thorndike was in no mood to strike up a friendship with Watson. Watson was never an easy man to relate to, except on his terms.

The review of the impact of Watson on philosophy and social thought, by Birnbaum, concluded that Watson attracted the attention of many philosophers because of the close tie between philosophy and psychology at the time. Watson was extremely antagonistic to philosophy, seeing a close tie between philosophy and religion. Watson did conceive of a role of a discipline that might be described as history of scientific thought, which comes near to what today is called philosophy of science. The strange feature of the writings of Watson is that they become progressively more philosophical, and yet proclaimed antagonism to philosophy. Although an antirationalist, his dogma concerning what should be the nature of a psychological science was derived, rationally, from the nature of successful sciences. His view that philosophy should be a particular form of synthesis of empirically based knowledge was warmly received by Bertrand Russell, disillusioned by the failure of philosophers to solve any of the traditional problems of philosophy. However, when Russell came to write his *History of Western Philosophy* (1945), he mentioned Pavlov, but not Watson. By that time he was no longer impressed with Watson's contribution to philosophy. Russell's analytic empiricism was vastly more sophisticated than anything of which Watson had dreamed.

John Dewey, undoubtedly intrigued by the ingenuity of this young man who was shaking up the whole field of psychology, gave Watson lukewarm support for a time, but it was not enduring. It could hardly have been, because Watson's naive epistemology, which reduced knowledge to a system of classically conditioned responses, was quite incompatible with the epistemology of Dewey. Dewey's concept of uncertainty and the reduction of uncertainty could find no place within Watson's system. Neither did Watson provide any place for the organization of knowledge through what Dewey called *assimilative processes*. Dewey's initial support of Watson must be regarded as an act of academic charity of a well-established academician towards a beginner.

Birnbaum suggested that Watson may have influenced the Vienna Circle philosophers. This hardly seems likely, for their approach bore little relation to American psychology of the time.

The influence of Watson on professional philosophy seems to have been transitory, if it ever was a real influence at all. Watson did have, nevertheless, a subtle and long-term influence on popular social philosophy. How schools and other social institutions came to be viewed by individuals and by a large section of the public ultimately came to bear the marks of a Watsonian view of life.

THE QUIET PERIOD OF BEHAVIORISM

The 20 years following Watson's demise at The John Hopkins University represented a time when the academic world produced a great array of ideas related to behaviorism, but during that time neither

Watson nor any of his followers had more than minimal contact with education. During that period, Watson wrote a number of flamboyant articles for publication in popular magazines, but these fell on ears tuned to other matters. The public's response to Watson's diatribes on traditional ways of rearing children was one of boredom. The academic world, too, turned away from Watson but gave birth to a new set of ideas that would ultimately produce a revival of behaviorism as a social philosophy.

The most notable related development on the academic scene was the appearance of a group of philosophers, referred to as the *Vienna Circle*, who sought to develop a philosophical system and a conception of science that ultimately became the foundation for a revival of behaviorism. The Vienna Circle consisted of a group of mathematicians, sociologists, philosophers, and others who met in Vienna in the 1920's for the purpose of investigating problems related to the use of language in science and the nature of scientific methodology. The enterprise they sought to develop has been given various names, including those of logical positivism, scientific empiricism, neo-positivism, and the unity-of-science movement. The movement included such men of distinction as Rudolf Carnap, Herbert Feigl, Gustav Bergmann, and Kurt Gödel. Most of the central figures in this movement came to occupy professorships in American universities during the 1930's and thereby came to exert powerful influence on American thought and American psychology. The best known direct influence was that of Gustav Bergmann on the thought and work of psychologist Kenneth Spence at the University of Iowa, who was a proponent of the new behaviorism of the 1930's and 1940's.

A basic concept of the Vienna Circle philosophy was that all statements, to be meaningful, had to be reducible to empirical statements, that is, to statements in which the terms pertained to verifiable observations. The statements of a science had to be reducible to statements that could be verified from publicly observable data. The concept of the unity of science was introduced through the idea that all the statements involved in the scientific social, and historical disciplines could be reduced to statements involving physical observations of the real world. The views expressed by the members of the Vienna Circle in their writings were at a sophisticated level.

Although most of the participants in the Vienna Circle had to retreat considerably from their original position during their lifetimes, their original position continued to have a lasting impact on psychology and education. The new generation of psychologists was reared in an academic atmosphere in which the only definitions acceptable were operational definitions. Doctoral students both in psychology and education were rigidly disciplined in operationalism during the 1930's, despite the fact that, by mid-century, Gustav Bergmann had clearly shown that some terms used in scientific discourse cannot be operationally defined.

Nevertheless, the influence of the Vienna Circle and operationalism on the development of educational research was, for the time, a healthy one. Schools of education had been far too permissive in the vague language that they had allowed in doctoral dissertations and theses. Even textbooks for students of education had acquired the reputation of sloppiness in their use of language. Vague terms had come to be used as broad umbrellas to cover entire educational philosophies. Thus, the U.S. Office of Education in the 1920's had sponsored something vaguely called "adjustment" education, that every school was able to interpret in its own way. There certainly was a place for the kind of operationalism that did not permit the use of such terms. This same influence extended also to the design of curricula for schools, an area that had been dominated by the use of vague terms to identify, supposedly, major objectives. The chapter on assessment and evaluation, Chapter 3, discusses at length the impact of operationalism on both curriculum design and the evaluation of outcomes, and points out that the impact was great and lasting.

Except for Watson, behaviorism of the early part of the century lacked the evangelistic zeal necessary for it to continue to have influence on education. The neo-behaviorists who immediately followed Watson had no evangelistic zeal whatsoever, and neither had the members of the Vienna Circle. Behaviorism was to have a strong revival after the quiet period we have just considered, and it was to be promoted with a zeal far beyond anything that John B. Watson had ever shown, even in the moments when he emulated his ancestor John Broadus, the Baptist evangelist. It is to the great revival of behaviorism as a social force that we must now turn.

BEHAVIORISM AND EDUCATION -- PHASE 2

During the first half of the present century, the influence of psychology on education depended upon the intense efforts of a few research-oriented psychologists. Psychologists such as Lewis M. Terman, Edward L. Thorndike, and Charles H. Judd were not only dedicated research workers, but they also were dedicated to bringing the attention of their work to teachers and school administrators. Without such dedication, their work would have remained only as a part of academic knowledge. These men did not want their knowledge to be filed away in an ivory tower, so they prepared versions of it which would attract the attention of school personnel. John B. Watson had also tried to do this, but with very little success. His extreme radicalism of thought, coupled with a quite abrasive personality, gave him visibility but little acceptance. He had none of the personal charm of a Terman or a Thorndike, and he lacked the personal charisma of a Judd. The full impact of behaviorism had to await the appearance of a psychologist of distinction able to bring behaviorism to education in the same way in which Terman, Thorndike, and Judd had brought their concepts of psychology to bear on school problems. The figure who ultimately emerged to do that was Burrhus Frederic Skinner (1904-   ).

Skinner is more difficult to discuss than most of the other figures presented in this volume, partly because he is still alive and is still a productive scholar. The position of an individual in his science and in its applications cannot be seen with any great objectivity until sometime after his death. An author writing about Thorndike and his work while he was still alive, would probably have seen him very differently from the way in which he is seen today. Nevertheless, a treatment of Skinner is necessary in that much of his most important work was undertaken during the period covered by this volume, and, by mid-century, Skinner had become a force to be considered in viewing education.

Skinner, as the main source of the impact of behaviorism on education, provides an extraordinary contrast with Watson. Indeed, Skinner has shown all of the admirable personal qualities that Watson lacked. Although a parent early in the century might have said to himself, "I don't want my child to grow up to be anything like John B. Watson," a modern parent who had some knowledge of Skinner might see in him the admirable personal qualities that a parent would like to see a child possess. Skinner brought to parents a conception of behavioristic child-rearing and education in a manner that would be quite acceptable to them, and in a way that Watson could never have done. Skinner shares with Thorndike and Terman kindliness and benevolence, and shares with Judd public charisma. Just as Thorndike, Terman, and Judd were successful in bringing their ideas into the public forum because of their admirable personal qualities, so too has Skinner been similarly successful because of his personal qualities.

Skinner has provided a much more complete autobiography than any of the other psychologists considered in this volume (*Particulars of My Life*, 1976, and *The Shaping of a Behaviorist*, 1979). Watson's short autobiography leaves one with the impression that he was a peculiarly nasty little boy and gained few redeeming personal qualities until he was a young adult, but Skinner's account of his childhood gives one the impression that he was a pleasant child, much like the best behaved that one could find anywhere in suburbia. Watson may not have been as bad as the "nigger fighting" kid he described himself to be. Perhaps, in writing his autobiography, Watson wanted to make himself out to have always been the *enfant terrible* that he was as an adult. Skinner never appears, whether in his adult personal contacts or in his childhood, anything other than the agreeable, kindly, and idealistic person that he has been all of his life.

Skinner's autobiography presents in great detail what can be described briefly as a middle-class and quite uninteresting childhood. His father was a lawyer, and self-made man, who had established his offices in Susquehanna, Pennsylvania, where Skinner was born. So many psychologists discussed in this volume came from the families of ministers that one is almost surprised to find one coming from the family of a lawyer. His father was successful as a lawyer, but failed to achieve some of his political ambitions, partly because of a lack of aptitude for political craft and partly because he provided legal services to politically unpopular clients. He had some musical talent and played the cornet as a young man, but his later life seems to have been extraordinarily devoid of any overwhelming leisure-time interests. Skinner's father seems to have had difficulty in relating to his children. He neither punished them nor showed much warmth towards them. In fact, his relationship was remote.

Skinner's mother was a woman of particular charm and seems to have had social skills that his father lacked. She too was interested in music and had a fine contralto voice. Skinner wrote much more warmly of hs mother than his father. She, like her husband, does not seem to have been any kind of religious zealot. Indeed, much of what Skinner described as his home background seems to be summarized by saying that it was quiet, devoid of any religious or political extremism, and not much different from that of other middle-class children in the Eastern states early in the century. One has difficulty in holding one's attention to Skinner's description of his childhood in Susquehanna because it was so commonplace. One can read 50 pages of it and then pause to wonder whether one remembers anything of it. Although Skinner's adult life is a topic of the greatest interest and of considerable consequence, the story of his childhood is wholly lacking in material of any interest whatsoever.

At the age of 18, Skinner went to Hamilton College, a fine private New York institution. During his freshman year, he wrote poetry prolifically, though he had hardly attempted to write any in high school. He wrote for the *Hamilton Literary Magazine* and the school newspaper, and much of what Skinner had to say about college pertains to his literary efforts. His program seems to have been broadly liberal arts, including considerable work in Greek and French and some Spanish. He also mentioned speaking engagements and considerable interest in the theatre.

In his senior year, he sent two short stories he had written to Robert Frost, who, after considerable delay, wrote back a quite flattering commentary. In this commentary, he stated that Skinner's writing was "worth twice anyone else I have seen in prose this year" (p. 249). He also said that he, Frost, did not know whether Skinner should go on and try to make a career of writing. Frost's letter is difficult to interpret, but Skinner seems to have taken it to mean that he should try and make a career of writing. Perhaps there were some doubts in his mind about his literary future, for he discussed the Frost letter with a friend. What Skinner probably needed most was hard-nosed criticism from faculty competent to judge literary effort. This, apparently, the young Skinner did not manage to receive. On graduating from Hamilton College, he set out to become a writer.

His parents were supportive of his ambitions, and Skinner could have spent a year developing whatever talent he had. However, after 3 months of effort he decided that writing in the surroundings of his family and his home would not be productive. He commented in his autobiography that he was good at writing about writing, even if his short stories and poetry were not successful. He said that he found it easy to be distracted from the life of a writer, because what he needed were activities that produced more immediate rewards.

One reads with pleasure in Skinner's autobiography that he decided to abandon the idea of a literary career, for the autobiography is peculiarly lifeless. Watson's autobiography, though completely factual and written in the style of objectivity that one would expect of a behaviorist, is never dull. Skinner's is dull, and yet one realizes that Skinner, unlike Watson, was a very fine young man of gentle disposition and whose values were thoroughly humanitarian. Even his rather prosaic collegiate writings, both in verse and prose, mark him as a thoroughly agreeable person. But perhaps the feature most lacking in all of these writings, as well as his later writings, is a lack of humor, in the broader sense of the term.

Skinner's decision to enter psychology seems to have been made slowly, for he graduated from Hamilton College in 1926 and did not enter Harvard for the purposes of studying psychology until 1928. He could have entered Harvard a semester earlier if he had known the ropes. His introduction to psychology was a slow one. Hardly any psychology had been taught at Hamilton, though, by the time that Skinner had gone there, psychology had reached some degree of maturity as an experimental science, but the college still emphasized philosophy. Skinner had read some of Bertrand Russell's writings from the period of Russell's life when he was reacting positively to Watson's emphasis on objective facts as a basis for a science of psychology. One should note that although Russell endorsed Watson's emphasis on collecting objective data, he realized, as Watson had not, that a science consisted of far more than objective data. The young Skinner was probably unaware of the major differences between the position of Russell and the position of Watson.

Then Skinner read an article in the *New York Times Magazine*, by H. G. Wells, in which Wells contrasted the approach of Pavlov to the understanding of behavior with that shown by playwright George Bernard Shaw. Wells was able to see virtue in the approaches of both these men. Perhaps Skinner was able to see himself as bridging the gap between Shaw and Pavlov, but he did not say. The Wells article led him to inquire about schools where he could study psychology and he was advised to go to Harvard which, in fact, had declined from its zenith as a center of psychology in the earlier part of the century. Skinner completed his master's degree in 1930 and his doctoral program in 1931. Then he stayed on at Harvard in various capacities until 1936. The years at Harvard were particularly productive for him.

Skinner's time at Harvard, throughout most of the 1930's, was the period when Watsonian behaviorism was having its greatest impact on thought and when the Vienna Circle was influencing American conceptions of science. Skinner was obviously enormously influenced by the prevailing intellectual atmosphere of the age. As soon as he had acquired some competence in his new field of specialization, he began to develop systematically the ideas which were to dominate his life. His first paper, "The Concept of the Reflex in the Description of Behavior" (1931), is a remarkable discussion of the history of the reflex and its value as a concept. Skinner noted that Descartes had stressed the automaticity of animal behavior and had recognized that the stimulus controlled behavior, but he had not recognized the existence of the reflex. Skinner pointed out that the concept of the reflex soon acquired a considerable amount of surplus meaning by those who insisted on including in their definitions of a reflex such ideas as that a reflex was unconscious, and non-voluntary. Skinner viewed such elements in the definition as involving unnecessary subjective elements. He proposed that the reflex should be defined strictly in terms of stimulus correlated with a response. In his first scientific paper, Skinner was already adopting the view that a science of behavior should confine itself to observables. He appears to have viewed the reflex and the development of knowledge about the reflex as a model after which a science of behavior might be developed.

Skinner was very much influenced by the prevailing view of the 1930's that discussion had to begin with the development of a set of operational definitions of terms. Skinner was deeply concerned with this matter and went to great lengths to provide operational definitions for all of the major terms used in his papers. Skinner's followers, down to the present day, have placed a similar emphasis on the use of operational definitions. Critics of Skinner and his followers have claimed that little has been achieved through this emphasis, and that the use of operational definitions has created an illusion of precision, rather than real precision. When the followers of Skinner began to attempt to apply their knowledge to education, they found there the followers of Ralph Tyler with similar views about the importance of defining terms operationally. The ideas of Skinner and Tyler, with respect to definitions, had a common source in the work of the Vienna Circle philosophers.

Skinner's early studies involved studies of the reflex, and specifically the relation between deprivation from food and the solving of what he called a *problem box*. The problem box was described in precise detail in the second of his articles relating food deprivation to what he called *reflex behavior* (he still used the term *drive*, rather than food deprivation, at that stage of his career). The article carried the title "Drive and Reflex Strength: II" (1932). The problem box described is what today would be called a *Skinner box.*

What Skinner called a problem box was a device mechanically far superior to any that Thorndike had ever produced, for Thorndike was all thumbs when it came to constructing equipment, while Skinner was a fine craftsman. The equipment also had scientific advantages over any that Thorndike had constructed over 30 years earlier. It involved a lever that could be pressed by a rat, and the pressing of the lever could result in the delivery of a pellet of food. A record could be kept of the lever-pressing, and the frequency and amount of food delivered could also be controlled. Apart from these advantages, the Skinner box comes in direct lineage from the Thorndike puzzle box, which, until the arrival of Skinner on the scene, had not been improved in all the intervening years.

During the 1930's, Skinner used his problem box to generate a very large quantity of data that he began to put together into a theory of behavior. Skinner was producing contributions to the scientific literature even before he completed his doctoral degree, and after his degree was completed he contributed five or six papers a year to scientific journals for the next 15 years. These contributions represented not a collection of separate and independent contributions, but an orderly accumulation of knowledge. The culmination of this effort came with the integration of the various components of his research into his classic work, *The Behavior of Organisms* (1938). The book was published shortly after Skinner left Harvard and had become assistant professor of psychology at the University of Minnesota.

The title of the book is, in itself, significant. Although the book is based on the study of a single type of organism, the laboratory rat, and this single organism was studied solely in Skinner's lever-pressing box, the title implies that the results can be applied to all organisms in all situations. The implication is that behavior, in all organisms in all situations, shows certain basic properties that can be demonstrated on a single organism in a single situation. In writing the book, Skinner was set to generalize his findings anywhere and everywhere he wished. This he has done throughout his life.

The initial techniques of experimentation of Skinner were strictly Thorndikian, a fact he acknowledged later in a letter to Thorndike (see Geraldine Joncich's *The Sane Positivist: A Biography of Edward L. Thorndike*, 1968), but the initial pages of Skinner's *Behavior of Organisms* are strictly Watsonian in approach. He repeated Watson's position that the data of psychology have to be observable events -- specifically, stimuli and responses -- and that a science of behavior should not introduce "fictional explanations" (p. 40) such as mental processes or fictions about the brain and its physiology. Psychology, he claimed, had to rid itself both of what he termed *psychic fictions* and *physiological fictions*. The relationship between stimuli and responses in which Skinner claimed to be interested was what he called the *reflex*, and he attempted to describe a set of laws pertaining to that reflex.

Although the conception of a behavioral science presented in the early part of the book contained absolutely nothing new, an important new idea was presented in the middle of the first chapter. This was the idea that some behavior shows a close correlation with the incidence of particular stimuli. Such behavior is referred to as *respondent behavior*. However, certain behaviors do not show this close relationship to specific stimuli. These were referred to as *operant behaviors*.

Through the introduction of the concept of the operant, Skinner suggested a way of overcoming a major difficulty of earlier stimulus-response theories of psychology. Such theories had posited the idea that for every behavior there was a particular stimulus, but the difficulty was that some behaviors appeared to occur with no identifiable specific stimulus. Skinner postulated that some behaviors were *emitted* by the organism and that these emitted behaviors could become tied, through conditioning, to particular stimuli. Skinner had observed that a rat placed in the problem box would, eventually, seem to emit many responses, including that of pressing the lever. The experimenter then went about arranging conditions so that the lever-pressing response that released food came to be strengthened and elicited by the stimuli provided by the box. The essential condition for learning was that reinforcement had to be contingent on the response to be strengthened. Once the response of lever-pressing had been strengthened, it could be reduced in strength, or extinguished, through the withdrawal of the reinforcing contingency.

The rest of the book provided information on the techniques used by Skinner for the study of the conditioning and extinction of the single operant of lever-pressing in the laboratory rat, and also a massive amount of data concerning various conditioning experiments. Virtually all of the materials had been published previously in journal articles. The new contribution of the book, and an important contribution, was the attempt in the early part of the work to extract from the material a general theory of behavior. The title of the book, *The Behavior of Organisms*, implied that Skinner had in mind the development of a theory of behavior that would apply to all organisms in all situations.

The belief that the theory outlined applied to all organisms, under all conditions, was a complete act of faith. The theory was presented as though it were on the same plane of generality as Newtonian physics, with application to a very broad spectrum of phenomena. To some extent, the belief that the laws of behavior, derived from a single organism in a single situation, were universal found some support in Darwinism. The continuity of all animal life and hence animal behavior was implied in evolutionary theory, but evolutionary theory was hardly a license for the gross overgeneralization found in Skinner's major work.

The word *overgeneralization* was selected for use here by the author. The followers of Skinner did not interpret his work in such terms. Indeed, the most devoted adherents to Skinner's position took the view that Skinner had, at last, managed to found a science of behavior and that Skinner's science of behavior was the only science of behavior that could be given any credence. Those who took such an extreme view were few in the 1940's, but managed to exert considerable influence. Thus, the psychology department at Columbia University adopted the position that only this new and true science should be taught to students, and developed a program strictly along the lines of operant psychology. There were, of course, dissenters within the department, whose views carried little weight, and the program of the department became one of training students in the viewpoints and findings of operant psychology. A few departments in other universities followed suit after mid-century, but these were few in number. Students who went through such programs graduated believing that they had found the true and only acceptable form of a science of behavior. Many believed that they were now equipped to apply a set of universally true behavioral science principles to the practical problems of living. Before considering the impact of the new generation of operant psychologists in disseminating and applying the principles they believed to be universally true, a little more needs to be said about Skinner's subsequent work.

Most of Skinner's important research was undertaken prior to World War II. During the war, he became intrigued with the behavior of the common pigeon and developed techniques for controlling its behavior. In many respects the pigeon has advantages as an organism to study because of the ease with which control can be exerted over its behavior. This fact was not new, for those who in the Middle Ages hunted through the use of falcons knew much about the ease with which the behavior of birds can be controlled. Pigeons are not falcons, but they are equally readily controlled.

When the pigeon became the second organism on which the laws of the behavior of organisms were to be based, questions were raised about whether the organisms were chosen to fit the laws. That is an issue that has never been settled. One can, of course, select both organisms and situations that will demonstrate particular laws, but that does not mean that the laws, thus demonstrated, can be applied to other organisms and other situations. Neither Skinner nor his followers ever seem to have doubted the reasonableness of their faith in applying what had been learned with one or two organisms in small variations of a single problem situation to other organisms and other situations.

Skinner demonstrated his point of view when he wrote what was presented as essentially a general textbook of psychology. The book was entitled *Science and Human Behavior* (1953), but the content goes far beyond the title in that it discussed a great range of applications of Skinner's principles of behavior.

The first half of the book presented his system, but the last half of the book was concerned almost entirely with what Skinner believed to be the applications of his theory of behavior. In this second half, Skinner wrote with the conviction of a prophet, and the conviction that has characterized most of his followers. The applications of his theory of behavior were extended to a discussion of such diverse areas as government and religion, psychotherapy, economic control, education, the design of a culture, group control, and personal control. Since the first part of the book was presented with virtually no reference to data, the sophomore college student and naive reader may reach the chapters on applications without realizing that Skinner was writing about a theory of behavior based mainly upon studies of the laboratory rat in a problem box. Such a naive reader may be persuaded that Skinner was writing about some eternal truths that have a broad data base and may then, because of his ignorance, be ready to accept the equally broad and sweeping applications that Skinner proposed. The reader is likely to be swept away with the conviction of Skinner's own convictions. The naive reader is also not likely to note that Skinner's book fails to follow the format of other books on general psychology of the time in that it is devoid of any references to scientific data and experiments to support what is said. Indeed, the format of the book is very much like the books of a half-century earlier that also neglected to document a single statement in terms of evidence and sources.

Nevertheless, the book had great influence, because it was used extensively with naive and uncritical readers, often in classes taught by almost equally naive instructors. It was widely used as a reference work in classes in education for those who wanted to find out about new trends in psychology. Such audiences were all too willing to accept statements on faith from professors.

In many ways, Skinner's technique of persuading his readers of the absolute truth of what he had to say was the same as that of Watson. Both insisted in their writing, again and again, that they represented the only scientific approach to the study of behavior. The prestige word *science* was used by both to give credibility to what they were doing. Watson was as short on data as was Skinner, but at least Watson had a small amount of data on human behavior, even though much of it has not stood the test of time. Both used a polemic style to persuade readers. Watson's seems to have been derived from his experience with religious polemics in his youth, but Skinner's was a reflection of his literary development. Both wrote with the conviction that they had found the only real truth about the nature of human nature.

Skinner's greatest effort to apply his theory to a field distant from his original data is found in his book *Verbal Behavior* (1957). Psychologists, physiologists, and others had long attempted to fit verbal behavior into some simple concept of behavior, such as conditioning. Pavlov had mentioned the difficulty involved, and had taken the position that the verbal system in humans represented a signaling system that increased enormously the complexity of human behavior. Skinner attempted to reduce the learning and the use of language to fit his conception of operant psychology. Verbal behavior represented instrumental behaviors that could be conditioned and become elicited by particular stimuli. This idea had been widely discussed before Skinner published his book, and linguists had commonly discarded the idea. When the book appeared, it was given a devastating review by Noam Chomsky ("Review [of Verbal Behavior]," 1959). At the same time, Chomsky presented a caustic critique of Skinner's theory of learning. Since the appearance of Chomsky's review, attempts to develop evidence to show that language is learned or modified by a simple conditioning process have not been able to provide any very convincing evidence that this is so. Indeed, verbal conditioning experiments have been fraught with so many difficulties, and the data produced have been so unclear, that such studies have virtually ceased -- at least, for a time. Furthermore, a vast amount of evidence has been accumulated to show that the acquisition of language in infancy takes place through a process far different from any described by Skinner. That is hardly surprising, in view of the fact that Skinner had no direct evidence with which to back up his claims. Indeed, what he had to say was largely an extension of what he had had to say about the laboratory rat.

Operant Psychology and Education

Skinner devoted a chapter to operant psychology's contribution to education in his *Science and Human Behavior,* which did little more than reiterate the belief that the improved use of reinforcements would result in the increased efficiency of education. Over the years he has contributed many easily read and, one might say, popularized papers on the subject that have been reproduced in books of collected papers. Most of what he said and undertook in relation to education occurred near to mid-century, and he has added little since that time. Thus, his contributions to education come within the scope of this volume, though they can be looked at with modern eyes that see them in a rather different light from the way in which they were regarded at the time when they appeared. Let us consider each of the central ideas that tended to be stressed by operant psychologists toward mid-century.

Reinforcement. Skinner believed that reinforcement was not adequately used in schools. He believed that if the behavior to be achieved, or some approximation to it, were reinforced systematically and without delay, that learning would be improved. The stress on immediacy of reinforcement was derived from animal studies, and from some word association studies with humans, but the evidence was derived from situations remote from the kinds of learning that took place in the classroom. The latter did not disturb the mid-century operant psychologists because of their firm and unshakeable belief that whatever was discovered on any species in any situation could be applied to other species in other situations. Learning processes were believed to be simple, identifiable, and universal. Some attempts were made around mid-century to demonstrate that learning could occur without reinforcement, but these attempted demonstrations generally had experimental weaknesses that were not circumvented for a long time to come. Later, when operant psychologists were faced with strong evidence that learning could take place without reinforcement, they tended to take the position that whatever learning occurred without reinforcement could not be learning. In other words, their definition of learning involved the concept of reinforcement.

Later evidence showed that not only was reinforcement not a necessary condition for what most psychologists referred to as learning, but that for many of the forms of learning involved in schools, immediacy of reinforcement or feedback was not important. Indeed, under some conditions a delay in reinforcement might be advantageous. In some situations the importance of immediacy of reinforcement was evident, notably in the acquisition of motor skills. A person would never learn to throw a basketball into a basket if the lights went out immediately after each throw, so that he could not see the result, and if he were told next day how well he was doing. There are a few activities, usually involving rote learning, in which immediacy of reinforcement may be important or even vital, as for example spelling, but in the case of much that is learned in elementary school and high school, delay in reinforcement is probably not important.

Ordering of subject matter. Skinner revived the central preoccupation of the medieval schoolmen, namely, the preoccupation with the ordering of subject matter. This was a matter that St. Augustine had been concerned with in his invention of cathechismic teaching. Catechisms were more than just inventories of the subject matter to be learned, presented in a question-and-answer form, for the development of the catechism as a teaching device raised the problem of the ordering of subject matter. Indeed, the optimum ordering of the subject matter was the problem that the curriculum builder of the Middle Ages tried to solve. Subject matter was generally ordered in terms of a logical conception of how it should be developed.

Skinner tied the ordering of subject matter within a curriculum to his conception of the analysis of behavior. He believed that curriculum builders should first identify what were called the "terminal behaviors" to be achieved. These were broken down into component behaviors, and the component behaviors were then arranged in what was believed to be an optimum order for their achievement. The concept of analysis of behavior is taken over from the physical sciences, where the concept of analysis has several distinct and quite precise meanings. The use of the word *analysis* provides the illusion that behavior can be analyzed with the same precision as, say, a chemical compound or the forces acting on an interplanetary vehicle; but the elements involved in a child solving an arithmetical problem are not easily determined, for how he solves the problem may depend upon how he has been taught. If the child has learned to solve the identical format of the problem by rote, then he engages in one set of behavior. On the other hand, if he has learned only the logic necessary to solve the problem, then the elements involved in solving it are quite different. One may have great difficulty in finding out just how a particular child solves a particular problem, if one can do it at all. Although a chemical compound can contain only certain elements combined in specific ways, a "terminal behavior" may consist of a variety of components, assembled in a variety of ways. Thus, there may be many ways of acquiring a particular "terminal behavior."

Much of what has been said and written about the analysis of behavior in relation to education makes assumptions about the structure of knowledge. The analysis of a chemical compound involves a knowledge of chemical structure. Indeed, before knowledge was available about chemical structure, there was no way of making a chemical analysis. The kind of analysis that preceded the work of Antoine Lavoisier involved the analysis of compounds into such attributes as floweriness, abrasiveness, corrosiveness, and so forth. The results of such analyses that preceded an understanding of chemical structure were absolutely worthless. One suspects that much of what is called analysis of behavior is at the pre-Lavoisier level, for it involves absolutely no understanding of the nature of knowledge reflected in behavior.

Operant psychologists are not dismayed by this criticism because of their Vienna Circle outlook and belief that they should stay with only that which is strictly observable. If chemistry had followed a similar policy, knowledge would still be at the alchemist level. Within the operant framework, the only discernible structure of knowledge that is discussed at all is an associationistic structure, which comes from both the tradition of the Russian physiologists, who saw linkages in the nervous system as corresponding to associations, and from the British empiricist philosophers, who viewed ideas and their associations much like atoms and chemical bonds. Neither of the latter views of knowledge has proved to be useful, as is evident from the research involving the computer stimulation of human intellectual behavior. Much knowledge has also been acquired in recent years about the development of such basic structures of knowledge as those of logic, time, and space, and considerable information has been acquired that may be useful in designing a curriculum. We appear to be near to the point where we have a sufficient understanding of the structures of knowledge, of which there are many, to begin to contemplate the possibility of making analyses of behavior related to school-learning. The problems involved are extremely complex, for they are probably far more complex than those involved in the analysis of chemical compounds. Claims that behavior can be easily analyzed should be regarded as premature, particularly in view of the fact that chemical analysis required a century to evolve, after some knowledge had been developed about the basic structure of matter.

Teaching machines and programmed learning. In order to provide an efficient learning situation for children, in which problems could be presented, responded to, and where appropriate responses could be reinforced, Skinner adapted the idea of his problem box to the classroom. This involved a reinvention of teaching machines that had been developed extensively, previously, by Sidney Leavitt Pressey (1888-1980), who in the early 1930's had predicted that the Industrial Revolution would come to education with the introduction of mechanical devices into the classroom (see "A Third and Fourth Contribution Towards the Coming 'Industrial Revolution' in Education," 1932). Pressey had been working on the problem for many years, having published articles on machines that tested and scored and provided feedback even as early as 1926. Pressey was fully familiar with the work of Thorndike and realized the importance of providing feedback in a learning situation, and his early machines, now exhibited in the Smithsonian Institution, did just that. During World War II and for some years after the war, Pressey worked with the U.S. Navy Department on the development of teaching machines that would instruct seamen in routine items of knowledge. Pressey realized that there was much more to education than that which could be provided by a mechanical device, but he also believed that mechanical devices should represent one teaching technique among many. Pressey was particularly interested in the use of such devices for helping the student to check up on what he knew and what he did not know, but Pressey's interest was much broader.

Skinner took the position that his form of teaching machine was fundamentally different from that of Pressey. For one thing, Skinner believed that his machines were based on a true theory of learning, though this is a matter that has always been open to question. In addition, Skinner and those associated in the work conceived of entire curricula being presented in the form of a program. One result of such thinking was the development of a theory of how a program of instruction should be constructed. Quite elaborate theories were developed concerning how particular frames of a program should be written and how branching programs should be introduced; later, computers were introduced to present the materials, score the responses, provide extra practice where necessary, and so forth. Critics who viewed pupils working on such materials pointed out that often the machine functioned only like a mechanical device for turning the pages of a textbook and that the material could be published in book format. Others argued that the machine prevented the pupil from cheating by not turning the page to the right answer until the pupil had made his response. The upshot of this controversy was the appearance of the programmed textbook, which retained the concept of programmed learning but without the use of a machine.

Programmed textbooks attracted some publishers, but were never a financial success. One can only speculate on why they were not the enormous advance that they were promoted to be. One can raise questions about whether they were perhaps based on an unsound theory of knowledge and the acquisition of human knowledge. A common criticism of them was that they were written in a completely task-oriented and humorless style and failed to arouse reader interest. The materials were also extremely bulky and costly. Research neither gave them any consistent support nor suggested that they be eliminated. Perhaps the strongest factor that accounts for their ultimate decline and almost total elimination is that programmed learning was originally proposed as a means of increasing the efficiency of education many times. Disillusionment inevitably followed such claims.

BEHAVIORISM'S OVERALL IMPACT

A serious difficulty in evaluating the impact of behaviorism on child-rearing and on the schools is that the movement became intertwined, at the practical level, with other movements. The emphasis of behaviorism on the reduction of complex behaviors into components was conceptually closely related to the ideas advanced by Tyler in the 1930's, but from a very different perspective. The background of Tyler's approach was operationalism and the impact of the Vienna Circle, but the background of behaviorism was a genuine disillusionment with traditional approaches to psychology and the hope of building a science of behavior instead of a science of mind. The Vienna Circle also lurked in the background of behaviorism, but its influence never seems to have been acknowledged, perhaps because behaviorists have generally had a negative attitude towards philosophy. The evaluation movement before mid-century and behaviorism had close ties in that both sponsored a reductionist view of behavior that seemed well-suited to the goals that each attempted to achieve.

Both behaviorism and the early evaluation movement had features that made them very attractive to educators. Both held out the tempting idea that there were very simple solutions available to the very complex problems of education. Both offered, in fact, a formula for solving the problems of schools that any educated person could easily understand. Complex behaviors could be analyzed into simple components. The simple components could be viewed as trainable elements, and the extent to which training was effective could be readily identified. Education no longer had to think in terms of vague generalities, but thought could now achieve a precision that had not been possible in the past. The idea of precision in educational thought was attractive to administrators and academicians and, to a lesser extent, to teachers. Precision in educational thought presumably led to efficiency, and nearly everybody was in favor of efficiency in schools.

Both the evaluation movement and behaviorism provided commendable efforts at achieving an increased degree of precision within their fields of activity. Attempts to achieve precision, or what critics have often called the illusion of precision, have had a long history in psychology. An immensely attractive feature of the psychology of Johann Friedrich Herbart, a century and a half earlier, was his attempt to develop a precise science of psychology, even attempting to reduce psychology to a mathematical science. Herbart may well have made a contribution to improving the precision of thought of psychological literature, and behaviorism may have made a similar kind of contribution, though it might be difficult to demonstrate that it had. Illusions of precision are very difficult to differentiate from real precision. Certainly, there was research before John B. Watson's time that had as much precision as any he undertook, and some of that research had at least as much impact as that of Watson- and post-Watson-vintage psychologists.

The reductionism of behaviorism has been largely accepted by educators, just as Tyler's reductionism was, yet it is this reductionism which seems to lead to some of the most ludicrous applications. Thus, after mid-century, school systems became involved in the detailed definition of objectives. In many cases, thousands of behaviors were believed to be identified related to progress through a curriculum. A mathematics curriculum for the grade school might involve 10,000 or more behaviors, depending upon how specific the analyzer thought specific behaviors should be. Such a list might have value for designing a test, but it might provide the teacher with little more than confusion. Teachers might be far better off understanding the relatively few basic mathematical understandings that children need to acquire than 10,000 different forms of problems that children should be able to solve.

The concept of reinforcement also became embedded in the language of educators and carried with it the belief that if the right reinforcers were handed out, then there would be no educational problems. Problems of discipline became discussed in terms of manipulating reinforcements. Reinforcement was treated like a new wonder drug. Operant psychologists cited in almost every textbook the importance of not reinforcing attention-seeking behavior. This turned out to be a gross oversimplification of the problem, for child development psychologists soon demonstrated that young children who were picked up when they cried, cried less than those who were left to cry, although the reinforcement paradigm suggested that the reverse should be the case. Still later, books appeared on the deleterious effects of some forms of reinforcement. The very simple formula provided by the operant psychologists was not the simple device for reforming education that it had been promoted to be.

The simplicity of the formula provided by operant psychologists accounts for the way in which it was widely embraced, but Skinner's persuasive style was also a contributing factor. Skinner was an effective persuader, partly because he wrote from deep conviction of the truth of the message he wanted to communicate, partly because what he had learned in his efforts to become a writer had taught him something about persuasive style, and partly because he was a person clearly dedicated to producing a better society. None of these components of Skinner's effectiveness has anything to do with the scientific value of the theory that was being promoted.

Finally, a few words must be said about the impact of behaviorism on educational philosophy. Like so many antiphilosophical movements, the impact of behaviorism was more often through its implied philosophy than through its findings. Indeed, the impact of behaviorism as a philosophical system is so marked that many believe that Skinner's place in history will be as a social philosopher rather than as a scientist. The extension of Descartes' mechanical view of behavior to the human, an extension that Descartes did not make, means that pupils are viewed as completely controllable by environmental conditions. The design of an educational program requires that an environment be designed that will produce the desired behaviors in the pupil and in a sequence that will permit the production of more complex behaviors. If learning in the child is automatic and, in some sense, mechanical, then the technologist designing the program does not have to make provision for pupils making decisions. Skinner did write on such topics as *self*-control and *self*-reinforcement, which seems to imply that individuals can make choices and that there is an executive, decision-making system in each individual. Yet such a system hardly seems to fit Descartes' conception of behavior as mechanical. The philosophical position of Skinner and his followers on this philosophical issue is, at the best, vague and, at the worst, hopelessly inconsistent. The common interpretation found among those who claim to be operant psychologists, and who are working in schools, is that the pupil's behavior should be completely controlled by the educational environment and that the only decisions made are those that pertain to whether a response is a "right" or a "wrong" response. The educational technologist does, presumably, make decisions at a more complex level, or perhaps he is just doing whatever he has been reinforced to do in his course work in operant psychology. Educational technologists trained in operant work do not usually consider themselves as mere victims of the reinforcements provided by their work in college. Indeed, they protest that they are the bearers of important truths, yet the concept of truth obviously has no place within the system. Such difficulties are generally resolved by viewing the educational technologist as a free agent, armed with vital truths about behavior that can be applied to the improvement of instruction, and the pupil is viewed as a strictly mechanical system. The latter is a very traditional way of viewing instruction. It was the way in which the monastic schools viewed the training of novices, who were expected to absorb completely, and without question, the catechismic teaching of their elders.

This raises the important question about what are the consequences of treating a child as a mechanical device. One knows, of course, that the adult thus treated rebels at the treatment, as many dictators have discovered. Adults have to be treated as though they were free, decision-making individuals, capable of controlling their own destiny. Children probably do not rebel to the same degree, but the long-term effects of treating them as Cartesian automata might well be dramatic. On this central point of impact of operant psychology on education, operant psychology has nothing to say.

A final point to note is that the view of operant psychologists has been used as the basis of a number of court cases in which school systems have been sued by pupils and former pupils. The cases involve the claim that the schools failed to educate the defendant. The essential argument in such cases is that the pupil is not responsible for learning, but the school is responsible for conditions that will produce learning. The argument embraces the operant psychology assumption that all behavior is controlled by stimuli provided by the environment. If learning does not occur, it is a result of the failure of the school to provide appropriate stimuli.

The courts have not been persuaded by the argument. Indeed, common sense tells one that a school, in which pupils claimed no responsibility, would be a school in which little learning occurred. It would be a school similar to an animal trainer's cage in which animals were slowly and laboriously taught tricks.

A final matter to note is that the views discussed in this chapter, derived from the strange mixture of behaviorism and Vienna Circle philosophy, have had some long term impact on education. An example of such an effect was the development of the movement in the 1970's to define teacher competency in terms of specific classroom behaviors. This was an application of the Vienna Circle idea that all definitions should be operational, and also the idea of behaviorists that any complex behavior could be analyzed into a set of fundamental component operants. The so-called competency movement seems to have been little aware of the now well-accepted fact that not all useful terms can be operationally defined, and that not all complex behaviors can be analyzed profitably into a set of components. The teacher-competency movement was based on a set of ideas, attractive because of their simplicity, that did much to lead education into unproductive activities.

G. STANLEY HALL

Photograph courtesy of Clark University

CHAPTER 9

Child Development Research as a Basis for Education

The education of children began quite late in the history of civilization. Throughout most of history, the period of growth was looked upon as a time during which the natural process of development took place, permitting some formal training during adolescence. Most children, of course, worked during the period of growth. Only the children of the privileged few lived a life of relative leisure but, even for them, some informal instruction must surely have been given by the servants hired to care for them. Formal instruction for the children of the elite, where there was formal instruction at all, came during and after adolescence.

The teaching of reading to children was probably introduced after the Bible had been printed and was widely distributed among the wealthy of Europe. The reading and understanding of the Bible was viewed as an essential step for the achievement of salvation, so the earlier the children could learn to read the Bible, the sooner they would be placed on the road to a beautiful eternal life. Whatever education the children of the aristocracy received focused for hundreds of years on the reading of the Bible. When the Puritans established common schools in 1647, the primary purpose was to teach the children to read the Bible, to achieve salvation in the next world, and to read the laws to achieve salvation in this. The issue of how old a child should be before he could learn to read hardly seems to have been raised. Child development, and child learning, was not considered a matter worth thinking about or studying. The ways of childhood, whether the laboring of the serf's child, or the relative idleness of the child of the aristocrat, seemed to be a part of the natural order of events, ordained by the Creator.

EARLY STUDIES OF INFANTS AND CHILDREN

Physicians of the Nineteenth Century wrote for parents tracts which attempted to transmit some of the practical wisdom about child rearing accumulated during medical practice, but actual studies of child behavior seem to have had a different origin. The earliest study of infant or child behavior seems to have been undertaken by Dieterich Tiedemann (1748-1803), sometime before 1803, when Tiedemann died. Tiedemann was a German philosopher, who had specialized in analytic approaches to the study of the human intellect, but his place in history derives from his pioneer study of the infant.

Little seems to have been done to develop Tiedemann's ideas of infant study and child study until the middle of the 19th Century, when the area blossomed into a major intellectual enterprise of the new German pedagogy. The developments in child study in Germany in the last half of the last century have been well documented in the Report of the Commissioner of Education for the year 1900-1901, a report undoubtedly stimulated by Commissioner Harris' interest in the pursuit of new knowledge.

Of particular interest with respect to the child study movement in Germany was that it seemed to have centered on education, and did not derive from the study of pediatrics. Hardly surprising was it that the new approach to understanding of children should have been centered in Jena, where Professor Stoy began to study children in the practice school, connected with the teacher training seminary, and to give examinations designed to explore intellectual development. The findings do not seem to have been published, but were probably viewed as exercises for the teachers in training. Although Professor Stoy's enterprise did not leave any recorded addition to human knowledge, it may well have been the stimulus for some of the inquiries that took place in other educational situations and which have left a better historical record.

The next landmark event in the child-study movement took place in Berlin by a group of teachers who, much like modern teachers, had come together in discussion groups to study for their own advancement. These teachers decided that they would like to make a study of the 6-year-olds entering the schools. The study was probably undertaken in 1869. The direction of the study was what one might have expected at that particular place and time. The emphasis was on the intellectual development of the child, and the approach was through a study of the content of consciousness.

The teachers sought to discover what ideas the children had already formed. Did they understand what it was for a frog to hop or for a toadstool to grow in the woods? What did they know about their geographical surroundings and did they know anything of the suburbs that surrounded Berlin? Did they know at what their father worked? How many could recite a poem, or sing a song?

This new research on the psychology of childhood soon ran into trouble. When the data collected by teachers began to be assembled, some of the data were suspect. Children who had been questioned in class-size groups concerning what ideas they had, said that they knew far more than those questioned in small groups. When a teacher asked a group of 30 children to raise their hands if they knew what a rabbit was like, most of the children raised their hands. The children had already learned that the chances of being asked to answer were small, and the raising of a hand made one look knowledgeable even if one was not. Thus much of the data had to be discarded. Nevertheless, this persistent group of early research workers did manage to salvage over 1,000 cases for further analysis.

The findings of the study were of considerable interest to teachers and others, a fact that may well have led to the development of further studies. These city children knew very little about the countryside and, indeed, had visited very few places within their own city and its suburbs. Particularly interesting was the difference between the children who had had experience in kindergarten in comparison with those raised only in their own homes. The children in kindergarten were markedly more knowledgeable than the home group. Although the reader might wonder whether the difference was due to the fact that the more educated families sent their children to kindergarten, the data suggests to the author that that is not the explanation. The kindergarten children showed evidence of having been taken to the kinds of places that kindergarten children might visit. For example, the kindergarten children knew what a zoo was much more frequently than the home-reared children, and they also knew about city landmarks. The kindergarten children also provided evidence of some formal learning having taken place in that they had some knowledge of such concepts as that of a cube and a circle. The study was, in some respects, a rather interesting evaluation study of the then new kindergartens that had come to flourish through the influence of Froebel. The children reared in creches also performed better than the home-reared children, suggesting that formalized training in Germany produced better results than home training.

The report showed that the teachers were quite entranced with the idea of expressing the content of the minds of children in statistical terms. The teachers who produced the study also recognized that the statistics provided information about where instruction should begin. Indeed, the teachers suggested that each child entering school should be studied systematically in this way, to determine where instruction should start. The teachers also recognized that the study needed to be extended to determine the extent to which children could perform such formal operations as counting, and the identification of geometrical forms in terms of their formal properties.

At least one further inquiry, along the same lines was undertaken in Saxony about 10 years later and with very similar results. This later study, also brought out the lack of contact that little girls have with their environment in comparison with boys.

THE EMERGENCE OF CHILD DEVELOPMENT RESEARCH

The Expansion of the Child Study Movement

The beginnings of child study in Germany were a part of a movement throughout Western civilization to give greatly enhanced attention to childhood, to child rearing practices, and to the relationship between education and knowledge of child development. The initiative for this new development, though it came first from teachers, soon expanded to parents. The movement was not one initiated by any idea that child study should be conducted by scientists, but the belief was widely voiced that any parent or teacher could benefit by systematically studying the child. The concept of inquiry underlying the movement was that an understanding of all children could be enhanced by observing children. The common conception of science in the last century was that the scientist was no more than an accurate observer and recorder of precise data, and that anyone could be a scientist by taking time to systematically observe.

The idea that observation was necessarily scientific dominated the early child study movement. It was implicit in the work of the Berlin teachers who sought to identify what knowledge children had. This idea dominated the early child-study movement in America. The *Child Study Association of America* was formed with just such an idea in the minds of its founders. The initial action in the formation of the Association involved the meeting of a group of 3 mothers in 1888 in New York City, The mothers decided to meet throughout the year in order to study child psychology and the new methods of education that were coming out of Germany. In the following year the group had expanded to 5 mothers. An additional year later, the group had expanded to more than 30 and adopted the title of *Society for the Study of Child Nature.* This society later became the *Federation for Child Study,* but it was not until 1924 that the Society was incorporated under the title *Child Study Association of America.*

A rather similar movement, at about the same period, was that which became incorporated as *The National Congress of Parents and Teachers.* When it was founded in 1897, it was called the *National Congress of*

Mothers and it had as its main objective that of changing conditions outside of the home that influenced the development of children. The main focus came to be on the school. From the attempts to influence education there emerged the parent-teacher association, with its capability of providing ideas related to how schools should be run. The organization produced a magazine *Child Welfare,* that first appeared in 1906, and later published as the *National Congress of Mother's Magazine.*

Although parent activities related to the study and application of child development appear to have emerged from the widespread interest in the matter among teachers of the era, the new organizations may also have had a link with the past. Activities, collectively referred to as parent education, had had a long history in the United States and may well have provided the fertile soil on which ideas related to the new child study movement could grow. Meetings of parents to discuss problems of child rearing were, apparently, common in the early part of the nineteenth century, and "Maternal Associations" were formed to develop these programs. This movement was not limited to the United States, but was part of a movement throughout Western civilization.

Hall and the New Child Development Research

The research on child development initiated by teachers in Germany slowly began to exert an influence in the United States, where there was an eagerness on the part of educators to grasp at new ideas derived from research. At the focus of the new child study movement in the United States was an impressive figure, Granville Stanley Hall (1844-1924).

G. Stanley Hall was one of the more colorful characters in the history of American psychology. He was the son of a New England farmer, who must have been well-to-do, for he was able to send the young Hall first to the well-known Sanderson Academy, and later to Williams College where Hall was awarded a bachelors degree in 1867. In 1878 he received the first American Ph.D. from Harvard University, which was just beginning to develop a graduate school. His initial vocational goal seems to have been that of entering the ministry and he spent a year after leaving Williams College attending the Union Theological Seminary. Through the patronage of Henry Sage, Hall went to study in Europe, where he stayed from 1868-1871. He went first to Berlin where he surely must have had some contact with the developing child-study movement, as well as with the new and controversial programs of education in the Prussian schools. Then he moved from Berlin to Bonn in order to study under Eduard Zeller, Isaac A. Dorner and Friedrich Trendelenburg, all of whom had notable positions in the field of philosophy in which Hall was primarily interested.

After returning to the United States in 1871, he spent a year completing his work at the Union Theological Seminary. Next year, 1872, he accepted a position at Antioch College teaching literature and philosophy. He stayed at Antioch for four rather undistinguished years and then, in 1876, resigned to accept an instructorship in English at Harvard. He still had not found his vocation, and resigned his Harvard position in 1878 in order to return to Germany where he worked again in Berlin and Leipzig, and then he later visited London. On this second period of study, Hall seems to have been interested in contacting leaders in the newly emerging sciences of biology and psychology. He had contact with Herman L. F. von Helmholtz, Wilhelm Wundt and Jean Martin Charcot. However, his contacts were not of the close kind that Judd or Cattell had enjoyed. Indeed, Hall was still searching for a goal in life and he seems to have conducted his search over a wide intellectual territory.

After returning to the United States in 1882, Hall was appointed lecturer in pedagogy at Harvard. Although by modern standards, Hall hardly seems to have qualifications for the job, he was well qualified by the standards of his age. A background in philosophy was considered to be an essential preparation for the teaching of pedagogy. Furthermore, Hall had presumably had some contact with the new European ideas on education, and the United States looked to Europe for ideas through which to develop the American school.

Although Hall had not participated actively in the new experimental psychology, and never did, he was provided the opportunity in 1882 of establishing the first American psychological laboratory at The Johns Hopkins University. In order to do that, he was given a special lecturship and 1,000 dollars for equipment. He must have created an excellent impression for in the next year, 1883, he was appointed professor of psychology and pedagogy. His extraordinary rise to emminence in the academic world can hardly be accounted for in terms of any scholarly contributions he had made up to that point in his career.

Hall was appointed President at Clark University in 1888, before this new institution had even opened its doors to students. Indeed, Hall was given almost a year in which to prepare himself to head the new university, and to discover what the new trends in instruction were. Clark University was founded as a graduate school, and that, in itself, was an important innovation on the American scene. Even the major American universities were, at that time, primarily undergraduate teaching enterprises. Only later did Clark University introduce an undergraduate program.

The compilation made by Louis N. Wison, librarian of Clark University, in 1914 (see *G. Stanley Hall: A Sketch*, 1914) showed that Hall had published 328 items up to that time. However, Hall was still writing prolifically, so one must assume that his published works must have reached 400 before he died. A point to note is that Hall had only about 40 publications to his credit when he was appointed to the presidency of

Clark University. Also, none of these early publications included those that made Hall a distinguished academician. Many of them had to do with religion, reflecting Hall's early interest in the ministry. Many were formal philosophical tracts. Several papers dealt with the then popular motor theories of thought. A single paper in 1883 dealt with the subject of "The Contents of Children's Minds," and was the only indication that Hall would later spend his life studying children.

Hall had a long history of founding and developing psychological journals. While at The Johns Hopkins University he founded the respected *American Journal of Psychology.* Shortly after arriving at Clark University, he founded the *Pedagogical Seminary,* which survives until today under the name of *Journal of Genetic Psychology.* He also edited the latter for 32 years from 1892 until his death in 1924. He edited the *Journal of Applied Psychology* from 1917 to 1924.

The way in which Hall ran both his seminars at Clark University and the university itself have been well described by Lewis M. Terman in his short autobiography cited in Chapter 4. The atmosphere of Clark University combined one of informality for the student combined with rigorous academic standards. Registration required no more than leaving one's name with President Hall's secretary. From that point on the student was free to attend whatever might happen to interest him on the campus. The student was very much responsible for preparing himself for the qualifying examinations that were required of a graduate degree, but the courses he took, and his presence or absence at those courses were the student's own business. Although Hall was President of the University, one of the important events on the campus was Hall's weekly seminar, held in the comfortable surroundings of his home. At those seminars all the latest developments in child psychology were discussed.

The Research Contribution of Hall and His Students

Hall undertook his first study in the field of child development shortly after he returned from Germany in 1882. It followed strictly the line of research that he had seen in Leipzig and Berlin, and sought to determine the concepts that young children had on entering school. The samples tested included 300 children in Boston and 678 in Kansas City, Missouri. The study was a slight improvement over the German studies in that each teacher tested only 3 children at a time. Of course, the study would have been better still if the interviews had been conducted with only one child at a time. Little attempt was made to standardize the interviews. The Boston children were 4 to 8 years old, but the Kansas children were identified only as those in the lowest primary grades. The study showed some quite fascinating differences between boys and girls. The girls tended to be more knowledgeable about objects in their immediate home environment, but the boys knew much more about things and objects distant from the home. The main implication of the findings was that the teacher could not assume that the children had any particular item of knowledge, even if it pertained to a common object. A second implication was that parents should instruct their children in the preschool years, bringing them into contact with common objects, and with the sights and sounds of nature. A third implication was that teachers could well begin work with a new class by exploring the minds of the children to determine what they knew and what they did not know.

The work on the contents of children's minds must have had some impact, for the material was reproduced in several other publications over the years, and was still being reproduced in 1908. Much of the data were also reproduced in the Report of the Commissioner of Education for the year 1897-1898 and, thereby, given extensive circulation. However, one should note that most of the reproduction of the original article took place after Hall had become famous for his contributions to child psychology. But for that fame, the original article might have remained unnoticed.

The study cited is one of the few researches in child development which Hall published under his own name. Most of the work on child study and child development, that came out of the Clark laboratory, was undertaken by Hall's graduate students, and the student published the results under his own name. The concept of joint authorship of student and professor had not yet become a common practice in American universities. Nevertheless, Hall had a substantial investment of both his time and thought in every study that came out of the Clark department. Sometimes the questionnaire used in a study would be sent out by Hall, with all of the prestige of his academic presidency behind it, but the student would do the work of assembling and interpreting the data and publishing the results. Hall reserved his efforts for other forms of publications, and particularly for the preparation of syntheses of knowledge and the creation of theories of child development.

Many of the investigations dealt with problems that were widely discussed among pedagogs of the time. Imitation was one such topic, and believed to be at the very core of the processes involved in education. Indeed, much education at the lower elementary grades involved little more than the teacher requiring the pupils to imitate the teacher, as the teacher said and pronounced words. The early studies of imitation went far beyond mere verbal imitation, and explored the extent to which children and adults could imitate physical objects such as an engine, a water pump, and so forth. The studies seemed to point away from the idea that imitation was an unlearned form of behavior and did suggest that teachers should reconsider the whole matter of what children could be expected to imitate profitably at particular ages.

Of greater interest to Hall were studies of the sources of the moral influences exerted on children, the play of children, and the interests of children. A quite extensive study was undertaken of moral development through the Clark University department. The study dealt with such very practical matters as the occasion on which a child had been punished and felt that he had benefited from it. Hall was always interested in how the child viewed the particular situation. Hall's approach was very much derived from the traditional German approach of studying psychology through the study of the content of consciousness. That had been the approach of Wundt, except that Wundt had developed his through an experimental method. Hall had little interest in experimentation, even after founding the first American psychology laboratory.

The study of morality came up with some tantalizing conclusions, even if these conclusions could not be fully substantiated through later inquiry. One conclusion was that conscience played no part in moral decisions before the age of 9 and very little before the age of 13. This was an interesting finding in that it corresponds with more recent research indicating that children cannot reach a high level of moral development until they enter the intellectual phase of formal operations. Of course, Hall and his students had difficulty in defining what was meant by conscience. Many of the findings do not correspond with those of modern research workers. For example, a large percentage of the boys interviewed claimed that direct religious instruction had produced moral development in themselves. Religious training probably has long term impact on the individual, but probably not the direct impact that Hall's students claimed to have found.

The study of the development of morality was further extended by studying the influence that other people had on the moral development of the child. The claim was made that the data showed that the child was influenced in his moral development by teachers, and that somehow the teacher's personality could radiate qualities that could influence the character of the pupil. The study claimed that although pupils were influenced by the superficial behavior of the teacher, such behavior surely flowed from deeper moral strength.

The children claimed that they were influenced, both positively and negatively, by their companions. Children aged 10 to 15 seemed to be particularly influenced by their companions, at least that is what the children said. Of interest was the finding that few boys were influenced by girl companions and girls were not influenced by boy companions, at least not within the school age that was studied. This is the kind of finding that fitted Hall's prejudice against coeducation that he strongly voiced in some of his works.

The study also covered the ethical relations of the children with their parents, an aspect of research that would be taboo in modern times. The conclusion was that relations between parents and children were viewed, generally, as good by the children. Another conclusion was that the influence of the one parent was about as important as the influence of the other. A conclusion, reflecting Hall's own bias, is that the parents do not provide direct moral influence but permit the child's nature to unfold. The idea is reminiscent of Rousseau.

The report of the research on moral development ends with a very interesting discussion of human rights, a topic that came up from time to time in the Clark research program. The rights that the Clark research had in mind were such matters as the right to stand first in the affections of their parents, the right to have proper food and clothing, and a right to what was referred to as mental and moral adjustment. Such rights are very different from the rights of children discussed today.

Play was a topic that the Clark group was interested in studying. Hall viewed play as of vital importance in the entire pattern of human development and wanted to explore the precise relationship of play to the needs of the developing child.

Although biography had long been the basis of much literature, the new child study movement saw biography as data that could be used for scientific purposes. The study of the biographies of the great was seen as a way of discovering the conditions of childhood that permitted great minds to emerge. Biography also provided a rich source of knowledge about human development in that a well-written biography can take the reader over an entire lifetime in a few hours. The biography compresses time to proportions that can be grasped.

Although the inquiries undertaken at Clark University into child development had a romantic atmosphere about them, there was also much research in other places on far more pedantic problems. Numerous investigations were carried out to determine norms for height and weight and the relationship of these two characteristics. The Commissioner of Education's annual report for the year ending 30 June 1902 described at length a very extensive study of the physical characteristics of children undertaken in the Chicago school system. The report of the Chicago study is of interest in that it showed the impact of the new instrumentation introduced into anthropometry and psychology. An illustration of the instrumentation showed the use of quite sophisticated apparatus for measuring vital capacity, auditory acuity, and an ergograph for determining strength, fatigue and other muscle work factors. Children were tested over the age range of 6 to 18. The school system was interested in establishing standards that pupils should meet, and there is an interesting statement (p. 1097) that evolutionary theory implied that the average represented an ideal type. One wonders where that idea arose, but educational thought of the period was influenced by evolutionary doctrine, even though the influence was largely in ways that were damaging.

The Chicago study sought to determine the relationship between scholarship and physical characteristics. The finding was that the brighter children were generally superior physically, but the relationships found were quite small. Nevertheless, the data were quite contrary to the prevailing view that very bright children tended to be inadequate in other respects, a view that was ultimately disposed of by Terman. The report also provided interesting data on the pubescent spurt in growth for boys and girls, a finding that was quite new at the time in terms of concrete data, though already well-recognized by physicians.

Problems of determining norms for physical characteristics were numerous. There was considerable interest in comparing the children in one community with those in another. Differences from one generation to the next also became a matter of interest, bringing out the fact that diet and conditions of child rearing were of importance in determining adult height.

The normative approach to the study of childhood development began with the study of such obvious physical features as height and weight. Each new generation introduced a higher level of sophistication, with the highest level of the normative approach being found in the laboratory of Arnold Lucius Gesell (1880-1961). The Gesell approach to the normative study of child development was much more sophisticated than that of any of his predecessors, particularly in that Gesell attempted to interpret his observations in terms of a theory of development, derived from his study of embryology, physiology and neuroanatomy.

Hall's Theory of Child Development

Although Hall is commonly described as the founder of the child-study movement, he was not. He found the movement active on the educational scene of his time, and encouraged an expansion of research in the area, though other individuals and groups were also encouraging the development of research. Hall's most impressive contribution to the movement was through his ability to weld the outcomes of research and observation into what appeared to him to be a consistent picture. Hall did this through producing a theory of child development into which he could fit all of the facts.

As a theorizer Hall suffered from the limitations found in the theoretical work of most of his contemporaries. His experience, training and background, as a preacher, had given him an expansive style of writing which interfered with any concise and brief presentation of his theoretical formulations. His style shows the same kind of evangelism that characterized the style of John B. Watson. Even Edward L. Thorndike, in many of his works, seemed to reflect the style of his father's evangelism, and even the cold and intellectual Charles H. Judd reflected some of the qualities of his missionary parents. Hall's evangelistic style of writing was quite characteristic of the other great psychologists of the early part of the present century whose impact on education has been discussed in this book. Hall also had a flair for writing and was a master of using colorful metaphor. The only time that the writings of Hall became dull was when they became cluttered with the details of studies that had been undertaken, for often these details seem to have little relevant connection to the main trend of the discourse. Hall is at his best when he manages to bring together studies and fit them into a theoretical framework.

The relationship between data, and the conclusions drawn by Hall from the data, was usually a little remote. Most of Hall's theorizing was not derived from the results of specific studies, but found its origins in the major ideas of the times, and particularly in the work of Darwin. One can understand why Hall, and psychologists contemporary to him, believed that important generalizations about behavior could be derived from small amounts of data, for had not the physicist been successful in doing just that. Newtonian physics had been based on a quite small amount of data on the motion of the planets in the solar system, and the wave theory of light had been supported by a few such phenomena as interference bands. The physicist had been successful in deriving very important generalizations from very minimal, but significant, observations. The psychologist of the later 19th century sought to do likewise in the social and behavioral area. Indeed, psychologists have attempted to do that down to modern times, though most have learned the dangers of so doing.

Hall has among his 400 or more publications two major works which capture his entire theoretical position in relation to child development and education. The last to be written of the two major works was his ponderous 2-volume work entitled *Educational Problems* (1911). This work is spread over 1424 pages, and was written over a period of 25 years. Hall told the reader in the introduction that the volumes summarize his Saturday morning lectures on education given over a quarter of a century. One suspects that these lectures were directed primarily at teachers, which is why they were scheduled for Saturdays. Nicholas Murray Butler had also delivered his lectures to teachers on Saturday mornings. The volumes not only deal with topics dear to Hall, such as moral development and sexual development, but they also cover the more prosaic matters of the teaching of reading, arithmetic, and the other school subjects. Some of the material involved the presentation of massive amounts of data but, in contrast, some of the chapters were quite discursive, as was the one that discussed "Pedagogy and the Press." Although the latter chapter suggested ways in which the schools and the press need to work together, the tone of the chapter towards the press was quite hostile, perhaps reflecting negative experiences that Hall had had. There was hardly a topic in the entire field of pedagogy that was not touched upon in the two volumes.

The second major work through which Hall has achieved some permanent fame, was his work *Adolescence* (1904). The full title of the work reads *Adolescence: Its Relation to Physiology, Anthropology, Sex, Crime, Religion and Education,* a title that reflects Hall's typical expansiveness. The two volumes were just short of 1,400 pages in length. In his preface Hall described it as his first book and stated that the volumes slowly grew out of his lectures to graduate students. Hall described himself as (P.XVIII) "an almost passionate lover of childhood and a teacher of youth," but he had found that development during adolescence as the theme that fascinated him most. Indeed, for Hall adolescence was worthy of "reverence," to use his own word. The two volumes covered every aspect of adolescent development, from matters of physical growth to the adolescent's grasping for religious concepts and attempts to understand the Universe. Hall even attempted to show how the seeds are sown in the adolescent for the development of superbeings, which Hall believed reflected the potential of the adolescent.

The work *Adolescence* was accepted as the authoritative work on the subject in its time, and Hall believed that the content should be made more widely available to teachers and parents. To achieve that goal, Hall prepared what was essentially a condensed version entitled *Youth: Its Education, Regimen, and Hygiene* (1917). The book was successful and new printings and new editions were produced through 1928. The book must surely have reached an education-related public and was probably used in teacher training.

Hall's theory of development in childhood has three central characteristics. The theory was thoroughly Darwinian in approach; it was strongly anti-intellectualistic, and, finally, it was genetic and mechanical. Let us consider each of these characteristics.

The Darwinian Developmental Model. If a modern student of psychology or education knows anything at all about G. Stanley Hall, it is that he developed the theory that ontogeny recapitulates phylogeny. Hall may have coined the phrase, and it may be hidden in one of his 400 or more publications. The author could not locate the phrase in Hall's major works. The basic concept was that the behavior of the developing child replays the biological history of the species. Charles Darwin and Darwinians had been immensely impressed with the fact that the developing embryo shows, at certain stages, characteristics of lower species. Thus the human embryo shows the anatomical relics of gill slits in an early stage of its development, and these vanish long before the baby is born. Embryology is full of the vestiges of the biological past, and the nineteenth century embryologists and anatomists saw the developing organism as recapitulating the biological history of the species. Hall lifted this idea from the field of embryology and applied it to the development of behavior. He proposed that the developing behavior of the child also recapitulates the historical behavior of the species. Hall did not recognize that the theory of biological recapitulation, as developed by biologists, seemed to apply only to the earliest stages of embryonic development, and that the baby after birth cannot be viewed as recapitulating *physiologically*, in any way, the history of the species. Hall either did not recognize this fact, or did not think that it was relevant. He saw childhood only in terms of developing patterns of behavior that had characterized the long ancestry of the species, going back even before the first hominid strode across the plains.

Hall mapped out child development into three main phases. These phases corresponded to the behavior of subhuman primates, the behavior of what Hall called savages, and the stage of the dawn of civilization. In order to understand Hall's theory, one must recognize that Hall viewed what he called the savage as an intermediate between the modern civilized human and the primate ancestor. Hall, like Karl Pearson and most of his academic contemporaries, viewed the white European as the superior human race. All other races were viewed as inferior. Such a theory did not die easily, for the Hitler youth, raised more than a generation later, embraced a similar view. However, one should hasten to add that there was nothing malicious about Hall's view of race, even though, at times, it was patronizing.

Hall viewed child development as involving three basic stages, corresponding to the evolutionary stages of the ape, the savage, and the early civilized human. These correspond to the preschool level, the elementary school level, and the adolescent level. The stages correspond roughly in age to more modern stages of development, but there the relationship ends. The stages were not stages of intellectual development, but stages that prepared the individual to play an intellectual role in adult society. Hall could see little intellectual role in either of what he called the ape or the savage. One must keep in mind that anthropologists had not yet studied so-called primitive peoples to the point of discovering the marvelous ingenuity through which they managed to live. The stages of the ape and savage were stages through which the child must mature to be able to undertake productive thinking, but during these stages little thinking is manifested.

The earliest stage was believed to be characterized by rapid growth and an enormous amount of muscular activity. Hall wrote about the child growing from within at this stage, and he loved the word *kindergarten*, coined by Friederich Froebel, for it conveyed to Hall the idea of a garden in which children could grow naturally, much as plants grow, but that was as far as Froebel and Hall could travel together.

Hall wanted nothing of the formal training materials, such as cubes and spheres, suggested by Froebel. He thought that children should play freely, and play out the history of their simian ancestors. He approved of kindergarten children playing out animal roles, in that this was one of the ways in which the history of the ancestry could be turned to good purpose. Play, guided by what Hall termed instinct, was believed to be the very essence of education in the early years.

In the ape-like stage of development the child was seen to have a high need for expressions of affection and a high level of obedience to the adult; at least that was the picture provided by Hall. This stage was supposed to reflect the behavior within the primate band where there is a close infant-mother relationship until weaning, and an obedience that is necessary for survival. One should note that in Hall's era very little was known about the life of primates, and Hall's view of the relationship of child behavior and ape behavior was based largely on ignorance.

Hall opposed the pragmatism of John Dewey and objected to the design of kindergartens as communities. The recapitulation theory had no place for the idea that the young child was capable of learning to live within the social framework of a community. The best that could be hoped for was that the young child should be able to participate in the relatively unstructured life of the primate band.

Motor development was considered a crucial aspect of all child development and particularly in the nursery school and kindergarten. The importance that Hall places on motor development stems from his acceptance of the motor theory of thinking that was popular in his day. Thinking was believed to be none other than a set of muscle actions that expressed thoughts, in an almost imperceptible way. Thus the thought of a hostile act against another might be expressed by a very slight clenching of the fist and the slight movement of the arm that would be a preliminary to the striking of a blow. Hall argued that motor development was necessary for the development of effective thinking skill. He also noted that what he called the natural course of development showed a progression from gross muscular activity to the fine coordination of the fingers, and that education must make provision for muscular development at all degrees of grossness and fineness. Hall thought that dance activities should form an important part of the education of young children since they fostered the development of muscular coordination at an overall level. He had other plans for developing finer muscular coordination during the elementary school grades. He also viewed music as derived from the pleasure of making rhythmical movements, and saw music as an effective tool for helping the child to develop dance skills. The relationship of music to dance, and of dance to muscular skill, and of muscular skill to thought, was presented within Hall's theory as a matter beyond speculation. Like so many psychologists, not just of his era, he propounded his views as though they represented well-tested theories.

Hall's statements on the importance of music and dance were always presented by him as a part of his recapitulation theory of childhood. The dancing of the kindergarten children, and the crude music that such children make with percussion instruments, were seen by him as a recapitulation of the tribal dances and music of the people he described as "savages." Hall viewed dancing as one of the ways in which music becomes understood, reflecting again the idea that understanding of the world, and thought about it, are achieved only through muscular activity. This also led Hall to see pantomine and the art of gesturing as important elements to be brought into education. Through such activities children were believed to learn to express thoughts that otherwise could not be expressed. Thus, learning to express thoughts through the musculature, other than the vocal cords, lies at the very core of Hall's concept of early education.

Hall was quite firm in the position that the lack of the development of motor skills would result in permanent impairment of the capacities of the child. Thus he claimed that children had to acquire the pronunciation of a foreign tongue, performance on a musical instrument, drawing, dancing, singing and other skills that had a strong motor component at an early age, or they would never acquire proficiency. Hall believed that lack of training in motor skills was already resulting in a degeneration of the "race" (*Youth*, p. 27). Hall clung closely to Pestalozzi's dictum that there was no knowledge without skill, meaning that knowledge always had an action component.

The transition from the ape-like or simian stage to the savage stage was claimed to take place around the age of 6 or 7. Hall described the second major stage as the preadolescent stage. The stage was not cut off sharply from the first stage of development, perhaps reflecting Hall's belief that the so-called savage was much more like the subhuman primate than like the Western Caucasian. In this second stage the child must live through the emotional life of the savage, and whatever intellectual life Hall believed the savage to have. Quite minimal intellectual capabilities are attributed to the child in the preadolescent stage.

The following quotation from Hall describes the kind of education that he thought most appropriate for the preadolescent (*Adolescence*, Vol. 11, pp. 451-452):

> Just as about the only duty of young children is implicit obedience, so the chief mental training from about eight to twelve is arbitrary memorization, drill, habituation, with only limited appeal to the understanding. After the critical transition age of six or seven, when the brain has achieved its adult size and weight and teething has reduced the chewing surface to its least extent, begins an unique stage of life marked by reduced growth and increased activity and power to resist both disease and fatigue, which, as was set forth in Chapter I, suggests what was, in some just post-simian age of our race, its period of maturity. Here belong discipline in writing, reading, spelling, verbal memory, manual training, practise of instrumental technique, proper names, drawing, drill in arithmetic, foreign languages by oral methods, the correct pronunciation of which

> is far harder if acquired later, etc. The hand is never so near the brain. Most of the content of the mind has entered it through the senses, and the eye- and ear-gates should be open at their widest. Authority should now take precedence of reason. Children comprehend much and very rapidly if we can only refrain from explaining, but this slows down intuition, tends to make casuists and prigs and to enfeeble the ultimate vigor of reason. It is the age of little method and much matter. The good teacher is now a **pedotribe**, or boy-driver. Boys of this age are now not very affectionate. They take pleasure in obliging and imitating those they like and perhaps in disobliging those they dislike. They have much selfishness and little sentiment. As this period draws to a close and the teens begin the average normal child will not be bookish but should read and write well, know a few dozen well-chosen books, play several dozen games, be well started in one or more ancient and modern languages, if these must be studied at all, should know something of several industries and how to make many things he is interested in, belong to a few teams and societies, know much about nature in his environment, be able to sing and draw, should have memorized much more than he now does, and be acquainted at least in story form with the outlines of many of the best works in literature and the epochs and persons in history. Morally he should have been through many if not most forms of what parents and teachers commonly call badness and Professor Yoder even calls meanness. He should have fought, whipped and been whipped, used language offensive to the prude and to the prim precisian, been in some scrapes, had something to do with bad, if more with good associates, and been exposed to and already recovering from as many forms of ethical mumps and measles as, by having in mild form now he can be rendered immune to later when they become far more dangerous, because his moral and religious as well as his rational nature is normally rudimentary.

The child was assumed to be incapable of reason, to be highly action oriented, and physical development was viewed as being much more important than intellectual advancement. At the savage stage there continued to be the same stress placed on the use of muscles. At the age of elementary schooling Hall believed that the large muscles should be developed through calisthenics, and the muscles involving small and fine movements should be exercised through manual training. Hall's theory was closely tied to the manual training movement that Nicholas Murray Butler and others so vigorously sponsored. Hall was in favor of teaching the basic skills through routines that involved considerable doses of drill. Although the use of drill seems to be out of keeping with the free-wheeling play of the kindergarten, Hall viewed drill conducted in an authoritarian fashion, as quite appropriate for the preadolescent, who was viewed as willing to show implicit obedience to the tribal leader. Hall was interested in the psychology of reading and seems to have been familiar with the research of his day, and extracts from it some useful advice on how reading should be taught. He advanced strong arguments against the practice of starting reading instruction with the learning of letter names, and he was strongly opposed to teaching reading by first starting the child on spelling. No method of instruction seemed appropriate from Hall's point of view before the third grade. Reading, writing, and spelling were all regarded as skills to be acquired strictly through drill, but Hall does concede that the amount of drill should be limited to very short periods each day.

Hall's view of elementary mathematics was that it is not rooted in reason, but rooted in habit. He conceded that mathematics does involve the idea of seriation, an abstract concept, but the rest of elementary mathematics involves no more than a set of automated habits. Hall sought to tie the teaching of elementary mathematics to other activities involving movement, and saw the value of counting to rhythmical movements, and even integrating the number series with dance. Children should be interested in mathematics with puzzles and all kinds of measuring scales and measuring equipment, but mathematics should be kept at a practical level. Geometry should be taught early, perhaps reflecting the fact that Hall's savages did use geometry in their art and building, and the teaching of geometry in children should be related to drawing and art. Very little time each day was to be devoted to arithmetic, and the time was not to include much in the way of abstraction. Mathematics instruction for the elementary grades was not to be designed by mathematicians.

Thus the elementary school curriculum was to be characterized by a strange mixture of authoritarian rule by the teacher, the tribal leader, who would instill the habits involved in the learning of the basics, and opportunities for physical development provided in such forms as dance and physical exercise, representing tribal ceremonies. Physical development was to take place over intellectual development, since maturity of the muscular system and the related nervous pathways was believed to be a prerequisite for intellectual development.

A final point about Hall's concept of how the elementary school should be run relates to the use of catharsis. Hall was impressed with the work of Sigmund Freud, and so much so that he invited Freud to visit Clark University and to deliver a set of lectures there in 1909. Hall believed that the Freudian mechanism of catharsis should be used in schools to dissipate hostility and other undesirable emotional responses.

The next stage in the recapitulation theory of child development was that of adolescence. This stage did not fully bring the individual through the historical period of enlightenment, but it was seen as a stage of transition from the savage to the moderately civilized human. Hall referred to the emergence of adolescence as a rebirth, for the born-again human seems to be starting a new life. The stage also did not result in the full development of the intellect. Indeed, Hall was so obsessed with the importance of emotional development during adolescence, that he seemed to be quite blind to the extraordinary intellectual growth that accompanied the stage. His views about adolescence have been well-summarized by him in the following paragraphs (*Adolescence*, Vol. 1, pp. XIII-XV):

> Adolescence is a new birth, for the higher and more completely human traits are now born. The qualities of body and soul that now emerge are far newer. The child comes from and harks back to a remote past; the adolescent is neo-atavistic, and in him the later acquisitions of the race slowly become prepotent. Development is less gradual and more saltatory, suggestive of some ancient period of storm and stress when old moorings were broken and a higher level attained. The annual rate of growth in height, weight, and strength is increased and often doubled, and even more. Important functions previously non-existent arise. Growth of parts and organs loses its former proportions, some permanently and some for a season. Some of these are still growing in old age and others are soon arrested and atrophy. The old moduli of dimensions become obsolete and old harmonies are broken. The range of individual differences and average errors in all physical measurements and all psychic tests increases. Some linger long in the childish stage and advance late or slowly, while others push on with a sudden outburst of impulsion to early maturity. Bones and muscles lead all other tissues, as if they vied with each other, and there is frequent flabbiness or tension as one or the other leads. Nature arms youth for conflict with all the resources at her command -- speed, power of shoulder, biceps, back, leg, jaw, -- strengthens and enlarges skull, thorax, hips, makes man aggressive and prepares woman's frame for maternity. The power of the diseases peculiar to childhood abates, and liability to the far more diseases of maturity begins, so that with liability to both it is not strange that the dawn of the ephebic day is marked at the same time by increased morbidity but diminished rates of mortality. Some disorders of arrest and defect as well as of excessive unfoldment in some function, part, or organ may now, after long study and controversy, be said to be established as peculiar to this period, and diseases that are distinctly school- and city-bred abound, with apparently increasing frequency. The momentum of heredity often seems insufficient to enable the child to achieve this great revolution and come to complete maturity, so that every step of the upward way is strewn with wreckage of body, mind, and morals. There is not only arrest, but perversion, at every stage, and hoodlumism, juvenile crime, and secret vice seem not only increasing, but develop in earlier years in every civilized land.
>
> The functions of every sense undergo reconstruction, and their relations to other psychic functions change, and new sensations, some of them very intense, arise, and new associations in the sense sphere are formed. Haptic

> impressions, appetite for food and drink, and smell are most modified. The voice changes, vascular instability, blushing, and flushing are increased. Sex asserts its mastery in field after field, and works its havoc in the form of secret vice, debauch, disease, and enfeebled heredity, cadences the soul to both its normal and abnormal rhythms, and sends many thousand youth a year to quacks, because neither parents, teachers, preachers, or physicians know how to deal with its problems. Thus the foundations of domestic, social, and religious life are oftenest undermined. The youth craves more knowledge of body and mind, that can help against besetting temptations, aid in the choice of a profession, and if his intellect is normal he does not vex his soul overmuch about the logical character of the universe or the ultimate sanction of either truth or virtue. He is more objective than subjective, and only if his lust to know nature and life is starved does his mind trouble him by in-growing. There are new repulsions felt toward home and school, and truancy and runaways abound. The social instincts undergo sudden unfoldment and the new life of love awakens. It is the age of sentiment and of religion, of rapid fluctuation of mood, and the world seems strange and new. Interest in adult life and invocations develops. Youth awakes to a new world and understands neither it nor himself. The whole future of life depends on how the new powers now given suddenly and in profusion are husbanded and directed. Character and personality are taking form, but everything is plastic. Self-feeling and ambition are increased, and every trait and faculty is liable to exaggeration and excess. It is all a marvelous new birth, and those who believe that nothing is so worthy of love, reverence, and service as the body and soul of youth, and who hold that the best test of every human institution is how much it contributes to bring youth to the ever fullest possible development, may well review themselves and the civilization in which we live to see how far it satisfies this supreme test.

An important point to note about the description of adolescence given by Hall is that he made no mention of the adolescent's new intellectual powers. There was an emphasis on the achievement of physical and glandular maturity and the resulting behaviors that seem to result. There was a considerable importance given to sexual development, a matter that Hall was interested in to almost an obsessive extent. Note that he stated that "sex asserts its mastery in field after field," a very strong expression. Sexual development, and the creation of a sex role was important in his concept of education, and he believed that boys and girls should be educated separately during adolescence in the presence of good sex role models. Sexual education, in the broadest terms, was almost central to the educational program proposed.

The Anti-intellectual Nature of the Model. The model of child development had little to say about intellectual development and, in fact, minimized the role of the intellect. The model was anti-intellectual in the sense that Rousseau's model was. The model assumed that somehow the good features of the intellect will shine forth in maturity, if only childhood permits the intellect to unfold, like a flower unfolding from a bud. The training of the intellect was hardly a matter to be undertaken during childhood and Hall even expressed fears that attempt to encourage intellectual development in the young might blight development. Physical development was vastly more important than any attempt to produce mental development. The sterile elementary school curriculum proposed by Hall is a model of dull disciplined routine. Nevertheless, out of the adolescent there is believed to emerge an elegant and mature intellect.

Hall took the position that most races never develop beyond the adolescent stage. He believed, as so many of his contemporaries believed, that the Caucasians of Western European origin were the only humans who had achieved a high level of intellectual development. He also conceded that evolution was a continuing process, and the human species might someday evolve a race of superhumans with superhuman intellectual powers. He was not optimistic about that possibility in that he viewed Western civilization as pocked with marks of degeneracy, a view also held by Karl Pearson and many other of his contemporaries. Hall believed that intellectual improvement could take place through the application of eugenic measures, including the sterilization of the mentally retarded, the insane, and habitual criminals. He did concede that the first offender criminal might be an otherwise normal individual.

The Genetic and Mechanical Features of the Model. The determinants of development within the Hall model are the hereditary mechanisms. Heredity was, for him, a form of memory, and that memory of the species history resulted in the developing individual living through species history, but in a contemporary environment. The entire pattern of psychological development was controlled by the mechanism of heredity. The environment may frustrate the normal pattern of development and cause abnormalities of behavior in the adult but, like Rousseau's *Émile*, the ingrained nature of the human must be given opportunities to unfold. The process of unfolding was strictly mechanical. There was absolutely no place in the model for the individual to take hold of his own development and to give it direction. The model did not emphasize learning, and, hence does not make provision for active intervention in the developmental process.

Hall's Impact on Education

Hall was certainly known to teachers throughout the United States during the years when his major works were appearing early in the century. His works were widely cited and discussed in journals distributed to teachers. One suspects that rigid drill-oriented teachers at the elementary level found comfort in his doctrine that children at that level should have their work in basic skills highly routinized. These same teachers probably forgot about what Hall had to say about the importance of free play and the value of acquiring real skill in the manipulation of real objects. Hall had emphasized Pestalozzi's dictum "no knowledge without skill," but little of that influenced the schools. Materials designed for the training of teachers in child study also included considerable material from the work of Hall and his students, and Hall was recognized as the leading synthesizer of the material. However, those in education who stressed intellectual development were far from happy with the developments that were taking place at Clark University. Neither Thorndike nor Judd had a good word to say about Hall and ignored him in their writings. Even William Torrey Harris, always attempting to give encouragement to new ideas, gave Hall only footnote status when he came to write his *Psychological Foundations of Education* (1898). Hall was identified correctly by his academic contemporaries as anti-intellectualistic. The time for the growth of the impact of Hall's anti-intellectualism was to come after World War I, when the U.S. Office of Education became the chief sponsor and proponent of what was then called "adjustment" education. That movement must have found far more comfort in Hall's view of the nature of childhood than in Dewey's views with which it has been mistakenly associated. The recapitulation theory, and its emphasis on emotional and physical development as a precursor of intellectual development, was quite unacceptable to those who viewed education as an instrument for intellectual growth.

Hall also provided some groundwork for those working in clinical psychology to have some minimal impact on education. Reference is made here to such writers from the psychoanalytic field as Karen Horney, Melanie Klein and Anna Freud. Whatever impact these writers had was completely minimal in that their ideas hardly entered the mainstream of educational literature and the magazine articles that teachers read. Hall wrote articles in such widely read periodicals as the *Forum, Good Housekeeping, Mother's Magazine, The School and Home, Harper's Magazine*, and others. Through such publications his voice echoed the prejudices of the day, including the view that society should seek to improve itself through an elite taking charge, and the genetic stock should be improved through a program of eugenics. Hall, like his other most distinguished contemporaries in the field of psychology, worked hard to have his ideas accepted among those teaching and administering education.

It is easy to arrive at a snap judgment of Hall's work and conclude that his central ideas were basically unsound. His form of recapitulation theory certainly was, but it has led to some more sophisticated forms of recapitulation theory on the modern scene, which are intellectually oriented, rather than anti-intellectual. Hall did help develop the field of research on the psychology of childhood with originality and imagination. He recognized in a way that had not been recognized before that what children think is important, and should be studied. Hall was able to bring to teachers and parents the idea that the child's point of view must be taken into account. Earlier generations had viewed the child's point of view as quite unimportant. Hall represented a new departure in terms of approach.

On the other hand, Hall's contribution as a theoretician is quite minimal. Like most of his contemporaries, including Thorndike and Watson, there is just the most flimsy intellectual structure that ties theory to the research on which it is supposedly based. The relationship of Hall's recapitulation theory to Darwinian theory is little more than a metaphor. Hall's work suffers from overgeneralization, but many would say that psychologists of a half century later also produced work that suffered from the same defect. Nevertheless, Hall's theory of recapitulation did not just fade away. It has now been revived in a much more acceptable format than Hall's. The new format ties it to intellectual development, but the new recapitulation theory is not a strong theory. History does not show clearly the kind of intellectual progression over the centuries that the child shows. Sometimes there is a quite unclear and dim picture of such a progression, but when one grasps such a glimpse, one is still left wondering whether the misty picture was real or a mere figment of the imagination.

Despite the extreme weakness of Hall's position, he was, nevertheless, a man of influence in his day, and one is tempted to attribute to him the strong element of anti-intellectualism that had impact on education, particularly during the 1920's. Other champions of anti-intellectualism emerged to keep his movement alive after he died, but none had the academic stature and international prestige that he had.

OTHER APPROACHES TO CHILD DEVELOPMENT

Montessori's Ordered Subject Matter

Although Hall's attempt to guide education through research on child development had considerable impact in the United States, there was at least one other notable attempt to do that, the impact of which was worldwide. Maria Montessori (1870-1952) represents by far the most notable attempt to do just that. Montessori was not a research worker herself, but she did have access to the most recent medical literature on child development and was impressed with what she had read. She was highly critical of the European school of anthropometry which had attempted to design school furniture scientifically, with the net result that the child became a slave to the system. She saw such a "scientific" approach to education as resulting in the preservation of decadence, a problem that has not disappeared. However, she was impressed with the work of Edouard Seguin who worked with what today we would call mentally handcapped children. Seguin had understood the physical process of development in physiological terms. He understood that development called for a progression of coordinations of the muscles and also sensory development, and he planned a program for the mentally handicapped children that took them through such a progression of physical development. He realized, as Hall had, that physical development was intimately related to psychological development, and he also realized that there was a certain sequence of development that all children had to pass through. He was not a devotee of recapitulation theory. Montessori saw in Seguin's work a basic model for instruction of normal children. She had had experience teaching in special education programs in both London and Paris, where she had acquired some skepticism concerning the way in which children were classified for such programs.

Montessori's great opportunity to develop her own program came when she was invited to establish what today would be called a day care center for children in one of the worst slums of Rome. There she established the Casa dei Bambini.

Her program for the school follows, to some degree, the physiological developmental model of Edouard Seguin, but, in many respects, the influence of the German school of experimental psychology is far more obvious. On the very first page of *The Montessori Method* (New York: Schoken, 1964 [tr. 1912]), Montessori acknowledges her debt to Weber, Fechner and Wundt, and one does not have to read far into the book to see how much she had been influenced by the new German experimental psychology. For example, a central feature of the curriculum she designed involved what she called the "education of the senses." Today, it would be called the training of perceptual processes. Montessori showed through the design of her curriculum that she was familiar with the basic ideas of the German psychologists such as stimulus differentiation, threshold, form perception, and so forth. She also clearly understood that sensory education had to involve more than vision and hearing. She claimed that the educational materials she used looked very much like "psychometric" material (p. 167), and, in fact, they could have come directly out of the laboratory of Wundt or Fechner. They consisted of quite formal materials, she referred to as stimuli, to which the child was to make a response. She also used graded series of stimuli, much like those that Fechner used.

Despite the emphasis of Montessori on sensory training, she also understood that mere exposure did not produce learning, but that a response to the materials was necessary. To some degree she accepted the motor theory of thinking of the day and, like Hall, believed that muscular development must be a prime objective of elementary education. She called the latter "muscular education." One can understand her acceptance of the idea that muscular development was essential for intellectual development, for there was no alternative theory that had any credibility at that time.

Another important feature of the Montessori materials was that they represented a graded series in terms of complexity. Here again the influence of the new German psychology is obvious. In the Wundt laboratory tasks had been analyzed in terms of complexity, often for the purpose of identifying tasks at a suitable level of complexity for undertaking particular experiments. Montessori took over the concept of graded perceptual tasks in the design of her curriculum, and made the correct assumption that each task in a series could be a prerequisite for a more complex task.

Although Montessori's curriculum was solidly rooted in the new experimental psychology, Montessori also made assumptions about human nature that were derived from her personal philosophy. Thus the child is viewed as a free and independent being, and that freedom and independence has to be respected. In keeping with this philosophy she was one of the earliest to dispose of fixed furniture in the classroom. She deplored available school furniture, designed after careful anthropometric studies of the dimensions of children. She viewed such supposedly scientifically designed furniture as a device to make the child a prisoner of the teacher. Freedom of movement was an essential ingredient for her program, yet, the teacher did exert indirect control over the child, by drawing the child's attention to particular "stimuli" and eliciting appropriate "responses" from the child. Montessori assumed that the stimuli were sufficiently interesting that merely directing the attention of the child to the stimuli would result in sustained activity in relation to the objects presented. Although the materials emphasized form rather than content, they were attractive and seem to have functioned in the manner expected.

In many respects the Montessori curriculum is one of the best examples of the development of an educational product, to use a modern term, through the application of major scientific ideas of the day. The survival of the materials over the best part of a century is testimony to the persuasiveness of the logical arguments and the scientific ideas on which they were based. One wonders whether any curriculum produced today will survive as many years.

Gesell's Physiological Model

Although this chapter has focused on Hall and Montessori, and their students, there were others who were initiating work on child development in novel directions. The work on infant development, begun with Dieterich Tiedemann at the start of the nineteenth century, was not followed up by others for many decades. Few thought that the infant was worth studying, though not all thought that way. Charles Darwin studied the development of behavior in his own infant during its first year of life. Such studies had little impact because of the view that infants were uninteresting objects, who learned what they had to learn with little adult intervention, and who were incapable of profiting from organized forms of instruction. Only in our present century has there been widespread recognition that the experiences of infancy and early childhood may be of vital importance to the rest of life. Even the classic work of Arnold Lucius Gesell (1880-1961) had relatively little impact on such practical matters as the running of schools. Nevertheless, a short statement about the work of Gesell is included because he influenced parents and the informal education provided in the home.

Gesell began his adult work as a psychologist. He was a student of G. Stanley Hall at Clark University, where he first became interested in child development. While at Clark, he wrote a book together with his wife, Beatrice Chandler Gesell, on *The Normal Child and Primary Education* (1912). The book shows a very strong influence of Hall, particularly in its emphasis on biological inheritance, which was to play such an important part in Gesell's later theorizing. The volume lacks the meticulous base of empirical observation that characterized Gesell's later work. In many ways it is a common sense volume, despite its claim to have a scientific base. It was the last work of Gesell that focused on elementary education.

He founded the Clinic of Child Development at Yale University in 1911, but then decided that medical training was essential for understanding child development. He completed the work for the M.D. in 1915. The prime focus of Gesell's work was on the retarded child and the diagnosis of the sources of retardation at an early age, but, as his work progressed, he became convinced that the study of the normal child was of crucial importance for understanding the retarded. His work then became centered on the description of the developmental pattern of the normal child.

The Gesell clinic and laboratory was an early user of film technique for recording child behavior, and many millions of feet of film recorded the behavior of children. Indeed, nobody has ever filmed as much child behavior as Gesell filmed.

The Gesell clinic produced norms for behavior of infants and children, and these became a center of interest for middle-class parents. Gesell warned the public that the norms of behavior should not be taken as standards that all children should meet, but his warnings were of little avail. The norms were widely used by parents, who believed that these provided a means of determining whether the child was or was not normal. Undoubtedly, many parents drilled their children on the criterion tasks to reassure themselves that they had a normal child.

Teachers, and educators outside of colleges, paid little attention to the work of Gesell. He received none of the publicity in educational journals and magazines that was given to Thorndike, Judd, or Hall. One suspects that the physiological orientation of Gesell's theorizing may have turned off his potential audience in education. Perhaps also, the heyday of the normative work of Gesell came at a time when people in education were rejecting normative approaches to the study of the child. The Progressive Education Movement was at its height in the 1930's when his work was having the peak of its impact on the middle-class parent. Gesell had nothing of the flamboyant style of Hall, and neither did he have Hall's desire to play the role of a social reformer. He also did not have Montessori's skill of converting scientific knowledge into useful educational products and procedures. Thus Gesell's influence on education was inevitably limited.

THE PERIOD OF DECLINE

The late part of the nineteenth century showed an extraordinary and rapid rise of research on child development. Enthusiasm was widespread throughout Western Europe and the North American Continent. Parents, teacher, and academicians engaged in child development research, for anyone could become an expert. All one had to do was observe children and record the results of observation. Perhaps research has to begin that way, and the collectors of unsophisticated observations have to learn through this process the kinds of expertise needed to undertake research with durable results. The early research on child development was contaminated with myth. One of the age old myths about child development was that the young child had little intellectual capability, and that childhood was purely a period of growth. The result of this contamination of research with this myth was the anti-intellectual approach to child development, which had little appeal in a culture that emphasized intellectual growth. A consequence of this was an inevitable decline in concern for the area. By the time of World War I, the rising stars of Thorndike and Judd were to draw attention away from the research that Hall promoted. Both Thorndike and Judd had a certain amount of contempt for research of a descriptive nature which added to the decline.

A further factor that contributed to the decline of child development research throughout the first half of the present century was the nature of the theorizing on which it was based and which permeated it. Hall's Darwinian and biological approach seemed remote from what common sense said should be at the core of education. Gesell's physiological approach was even more remote. Common sense was, perhaps, right. Darwinian biology and physiology may well be inappropriate bases for building a theory of child development on which a useful theory of education can be based. Indeed, Darwinian theory, though an excellent biological theory in its age, seems to have damaged rather than contributed to education over the century during which it has been applied.

Apathy with respect to research on child development in the United States continued until the 1960's. Then came an extraordinary revival, partly produced through the invention of new techniques for the study of infant behavior, and partly through the growing interest in the work of Jean Piaget. The revival was focused on intellectual development and led to suggestions of how the child caretaker might promote the development of intellectual growth. This new start seems to have had a more solid foundation, and a more acceptable purpose, than that proposed by Hall.

PART IV

Some Direct Approaches to Educational Problems

Those who attempted to produce educational innovations, through laboratory studies, achieved notable success in changing education in the early part of the present century. Despite that success, the approach of laboratory psychologists to educational reform had its critics. Particularly critical were some professors of pedagogy who claimed that schools and classrooms should be studied directly. They believed that much more could be accomplished by a direct approach to educational problems than through the indirect approach advocated notably by Thorndike and Hall, and to a lesser extent by Judd. The professors of pedagogy took the quite defensible position that they could bring their expert knowledge to bear directly on the problems of the schools. What had to be done, they claimed, was to go out into the schools and discover what was happening there. Once the facts were collected, then recommendations could be made for improving education. The argument was persuasive and hundreds, if not thousands, of studies were undertaken of classroom teaching, mainly by doctoral students of education.

This part of the book examines some of the studies of schools and teaching that were undertaken in the first half of the present century. In the judgment of the author, the most significant of those studies are the two reviewed in the next chapter. These two studies show how the school can become an instrument for changing the entire economic structure of a community. The two studies have an imagination and boldness of incomparable quality which should surely give them a meritorious place in any history of educational research. They represent a frontier of research, where the discipline of economics touches the art of education and, indeed, represent the only direct influence that economists have had on educational practice.

The second chapter discusses the familiar studies of teaching that have appeared a thousand times over. The chapter is brief, despite the large number of studies that have been conducted on events in the classroom. The massive effort to investigate classrooms may not have demonstrated how to conduct a more effective schoolroom, but collectively led to some important knowledge of a different kind.

CHAPTER 10

Economic Research and Attempts to Change the Economic Base of Communities

THE DISCIPLINE OF ECONOMICS AND EDUCATION

The relationship of the discipline of economics to education has been a very different one from the relationship of psychology. For about a century there have been leading psychologists who have devoted their entire lives to the study of problems related to education, as much of this volume demonstrated. In contrast, the great historical names associated with the development of economics have had hardly even a marginal interest in that part of society that constitutes the educational enterprise. Furthermore, although numerous psychologists have had appointments in schools and colleges of education since the start of the century, economists have not had comparable positions. Indeed, Harold F. Clark (1899-), professor at Teachers College for nearly half a century, had the unique distinction of being a professional economist appointed to a college of education. The administrations of schools and colleges of education saw little value in the employment of professional economists.

Economics was also separated from education in another respect. Although many psychologists, appointed to academic departments of psychology, wrote extensively about educational problems and often undertook research in educational settings, economists in comparable positions had virtually no interest in education. The professional interests of economists did not include anything closely related to education. Thus, although psychologists adapted their psychological theories to account for the impact of education on the socialization and intellectual development of the child, economists only very rarely explored the use of economic theory for understanding how education came to be financed, and how that investment produced a later economic return. During the period covered by this volume, no theory of the economics of education developed that was in any way comparable to the many psychological theories that attempted to account for the development of the child through schooling.

School Finance and Economics

The absence of research in education by professional economists is demonstrated by the fact that the *Review of Educational Research,* published since 1930, and covering an immense range of research topics, has never had a complete section on economic research related to education. The latter journal has produced issues that provide a superficial resemblance to the application of economic theory to the understanding of educational phenomena, but this resemblance is only superficial. For example, the seventh issue of the *Review,* published in 1932 covered the topics of *finance* and *administration.* The authors were mainly individuals in colleges of education who functioned as experts on school administration and included such well known names in that field as Arthur B. Moehlman, Carter Alexander, Ward G. Reeder, and Floyd W. Reeves. The issue of the *Review* did not include a single professional economist, though many of the problems discussed bordered on problems that lie near to the heart of economics. In the latter category are such problems as the equalization of education across school districts and across states and regions, and the measurement of educational need. The latter topics were not of focal importance in the document, much of which centered on such practical matters as the establishment of school budget categories and the practicality of financing education in various ways, and the feasibility of various taxation plans. Much of this work had more to do with the identification of problems, rather than with their solution. The basic underlying philosophy seems to have been that once the problems were identified, they would then become amenable to solution. History has not justified that optimism.

The kind of fact finding displayed in the issue on finance and administration, was viewed as research by that generation of educational research workers. Theory had no function within that particular framework of thought. There is, of course, a place for fact finding, but until the facts are incorporated into a framework of theory, in such a way that they have organization and coherence, the facts have only the most limited value. Information collected on the financing of schools was never incorporated into a general framework of economic theory by the hundreds of students who sweated out dissertations in departments of educational administration. Yet, there were a few who were uncomfortable with the absence of economic principles from the field of school finance. Paul Mort (1894-1962) was one who voiced such concern.

Later issues of the *Review of Educational Research* were also devoted to finance and administration as the topic came up in the cycle of issues. The basic approach to finance in these subsequent publications remained very much the same for the next twenty years. One might, perhaps, blame the editors of the *Review* for omitting to report other more productive approaches, due to their parochial vision, but that would not be a fair charge. The absence of economic research of the kind that economists might undertake is all too obvious. This is evident from a perusal of the 1941 first edition of the *Encyclopedia of Educational Research.*

In the first edition of Walter S. Monroe's *Encyclopedia of Educational Research,* research related to education by economists was notably absent. The volume did contain a long article by William G. Carr (1901-) on school finance. Carr's background, one should note, had not been in economics and neither had it been in school administration. He had spent a year as a teacher after graduating from Stanford University in 1924. He then became involved in the California Teachers Association and from there moved to the National Education Association, where he spent much of his life developing it as a teacher-oriented organization. He played a central role in the development of the United Nations Educational, Scientific, and Cultural Organization. His approach to the subject of school finance was obviously not that of the economist, and yet it represented the approach of the practical school administrator of the time. The concluding section of Carr's article enumerated problems that need to be investigated but none of these touched on economic theory in relation to school finance. That is hardly surprising, for experts on finance have even in modern times received an entirely different background and training from that received by professional economists.

The first edition of the *Encyclopedia* did contain an article by Harold Clark on the money value of education. The editors, apparently, did not conceptualize the article as a contribution on economics. Since the article was expanded in the second edition of the *Encyclopedia,* only the expanded version will be considered here.

Economics Enters the Educational Scene

The 1952 revised edition of the *Encyclopedia* included the first articles that could be viewed as a contribution from economics. Another had only marginal significance in this respect. The latter article *Economic Cycles and Education* by Jesse B. Sears (1876-c.1945) carried a suggestion in its title that economists were at last beginning to study problems of education, but much of the work reviewed was historical rather than economic, focusing on the effects that depressions had had on education through the previous century. Depressions have deep impact on every aspect of education, besides the financial, for they may influence educational philosophy and the values that underlie the curriculum. The great depression of the 1930's also had an influence on the courses in which college students enrolled, with many students seeking to mold a college program into a vocational training program. These influences of economic conditions during the depression on education represent psychological studies, rather than economic studies.

Nearer to the approach of the economist was the short article in the same edition of the *Encyclopedia* on the topic *economic aspects of education.* The article by Harold F. Clark was an expansion of the article he had written in the first edition of the *Encyclopedia* on the *money value of education.* His article, covering the entire area of the economic aspects of education, was less than 2 pages, a fact which suggests that the editors of the *Encyclopedia* did not think much work had been done in the field or that it was of only marginal importance. Unlike those who wrote on school finance, Clark was a professional economist, having studied economics both at Columbia University as a student and having taken postdoctoral work at the London School of Economics. Although Clark spent most of his professional life as a professor of educational economics at Teachers College, he was extremely active in all kinds of professional organizations related to education, where he was much in demand because of the unique position he held in the academic world. If an organization needed advice on some economic problem related to education, there was nobody else to whom they could turn.

The Clark article in the *Encyclopedia* summarized the little that had been done on the economics of education. He pointed out that Horace Mann had written extensively, and perhaps speculatively, on the economic value of education both in his 1841 and his 1848 annual reports. Mann did not have carefully collected data to back up his contentions, but his arguments were quite tight and persuasive. Attempts to study this problem systematically were first undertaken in the early part of the present century, though the studies were generally filled with flaws.

The great difficulty in the conduct of such studies is the equating of groups that are exposed to different amounts of education. Although hundreds of studies have been undertaken in this area, none are beyond criticism in this respect, and, probably cannot be. Nevertheless, evidence from many directions converges on the conclusion that education has an immense impact on the economic status of a community. Even a small increase in the level of education in a third world country, for example, might be expected to produce a large economic gain over subsequent decades in terms of the production of goods and, without such an increase in education, little gain might be expected. Economists have also pointed out that when training programs are expanded, to produce an oversupply of workers with a particular skill, then the wage of those workers tends to drop and the oversupply produces a disruption in the system. Relationships between education and economic conditions are complex. Nevertheless, the evidence is clear that differences in economic productivity between nations is far more a result of differences in education than differences in natural resources.

Clark held the view that, in order for education to have maximum economic benefit, it had to be free. A person, who drops out of school because the expense of staying in school is too high, may be depriving the society of a person with fully developed skills, and hence, lowering the productivity of that society. Clark's view was that only when education was completely free, and with no hidden expense, could it contribute to a maximum extent to economic development. Clark's essential argument is that a free market place should determine who is trained for what. Clark proposed the general principle that education should be increased so long as there was a corresponding increase in the output of goods and services that was greater than the cost of education. Such a principle would be contested by those who view education as contributing far more than goods and services.

Clark also worked on the issue of how vocational education should be distributed across different occupations. Although he concluded that the distribution should be such that it would maximize the output of goods and services, the problem of maximizing the output would be a very difficult mathematical problem to solve, even if all the data necessary for solving it were available.

The concept of maximizing the output of goods and services as a goal for educational planning was used by other writers in the same era. John Kelley Norton (1893-unknown) wrote the volume *Education and Economic Well-Being in American Democracy* in 1940 for the Educational Policies Commission of the National Education Association, and that volume stressed that (p. 126) "from the economic standpoint the quantity and quality of schooling should be determined primarily by the contribution it makes in increasing total national income." The committee that approved the Norton volume included many of the best known leaders of education of that age. The depression years must surely have left those who lived through them with a deep awareness of the importance of goods and services to the achievement of the good life. Other volumes produced by the Educational Policies Commission placed heavy emphasis on the related issue of expanding vocational education. Although this series of publications bore deep marks left by the depression, and the idea that the good life was to be achieved through expanding the availability of goods and services, other goals of education were not completely neglected.

Economic Policies and Education

The thought of economists, reflected in the previous pages, probably had little impact on education. Vocational education expanded in the years following the depression, but not because of the argument that this would expand the available goods and services. The supporting argument for such expansion was more frequently that such training would relieve unemployment or that it satisfied a demand for training. School administrators did not attempt to set quotas for training in particular fields in terms of any concept of maximizing goods and services. Other immediate considerations seemed to be of far greater importance. The economist's view of education as a mere tool for generating goods and services was a narrow one that had little appeal to those responsible for formulating educational policies.

ATTEMPTS TO CHANGE THE ECONOMIC BASE OF COMMUNITIES THROUGH EDUCATION

Economists have not generally been able to conduct economic experiments in order to provide data to support or reject their theories. The field of education offers some possibility for studying the economic impact of education in that experiments can be undertaken with small isolated communities in order to determine whether changes in the school program can change economic conditions. One such experiment was carried out under the direction of Harold F. Clark and will be considered later in the chapter. First, attention must be turned to an economic experiment in an educational context that was initiated with the sponsorship of the Federal Bureau of Education before the beginning of the present century.

Educating People to Use New Resources

Nearly a hundred years ago, the Federal Bureau of Education became involved in one of the most remarkable research and development enterprises found in the annals of educational research. The term *research and development* was not used in connection with it, for the activity involved had not yet been dignified with any such label. Nevertheless, the project involved both research and development, and involved the collection of extremely interesting data over a period of nearly half a century.

The enterprise found its seeds in the work of Sheldon Jackson

(1834-1900), one of the remarkable men of the last century. Jackson had spent much of his life as a Presbyterian minister and missionary, but he was a man of adventuresome disposition, and of extremely broad knowledge. He traveled extensively through the northwest of the continent. Among his unusual accomplishments was an exploration of the Yukon Valley, to determine for the United States government the possibility of developing the region agriculturally. In 1879 he was appointed to a special commission to study the condition of the natives in Southeast Alaska. In 1883 he established the first canoe service for mail in Alaska. In 1884 he introduced the first public school system into Alaska, and in 1885 became the first federal agent for education in Alaska, a position that he retained until his death. In that position he wrote a yearly section on Alaskan education for the Commissioner of Education's report. What has been said here reflects only a few of Jackson's remarkable accomplishments during a remarkable life.

In 1890 Jackson reported to the Commissioner of Education the deplorable economic conditions that existed in Alaska. American whalers had contributed much to the destruction of the Alaskan economy in that the basic food supply, consisting of whales, walruses, seals, and small fur-bearing animals, had been virtually destroyed. In addition, the introduction of the rifle to the natives of Alaska had resulted in the almost total destruction of many sources of food, including the caribou.

Jackson was impressed by the fact that the natives of neighboring Siberia, living in very similar environment, had a relatively thriving economy. At least, nobody on the Siberian side of the Bering Straits was starving. Jackson saw that a properly managed ecology would permit the natives of Alaska to derive from it the necessities of life. He proposed that reindeer be introduced into Alaska, to provide immediate relief for the food shortage, and as a possible basis for providing a permanent and prosperous industry. Apparently, the natives of Eastern Siberia had a prosperous reindeer business and Jackson viewed the reindeer as a new source of Alaskan economic vitality.

The Commissioner of Education was fully in support of Jackson's proposal and urged the Congress to appropriate money for the introduction of reindeer into the territory, but Congress was slow to act. In the meantime, the public press became interested in the idea and proposed that the program be initially funded through public subscription. The sum of $2,146 was raised, and 16 reindeer were purchased in Siberia in the summer of 1891 and were shipped to Alaska. They survived the winter in Alaska without any difficulty and, as a result of this small success, 171 reindeer were purchased the following year and were shipped to Port Clarence. Then, in 1893 Congress at last voted $6,000 for the enterprise.

The early work on the project involved only the introduction of the reindeer, but this involved many difficulties. Those who shipped the animals had little conception of how to care for them on-board ship, and on many shipments nearly all the reindeer died during transportation. The animals had been domesticated by the Siberian natives, and there should have been little difficulty in transporting them, but they were crowded into hot ship holds without adequate water and food, and under unsanitary conditions.

The success of the enterprise depended upon the bringing about of major changes in the way of life of the Alaskan Eskimo. These people, unlike the Siberians, were not herders who lived in villages, but their way of life seems to have been more nomadic. In order for the Eskimo to develop the new reindeer resource offered, groups of Eskimos had to learn to have quite fixed abodes. The program required a total reeducation of the population. To some degree the economic incentive was there, though the Eskimo at the turn of the century was probably not as badly off as he may have appeared to be from Jackson's viewpoint.

The herding of reindeer is not a simple matter that a person can learn in a few minutes. Almost every part of the reindeer is useful for some purpose. Most of the males could be killed for food, and the skins could provide clothing. The horns had been used by the Siberian natives for the making of runners for sleds. The females provide a highly nourishing milk which has to be diluted for human use, and the milk can be converted into butter and cheese by those who know how. In addition, reindeer trained to pull sleds and obey commands provide excellent transportation. All these goods and services could be produced by reindeer who lived off the lichens on the tundra and who needed no food supplements. However, to use these resources, the native Alaskans needed training.

Jackson solved the problem of training by bringing in herders from Siberia and Lapland. The plan was to assign a small herd to a native, instruct him in its use, and then supervise him for a few years. When he became proficient in the herding of reindeer, he was allowed to keep the herd, less the number of animals with which he had started. The number taken back was then to be used to start another native as a herder. Thus, through a combination of education in herding and the provision of basic resources, a man was provided with the opportunity of becoming independent and self-supporting.

In 1902 the Russian government withdrew its permission to transport reindeer to Alaska, but by that time the Alaskan herd had grown to nearly 5,000 and was doubling in size every 3 years. The imported instructors were becoming progressively of less importance, for the government introduced a policy of requiring each herder to have an apprentice, who would ultimately become an independent herder.

The apprentice system became widespread in 1907 when the Congress introduced a provision whereby all government-owned herds should be turned over to the natives or to missions as soon as possible. The missions were to hold the herds in trust for the natives, and the income from the herds held in trust was to be used to support the apprentice herders. The entire stock of reindeer in an area came under the supervision and ultimate control of the district leader.

The decision to turn over the entire industry to the natives seems to have been a successful one. Eskimos, engaged in reindeer herding, began to organize and held their first convention at Igloo in 1915. And Eskimo Reindeer Men's Association was formed in 1917, and by that time the herds had reached nearly 100,000 head. In the meantime, other aspects of the industry had developed. As early as 1909, the Department of Agriculture had taken steps to facilitate the export of meat, hides, and horns, and in 1911 the first shipment of these products reached Seattle. There seemed to be almost no limit to the number of head that could be raised on the Alaskan tundra. It might take as much as 100 acres to support a single reindeer, but there were millions of acres available.

The Bureau of Education remained in charge of instruction of the herders. In a bulletin on the subject published by the Bureau (1919, No. 40), the apprenticeship system is described. The apprentices were taken on by the herders for four years; for each year they received, in succession, 6, 8, 10 and 12 reindeer. At the end of the four years, if the apprentice had served satisfactorily, he became a herder himself, obtaining a herd either from a mission or a school district. He was then required to take on an apprentice for four years, and, thus, an expansion of the system was ensured.

The government continued to regulate the industry to some degree. No female reindeer could be killed without government permission. Government agents and teachers had to be particularly concerned with preventing native herders from selling their herds. To some extent, this was controlled by prohibiting the sale of female reindeer. Since 80 percent of the herds were female, this regulation provided strong control.

Frank Dufresne, Governor of Alaska after it achieved statehood, has described in his colorful autobiography his visit to a reindeer camp shortly after 1920 (*My Way Was North*, 1966). The reindeer industry at that time had almost reached its peak and the animals numbered near to a quarter of a million head. At the camp, the Eskimos were in the process of dividing up the new reindeer among about 50 herders. The animals were to be marked with slots cut in their ears to indicate ownership, and the young bulls were to be transformed into steers. In addition, some of the reindeer were to be slaughtered for meat and other products. The Eskimos had fashioned cold-storage facilities by digging into the tundra, 20 feet down, where the temperature was 24°F. Racks had been built to hold the carcasses in permanent cold storage, though the temperature was not low enough to hold the meat in good condition over long periods. At that stage of the development of the industry, the production of meat far exceeded the needs of the Eskimo, and the plan was to develop an export industry. The difficulty of doing this was beyond that which could be developed through the simple educational program that had brought the reindeer industry to the point of success that it had already achieved. What the industry needed were capital and equipment that would permit the handling of very large quantities of meat, the storing of the meat at low temperatures, or the canning of meat. The industry was not able to attract that kind of capital from the free-enterprise system of the United States. The export of reindeer meat never became an important factor in the Alaskan economy.

The reindeer project, for its first 40 years, was the most remarkable example of how a well-designed educational program can transform a society. The initial investment in the purchase of reindeer amounted to only a few thousand dollars, and most of the actual expenditure came from the education funds invested in both instruction and the administration of the program. The program also had built into it a clear criterion of success, namely, the size of the reindeer herds. William Torrey Harris, Commission of Education during the early years of the program, used to say that his most important task was to herd reindeer in Alaska. Although he would make this remark as a humorous reflection of his job, the fact remains that the project was one of the most important ones that he administered, and one of the most brilliantly imaginative.

Data on the reindeer project have continued to be collected down to the present time. The massiveness of the data is reflected in the fact that when the Institute of Arctic Biology at the University of Alaska prepared an annotated bibliography on the subject in 1977, hundreds of items were reviewed in the 166-page document (*A Selected Annotated Bibliography of Sources on Reindeer Herding in Alaska* [Occasional Publications on Northern Life, No. 2], compiled by Richard Olav Stern). The bibliography documents well the decline of the industry after 1930. Many problems produced this decline. There seems to have been a selling-off of the herds to nonnatives. Then there was a migration of the native Alaskans to the cities. The items listed in the bibliography emphasize again and again the difficulty experienced by the industry in the attraction of capital. The main decline seems to have taken place during the years 1930-1950. During this period, herders found it necessary to restrict production of reindeer products because of the lack of a broad market through which they could be distributed. The local market had a very limited capacity to use the products. Thus, an Eskimo living on a range capable of supporting 200 reindeer might have only half that number, because that number produced all the meat and hides that he could sell. A further problem arose as the white settlers in Alaska took over the herds from the Eskimos. Indeed, by mid-century the latter problem had become acute, and the Eskimos had virtually ceased to own reindeer. In addition, the new white managers attempted to squeeze every dollar they could out of their investment, and the result was overgrazing and damage to the range. Indeed, the new owners thoroughly mismanaged the industry. In order to remedy this problem, the Bureau of Indian Affairs purchased all reindeer from the whites in order to bring them back into the hands of the natives. Under the new system, an attempt was made to locate new herds near Eskimo villages so that there would be an easily accessible market for the products, and so that the products would provide the necessities of life for the inhabitants. The Bureau was also concerned about the old problem of giving the native herders access to a larger market than that provided locally. This would have involved the development of roads and the machinery needed to transport, store, and market the products. Once again, the necessary capital was not forthcoming.

The full revival of the industry was not possible, for the world was changing. Eskimos were migrating to the cities and abandoning their traditional way of life on the range. The new city-bred generations, reared on an intellectual diet of Dick and Jane, had no conception of the life that the open range could provide. The new generation of educators had no understanding of the immense impact that a suitable educational program might have on the native Alaskan economy. Even the federal government had not learned any lessons from Alaska's past, for when the government produced a set of readers specifically for use among Eskimo children, they were little more than Dick and Jane readers using beavers as the main characters in one of the books. What the new program lacked most was a man with the vision of a Sheldon Jackson.

Perhaps a main lesson to be learned from this most extraordinary effort on the part of educators to change an entire economy, through the instrument of education, is that a program cannot remain static. As times change, the program has to be modified or new programs have to be introduced. The economic problems also go beyond those that can be solved by education. Education does not directly create capital, and such an enterprise needs capital if it is to develop beyond a primitive stage. Also, all rural programs have difficulty in competing with the rather superficial glamour offered by life in the city.

There has been at least one other attempt to introduce a major change into the life of the Alaskan native through the introduction of a new means of earning a living. During the last decade, an effort was made to reintroduce the musk ox into the coastal economy of the Alaskan natives. This effort has come about largely through the work of John J. Teal, Jr., whose enterprise has been supported by the W. K. Kellogg Foundation and the University of Alaska.

John J. Teal was director of the Institute of Northern Agricultural Research in Vermont. In 1954 he became interested in studying the musk ox and developing the animal as a natural resource. Earlier in the century, the animal had become almost extinct. Hunters had found that they could virtually walk up to a herd and shoot every animal. The musk ox had become extinct in Alaska through this process by 1850, but fortunately some herds still existed in remote regions of Canada.

Eventually, the Canadian government gave the musk ox total protection. If it had not, the species would now be extinct.

The musk ox has immense potential for contributing to an arctic community, but one feature of the animal is more valuable than anything else it has to offer. That feature is the production of a wool of intensely fine quality, rivaling the cashmere of the goat. The wool, called *qiviut*, grows on the underside of the animal and is shed in thick clumps each spring. An animal may produce as much as 6 pounds, which may not seem much until one learns that an entire garment produced from it may weigh only a few ounces.

Teal has described his work on domesticating the musk ox and introducing it into the economy of Alaska in a fascinating article, "Domesticating the Wild and Woolly Musk Ox" (1970). In 1954 and 1955, Teal organized expeditions to the northern reaches of Canada, where a number of musk ox calves were captured and brought back to Vermont for study. After a decade of study, the staff of the institute concluded that the animals were suitable for domestication and provided a valuable product in their wool. Not only did the animals appear to be economically valuable, but they had the same kind of endearing qualities that make the porpoise loved by all except tuna fishermen. They are playful and love to engage in human games with balls and other paraphernalia. They develop an intense affection for their herders, even to the point of protecting them in the same way as a dog will protect its master. In addition, they have the extraordinary capacity of thriving on terrain which cannot support most other animals of that size. In captivity, they can produce a calf every year.

The establishment of the musk ox as an Eskimo industry in Alaska has involved all of the problems that were involved in the original establishment of the reindeer industry. The people had to be taught to herd the animals, but the musk ox is much easier to herd than the reindeer. The musk ox will stay within a short range of its herder and easily learns to come when called by its name. However, the use of the product requires that the natives acquire skills related to the spinning of the wool and the knitting of the spun product into items. Teal reported the development of marketing cooperatives and the development of a cottage industry. At the time when Teal was writing his article for the *National Geographic*, he reported that there were about 150 knitters in Alaska, and that a knitter could easily produce a scarf a week that would sell for $25 to wholesalers. The products were destined for a luxury market, very much as the Shetland Isles have developed a superlative woolen product famous throughout the world. The wool of the musk ox has one important advantage over the wool of the sheep in that it does not shrink when boiled.

The Appalachian Experience

Neither Sheldon Jackson nor William Torrey Harris nor those who exercised leadership later in the reindeer project thought of themselves as research and development workers, and yet their work constituted one of the most significant research and development projects not only of the last century, but of the present one. The project was a clear demonstration of the enormous impact of education on economic welfare that Horace Mann had spoken about a half-century earlier. The key to the project was education of the potential herders, but the schools and teachers of Alaska provided administrative support for the enterprise well into the present century. Only as the enterprise found independence from education did the enterprise decline, though there were factors other than the withdrawal from education which caused its demise. The project was also well designed in terms of modern concepts of evaluation, for the success of the enterprise could be measured in terms of the increase in the size of the herds once the initial few hundred head had been brought from Siberia. Modern evaluators might have introduced other criteria such as measurements of the extent to which the diet of the Eskimo in Alaska was favorably affected by the introduction of the reindeer. The principal developers of the project also had the advantage of not expecting results in 2 or 3 years. In modern times, the enterprise might have been funded for 3 years and then abandoned because of lack of results. The promoters of the reindeer project realized that the effectiveness of the enterprise could be evaluated effectively only after a rather long span of years. Sheldon Jackson died in 1900, after the project had been in progress for less than 10 years, but there were already signs that it was a success.

Few workers in modern times have had the vision of Sheldon Jackson in developing such far-reaching research and development projects in education, and most commissioners of education who followed Harris would not have had the initiative to give such ideas administrative support. Nevertheless, the field of intervention in the economics of a community through education has attracted at least one later significant enterprise.

During the 1930's, curricula materials showed a trend towards the practical, partly through the influence of the progressive education movement. Children in at least some schools were encouraged to study problems related to the improvement of their communities, and the field trip became established as a recognized educational technique. Some social studies materials encouraged children to obtain objective evidence of what was wrong with society. The curricular materials developed under the sponsorship of the Progressive Education Association showed this trend and provided many valuable suggestions for teachers. There were also attempts to develop reading materials that attempted to teach children how to improve their diet and solve some of their health problems. One such series of readers was developed by D. F. Folger, of West Georgia College. The West Georgia project included efforts to help communities develop cooperatives for the growing and canning of food. Folger's article, "We Venture in Teacher Education" (1945), provided some anecdotal material on the success of the enterprise, but hard evidence was lacking.

By far the most significant enterprise related to helping individuals help themselves economically during this period was the work of Maurice F. Seay (1901-   ), who worked closely with economist Harold F. Clark. Seay came to educational research through a career in educational administration. His first job after completing his bachelor's degree at Transylvania College in 1924 was that of superintendent of schools in Crab Orchard, Kentucky. Later, he became principal of the high school in Danville, Kentucky. An important advance in terms of the development of his ideas was his appointment to the educational division of the Tennessee Valley Authority, where he worked from 1934 to 1937. From that position he moved to the University of Kentucky in 1937, where he was Director of the Bureau of School Service for 9 years and where he conducted the significant work discussed in this chapter. As director, Seay was in charge of what became known as the Sloan Experiment in Kentucky, as well as other projects. When Seay worked with the Tennessee Valley Authority, he was in charge of setting up new educational programs to take care of the new communities that emerged as dams were built to produce hydroelectric power. These programs called for considerable vision, in that the people living in the communities could expect that their lives would be changed radically through the electrification of the area. The people in the communities had to be prepared to live in a technically oriented society, entirely different from the simple agrarian society in which their parents had lived. This led Seay to conceive of a program to help the rural poor in Eastern Kentucky, outside of the reach of the new Roosevelt programs. The program which Seay conceived is discussed here because of its potential significance, rather than in terms of any strong evidence available concerning its accomplishments. Although the program was originally developed with a quite well-worked-out method for discovering the impact of the educational program that the project introduced, the entry of America into World War II virtually precluded the completion of the evaluation study.

The focus of Seay's project, developed when he was at the University of Kentucky, was on the rehabilitation of rural communities in Eastern Kentucky through the use of education to stimulate self-help. Charles H. Judd, in his *Education and Social Progress* (1934), had considered the role that education should play in the improvement of conditions in Appalachia and had concluded that economic change and innovation were outside the scope of the schools. Indeed, Judd seems to have considered that the use of the school for economic change involved dangerous radicalism. Judd was wrong, for the kinds of changes proposed by Seay were extremely conservative in character. Seay believed that individuals should help themselves, a concept that has been the very core of conservative social reform. Nevertheless, individuals obviously had some difficulty in the initiation of the kind of self-help that would improve their lives, and Seay developed the idea that the school had to become the instrument through which the individual could be guided to help himself.

The first step in the Seay study was to identify four poor rural communities in the mountains of Eastern Kentucky that were essentially equivalent in size, economic status, and potential for development. Two communities were to be experimental communities and the others, the control. Then, both communities were surveyed to determine the economic status of individuals and families in the communities, to provide a base line from which changes could be measured. The survey provided data concerning the health, nutrition, housing, and clothing of the inhabitants and the natural resources of the community. Experts then reviewed the data and drew conclusions concerning the changes that the people needed to make in their ways of living in order to improve their standard of living. Then materials were designed, for use in schools, which would explain to children how to pursue the new lines of activities that would better their lives.

The essentials of the study are described in two bulletins issued by the Bureau of School Service, University of Kentucky. The first, by Maurice F. Seay and Harold F. Clark, was entitled *The School Curriculum and Economic Improvement* (1940) and described the Kentucky community in which the experiment was conducted, with particular emphasis on nutrition and health. The bulletin also described the kind of teaching found in the school at the start of the experiment. A film record of the teaching in the one-room school showed the children attempting to read *The Canterbury Tales*, and the teacher telling the story of the heroic boy who saved Holland from flooding by placing his arm in a dike. The film also showed the disinterested attitude of the children towards the entire school enterprise, and the boredom and listlessness of the students. Then the film showed the children eating the contents of their lunch pails, consisting of corn bread and pork fat. The children were undernourished and showed signs of scurvy from a lack of vitamin C.

On the basis of the data initially collected, Seay and his associates developed reading materials for the experimental schools. The plan was to develop reading materials for the first few grades that would tell the children about the changes that needed to be made in their way of life in order to improve their nutrition, health, and standard of living. For example, the study of the community by agricultural experts showed that the people were raising the wrong animals and crops to provide them with an adequate diet. They were attempting to raise pigs on hillsides that provided little for the animals to eat. The inhabitants had brought with them from their countries of origin the pig-farming enterprise, but what they should have been doing was to change their practice and raise goats that could live off the terrain. The community needed to change from a pig-rearing community to a goat-rearing community. The goats would not only provide meat, but would also yield milk and cheese and thrive well on the steep hillsides. Readers were developed which explained to children the advantages of raising goats and the techniques involved in the care of goats.

Altogether, 31 readers were produced together with a teacher's guide. The books were all related to one or another practical theme, and the practical themes all shared the common goal of improving the quality of life in the community. The books on the raising of goats represented one way of improving rural life. Other books focused on the development of a garden for the raising of vegetables. The initial survey had shown that the children in the community lacked vitamin C. Families could not afford to purchase citrus fruits, but conditions were ideally suited to the raising of tomatoes, and tomatoes could be canned for use in the winter months. The books for the children explained how a large part of their food needs could be provided by the raising of a vegetable garden, coupled with the use of canning. The hope was that the children would discuss with their parents what they had learned in school, and even that the parents would want to borrow the books to read. Some attempt was made to introduce into the school some of the actual activities described in the readers. Thus, the children planted seeds in boxes in the school and then watched the seedlings grow until they were large enough to plant outside as the spring weather became warmer. The books on how to raise a garden began with the very practical details of clearing the land of rubble and preparing the soil for planting. They then discussed planting and the thinning of the seedlings, the elimination of pests, and the final harvesting of the products. Further readers dealt with the preservation of the garden products for winter use. The latter materials included descriptions of the digging of a storage cellar in the hillside for root vegetables, the dehydration of vegetables, as well as the more conventional methods of canning.

The books suggested ways of raising animals other than goats to improve the diet. Several books dealt with the raising of chickens and included sections on the candling of eggs. Then there was a rather interesting book on the development of a fish pond on the farm. At that time the federal government would finance the building of a dam on a farm as a way to prevent erosion and as a means of providing irrigation. Once a dam had been developed, fish could be raised in the pond and the fish could supplement the diet of the farmer and his family. The reader discussed the development of fish ponds within the context of a father and his son undertaking just such a project. One suspects that the writer of the book hoped that the story would prompt the children to discuss the development of a fish pond with their parents.

The materials developed for the children also attempted to incorporate within them some of the more traditional activities such as singing, but the songs had a special twist. The song "She'll Be Comin' Round the Mountain" was converted into lines such as "She'll Be Cannin' Ripe Tomatoes When She Comes." The children were encouraged to develop other lines and other themes for the song. The songs collectively summarized much of the substantive knowledge related to nutrition that appeared in the other readers.

The plan for the program was to develop materials in the areas of health and nutrition, housing, and clothing, but most of the Kentucky materials pertained to the first category. One reader did deal with the matter of purchasing a farm, and the various agencies that would help in such an enterprise. The reader also explained how loans were obtained and how farms were purchased. Further chapters in the reader explained how the farmer could obtain help from various federal agencies in the working of his farm and in planning his crops and marketing them. Practical details were also outlined on how the United States Forest Service would help a landowner forest his property, virtually without cost. The book was an interface between the government and the people to be served.

The evaluation study conducted in relation to the enterprise involved an appraisal of the children in the experimental and control communities in the summer of 1940 and then again, two or three years later. The evaluation study connected with the experiment was reported in a monograph by Maurice F. Seay and Leonard E. Meece entitled *The Sloan Experiment in Kentucky* (1944). The initial data showed that the children in both communities were approximately the same in mean intelligence quotient at the start of the experiment. Both groups of children had mean intelligence quotients of 76. The rather low mean appears to reflect the combination of deprived social and economic circumstances and perhaps also the failure of the school to provide a curriculum that stimulated the children in any way. Over the three-year period of the study, the children in the experimental group gained an average of 30 points in intelligence quotient and the control children, 15 points. This difference appears large, but barely reaches the 10 percent level of significance. In the case of the achievement tests, the main gain of the experimental group over the control group was in reading comprehension, reflecting the fact that if one gives children interesting material to read, then they improve their reading skills. The difference was at about the 10 percent level of significance. One has to remember that the investigators were dealing with rather small groups of children that rarely exceeded 50.

Of special interest were the attempts to measure changes in the diet of the pupils over the period of the experiment. A 2- or 3-year time span was probably unsatisfactorily short in that the impact of the curriculum required a long chain of events before it could have real impact. A child who read about growing tomatoes would have to take the information home, and the information would have to have impact on the parents before it could result in a change of diet, and the parent might not start growing tomatoes for another year.

The original plan of the experiment involved the collection of extensive data on the diet of the children. However, the data that were actually collected were unsatisfactory, for they related to changes during the 5-month period of December, 1940 to May, 1941. Data collected over that period were related to such matters as the foods that were served on one particular day in the homes of the children. There were no notable differences between the diets of the two communities. The data suggest that the food served depended upon what happened to be available in the particular communities at that time. The reason for the lack of data after May, 1941 is that the war intervened and prevented the pursuit of the research. A similar problem existed with the detailed information concerning the serving of eggs and milk. Data were also collected on the number of families producing certain food items, but the data were available only for the 1940 bench mark. The project staff also began to collect data on the activities of the families related to the storage of food. A later set of data were obtained from the diaries that the children were asked to keep, on which they recorded the food eaten during a 5-day period. The overall appearance of the data thus derived suggests that the experimental children received a rather better diet, with a greater emphasis on lean meat and green leafy vegetables, and a decline in the consumption of fatty pork products.

An attempt was made to collect data on the health of the pupils. These data were available mainly for 1942 and 1943. The assumption seems to have been made that the base line for health factors for the two communities would have been the same. The data do not show any striking differences between the communities, except that certain accidents of health seem to have affected the one community more than the other. For example, the control community was stricken with an epidemic of measles that the experimental community did not have. Here again, one must point out that the time span was probably much too short to influence the health of the communities to any degree.

The conclusion of the report was that the data provided base lines from which future changes could be measured. However, there were problems that prevented a follow-up to determine further changes. The entry of America into World War II radically changed life for the people in the communities. The draft and the great need for factory workers changed the entire character of American life, though life in rural Appalachia was to drift back, after the war, to where it had been earlier. There was no way in which the study could have been re-initiated at a later date. Because the data provided by the enterprise were so incomplete and inconclusive, they have tended to be relegated to the archives of research and forgotten. They should not have been thus buried, for the basic idea underlying the research was brilliant, and represented an extraordinary innovation which should not be lost in the files.

Perhaps another reason for the lack of any follow-up of this enterprise is that the times are no longer receptive to what the research tried to accomplish. The idea behind the project grew towards the end of the Depression, a time when most of the help that an individual could find had to come from his own initiative. That is to be contrasted with the era of 1950 to 1980. After the war, the idea of self-help seems to have foundered through the development of programs designed to help the individual. The idea that the government should be the source of help rather than the individual's own initiative, perhaps prompted by social agencies, changed the way of looking at society. No longer were individuals expected to help themselves, and programs that helped the individual to do that seemed out of place and lacked support. A change in social and government philosophy may well be on the way at the time of writing and, when it comes about, there may be support for research on helping individuals to help themselves.

The Kentucky experiment was sponsored by the Alfred P. Sloan Foundation, which also sponsored two additional and related enterprises that have left little trace behind them. One of these related enterprises was a project on housing, developed by the University of Florida. The project had the same format as the Kentucky project, except that the materials developed for schools focused on improvement in housing. A third project was developed by the University of Vermont on clothing. These latter projects seem to have left no formal record behind them, a not uncommon feature of curriculum development projects. Then, in 1943, the schools of Greensburg, in Green County, Kentucky, used all three sets of materials in an effort to help the community help itself.

SOME CONCLUSIONS

The studies reviewed in this chapter offer powerful hope that the schools can become the instruments for improving the economic status of communities. Most communities, and particularly small ones, perpetuate a way of life that may have been, at one time, successful, but which no longer meets the needs of modern times. The knowledge necessary for bringing about a new economic base, with a resulting new way of life, can be brought to the people through the schools. The children not only use that knowledge as they grow up, but the knowledge filters through to the parents who may see in it the vision of a new future.

In order to undertake this kind of change through the schools, very knowledgeable and creative individuals must be involved in the planning stage. That is where economists can play a vital role, and so too can the agricultural experts, biologists, geologists, and others. The identification of the potential resources of a community, and the development of plans to use those resources, calls for the best intelligence available. When expert advice is properly used, almost any community can gain prosperity. A supreme example of the latter is the country Denmark, which has little to offer its people except a sandy peninsula, located in a drab climate. Yet, through great intellectual ingenuity and hard work, Denmark has become one of the most prosperous countries in the world. Little communities in the United States, that have little to offer except poverty and an absence of natural resources, can be offered a real hope of achieving the abundant life. The first step has to be a discovery of what the hidden potentials of the community really are. The second step is to change education in such a way that the community can begin to achieve its potential. The materials discussed in this chapter offer promise of what can be done. Perhaps the missing element on the current scene is a William Torrey Harris who can initiate action at a high level of power.

The role of the educational research worker in such enterprises is to begin by coordinating the work of the many experts that must be brought in for surveying the community resources and designing new school materials. Later work involves the planning and execution of evaluation studies to determine the success of the enterprise. The educational research worker gives continuity to the enterprise as the other resource individuals come and go as they are needed.

CHAPTER 11

Research on Events in the Classroom

TEACHER SUPERVISION AND APPRAISAL

Changing Concepts of Teaching

Classroom research finds its beginnings in such events as the survey of achievement undertaken by the Boston School Committee in 1845, attempts in the last century to design particular teaching procedures in terms of what were believed to be sound learning principles, and the work of Joseph Mayer Rice in his efforts to demonstrate the inadequacy of the teaching methods of his contemporaries. Research undertaken in the context of the classroom slowly grew as the behavioral and social sciences grew. Sometimes there was quite close contact, but all too often there was parallelism in the development of behavioral and educational research, but without the contact that would have benefited both enterprises. An earlier chapter in the book discussed the development of surveys of achievement that led to the emergence of the present evaluation movement, but there is also a whole realm of research related to events in the classroom that has not been touched upon elsewhere in this volume. Omitted from previous discussion have been those inquiries concerned with relating what happens in the classroom with the intellectual and social development of the pupil. A spinoff from such studies has been the slow refinement in the concept of teacher effectiveness. Another has been the concept that learning environments can be designed in terms of principles, and that such planned environments are assumed to be more effective than those that have emerged as a result of vague historical forces. Let us consider the emergence of classroom research related to teacher effectiveness as this has occurred during the present century.

Throughout most of history, those who wrote about teaching wrote as though they knew precisely what was meant by the effectiveness of the teacher. When Charles Hoole wrote in 1659 a complete guide to the running of a grammar school, he had a clear idea about what constituted an effective teacher. In terms of the grammar school of the day, the teacher's functions were primarily managerial. Instruction was largely individualized and each child worked on an assigned task. When the assignment was completed, the learning of the pupil was checked either by the teacher or the usher, before the next assignment was given. There was virtually no discussion. The only interaction with the pupil was at the point of giving the assignment and the point where the pupil's achievement was appraised. A teacher might be criticized for failing to give the right assignment or in failing to check pupil achievement, and also in failing to maintain the order and discipline necessary for such a system to function. In addition, the teacher was responsible for maintaining the dignity of the school in the eyes of the public and in handling, and even subduing, any members of the community who dared voice negative comments about the school. Such schools in England were private enterprises, and although the ushers might have been rated by the master, there was nobody to rate the master. The criterion of his effectiveness was whether the school did or did not survive.

The common schools of Puritan New England presented special problems related to the assessment of the efficiency of the teacher. Most of these schools were one-room schools, overseen by a locally appointed committee. The school committee had the task of appointing the teacher and supervising the way in which the schools were run. If the school committee objected to the practices of the teacher, then the committee could fire him. The word *him* is appropriately used in that most of the teachers in the Puritan schools were men. Few school committees in New England ever exercised their prerogatives, and their main task was more often that of persuading the teacher to stay on as long into spring as possible. All too often the teacher was a farmer who attempted to earn a living in winter by taking whatever jobs were available, and teaching jobs were readily obtained by those who had had some education. Two centuries later, when Horace Mann encountered this problem in the schools of Massachusetts, he urged that school committees employ women so that the schooling could be prolonged into springtime. In such situations little attempt was made to assess teachers for their effectiveness, and the concept of paying in terms of merit had not yet emerged. Indeed, the idea of merit pay seems to have been entirely a product of this century in this country, although it had been introduced, with disastrous results in England in the previous century.

The concept of a good teacher was, until near to a century ago, that of a good classroom manager, a concept that has more recently been revived by operant psychologists. The tasks of the teacher were largely managerial, and could not be otherwise so long as a classroom consisted of a group of children of widely varying ages and backgrounds. A teacher, like the one described by Horace Mann, who had in his classroom 50 children aged from 2½ to 25, could do little more than spend a few minutes each day giving each child a task from which the child could learn. Such a teacher had to be, above all, an organizer. Running such a classroom was a problem in management. The task of the Puritan teacher was something like that of the operant oriented teacher of today, who hands out packaged materials to each child on an individualized basis.

The great change in the functions and potential scope of teaching came with the introduction into American schools of the Prussian system of graded classrooms. This system had already been widely adopted in Europe before it became used in America. The idea of dividing children up into groups in terms of their age was also coupled with the idea that all children were equally able to learn. These two ideas together led to the further idea that children thus grouped could all be given the same assignments and the lockstep system of education emerged. This produced a radical change in the way in which a teacher used the time available. No longer did the teacher have to give 30 or more different assignments, but the Prussian plan of graded classes made it seem practical to give a single assignment to all students, releasing the teacher's time for other activities.

The immediate impact of the introduction of graded classes was for the teacher to make the recitation aspect of teaching a public matter. When there were individual assignments, pupils were checked individually. Recitation was the method of checking, and it was thus named because the student was typically required to recite back whatever he had learned by heart. Under the new Prussian system a teacher might just check a few students to sample the performance of the class, for to ask every child to recite back the same lesson introduced much tedium. Only slowly did the modern concept of recitation as a form of discussion and interaction emerge.

The change to the graded system, expanding as it did the two-way interaction of pupil and teacher, changed the task of the teacher and the criteria that could be used in evaluating teacher effectiveness. The teacher's functions were now enlarged to include elements other than those related to the managerial. The teacher now was viewed as a person who had a role in stimulating the student, in imparting information, in helping the student clarify his ideas and so forth. Such conceptions of teaching had not had a place in Western education though they had been the very core of the concept of education developed by Socrates and Aristotle. Western education, dominated by the ideas of Augustine and the set curriculum to be mastered item by item, was slow in finding a place for the form of inquiry that had been the very heart of education in the Lyceum.

Those who wrote about the evaluation of teaching near the turn of the century did not include such criteria in their systems of appraisal. William Torrey Harris, with his long experience as a principal, a superintendent, and as Commissioner of Education, generally took the position that the teacher had to maintain an orderly structured classroom in which the pupils were working on their assigned tasks. Harris even suggested that those teachers who departed from these standards for a well-managed classroom should be laid off for a week or more at a time as a punishment. Although Harris was a professional philosopher, he had little use for the informality of an Aristotle discussing the nature of the world with a group of students in a classroom. Teachers, in the time of Harris, were probably evaluated in terms of the kind of managerial criteria that he proposed.

In some of his later writings on the subject Harris's position was toned down. In an address before the American Institute for Instruction in 1906, he suggested that one criterion of effective teaching was whether the teacher was able to extract from the pupil a statement, in the pupil's own words, of the meaning of the lesson. The pupil should also learn to understand that the meaning he extracts from the lesson may be different from the meaning extracted by other pupils. The teacher should help the pupils synthesizing these partial views, an approach consistent with the Hegelian philosophy of Harris. Harris praised the virtues of the group recitation possible in the graded school, that was not possible in the ungraded (See "How the Superintendent may Correct Defective Class-Work," 1906). A new concept of teacher effectiveness was emerging. Harris did not relate to the new efficiency movement in education, but others did.

The Efficiency Movement

Criteria of teacher effectiveness, in the first fifteen years of the present century, became contaminated with ideas from the new movement to make schools and teachers as efficient as businesses were alleged to have become, under the influence of time and motion study. Journals read by teachers included numerous articles on the new efficiency movement in schools. Even President William H. Taft gave speeches on the subject (*Is a National Standard of Education Practical,* 1915). The speech hardly provided new solutions to problems, but proposed only that teachers be carefully rated and that the ratings be carefully discussed with the teachers themselves. Little was said about what should be the basis for ratings. Superintendent Green in a 1915 article echoed what other educational administrators had stressed, namely, that only the supervisor should rate the teacher, and that claims by parents or pupils of the teacher's efficiency should be disregarded. The article went on to discuss the practice of promoting teachers through examinations, a practice that was not uncommon at that time. The examinations were much like the modern National Teacher Examinations, covering methods of teaching in the various subject matter fields. The author of the article had in mind a set of levels of competency for teachers based upon performance on the examinations.

The efficiency movement did little to help clarify the concept of teacher effectiveness, but it had one positive outcome. Some of those preoccupied with the efficiency movement suggested that an important function of the teacher was to develop efficient methods of study on the part of the pupil. This represented the birth of the idea that the schools should develop in pupils efficient ways of learning. The movement did not say much about what efficient study habits were, for many of these had to be derived from later empirical research. Nevertheless, there was a common-sense core of habits that constitute good study habits, and teachers knew what the pundits of efficiency were discussing.

Nevertheless, the efficiency movement did little for education, neither clarifying to any degree the concept of teacher effectiveness, nor making the schools more efficient in some broad sense of the term. The failure of the movement was inevitable, because it failed to learn from business the lesson that was supposed to be applied to education. The efficiency movement in business came into being through an empirical approach to problems of productivity. The very foundation of the movement was the observation of worker performance and the careful recording of data related to what the worker did. In addition, the efficiency movement in business and industry involved experimentation, through which the most efficient procedures were discovered. Thus, rest periods were found to be extremely important in work involving physical effort, and experimentation at industrial sites established the length and the timing of the rest periods that made for maximum worker output. None of these techniques of observation, research and experimentation, were carried over into the schools but the efficiency movement in the schools produced little more than rhetoric up to 1915 when it hit its peak before declining. Academicians, who could have supplied the empirical methods, were too busy in their own enterprises, and believed that what they were doing would contribute to efficiency in the schools, though they did not generally use the term.

The basic reason why the efficiency movement, when applied to education, failed to provide a base of empirical data from which to promote efficiency, was that educators believed they knew exactly what needed to be done in the classroom. Those who wrote on the problem of assessing teacher effectiveness early in the century wrote as though the answers to all the problems were available. Superintendents and supervisors believed they knew what a teacher had to do in order to promote learning in pupils, and the writings on the subject reflected few doubts in the minds of the authors. The practical administrator was quite unmoved by the writings of John Dewey, who suggested that most of what teachers did in schools was quite ineffective. Dewey was passed off as an academician who knew little about the management of public schools, even though he had had a brief encounter with the operation of a private school.

The first attempt to bring together systematically what was believed to be the knowledge available in the area was published in the *Fourteenth Yearbook of the National Society for the Study of Education, Part II* by Arthur C. Boyce, dealing with the appraisal of the teacher. The document is of interest in that it presents thinking on the subject of teacher ratings at the height of the school efficiency movement. The document opened with a section on the use of examinations for the promotion and evaluation of teachers. The document implied that this was a common practice in the large city systems, but the document also reported that examinations were never the sole basis for assessing the merits of teachers. A strong argument for the use of examinations was that teachers were forced by the examination to keep abreast of the new literature on education and to familiarize themselves with the new ideas. Superintendents varied in the extent to which they had faith in examination methods. There had been no investigations of the use of teacher examinations, which were justified in terms of the rationale that there was surely a body of knowledge that teachers needed to master, and that they should be able to show their mastery of that knowledge on an examination. Such logic, based on the new concept of teaching emerging at that time, seemed unassailable. At least, no one dared attack it.

Teacher Rating Studies

The remainder of the second part of the Yearbook, dealing with teacher efficiency, was concerned with the rating of teachers. This was viewed as the primary method of evaluation. Indeed, in order to be eligible to sit for one of the examinations, the teacher usually had to be rated first by a supervisor. Boyce sent letters to about 100 city systems to determine how they assessed the efficiency of teachers. The letters that came back showed a country-wide faith in rating systems, but the letters also showed that the methods used manifested "indefiniteness and looseness" (p. 14). Boyce also presented what he claimed to be 22 typical statements from the respondents. These statements are interesting in that they reflect a confident attitude with respect to the validity of what was being done. They generally give the impression that the superintendent rated each teacher for efficiency and that the superintendent believed that he knew what he was doing.

Boyce did what was commonly done in his time. He sought to determine whether the rating systems manifested a common core of ideas. When he first sorted through the letters and rating devices he prepared a list of 150 factors that were included in all of the scales and devices. Boyce first reduced this list to 53 by eliminating those that overlapped. Then he reduced the list still further to 25 to include what he considered to be the most important characteristics of the effective teacher. He presented these in a table, which is of interest in that it presents the views of his age concerning the elements that made for an effective teacher.

The list places at the top "discipline," but factors such as "skill in questioning" and "personal influence" come near to the bottom of the list. Also high on the list were "instructional skill" and "scholarship and education."

Boyce, like his contemporaries, saw the defects in the system to be a matter of language. What had to be done was clear up the indefiniteness and looseness of the rating system, and then the problems would be solved. Terms had to be defined, and raters had to know exactly what they were rating. Boyce urged that ratings should not be based on personal opinion, but that the rating device should be such that the rater should be able to record information about the teacher with objectivity and precision. Little did Boyce know that the issues he raised would not be settled a half century later. Boyce never raised any questions about whether the appropriate traits were being assessed. Questions about what constituted good teaching still had to be raised, though Horace Mann had raised the issue half a century earlier.

Boyce provided a long discussion of how ratings should be used by administrators. He pointed out that teacher ratings had four main uses. These were for the making of salary adjustments, for determining promotions, for helping the teacher improve, and for the private use of the superintendent. One presumes that the latter use was related to such matters as the handling of complaints and in defending particular teachers against attack by parents and school board members. Sometimes the rating system was used in ways that were nothing short of ridiculous. The Philadelphia superintendent distributed a circular in which he proclaimed that all teachers must achieve a rating of at least 80 per cent in order to be regarded as "competent." He did not say that those with a lower rating would be fired, for there was a teacher shortage at that time. He also never explained the 80 percent or said what it was a percentage of.

It is to Boyce's credit that he seems to have been the first to open up the way for empirical studies of teacher effectiveness. Indeed, one suspects that he had been invited to prepare the Yearbook because he was already engaged in the study of rating teachers, having first worked on this problem while he was a graduate student at the University of Illinois and later at the University of Chicago. What Boyce did in his study was to prepare a consolidated list of teacher characteristics supposedly related to "efficiency" and to convert the list into a rating scale. In his first attempt to do this he used a 20-point rating scale, but found that this involved finer discriminations than judges could make or use, so he reduced the rating categories to 10. Then he attacked the problem of the lack of precision of terms, by providing a definition of each of the characteristics listed. One has to remember that the simplest matters related to the design of rating scales had not yet been studied. Boyce's apparently naive exploration was the kind of enterprise that has made it possible for research workers to acquire some degree of competence in the development of rating systems. He also prepared a set of directions for raters, and that was also an innovation. Then he began to ask important questions related to the use of rating scales.

One question he asked was whether ratings made by judges at different times on the same teacher showed agreement. Another was whether judges agreed on the rating assigned to a group of teachers. Boyce was asking questions about the reliability of the instrument, questions that had not been asked before. He did not use the term reliability, but he was on the right track and asking the right questions. He was able to find a good correlation between judgments made by different judges, and judgments made by the same judges on different occasions, but was disturbed by the fact that some judges were generally high raters and some low. In other words, raters seemed to be characterized by a personal constant, which indicated the extent to which they were high or low raters. Boyce saw the importance of this personal constant and identified it as a serious problem in the rating of teachers. One rater might rate a group of teachers as poor or mediocre, but another might rate them as good, depending upon the standards applied. Boyce had no remedy for this practical difficulty in the application of rating to field situations.

Boyce then went on to study the relationship between various traits to a rating of what was described as general merit. Boyce made the assumption that a rating of general merit was a valid measure of what was widely called "teaching efficiency." Boyce did not question the idea, widely accepted at that time, that any administrator could make valid judgments of teaching effectiveness. His acceptance of this idea led him to attempt to determine the components of teacher effectiveness. That was an attractive idea in those days, as it is today, but the difference was that Boyce sought the components in terms of traits, but the emphasis today is in terms of skills. Both concepts may have some utility.

Boyce found a very large halo effect, but did not know how to interpret it. The highest correlations with general merit were with the characteristics described as "results" and "technique of teaching." Those least associated with general merit were "professional and academic preparation" and "health, general appearance, and voice." To some degree the results fitted the prejudices of administrators of his age. The research represented a closed system of ideas and, inevitably, produced results consistent with the content of that closed system. The breakaway from that closed system was to be accomplished only very slowly, requiring almost another half century. During most of that subsequent half century, a massive amount of research was to be undertaken within that closed system.

Before leaving Boyce's contribution, a rating scale for teachers, appended to his report, must be mentioned. The rating scale had been produced by the New York Bureau of Municipal Research, a component of the New York City school administration. The rating scale is remarkable in that it is a complete departure from the thinking of the period, including the thinking of Boyce, which is perhaps the reason why he included the rating procedure without comment. Whoever prepared the rating scale must have been aware of the writings of John Dewey. The scale called for an analysis of the teacher's questions, in terms of whether they were thought provoking, calling for facts, irrelevant, and so forth. The scale also called for an analysis of the recitation material in terms of whether it was confined to the text, adapted to children's present and future needs, related to children's lives and experiences, and worthwhile. The observer also had to make an analysis of teaching in terms of such categories as rambling, formal and mechanical, stimulating, calling for independent thinking and resourcefulness, requiring cooperation, resulting in clarification, and other features. Nearly every item in the scale can be found in modern instruments that attempt to measure characteristics related to teacher effectiveness. Yet the instrument seems to have had little impact, for the research that characterized the next quarter century was confined largely to the approach that Boyce had taken, with an emphasis on rating personality traits that seemed to have some relationship to teaching.

Although Boyce initiated the study of teacher ratings, another aspect of teacher effectiveness had been studied since the end of the previous century, when G. Stanley Hall's students had begun to study what children thought about the instruction given them. The work does not seem to have been of any notable significance. Another line of study that preceded that of Boyce was the investigation of why teachers were classroom failures. These latter studies offered some promise.

From the year 1915, and down to the present day, studies related to the rating of teachers have proliferated. Most of these studies were undertaken by unsophisticated doctoral students, who were often, sad to say, supervised by faculty who had had little training or experience in research. The number of studies produced was quite stupendous. Simeon J. Domas and David V. Tiedeman compiled a list of these studies up to

1950 in the document *Teacher Competence: An Annotated Bibliography* (1950). The material listed in the bibliography is massive, but its utility is limited by the fact that, although studies are coded into groups, no attempt was made to synthesize the knowledge that could be derived from each group of studies. A more useful attempt to bring together the research on teaching efficiency up to the midcentury was made by Arvil Sylvester Barr (1892-1962) in his monograph *The Measurement and Prediction of Teaching Efficiency: A Summary of Investigations* (1948). The monograph was at least selective in the studies he included, and Barr attempted to synthesize the knowledge that could be extracted. Barr was a scholar who realized that most of the published material lacked scholarly merit, so he was quite selective in what he presented in his report. He also provided an excellent discussion of the many meanings of *teaching efficiency*, and he made an excellent attempt to extract from the studies the various meanings of the terms that were implied. He pointed out that *teaching efficiency* referred in some studies to the personal qualities of the teacher that were assumed to be associated with teaching success. Other studies defined teaching efficiency in terms of the way in which the teacher exercised controls over behavior. In this connection Barr used the term *teaching competencies* that was to appear on banners 25 years later. Barr also pointed out that a third major use of the term *teaching efficiency* was in connection with pupil growth and achievement. This latter use reflected the new emphasis in educational thought on the role of the teacher in influencing learning. This was a departure from the nineteenth century idea that the teacher merely provided conditions that permitted children to learn, and that it was the choice of the child either to learn or not to learn. In the new way of thinking, the teacher, and not the pupil, made the choice. The trend in research reflected this new way of thinking. The research on teacher effectiveness reviewed by Barr reflected the trend that emphasized teacher responsibility for pupil learning, beyond that produced by a good classroom manager.

While Barr was undertaking his review and synthesis of research related to classroom teaching, another review was being conducted by Joseph E. Morsh and Eleanore W. Wilder (*Identifying the Effective Instructor: A Review of the Quantitative Studies.* 1900-1952, 1954). The latter review is rather more useful than that provided by Barr for our present purpose, though it does not have the sophisticated understanding of the history of pedagogy of the latter. Morsh and Wilder's review covered 392 studies, though many of these studies included little data. They brought together studies with similar purpose and arranged them chronologically. Let us consider some of these tables which illustrate well the history of the era.

Table 1 in the Morsh and Wilder monograph listed 26 studies in which an attempt was made to determine the reliability of administrative ratings of teacher effectiveness. Of interest is the fact that the first of these studies was published in 1927, at least a quarter century after such ratings had become widely used. The need for such research had not been evident at all, for nobody had doubted the sterling quality of administrative ratings. A second interesting point about the table is that research workers continued to produce studies of the consistency of an administrator in rating teachers for a period of at least ten years. One finds study after study that demonstrated that administrators could consistently rate the same teacher in about the same way. The use of the two different observers and a comparison of the ratings of the two different observers did not seem to be introduced until the mid thirties. Still later attempts were made to compare ratings of teacher effectiveness derived from different rating scales. A modern reader of the studies has difficulty in understanding that the issue of the capability of the administrator to rate his teachers consistently was a burning issue and a controversial one for nearly a quarter of a century. Once it had been established that administrators could rate teachers consistently, administrators began to feel confident in what they were doing.

The second table in the report listed studies in which administrative ratings were compared with other measures of teacher effectiveness. Of interest is the fact that pupil gain measures had been used as far back as 1921, and that these continued to appear throughout the period covered. The correlations reported with teacher ratings were generally small and positive. Morsh and Wilder were not impressed with them, and yet the data strongly suggest that administrators are not wholly ignorant about the effectiveness of teachers in producing learning. The correlations are at least as large as the correlations one finds in other fields between, say, measures of job knowledge, and criteria of effectiveness in performing the job.

Table 3 of the report summarized research that has attempted to relate characteristics of teacher behavior and ratings of teacher effectiveness. These studies made the assumption that overall ratings of teacher effectiveness are valid and that this global characteristic can be divided into a set of components. The studies reflected the viewpoint of reductionism that characterized educational research until quite recently. The first study identified was published in 1910. The early studies were typically attempts to identify the causes of what was called failure.

Although studies of the components of teacher effectiveness still continue to be made, they show remarkably little progress over the period covered by the Morsh and Wilder report. Different studies list different components of teacher effectiveness, and most show quite high correlations with overall ratings. The latter is hardly surprising today in view of the fact that the halo effect in ratings is well established and well known. Attempts have been made to reduce the enormously long list of characteristics of teacher behavior. Boyce did this in his 1915 study, and when Barr put together the knowledge available in 1948, he also attempted to develop a consolidated list of traits. Barr's list enumerated 200 characteristics, and these he grouped into seven categories and then, by the elimination of overlaps, reduced the number to 53. His broad categories were those of classroom management, instructional skills, personal fitness for teaching, scholarship and professional preparation, effort towards improvement, interest in work, and ability to cooperate with others. Barr's classification did little to help work in the area because it did little more than set up broad categories in terms of which his inventory of traits could be sorted. It did not do what a scientific classification should do, namely, develop a theory of the events involved, and then classify the events in terms of the theory. Indeed, the area of teaching research, during the period covered by Barr, was notoriously lacking in any kind of theory, and it was this lack which accounted for the lack of any accumulation of knowledge. Each new research seemed to provide another piece of the jigsaw, but the pieces never fitted together to provide any overall picture of teaching.

The studies of teacher characteristics showed an increasing emphasis over time with the impact of what were termed personality variables. Psychologists had become interested in developing theories of personality, and this interest had impact on educational research. However, even up to the present time, theories of personality have represented very primitive constructs, and so primitive that they have had little value as a foundation for research. The impact of these primitive personality theories on classroom research related to teacher effectiveness probably added obscurity rather than clarification. Although personality theories may not have added to knowledge about teaching, the introduction of such theories opened the way for the development of hundreds of quite worthless doctoral dissertations. Educational research workers, at the doctoral level, have also had the difficulty of not being trained in the area of personality theory, and have been unable to cope with such theories critically. One only has to look down the lists of studies presented by Morsh and Wilder to realize the unsophisticated nature of the research that was undertaken on teacher personality in the first half of the present century.

Tables 4 and 5 of the Morsh and Wilder report summarized data on the relationship of peer ratings to other measures of instructor effectiveness. Such studies began in the early twenties. Once again the data were of little consequence, because of a lack of any theoretical basis for the inquiries. Peer ratings of teachers for teacher effectiveness are odd, in that teachers do not typically visit one another. The rating by peers has to be based on some kind of inference about whether the teacher rated has the kinds of characteristics that make for good teaching. Nevertheless, whatever was being rated correlated positively and substantially with supervisor ratings of teacher effectiveness.

There would be little point in discussing each of the remaining tables, for we have presented enough to indicate the fact that the early research workers were floundering once they had established the fact that administrators could rate teachers with considerable reliability. To demonstrate much else seemed impossible at the time the studies were undertaken. One is often left with the impression that investigators were willing to correlate any variable with any other variable, just to produce a table of figures. Such a table provided the illusion of bringing order into chaos. The rows of correlation coefficients also provided an illusion of precision. Morsh and Wilder rightly pointed out that most of the computation involved in most of the studies was a waste of time (p. 57). Although there were a few sophisticated research workers in the area, such as A. S. Barr, the majority of studies were undertaken in an atmosphere of complete incompetence.

THE STUDY OF CLASSROOM PHENOMENA AS THE BASIS FOR TEACHER EDUCATION

Research on events in the classroom led to a new interest in the design of programs for the education of teachers. By the mid twenties, there was a realization that the courses in pedagogy, that found their roots in Herbartian theory, did not prepare teachers adequately. New approaches were sought. For this purpose, the Commonwealth fund provided the University of Chicago with $43,000 to develop a new approach to teacher training under the leadership of W. W. Charters and Douglas Waples. Their report of the resulting study appeared in what should be considered to be a landmark publication *The Commonwealth Teacher Training Study* (1929). The study is remarkable in that it introduced the concept of training teachers in what were believed to be the basic competancies required of the teacher in the classroom. In that study competency based teacher education was born.

Charters and Waples based their study upon the idea that teacher education should train teachers to undertake effectively the tasks they would be required to undertake in the classroom. The approach in curriculum development was similar to that proposed by Franklin Bobbitt for elementary and secondary schools, but extended the idea to professional training. In order to develop a new teacher education curriculum, Charters and Waples set out to discover what teachers actually did. They were not able to visit classrooms and spend hundreds of hours making a job analysis of the work of the teacher, but what they did was to distribute questionnaires to teachers asking them to outline their classroom activities. The lists were then consolidated and a teacher education curriculum developed on the basis of the consolidated list. The basic list included over one thousand activities. The new curriculum was based partly on revisions of old courses and partly on the development of new courses.

THE CONCEPT OF TEACHING METHOD AND THE STUDY OF THE CLASSROOM

Through the period of World War I, research related to the classroom was dominated by the idea that supervisors understood the nature of effective classroom teaching and the way in which effective teachers acted. The only research problem was that of quantifying the activities of the effective teacher. Educational administrators seemed satisfied with their position and paid little attention to critics within the universities who doubted that the traditional pattern of teaching, endorsed by the educational establishment, was the only possible pattern of effective teaching. The voices of critics had loudly proclaimed their message that the time had come for a new conception of effective teaching. Dewey had written forcefully on the subject since the turn of the century. His books had been widely read, at least by an academic audience, but his message had not penetrated the circles of educational supervisors. Teachers College had begun to train a new generation of supervisors, aware of the possibility that new patterns of teaching might be more effective than those that had been traditionally endorsed, but these new supervisors, scattered over the entire United States, were not to have their voice heard until the 1920's. Then, as now, the educational establishment held on to tradition with a firm hand, and prevented classroom teachers from deviating from that which had been traditionally approved.

The 1920's saw a world-wide movement to change the pattern of classroom teaching and to question the value of the traditional pattern. This movement not only raised questions about the value of traditional approaches to teaching but, at the same time, raised questions about the usefulness of the research that had been undertaken on the rating of teachers. Perhaps the latter research had resulted merely in the development of more reliable methods of rating the wrong qualities. The new conception of teaching, that was being produced by the Progressive Education Movement in the United States and parallel movements in European countries, stressed qualities that were not included among the qualities listed in the commonly used rating scales. The new ideas related to teaching not only questioned the value of the then current teaching practices, but raised questions about the value of the research that had been undertaken as a part of the efficiency movement in education. The research no longer appeared to be the panacea that it had been promoted to be, but now it was seen as being on the wrong track and producing results that were misleading. Classroom research, if it were to survive at all, would have to move along an entirely different track.

Teaching Method Studies

The new track for educational research was that of discovering the relative effectiveness of different teaching methods. The new approach was slow in developing for a number of reasons. Perhaps the strongest reason was that schools were slow in the innovation of new teaching procedures. Superintendents tended to suffer from attacks of nerves when a new way of teaching was proposed. The public tended to endorse very traditional approaches to teaching, and viewed innovation with suspicion. Another reason was that the logic underlying the proposed new teaching methods was not always easily identified by an undiscerning and unknowledgeable public. Furthermore, a majority of parents viewed the schools as a place where all children acquired a fixed body of knowledge and a number of well-recognized skills, and few were willing to concede that traditional ideas about education might be wrong.

Despite the staunch support that existed for traditional concepts of education, new ways of teaching began to appear, mostly related to the ideas about which Dewey had written a quarter of a century earlier. The introduction of such innovations often required the presence of a strong and determined superintendent, whose powerful presence withered opposition. Such a person was Carleton Washburne at Winnetaka, who wrote about the manner in which he was able to overcome opposition to innovation. Washburne was a tall and massively built man with a stentorian voice, whose very presence seemed to overwhelm opposition. He provided detailed accounts of how he overcame opposition to innovation at Winnetka. His accounts suggest that his success was a result of his ability to discuss the matter rationally, but far more was involved. He probably was not aware of the part played by the force of his personality.

Washburne understood the value of facts and figures as a means of overcoming opposition, and he also realized that facts and figures had to be collected by experts if they were to be credible. In order to demonstrate that his innovative program of teaching was at least as good as the traditional program, Washburne established a research program and employed a talented young man, Louis Raths, to conduct the enterprise. For a time the combination worked well and studies were undertaken showing that the then notorious Winnetka program produced results, in terms of achievement, that were comparable to those achieved by more traditional methods. The Washburne and Raths team survived for only a short time, though it is surprising that it survived at all.

Washburne was intensely concerned with the public relations value of the data collected, but the more scholarly oriented and intellectually profound Raths was interested in the implication of the data for the development of theory of education and knowledge about the nature and effects of the teaching process. Hardly surprising was it that, after a few years at Winnetka, Raths left for The Ohio State University where he provided much of the scholarship underlying the Eight Year Study.

The new classroom experimentation of the 1930's was intensely practical in orientation, but was a step forward in that it introduced the possibility of genuine experimentation in schools, in contrast to the earlier research that had not involved experimental methods. Despite the progress that the introduction of an experimental approach to education seemed to imply, the full development of the approach was hindered by fuzzy thinking on the part of both researchers and educational administrators at the state and Federal levels.

Considerable confusion was injected by the Federal Office of Education that became enamoured with the idea of "adjustment education" during the 1920's and 1930's. Just how the Federal government became involved in the sponsorship of such a vague idea is not clear, but it did produce bulletin after bulletin which promoted the idea that the concept of adjustment was the very key to effective education. The concept does not seem to have been derived so much from the work of Dewey as from the emerging field of psychotherapy, which tended to view the teacher as a potential therapist. The implication was that the well-adjusted child was one who would learn rapidly. Hence the promotion of the adjustment of the child would promote effective learning. The only data to support the position came from therapists who claimed that any improvement in the adjustment of the child was accompanied by an improvement in the child's effectiveness as a learner.

The most notable proponents of the new experimental approach to classroom research were in the Eastern part of the country, and the name of J. Wayne Wrightstone (1904-   ) was connected with much of that activity. Wrightstone came up through the educational ladder by a quite conventional path, having taught at the junior high school level and then becoming a principal. Then, in 1932, he went to Teachers College to obtain advanced training and a higher degree and worked there in the Institute of School Experimentation, where he came under the influence of Otis W. Caldwell (1869-1947). The institute had done little that would be described as experimental, in the scientific sense of the term, but it provided an atmosphere in which a young person could have freedom to develop new ideas. Caldwell himself was acutely aware of the need to develop genuine experimental methods in the social and biological sciences and hoped to see these methods extended to school settings. Caldwell understood the differences between the establishment of what was called an experimental school and the conduct of a scientific experiment, even though many of his colleagues did not understand the difference.

A major product of the Institute of School Experimentation was the study by Wrightstone entitled *Appraisal of Newer School Practices in Selected Public Schools* (1935). In this study, outcomes were compared for schools sponsoring a traditional curriculum and schools that claimed to have what was called a "newer" type of curriculum. The great political importance of this comparison in establishing school policy overshadowed the fact that the two categories of schools were only fuzzily defined. Indeed, this kind of experiment would be comparable in the agricultural field to making a comparison between the effect of cow manure and horse manure, on the quality of a crop. Such an experiment, if it can be called an experiment at all, might yield a certain amount of practical knowledge, but could not possibly produce the kind of organized knowledge that constitutes a science. Although educators needed to know, for the purposes of policy making, whether newer practices lowered or raised level of achievement in traditional subject matter categories, the knowledge that was needed, for designing new curricula, was the relationship between specific practices and level of achievement. Research workers in the late 1930's had not yet conceptualized this difference. Indeed, for a long time to come educational research workers were to conduct studies that compared some vague complex of practices referred to as Method A with another vague complex of practices referred to as Method B. Such studies turned out to be quite unproductive.

It is easy to be critical of the school experimentation of the 1930's from today's point of view. Yet the studies of which one can be critical today were conducted by extremely capable individuals who brought educational research some distance along the road of progress. One can be sure that studies conducted in the 1970-1980 period will seem to be equally filled with flaws by those who will view them with the wisdom accumulated by the year 2000. The early studies, such as those of Wrightstone, did much to identify the difficulties of conducting such research, and did much to focus on the need for developing new instruments that would measure outcomes related to specific curricula. The studies also focused on the need to describe more precisely what was meant by a teaching method and introduced new approaches to classroom observation that attempted to identify teacher variables related to particular approaches to teaching. The early studies of classroom experimentation did much to identify the difficulties involved in such work and to establish what became known as the quasi experiment. Less wise followers of the movement unfortunately became involved in the notorious pseudo experiment.

Although the Wrightstone studies were the most ambitious published in the field of classroom experimentation during the 1930's, there were other less ambitious enterprises that attacked the same problem in various school districts throughout the country. The knowledge derived from these studies was assembled by an informal committee appointed by the Progressive Education Association. The chairman was G. Derwood Baker, Superintendent of Schools in Boulder, Colorado, but the committee included the names of such notables as Ralph Tyler, J. Wayne Wrightstone, P. J. Rulon and Irving Lorge. The report of the committee was published as a pamphlet entitled *New Methods Versus Old in American Education* (1941).

The report of the committee, summarizing the results, reached conclusions that might have been reached today. Differences in outcomes between children in schools designated as "experimental" or "progressive" and children in schools designated as traditional were negligible. Sometimes the differences favored the new curriculum and sometimes the old. Basic skills, such as reading seemed to be acquired about as well over the elementary grades by children in the one class of curricula as in the other; though the children in the curricula designated as "new" seemed rather slower in learning to read, they managed to catch up by the time they had arrived at the upper elementary grades. The evidence generally showed that the practice advocated by the Progressive Education Movement had not had the disastrous effects on traditional forms of academic achievement that the critics had claimed it would have. On the positive side, there seemed to be some evidence that the newer types of school program did seem to facilitate the social development of the individual and the understanding achieved related to contemporary society. The gains in these peripheral areas were claimed to justify the newer practices.

The report could be regarded as a political document rather than a scientific one. The conclusion provided a defense for the newer educational practices, even though these were vaguely defined. In order for the studies to have provided a scientific basis for the new education, they would have had to have shown how the newer practices fitted a theory of learning and instruction that would have predicted the superiority of the progressive practices. The studies provided no data that could have been used for such a scientific purpose, for the newer practices remained as ill defined as the older ones. Such limitations were not recognized in the 1930's, when such studies were viewed as highly innovative and a worthwhile new direction for educational research.

Nevertheless, the atmosphere for classroom experimentaton was highly favorable in the 1930's, for at last individuals with a scientific training were becoming involved in the enterprise. The idea, of course, was not new. The New York Society for the Experimental Study of Education had been formed in 1918 for the purpose of encouraging teachers to conduct what were called classroom experiments. Teachers were prime movers in forming the society. Those who sponsored the society probably had little concept of what an experiment involved, and there seems to have been little understanding among members of the society that experimentation in schools involved any competencies other than those possessed by the classroom teacher. The original membership was 78, but by the mid-twenties the membership had reached the 1000 mark. An odd feature of the society is that its presidents, at least up to midcentury, were individuals whose names are wholly unfamiliar to those with a knowledge of the history of educational research. Despite the vacuum at the top, the society had some highly competent and well-known Vice Presidents, including Harold O. Rugg, William A. McCall, and Percival M. Symonds. Apparently, competence was not permitted to contaminate the top echelon of the society during those early years. The work of the society seems to have remained outside of the mainstream of educational research. It may well have played a role in the encouragement of innovation on the part of teachers in schools, but it played no role in the development of scientific experimentation in schools.

The New York Society for the Experimental Study of Education probably encouraged few actual studies in schools, but it had some impact on teachers through its meetings at which innovations in the classroom were discussed. Much more effective in actually conducting classroom experiments related to new ways of teaching was the New York City Department of Education. The City introduced an experimental program of education, referred to as an activity program, into 70 elementary schools in the late thirties, and undertook an ambitious program for comparing the outcomes of that program with those of a more traditional curriculum. In order to encourage such evaluative efforts the Bureau of Reference, Research and Service had brought in J. Wayne Wrightstone, who had already made a reputation for himself at The Ohio State University, where he had worked as assistant director of the Evaluation Staff of the Eight Year Study. It is of interest to note that Wrighstone obtained his position with New York City through taking a competitive examination, in which he had to compete with some of the outstanding young men in the field of psychology. One can hardly imagine such a formal examination being given today.

The enthusiasm for experimentation in the New York City schools in the 1930's was short lived. It did survive long enough for the study to be made of the 70 experimental schools. However, the latter was conducted with outside funds and an outside professional staff. The study appeared under the authorship of a group of researchers headed by A. T. Jersild and R. L. Thorndike (A. T. Jersild, R. L. Thorndike, B. Goldman, and J. J. Loftus, "An Evaluation of Aspects of the Activity Program in the New York City Public Elementary Schools," 1939).

New York City was not alone in its sponsorship of an experimental elementary school curriculum along the lines proposed by John Dewey. The City of Los Angeles had made similar efforts to change the curriculum and had attempted to do this on a system-wide basis. The City of Los Angeles also had an Education Research and Guidance Section, not as well staffed as the corresponding organization in New York City, but, nevertheless, adequately staffed. The research organization attempted to relate changes in test scores over the years to changes in the curriculum. The data appeared to indicate that the introduction of new methods had not adversely affected performance in the three Rs. However, the results could not be interpreted easily since the change in the curriculum had also been accompanied by other changes in the schools and in the populations they served.

The New Media Studies

The kinds of experimental curricula that were introduced by school systems during the 1930's faded into oblivion with the outbreak of World War II. School systems had difficulty maintaining their staffs, with the draft of men into the army and the drawing of women into highly paid jobs in war industries. The emphasis in curriculum development was on the development of practical skills. Many of the more innovative administrators were recruited for work with the armed forces where they helped design a magnificent array of training procedures. The schools became impoverished of the talent needed to continue the development of the new curricula, begun in the 1930's.

The war brought an emphasis on a different type of educational experiment in classroom situations. The armed services were interested in developing teaching devices that would permit the training of a large number of men and women for particular jobs. The new training devices appeared to open the way for teaching very large numbers of individuals with only a skeleton force of training personnel. The armed forces, and particularly the United States Navy, developed large organizations for developing training devices and, late in the war and during the post war years, initiated a research program to investigate the utility and improvement of these training devices. The most notable of these research programs was that developed by the Navy's Training Service Center at Port Washington, New York. The trend of this research was to compare the outcomes of instruction using a particular training device, such as a film, with similar instruction without the use of the device. Another model of research involved a comparison of different versions of the training device or a comparison of different ways of using the device.

This form of classroom experimentation was much better designed to develop systematically knowledge about education than was the kind of experimentation that had taken place in relation to the development of new curricula or new teaching methods. The training devices research dealt with precisely identified conditions, and not the vague generalities that had enshrouded curriculum research. The research was designed to discover specific pieces of knowledge about techniques of instruction, that could be applied to the design of methods for the training of service men. The research was based upon the idea that there were specific competencies related to the effective use of training devices.

One should also note that this form of classroom research involved conditions that could be readily controlled. Research involving the mode of behavior of the teacher has always been very difficult to control, because teachers are human and produce spontaneous variations in behavior that may influence outcomes in unexpected ways. Research on teaching devices did not suffer from this defect.

This form of classroom research was not new, but it had not been widely pursued. Research on the use of slides for instructional purposes had been undertaken at the end of World War I, but this form of study had not attracted the attention of many academicians, and had even been regarded as research into trivia, perhaps because training devices, including slides and films, had been viewed as frills rather than as important contributors to education.

The Training Device Center of the U.S. Navy, also known later as the Special Devices Center pursued its research after the war largely through contracts negotiated with universities. It had contracts on the use of teaching machines with The Ohio State University where Sidney Pressey had long developed work in the area, but in a small way. During the war Pressey had been active in assisting the Navy develop mechanical devices for training enlisted men in such matters as technical vocabulary. Pressey pursued this line of research for a short time after the war. The largest of the contracts related to media was with Pennsylvania State University, which at that time was just a college, where C. R. Carpenter had long been engaged in research related to innovative classroom practices and materials at the college level.

Clarence Ray Carpenter (1905-1974) was an unusual man who was a scholar in many fields. Some of his early work was in primate behavior, and he spent a year running the primate colonies at Columbia University. After the war he settled into a career in the field of instructional research at what was then Pennsylvania State College. In many respects the program was, in its time, one of the most distinguished enterprises of its kind. Carpenter ran it with competence and imagination. The focus of the program was on the discovery of means of using instructional devices effectively in the classroom.

The Carpenter studies sponsored by the Special Devices Branch began with a thorough review of the research that had been undertaken on the use of films for educational purposes, as far back as 1918. The amount of research that had already been done was quite impressive. Carpenter thought it was a sufficient basis for deriving 10 principles describing the influence of films on learners. These principles were as follows:

> 1. Films have greatest influence when their content reinforces and extends previous knowledge, attitudes, and motivations of the audience. They have least influence when previous knowledge is inadequate, and when their content is antagonistic or contrary to the existing attitudes and motivation of the audience. (p. 9-3)
> 2. The influence of a motion picture is more specific than general. (p. 9-3)
> 3. The influence of a motion picture is greater when the content of the film is directly relevant to the audience reaction that it is intended to influence. (p. 9-3)
> 4. Reactions to a motion picture vary with most or all of the following factors: film literacy, abstract intelligence, formal education, age, sex, previous experience with the subject, and prejudice or predisposition towards the subject. (p. 9-4)
> 5. The influence of a motion picture is primarily in the strength of the visual presentation, and secondarily in the narration or commentary. It is relatively unaffected by "slickness" of production as long as meaning is clear. (p. 9-5)
> 6. An audience responds selectively to motion pictures, reacting to those things which it finds familiar and significant in the pictorial context in which the action takes place. (p. 9-6)
> 7. Individuals respond to a motion picture most efficiently when the pictorial content is subjective for them. (p. 9-7)
> 8. Rate of development influences the instructional impact of a motion picture on its audience. (p. 9-7)
> 9. Established instructional techniques, properly built into film or applied by the instructor, substantially increase the instructional effectiveness of a film. (p. 9-7)
> 10. The leadership qualities of the instructor affect the efficiency with which his class will learn from the film or filmstrip. (p. 9-8)

Several very competent research workers, in addition to Carpenter, developed the program of research at the Pennsylvania State College, notably L. P. Greenhill, who was key man in the enterprise, and who had direct responsibility for much of the work. The program of research included a great range of variables including the rate of development of instructional films, the effects of repetition, the demonstration of errors of performance, the use of audience participation, the amount of commentary, the use of stereoscopic effects, the density of ideas, to mention a few.

The program of research resulted in a series of conclusions of considerable practical value. Such research led to such findings as that many motor skills could be readily taught by means of films, that instructional films should be designed with particular audiences in mind, that films might release the time of instructors for helping individuals with particular difficulties, that instructional films should have a straightforward approach, that films should develop ideas slowly, that the camera angle should show the task to be learned from the learner's physical position in space, and many others. Altogether 65 major conclusions were drawn. Many of these conclusions disposed of such prejudices of film makers as that special effects and dramatizations were of value, and music was also shown to be quite ineffective in promoting learning. The conclusions are outlined in the final volume of *Instructional Film Research Reports,* published in 1956, covering research pursued over many years.

The research had surprisingly little impact on those who produce instructional films for schools, though some of the university centers of instructional film production, such as that at Indiana University, were influenced. The typical commercial producer of instructional films still continued to introduce unnecessary drammatizations, and tended to be guided by what might be termed aesthetic insight. The wisdom derived from the Pennsylvania State College studies was not assimilated into educational practice, perhaps because instructional films have to be made attractive to teachers and purchasers rather than useful to students.

While Carpenter was developing his experimental studies of the use of motion pictures for classroom instruction, a second program of research was in progress on the use of television for instruction. The latter was under the direction of Robert T. Rock at Fordham University. Rock had been a student of Thorndike's at Teachers College. Then he moved to Fordham University where he had worked in the Department of Psychology and served as chairman for many years, but he never became a particularly productive research worker.

Rock did not have to undertake the ponderous review of previous research that Carpenter had to undertake in developing his enterprise, for television was new and research on its instructional uses was new. What Rock did was to develop a rather large research enterprise to explore the usefulness for the military of television instruction in contrast with traditional forms of instruction. The final report concluded that television instruction could be used effectively to develop many military skills (Instructional Television Research Reports No. NAVTRA DEVCEN 20-TV-4. (1956).

The study of specific classroom techniques and classroom materials, in classroom settings, was a successful enterprise, in that it produced findings that had important practical applications, even though the applications were not always made. The research demonstrated that inquiry in classroom settings could be valuable, even though previous efforts had not led to any success. Research has continued through to modern times along such lines, though few devices have shown themselves to be as useful as the motion picture.

WHATEVER HAPPENED TO STUDIES OF TEACHING METHODS!

The advent of peace in 1945 did not bring a return to the enthusiasm for innovation of the previous decade. There were scattered efforts in the United States to move away from regimented classroom procedures, and a few efforts to compare the outcomes of these new curricula with the outcomes of more conservative methods. But the studies that had been undertaken had produced a pervasive atmosphere of disillusionment concerning the value of educational research as a means of supporting educational change. Indeed, by 1950, systematic attempts to establish the worth of new methods of teaching in classroom situations had been largely abandoned in the schools, though college professors became interested in the study of college teaching.

The decline in studies concerning the worth of innovative curricula in schools came to an end, not because of any lack of financial support, but because the results appeared so unpromising. The hope of research workers had been that research would show that some educational practices were more effective than others in achieving particular goals. The research had not shown anything like that. Any practice seemed to be about as effective as any other. The comment was voiced that any practice designated as "experimental" seemed to be a little more effective than whatever practice was designated as traditional. That was hardly a surprising result for educational administrators have long known that any innovative program energizes teachers. Yet despite the failure of research to produce evidence that one method of teaching might be better than another, the educational establishment seemed convinced that there were important differences in outcomes, though research methods were too crude to demonstrate differences.

Disillusionment with research on newer educational practices was accompanied in the public sector by disillusionment with those practices. Strong attacks were launched, from midcentury on, against anything that might be associated with the Progressive Education Movement. Loud and often eloquent voices urged that schools return to traditional methods with an emphasis on basics. What the advocates of a return to traditional classroom procedures do not seem to have recognized was that few schools had ever departed from a very traditional approach to teaching. Nevertheless, in such an atmosphere educational administrators were fearful of introducing any innovation, and those interested in research had few classroom situations in which they could conduct experimental studies. Some classroom research developed that avoided such sensitive matters as the virtues of progressive education. One line of research that propspered at the college level was a comparison of lecture methods and discussion methods of teaching. The latter research was important, but it did not carry the appeal of the earlier research that had sought to attack the core issues of educational reform. Classroom experimentation had lost much of its glamour.

PART V

Since Midcentury

This last chapter has been reserved for a discussion of educational research during the last 30 years. Such a discussion is particularly difficult because the work has not yet stood the test of time. Research may be backed by the enthusiasms of the age in which it is undertaken, and later fail to meet the approval of subsequent generations. The history of educational research shows, again and again, the pouring out of enthusiasm for some research-based innovation, only to be followed by the rapid disappearance of the innovation. The worthwhile contributions of research workers persist. Time is a powerful test of the value of research findings and application. Thorndike's concept of the importance of knowledge of results has survived the test of time. Almost nothing of the educational reforms suggested by John B. Watson have survived, largely because they have been demonstrated to be wrong. There is no way in which to speed up the test of time. That is the central difficulty in reviewing research of recent decades.

The volume was originally planned to end this historical review around the year 1950, but most critics of the initial drafts of the manuscript insisted that a final chapter should be added, that presented the salient features of educational research of the last few decades. So this chapter came to be written.

Were the educational research organizations, developed by the Federal Government successes or failures? Did the inflow of large amounts of money into the educational research enterprise increase substantially the knowledge available? Did the new Federally-sponsored enterprises improve the quality of educational research? What have been the sources of recent research influences on schools? Final answers to such questions cannot be given yet, but the reader may draw some tentative conclusions after reading this chapter. The answers, arrived at by the reader, can be only very tentative, for good answers cannot come until this entire century has become a part of history.

CHAPTER 12

Recent Trends and Future Promises

THE NEW SOCIAL STRUCTURE OF EDUCATIONAL RESEARCH

Educational research since midcentury has changed for at least two major reasons. First, it has changed because of the intervention of government. This intervention has resulted both in increasing funding and a change in the locus of control. Second, educational research has changed because the outstanding figures in psychology who influenced the course of research in the first half of the century have faded into history. New figures have emerged, with new concepts of the nature of the human. Some influence still lingers from Thorndike, Judd, Terman, and the other leaders of earlier times, and some of the influences they have left with us have become engraved on the schools, but there are new figures with new influences. The central and influential ideas of psychology have changed and, indirectly, produced changes in educational research.

NEW WAYS OF ESTABLISHING RESEARCH POLICIES

Research related to education developed in the early part of the century, through scholars becoming fascinated with exploring the educational implications of some of the ideas that dominated the expanding frontier of social research. These research enterprises were the product of individual initiative. In contrast, much of the contemporary research related to education is not a product of individual initiative, but a consequence of government policy.

The first move in the direction of the government taking the initiative in setting research policies related to education came through the Cooperative Research Act of 1954. There had been some government influences before that time. The Federal government, for nearly a century, had emphasized data collection as a means of discovering where improvements needed to be made in education. States and cities had, since very early in the century, supported research bureaus. The bureaus of research generally undertook quite prosaic tasks of data collection. They pursued the kinds of empirical methods that had been a part of the work of Horace Mann in Massachusetts and Henry Barnard in Connecticut. The bureaus were not innovative, and were not designed to be, but schools were probably better administered because of their existence. Educational research, as an innovative activity, was a product of academicians.

THE COOPERATIVE RESEARCH ACT

After midcentury, the Federal government sought to encourage the innovative educational research of academicians that had done so much for the transformation of education in the past. The Cooperative Research Act of 1954 was developed with skill and insight. The act sought to encourage educational research in the academic world in which research had been successfully developed in the past. The Act provided funds for the development of research within an academic setting. Academicians were encouraged to submit proposals, and those who had good qualifications to undertake research, of which there were few, were likely to have their projects funded. The money also served the important function of developing research talents in graduate students, for graduate students of education were thereby provided opportunities for participating in ongoing research projects.

When the Cooperative Research Act was passed, it was an enabling act but without any funding. The next year, the Congress provided one million dollars, but two thirds of the sum was earmarked for research on the retarded. In later years this restriction was dropped. However, the way was not open for the development of a research program in terms of the ideas of those capable of conducting research in academic institutions. A conflict developed between the staff of the office of education on how projects should be selected. The staff looked upon the funds as enabling them to do the kinds of surveys that they had been doing since the days when Charles Judd exercised power. The Research Advisory Committee wanted to see research expanded into new areas. The immediate winner in that contest was the Research Advisory Committee, backed by the Commissioner of Education. The Cooperative Research Program, under the sponsorship of the Research Advisory Committee, acquired considerable prestige and by 1959 was receiving an appropriation of 2.7 million. The conflict related to the control of the Cooperative Research Program is of interest in that the years that followed showed an intensification of that conflict. Nevertheless, so long as the Cooperative Research Program was guided by the Research Advisory Committee it had some excellent products, and yet the program was criticized for a lack of products.

The amount of money invested in educational research through the Cooperative Research Act was quite minimal, but the products were of considerable significance. Most of those who undertook research in the program were well established research workers. The Act permitted these individuals to expand what they were doing by employing doctoral students. The choice of problems for research remained almost entirely in the hands of research workers. The Act did much to encourage research in classrooms and resulted in the development of many instruments for assessing aspects of teaching. Under the auspices of the Act there were many worthwhile developments. Ned Flanders developed extensive research on his system of interaction analysis, Marie Hughes developed a more elaborate system of interaction analysis, B. Othanel Smith explored the use of logical structures for categorizing pupil-teacher interactions, Hilda Taba developed work on teaching strategies, and there were other significant contributions.

More than anything else the program became a stimulus for the development of research within schools and colleges of education. These institutions needed this kind of stimulus and support for them to fulfill their functions as centers of innovation. A few colleges of education had, in the past, emphasized research and scholarly work, now other institutions saw that they had opportunities to provide similar leadership. The future of academic institutions for the graduate training of educational personnel became even brighter when the Congress passed further legislation to facilitate educational research as a part of the hastily drawn up National Defense Education Act of 1958. Title VII of the Act was designed to promote research into such areas as the development of visual aids and the technology of instruction.

Dershimer in his fascinating book on *The Federal Government and Educational R & D* (1976), states that the section of the bill that promoted research into educational technology was inserted by congressmen without any expert advice. The latter seems to have been the beginning of a trend that would later shape the policies related to the initiation of research policies. Despite the fact that the Title VII proposal was born of a combination of enthusiasm and ignorance it was one of the better ideas that the Congress has initiated in the educational research field.

Thus by 1960 substantial funds were available for educational research. The Cooperative Research Program was now funded to the extent of 3.2 million, and the total available for educational research in all programs was over 10 million. By 1964 the amount available had grown to nearly 20 million. These appear to be very large sums of money, but in some respects they do reflect the state of affairs in educational research. Although the funds had grown substantially, the number of accepted proposals from colleges of education had not grown. The expanding funds available had attracted research workers from related fields, who managed to give their research projects a twist that often produced the illusion that the enterprises had important implications for education. Few of these research workers on the periphery continued to show any interest in education once the funds dried up, though a very few did.

RESEARCH CENTERS AND LABORATORIES

The staff of the Office of Education, and a sequence of Commissioners had long felt dissatisfaction with the university-based focus of the decision making process related to what research should be undertaken and how it should be undertaken. In the early 1960's Sterling McMurrin was Commissioner of Education, and he had other plans for the growth of educational research which included the revival of the old idea of a half century earlier of the development of Research and Development Centers. This was far from a popular idea within the staff of the Office of Education, in that such centers implied that control would also lie outside of the Office. Nevertheless, despite opposition, McMurrin appointed committees to consider the possibility of developing Research and Development Centers related to education.

Eventually McMurrin found an advisory panel that produced the plan he wanted. The panel chaired by Ralph Tyler recommended that Research and Development Centers be established for the purpose of bringing to bear financial and intellectual resources to the solution of educational problems. The Centers were also expected to innovate, disseminate knowledge, and to conduct research along the entire range from basic to applied and administrative. Although McMurrin's panel members held important positions, the only one who had had any recent experience with the conduct of research was Benjamin Bloom. In many respects the panel reflected the views commonly held by the public in the 1960's rather than the views of professional research workers. Such views were at that time overwhelmed by the wartime success of the Manhattan project. From that project there emerged the view that any practical problem could be solved by bringing together a group of scientists and providing them with whatever resources were needed to solve the problem.

There was a basic fallacy in such thinking. The Manhattan project was successful because it was based upon a very advanced state of knowledge of nuclear physics. All the essential basic knowledge was there for the development of an atomic bomb, but some very difficult technical problems had to be worked out in order to make the bomb an actuality. A similar state of affairs did not exist in education. Behavioral sciences were still in a very primitive state, and could not provide the intellectual backing for Research and Development Centers of the kind that physics provided for the Manhattan project. The kind of development that was needed in the field of education could not possibly be based on a parallel with successful developments in the physical sciences.

An important feature of the design of the proposed centers was that they should be comparable in some respects to the agricultural research stations. The analogy between educational and agricultural research had long been used and can be traced back to the 1920's when the Office of Education had previously attempted to develop educational research centers. The centers had not survived. The analogy with the agricultural centers focused on the idea that there was a body of knowledge available that needed to be passed on to practitioners. The agricultural experiment stations were established under the Hatch Act (1887) for the purpose of diffusing "practical information on subjects connected with agriculture and to promote scientific investigation and experiment respecting the principles and applications of agricultural science." States were originally required to match Federal funds but later became the major contributors, for the stations were an enormous success. Educational Research and Development Centers were expected to have a similar success, but this hope was based upon a false analogy.

Enthusiasm for the new centers for undertaking research and development within the Office of Education knew no limits. Even before some of the new centers had been started, a new type of center was established, described as a Policy Research Center, and that was soon followed by specialized centers for undertaking work in early childhood education and vocational education. The hope was that what was believed to be the slow pace of educational progress would be rapidly accelerated through this unprecedented concentration of talent for research in a few localities. The Manhattan Project for Education was now in full swing, but the critics claimed that it could produce nothing more than a puff of smoke.

Critics there were. The only real supporters of the new enterprises were just a few universities to which a minority of the research centers were attached. These were the beneficiaries of the Office of Education's newly found power. In other institutions, that had gained from the Cooperative Research Program but lost from the new program, there was much less enthusiasm. They saw the new centers as draining away the funds that had enabled them to initiate a research program. They were right. Schools and Colleges of Education were to lose most of their support for the research they needed to make them genuinely centers for graduate training, though schools such as those at the University of Chicago and Teachers College, Columbia, would, of course, continue to undertake research. Also, even the new centers that were located in universities, were not components of schools and departments of education, but were independent enterprises.

The move to establish centers made by the Office of Education was not the only move that tended to further isolate schools and colleges of education and the teaching profession from the research enterprise. While the Office of Education was developing its center program, the American Educational Research Association was severing its connection from the National Education Association. The Association had shown great expansion during the 1960's as a result of the influx of Federal money into educational research and development. This new membership provided strong backing for taking the Association out of the National Education Association and to make it an independent scientific and scholarly organization. The new membership had little in common with those who formed the core of the National Education Association. They thought of themselves as a part of scientific community, dedicated to the advancement of knowledge and the application of scientific knowledge. The severing of ties permitted this new image to grow, and at least to provide an image of a new maturity. The move of educational researchers to achieve independence from those in other aspects of education received almost unanimous support within the educational research community.

Still a further idea emerged in the Office of Education. That was the idea of developing a national chain of what were to be called regional laboratories. The idea had received the endorsement of the usual blue ribbon committees. The year 1966 seems to have spawned Office of Education committees related to the proposed new program of regional laboratories, and the decision was made to fund 20 laboratories. Edith Green, who chaired the related congressional committee, wanted only one or two centers started on a trial basis, but was outvoted by her committee. Her position was that there were enough trained personnel for only a modest beginning.

The Office of Education took steps to ensure a greater certainty for the future of the laboratories by appointing a still further committee to investigate the early activities of those that had been established. The new committee was chaired by Francis S. Chase and seems to have been generally in favor of the regional laboratory idea. The committee members had virtually no credentials as research workers, and were quite unknown to research workers in the field. The Office of Education staff did not seem to care much about who made recommendations so long as they were consistent with Office of Education policy. The Chase committee kept the laboratories alive in their early stages. Later, when Chase was sent out to evaluate particular laboratories, his favorable reports also served to extend the life of the institutions.

The reader should note that Francis Seabury Chase (1899-) had been chairman of the Department of Education at the University of Chicago from 1951-1968, a position to which Judd had given considerable prestige. However, Chase had had only the minimal kind of experience in research that a professor of education typically has. He had spent many years in the principalship of schools and was a recognized authority on school administration about which he had written extensively. He had the kinds of sympathies related to research that the Office of Education endorsed, even if he lacked the qualifications needed to make him competent to judge the merits of research policies. His prestige as a practical administrator made him useful to the Office of Education as the contact with schools where his views on research seemed to be appreciated, even if they were not appreciated by research scholars in the academic community. Despite Chase's limitations in the field of research, his influence in the late 1960's was considerable. Indeed, without his influence, the centers and laboratories would probably not have survived.

Nevertheless, at least half of the laboratories were doomed to failure and represented planned failures on the part of the Federal government. The bureaucracy had not wanted to establish 20 laboratories, but a number closer to 10 seemed about right in terms of the money that could be expected. However, in order for the program to be funded at all, every congressman had to be able to point to a laboratory reasonably close to his constituency to which problems could be referred. The existence of 20 laboratories ensured that kind of proximity. Once the Congress had approved the program there would then be little difficulty in whittling down the number to 10 or fewer. The time was propitious to have such a program funded, for the enthusiasm for the Great Society ensured that the Elementary and Secondary Education Act would slip through Congress with the proposal intact. Authorization for the laboratories was in Title IV of the Act. Over a year elapsed between the passage of the enabling act and the negotiation of the preliminary contracts for laboratories. The Office of Education was already planning the demise of some of the organizations almost as soon as they were developed. By August 1969 five of the laboratories were dropped. Within 4 years of the initiation of the program the number of laboratories had been cut in half.

Throughout the documents related to the development of the laboratories and other forms of centers is the notion that items of scientific information are waiting to be picked up and used by practitioners, and that the new educational research organizations could mediate the transfer of that information. This is a great oversimplification of how knowledge influences education. In embracing this oversimplification the cause of education has not been helped. First, one must notice that what is called "knowledge" in the behavioral sciences does not have the secure footing that, say, Newtonian physics has. Indeed, a "discovery" in the behavioral sciences hardly qualifies as knowledge until the work on which it has been based has not only been repeated, but has been repeated by different groups of scientists working in different settings. There are too many examples of work, coming out of one laboratory, and with completely consistent results, that cannot be repeated elsewhere. The behavioral sciences are frequently led along false paths by will-o-the-wisps, that not only lead nowhere, but which vanish. There is much solid knowledge, but it has sometimes taken a quarter of a century or more to find out whether knowledge is solid or a will-o-the-wisp.

Personnel in the Office of Education had little understanding of the nature of knowledge in the behavioral sciences and even less knowledge of the problem of applying that knowledge. Associate Commissioners for Research had typically no qualifications in the field though they may have had experience in administration. Perhaps the cue for such appointments may have come from the memory that the Manhattan Project was run successfully by General Groves who had no reputation as a scientist. The analogy was hardly a productive one, for Groves was closely advised by the top scientists in the country. Associate Commissioners for Research in the Office of Education had no such entourage. They remained isolated from the research community. Yet despite this isolation, the personnel of the Office of Education in the Bureau of Research came to assume ever increasing power in the establishment of research policies and decisions related to whether particular projects should, or should not, receive support.

In 1966, a meeting was arranged in Washington between the staff of the Office's Bureau of Research staff and research workers across the country. At that meeting the policy was announced that all decisions related to the use of research funds would be made by a committee consisting of the heads of the various divisions of the Bureau. Questions were, of course, asked about whether the department heads had had sufficient experience with research to make judgments, but the questions led nowhere. The new policy remained in force for many years, until the programs were ultimately transferred to the National Institute of Education. Whether there was, or was not, a policy of having all decisions related to educational research made by the bureaucracy made little difference. The bureaucracy had already learned that carefully selected committees would endorse almost any viewpoint the bureaucracy wanted. The formation of committees can be manipulated.

CONGRESS AND THE NEW EVALUATION MOVEMENT

Educational research has also been influenced by Federal legislation in other important ways. For the last decade, virtually every bill authorizing particular educational programs has included a requirement that the particular programs be evaluated to determine whether the program was worth the money spent upon it. The idea was that, if a program could be shown to be worth the money, then continued support should be legislated, otherwise it should be scrapped. The argument has appeal to those who know much about legislation, but little about evaluation. It is based upon the assumption that techniques are available for determining the worth of particular educational programs, and that the result of the application of those techniques can be used to decide whether to continue or drop a program or to continue it in a modified form.

The logic of the proposed educational evaluation was very much the same that was applied to the evaluation of medications. However research workers have now discovered that the effect of a drug might not be evident for as long as 25 years, and might be apparent only in the next generation. The same difficulties are now apparent in the evaluation of educational programs. There is no simple way of determining whether a program is or is not a worthwhile element in the life of the individual. A quick method of teaching a child to read could, conceivably, lead the child to dislike reading in such a way that he might become a nonreader as an adult. Immediate outcomes of education may bear little relationship to long-term outcomes. The problem of the evaluation of educational programs is a very difficult problem, and as difficult as that of evaluating the effects of medication. Legislators may want quick answers to questions and are likely to receive answers contrived for political purposes rather than real answers. Merely including a requirement for evaluation into a Congressional bill, does not ensure that a genuine evaluation can be made. Indeed, when included as a requirement, the practice is likely to encourage what might be termed counterfeit evaluation studies.

Despite the fact that legal requirements for evaluation of new federally funded educational programs were based on false logic, the legislation did have an indirect positive outcome. Although evaluation studies had virtually ceased to exist in the late 1930's, the new money that was poured into evaluation in the 1970's led to a revival of exploration in the area. The difficulties that had led to the virtual abandonement of evaluation studies thirty years earlier had not been overcome in the intervening years, and had not been studied. At least there was now a cadre of competent academicians who were willing to wrestle with the problems. Few seem to have recognized, what comes out so clearly in this volume, that evaluation activities over the past century have tended to stultify innovation in education. The techniques are too crude to provide much evidence of immediate gains and wholly unable to identify any long term effects that particular programs may have. The evidence thus produced tends to be biased in the direction of producing false negatives.

Evaluation studies also appear to have the strange effects of encouraging educational programs that fit the evaluation techniques. Thus if the techniques of evaluation involved traditional forms of paper-and-pencil tests, then decisions based on the evaluation results tend to lead to the retention of programs that produce skills in taking paper-and-pencil tests. Very little is understood about these problems, but much more would be known if the Congress had supported the development of evaluation techniques, rather than requiring evaluations of particular programs.

THE NATIONAL INSTITUTE OF EDUCATION

Once the first wave of enthusiasm for the new centers and laboratories had faded, the Washington bureaucracy had considerable difficulty in maintaining support for the new programs. Indeed, support within the Department of Health, Education and Welfare seems to have dwindled. The latter is evident from the fact that the staff of the Bureau of Research was cut in half from the year 1967 to the year 1971. Congressional support was also dwindling. Then Nixon was elected to the Presidency and the new administration sought to cut spending on education, since the Vietnam war was absorbing far more than the government had to spend. However, Nixon had proposed during his campaign to be elected that a National Institute for the Educational Future should be created (see Dershimer, p. 128). Nixon also wanted to see all programs cut out that could not be justified in terms of results, and that would have involved the entire array of new research organizations. Since Nixon had proposed the National Institute of Education, this seemed to be a way to salvage the entire program of research that had grown up under the Johnson administration. A new National Institute of Education could appear as a new start, with no questions asked about whether the ventures of the past had or had not been successful.

The new National Institute of Education was scarcely discriminable from the Bureau of Research in the Office of Education. There was no freshness of viewpoint of the kind that some had anticipated. Nevertheless, the creation of the Institute was a successful bureaucratic ploy, for it had saved both the research laboratories and centers and the related bureaucracy from destruction. For some this seemed a worthwhile outcome, but those who believed that a change was necessary were left with disappointment. The new Institute continued the programs of the past even though it had difficulty in keeping them alive.

There are many different opinions about the worth of the centers and laboratories, but a defensible evaluation is impossible to find. Any estimation of the worth of the organizations has to take into account the fact that they were conceived without any thoughts about whether they could, or could not, be staffed. The new organizations were able to offer no employment advantages to research workers of repute, and the fact that only half of the laboratories had a 5-year survival rate shows how little they had to offer to prospective employees. Many would say that, taking into account the difficulties they had in staffing, they have done quite well.

Anyone who wishes to take a quick look at what the organizations have produced should turn to the publications of the Council of Educational Development and Research. The latter is a coordinating organization for the centers and laboratories. One of its functions has been to compile a catalog of the products of the participating organizations. This compilation is referred to as the *Cedar Catalog.* The *Cedar Catalog* appeared annually through 1974, but was not prepared after that date in view of the fact that the National Institute of Education planned to take over the task. However, the National Institute of Education has so far never produced a complete catalog, but has put out partial lists of products in particular areas.

In the *Cedar Catalog* the products were classified into the categories of school organizations, early childhood education, elementary education, secondary education, career education, higher education, teacher education, basic research, and school organization and administration. A first point to note about this compilation is that the category of basic research is the smallest. The category includes such products as "*Promising School Practices for Mexican Americans.*" However the Wisconsin Research and Development Center has a bibliography of nearly 450 technical reports and theoretical papers, which implies that the center did encourage basic research, presumably among the young doctoral candidates that worked there.

Much of the remainder of the products listed are packaged programs. Some of these packaged programs are materials for children. Others are packages related to such matters as how to develop a school consortium within a state, or how to diffuse educational innovations. The catalog also lists a number of books that have been produced and published by the centers and laboratories.

The catalog shows that the centers and laboratories were producing materials and programs for use in schools. The early materials were designed so that they could, supposedly, be used by teachers without special training in the use of the materials, but that did not work. One cannot criticize the research organization for failing to produce evidence that the programs were more effective than those in use, for there is probably no way to demonstrate immediate superiority, even if such superiority exists. Long-term superiority is what really counts and time does not permit long-term follow-up studies, and short-term follow-up studies might well be misleading. The materials listed in the *Cedar Catalog* probably represent products that are well-designed in terms of available knowledge. Although the centers and laboratories were established to do research and provide tested products for schools, they have not been able to provide tested products. Indeed, the idea of a tested educational product, except in a very general sense, is almost an obsolete one.

In many areas the products of the organizations did not have to compete with commercially available products. For example, a commercial publisher probably would not invest in a publication related to the development of school consortia, but a center or laboratory could. Where they had to compete, they had difficulties in reaching a national market.

When one considers the fact the centers and laboratories were poorly conceived in the first place, they did surprisingly well. In view of the misdirection provided by the Congress, the Office of Education bureaucracy, and the various advisory committees that established them, they have shown at least some productivity.

If one allows oneself to be critical in terms of the limited evidence on which one can base such criticism, one would probably focus on the lack of originality of most of the materials that have been produced. The materials developed by the centers and laboratories tend to be quite prosaic and tied to whatever happens to be the leading idea of the moment. Thus the 1974 vintage showed a substantial emphasis on the ideas of competency analysis and program planning and budgeting systems. The materials showed a shortage of new ideas, but that is hardly surprising in view of the shortage of the talent of originality, and the difficulty that the laboratories had in attracting such talent.

The rather bland evaluation of the centers and laboratories that has been presented here cannot be left without pointing out that a large section of the academic community of educational research workers reviews the accomplishments of the organizations in different terms. A paper by Orlich ("Federal Educational Policy: The Paradox of Innovation and Centralization," *Educational Researcher*, 1979, 8(7), 4-9) reflects a common critical position. The key paragraph in the article is the following (p. 8):

> There is a tendency to fund poorly conceptualized and politically motivated R & D projects, rather than to fund well-planned research proposals. The USOE is looking for quick payoffs which never tend to materialize.

The paragraph represents a widely-held opinion, but the basis of the opinion could probably be readily documented. There are also other, equally devastating criticisms of the way in which projects were funded by the Federal Government that are well documented in terms of fact. For example, Orlich points out that there is evidence that (p. 4) "the size of a project is unrelated to its success," and that small grants had as much impact as the larger ones. Yet the government persists in funding very large enterprises that absorb much of the money available for educational research.

There was also another widely voiced criticism of the then current methods of distributing research and development funds. All too often organizations are established, both in school systems and elsewhere, for the sole purpose of obtaining federal funds. The object of the organizations is not to do research or develop new ideas or to apply old ones. The primary purpose is above all to obtain money. Whatever money is available is applied for, but it is not applied for out of a burning desire to solve some problem. When the money is obtained some attempt may be made to solve the problem for which the money was given but the research project officer may have no particular interest in the problem. Hardly surprising is it that the money thus obtained produces few solutions to problems. Very difficult problems are solved by those who have both the drive and the enthusiasm to solve them, and not by those whose primary interest is in grantsmanship.

The survival of educational research, over the long term, depends upon the support of the talent that can make it a success. Such talent has to acquire a strong voice in policies related to what is undertaken. Government committees of worthy and distinguished business executives and university and foundation presidents cannot provide the guidance needed. They simply do not understand what educational research can and cannot accomplish. The control of educational research, like the control of research in the biological and physical sciences, must come from those who are professionally identified with it. Congressmen have to be persuaded that much more than good intent is needed in designing legislation to develop education through research. The task of changing the attitudes of congressmen seems easy compared with the task of convincing the Federal bureaucracy that some of their control should be relinquished, because to relinquish control is to lose supervisory functions, and to lose supervisory functions leads to the downgrading of jobs and the lowering of salaries. The control of educational research, since midcentury, has been caught in a quagmire of politics, from which escape seems to be nigh impossible. Yet escape is essential.

SOME OF THE NEW SOURCES OF KNOWLEDGE RELATED TO EDUCATIONAL RESEARCH

Although the new centers and laboratories did little to create a body of new knowledge relevant to education, the period since midcentury has been one that has presented a glittering pageant of new ideas, coming from outside education, that have had important implications for education. These ideas have come from a variety of sources including psychology, sociology, biology, pediatrics and child development, and linguistics. The discussion that follows of some of these new sources of ideas important for education can cover only what are judged by the author to be some of the significant trends. The discussion is provided to point out the wealth of new knowledge that has been accumulated and can influence education.

Perception, Memory, and Brain Models

The psychology of perception has long been a source of influence on education. Indeed, one of the earliest scientific influences on educational thought was the development of the study of perception by Herbart. A century later James McKeen Cattell was to initiate his experimental studies of perceptual problems in reading. The latter work, neglected during much of the present century, was taken up again after midcentury. The work was supported by the Federal Government in the 1960's when funds were given to academicians interested in exploring psychological problems related to education, but the support did not continue into the 1970's when the Federal government became interested in supporting the research organizations it had created.

The work on perceptual processes in reading could well have been extended into the study of perceptual difficulties of those who are poor readers, or late readers, or nonreaders. The claim is often made that a considerable fraction of reading difficulties are a result of perceptual difficulties, but the way in which those perceptual difficulties can be understood in terms of a general theory of perception still needs to be worked out.

Research on the psychology of perception has also introduced radical changes into our present concept of learning. Up to midcentury, just a few psychologists held the position that learning could not take place through mere exposure to the phenomenal world, and without reinforcement, those working on the psychology of perception have now been able to demonstrate that learning without external feedback or reinforcement does take place. Such demonstrations have produced radical changes in our concept of how the infant learns and discovers structure in his environment. Though nobody would abandon the idea that the acquisition of knowledge in the infant is tied, to a considerable degree, to action, the new research on perception opened up the way for the inclusion of perceptual learning, not tied directly to action. Psychologists, who had earlier rejected the idea that learning could not take place efficiently by expository methods, were now forced into a defensive position through the discovery that perceptual learning is a reality.

Research on perception and perceptual learning has emphasized the fact that the channel of entry of information into the human processing system is a channel of limited capacity. Indeed, the current model of perceptual processing is much like that adopted by Maria Montessori in designing her learning procedures. Montessori assumed that the child has a limited capacity for processing information and must be given a limited amount of information at any one time. Although the capacity of the human memory is very large, information can be placed there, or retrieved, only through a limited capacity system.

Research on perception has provided a new foundation for designing audiovisual materials for instructional purposes. The first half of the present century laid the foundation for the design of verbal materials for instruction, but provided little that could lead to the improved design of instructional materials involving nonverbal materials. Research on perception also provided a useful understanding of what happens in the learner when information is provided through more than one channel. Classical information theory, developed in the medium of electronics and physics, has been particularly valuable for providing a structure within which some aspects of perception can be understood.

The study of perception in infancy has been advanced through the application of classical and operant conditioning techniques. Although operant conditioning, as a theory of behavior, has had little influence on the accumulation of knowledge about infant behavior, operant techniques have contributed to experimentation in the area. The understanding of the intellectual development of the young infant has always been hampered by the lack of outputs of behavior on the part of the infant. This lack of outputs has led, in the past, to interpretations of infant behavior that grossly underestimated intellectual achievements. The newer techniques of studying infants have provided a much richer, and more correct, view of early intellectual development.

Our recently acquired understanding of learning and perception in infancy has led to the beginning of an understanding of the role that education can play in the early years. Those who lived in antiquity believed that the period of growth that preceded adolescence were just years of growth calling for no formal training. Schools were for adolescents and for young adults. Only slowly has humanity come to realize the infinite importance of learning in childhood. Slowly, the age at which formal methods of education are begun has been pushed to a lower and lower age. Now research has led us to understand that a wealth of learning must take place in infancy if the individual is to develop to a maximum. Research in this area is of the greatest importance to education.

Models of the brain have shown considerable development in the last few decades, and particularly in relation to perception. The concept of the perceptual mechanisms of the brain involving specific analyzers was one important development. A second has been the introduction of the idea that the brain is far more than an analyzer of information and a maker of associations, for the brain is capable of simulating external events. Thus when the brain is thinking about how a piece of machinery works, it performs internal operations analogous to the working of the machine. The recognition of the fact that the brain can simulate external conditions accounts for the fact that an individual viewing an object can imagine what the object would look like if turned in different positions. The brain is also capable of imagining events that have not yet occurred, and from those imaginings the individual may be able to predict outcomes. This form of brain function seems to develop with age and preschool children show little capacity for it. Whether maturation is the chief factor in this transition and development still has to be determined, but the significance of the idea for the design of curricula is obvious.

Other developments of brain models are better known to educators, even though their implications for education are far less clear. Much has been written on right-versus-left side brain functions, though the picture that is now emerging is far less clear than that which seemed to emerge from the initial research. Unfortunately, educators seized on the initial findings of right and left brain differences and made applications to education that were probably unjustified. Perhaps the lesson still has to be learned that the path that leads from the laboratory to the field application has to be followed slowly and cautiously.

Perception and memory are intimately related, as James J. Gibson has reminded us throughout his lifetime. Perception is information processing, and memory is information storage. The way in which information is processed has to be related to the way in which information is stored, for some of the information that is processed is stored. The processing of information has to leave it in a form compatible with the storage system. Thus the study of memory and percetion are intimately related.

Since midcentury extensive research has been undertaken on memory, much of it related to the problem of understanding the nature of the storage system. Studies of memory of the last century suggested significant ways in which the memorization of materials might be facilitated in schools. The newer trend in research on memory has much broader implications. A valid model of the human memory would indicate how human knowledge is organized. An understanding of how human knowledge is structured in memory should suggest how the curriculum should be planned to facilitate the entry of information into memory. Yet curriculum workers seem to be largely unaware of the research that has been undertaken on human memory and the implications of that work for curriculum construction.

Thought related to the structure of human memory has been facilitated by the fact that computers have memories, and the computer permits the research worker to experiment with models of memory systems that may be built into computers. The research worker no longer has to imagine how a particular model of memory would work, for he can simulate a model of memory with a computer and then watch it work. However, such models still fall far short of the capacity of the human memory to identify a particular piece of information almost instantly and transform it into a verbal output.

Research on perception has had very important implications for the development of an understanding of the difficulties of those who have sensory and perceptual handicaps. Not until blind infants were studied were the full difficulties of the person born blind fully understood. The study of the perceptual problems of the hearing impaired and the deaf have led to a greater understanding of the problem of developing language skills in such individuals. The understanding of the Spitz hospitalism syndrome in foundling home children has also been expanded through research on perception.

Research on Language

This category of research has been selected for brief discussion here because it has such obvious and important implications for education. Few areas of psychology have shown such a radical transformation of ideas since midcentury. The revolution that has taken place in our understanding of language was the product of one thinker, and one thinker alone, namely Noam Chomsky. The word *thinker* has been carefully selected for this context in that Chomsky is first and foremost a thinker and not an empirical researcher, and yet his work has had far reaching impact on research. But the impact of Chomsky has gone far beyond research in linguistics, for it has influenced anthropology, and has even opened up new avenues of thought in philosophy.

At various points in this volume there has been a discussion of the influence on education of aspects of research related to language in the period before the revolution in linguistics. The research dealt with such matters as the vocabulary of very young children at different stages of language development, what was believed to be work on the shaping of the babbling of the child into recognizeable words, length of sentence, second language learning, and so forth. The new emphasis in research is on entirely different matters, and especially the creative aspect of language reflected in the fact that an infant can produce novel sentences, even in the second year of life. The new research seeks to discover how the speaker acquires a knowledge of the structure of language, that permits new sentences to be created. The competence of a speaker has to be understood in terms of the speaker's knowledge of the rules involved in the production of language, even though the speaker cannot state those rules. The discovery of these implicit rules provides a scientific description of the nature of language. The grammar described by these rules must be such that it can account for an infinite set of sentences that can be included in the language. Within such a context, the task of the psychologist is to discover the way in which the rules emerge and the conditions necessary for the acquisition of competence in a language. The research undertaken to date has not resulted in a complete theory of language, because language is perhaps the most complex form of behavior, or form of anything, ever studied. Nevertheless, considerable progress has been made and far more is known today about human language than was known a quarter of a century ago.

New techniques for studying young children have made it possible to study the perception of speech sounds in young infants. A great deal is now known about the development of the perception of speech in infants, and apparent attention given by infants to speech sounds suggests a specialized aspect of perception related to speech that may well be innate. The child obviously has considerable expertise in speech perception before it utters its first word. Research in this area should eventually provide information about the kind of verbal environment that favors the development of pre-speech competencies in infants. In this connection the role of babbling remains obscure. It does not seem to be a practice period for communicative speech, but it may have other more obscure functions. The now well-established fact that speech is not slowly shaped out of babbling has changed the character of research related to early speech development.

Related to research on the development of perception of speech, is research on single-word speech that characterizes the infant around the first year. The traditional view has been that the single word generally seems to refer to a category of objects, or it places a particular object in a category. The categories are generally much broader than those used by an adult. Thus the word "doggie" may be used to refer to any animal. Only through a long period of learning does the child learn the discriminative features of the category as it is used by adults. Here again the findings have important implications for education that need to be explored. For example, do children from underprivileged environments, provided with little verbal interaction, fail to narrow the categories to which words refer, so the child continues to use words with reference to his own individualized categories. There are also interesting questions as to when the adult should attempt to expand the young child's one-word utterances. The child in the one-word stage attends to one-word utterances of adults, rather than multi-word utterances, which suggests that she attends only at the grammatical level to that which she understands. Attention to utterances of more than one word would appear to require an understanding of grammar.

The early development of grammar is a particularly controversial area, and yet one that has potentially important implications for helping the child acquire a first language. Early attempts to formulate the grammar of the child in his second year have not been particularly successful, and have even been misleading. The problem appears to be an extremely complex one, and yet one that must be understood, if preschool language programs and the programs of day-care centers are to be successful.

At the two-word stage of development much as been accomplished in describing some of the speech mechanisms involved. At this stage the child can express actor-action relationships that cannot be expressed with one word. The use of two or more words reflects an expansion in the meanings that the child is able to express.

Much has been learned about the child's learning about specific features of utterances that give them particular meanings. Thus, the child acquiring English learns quite early that word order is important. He also learns such features as plurals, and learns the use of intonations to imply a question. Such understandings involve the discovery or invention of general rules. Researchers have commented on the telegraphic characteristics in the speech of young children, a fact which reflects the omission of function words. Embedded clauses are absent from the young child's speech and reflect his inability to understand such structures.

The new knowledge of language learning has already had a profound impact on education. One only has to examine any modern program for the development of language in the preschool child to see how influential the ideas have been. No longer does one find the adult teacher giving the child examples of speech to master that the child is expected to imitate with precision, but rather is there an attempt to encourage young children to express their ideas and to talk about whatever they want to talk about. The emphasis is on expression and encouragement for expression rather than on imitation and reinforcement. The new emphasis is on the creation of linguistic forms rather than on copying models. What is still really not known is the kind of language input that is most effective in helping the child. There obviously has to be an input, and the input has to begin long before there is even a single word of speech, but just what that input needs to be is a crucial matter for education. Research workers have not yet been able to specify what that input should be.

At the level of the elementary and secondary school the influence of the new science of language has been much more indirect. It has led to teachers of English questioning the traditional methods of attempting to teach language competence through the study of grammar. There has been an increasing awareness that a student who does not have the deep structures necessary for understanding a sentence may not have the structures necessary for generating a sentence with particular semantic properties. Although one traditional approach to the learning of the writing of a language has been to expose that student to models of effective writing, the potential effect of such models may be lost if the individual does not have the structures necessary for comprehending the structure of what is read. The problem of teaching written English in American colleges is far more complex than it was thought to be 50 years ago. The concept of reading has also shown a corresponding change, with the mere translation of the written symbols into phonemes seen as only a small component of reading. Much more difficult in the development of reading is the analysis of the material read into components from which meaning can be derived. A person may be able to read material in his native language word by word and yet be so deficient in the analysis of the material that virtually no meaning can be derived from it. The structures needed for the analysis of a sentence may not be there. Comprehension results when analysis leads to semantic information that can be assimilated.

Research has moved a long way towards identifying the kinds of mechanisms that are involved in understanding or generating a sentence in English. As that knowledge develops it will provide a basis for instruction.

One cannot leave this brief discussion of the potential and actual impact of the new work in linguistics on education without mentioning that the research is also leading the way to a better understanding of speech disorders. Present attempts to study the aphasic disorders, for example, are clearly guided by the different levels of analysis that linguistic science has introduced. Thus some aspects of aphasia can be understood in terms of the individual's failure to make phonemic discriminations, but other difficulties involve deficiencies in grammatical structures.

New Conceptions of Reasoning and Problem Solving

Most of those who have attempted to design curricula for elementary and secondary school children since World War I have emphasized the importance of problem solving skills. Efforts to develop high level thinking skills were based, until recently, on a common sense approach, and could not have been based on anything else, for the theories of problem solving of psychologists in the early part of the century were nothing short of primitive. The connectionist theory of Thorndike had little to say about problem solving except that those who had a rich inventory of connections had a better chance of solving problems than those who did not. Watson's attempts to reduce problem solving to classical conditioning led to difficulties that he, Watson, did not recognize, though Pavlov was fully aware of the difficulties. The common sense notion that logic was the core to problem solving, and that logic was quite different from making associations, appealed to the curriculum makers, even if it did not appeal to the antiphilosophical psychologists of the era.

Connectionist and Watsonian theories of problem solving were reductionist in nature. That is to say they attempted to reduce complex behavior to chains of small components. A complex behavior, in contrast with a simple behavior, involved a longer chain of components. The chain theory fitted well into stimulus-response forms of theory in that each link in the chain could be viewed, not only as a response to the previous link, but also as the stimulus for the next link. Such a theory provided a plausible account of some complex forms of behavior, such as that of playing a piano concerto, but the plausibility soon broke down when subjected to careful study. The theory survived as long as midcentury, only because there were no defensible alternatives.

In the 1970's educators began to view problem solving in terms of the theory of intellectual development of Jean Piaget. In contrast to earlier theories, Piaget's is a nonreductionist theory of problem solving behavior. The theoretical position of Jean Piaget is having the same kind of impact on education and educational theory that individuals such as Thorndike, Judd and Terman had earlier in the century.

Piaget was able to bring together certain disciplines in a way that made the resulting system of thought appear to be highly relevant for education. These branches of knowledge that Piaget fused are epistemology, logic, and child development. Piaget has been able to weld them into a form that provides a highly plausible picture of how the human develops, acquires knowledge, and fits that knowledge into a logical system. Piaget describes the result of this amalgamation as genetic epistemology.

Piaget does not deny the existence of phenomena of the type that Skinner and his associates have discussed, and he refers to these as regulatory mechanisms. However, he regards these as quite trivial phenomena. The centrally significant aspect of development, for Piaget, is the emergence of the human as a logical thinking system. The main product of Piaget's life work is a detailed description of how this occurs, based upon a massive amount of experimental evidence. His model has important implications for education at all levels, and suggests how education can be planned, in order that the person that emerges from it may be an effective problem solver. The model has many limitations that cannot be discussed here, but it is still more useful than any other so far produced. It has had substantial impact on the development of educational materials.

One of the most interesting contributions of Piaget is that he has been able to advance the development of the old idea of the psychology of a subject matter field. Piaget's contributions in this respect have been limited to those subject-matter areas related to problem solving in mathematics and science. The dream of Herbart in the early part of the last century of developing a psychology of each subject matter field, and the same dream of Judd in the early part of the present one, was brought by Piaget a step nearer realization. Piaget is the main contributor of his generation to the development of psychologies of particular subject-matter fields. Earlier in the book, mention was made of the impact of Piaget on our understanding of how children acquire the logic of arithmetic. His later work on the development of the child's understanding of the geometry of space, and the transition from a topological to Euclidean geometry is almost a model example of how a psychology of the learning of an academic discipline should be developed. The work would have delighted both Herbart and Judd.

In more recent times Piaget has also laid the foundation for developing the psychology of acquiring scientific knowledge. His research on formal reasoning, though not as complete and thorough as his research with younger children, shows how certain forms of scientific understandings are acquired, and how logical operations necessary for the acquisition of those understandings are developed. Some of his work has been used as a basis for the development of programs of science teaching in schools. Piaget's work on formal operations is not as complete as his work on the psychology of learning the geometry of space, but it is nevertheless a step forward from anything that existed before.

A third area in which the work of Piaget has helped to develop a psychology of subject-matter learning is at the preschool level, where his work on infralogical and perceptual operations has had enormous impact. The term *subject matter* is used here in the broadest sense to cover the content of the preschool curriculum.

Finally, the emerging impact of the ideas of Piaget on American education have tended to deemphasize much that has been called the technology of education. The epistemology of Piaget calls for an education in which young children interact with the real world. In contrast educational technology introduces an artificial interface through which the child engages in an indirect interaction with the world of physical reality. One presumes that Piaget would not throw out all technology related to education, for obviously books have their uses, but to mechanize the classroom is no substitute for filling the classroom with interesting objects to be explored.

In contrast to operant theories of learning, the genetic-epistomology approach to curriculum design has much to say about the content of the curriculum. Curricula, based on operant views of learning, have all uniformly included a very traditional content. The operant psychologists did not see the content to be a problem of consequence. The followers of Piaget have concerned themselves with finding new content for the elementary school curriculum, not just for the sake of introducing novelty, but in order to design a curriculum that will conform to the conditions of effective learning that Piaget has outlined.

Since a fundamental proposition of Piaget's epistemology is that knowledge at the basic level is *action on an object*, the curriculum maker at the elementary and lower levels of education must find objects on which the child can perform some action. The actions that are to be performed should be related to the discovery of the fundamental properties of the environment. Thus the 18 month old child may spend time fascinated by the task of putting objects inside a can, and then spilling them out. Piaget would say that the child is fascinated by this task because he has already learned that two objects cannot occupy the same part of space, but he has now discovered that sometimes this principle is violated and two objects can occupy the same space.

Considerable effort has been expended on the selection of content through which the intellectual development envisaged by Piaget can be achieved. The best example of such assemblies of content is found in the materials developed through the support of the Nuffield Foundation in Great Britain by the Schools Council. The materials have been published by Macdonald Educational in the form of a series of booklets for teachers. The booklets describe ways in which common materials can be used to help children derive knowledge for themselves and study scientific and mathematical principles. Separate booklets cover such topics as (1) *Science, Models, and Toys,* (2) *Working with Wood,* (3) *Holes, Gaps and Cavities,* (4) *Children and Plastics,* and so forth. The series does not provide things for children to learn as much as things *from which* children can learn. At the end of each book, the various tasks are analyzed in terms of the intellectual level needed to solve each problem. The levels described are those that Piaget discovered.

The Slowly Emerging Sociology of Education

Most of the research discussed in this volume has been conducted either by individuals whose main affiliation was either with education or with psychology. Not one has been mentioned in the present century whose background or whose interests lay in sociology. Yet sociologists have been interested in education and, in the last century, Herbert

Spencer had a powerful indirect influence on education through his social Darwinism. In the present century, sociologists have written books for educators pointing out the strong implications that sociology has for the management of educational enterprises. Examples of this interest in the sociology of education are illustrated by George Herbert Betts' *Social Principles of Education* (1912), Robinson Smith's *Principles of Educational Sociology* (1917) and Charles Clinton Peter's *Foundations of Educational Sociology* (1924).

Since midcentury the field of educational sociology texts has been dominated by the name of Wilbur B. Brookover, whose first edition of *A Sociology of Education* (New York: American Book Company, 1955) appeared in 1955, and which he has since produced in new editions with coauthors David Gottlieb in 1964 and Edsel Erickson in 1975. There has also grown a body of research literature on the sociology of education including such landmark studies as George S. Counts' *The Social Composition of Boards of Education* (1927).

Social psychology, a close relative of sociology, has had some impact on education through the work of Kurt Lewin (1890-1947), who studied experimentally the conditions that influenced the work output of groups. The famous experiment that Lewin undertook together with Ronald O. Lippitt and Ralph K. White was probably more familiar to teachers during the 1950's than any other psychological experiment. Lewin himself became deeply interested in the dynamics of groups in the last years of his life which came to an abrupt end in 1947, but Lewin left behind a group of dedicated followers, trained in his laboratory, who sought to apply Lewin's theory of group organization and group process to the solution of problems in schools and businesses, and particularly problems of leadership. The impact of Lewin's group dynamics on education came through the creation of the National Training Laboratory, in which teachers, administrators, and others, received training claimed to make them more effective in handling group situations. The form of training that emerged from Lewin's concept of group process has been promulgated under many names, but the term *sensitivity training* has been most widely used.

The difficulty of establishing the value of this form of social training is substantial. Indeed, the difficulty is so great that the task of evaluation cannot be undertaken at this time with results that could ever be regarded as fair, either one way or the other. The generally negative findings that characterize such evaluation studies are all too likely to destroy an interesting idea before it has had time to bear fruit.

Sociology has obviously produced knowledge of the greatest significance for education. Through the work of sociologists we have begun to understand the inertia of educational practices and the difficulties and problems related to the introduction of innovations. We have learned about the social class affiliations of teachers and the slant that this may give to education. We have come to view education as a process highly controlled by particular segments of the community and have learned that the broad base of community control envisaged by the Puritans has never been achieved. We are beginning to learn about the social conditions that lead to effective control of pupils by teachers, and the difficulties in our society of providing the teacher with sufficient status to maintain an effective relationship with pupils. Sociologists and social psychologists have provided a wealth of information concerning how attitudes and values are acquired. Such a list of potential contributions could be extended over many pages. There is absolutely no question that sociology can make important contributions to education, and the question is why it has not? Except, perhaps, in the rare instance of the Coleman Report, the value of which remains highly controversial and the work of Herbert Spencer, sociology has had little impact.

A first reason is that sociologists have had appointments outside of the educational establishment. Only in quite recent times have sociologists been appointed in schools and colleges of education, and even then the appointment has typically been on a part-time basis.

There have been a few educators who have turned sociologist. Notably among these was George S. Counts, but the interest of professors of education in sociology has been minimal. Most graduate schools of education still do not have a course on the sociology of education, though courses in the social foundations of education have long been common. The latter courses are only rarely taught by sociologists, but have generally been assigned to professors of pedagogy.

A second important reason for the apparent lack of impact of sociology on education is that knowledge developed by sociologists has no clear channel through which it can lead to action in education. The psychologist has such channels. For example, suppose a psychologist has worked on the development of mathematical concepts in children and has made discoveries that he believes have important implications for teaching materials. He can have them marketed through ordinary publication channels. That is what Thorndike did. This channel of influencing education has been widely used by psychologists throughout the present century, and it has been a major means through which psychological research has influenced education. The sociologist cannot use the channel of publication and distribution of teaching materials, for his ideas are important for other aspects of education. The findings of sociology have broad implications for policy making at the highest administrative levels, but these levels of education are not likely to be touched by the writings of sociologists. Consider the typical composition of a school board, found by Counts a half century ago, and certainly not too different today. That school board typically consisted of a banker, a manufacturer or business executive, a physician, a merchant, a lawyer and a housewife. These fine people are hardly likely to be consumers of the writings of sociologists, and yet they are the people who make high level policy decisions. Even higher levels of decision making related to the educational policies are unlikely to have contact with sociological work, except when it has been specially commissioned by the higher level policy makers. For example, many decisions related to education are now made at the congressional level, but these decisions have been notoriously devoid of any input by social scientists.

EPITOME

When one looks back over the story of educational research, one is struck by the fact that perhaps the most resplendent period of the enterprise was the first quarter of the present century. During that period there was enthusiasm for educational research in every corner of the educational enterprise. School systems welcomed research workers with open arms. Famous educational research workers were given top billing at such conferences as the annual meeting of the National Educational Association. Superintendents of schools were forming associations to promote research. Bureaus of research were developed across the country, both in school systems and in universities. Research in schools was conducted by nationally known professors. The hope was widely voiced that all important educational problems would soon be solved through the intervention of the research worker, whose newly emerging presence gave high expectations for the future of education. During that period great advances were made in the way in which educational problems were conceptualized and there was a considerable accumulation of empirically based knowledge about learning and instruction.

The first quarter of the present century was an age of enthusiasm for educational research, and a productive one. But educational research could not possibly be as productive as the enthusiasts in the schools expected it to be. It could not live up to expectations. The result was a later disillusionment among school administrators, a disillusionment that has lingered on until the present day.

Despite the failure of educational research to live up to its expectations, the enterprise continued to grow in vigor during the second quarter of the century. A few graduate schools of education trained research workers, and without such a body of trained personnel, educational research could not possibly achieve any of its goals. Progress was steady, despite a lack of financial support. By the later 1930's, the American Educational Research Association had grown to over 500 members, and the academic research workers were largely in control of policies. This transition of control to the academician was probably not a result of any power seizure, but a result of the waning of interest of administrators in school systems. The school survey continued to be used by educational administrators, but it was no longer viewed as a research technique but as a routine means for identifying deficiencies. Individuals trained in survey techniques often formed themselves into firms of educational consultants and offered services to schools.

During the second quarter of the century educational research showed expansion in universities even if it showed a constriction in school systems. Such an expansion was needed, for without well-trained graduate students research could not assume the place in education that the early pioneers had visualized. Colleges of education were particularly fitted for turning out specialists in statistics, but often neglected other aspects of research. By midcentury the future of educational research looked bright, except for the scepticism found among some school administrators, who took the position that educational research was a failure.

If educational research had been built upon the foundation that had been laid by 1940, it might well be today far in advance of where it is. However, decisions in Washington attempted to give educational research a new thrust. The intentions of the Congress, the Washington bureaucracy, and the advisory committees, on which decisions were made, were excellent, even if the results were not. Centers and laboratories were created without any careful study of how education could best be developed over the years. The emphasis was on producing rapid educational change rather than on building up research facilities through the extensive training of educational research workers. The political power had to learn, what the educational administrative establishment had learned 50 years earlier, that there are no sure and speedy ways of producing effective educational change.

Just as school administrators had become disillusioned with research in the 1920's, the political powers in Washington became disillusioned in the late 1970's. The basic mistake of both the school administrators and politicians was in viewing research as a quick fix for educational problems. There can be no quick fix. Only patient, persistent effort, aided at times by a touch of genius, can bring progress.

The history of educational research provides a basis for planning the enterprise in the future. There can be no doubt that research can be a powerful means of influencing education, mostly for the better. The planners of educational research should now face the future with the light of sunrise in their eyes, and the wisdom from the past engraved in their actions.

Sources

GENERAL SOURCES

Certain general sources were valuable in preparing the author to write sections of the book. Henry Barnard's *American Journal of Education* (1855-1882) is a basic source of information related to American education in the last century. It is a completely fascinating collection of papers that might well make much modern educational literature seem dull. Another useful source of information about education in the last century is the 1891 Chicago reprint edition of the *Encyclopaedia Brittanica*. Other worthwhile general sources of information include *A Cyclopedia of Education*, edited by Paul Monroe and published in 1911 (New York: Macmillan). The modern counterpart of the latter work, edited by Lee C. Deighton, was also valuable (*Encyclopedia of Education*. New York, Macmillan, 1971).

The *Encyclopedia of Educational Research*, edited by Walter S. Monroe in 1941 (New York: Macmillan) provided useful bibliographies related to educational research early in the century.

The *Yearbooks of the National Society for the Study of Education*, beginning in 1902, provide a history of educational thought, and particularly educational thought that had a foundation in educational research. Indeed, the volumes represent an excellent and extended history of educational research and its impact on thought and practice.

Preparation for writing some of the material concerning the last century included a study of the short-lived *Academician* (1818-1820) which died through a lack of subscribers, *The Common School Journal*

(1838-1852) which became the medium through which Horace Mann addressed his educational public, and *The Connecticut Common School Journal and Annals of Education* (1838-1866, with some missing years when publication was suspended). The study of these materials provided a completely fascinating period of study for the author, which prepared him for work on this volume. Much of this material was new to the author and occupied him during the first years of work on the enterprise.

A further general source of information on education towards the end of the last century and the early part of the present century was Nicholas Murray Butler's *Educational Review.* The latter must surely have been inspired by Henry Barnard's *American Journal of Education* which had expired a decade before Butler began his enterprise. Butler's *Educational Review* was carefully scanned.

The enormous proliferation of educational journal literature in the early part of the present century made it difficult to decide upon the materials to inspect. Judd commented in his editorial in the *Elementary School Journal* (1914-15, 15, 68) that there were over 100 periodicals devoted to education in the United States at that time. Judd stated that almost every state had an educational journal and, in addition, there were local and national journals. Although Judd acknowledged that the journals were useful means of distributing news, they generally lacked substantive suggestions regarding the improvement of education. Judd attempted to remedy this deficiency through his journal *The Elementary School Teacher.* This journal was edited by Judd from 1909 to 1914, and he used it as the medium for disseminating his ideas. His unsigned editorials are clearly the products of his thinking. The pages of this journal through 1925 were scanned, not just to discover trends in thought at Chicago, but to identify professional activities related to research throughout the country.

Special attention was given to the *Journal of Education,* particularly in the early part of the century when it reported activities of professional teacher organizations. Also, during the 1900 to 1925 period, the journal was the main medium through which teachers were familiarized with the new empirical knowledge developing about education.

Among other early journal literature searched was the *Mathematics Teacher, School Science and Mathematics, Teachers College Record,* the *English Journal,* and the *Pedagogical Seminary.* Journals of rather later birth that were scanned were *School and Society,* and the *NEA Bulletin.*

Considerable use was made of standard biographical sources including the *National Cyclopaedia of American Biography,* the *Dictionary of National Biography,* and *Who's Who in America.* The documents in the archival section of the University of Chicago Library, the Columbia University Library, the Boston Public Library, and the Library of Congress were of value at particular points in the preparation of the work.

A search for materials was also undertaken in such popular magazines of the last century as the *Atlantic Monthly* and the *Forum.* Such materials provide some indication of the educational issues that the reading public was thinking about and discussing.

Some time was spent in scanning Board of Education reports both in New York City and Boston. Except for the early reports of the Boston School Committee, the material was quite noninformative of what new ideas were influencing education, since the reports were completely dominated by problems related to school plant.

The annual reports of the Commissioner of Education, from the time of the founding of the Bureau of Education through to modern times, were rather carefully studied. Those published before 1910 were interesting material to study, but those of a later date radiated bureaucratic dryness.

SOURCES: CHAPTER 1

A most useful source of the early Massachusetts statutes related to education is found in the Report of the Commissioner of Education for 1892-1893, Volume 2, pp. 1225-1893. This was a report produced under the direction of W. T. Harris, and almost every report of his commissionership has some important materials related to the history of education. *The Evolution of the Massachusetts Public School,* by G. H. Martin (Boston: N. Sawyer & Sons, 1893), is a more general source of information on the early common school movement. An article by George B. Bush entitled "The First Common Schools of New England," in the Report of the Commissioner of Education for 1896-1897, Volume 2 (published in 1898), is particularly interesting to those concerned with the financing of schools.

Horace Mann and the Common School Revival in the United States, by B. A. Hinsdale (New York: Scribner, 1898), is not only an interesting source of information on Horace Mann, but provides an excellent background of information of the history of the common school in Massachusetts during the 200 years that preceded the work of Horace Mann.

Louise Hall Tharp's book *Until Victory: Horace Mann and Mary Peabody* (Boston: Little, Brown and Company, 1953) provides insight into the inner life of Horace Mann by drawing heavily on his correspondence and the diary that he later began to keep. It is a good source for understanding Horace Mann as a person, but provides little information concerning his work and ideas. The Frenchman Gabriel Compayré wrote *Horace Mann and the Public School in the United States* in 1890, which was translated by Mary D. Frost (New York: Thomas Y. Crowell, 1907).

The translation is excellent and readable.

Mary Peabody Mann, Horace Mann's wife, wrote *Life of Horace Mann* (Boston: Walker, Fuller and Company, 1865), which reproduces many letters written by Mann. The book also provides a valuable impression of Mann as a human being in a daily struggle to handle human relationships effectively.

The famous Annual Reports of Horace Mann as Secretary of the Board of Education are, of course, primary sources of vital information about Horace Mann's ideas and the times that involve them. The last facsimile reproduction of these important documents was undertaken by the National Education Association in 1937. They are not available for purchase in any form at the time of this writing, so many libraries have only broken sets.

An excellent short biography of Henry Barnard, by A. D. Mayo, can be found in the Report of the Commissioner of Education for 1896-1897 (chapter 16, pp. 769-810). The Commissioner of Education's report for the year ending June 30, 1902, has an interesting collection of materials related to Henry Barnard. One suspects that these materials were published in honor of his 90th birthday. They include a reproduction of some remarks made 5 years earlier by W. T. Harris, and a further discussion by A. D. Mayo of Barnard's career, summarizing Barnard's work as Commissioner of Education. An additional article by W. T. Harris describes Barnard's role in establishing the office of Commissioner of Education. An appendix to the latter Harris article reproduces many interesting documents related to the establishment of the commissionership.

Henry Barnard's ideas related to education can be studied through his own writings, which he published in the *American Journal of Education.* The total mass of material in the 40 volumes reflects what he attempted to do, namely, to provide a professional literature of education.

The main source of materials on William Torrey Harris is derived from Kurt F. Leidecker's work, *Yankee Teacher: The Life of William Torrey Harris* (New York: Philosophical Library, 1946). Work on the latter volume was initiated by the American Philosophical Society at the time of the centenary of the birth of Harris.

A complete list of the Harris publications was printed in the Report of the Commissioner of Education for the year ended June 30, 1907. The publications, 479 in all, are chronologically arranged and indexed. The titles reflect the enormous range of interests and competencies that Harris had, and the chronological order reflects the development of his thought over nearly 50 years.

The Report of the Commissioner of Education for the year ending June 30, 1894 (chapter 10, pp. 426-445), is a collection of papers entitled *The Psychological Revival,* some of which are discussed in the chapter. The paper by Harris is of particular interest. A further understanding of the position of Harris in this matter was derived from his book *Psychologic Foundations of Education* (New York: D. Appleton and Company, 1904). The latter book carries the stamp of Harris thinking.

The circular cited concerning criminality and the insane is one edited by Arthur MacDonald, entitled *Abnormal Man, being Essays on Education and Crime Related Subjects* (Bureau of Education Circular of Information No. 4; Washington, D.C.: Government Printing Office, 1893).

Joseph Neef's remarkable document *Sketch of a Plan and Method of Education,* originally published in 1808, has been reproduced in facsimile in the volume *American Education: Men, Institutions and Ideas* (New York: Arno Press and The New York Times, 1969). It was the first, but not the only medium that brought the ideas of Pestalozzi to the American continent.

SOURCES: CHAPTER 2

The writings of Johann Friedrich Herbart concerned with education have been translated into English, though translators have often had difficulty with particular words. The major works are *The Application of Psychology to the Science of Education* (trans. B. C. Mulliner; New York: Scribner, 1898 [c. 1835]); *Outlines of Educational Doctrine* (trans. A. F. Lange; New York: Macmillan, 1904 [c. 1806]); *Herbart's ABC of Sense Perception* (trans. W. J. Eckoff; New York: D. Appleton, 1903 [1802]); *Letters and Lectures on Education* (trans. H. M. & E. Felkin; London: Swam Sonnenschein, 1898 [various dates throughout Herbart's life]). Herbart's *Textbook in Psychology* appears in many translations. The one I used was translated by M. K. Smith (New York: D. Appleton, 1891 [1816]). The first of the Herbart volumes cited provides an interesting biography of Herbart that was used as a basis for the paragraphs written about him. The information provided in this source corresponds closely to that found in encyclopedias.

A primary source of information about Wundt is found in E. B. Titchener's article "Wilhelm Wundt" (*American Journal of Psychology,* 1921, 32, 161-178). The article may be described as Wundt as seen by a Wundtian. It is a rather cold account. Most of those who studied with Wundt, such as C. H. Judd, wrote of him in much warmer terms, but Titchener could not escape from his cold academic style of writing.

Edwin G. Boring's description of Wilhelm Wundt was a particularly valuable source especially since Boring had an intimate knowledge of Wundt's work. Boring's *History of Experimental Psychology* (2nd ed.; New York: Appleton-Century-Crofts, 1950) reflects not only Boring's excellent knowledge of Wundt's work which he, Boring, has obviously read in the original German, but Boring's long association with Edward Bradford Titchener, who knew Wundt and his psychology so well, provided him with a special source of understanding in the matter. Our own familiarity with Wundt's position has been through C. H. Judd's translation of the *Grundriss der Psychologie*, which appeared under the title of *Outlines of Psychology* (London: Williams and Norgate, 1907 [1896]). Judd provided an interesting glossary giving his translation of particular German words. The latter is a real problem in the translation of German psychological and philosophical works, as Boring brought out so well in his history.

The available translation of the *Physiologische Psychologie* was the fifth German edition (1902) translated by E. B. Titchener and entitled *Principles of Physiological Psychology* (2 vols.; 2nd ed.; New York: Macmillan, 1910).

James Sully's works are of considerable interest in that Sully was, above all, a textbook writer who attempted to assimilate the new to the old. The main work cited was his *Teacher's Handbook of Psychology* (New York: D. Appleton, 1886). William James's *Talks to Teachers* (New York: Henry Holt and Company, 1924) appeared 13 years after Sully's textbook appeared. The first edition was published in 1899.

Among the new generation of textbooks for teachers at the turn of the century James Mark Baldwin's is especially distinguished. The book *Mental Development in the Child and Race* (New York: Macmillan, 1895) deserves special mention. Others include Hugo Münsterberg's *Psychology of the Teacher* (New York: Appleton, 1910) and Conway Lloyd Morgan's *Psychology for Teachers* (New York: Scribner, 1911).

The important works of Ivan Sechenov have been published in English, in Moscow, under the title *Selected Physiological and Psychological Works* (Foreign Language Publishing House, c. 1965). The latter collected works include a biography of Sechenov by K. S. Koshtoyants. The latter author also wrote an interesting biography of Ivan Pavlov in the collection of Pavlov's writings published as *Experimental Psychology and Other Essays* (New York: Philosophical Library, 1957). Koshtoyants also wrote an introduction to a volume entitled *I. P. Pavlov: Selected Works* (Moscow; Foreign Languages Publishing House, c. 1965). The latter volume also includes Pavlov's autobiography. The Koshtoyants writings trace the relationship between the thinking of Sechenov and Pavlov in some detail. They also discuss the relationship of that line of thinking to post-revolutionary Russian thought.

SOURCES: CHAPTER 3

A convenient source of material on the Boston Survey of 1945 is the volume of Otis W. Caldwell and Stuart A. Courtis (*Then and Now in Education.* 1845: 1923. Yonkers-on-Hudson, New York: World Book Company, 1924). The latter volume reproduced the report of the Boston School Committee and also the complete examinations given to the Boston Schools in 1845.

The records of the Boston School Committee, from 1945, can be viewed on microfilm in the Boston Public Library. All official Boston City documents were printed and filed in sequence, so the School Committee documents are found among other City documents. The Boston School Committee reports were concerned largely with reports of school visitations. Other matters pertaining to schools, such as the need for new buildings, seem to have been taken up by the city council. The general structure of the Massachusetts schools at the time was derived from extensive reading of the *Common School Journal* in the volumes published during the 1940's. The latter publication also provided the source of Horace Mann's comments on the new survey method.

Material on the history of examinations in schools and the various uses of examinations is derived from early editions of the *Encyclopedia Brittanica*, particularly the 10th edition, published in the U.S. in 1891 and the 11th in 1911. The *Encyclopedia Americana*, 1977 edition, is the source of material on the development of writing materials and the steel pen.

Common sources of biographical information yielded little about Joseph Mayer Rice. He came from obscurity and moved back into obscurity long before his death. Rice was not even considered worthy of an obituary in the *New York Times.* Rice's articles on the reform of education and the results of his surveys of children's achievements are readily available. Rice's major articles, cited in the text, are as follows:

"Need School be a Blight on Child-Life," (*Forum*, 1891, *12*, 529-535).

His articles of 1892 and 1893 have been reproduced in book form as *The Public School System of the United States*, New York: Century Company, 1903, and reprinted by Arno Press, 1969.

"The Futility of the Spelling Grind," (*Forum*, 1897, *23*, 163-172 and 409-419).

"Educational Research: A Test in Arithmetic," (*Forum*, 1902, 281-297).

"Educational Research: Causes of Success and Failure in Arithmetic," (*Forum*, 1903-*34*, 437-452).

"Educational Research: The Results of a Test in Language," (*Forum*, 1903, *35*, 269-293).

"English (continued): The Need of a New Basis in Education," (*Forum*, 1904, *35*, 440-457).

"The Need for a New Basis in Supervision," (*Forum*, 1904, *35*, 590-609).

"Why Our Improved Educational Machinery Fails to Yield a Better Product," (*Forum*, 1904, *36*, 6-114).

Rice's final publication was *The People's Government: Efficient, Bossless, Graftless* (Philadelphia: J. C. Winston, 1915).

The descriptions of the Gary schools are based on the account provided by Randolph S. Bourne (*The Gary Schools.* Boston: Houghton Mifflin, 1916, reproduced in 1970 by the M.I.T. Press). The volume by John Dewey and Evelyn Dewey (*Schools for Tomorrow.* New York: E. P. Dutton and Company, 1915) provides a short and uncritical account of her brief and hurried visit to Gary.

The inquiry into the Gary schools, financed by the General Education Board is summarized in the volume by Abraham Flexner and Frank P. Bachman (*The Gary Schools: A General Account.* New York: General Education Board, 1918). In addition, the following 7 volumes were published simultaneously about the Gary study and provided the data from which Flexner and Bachman drew their conclusions:

George D. Strayer and Frank P. Bachman, *Organization and Administration*

Frank P. Bachman and Ralph Bowman, *Costs*

Charles R. Richards, *Industrial Work*

Eva W. White, *Household Arts*

Lee F. Hammer, *Physical Training and Play*

Otis W. Caldwell, *Science Teaching*

Stuart A. Courtis, *Measurement of Classroom Products.*

These volumes represent excellent work and should have set a standard to be followed by the developers of later evaluation studies. All volumes were published by the General Education Board in 1918.

The Gary system was extensively discussed in the *New York Times* during the months of September, October, and November, 1917, when the adoption of the Gary plan was a high political issue for New York City. Adeline and Murray Levine have presented a quite full discussion of the matter in their article, "The Social Context of Evaluative Research," (*Evaluation Quarterly*, 1977, 4, 515-539). The conclusions of the chapter with respect to the Gary episode do not entirely agree with those of the Levines.

The collected papers of Abraham Flexner are in the Library of Congress. These consist of his professional correspondence after 1920. Apparently his professional correspondence before 1920 either was not kept or was destroyed. There are some personal letters, written to his family before 1920, but these throw little light on the Gary program and the political entanglements in which Flexner and the plan became embroiled. The absence of the professional papers and Flexner's failure to discuss the Gary incident, and its relationship to New York City politics in his autobiography, suggests that the Gary matter was one that Flexner hoped would be forgotten. Flexner's correspondence after 1920 is enormously voluminous, a fact which stands out in contrast with the absence of correspondence from the previous years about the Gary experience.

The material on the development of research bureaus was derived largely from scanning educational publications of the 1900-1925 era. Particularly useful for this purpose were the *Elementary School Teacher, Elementary School Journal, Educational Review,* and the *Journal of Education.* The *Encyclopedia of Educational Research* (New York: Macmillan, 1941) edited by Walter S. Monroe provides useful material on the development of testing in schools early in the century. The yearbooks of the National Society for the Study of Education were searched for material related to the early uses of tests in schools. The 16th Yearbook proved useful, in that it was devoted to the topic of the new efficiency movement in schools. One can also see from an examination of the Yearbook that the new efficiency movement was supported by the most influential academicians in education.

Many sources provide extensive information on the growth of school surveys during the 1900 to 1920 period. The Annual Reports of the Bureau of Education devote considerable space to the surveys in which the Bureau played a considerable role. The *Journal of Education* and the *Elementary School Teacher* report survey after survey. An examination of the correspondence of Charles Hubbard Judd showed that he was deeply engaged in that activity, but liked to conduct surveys near to Chicago because he did not want to lose time in travel. Edward L. Thorndike did not become involved in surveys, but Ellwood P. Cubberly at Stanford University was very active in the area. The survey method of producing educational improvements was viewed with great hope and was widely discussed. The concept of the standardization of education also received considerable coverage in the literature of the time. The thinking in this area was also influenced by the writings of Edward L. Thorndike, and particularly those aspects of his writing that identified science with fact finding.

An excellent source of information about the early use of tests in schools, including achievement tests is provided by the volume compiled by Gertrude H. Hildreth (*Bibliography of Mental Tests and Rating Scales.* New York: Psychological Corporation, 1939). Unlike the compilations of Oscar K. Buros, the Hildreth bibliography lists tests whether they were still available or not. The bibliography is far from complete, and yet it does indicate the extensive use of achievement tests in the early part of the century. The tests used in the Pennsylvania Study were reproduced in full in the report by William S. Learned and Ben D. Wood (*The Student and His Knowledge.* New York: Carnegie Foundation for the Advancement of Teaching, 1938).

In order to understand Tyler's operationalism and the operationalism of educational thought at the time of the *Eight Year Study,* one should read Percy Williams Bridgman's classic book on the subject (*The Logic of Modern Physics*. New York: Macmillan, 1927). Tyler's papers, on the problem of defining objectives, (*Constructing Achievement Tests*. Columbus, Ohio: The Ohio State University, 1934), are also valuable in providing insight into his views on how educational research should proceed.

Sometimes the absence of a literature is as important as the presence of one. The absence of published materials related to evaluation during the period 1950-1965 is extraordinary. One suspects that this absence reflects the disillusionment felt by academicians concerning the accomplishment of evaluation studies in the earlier decades. One also suspects that the presence of high interest in the area would not have emerged, except for the availability of Federal and State funds.

There is no comprehensive history available on state-wide testing programs, but information about them has to be gleaned from brief notes concerning them in journals distributed to teachers and academicians. The 1941 edition of the *Encyclopedia of Education* has some information on the topic. There are good reasons why such an inconsequential aspect of the application of measurement techniques to education should be avoided, for identifyable consequences of such programs are hard to find. Yet the subject deserves better treatment because of the large sums of money that such programs have involved and still involve.

Harold O. Rugg's article that describes the development of research bureaus is "How I Keep in Touch with Quantitative Literature in Education," (*Elementary School Journal*, 1917-18, 18, 301-320).

A book by Harold Benjamin Chapman is a highly useful source of information on the development of institutionalized forms of educational research (*Organized Research in Education*. Columbus, Ohio: The Ohio State University Press, 1927). Chapman's inquiry is detailed. The only element lacking in his report is a detailed discussion of what the various bureaus did. Chapman must have assumed that what educational research bureaus did was a matter of common knowledge.

The *Eight Year Study* has been well described in the 5-volume work published by Harper in 1942 under the general title of *Adventure in American Education* (New York: Harper, 1942). The volumes have the following authors and titles:

Wilford M. Aiken, *The Story of the Eight Year Study*

H. H. Giles, S. P. McCutcheon, and A. N. Zechel, *Exploring the Curriculum*

Eugene R. Smith and Ralph W. Tyler, *Appraising and Recording Student Progress*

Dean Chamberlin, Enid Straw Chamberlin, Neil E. Drought, and William E. Scott, *Did They Succeed in College*

Contributors from the participating schools, *Thirty Schools Tell Their Story*

The tests used in the *Eight Year Study* were made available to the Educational Testing Service which, in turn has made them available to a number of users. However, the tests do not seem to have been used for any large scale inquiries.

In some respects the blueprint for the evaluation work in *The Eight Year Study* is found in an earlier volume by Ralph W. Tyler and Douglas Waples (*Research Methods and Teacher Problems.* New York: Macmillan, 1930).

SOURCES: CHAPTER 4

An excellent summary of the early history of the mental testing movement has been provided by Kimball Young in his article "The History of Mental Testing" (*The Pedagogical Seminary,* 1923, 31, 1-48). Another source, written at about the same time, is the historical material in Rudolph Pintner's *Intelligence Testing: Methods and Results* (New York: Henry Holt & Co., 1923).

The definitive work on Francis Galton is that by Karl Pearson, entitled *The Life, Letters and Labours of Francis Galton* (London: Cambridge University Press, 1914-30). The latter consists of four volumes and includes many of Galton's letters to other eminent scientists. A short account of Galton's life, based largely on Karl Pearson's biography, is found in C. P. Blacker's book, *Eugenics: Galton and After* (London: Duckworth, 1952). Blacker's book provides a complete listing of the written works of Galton which span a period of 61 years. Galton's *Inquiries into Human Faculty and Its Development* (London: Macmillan and Co., 1883) has been reproduced many times and is purchasable at the time of this writing.

Karl Pearson's voluminous writings were mainly mathematical, but he made many excursions into other fields. Outside of mathematics he is best known for his *Grammar of Science* (London: W. Scott, 1892). His arguments for eugenics is presented forcefully in many publications, the most accessible of which is his lecture *National Life from the Standpoint of Science* (London: Adam and Charles Black, 1901).

A major source of information about Alfred Binet is Theta H. Wolf's book, *Alfred Binet* (Chicago: University of Chicago Press, 1973). Theta Wolf spent 8 months in Paris and had access to the Bibliothèque Nationale, which houses many of Binet's papers. In addition, Theta Wolf had an interview with Theodore Simon, who was then 86 years of age. Binet's works have not been extensively translated into English, but his French is easy to read. Two works seem to have had the greatest impact on education in the English-speaking world. The most famous is his

L'étude expérimentale de l'intelligence (Paris: Schleicher Freres, 1903. Later reprints by other publishers are also available.) His other work which had impact on American education, written in collaboration with Victor Henri, is *La fatigue intellectuelle* (Paris: Schleicher Freres, 1898).

The previously cited article by Kimball Young provides information about Emil Kraeplin's excursions into measurement. Further information on Kraeplin was derived from the volume produced on the centennial of the birth of Emil Kraeplin. The volume, edited by Benjamin Passamick, is entitled *Epidemiology of mental disorder* (Washington, D.C.: American Association for the Advancement of Science, Publication No. 60, 1959).

James McKeen Cattell refused to contribute an autobiography to various volumes. He sat down in 1936, at the age of 76, and wrote a brief autobiography, which was not published until Michael M. Sokal found it among the Cattell papers in the Library of Congress (see Michael M. Sokal, "The Unpublished Autobiography of James McKeen Cattell," American Psychologist, 1971, *26*, 626-635).

The volume *James McKeen Cattell, Man of Science* (2 vols.) Lancaster, Pa.: Science Press, 1947) was produced under the general editorship of A. T. Poffenberger. The volumes include an introduction by Robert S. Woodworth, who was a colleague of Cattell at Columbia University. In addition, the volumes include most of Cattell's scientific papers and a complete list of his publications. Another important source on Cattell is a monograph edited by Robert S. Woodworth, "The Psychological Researches of James McKeen Cattell" (*Archives of Psychology*, no. 30, 1914). Most of the articles in the latter publication were written by Cattell's students and close associates.

No biography or autobiography by Henry Herbert Goddard could be found, so what can be said about him as a person is limited. His prolific writings provide an excellent chronicle of his work. There are at least two important historical documents from The Training School at Vineland. One of these, *The Research Department: What It Is; What It Is Doing* (Vineland, N.J.: The Training School, 1914), describes the work of the laboratory established by Goddard. The second publication, *The Binet-Simon Measuring Scale for Intelligence* (Vineland, N.J.: The Training School, 1911), presents Goddard's American version of the famous scale. His work with New York City is described in considerable detail in *School Training of Defective Children* (Yonkers-on-Hudson, N.Y.: World Book Company, 1914). His famous study of the Kallikak family appears with a title which shows Goddard's personal bias, *The Kallikak Family: A Study in the Heredity of Feeble-Mindedness* (New York: Macmillan, 1912). His brief excursion into the problem of the training of the gifted is described in a study of the Cleveland Public Schools entitled *School Training of Gifted Children* (Yonkers-on-Hudson, N.Y.: World Book Company, 1928).

Lewis M. Terman's charmingly written autobiography provides an excellent picture of his personality (in C.E. Murchison [Ed.], *A History of Psychology in Autobiography*, Vol. 2. Worcester, Mass.: Clark University Press, 1930, pp. 297-331). Terman's major written works show progressive development in his thought concerning school applications in the following sequence: *The Measurement of Intelligence* (New York: Houghton Mifflin, 1916); *The Stanford Revision and Extension of the Binet-Simon Scale for Measuring Intelligence* (Baltimore, Md.: Warwick and York, 1917. In this latter volume, Terman listed as coauthors all the graduate students who helped with the development of the scale); *The Intelligence of School Children* (New York: Houghton Mifflin, 1919); and *Intelligence Tests and School Reorganization* (Yonkers-on-Hudson, N.Y.: World Book Company, 1922). In the latter book only the first chapter is by Terman, but the rest was collected and edited by him. Terman's final revision of the scale, together with the production of a second form, is described in Lewis Terman and Maud A. Merrill's book, *Measuring Intelligence -- A Guide to the Administration of the New Revised Stanford-Binet Tests of Intelligence* (New York: Houghton Mifflin, 1937). The results of the work of Terman and his associates on the gifted are described in a series of volumes edited by Terman and collectively entitled *Genetic Studies of Genius* (5 vols.; Palo Alto, Calif.: Stanford University Press, 1925, 1926, 1930, 1949, 1959).

Sources of information on Cyril Burt include his autobiography in *A History of Psychology in Autobiography*, Vol. 4, edited by Edwin G. Boring and others (Worcester, Mass.: Clark University Press, 1952, pp. 57-73).

Leslie S. Hearnshaw has been helpful in answering questions about Burt through correspondence. His biography of Burt, *Cyril Burt, Psychologist* (Ithaca, N.Y.: Cornell University Press, 1979), arrived after the chapter had been drafted. When the content of the chapter was checked against Hearnshaw's account, close agreement was found.

The article by D. D. Dorfman, "The Cyril Burt Question: New Findings," (*Science*, 1978, *201*, 1177-1184) raises important issues with respect to the Burt problem.

I have also drawn heavily on my personal knowledge of Burt and on knowledge derived from those who associated with him during the 1930's. Much of his work with the London County Council is reflected in his volume *Mental and Scholastic Tests* (London: P. S. King, 1921). The full title of the latter volume, that is never used, is *London County Council Mental and Scholastic Tests* (London: P. S. King and Son, 1921). The volume includes a disclaimer of all responsibility for the tests, which is an odd inclusion. Burt's *The Young Delinquent* (London: University of London Press, 1921) ran into many editions and many printings. It is not only an excellent study in itself, but it also reflects the extraordinary thoroughness of the work of Burt as a young man. *The Backward Child* (London: University of London Press, 1937) also brings together much of the data collected while with the London County Council, as well as research accomplishments elsewhere. Later editions of that book, like later editions of other works by Burt, do not show substantial change, but rather, they reflect the effects of changes in government policy on the handling of delinquents. Burt's final work, published posthumously, is the final source of Burt's vision of a new Platonic world (*The Gifted Child.* New York: Wiley, 1975).

The six initial articles in *The New Republic* series attacking intelligence tests were as follows: "The Mental Age of Americans" (1922, 32[412], 213-215); "The Mystery of the 'A' Men" (1922, 32[413], 246-248); "The Reliability of Intelligence Tests" (1922, 32[414], 275-277); "The Abuse of the Tests" (1922, 32[415], 297-299); "Tests of Hereditary Intelligence" (1922, 32[416], 328-330); and "A Future for the Tests" (1922, 33[417], 9-11).

Terman's reply to Lippmann is contained in the article "The Great Conspiracy" (*The New Republic*, 1922, 33[420], 116-120). Lippman's rebuttal is entitled "The Great Confusion" (*The New Republic*, 1923, 33[422], 145-146). Lippmann's rebuttal was followed by his two *New Republic* articles discussing the work of Cyril Burt: "Mr. Burt and the Intelligence Tests" (1923, 32[439], 263-264); and "A Judgment of the Tests" (1923, 34[440], 322-323).

John Dewey's two critiques in *The New Republic* of the use of intelligence tests were as follows: "Mediocrity and Individuality" (1922, 33[418], 35-37); and "Individuality, Equality, and Superiority" (1922, 33[419], 61-63). Edwin G. Boring's concluding article in the series was "Intelligence as the Tests Test It" (*The New Republic*, 1923, 35[443], 35-37).

The contribution of Edward L. Thorndike, *An Introduction to the Theory of Mental and Social Measurements* (New York: Science Press, 1904), was a landmark in the history of measurement in education. The book had a long life, being reprinted with only minor changes a decade later. The book remained a standard American text for the best part of 20 years. Guy M. Whipple's *A Manual of Mental and Physical Tests* (Baltimore, Md.: Warwick and York, 1910) was also a book of prolonged influence which was used by students for at least 20 years. Neither of the two volumes had any competitors in their time.

Whipple's remaining publication is of considerable interest. Its title was *Relative Efficiency of Phonetic Alphabets. An Experimental Investigation of the Comparative Merits of the Webster Key Alphabet and the Proposed Key Alphabet Submitted to the National Education Association* (Baltimore: Warwick and York, 1911).

William Stern's book *The Psychological Methods of Testing Intelligence* (trans. Guy M. Whipple. Baltimore, Md.: Warwick and York, 1914) probably had more impact in Europe, in its original German edition, than it had in the United States. By the time it reached America, Lewis

M. Terman and Henry H. Goddard were busy at work and writing about intelligence tests, and Stern's writing must have seemed as only the contribution of an obscure German academician.

The next generation of books on measurement had many competitors. Best known among these were the following: Rudolph Pintner, *The Mental Survey* (New York: Appleton, 1918); Sidney L. Pressey and Luella C. Pressey, *Introduction to Standardized Tests: A Brief Manual in the Use of Tests of Both Ability and Achievement in the School Subjects* (Yonkers-on-Hudson, N.Y.: World Book Company, 1922); William A. McCall, *How to Measure in Education* (New York: Macmillan, 1922); and Walter S. Monroe, *Educational Tests and Measurements* (Boston: Houghton Mifflin, 1917). The contributions of Lewis M. Terman and Cyril L. Burt played an important role. The titles of these works were cited in relation to the previous chapter. The later vintage of books on testing, towards the end of the 1920's, tended to emphasize a how-to-do element in their titles. Thus, William A. McCall wrote *How to Classify Pupils* (New York: Columbia University, Teachers College, 1928).

A very useful reference on the history of testing is a brief volume by Kathryn W. Linden and James D. Linden, *Modern Mental Measurement: A Historical Perspective* (Boston: Houghton Mifflin, 1968).

The two early yearbooks of the National Society for the Study of Education concerned with testing were as follows: *The Fifteenth Yearbook: Standards and Tests for the Measurement of the Efficiency of School Systems* (Bloomington, Ind.: Public School Publishing Company, 1916); and *The Twenty-First Yearbook: The Nature, History, and General Principles of Intelligence Testing* (Bloomington Ind.: Public School Publishing Company, 1923). Thomas S. Kuhn's *Nature of Scientific Revolutions* (Chicago: University of Chicago Press, 1970) provided a framework for understanding the historical inertia of some of the ideas discussed in this chapter.

Robert M. Yerkes was responsible for editing much of the material that came out of the World War I army testing program. Particularly significant is the volume he edited entitled *Psychological Examining in the United States Army* (Vol. 15 of *Memoirs of the National Academy of Science*. Washington, D.C.: Government Printing Office, 1951). The latter volume includes data on the differences between various groups in measured intelligence.

The book edited by Otto Klineberg, entitled *Characteristics of the American Negro* (New York: Harper, 1944), summarizes his work in the area which goes back to the mid-1920's. The book is fully documented and is an excellent source for finding the titles of his earlier monographs and other articles on the topic.

Beth L. Wellman published many papers, but her 1934 paper summarizes much of her previously published work. The paper repeats much that she had already published. It has the title "Growth in

Intelligence Under Differing School Environments" (*Journal of Experimental Education*, 1934, 3, 59-83).

Piaget's book *The Psychology of Intelligence* first appeared in French in 1947, and the American edition was published shortly afterwards in 1950 by Routledge and Kegan Paul. The quick translation indicates the high degree of interest in the topic.

SOURCES: CHAPTER 5

Information on the founding of Teachers College is based on the account given by Lawrence A. Cremin, David A. Shannon and Mary Evelyn Townsend in their book *A History of Teachers College, Columbia University* (New York: Columbia University Press, 1954). Another source is Lawrence A. Cremin's book *The Transformation of the School* (New York: Knopf, 1961). A rather disappointing source of information on this topic is Nicholas Murray Butler's autobiography *Across the Busy Years* (New York: Scribner, 1939). One suspects that Butler viewed the founding of Teachers College as a small enterprise compared with the transformation of Columbia University into a major school and in bringing to the University over 120 million dollars. A book by Richard Wittemore, *Nicholas Murray Butler and Public Education* (New York: Teachers College, Columbia University, 1970), provides a good account of Butler's early role related to public education and the founding of Teachers College.

The papers of Nicholas Murray Butler are housed at the Columbia University main library in over 500 boxes. Of most interest for the purpose of this book was a printed document outlining the course on education that Butler gave, before Teachers College had even been conceived. This outline developed the idea of a science of education that was in keeping with thought on the subject 75 years later. The early correspondence with Grace Dodge was not particularly illuminating for our purposes here, but Butler's Annual Reports of the Industrial Education Association were.

There is no useful collection of Thorndike papers that one can consult. Thorndike culled through his papers before he died, throwing away most of them. The few remaining papers were left in the keeping of his daughter, Frances Cope, who gave them to the Library of Congress in 1964. The collection consists of only two letters written by Thorndike and the typescripts of some of his published articles. Thorndike did not usually dictate answers to correspondence, but wrote his reply on the letter he had received, which he then sent back to the sender. Thorndike also wrote many short personal notes in his own handwriting, and these are scattered through many collections of papers. Thus the papers of Nicholas Murray Butler contain several personal notes by Thorndike.

The author worked in Thorndike's Institute of Educational Research as a research assistant during the year 1938-39. This contact provided information about Thorndike and his associates. The author also has a large personal collection of Thorndike's publications. The author's wife, formerly Norma Colcaire, served as secretary to Thorndike during the years 1936-40 and was closely familiar with his ways of working. Two bibliographies of Thorndike's publications provide a quite complete listing of his publications. The first of these, listing his publications up to 1940, was prepared by John Boldyreff, and was published anonymously under the title "Publications from 1898 to 1940 by E. L. Thorndike," (*Teachers College Record*, 1940, 41, 699-725). The second, published under the authorship of Irving Lorge is "Edward L. Thorndike's Publications from 1940 to 1949," (*Teachers College Record*, 1949, 51, 42-45). These two bibliographies list 507 titles.

The only autobiography that Thorndike wrote is a short one in the volume edited by Carl Murchinson *A History of Psychology in Autobiography*, Volume 3 (Worcester, Mass.: Clark University Press, 1936, see pages 263-270). A first reading of the document leaves the impression that the autobiography says little, but on further reflection one realizes that it is highly reflective of Thorndike's character. The shortness of the autobiography reflects his modesty and unassuming role in life. Eight pages is a very short history of one who accomplished so much. He undoubtedly gave the project a very low priority in his busy schedule of writing, and he probably wrote it at a time when he was too tired to do much else. The biography of Thorndike by Geraldine Joncich, *The Sane Positivist: A Biography of Edward L. Thorndike* (Middletown, Conn.: Wesleyan University Press, 1968), is based on a very detailed study of the papers of Thorndike that are mainly in the hands of his daughter, Frances Thorndike Cope of Montrose, New York. Other Thorndike papers are mixed with other collections of papers of psychologists of his era. The Joncich volume is heavy reading, weighted by the enormous volume of documents on which it is based. It does not look deeply into Thorndike's work nor does it relate his work to that of his contemporaries, in that it is a work of a historian and not a psychologist. In the discussion presented in this volume I have placed far more emphasis on the impact of his work, on the thought and practices of his age, than on the material emphasized by Joncich. Thorndike's monument is his 507 publications, and not his correspondence.

Since a reader should have easy access to the complete list of Thorndike's publications, those cited in the text, in an abbreviated form, are not listed here. Readers interested in exploring further any work mentioned can find the full citation in either the Boldyreff or the Lorge bibliographies. Just a few references are cited in full here to provide ready access to them in that they may be of special interest to readers. The Thorndike and Woodworth article entitled "The Influence of Improvement in One Function Upon the Efficiency of Other Functions," *Psychological Review,* 1901, *8,* 247-261, 384-395, 553-564) is of contemporary interest. The devastating review of Thorndike's views prepared by Titchener is in *Elements of Mind* (1905, *14,* 552-554). Other difficult to locate items are Morgan's *Psychology for Teachers* (London: Scribner, 1911) Münsterberg's *Psychology and the Teacher* (New York: D. Appleton, 1914), and the three important volumes by Mark A. May and Hugo Hartshorne: (1) *Studies in Deceit* (New York: Macmillan, 1928), (2) *Studies in Service* (New York: Macmillan, 1929), and (3) *Studies in the Organization of Character* (New York: Macmillan, 1930). The Woodyard monograph *Education at a Price: A Study of Private Correspondence School Offerings* (New York: American Association for Adult Education, 1940) is also of contemporary interest.

SOURCES: CHAPTER 6

A primary source of information on Charles Hubbard Judd was his collection of papers in the archives of the University of Chicago. Unfortunately, the papers that Judd left behind include no documents before 1925. Judd's second wife, Dorothy Hubbard Judd, told me that the Judd papers prior to 1925 were stored during the 1930's in the basement of the education building on the Chicago campus, but they disappeared. One suspects that they were removed by an overzealous janitor who could see no point in keeping some boxes of old correspondence that nobody seemed interested in using. Nevertheless, the papers from 1925 on are voluminous and provide an excellent basis for describing Judd's interests, professional pursuits, and personality.

The library of the University of Chicago includes in its holding what appears to be a complete listing of Judd's publications. The list includes 685 items and I know of no omissions. The bibliography was prepared by the education librarian. A memorial symposium was held at the University of Chicago shortly after Judd's death (*Conference on Education held on the Occasion when Charles Hubbard Judd Hall was Dedicated in his Honor,* 15 April 1948. Copy in University of Chicago Library).

The papers to the symposium provide quite a useful account of Judd's main contributions to education. However, the symposium did not impress the present writer as giving an adequate account of Judd's remarkable contribution either to his institution or to American education.

Judd's own short autobiography (Carl Murchison [Ed.], *History of Psychology in Autobiography.* Worcester, Mass.: Clark University Press, 1936, pp. 207-235) provides insight into goals, ideals, and strivings. Judd put much of himself into the writing of this autobiography.

A single dissertation was located that focused on the work of Judd. The dissertation by Margaret Louise Walton Clark, entitled *Charles Hubbard Judd: Educational Leadership in American Secondary Education* (Stanford University, 1960, Microfilm 60-6701), might be useful to others but added little to the rich sources available to the author at the University of Chicago.

Judd's study of *Research in the United States Office of Education,* prepared for a Presidential Advisory Committee on Education (Government Printing Office, House Document No. 529, Seventy-Fifth Congress, Third Session, 1939), reflects Judd's views on research in education, particularly as it relates to the use of the school survey.

The main works of Judd are books in which he summarized his thoughts presented in hundreds of articles. His main books, closely studied in the preparation of this volume, were the following:

Genetic Psychology for Teachers (New York: Appleton, 1903).
Laboratory Equipment for Psychological Experiments (New York: Scribner, 1907).
Psychology of High School Subjects (New York: Ginn, 1915).
Introduction to the Scientific Study of Education (New York: Ginn, 1918).
Democracy and American Schools (Chicago, Ill.: University of Chicago Press, 1918).
The Evolution of a Democratic School System (New York: Houghton Mifflin, 1918).
The Psychology of Social Institutions (New York: Macmillan, 1926).
Psychology of Secondary Education (New York: Ginn, 1927).
Problems of Education in the United States (New York: McGraw Hill, 1933).
Education and Social Progress (New York: Harcourt Brace, 1934).
Educational Psychology (New York: Houghton Mifflin, 1939).

SOURCES: CHAPTER 7

The literature on the psychology of school subjects has had a history that goes back nearly 200 years. The basic materials related to this topic, developed by Herbart, are cited in the sources related to Chapter 2. An existensive and scattered literature on the topic was produced throughout the last century. During that period, a writer on education could scarcely avoid the topic, in view of the prominent place that

Herbart had given it in his pedagogy.

A search for materials related to the development of reading research was conducted in the *Elementary School Teacher*, the *Elementary School Journal*, the *Supplementary Educational Monographs* and the *Journal of Education*. The first three of these showed the heavy influence of Judd during much of the time when he was in Chicago, but these publications did not exclude contributions from other institutions.

The works of James McKeen Cattell on reading have been brought together and described in a monograph, honoring Cattell's work, and edited by his close associate Robert S. Woodworth ("The Psychological Research of James McKeen Cattell," *Archives of Psychology*, 1914, No. 30). Edwin G. Boring (*History of Experimental Psychology*, New York: Appleton-Century-Crofts, 1929) provided an excellent account of Cattell's early work and particularly his experiences in Wundt's laboratory at Leipsig. Considerable reliance was placed on Edmund Burke Huey's book *The Psychology and Pedagogy of Reading* (New York: Macmillan, 1908) for an account of the early research related to reading. The Huey book covers much that is quite unaccessible otherwise since it has long since been buried in European publications that are not available even in the Library of Congress. The remarkable feature of Huey's book is that it would still be a sound and valuable book on the psychology of reading three quarters of a century after it was published.

The great classic work of Eleanor J. Gibson and Harry Levin, *The Psychology of Reading* (Cambridge, Mass.: The M.I.T. Press, 1975) was valuable with respect to all aspects of understanding the development of the psychology of that area. Judd's article "Reading Tests," (*Elementary School Journal*, 1913-14, *14*, 365-373) reflects the views related to standardized tests that were prevalent at the time. Gray's viewpoint with respect to the latter issue is presented in his article "Reading in the Elementary Schools of Indianapolis," (*Elementary School Journal*, 1918-19, *19*, 336-353, 419-444, 506-531). The practical orientation of the Gray program in Chicago is shown particularly in the writings of Ruth Monroe whose works included *Children Who Cannot Read* (Chicago: University of Chicago Press, 1932) and *Before We Read: Developmental Activities for the Pre-Reading Period* (Chicago: Scott Foresman, 1937). Frank Smith's book *Understanding Reading* (New York: Holt, Rinehart and Winston, 1971) also provided useful information.

This literature reflects the very practical orientation of the reading research at the University of Chicago, and yet the research must be viewed as highly disciplined inquiry. The thinking that provided the foundation for the research program came out of the psychological laboratories of the day and bears the stamp of scientific research. The research enterprise has none of the flavor of the more recently developed action research.

The initiator of the reading research program at the University of Chicago was Charles H. Judd. His views on reading are summarized in his article "Reading Tests," (*Elementary School Journal*, 1913-14, 14, 305-373). Gray's later article "Reading in the Elementary Schools of Indianapolis," (*Elementary School Journal*, 1918-19, 19, 336-353, 419-444, 506-531) reflects much of Judd's earlier thinking.

Huey provides an account of the early attempts to record eye movements, including his own attempts. A thorough discussion of the early efforts to do this is provided by Alfred L. Yarbus (*Eye Movements and Vision*. New York: Plenum Press, 1967). Yarbus wrote from the University of Moscow and had access to the early European literature on the topic. Yarbus, one may note, was not particularly interested in reading, but in the more general problem of the way in which the eye scans the environment.

Gray was a prolific publisher. Much of his work tended to be summarized and consolidated into key books and articles published at various times during his career. Particularly significant in this respect were his articles in the 24th and 36th *Yearbooks of the Society for the Study of Education* (published in 1925 and 1937 respectively) and also his article on reading in the 1941 edition of the *Encyclopedia of Educational Research*. Gray's papers were donated to the archives of the University of Chicago, but funds have not been made available to classify them and make them available to historians. Gray left no autobiography.

Other significant works, related to reading, include the paper by Arthur I. Gates and Guy L. Bond "Reading Readiness," (*Teachers College Record*, 1935-36, 37, 679-685). The work of Marion Monroe was an important contribution and included *Children Who Cannot Read* (Chicago: University of Chicago Press, 1932) and *Before We Read: Developmental Activities for the Pre-Reading Period* (Chicago: Scott Foresman, 1937).

Material on revised and transitional alphabets was located in John A. Downing's book *Evaluating the Initial Teaching Alphabet* (London, England: Cassell, 1967) and also from his contribution to the *Encyclopedia of Education* (New York: Macmillan, 1971). There was also a considerable amount of material, particularly related to spelling reform, in the *Educational Review* and also in the *Journal of Education* during the years 1900 to 1915.

The most elaborate study of the initial Teaching Alphabet is that of F. W. Warburton and Vera Southgate entitled *i.t.a.: An Independent Evaluation* (London, England: John Murray and W. & R. Chambers, 1969). Another elaborate study is that of D. V. Thackray *Readiness for Reading with i.t.a. and t.o.* (London, England: Geoffrey Chapman, 1971).

Jeanne S. Chall's book *Learning to Read: The Great Debate* (New York: McGraw Hill, 1967) provides a good critique of the experimental studies comparing the results of one teaching method with another.

Sources of information on research related to mathematics education includes the extraordinary collection of 19th century textbooks in the Grand Rapids Public Library. This source provided the author with direct access to such classics as Warren Colburn's arithmetic as well as to later widely used books of the past century. A valuable and comprehensive history of mathematics education is provided by the *Thirty Second Yearbook of the National Council of Teachers of Mathematics* (Washington, D.C.: National Council of Teachers of Mathematics, 1970). The early textbooks in mathematics instruction are mirrors of the popular view of mathematics of the day. The typical instructional materials of the last century show no influence of the thinking of mathematicians. They seem to have been written by practical people for practical purposes. They reflect little understanding of the logical nature of mathematical thought. The journal *Mathematics Teacher*, founded in 1908, was searched for materials related to research. Further searches were undertaken of Judd's *Supplementary Educational Monographs* and the *Elementary School Teacher*. A particularly interesting source of information on the development of the arithmetic curriculum of the elementary school was the *Twenty-Ninth Yearbook of the National Society for the Study of Education* (Bloomington, Illinois: Public School Publishing Company, 1930).

Two books were found to be particularly instructive. The one was by Charles Davies entitled *The Logic and Utility of Mathematics* (New York: A. S. Barnes, 1850). This volume provided an extraordinary analysis of what is involved in the learning of elementary mathematics. Davies was one of the best respected mathematicians of his time, and yet had a deep understanding of the psychology of learning mathematics. The book came on the scene too early to exercise the kind of influence it should have exerted, for those who taught mathematics in school in his day were still largely oriented to it as a trade subject.

An equally interesting volume from the early part of the century is that by James E. McLellan and John Dewey on *The Psychology of Number* (New York: D. Appleton and Company, 1907). The volume does not reflect the mathematical understanding of the Davies volume, but is nevertheless a notable contribution that foresaw the future better than it influenced its present. The book reflects Dewey's pragmatic view and because of that viewpoint, might have been in better contact with the thought of the time about mathematics teaching than was the volume by Davies. The kind of program that McLellan and Dewey advocated is well illustrated by that in the Gary schools a few years later.

Reviews of research in the area are found in the sources already listed but also in *The Elementary School Teacher*, the *Review of Educational Research* and also in various government publications. The writing of reviews of research was widely undertaken during the first half of the present century. Indeed, the reviews were often of better quality than the items of research covered. Top academicians wrote reviews, a practice that top academicians rarely engage in today. Walter S. Monroe specialized in the study of Warren Colburn and published a series of articles that all carried the title "Warren Colburn on the Teaching of Arithmetic Together with an Analysis of the Arithmetic Texts," (*Elementary School Teacher*, 1911-12, *12*, 421-425, 463-480, and 1912-13, *13*, 17-24, 239-246, 294-302). David Eugene Smith, a great historian in the area, was also an important source. Particularly useful was his article "The Development of the American Arithmetic," (*Educational Review*, 1916, *52*, 109-118). An important source of material on early investigations in mathematics is the monograph by Charles H. Judd and Guy T. Buswell "Summary of Investigations Related to Arithmetic," (*Supplementary Educational Monograph*, 1925, *27*). Buswell brought together later research on learning mathematics in a chapter entitled "A Critical Survey for the Study of Education," (*Twenty-Ninth Yearbook of the National Society for the Study of Education*. Bloomington, Illinois: Public School Publishing Company, 1930, 445-470). Judd's own attempt to develop research in the area was published in his monograph "Psychological Analysis of the Fundamentals of Arithmetic," (Chicago: University of Chicago Press, 1927). William A. Brownell, a student of Judd's, attempted to develop the same thesis in "The Development of Children's Number Ideas in the Primary Grades," (*Supplementary Educational Monographs*, 1928, *35*). A very early developmental study, by D. E. Phillips, discusses prevailing views about learning mathematics. The latter article is entitled "Number and its Application Psychologically Considered," (Pedagogical Seminary, 1897, *5*, 221-281). An early article by Caroline Fisher "Arithmetic Reasoning in Children" (*Pedagogical Seminary*, 1912, *19*, 48-77) also discusses prevailing pedagogical views. Another source of material on the interest in reasoning related to arithmetic is the article by Willis L. Gard "A Preliminary Study of the Psychology of Reasoning," (*American Journal of Psychology*, 1907, *18*, 490-504).

The document criticizing the use of drill for teaching arithmetic in the Boston schools is "The Courtis Tests in Boston, 1912-1915: An Appraisal" (School Document No. 15, 1916: Bulletin No. 10 of the Department of Educational Investigation and Measurement. Boston: Boston Printing Department, 1916).

The yearbooks of the National Council of Teachers of Mathematics provide a history of thought related to mathematics instruction since World War I, but most of them have little to say about research that was relevant to our purposes here. The rationalist approach is deeply ingrained in the area, and hardly surprisingly so.

The Judd papers have very little to say about his interest in the teaching of mathematics.

The works by Jean Piaget cited in the chapter are now so readily available that specific sources will not be listed here.

A history of attempts to reform the spelling of English, back to Queen Elizabeth I, has been provided by R. E. Zachrisson, "Four Hundred Years of English Spelling Reform," (*Studia Nephilologica*, 1931, *4*, 1-69). The article does not consider the basic problems involved and the losses that would be incurred by the introduction of a simplified system.

Readers interested in research on handwriting are referred to the *Elementary School Journal* in the years 1905-1925. Frank Freeman was the major psychologist interested in this matter.

A major source of information on research related to the teaching of science is the *Thirty-First Yearbook of the National Society for the Study of Education* published in 1932. It was virtually the first major work on the subject, though not a notable beginning. The early issues of what was then the new *Review of Educational Research* include chapters on the subject. Of interest is the fact that the 1941 *Encyclopedia of Educational Research* included only 2½ pages on science education in contrast with 31 pages on the social sciences. The lengths of these two articles reflect the difference in development in the two areas.

In order to understand the development of the teaching of the social sciences, general documents of the subject were perused. Particularly interesting was the 1899 report on the Committee of Seven of the American Historical Association (*The Study of History in Schools: Report of the American Historical Association Committee of Seven.* New York: Macmillan, 1899). The 1899 report was followed by a committee study related to elementary education (*The Study of History in Elementary Schools: Report to the American Historical Association of a Committee of Five.* New York: Macmillan, 1911). Then two years later appeared the report on secondary education (*A Study of History in Secondary Schools: Report to the American Historical Association of a Committee of Five.* New York: Macmillan, 1911).

The long series of *Yearbooks of National Council for the Social Studies* were perused for materials but provided little material for the purposes of this chapter. Educational research did not apparently have much status among those who planned the yearbooks. The lengthy review of the area in the 1941 *Encyclopedia of Educational Research* is a remarkable and excellent discussion of the entire subject. The latter article is a classic contribution to the area. The writings of Franklin Bobbitt were of value because of his interest in curriculum development in the social sciences. I benefitted much in writing the section on the teaching of the social sciences from personal contacts with Harold Rugg thirty or more years ago. Although these contacts were often thoroughly abbrasive, they left one filled with admiration for the intellectual vigor of the man. At the time when I knew him, he had become disillusioned with research as a means of producing change in education, discarding his own past as a researcher as virtually worthless. Rugg was a restless romantic. A big landmark in his life was the publication he chaired in 1923 the *Twenty Second Yearbook of the National Society for the Study of Education* entitled "The Social Studies in the Elementary and Secondary School." The work on this landmark publication set the stage for the rest of his life. Ultimately, this interest was to fade and become displaced by an interest in art, architecture and literature as creative activities.

Rugg must surely have been influenced by Judd at the University of Chicago who was not only interested in the teaching of history and related subjects, but also in the relationship of the school to society.

The best known of Franklin Bobbit's work is *How to Make a Curriculum* (Cambridge, Massachusetts: Riverside Press, 1924). W. W. Charters' book on the curriculum, also published in 1924, was *Teaching the Common Branches* (New York: Houghton Mifflin, 1924). The latter book was a completely rewritten version of an earlier edition published in 1913.

SOURCES: CHAPTER 8

This chapter is nearer than many others in belonging to the present scene. Behaviorism is still alive as a movement in its more extreme form. The central characters in the development of behaviorism, with the exception of John B. Watson, are known to many contemporary psychologists. B. F. Skinner is still a very active force in psychology. On the other hand, the members of the Vienna Circle were known to only a few contemporaries, and virtually all are now dead. Also, the doctrines they promoted have not survived in their original form. Indeed, the Vienna Circle group showed flexibility, in contrast to the well-known rigidity of American behaviorists.

John B. Watson was not a self-revealing person, since he had a habit of talking about himself in behavioristic terms. His short autobiography in a work edited by Carl Murchison, *A History of Psychology in Autobiography,* Volume 3 (New York: Russell and Russell, 1931, pp. 272-281), provides an extraordinarily obnoxious picture of the young Watson. No biographer of Watson, with any sense of fairness, would have described him in such derogatory terms. A writer of history has difficulty in knowing what to make of such a document of self-denigration. Watson's second wife, Rosalie, wrote an article which, indirectly, speaks of Watson as a person, "I Am the Mother of a Behaviorist's Children." (*Parents Magazine,* 1930, 5[12], 16-18, 67).

The remarkable study of Watson by David Cohen entitled *J. B. Watson: The Founder of Behaviorism* (London: Routledge and Kegan Paul, 1979) appeared just after a first draft of the chapter had been completed. It proved to be an invaluable source of information, and also a completely fascinating book to read.

Lucille T. Birnbaum's doctoral dissertation, *Behaviorism: John Broadus Watson and American Social Thought* (Doctoral dissertation, University of California at Berkeley, 1964 [University Microfilms N. 64-12, 1964]), is an excellent study oriented towards the impact of Watson on social philosophy. It is also an excellent statement of the little that is known about Watson's childhood. Birnbaum visited the community where Watson was raised and consulted records and individuals there, but her research adds little except to bring out the influence of Watson's preacher grandfather.

Watson's major contributions include his doctoral dissertation, *Animal Education: An Experimental Study on the Psychical Development of the White Rat, Correlated with the Growth of Its Nervous System.* Watson had to borrow $350 to pay the University of Chicago to publish the document in 1903. Such payment was customary at that time. Perhaps his most significant scientific publication, the results of which have stood the test of time, is a short book entitled *Kinesthetic and Organic Sensations: Their Role in the Reactions of the White Rat to the Maze* (Baltimore: Review Publishing Company, 1907). A later work published with Karl S. Lashley, on *Homing and Related Activities of Birds* (Washington, D.C.: Carnegie Institution, 1915), was highly regarded in its time but made little long-term contribution to the area. Watson's work on comparative psychology, *Behavior: An Introduction to Comparative Psychology* (New York: Holt, 1914), represented almost the end of his career as a scientist. The research included in his later book, *Psychological Care of Infant and Child* (New York: W. W. Norton, 1928), represents work of very inferior quality in terms of its scientific contribution, understandably so in view of the fact that the work was cut short by what the press claimed to be the scandal surrounding Watson's personal life. Outside of the works considered, one must add Watson's famous paper "Psychology as the Behaviorist Views It" (*Psychological Review*, 1913, 20, 158-177), which created a limited stir among psychologists at the time that it was published. Today, it is viewed as a landmark paper in the behaviorist movement, but it was probably viewed in its time as an awkward and outlandish piece of writing.

The works cited up to this point probably did not have the impact that Watson's polemic writings had and which are contained in several volumes published in the later part of his professional life. These volumes are *Psychology from the Standpoint of a Behaviorist* (Philadelphia: Lippincott, 1919); *Behaviorism* (New York: People's Institute Publishing Company, 1924); and *The Ways of Behaviorism* (New York: Harper, 1928).

Most of the interest in the work of Watson was American. His works do not seem to have been translated into foreign languages. On the

American scene, Watson used rhetoric to fan the fire he had started. The heat of the debate in the late 1920's is shown in the debate between Watson and William McDougall (*The Battle of Behaviorism, an Exposition and an Exposure*. New York: W. W. Norton, 1929). The flamboyant title of the ensuing publication must surely have been to Watson's taste.

The main impact of logical positivism and the Vienna Circle on American psychology came through the work of Gustav Bergmann and his close association with the behaviorist psychologist, Kenneth Spence. There seems little point in listing here the quite prolific writings of Bergmann and his joint contributions with Spence. However, it is relevant to note that Bergmann showed a considerable retreat from the original position of the Vienna Circle. His late position, like the late position of other Vienna Circle philosophers, would give little comfort to those who embrace the philosophy of science of Skinner's contemporary followers. Those interested can read his *Philosophy of Science* (Madison: University of Wisconsin Press, 1958).

The contrast between the personalities of Watson and Burrhus Frederic Skinner is striking; indeed, their autobiographies are so extraordinarily different that one wonders how the two could have been attached to a similar conception of science. Skinner's biography, *Particulars of My Life* (New York: Knopf, 1976), is so boringly trivial in content that one wonders how it came to be published. The autobiography takes him up to his mid-20's, which may well have been the least interesting part of his life. His *Shaping of Behavior* (New York: Knopf, 1979) describes adulthood. The development of his scientific thought is found in his scientific papers. Like Watson, the early part of Skinner's career involved the development of his conception of behavior and, also like Watson, that conception, broad in scope, was derived from very narrow data. The culmination of that work came in a synthesis of it in *The Behavior of Organisms* (New York: Appleton-Century-Crofts, 1938). Later works explored the possible extension of the ideas developed to an understanding of a great range of social and individual behavioral phenomena. Skinner's *Science and Human Behavior* (New York: Macmillan, 1953) did this in a broad and bold way. His *Walden Two* (New York: Macmillan, 1948) used the style of fiction to expand on social applications. His *Verbal Behavior* (New York: Appleton-Century-Crofts, 1957) did the same for the verbal field. The speculative works, produced later than his scientific works, just like Watson's, are interesting to read.

A paper by Skinner that represents a foundation stone to his work is "Drive and Reflex Strength 11," (*Journal of General Psychology*, 1932, *6*, 38-47). His first published paper "The Concept of the Reflex in the Description of Behavior," (*Journal of General Psychology*, 1931, *5*, 427-458) is a classic.

Noam Chomsky's "Review of [Verbal Behavior]," (*Language: Journal of the Linguistic Society of America,* 1959, *35,* 26-58), is an extraordinarily complete criticism of Skinner's behaviorism, and covers virtually all the criticisms that have been published elsewhere.

Sidney Pressey's explorations of teaching machines are described in many of his publications, but he wrote on the subject with particular fervor in his article "A Third and Fourth Contribution Towards the Coming 'Industrial Revolution' in Education," (*School and Society,* 1932, *36,* 668-672).

Material that discusses attempted applications of operant psychology is massive in quantity. I have reviewed the material every few years and have summarized it in *Essentials of Learning* in its various editions (New York: Macmillan, 1963, 1966, 1972, 1977, 1982). These reviews have changed in tone as the outpouring of material has changed in its message.

Reference is also made in the chapter to Bertrand Russell's *History of Western Philosophy* (New York: Simon and Schuster, 1945), P.M. Symonds' *The Nature of Conduct* (New York: Macmillan, 1928), and Geraldine Joncich's *The Sane Positivist: A Biography of Edward L. Thorndike* (Middleton, Conn.: Wesleyan University Press, 1968).

SOURCES: CHAPTER 9

Two general sources were of value in obtaining perspective related to the early developments of the child study movement. These were the *Twenty Eighth Yearbook of the National Society for the Study of Education* (Bloomington, Illinois: Public School Publishing Company, 1929) edited by Guy Montrose Whipple. Like all of Whipple's other works, the volume is a massive compendium of information. Also of value was *The 1930 White House Conference on Child Health and Protection* (New York: Century, 1931).

The work of Dieterich Tiedeman in the eighteenth century has been reproduced in full by Bernard Perez under the title of *Record of Infant Life* (New York: C. W. Bardeen, 1890). Also of value is the history of child rearing in the chapter "Early Nineteenth Century Literature on Child Rearing," by R. Sunley in *Childhood in Contemporary Culture* (edited by Margaret Mead and Martha Wolfenstein. Chicago: Chicago University Press, 1955).

Particularly useful as sources of information about child study in the last century are the Commissioner of Education annual reports near the turn of the century. The Report for the year 1897-98, Volume 2, Chapter 25, pp. 1281-1385, prepared by Arthur MacDonald provides an extended review of child study, together with a bibliography of several hundred items. The research covered goes back to the early 1800's. Two other

Commissioner Reports also provide information of the early child study movement. One of these is the report for the year 1900-1901, Chapter 15, pp. 709-729, which discusses child-study work in Berlin. The author of the latter report is not identified, but the original was published in German. The other report is for the year 1901-1902, Chapter 27, pp. 1095-1137, and presents a study conducted in Chicago by a Fred W. Smedley, who directed a department of child study and pedagogic investigation of the Chicago schools. Incidentally, Smedley was a physiological psychologist who had received his training at the University of Chicago.

Several sources of information are available on the life of G. Stanley Hall. His own autobiography came out under the title *Life and Confessions of a Psychologist* (New York: Appleton, 1924). A short biography of Hall was written by Louis N. Wilson, the librarian of Clark University while Hall was there. Wilson worked closely with Hall, who acknowledged Wilson's help on many occasions. The biography is entitled *G. Stanley Hall: A Sketch* (New York: Stechert, 1914). The biography also includes a listing of Hall's 328 publications up to 1913. *The National Cyclopaedia of American Biography* has a lengthy and informative entry on Hall, probably written by Hall. The autobiography of Hall, which carries the flamboyant title *Life and Confessions of a Psychologist* (New York: Appleton, 1924) nevertheless is written in a style of modesty. The latter surprised me after reading *Adolescence* (New York: Appleton, Vol. 1, 1904, Vol. 2, 1905). Lorine Pruette has also written on Hall in her volume *G. Stanley Hall: A Biography of a Mind* (New York: Appleton, 1926). In addition to his *Adolescence*, his major works include a massive two-volume work *Educational Problems* (New York: Appleton, 1910) which consists of Hall's lectures on pedagogy. He also wrote a short work on education with the title *Youth: Its Education, Regimen, and Hygiene* (New York: Appleton, 1917), which is essentially a condensed version of his *Adolescence.*

Hall's article "The Contents of Children's Minds" (*Princeton Review,* 1883, 11, 249-272) represents the start of Hall's work. His ideas on morality emerged later and appeared in an article "Moral Education and Will Training" (*Pedagogical Seminary,* 1892, 2, 72-89). The empirical work on morality at Clark is reported in a study by J. R. Street, "A Study in Moral Education" (*Pedagogical Seminary,* 1897-98, 5, 2-40).

In the present context, the most important work of Maria Montessori is *The Montessori Method* (original translation 1912, and now reproduced by many different publishers). This work shows clearly her ties to German psychology and her orderly conception of intellectual development. The latter influence is obvious throughout her work. Less obvious is the source of her ideas discussed in *Spontaneous Activity in Education* (original translation 1917, and now reproduced in many sources). Her ideas in the latter volume seem to tie to the Froebel and Pestalozzi tradition, but she does not acknowledge any sources.

Gesell wrote up accounts of his observations in many forms during his long professional life. One suspects that the book that brought his normative approach to middle class parents, more than any other publication, was his *The Mental Growth of the Preschool Child* (New York: Macmillan, 1925). The book is not written in a popular style, but most of Gesell's writing is intelligible to typical middle class parents. A volume written with Helen Thompson *Infant Behavior, Its Genesis and Growth* (New York: Greenwood, 1969) provides norms of early behavior that was attractive to infant watchers of the late 1930's. The volume he wrote with Frances L. Ilg *Infant and Child in the Culture Today: The Guidance of Development in Home and School* (New York: Harper, 1943) probably had some influence on thought related to preschool programs. Much of his writing had to do with the handicapped and the application of his findings to the schooling of the handicapped, but one of his early books written with his wife, Beatrice Chandler Gesell, dealt with education in a broader sense. The latter book was entitled *The Normal Child and Primary Education* (New York: Ginn, 1915). Gesell's physiological theory of child development is presented in *The Embryology of Behavior: The Beginnings of the Human Mind* (New York: Harper, 1945).

Gesell's main consideration of child development in relation to elementary education was written before he developed his program at Yale. It was written while he was still at Clark University and was much influenced by Hall. The Volume bears the title *The Normal Child and Primary Education* (New York: Ginn, 1912) and was written with his wife Beatrice Chandler Gesell.

SOURCES: CHAPTER 10

Materials related to the content of this chapter were difficult to locate. A perusal of the annual reports of the Bureau of Education, during the years 1902-1907, brought to the attention of the writer the importance of the reindeer project in Alaska. During these years, when William Torrey Harris was in office, the reports made fascinating reading. The later, extremely dull reports of subsequent commissioners did not even mention the reindeer project, and provided no follow-up. Even though the enterprise was later taken over by other agencies, one cannot help but be surprised that the Bureau of Education was not interested in the long-term impact it had had. A summary of the project is available in Darrell Hevenor Smith's *The Bureau of Education: Its History, Activities and Organization* (Baltimore, Md.: The Johns Hopkins Press, 1923). For material related to the subsequent development and decline of the reindeer project, I am indebted to Richard Olav Stern, who compiled *A*

Selected Annotated Bibliography of Sources on Reindeer Herding in Alaska (Occasional Publications on Northern Life, No. 2. Fairbanks: University of Alaska, Institute of Arctic Biology, 1977). The descriptions of each article are sufficiently clear to provide a quite detailed account of what happened to the enterprise in subsequent years, and there is sufficient duplication of coverage to compare one source with another. A former governor of Alaska, Frank Dufresne, has picturesquely described the reindeer project in his autobiography, *My Way Was North* (New York: Holt, Rinehart and Winston, 1966).

Material on the musk ox project was found in the *National Geographic* article entitled "Domesticating the Wild and Woolly Musk Ox," by John J. Teal, Jr. (1970, 137 [6], 862-878).

The West Georgia College project has been reviewed by D. F. Folger in "We Venture in Teacher Education" (*Junior College Journal*, 1945, 15, 413-416). I have seen the materials put out by this project for schools, and have been favorably impressed with them. It is too bad that no evaluation of the uses of the materials was conducted.

The background for Maurice F. Seay's development of the Sloan Experiment in Kentucky is found in a monograph on *Adult Education*, edited by Seay (Lexington: University of Kentucky, Bureau of School Service, 1938, 10 [4]). This bulletin described the work undertaken by Seay and his associates in connection with the Tennessee Valley Authority. The development of the experimental school curriculum in the project was described in *The School Curriculum and Economic Improvement*, by Maurice F. Seay and Harold F. Clark (Lexington: University of Kentucky, Bureau of School Service, 1940, 13[1]). Another monograph, by Ruth Hillis, described *The Preparation and Evaluation of Instructional Materials on Community Agencies* (Lexington: University of Kentucky, Bureau of School Service, 1948, 21[2]). The final report on the project appears under the authorship of Maurice F. Seay and Leonard E. Meece and is entitled *The Sloan Experiment in Kentucky* (Lexington: University of Kentucky, Bureau of School Service, 1944, 16[4]).

SOURCES: CHAPTER 11

The Journal of Education, the most widely distributed journal for teachers in the early part of the century, was carefully examined up to the early 1920's. The journal has much to say about professional attitudes towards research during that period. What was learned from the *Journal of Education* has colored much of what is said in the chapter about the views of teachers and administrators with respect to research early in the century. The chapter cites only three specific articles from that journal.

One is by William Torrey Harris on "How the Superintendent may Correct Defective Class-Work," (*Journal of Education*, 1906, 64, 159-161). The second is the address by President William H. Taft on "Is a National Standard of Education Practical," (*Journal of Education*, 1915, 81, 260-261). The third article cited is that by a Superintendent Clyde C. Green, on the then focal topic of "The Promotion of Teachers on the Basis of Merit and Efficiency," (*Journal of Education*, 1915, 81, 482-483). Green's article is mentioned, not because Green was distinguished, but because he reflected the position of most superintendents of his age.

The post World War II years produced a number of summaries of research related to teacher effectiveness. The first of these was that by A. S. Barr, "The Measurement and Prediction of Teaching Efficiency: A Summary of Investigations," (*Journal of Experimental Education*, 1948, 16, 203-283). Barr was selective in what he included in his summary. His work was a summary and made no attempt to synthesize the results. Another and far more comprehensive summary was provided by Simeon J. Domas and David V. Tiedeman under the title "Teacher Competence: An Annotated Biography," (*Journal of Experimental Education*, 1950, 19, 101-218). The third and most useful attempt to bring together the results of classroom research is provided by the volume prepared by Joseph E. Morsh and Eleanor W. Wilder, the purpose of which is well described by its title "Identifying the Effective Instructor: A Review of the Quantitative Studies 1900-1952," (*Research Bulletin AFPTRC-TR-54-44*. San Antonio, Texas: Air Force Personnel and Training Research Center, Lackland Air Force Base, San Antonio, 1954). The Morsh and Wilder document is a thoughtful synthesis of the research.

The first attempt to summarize classroom research related to teaching is found in the *Fourteenth Yearbook of the National Society for the Study of Education.* The second part of the Yearbook is a monograph by A. C. Boyce on "Methods of Measuring Teacher's Efficiency," (Chicago: University of Chicago Press, 1915).

G. Derwood Baker's committee report on studies comparing traditional with progressive classrooms appeared as *New Methods Versus Old in American Education* (New York: Bureau of Publications, Teachers College, Columbia University, 1941).

J. Wayne Wrightstone's studies, which were perhaps the best examples of classroom research of his era were the following:

Appraisal of Experimental High School Practices. (New York: Teachers College, Bureau of Publications, Columbia University, 1936).

Appraisal of Newer Elementary School Practices. (New York: Teachers College, Bureau of Publications, Columbia University, 1938).

Appraisal of Newer Practices in Selected Public Schools. (New York: Teachers College, Bureau of Publications, Columbia University, 1935).

(With Joseph Justman and Irving Robbins) *Evaluation in Modern Education.* (New York: American Book Company, 1956).

The New York City research on the group of progressive elementary classrooms appeared in the following article: A. T. Jersild, R. L. Thorndike, B. Goldman and J. J. Loftus, "An Evaluation of Aspects of the Activity Program in the New York City Public Elementary Schools," (*Journal of Experimental Education*, 1939, 8, 166-207).

The W. W. Charters and Douglas Maples volume that describes their competency based teacher education program is entitled *The Commonwealth Teacher Training Study* (Chicago: University of Chicago Press, 1929).

The reports of research that came out of the Fordham project and the Pennsylvania State College projects were never sold, but were distributed to interested individuals and libraries that include government documents. Since the reports are difficult to trace through ordinary library catalogs, the Library of Congress Catalog number is given here as LB 1044 .P42. The series includes the following 4 volumes in which C. R. Carpenter is described as principal investigator rather than author, though his hand and style of writing is evident throughout the 3-volume series:

Instructional Film Research 1918-1950. Technical Report No. NAVEXOS P-977. Port Washington, New York: Special Devices Center, 1956.

Instructional Film Research Reports, Volume I. Technical Report No. NAVEXOS P-1220. Port Washington, New York: U.S. Naval Training Device Center, 1956.

Instructional Film Research Reports, Volume II. Technical Report No. NAVEXOS P-1543. Port Washington, New York: U.S. Naval Training Device Center.

Only the first of these two publications is a volume in the sense of being a unified work. The last two items listed are collections of mimeographed papers, produced over a period of many years. The third volume does list a set of conclusions derived from the motion picture research program.

The work on television instruction, organized by Robert T. Rock, is presented in the following volume, which is organized as a single unified document:

Instructional Television Research Reports. Technical Report No. NAVEXOS P-1544. Port Washington, New York: U.S. Naval Training Center, 1956.

SOURCES: CHAPTER 12

A key document in preparing the first part of this chapter was Richard A. Dershimer's book *The Federal Government and Educational R & D*

(Lexington, Mass.: Lexington Books, 1976). Dershimer interviewed virtually every person that had been involved in making policy decisions related to educational R & D during the 20-year period 1955 to 1975. The book has all the markings of an excellent historical study and should be studied by modern educational policy makers. The author, who has lived through this period has considerable knowledge of the behind-the-scenes action related to the Federal government and educational research and development, and the Dershimer book authenticates that knowledge derived from the grape vine.

Less impressive, and much less useful, is the Federal government's own version of how educational research and development was expanded during the 1950 to 1970 period. The Federal government's version is found in a document anonymously presented and entitled *Educational Research and Development in the United States* (Washington, D.C.: U.S. Department of Health, Education, and Welfare, 1970, Document Catalog No. HE5.212:12049).

The reports of the National Council on Educational Research were consulted in the hope of throwing light on the activities of the National Institute of Education, but these were peculiarly nonilluminating. The latter fact is hardly surprising since the members of the Council that supposedly oversees Federally sponsored educational R & D has many qualifications, but few that have to do with competence in research. These documents are of historical interest, reflecting the lack of input of research workers into the establishment of educational research policies.

The article by Donald C. Orlich was cited ("Federal Educational Policy: The Paradox of Innovation and Centralization," *Educational Researcher*, 1979, 8 (7), 4-9). This article presents a viewpoint commonly expressed by educational research workers. The article emphasizes the theme that comes out in the Dershimer book, namely, that Federal decisions related to research and development are much more likely to be influenced by political considerations than by intelligent appraisals of what can be accomplished.

The work of the centers and laboratories up to 1974 is presented in the publications of the Council for Educational Development and Research, entitled *Cedar Catalog* (Portland, Oregon: Commercial Educational Distributing Service, 1971-1974). The catalogs are dull inventories with virtually no evidence of the worth of the products and projects.

A typical report of a review panel on the laboratories and centers available to the author bears the date January, 1979. This short report reads very much like previous reports. The latter is hardly surprising in view of the fact that the panel consisted mainly of administrators, just as previous panels had consisted mainly of administrators. Only one member could be viewed as an expert on educational research (Panel for the Review of Laboratory and Center Operations, *Research and Development Centers and Regional Laboratories: Strengthening and*

Stabilizing a National Resource. Washington, D.C. National Institute of Education, 1979).

The second half of the chapter represents, inevitably, some personal opinions about the importance for education of particular frontiers of academic knowledge. No one could fail to be impressed with the work on perception during the last 30 years. The 10-volume work, edited by Edward C. Carterette and Morton P. Friedman, entitled *Handbook of Perception* (New York: Academic Press, 1974-1978) is impressive testimony of what has been accomplished in the area. One also has to be impressed by the classic work of Eleanor J. Gibson *Principles of Perceptual Learning and Development* (New York: Appleton-Century-Crofts, 1969). Ulric Neisser's *Cognitive Psychology* (New York: Appleton-Century-Crofts, 1967) has been a particularly influential book, particularly in that it links perception, cognition, and memory.

The original publication and distribution of the so-called Nuffield mathematics and science materials was undertaken in London, England, by Macdonald Educational. The materials were distributed in the United States through various distributors, but the interest in them seems to have been quite minimal.

The works of Noam Chomsky are so well known that they do not need to be listed here and their influence on language instruction at the lower levels is also evident in almost all materials published at the present time. However, any reviewer of such curricular materials must also be impressed by the failure of some of the producers of the material. One set of materials is advertised as combining the best in linguistics with the best in operant techniques, without understanding the incompatibility of the two approaches. Not all authors of such materials are as confused.

The works of Piaget will not be cited here in that he is the most prolific writer in psychology of his time. His chief disciplies in America have been John H. Flavell and David Elkind who have done an excellent job of conveying Piaget's message to educators. Whatever is said about Piaget in this chapter is based on a study of his original works.

The ancestor of all books on the sociology of education is Herbert Spencer's *Education: Intellectual, Moral and Physical* (New York: Appleton, 1961). The work was originally presented as a series of articles in various British periodicals. The book appeared in numerous printings through the early part of the present century, and was of obvious influence on those who wrote on the sociology of education in the early part of the present century. The latter include George Herbert Betts' *Social Principles of Education* (New York: Scribner, 1912), Walter Robinson Smith's *Principles of Educational Sociology* (Boston: Houghton Mifflin, 1917) and Charles Clinton Peters' *Foundations of Educational Sociology* (New York: Macmillan, 1924). These early books on sociology are not what would today be called sociology in that they include virtually no empirical research. Nevertheless, they took an analytic approach to the sociology of education, and provided a foundation for later empirical studies. Charles Hubbard Judd's *The Psychology of Social Institutions* (New York: Macmillan, 1926), though not written by a sociologist, is still a remarkable contribution to the sociology of knowledge, and can be read profitably today. The contemporary works of Wilbur B. Brookover and his associates can be easily located by interested readers.

Index of Names

Index of Subjects

Lewis and Clark College - Watzek Library
LB1028 .T722 1983 wmain
Travers, Robert Mor/How research has cha
3 5209 00336 6016